Handbook of
The Biology of Aging

The Handbooks of Aging

Consisting of Three Volumes

Critical comprehensive reviews of
research knowledge, theories, concepts, and issues

Editor-in-Chief
James E. Birren

Handbook of the Biology of Aging
Edited by Edward J. Masoro and Steven N. Austad

Handbook of the Psychology of Aging
Edited by James E. Birren and K. Warner Schaie

Handbook of Aging and the Social Sciences
Edited by Robert H. Binstock and Linda K. George

Handbook of
The Biology of Aging
Fifth Edition

Editors
Edward J. Masoro and Steven N. Austad

Volume Associate Editors
Judith Campisi, George M. Martin,
and Charles V. Mobbs

ACADEMIC PRESS
A Harcourt Science and Technology Company

San Diego   New York   Boston   London   Sydney   Tokyo   Toronto

The sponsoring editor for this book was Nikki Levy, the editorial
coordinator was Barbara Makinster, the production editor was
Paul Gottehrer, and the manufacturing manager was Brenda Johnson.
The cover was designed by Cathy Reynolds. Composition was done by
Inde-Dutch Systems (IDS), Chandigarh,
India and the book was printed and bound by Quinn-Woodbine, Inc.,
Woodbine, New Jersey.

Cover photo credit: Index Stock © 2001.

This book is printed on acid-free paper. ∞

Academic Press
A Harcourt Science and Technology Company
525 B Street, Suite 1900, San Diego, California 92101-4495, USA
http://www.academicpress.com

Academic Press
Harcourt Place, 32 Jamestown Road, London NW1 7BY, UK
http://www.academicpress.com

Library of Congress Catalog Card Number: 00-110673

International Standard Book Number: 0-12-478260-4

PRINTED IN THE UNITED STATES OF AMERICA
01   02   03   04   05   06   QW   9   8   7   6   5   4   3   2   1

Contents

Part One
Introduction

Part Two
Cellular Processes Influencing Organismic Aging
Edited by Judith Campisi

Section Three
Systemic Factors Influencing Organismic Aging
Edited by Charles V. Mobbs

Part Four
Models of Retarded Aging
Edited by George M. Martin

Part Five
Epilogue
Edited by Steven N. Austad and Edward J. Masoro

Contributors

Numbers in parentheses indicate the pages on which the authors' contributions begin.

Judd M. Aiken (114), Department of Animal Health and Biomedical Sciences, University of Wisconsin-Madison, Madison, Wisconsin 53705

Steven N. Austad (3), Department of Biological Sciences, University of Idaho, Moscow, Idaho 83844-3051

Chantal Autexier (246), Bloomfield Center for Research in Aging, Lady Davis Institute for Medical Research, The Sir Mortimer B. Davis Jewish General Hospital, McGill University, Montreal, Quebec, Canada H3T 1E2

Andrzej Bartke (297), Department of Physiology, Southern Illinois University School of Medicine, Carbondale, Illinois 62901-6512

Edwin Chen (246), Bloomfield Center for Research in Aging, Lady Davis Institute for Medical Research, The Sir Mortimer B. Davis Jewish General Hospital, McGill University, Montreal, Quebec, Canada H3T 1E2

Kelvin J. A. Davies (25), Ethel Percy Andrus Gerontology Center, University of Southern California, Los Angeles, California 90089-0191

Martijn Dolle (84), Department of Physiology, Cancer Research and Therapy Center, University of Texas Health Science Center and Department of Basic Research, San Antonio, Texas 78229

Rita Effros (324), Department of Pathology and Laboratory Medicine, University of California, Los Angeles School of Medicine, Los Angeles, California 90095-1732

Ari Gafni (59), Institute of Gerontology and Department of Biological Chemistry, University of Michigan, Ann Arbor, Michigan 48109-2007

Tilman Grune (25), Neuroscience Research Center, Medical Faculty, Humboldt University Berlin, 10098 Berlin, Germany

Eun-Soo Han (140), Department of Physiology, The University of Texas Health Science Center at San Antonio, San Antonio, Texas 78229-3900

William R. Hazzard (445), Geriatrica and Extended Care, VA Puget Sound Health Care System, Seattle, Washington 98108

Scott Hofer (423), Biobehavioral Health Department, Center for Developmental and Health Genetics, The Pennsylvania State University, University Park, Pennsylvania 16802

Nikki J. Holbrook (179), Laboratory of Biological Chemistry, National Institute on Aging, Gerontology Research Center, Baltimore, Maryland 21224

Peter Hornsby (207), Huffington Center on Aging, Baylor College of Medicine, Houston, Texas 77030

Mark A. Lane (297), Nutritional and Molecular Physiology Section, Laboratory of Neurosciences, National Institute on Aging, National Institute of Health, Baltimore, Maryland 21224-6825

Yusen Liu (179), Laboratory of Biological Chemistry, National Institute on Aging, Gerontology Research Center, Baltimore, Maryland 21224

Marisol Lopez (114), Program in Cellular and Molecular Biology, Department of Animal Health and Biomedical Sciences, University of Wisconsin-Madison, Madison, Wisconsin 53705

Edward Masoro (396), Department of Physiology, The University of Texas Health Science Center at San Antonio, San Antonio, Texas 78229-3900

Gerald McClearn (423), Biobehavioral Health Department, Center for Developmental and Health Genetics, The Pennsylvania State University, University Park, Pennsylvania 16802

Richard A. Miller (369), University of Michigan School of Medicine, University of Michigan Institute of Gerontology, Ann Arbor Veterans Administration Medical Center, Ann Arbor, Michigan 48109-0940

Mohammad A. Pahlavani (140), Department of Physiology, The University of Texas Health Science Center at San Antonio, San Antonio, Texas 78229-3900 and South Texas Veterans Health Care System, San Antonio, Texas 78284

Linda Partridge (353), Galton Laboratory, Department of Biology, University College London, London NW1 2HE, United Kingdom

Arlan Richardson (140), Department of Physiology, The University of Texas Health Science Center at San Antonio, San Antonio, Texas 78229-3900 and South Texas Veterans Health Care System, San Antonio, Texas 78284

Stephen C. Stearns (353), Department of Ecology and Evolutionary Biology, Yale University, New Haven, Connecticut 06520-8106

Mark Steinhelper (140), Department of Physiology, The University of Texas Health Science Center at San Antonio, San Antonio, Texas 78229-3900

J. Randy Strong (140), Department of Pharmacology, The University of Texas Health Science Center at San Antonio, San Antonio, Texas 78229-3900 and South Texas Veterans Health Care System, San Antonio, Texas 78284

Holly Van Remmen (140), Department of Physiology, The University of Texas Health Science Center at San Antonio, San Antonio, Texas 78229-3900 and South Texas Veterans Health Care System, San Antonio, Texas 78284

Jan Vijg (84), Department of Physiology, Cancer Research and Therapy Center, University of Texas Health Science Center and Department of Basic Research, San Antonio, Texas 78229

George Vogler (423), Biobehavioral Health Department, Center for Developmental and Health Genetics, The Pennsylvania

State University, University Park, Pennsylvania 16802

Johathan Wanagat (114), Medical Scientist Training Program, Program in Cellular and Molecular Biology, Department of Animal Health and Biomedical Sciences, University of Wisconsin-Madison, Madison, Wisconsin 53705

Eugenia Wang (246), Department of Biochemistry and Molecular Biology, School of Medicine, University of Louisville, Louisville, Kentucky 40292

James B. Young (269), Department of Medicine, Northwestern University Medical School, Chicago, Illinois 60611-3008

Foreword

This volume is one of a series of three handbooks on aging, *Handbook of the Biology of Aging; Handbook of the Psychology of Aging;* and the *Handbook of Aging and the Social Sciences.* The series is in its fifth edition and reflects the growth of research and publication about aging.

The handbook series is used by research personnel, graduate students, and professional personnel for access not only to the rapidly growing volume of literature but also for the perspectives provided by the integration and interpretations of the findings by experienced and well-informed scholars. The subject matter of aging has matured and expanded in recent years with much research and education being conducted. It has become a mainstream topic in the sciences ranging from the biological to the social and also in the many professions serving older persons.

One of the by-products of the exponential growth of the research literature on aging and the speed of access in the information age is an overwhelming amount of information quickly available to the individual. One result of such information overload can be an adaptive narrowing of interests and scope. This is particularly relevant to understanding of a complex field such as aging in which many factors interact. More than ever, students of aging need integration and interpretations from experts in adjacent subtopics to their special interests. The handbook series provides the opportunity of not only reading a topic of special interest but also reading about the adjacent subject matters that may have important implications. This is particularly significant in aging which is not a lock and key issue to be solved by one discipline or one study or insight.

The rapid changes of the 20th century are evidence that environmental factors can contribute much to the length of life, and also to the quality of life. Aging is a dynamic process as indicated by the shifts in the magnitudes of the contributors to the processes of aging. There is little doubt that our genetic background as a species and our individual heredity contribute to our prospects for length of life and life-limiting and disabling diseases. We can expect much more understanding of the genetic factors in aging as contemporary research continues to expand. However, environmental factors, both physical and social, and our behavior modulate the expression of our genetic predispositions. In a broad perspective, aging is a product of ecological forces. For this reason researchers and students of aging have to be aware of diverse contributing factors to phenomena of aging. The handbook series makes available interpretations of a wide literature and contributes to the integration of a highly complex but vital subject matter.

Public interest in aging has grown along with the impressive increases in life expectancy and rise in the numbers and proportion of older persons. This interest presumably has led to the increased support of research and scholarship by government and foundations. The subject matter of aging has become a topic in daily life discussions. Further improvements in our life expectancy and reductions in limitations on the quality of life with advancing age may be expected to emerge from the efforts of those who have written chapters for the series of handbooks on aging.

Without the intense efforts and cooperation of the editors and asssociate editors of the individual volumes, the series would not be possible. I wish to thank the editors, Edward J. Masoro and Steven N. Austad, of the *Handbook of the Biology of Aging* and their Associate Editors, Judith Campisi, George M. Martin, and Charles V. Mobbs; Robert H. Binstock, and Linda K. George, editors of the *Handbook of Aging and the Social Sciences*, and their Associate Editors, Victor W. Marshall, Angela M. O'Rand, and James H. Schulz; my co-editor of the *Handbook of the Psychology of Aging*, K. Warner Schaie, and the Associate Editors, Ronald P. Abeles, Margy Gatz, and Timothy A. Salthouse.

I wish to express my appreciation to Nikki Levy, the editor at Academic Press, whose long standing interest and cooperation have facilitated the publication of the series of handbooks on aging.

James E. Birren

Preface

The fifth edition of the *Handbook of the Biology of Aging* follows its predecessors in providing in-depth coverage of cutting edge research by leading investigators in biological gerontology. However, it differs from its predecessors, and most multiauthored books on this subject, in that it develops an overarching theme that integrates detailed, isolated findings of biogerontologic research within the context of organismic aging.

The book begins with a broad conceptual framework that includes a consideration of the evolution of senescence. This is followed by chapters that provide detailed coverage of recent findings on age-associated changes in cellular and systemic processes: oxidative stress and damage, protein structure and turnover, instability of the nuclear and mitochondrial genomes, DNA repair, gene expression, cellular signal transduction, apoptosis, cellular proliferation, the sympathetic nervous system, endocrine and neuroendocrine regulatory functions, and the immune system. Next, the importance of animal models in the study of aging is addressed in chapters on the genetics of retarded aging in *Drosophila* and mice, and the role of caloric restriction in the retardation of aging in rodents and possibly nonhuman

primates. The emphasis is on the future use of these and related models in the exploration of the basic nature of aging and in the development of aging interventions.

The penultimate chapter assesses the involvement of gene-gene interactions and gene-environment interactions in aging. Clearly, interactions between genes and environment play the major role in aging, and thus focus should be on "nurture and nature" rather than "nurture versus nature."

The book concludes with a broad consideration of the impact on geriatric medicine of research on the biology of aging. Although already evident, the benefits for geriatric medicine are just beginning.

The fifth edition, like the earlier editions, is primarily directed to those involved in aging research, including faculty and other senior scientists as well as postdoctoral trainees and graduate students. In addition, teachers of the biology of aging in the many gerontology programs in colleges and universities should find the book invaluable. And it will also admirably serve the needs of biologists and physicians who wish to learn more about aging.

The editors are indebted to the Associate Editors, Drs. Judith Campisi,

George M. Martin, and Charles Mobbs, for their help in developing the theme of the book. Moreover, their reviews of the scientific substance of the first drafts, as well as those of the reviewers they enlisted, and their constructive comments enabled each of the chapter authors to produce a final version of superb quality. To each and every author, we extend our grateful thanks.

Edward J. Masoro
Steven N. Austad

About the Editors

Edward J. Masoro

Dr. Masoro is Professor Emeritus in the Department of Physiology at the University of Texas Health Science Center at San Antonio, where from 1973 through May of 1991 he served as Chairman. He was the founding Director of the Aging Research and Education Center.

Dr. Masoro was the recipient of the 1989 Allied-Signal Achievement Award in Aging Research. In 1990, he received the Geriatric Leadership Academic Award from the National Institute on Aging and the Robert W. Kleemeier Award from the Gerontological Society of America. In 1991, he received a medal of honor from the University of Pisa for Achievements in Gerontology, and in 1993, Dr. Masoro received the Distinguished Service Award from the Association of Chairmen of Departments of Physiology. In addition, he received the 1995 Irving Wright Award of Distinction of the American Federation for Aging Research and the 1995 Glenn Foundation Award. He served as President of the Gerontological Society of America from 1994–1995, as Chairman of the Aging Review Committee of the National Institute on Aging (NIA), and as Chairman of the Board of Scientific Counselors of the NIA.

Dr. Masoro has held faculty positions at Queen's University (Canada), Tufts University School of Medicine, University of Washington, and Medical College of Pennsylvania. Since 1975, Dr. Masoro's research has focused on the influence of food restriction on aging. He has served or is serving in an editorial role for 10 journals, and from January 1992 through December 1995, he was the Editor of the *Journal of Gerontology: Biological Sciences*.

Steven N. Austad

Dr. Austad is a Professor of Zoology in the Department of Biological Sciences at the University of Idaho as well as Affiliate Professor of Pathology at the University of Washington. A Fellow of the Gerontological Society of America, he is also serving as current Chair of the Biological Sciences Section of that organization. He was previously an Associate and Assistant Professor in the Department of Organismic and Evolutionary Biology at Harvard University. His interests lie in the evolutionary and comparative biology of aging and his current research delves into the genetics of exceptional longevity in birds and wild-derived mice. He is the recipient of the Phi Kappa Phi/ University of Idaho Alumni Assocation's Distinguished Faculty Award, the Fifth Nathan A. Shock Award, and shared the Geron Corporation-Samuel Goldstein Distinguished Published Award with graduate student John. P. Phelan.

He was formerly on the Science Advisory Board of National Public Radio. His trade book, *Why We Age* (1997), on the biology of aging has been translated into seven languages besides English and he frequently writes for the general public on topics related to aging. He is on the editorial board of the *Journal of Gerontology: Biological Sciences, Aging* (Milano), *Biogerontology, Mechanisms of Aging and Development*, and *The American Naturalist*.

Judith Campisi

Dr. Judith Campisi is a Senior Scientist in the Life Sciences Division of the Lawrence Berkeley National Laboratory, and Head of the Center for Research and Education on Aging. Her research focuses on the molecular and cellular biology of cell senescence and the role of aging in cancer development and progression. She was on the faculty of the Boston University Medical School, where she received a Cancer Research Scholar Award from the American Cancer Society (1985) and Established Investigator Award from the American Heart Association (1988). Since moving to Berkeley, she received a MERIT Award from the National Institute on Aging (1995), the Allied-Signal Award for Aging Research (1997), an Ellison Medical Foundation Senior Scholar Award (1998), and the Glenn Foundation Award from the Gerontological Society of America. She served on the Biological and Clinical Aging Review Committee and Board of Scientific Counselors of the National Institute on Aging. She is currently a member of the National Advisory Council on Aging, Scientific Advisory Board for the Alliance for Aging Research, and Board of Directors of the American Federation for Aging Research. She serves on several editorial boards, including the *Journal of Gerontology* and the *Science of Aging Knowledge Environment*.

Charles V. Mobbs

Dr. Mobbs is an Associate Professor of Geriatrics and Neurobiology at the Mt. Sinai School of Medicine. In 1982 he received the George Sacher Award from the Gerontology Society of America. In 1989 he received the first Glenn Foundation Fellowship for research in gerontology and was appointed to the editorial board of *Mechanisms of Aging and Development* in 1990. He has served as a mentor for the Brookdale Foundation from 1997 to the present. Since 1996 he has served on the review panel of the American Federation of Aging Research and from 1999 to the present has served on study sections and special review panels for the NIH. In addition to publishing over 60 peer-reviewed papers and over 20 reviews, Dr. Mobbs has also edited two books, *Functional Endocrinology of Aging* and *Functional Neurobiology of Aging* with Dr. Patrick Hof.

George M. Martin

Dr. Martin is currently Professor of Pathology, Adjunct Professor of Genetics, and Associate Director at the Alzheimer's Disease Research Center, University of Washington. Dr. Martin's research has for many years been concerned with the development of genetic approaches to the study of aging and age-related diseases in mammals; one theme being the plasticity of the genome of somatic cells. Honors for his research have included the Brookdale, Kleemeier, and Paul Glenn Foundation awards of the Gerontological Society of America, the Allied-Signal Corporation Award, the Irving Wright Award of the American Federation for Aging Research, and the American Aging Association Medal. He has also received an Outstanding Alumnus Award from the University of Washington School of Medicine and is a Senior Member of the Institute of Medicine of the National Academy of Sciences. Dr. Martin has served on the National Advisory Council and the Board of Scientific Counselors of the National Institute on Aging. He currently serves on the Scientific Advisory Board of the Ellison Medical Foundation and is President of the American Federation for Aging Research.

Part One

Introduction

One

Concepts and Theories of Aging

Steven N. Austad

I. Introduction

Biological aging may be defined as a process of intrinsic, progressive, and generalized physical deterioration that occurs over time, beginning at about the age of reproductive maturity. Aging, defined at levels other than the organism, such as at the level of the organ, tissue, cell, or extracellular matrix, is a decrement in function that contributes to deteriorating function in the organism as a whole. Not all organisms age. Prokaryotes do not appear to age, nor do some protists and at least a few multicellular eukaryotes (Bell, 1982, 1984). However, aging is highly prevalent among multicellular organisms (Finch, 1990).

The rate of aging varies enormously among animal groups, with some species growing feeble and dying within days and others surviving more than a century (Finch, 1990). Some authors prefer to term the process of age-related deterioration "senescence" to distinguish it from simply growing older without deterioration (Finch, 1990). However, because relatively few animals fail to deteriorate with the passage of time, aging and senescence will be considered synonymous in this volume.

Aging is not synonymous with disease, however, even though the incidence of many (but not all) diseases increases exponentially over time as mortality rate often does (Finch, 1990; Simms & Berg, 1957). Rather, aging proceeds even in the absence of disease, although part of aging clearly includes increased *vulnerability* to disease. Indeed because the overwhelming majority of biomedical studies using animal models calculate patterns of age-at-death to assess aging rate (see the following), the presence of infectious disease leading to premature death in research animals can seriously confound such studies. This is why the model of choice for mammalian aging studies is animals known to be specific-pathogen-free, although some of the longest-lived mice reported were kept in clean, but not specific-pathogen-free, colonies (Weindruch, *et al.*, 1986). Not only infectious diseases, but even degenerative diseases may compromise aging studies in model organisms if the disease is too prevalent in the model used. The study then becomes primarily one of that particular disease rather than aging itself. For this reason, Weindruch and Masoro (1991) expressed concern about the widespread use of F344 rats in aging research. This rat strain is particularly prone to developing lethal kidney disease. A cogent discussion of the complex relation between aging and disease is given by Masoro (1995).

Observations that intrinsic aging has occurred among individuals are most convincing, in fact, when measures of physical and/or mental performance decline in the absence of detectable disease (McCarter, 1990; Albert, 1994). As a vivid example, age-specific world records of most athletic events requiring speed, strength, or endurance decline perceptibly by about age 30 in humans (Holloszy & Kohrt, 1995; Fig. 1). People holding such records are generally in superb health for their age-group, presumably free from any disease relevant to their performance and trained to near their physiological maximum. Yet performance declines ineluctably with age nevertheless.

II. Measuring the Rate of Aging

Despite its straightforward definition, the rate at which aging occurs in individuals has proven surprisingly difficult to measure. A major problem with interpreting direct measurements of the decline of specific physical or physiological parameters, whether at the cellular, tissue, organ, or organismal level, is that the decline occurs at a variety of rates, and these rates may have idiosyncratic relationships to one another among different individuals (e.g., Borkan & Norris, 1980). However, the rewards of being able to predict the remaining health, vigor, or longevity of individuals by taking one or a few measurements early in life are considerable. To the extent that such "biomarkers" make better predictions about the future of individuals than does calendar age, they have the potential to accelerate the pace of aging research enormously. To understand, for instance, whether an experimental manipulation or intervention influences aging rate, researchers would not have to follow treated individuals through the rest of

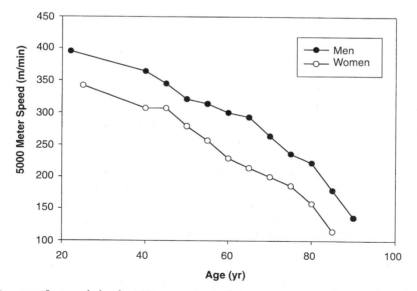

Figure 1. Age-specific records for the 5000-m run. Note that current men's and women's world records are held by athletes in their early to mid-20s. (Modified from Holloszy & Kohrt, 1995.)

their lives. They could assess the biomarkers at some appropriate interval after the treatment and evaluate the experiment at that point (Reff & Schneider, 1982; Baker & Sprott, 1988). This approach would also facilitate gerontological research on longer-lived animal models, such as those more closely related to humans than most current models.

With such rewards in mind, an extensive research program to identify potential biomarkers of aging in laboratory rodent strains was begun by the National Institute on Aging in cooperation with the National Center for Toxicological Research in 1988 (Sprott, 1999). Despite this considerable effort, as yet no measurement or panel of measurements made on living individuals achieves the original criteria for a successful biomarker, although promising candidate measures, such as glycoxidation of collagen (Sell, et al., 2000) or proportion of CD4 T-cells that display a memory phenotype, are beginning to appear for mice (Miller, 1997). Some researchers, moreover, believe that aging is such an intrinsically multifaceted and heterogeneous process that such "biomarkers" of aging rate will never be found (Costa & McCrae, 1980). Regardless, due to their undeniable utility for assessing the efficacy of putative therapeutic interventions in the aging process and their potential to obviate complete life span studies and therefore shorten experiments on mechanisms of aging, the search for such biomarkers continues to be something of a Holy Grail for biogerontologists and is still being pursued vigorously (Miller, 1997; Heller, et al., 1998).

The measurement of an aging rate within populations has proven considerably easier largely by ignoring functional changes in health and vigor and analyzing patterns in age-at-death. The advantage of age-at-death is that it is an unambiguous and easily measured end point. The implicit assumption behind using this surrogate measure for physiological decline is that patterns of age-at-death will parallel functional changes within a population. Experimental research on a variety of organisms suggests that this assumption is warranted. For instance, caloric restriction increases almost any measure of age-at-death and also prolongs function and vigor in laboratory rodent populations (see Chapter 15 of this volume). Genetic selection for extended life in both the nematode, Caenorhabditis elegans, and fruit fly, Drosophila melanogaster, has also been observed to prolong physical vigor (Duhon & Johnson, 1995; Service, 1987).

Patterns in age-at-death may be analyzed for either longitudinal or cross-sectional data. Longitudinal studies are those in which a cohort of individuals born within a small time interval is followed until death, whereas cross-sectional studies, record age-at-death of individuals dying within a small time interval, although those individuals were born at different times. Longitudinal analyses are much the preferred approach, all else being equal, because they do not confound changes due to age with unavoidable historical effects or environmental variability [see Arking (1998) for a detailed discussion]. As one wag put it, a cross sectional study will tell you that Floridians are born Cuban and die Jewish. Virtually all research with animal models is now performed longitudinally, sometimes with a fraction of animals sacrificed at intervals during the study. This approach combines the ability to assess animal subclinical pathology in a longitudinal fashion (e.g., Lipman et al. 1999).

The easiest, yet least informative, measures of this actuarial aging rate are point estimators, such as mean, median, or maximum age-at-death in a population.

Of these, mean longevity is the most useful because a measure of data dispersion such as standard error can be calculated simultaneously. For a crude analysis of population differences this measure may suffice, but it contains precious little information on age-specific changes, which is precisely how aging is defined. For instance, in modern technological countries women display anywhere from 5–10 years greater mean longevity than men (United Nations, 1990), yet this comparison reveals little about whether women physically deteriorate at a slower rate than men. In fact, over most of the adult life course, men's and women's death rates increase in parallel (Fig. 2B). Women, however, die at lower rates from birth to very old age. For reasons we do not understand, human females seem better designed for survival at all ages; they do not deteriorate more slowly. One weakness of mean longevity as a measure of aging is that it gives little information on maximum age, which can be somewhat informative about patterns of aging. For instance, voluntary exercise (wheel running) begun at 6 months of age in Long–Evans rats increased mean and median longevity, but failed to alter maximum longevity or the pathology profile at necropsy, suggesting that exercise retarded the onset of disease, but did not influence aging (Holloszy, *et al.*, 1985).

Maximum longevity is another frequently used measure of aging rate. Used as a point estimator, maximum longevity merely consists of the oldest reported age-at-death of an individual (*e.g.*, Sacher, 1959; Austad & Fischer, 1991). Its use in this sense is virtually always in the analysis of interspecies comparisons, where it is the only metric available for dozens to hundreds of species. Ideally, maximum longevity represents the age of a very old individual of a given species kept in protected conditions and, hence, will give some idea of the rate of physical deterioration of that species. However, to the extent that deaths occur from nonsenescent causes, the measure may be heavily dependent on the size of the population from which the data were compiled (Promislow, 1993), unless morality rate accelerates exponentially, in Gompertzian fashion, to the very end of life (Finch & Pike, 1996). The validity of this metric, regardless of sample size, also depends on the proficiency of existing husbandry procedures for that particular species. Poorly developed husbandry guarantees that deaths will likely be due to nonsenescent causes. Due to these complications, maximum captive longevity analyses should be interpreted with caution. In any case, maximum longevity should not be thought of as a theoretical boundary beyond which individuals of a species cannot survive (i.e., *sensu* Fries, 1980). Modern demographic studies have discovered that such boundaries are illusory (Carey *et al.*, 1992; Curtsinger *et al.*, 1992). Instead of mortality rate accelerating to infinity as it would have to for longevity to approach a fixed boundary, most detailed studies show otherwise (see the following discussion).

Maximum longevity may also refer to the mean longevity of a standardized sample from the longest-lived individuals in a population. For instance, it is sometimes implemented as mean longevity of the longest-lived 10% of a population in order to make within-species arguments concerning whether a given treatment, such as caloric restriction, exercise, or a dietary antioxidant, has affected aging rate itself rather than just specific disease processes (e.g., Iwasaki *et al.*, 1988).

A more informative method for comparing aging between populations is the analysis of survivorship, signified by demographers l_x, defined as the proportion of individuals born that are still alive at age x (Fig. 2A). As probably the most common way of portraying longevity data in the gerontological literature, survivorship, unlike previously mentioned measurements, portrays

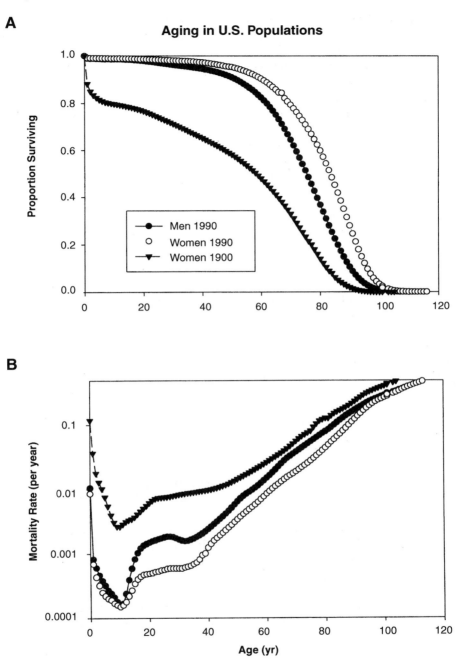

A

Aging in U.S. Populations

Figure 2. Two methods of presenting age-at-death data for the United States population. (A) Survivorship curve. Note that, in 1900, when the leading causes of death were infectious diseases, the survivorship curve lacked a pronounced right "shoulder." This pattern is often a sign that infectious disease rather than aging is dominating the shape of the curve. Note also that all survivorship curves appear smooth, such that the relatively abrupt alterations in age-specific mortality patterns observed in (B) are masked. (B) Age-specific mortality rate. Note that the difference between women in 1900 and in 1990 is most dramatic during the period of infant mortality and the child-bearing years. Note also the male pattern of rapidly increasing mortality through the late teens and twenties. This pattern is due to behavioral, not physiological, reasons. (Data from Faber, 1982.)

(albeit crudely) age-specific mortality patterns. For instance, a survivorship plot will indicate the extent to which deaths are clustered toward the tail of population longevity by the degree to which it exhibits a right "shoulder." Survivorship plots that fail to exhibit a substantial shoulder are likely to be heavily influenced by extrinsic mortality factors such as accidents or infectious disease. For instance, a comparison of the survivorship plot of American women in 1900, when infectious diseases formed the greatest causes of death (Smith, 1993), with that of American women in 1990, when degenerative diseases constituted the major causes of death, illustrates this point (Fig. 2A). Survivorship curves can also be easily statistically compared by a variety of nonparametric statistical procedures (Lee, 1992).

Because survivorship, by definition, is bounded by 0 and 1 and must decline monotonically with age, it is less useful for detecting detailed patterns of age-specific mortality. However, age-specific mortality rate, q_x, may be easily calculated from survivorship data:

$$q_x = 1 - (l_x + 1/l_x).$$

A plot of q_x versus age instead of l_x (Fig. 2B) reveals, for instance, that in the United States in 1990, mortality drops precipitously until it reaches a minimum at about the time of puberty and then increases approximately exponentially thereafter. It also reveals a relative slowing of mortality rate increase in women between about ages 20 and 40 and a dramatic increase in mortality in males during adolescence, patterns that were not evident visually in the survivorship curves. Similarly, age-specific mortality rate analysis of several thousand *Drosophila* allowed Khazaeli *et al.* (1997) to demonstrate that exposure to a brief heat stress increased mean longevity by

reducing age-specific mortality for anywhere from a few days to a few weeks immediately after the heat exposure, even though at later ages this mortality rate difference disappeared.

Age-specific mortality rates can reveal subtle patterns in large populations, such as the human population of the United States, but in smaller populations such as those used in laboratory research, where the number of individuals in an age-class may be limited to a few hundred to several thousand individuals, age-specific morality often changes erratically from age to age. For instance, Fig. 3 depicts age-specific mortality for DBA2/JNia mice fed either *ad libitum* or restricted to 60% *ad libitum* in the NIA/NCTR biomarkers of an aging colony (A. McCracken, personal communication, 1999). For this figure, sexes within a treatment were combined as there were no statistically significant sex-specific differences in longevity. Thus, the sample size of 112 individuals per treatment is quite large for a rodent study. Despite the erratic changes in age-specific mortality over the life course at this sample size, it is clear that the increased longevity of the calorically restricted group was due to a generally depressed mortality rate throughout life rather than a narrow age-specific effect. Importantly, age-specific mortality rate data for two groups may also be compared statistically by using maximum likelihood methods (Pletcher, 1999)

Age-specific mortality rate is, like survivorship, bounded by 1. It also varies in magnitude depending on the age interval used to construct it. For these reasons, many demographers prefer a parameter, generally denoted μ_x, which is variously called the force of mortality, the instantaneous death rate, or the hazard rate at age x. Conceptually, μ is the instantaneous mortality rate as the age interval is made infinitely small. Various formulae may be used to estimate μ_x from survival

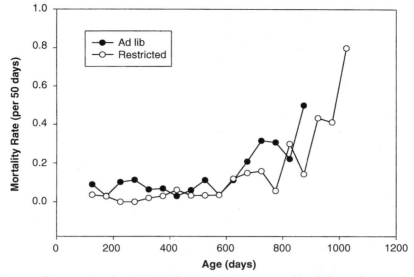

Figure 3. Age-specific mortality for 112 DBA/2JNia mice (sexes combined) for each treatment from the NIA/NCTR biomarker colony (A. McCracken, personal communication, 1999).

data, the most straightforward being $-\ln(l_x+1/l_x)$ or equivalently $-\ln(1 - q_x)$. Not only is this metric not bounded by 1, it is in principle independent of the width of age interval used. Like age-specific mortality, however, it tends to vary erratically when populations from some or all age-classes are relatively small. As a consequence, smoothing functions or fitting of the data to various analytic functions often is used to clarify patterns in the data (Carey, 1999).

Various explicit mathematical models of age-specific mortality rate patterns have been developed to which empirical demographic data may be fitted [reviewed in Carey (1999)]. The advantages of implementing explicit models are the following: (1) they reduce the complexity of mortality data to a few parameters, which facilitates comparisons between data sets; (2) to the extent to which they may represent real patterns underlying messy real-life data, they allow parametric statistical tests (such as standard linear regression techniques for Gompertz curves) to be implemented; or (3) they may yield insight into underlying

processes of aging [see Yashin, Vaupel, and Iachine (1994), who developed two mortality models with divergent biological assumptions that fit Swedish old-age mortality data equally well]. For instance, the Weibull model derives from reliability theory and describes how the failure of various configurations of subsystems relate to the failure of the overall system (Gavrilov & Gavrilova, 1986).

The most popular of these explicit models has been the Gompertz model, $m_x = m_0 e^{B}{}_{x'}$ where m is some age-specific mortality metric, m_0 is the mortality at or near sexual maturity, and B is the Gompertz slope, which measures the rate at which mortality increases with age. Note that this model assumes a constant, exponential increase in mortality rate throughout adulthood. The Gompertz model was empirically derived, although it turns out to be a special case of the Weibull model. It provides a rough fit to a surprising range of empirically observed mortality rates from animal species in both the laboratory and the field (Finch, 1990). Moreover, it has the merit of helping to disentangle differences in longevity due to differences in intrinsic vulnerability early in adulthood (measured by m_0) from those due to differences in the rate of deterioration (measured by B).

In detail, the Gompertz model usually fails to provide a completely satisfying fit to data early in adulthood (e.g., Fig. 2B). Also, analyses of large cohorts of several species have revealed that, at later ages, mortality rate may slow relative to Gompertzian expectation, or even plateau or decline (Vaupel et al., 1998). The meaning of this slowing, cessation, or decline of mortality rate increase is not clear, and the effect varies considerably among species. For instance, in laboratory C. elegans, Medflies (Ceratitis capitata), and D. melanogaster populations, mortality rate begins to plateau when a substantial fraction (20–25% or more) of the original population is still alive (Fig. 4). By contrast, although mortality rate increase slows slightly in modern human populations from technological countries relative to Gompertzian increase when about 50% of the population is still alive, a mortality plateau, if it occurs at all, does not emerge until age 105+ when fewer than 1 in 100,000 people is still alive (Vaupel et al., 1998). Mortality plateaus have never been reported in genetically homogeneous laboratory rodent populations, even at population sizes of several thousand (A. Turturro, personal communication, 2000). These population sizes still may not be sufficiently large to detect subtle late life effects or, equally plausibly, they either do not occur or occur so late in life that it would never be detected at population sizes available in captive rodent populations.

At least three interpretations of the mortality plateau phenomenon exist. First, it may represent population heterogeneity. That is, there is a spectrum of

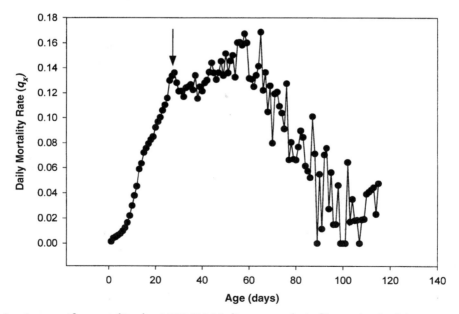

Figure 4. Age-specific mortality for 1,203,646 Mediterranean fruit flies maintained in group cages of approximately 7200 individuals initially. Mortality rates are shown only until the population had fallen to 40 individuals. The Arrow, signifying the first severe departure from Gompertz kinetics, represents the point at which 19% (225,101 individuals) of the original cohort remained alive. (Data from Carey et al., 1992.)

"frailty" within the population in which individuals within frailty classes die at increasing rates, yet differences between frailty classes mean that the most frail die first, leaving behind more robust individuals who die at a slower rate (Curtsinger *et al.*, 1992; Carey *et al.*, 1992; Yashin *et al.*, 1994). It is important to note that this heterogeneity need not have a genetic underpinning, because mortality rate leveling is found not only in genetically heterogeneous populations but also in both homogeneous outbred and homogeneous inbred populations (Carey *et al.*, 1992; Fukui *et al.*, 1996). It is of interest to note that even genetically identical individuals kept in as rigidly controlled conditions as possible still die at a broad range of ages from a variety of causes (Lipman *et al.*, 1999). It is also important to note that it is not clear whether sufficient heterogeneity in frailty exists to explain observed invertebrate data. For instance, Vaupel and Carey (1993) show that to fit an underlying, but heterogeneous Gompertz mortality to the Medfly data would require that the frailest subgroup had 5 billion times the chance of death at any age as the most robust subgroup.

Second, mortality leveling may result from slowed aging at the individual level, possibly due physiological or behavioral changes with age—factors, that are difficult to study in large populations of laboratory invertebrates (Carey *et al.*, 1992; Tatar, *et al.*, 1993). However, it is well-known that something as simple as reduced physical activity can slow aging rate in poikilotherms (Sohal & Donato, 1978). A related idea is that with increasing frailty, minor stochastic environmental events come to dominate mortality rates. All death becomes, in essence, accidental. This is well-known in field populations, where frequently no age-specific increase in mortality is observed (Promislow, 1991), because the environment is extremely hazardous

relative to the intrinsic mortality rate. Thus, although they have not been observed to exhibit actuarial senescence in nature, it seems highly unlikely that, in a protected environment like a zoo, wildebeests, for instance, would not age like all other mammals. Mortality plateaus in laboratory populations typically are observed at levels of extreme frailty, where mortality levels, for instance, approach two orders of magnitude or more above initial mortality rates (Vaupel *et al.*, 1998).

A third interpretation of late life mortality plateaus comes from reliability theory, where organisms are considered complex systems that fail, that is, die, when some configuration of their subsystems fails. Recall that it was such thinking that initially informed the Weibull mortality rate model. The implicit idea in these models is that there are good engineering reasons to expect that complex systems designed to last a specified length of time will not fail *en bloc* as soon as that time point is reached. So if natural selection has engineered organisms to survive and reproduce for about as long as the environment typically allows, senescent death is not expected to follow immediately. Several independently derived models of this type converge at predicting a deceleration and eventual leveling off of mortality (Vaupel, 1997; Wachter, 1999). Data compiled by Vaupel and Owens on mortality rates of automobiles (failure to reregister them) look remarkably similar to laboratory mortality curves of many invertebrate species.

None of the demographic or engineering models presented so far makes predictions about the absolute longevity or mortality rates of different populations or species. They do not, for instance, address why humans live longer than fruit flies or mice. For that type of prediction, more general theories must be pursued.

III. Theories of Aging

It is conceivable that no other field of
science is so littered with theories as the
field of biogerontology. Medvedev (1990),
for instance, was able to catalogue and
attempt to organize more than 300 theories of aging. Given the number of potential ways that organisms can deteriorate,
perhaps it is not surprising that each
research specialist might have a pet
theory, depending on the perspective of
his or her scientific specialty. However,
this does not mean that some order
cannot emerge from a seemingly chaotic
welter of theories. One useful approach to
categorizing aging theories is to sort them
by their level of explanation (Mayr, 1961).
What issue does each theory address?
One category of aging theory seeks to
answer the question of why the aging of
biological organisms exists at all and,
furthermore, why aging rate varies as it
does among species and populations.
Another distinct group of theories
addresses how, that is, by what mechanistic processes, aging proceeds. The
former category addresses "ultimate"
issues about aging, the latter "proximate"
issues. Each category will have subcate-
gories inevitably. An important point,
however, is that whereas specific research
findings may be relevant to the critical
evaluation of theories at either level, the
theories themselves only compete against
other theories addressing the same questions. Scientific theories need not, of
course, always be mutually exclusive, but
they must be, at least in principle, falsifiable. Moreover, the *power* of any theory
will be proportional to the breadth of the
phenomena it can explain.

A. Ultimate Theories

There seem to be three distinct categories
of "ultimate" theories of aging. The first
of these, will be called *thermodynamic
inevitability* theories. These theories are
nonevolutionary in the sense that they
posit, explicitly or implicitly, that aging
is inevitable—an inescapable consequence of the physical nature of matter
rather than the product of biological
evolution. Theories of this type make a
straightforward prediction that aging
should be universal among organisms,
and they are disproven in straightforward terms by the failure of bacteria,
amicronucleate ciliates, some other
protists, and at least some multicellular
eukaryotes to manifest aging changes
(Bell, 1988; Finch, 1990)

A particularly influential hypothesis of
this type was first advanced by Rubner
(1908), named (the "Rate of Living"
theory) generalized by Pearl (1928), and
elaborated by Sacher (1959). The idea,
in its most straightforward terms,
assumes that energy consumption limits
longevity. Therefore, implicitly, all organisms that consume energy will age. This
idea's mechanistic support comes from
the increasing consensus that the production of reactive oxygen species—
inevitable by-products of oxidative
metabolism—is causally involved in
aging (Sohal & Weindruch, 1996), and its
empirical support stems from the clear
and robust effect of altered metabolic rate
on longevity within species of poikilotherms. As many experiments have
confirmed, longevity in a population of
poikilotherms is inversely related to the
temperature at which they are maintained (Miquel *et al.*, 1976) or the amount
of physical activity they are allowed to
exhibit at a specific temperature (Trout &
Kaplan, 1970; Sohal & Donato, 1978).
Indeed, a current controversy among
biogerontologists using the nematode *C.
elegans* as a model system is how much
of the life extension found in an increasing number of single-gene mutants
discovered in that species is due to
anything more than a genetically reduced
metabolic rate (Van Voorheis & Ward,
1999; Vanfleteren & De Vreese, 1995). On

the other hand, that metabolic rate *can* affect aging rate is undeniable, but whether it *necessarily* does so is not. For instance, *Drosophila subobscura* maintained at high temperature early in adult life and then transferred to lower temperature later in life exhibited longevity statistically indistinguishable from flies maintained at the lower temperature throughout adult life (Clark & Maynard Smith, 1961). More recent work with *D. melanogaster* has shown that a brief exposure to elevated temperatures can actually slow aging rate for as long several weeks (Khazaeli *et al.*, 1997).

Additional evidence for the rate-of-aging theory has been adduced from multispecies analyses of the positive relationship between body size and maximum captive longevity combined with the negative relationship between body size and mass-specific basal metabolic rate, such that energy expended per gram per lifetime is approximately independent of body size in mammals and birds (e.g., Sacher, 1977; Calder, 1984). A weaker form of the same idea is that whereas mass-specific lifetime energy expenditure may vary considerably among large taxonomic groups such as birds or mammals, significant subgroups of eutherian mammals, for instance, have their aging rates constrained primarily by energetic expenditure (Cutler, 1978).

The rate-of-living theory in both its strong and weaker forms has been rejected by the following empirical evidence: (1) not all alterations in metabolic rate, even in invertebrates, alter longevity as expected (citations above); (2) environmental treatments such as chronically reduced energy intake dramatically affect aging rate in laboratory rodents without reducing whole animal mass-specific metabolic rate (McCarter *et al.*, 1985; Duffy *et al.*, 1989); (3) experimental enhancement of energy expenditure does not necessarily reduce longevity (Holloszy & Smith, 1986); and (4) detailed

analysis of species comparisons finds both major and minor exceptions to the body size, metabolic rate, and longevity relationships within both large and small taxonomic groups of birds and mammals (Finch, 1990; Austad & Fischer, 1991).

At least two types of theories exist that attribute aging to the workings of biological evolution. The first of these posits that aging is a process favored by evolution in the same sense that having acute senses or a functioning reproductive system is favored, because it is somehow beneficial to Darwinian fitness. It is difficult to see how physical deterioration can be beneficial to the fitness of individuals, except in special cases, so the argument implicitly is about populations or groups. "The elderly must die to create room and resources for the next generation. Without the turnover of generations, evolution will be unable to proceed" runs the logic. That is, it will be beneficial for this population or species if generational turnover exists. This idea at one time was widespread in biogerontology, but has fallen out of favor more recently because in most cases it is inconsistent with how modern biologists understand the workings of evolution. Evolution, as it is currently understood in most cases, favors traits that benefit the reproductive success of individuals rather than the success of groups, when a trait is favorable in an individual context and unfavorable in a group context (Williams, 1966).

In conjunction with this view of the evolution of aging arose the idea that aging might be programmed as part of a continuing ontogenetic program (Russell, 1987). Unfortunately, much of the debate over the idea of programmed aging devolved into disagreements concerning the definition of the word "programmed," rather than about more scientifically relevant issues (Rose, 1991). However, to the extent that "programmed" means something akin to development and morphogenesis, where natural selection has designed a genetic blueprint of stereotypical, sequential events leading to the formation of a highly functional adult, it is difficult to understand how the increasing disorganization of aging could be programmed in the same sense except in special circumstances. Development, even of genetically heterogeneous individuals of the same species in a range of environments, leads to approximately the same product—a functional adult. By contrast, aging, even of genetically identical individuals reared in environments as similar and controlled as possible, occurs in many different ways. The range of age at death is not much different from that among genetically heterogeneous individuals (Finch & Kirkwood, 2000), plus organs and tissues that have failed utterly in one individual will remain lesion-free in another (Lipman et al., 1999).

One of the special cases in which describing aging as a programmed event may be tenable is in semelparous organisms that die shortly after their first and only reproductive episode. Although uncommon among animals generally, this life history is probably more common than generally supposed. A nonexhaustive list of animals in which one or both sexes are semelparous would include many spiders, many octopus and squids, several lampreys and eels, Pacific salmon, and at least 10 species of small marsupials [reviewed in Finch (1990)]. In some species, such as the anadromous fish the American shad (*Alosa sapidissima*) and the dasyurid marsupial *Parantechinus apicalis*, individuals from some populations are semelparous, whereas those from other populations live to reproduce several times. In virtually all cases of semelparity in which the mechanism of death has been investigated, neuroendocrine changes seem to underlie the rapid deterioration following reproduction (Finch, 1990). For instance, in the shrewlike marsupial, *Antechinus*

stuartii, all males in a population die within about a 2-week period due to corticosteroid and, e.g. androgen-mediated immune system collapse (Bradley, 1980). However, it is not necessary to invoke natural selection at the level of the population or species to account for this phenomenon, nor is it clear that this sort of rapid deterioration and death is functionally similar to aging in a more typically gradual fashion.

An alternative evolutionary theory of aging, which has been supported by an avalanche of data from a variety of research paradigms, focuses on the age-related, gradual, and inevitable failure of natural selection to be able to mold traits with age-specific genetic effects (Medawar, 1952; Williams, 1957; Hamilton, 1966). The major insight behind this theory is that, because of the inevitability of death from stochastic environmental hazards such as predators, resource shortages, or infectious disease, progressively fewer animals will be alive at progressively later ages, irrespective of the existence of senescence. Consequently, young parents will be larger genetic contributors to succeeding generations than old parents. The logical consequence of this fact is that the later in life that genetic alleles with age-specific effects have their impact, the less contribution they will make to fitness, because it is less likely that individuals bearing those alleles will be alive for the effect to be manifested. The quantitative details of natural selection's waning power with age was derived by Hamilton (1966). Figure 5 shows the general pattern of this effect for a relatively high mortality human population of females from Taiwan in 1906 (life expectancy = 29.4 years) and a similar, but relatively low mortality, population from the United States in 1939–1941 (life expectancy = 63.1 years). In either case, natural selection has uniformly high power until the beginning of reproduction, after which it

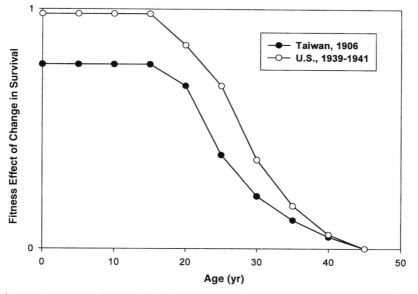

Figure 5. The waning power of natural selection estimated for two human populations. These estimates assume no post-reproductive contributions to fitness from "grandparent" effects. (Modified from Charlesworth, 1994).

declines toward zero as both fertility and survivorship decline.

According to this theory, senescence can evolve as a direct consequence of the ebbing power of natural selection via two potential genetic mechanisms: (1) mutation accumulation, or the passive genomic build up of alleles with deleterious effects expressed only late in life when such effects approach selective neutrality, regardless of their impact on physiological integrity (Medawar, 1952), and (2) antagonistic pleiotropy, or active selection favoring alleles with salubrious early life effects but pleiotropically harmful effects later in life (Williams, 1957). Such alleles are favored because the early benefits are under powerful selection, whereas the later deleterious effects are under weak selection. This latter genetic effect has been incarnated on the level of cellular energetic physiology as Kirkwood's (1977) "disposable soma" theory of aging, where cellular resources are subject to trade-offs between current versus future fitness.

Note that the two genetic mechanisms described earlier are not mutually exclusive and that they are theoretically *plausible*, not empirically observed, mechanisms. Current evidence much more strongly supports antagonistic pleiotropy than mutation accumulation (see below). It has been proposed that mechanisms of aging associated with mutation accumulation are likely to be "private," that is, idiosyncratic of certain lineages, populations, and species, because which allele frequency will be determined largely by random genetic drift. Mechanisms associated with antagonistic pleiotropy are more likely to be "public," that is, generally operational over a large range of organisms, presumably because there are a finite number of processes in which functions that are beneficial at one point in life become harmful later on and also because these alleles will be maintained by selection once they have arisen (Martin *et al.*, 1996).

This evolutionary theory of aging makes two clear and falsifiable predictions. First, for species, such as those that reproduce by binary fission, for which parent and offspring status cannot be assigned, there will be no population age structure, and therefore aging would not be expected to evolve. Williams (1957) originally cast this prediction in terms of the lack of distinction between a soma and germ plasm, but because age structure is apparent in some single-celled organisms such as budding yeast (*Saccharomyces cerevisiae*) that lack a soma–germ line distinction, the theory has been recast to more closely convey his meaning. As previously mentioned, prokaryotes, some (but not all) protozoa, and certain multicellular asexually reproducing invertebrates do not age (Bell, 1982, 1984; Finch, 1990). The difficulty with implementing Williams' prediction in all cases is some practical ambiguity about the determination of whether some single-celled organisms exhibit age structure, particularly the extent to which unequal cell division such as budding constitutes the existence of age structure. These definitional problems are discussed by Bell (1988) and Rose (1991).

Second, an easier prediction to evaluate empirically is that retardation of the rate at which the power of natural selection deteriorates with age will lead to the evolution of retarded aging rate. This may be done by reducing the environmentally induced death rate (Edney & Gill, 1968) or by making late life reproduction a larger component of fitness (Rose, 1991). A corollary of this prediction is that, to the extent that antagonistic pleiotropy is involved in the evolution of senescence, retardation of aging will be expected to reduce some component of early life fitness.

The most rigorous evaluation of this prediction has been from studies of laboratory evolution in *Drosophila* specifically designed for this purpose. All, if performed properly, have been successful at retarding aging and all have reported early life trade-offs, although the

nature of these trade-offs has ranged from a reduction in fecundity to an increase in development time to decreased larval survival or competitive ability (see Chapter 13 of this volume). In addition, the surprising variety of long-lived single-gene mutants discovered in laboratory populations of the nematode, *C. elegans*, has also been found to exhibit decrements in any of a number of components of early life fitness, such as ability to enter the larval dauer stage appropriately (Johnson, personal communication, 1999), retarded developmental rate, increased age at first reproduction, and reduced egg-laying rate (Van Voorheis & Ward, 1999). A recent study of direct competition between the long-lived *age-1* mutant and wild-type worms found that, under constant laboratory conditions, neither genotype eliminated the other. However, under conditions of fluctuating food availability, as is typical of natural populations, the wild type quickly predominated (Walker, *et al.*, 2000). Field research on two opossum populations from environments with ecological histories of differential environmental hazards were also found to exhibit retarded aging combined with reduced fecundity (Austad, 1993).

Relative susceptibility to environmental hazard also helps explain a number of otherwise puzzling trends in the comparative longevity among species. For instance, it may explain the general relationship between body size and longevity in eutherian mammals, why flying vertebrates, such as birds and bats, live much longer than expected for their body size (Austad & Fischer, 1991; Holmes & Austad, 1995), and why queens in highly protected eusocial insect colonies live so much longer than their closest solitary relatives (Keller & Genoud, 1997). Similar reasoning may explain the evolution of semelparity. Particularly in seasonally breeding organisms, if the odds of dying due to environmental hazards prior to the next breeding season are quite high, it may be evolutionarily advantageous to allocate somatic resources such that the current year's reproduction is maximized at the expense of somatic maintenance. This idea is, in principle, testable by assessing extrinsic mortality in different populations in species like American shad or the marsupial *Parantechinus apicalis*, which are semelparous in some populations and iteroparous in others.

The Medawar–Williams evolutionary theory of aging extracts coherence out of a welter of interspecies variation in aging rate and is also consistent with a large body of experimental evidence. Of the two potential genetic mechanisms of aging, antagonistic pleiotropy has received the most experimental support so far, with virtually any of the single genes found to be associated with increased longevity in *C. elegans* serving as specific examples. If, as hypothesized by Martin *et al.* (1996), the predominance of antagonistic pleiotropy suggests that there may be a manageable number of general processes modulating aging rates, then untangling the welter of hypothesized mechanisms of aging may turn out to be a more soluble problem than many researchers have supposed.

B. Proximate Mechanisms

Ideas about proximate mechanisms of aging account for the vast majority of theories in the field. Such a chaotic welter of theories arose mainly because of the complex phenomenology of the aging phenotype, but also because mechanistic theories are not necessarily competitive with one another. Many could be valid to some degree. Cross-linking of important macromolecules (Bjorksten, 1968; Kohn *et al.*, 1984; Cerami, *et al.*, 1987) may play a role in some aspects of aging, such as arterial stiffening. Somatic mutations in nuclear or mitochondrial DNA may influence other aspects of aging, such as loss of proliferative homeostasis in certain tissues or progressive muscle weakening. The challenge is to understand the relationship, if any, of such processes to one another. Mechanistic theories are judged not only by their empirical validity but by the breadth of phenomenology they can explain. For instance, the glucocorticoid cascade hypothesis of aging (Sapolsky, *et al.*, 1986) will not explain aging in organisms without glucocortioids as part of their stress response, and the replicative senescence model of aging (Norwood & Smith, 1985) is unlikely to yield insight into aging in largely postreplicative tissues like brain or in organisms composed primarily of postreplicative cells like flies and nematodes. However, because reviews of the mechanistic hypotheses and investigations of aging form the bulk of the remainder of this volume, such theories will be addressed here in only general terms.

Some mechanistic hypotheses, though no longer tenable, served a useful purpose in gerontological research. The metabolic rate hypothesis, though not valid itself, focused attention on how fuel usage might affect aging and clearly helped sire current work on how oxidative stress, that is, the imbalance between damage by reactive oxygen species and the prevention or repair of that damage, might affect aging—an idea that is not only still alive but looking more and more convincing as more data pour in (see Chapter 2). Similarly, the error–catastrophe (Orgel, 1963) and glucocorticoid cascade (Sapolsky *et al.*, 1986) hypotheses helped focus research in what are still promising research directions (see Chapters 3 and 11) even though the original hypotheses have been rejected.

A crucial issue in formulating research strategies into mechanisms of aging is whether aging rate is modulated by one, a few, or dozens and dozens of underlying mechanistic processes. If it is the latter, then many aging theories will likely be valid to varying degrees and the general process will resist full understanding. Biomedical modulation to any significant extent is unlikely (Hamilton, 1966). However, the evidence that aging is largely governed by one or a few primary processes is increasingly persuasive (Miller, 1999). In support of this view is the fact that a simple environmental manipulation such as caloric restriction can retard virtually all changes in the aging phenotype, at least in laboratory rodents (see Chapter 15). Also, single-gene mutations, which affect aging rate in model organisms from *C. elegans* to *Drosophila* (Lin *et al.*, 1998; Chapter 13) to mice (Brown-Borg *et al.*, 1996; Chapter 14) are now being discovered almost routinely. Furthermore, these genes seem to fall coherently into biochemical pathways involved in fuel utilization, stress resistance, and/or neuroendocrine regulation.

This is good news for researchers. As our ability to understand and manipulate genome increases, we will become capable of performing critical experiments to help us organize mechanistic aging hypotheses hierarchically, such that the direction of causation and interaction between the processes behind these theories become clear.

IV. Conclusions

Aging is easy to define and observe, but difficult to measure in individuals. Yet a critical goal in gerontological research is to develop methods of distinguishing individuals aging at different rates. In populations, demographic tools are now in hand to assess with exquisite subtlety the age-specific effects of different treatments or environments. Despite this, most demographic analyses of experimental populations implement less useful approaches, such as statistically comparing mean longevity or survivorship curves.

Over the past 15 years, experimental and comparative research has firmly validated a population–genetic approach to understanding the evolution of aging. A striking result of much of this empirical research is that retarded aging is generally purchased at the expense of one or more early life fitness benefits, as predicted by the postulated genetic mechanism of antagonistic pleiotropy. This is a heartening finding because it suggests that there is likely some manageably small number of primary processes underlying the aging phenotype and promises that we should eventually be able to identify and manipulate these processes by either genetic or pharmacological intervention.

As heartening as this finding is for the prospect of finally beginning to understand fundamental aging processes and for expectations of more rapid progress given our increasing knowledge of the genomes of model organisms and new techniques for analyzing and manipulating these genomes, it should be borne in mind that, due to antagonistic pleiotropy, all of the life-extending genes that have had their early life side effects investigated in detail have turned out to manifest such side effects. As we move toward the development of interventions in the aging process in the not-too-distant future, we must not forget this.

References

Albert, M. S. (1994). Cognition and aging, In W. R. Hazzard, E. L. Bierman, J. P. Blass, W. H. Ettinger, J. B. Halter Eds., *Principles of Geriatric Medicine and Gerontology*, 3rd Ed., (pp. 1013–1020), New York: McGraw-Hill, Inc.

Arking, R. (1998). *Biology of Aging*, 2nd ed., Sunderland, MA: Sinauer Associates, Inc.

Austad, S. N. (1993). Retarded aging rate in an insular population of opossums. *Journal of Zoology, 229,* 695–708.

Austad, S. N., & Fischer, K. E. (1991). Mammalian aging, metabolism, and ecology: evidence fro the bats and marsupials. *Journal of Gerontology: Biological Sciences, 46*, B47-B53.

Baker, G. T. III, & Sprott, R. L. (1988). Biomarkers of aging. *Experimental Gerontology, 23*, 223–239.

Bell, G. (1982). *The Masterpiece of Nature*, London: Croom Helm.

Bell, G. (1984). Evolutionary and nonevolutionary theories of senescence. *American Naturalist, 124*, 600–603.

Bell, G. (1988). *Sex and Death in Protozoa*, Chicago: University of Chicago Press.

Borkan, G. A., & Norris, A. H. (1980). Assessment of biological age using a profile of physical parameters. *Journals of Gerontology, 35*, 177–184.

Bradley, A. J. (1980). Stress and mortality in a small marsupial (*Antechinus stuartii*). *General and Comparative Endocrinology, 40*, 188–200.

Brown-Borg, H. M., Borg, K. E., Meliska, C. J., & Bartke, A. (1996). Dwarf mice and the aging process. *Nature, 384*, 33.

Calder, W. A., III. (1984). *Size, Function, and Life History*. Cambridge, MA: Harvard University Press.

Carey, J. R. (1999). Population study of mortality and longevity with Gompertzian analysis. In *Methods in Aging Research*. B. P. Yu, Ed., Boca Raton, FL: CRC Press.

Carey, J. R., Liedo, P., Orozco, D., & Vaupel, J. W. (1992). Slowing of mortlaity rates at older ages in large medfly cohorts. *Science, 258*, 457–460.

Cerami, A., Vlassara, H., & Brownlee, M. (1987). Glucose and aging. *Scientific American, 256*, 90–96.

Charlesworth, B. (1994). *Evolution in Age-Structured Populations*, 2nd Edn., Cambridge, UK: Cambridge University Press.

Costa, P. T., & McCrae, R. R. (1980). In S. G. Haynes & M. Feinlieb (Eds.), Functional age: A conceptual and empirical critique. *Proceedings of the Second Conference on the Epidemiology of Aging*, Washington, DC: NIH Publication No. 80–969.

Curtsinger, J. W., Fukui, H. H., Townsend, D. R., & Vaupel, J. W. (1992). Demography of genotypes: Failure of the limited life-span paradigm in *Drosophila melanogaster*. *Science, 258*, 460–463.

Cutler, R. G. (1978). Evolutionary biology of senescence. In: J. A. Behnke, C. E. Finch, & G. B. Moment, Eds., *The Biology of Aging*, New York: Plenum Press.

Duffy, P. H., Feuers, R. J., Leakey, J. A., Nakamura, K., Turturro, A., & Hart, R. W. (1989). Effect of chronic caloric restriction on physiological variables related to energy metabolism in the male Fischer 344 rat. *Mechanisms of Ageing and Development, 48*, 117–133.

Duhon, S. A., & Johnson, T. E. (1995). Movement as an index of vitality: Comparing wild type and the *age–1* mutant of *Caenorhabditis elegans*. *Journal of Gerontology A: Biological and Medical Sciences, 50*, B254–B261.

Edney, E. B., & Gill, R. W. (1968). Evolution of senescence and specific longevity. *Nature, 220*, 281–282.

Faber, J. F. (1982). *Life Tables for the United States: 1900–2050*, Actuarial Study No. 87, Social Security Administration Publication No. 11–11534. Washington, DC: U.S. Department of Health and Human Services.

Finch, C. E. (1990). *Longevity, Senescence, and the Genome*. Chicago: University of Chicago Press.

Finch, C. E., & Kirkwood, T. B. L. (2000). *Chance, Development, and Aging*. Oxford, UK: Oxford University Press.

Finch, C. E., & Pike, M. C. (1996). Maximum life span predictions from the Gompertz mortality model. *Journal of Gerontology: Biological Sciences, 51*, B183–B194.

Fries, J. F. (1980). Aging, natural death, and the compression of morbidity. *New England Journal of Medicine, 303*, 130–135.

Fukui, H. H., Ackert, L., & Curtsinger, J. W. (1996). Deceleration of age-specific mortality rates in chromosomal homozygotes and heterozygotes of *Drosophila melanogaster*. *Experimental Gerontology, 31*, 517–531.

Gavrilov, L. A., & Gavrilova, N. S. (1986). *The Biology of Life Span: A Quantitative Approach*. Chur, Switzerland: Harwood Academic Publishers.

Hamilton, W. D. (1966). The molding of senescence by natural selection. *Journal of Theoretical Biology, 12*, 12–45.

Heller, D. A., Ahern, F. M., Stout, J. T., & McClearn, G. E. (1998) Mortality and biomarkers of aging in heterogeneous stock (HS) mice. *Journal of Gerontology: Biological Science and Medical Science, 53A*, B217–B230.

Holloszy, J. O., Smith, E. K., Vining, M., & Adams, S. (1985). Effects of voluntary exercise on longevity of rats. *Journal of Applied Physiology, 59*, 826–831.

Holloszy, J. O., & Smith, E. K. (1986). Longevity of cold-exposed rats: A reevaluation of the "rate-of-living theory." *Journal of Applied Physiology, 61*, 1656–1660.

Holmes, D. J., & Austad, S. N. (1995). The evolution of avian senescence patterns: Implications for understanding primary aging processes. *American Zoologist, 35*, 307–317.

Iwasaki, K., Gleiser, C. A., Masoro, E. J., McMahan, C. A., Seo, E. J., & Yu, B. P. (1988). Influence of the restriction of individual dietary components on longevity and age-related diseases of Fischer rats: The fat component and the mineral component. *Journal of Gerontology, 43*, B13–B21.

Keller, L., & Genoud, M. (1997). Extraordinary lifespans in ants: A test of evolutionary theories of aging. *Nature, 389*, 958–960.

Khazaeli, A. A., Tatar, M., Pletcher, S. D., & Curtsinger, J. W. (1997). Heat-induced longevity extension in *Drosophila*. I. Heat treatment, mortality, and thermotolerance. *Journal of Gerontology: Biological Science and Medical Science 52A*, B48–B52.

Kirkwood, T. B. L. (1977). Evolution of aging. *Nature, 270*, 301–304.

Kohn, R. R., Cerami, A., & Monnier, V. M. (1984). Collagen aging *in vitro* by nonenzymatic glycosylation and browning. *Diabetes, 33*, 57–59.

Lee, E. T. (1992). *Statistical Methods for Survival Data Analysis*, New York: John Wiley & Sons.

Lin, Y. J., Seroude, L., & Benzer, S. (1998). Extended life-span and stress resistance in the *Drosophila* mutant *methusaleh*. *Science, 282*, 943–946.

Lipman, R. D., Dallal, G. E., & Bronson, R. T. (1999). Lesion biomarkers of aging in B6C3F1 hybrid mice. *Journals of Gerontology: Biological Sciences & Medical Sciences, 54A*, B466–B477.

Martin, G. M., Austad, S. N., & Johnson, T. E. (1996). Genetic analysis of ageing: Role of oxidative damage and environmental stresses. *Nature Genetics, 13*, 25–34.

Masoro, E. J. (1995). Aging: current concepts. In E. J. Masoro, (Ed.). *Aging, Handbook of Physiology*, Section 11. Oxford, UK: Oxford University Press.

Mayr, E. (1961). Cause and effect in biology. *Science, 134*, 1501–1506.

McCarter, R. J. (1990). Age-related changes in skeletal muscle function. *Aging, 2*, 27–38.

McCarter, R. J., Masoro, E. J., & Yu, B. P. (1985). Does food restriction retard aging by reducing the metabolic rate? *American Journal of Physiology, 248*, E488–E490.

Medawar, P. B. (1952). *An Unsolved Problem of Biology*, London: H. K. Lewis.

Medvedev, Z. A. (1990). An attempt at a rational classification of theories of ageing. *Biological Reviews, 60*, 375–398.

Miller, R. A. (1997). When will the biology of aging become useful? Future landmarks in biomedical gerontology. *Journal of the American Geriatrics Society, 45*, 1258-1267.

Miller, R. A. (1999). Kleemeier award lecture: Are there genes for aging? *Journal of Gerontology Series A: Biological Science and Medical Science, 54*, B297–B307.

Miquel, J., Lundgren, P. R., Bensch, K. G., & Atlan, H. (1976). Effects of temperature on the life span, vitality, and fine structure of *Drosophila melanogaster*. *Mechanisms of Ageing and Development, 5*, 347–370.

Norwood, T. H., & Smith, J. R. (1985). The cultured fibroblast-like cell as a model for the study of aging. In: C. E. Finch, & E. L. Schneider, (Eds.). *Handbook of the Biology of Aging*, 2nd ed., New York: Van Nostrand.

Pearl, R. (1928). *The Rate of Living*. New York: Knopf.

Pletcher, S. D. (1999). Model fitting and hypothesis testing for age-specific mortality data. *Journal of Evolutionary Biology, 12*, 430–444.

Promislow, D. E. L. (1991). Senescence in natural populations of mammals: A comparative study. *Evolution, 45*, 1869–1887.

Promislow, D. E. L. (1993). On size and survival: Progress and pitfalls in the allometry of life span. *Journal of Gerontology: Biological Sciences, 48,* B115-B123.

Reff, M. E., & Schneider, E. L., Eds. (1982). *Biological Markers of Aging,* NIH Publication 82–2221. Washington, DC: U.S. Department of Health and Human Services.

Rose, M. R. (1991). *Evolutionary Biology of Aging.* Oxford: Oxford University Press.

Rubner, M. (1908). *Das Problem der Lebensdauer.* Munich: Oldenbourg.

Russell, R. L. (1987). Evidence for and against the theory of developmentally programmed aging. In: H. R. Warner, R. N. Butler, R. L. Sprott, & E. L. Schneider, Eds. *Modern Biological Theories of Aging.* New York: Raven Press.

Sacher, G. A. (1959). Relation of lifespan to brain weight and body weight in mammals. *CIBA Foundation Colloquium on Aging, 5,* 115–133.

Sacher, G. A. (1977). Life table modification and life prolongation. In C.E. Finch & L. Hayflick (Eds). *Handbook of the Biology of Aging.* New York: Van Nostrand Reinhold.

Sapolsky, R. M., Krey, L. C., & McEwen, B. S. (1986). The neuroendocrinology of stress and aging: The glucocorticoid cascade hypothesis. *Endocrinological Reviews, 7,* 284–301.

Sell, D. R., Kleinman, N. R., & Monier, V. M. (2000). Longitudinal determination of skin collagen glycation and glycoxidation rates predicts early death in C57BL/6NNIA mice. *FASEB Journal, 14,* 145–156.

Service, P. M. (1987). Physiological mechanisms of increased stress resistance in *Drosophila melanogaster* selected for postponed senescence. *Physiological Zoology 60,* 321–326.

Simms, H. S., & Berg, B. N. (1957). Longevity and the onset of lesions in male rats. *Journal of Gerontology, 12,* 244–252.

Sohal, R. S., & Donato, H. (1978). Effects of experimentally altered life span on the accumulation of fluorescent age pigment in the housefly, *Musca domestica. Experimental Gerontology, 13,* 335–341.

Sohal, R. S., & Weindruch, R. (1996). Oxidative stress, caloric restriction, and aging. *Science, 273,* 59–63.

Sprott, R. L. Biomarkers of aging. *Journal of Gerontology: Biological Sciences, 54A,* B464–B465.

Tatar, M., Carey, J. R., & Vaupel, J. W. (1993). Long-term cost of reproduction with and without accelerated senescence in *Callosobruchus maculatus*: Analysis of age- specific mortality. *Evolution, 47,* 1302–1312.

Trout, W. E., & Kaplan, W. D. (1970). A relation between longevity, metabolic rate, and activity of shaker mutants of *Drosophila melanogaster. Experimental Gerontology, 5,* 83–92.

United Nations. (1990). *Demographic Yearbook, 1988.* New York: United Nations, Department of International Economics and Social Affairs.

Vanfleteren, J. R., & De Vreese, A. (1995). The gerontogenes *age–1* and *daf- 2* determine metabolic rate potential in aging *Caenorhabditis elegans. FASEB Journal, 9,* 1355–1361.

Van Voorheis, W. A., & Ward, S. (1999). Genetic and environmental conditions that increase longevity in *Caenorhabditis elegans* decrease metabolic rate. *Proceedings of the National Academic of Science, USA, 96,* 11399–11403.

Vaupel, J. W., & Carey, J. R. (1993). Compositional explanations of medfly mortality. *Science, 260,* 1666–1667.

Vaupel, J. W., Carey, J. R., Christensen, K., Johnson, T. E., Yashin, A. I., Holm, N. V., Iachine, I. A., Kannisto, V., Khazaeli, A. A., Liedo, P., Longo, V. D., Zeng, Y., Manton, K.G., & Curtsinger, J. W. (1998). Biodemographic trajectories of longevity. *Science, 280,* 855–860.

Wachter, K. Evolutionary demographic models for mortality plateaus. *Proceedings of the National Academic of Sciences, USA., 96,* 10544–10547.

Walker, D. W., McColl, G., Jenkins, N. L., Harris, J., & Lithgow, G. J. (2000). Evolution of lifespan in *C. elegans. Nature, 405,* 296–297.

Weindruch, R. H., Walford, R. L., Fligiel, S., & Guthrie, D. (1986). The retardation of aging in mice by dietary restriction:

Longevity, cancer, immunity, and lifetime energy intake. *Journal of Nutrition, 116,* 641–654.

Williams, G. C. (1957). Pleiotropy, natural selection, and the evolution of senescence. *Evolution, 11,* 398–411.

Williams, G. C. (1966). *Adaptation and Natural Selection. A Critique of Some*

Current Evolutionary Thought. Princeton, NJ: Princeton University Press.

Yashin, A. I., Vaupel, J. W., & Iachine, I. A. (1994). A duality in aging: The equivalence of mortality models based on radically different concepts. *Mechanisms of Ageing and Development, 74,* 1–14.

Part Two

Cellular Processes Influencing Organismic Aging

Edited by
Judith Campisi

Two

Oxidative Processes in Aging

Tilman Grune and Kelvin J. A. Davies

I. The Oxygen Paradox

Oxygen is both necessary for aerobic life and yet highly dangerous to all living creatures: the Oxygen Paradox. An oxygen environment causes iron to rust, oils and meats to turn rancid, and vegetables to spoil. On the other hand, oxidation reactions make multicellular life possible due to the high efficiency of energy extraction from foodstuffs by mitochondrial oxidative phosphorylation. Life for all aerobic organisms is unavoidably associated with the formation of activated oxygen species, and various systems have evolved to permit their detoxification and to catalyze the removal or repair of oxidant-induced damage. Because reactive oxygen species are dangerous to cells and organisms, the effectiveness of antioxidants and of damage removal and repair systems is of vital importance. Constant exposure to oxidative stress as an unavoidable consequence of aerobic life and the activation of molecular oxygen during cellular metabolism make this one of the major factors influencing the fate of cells, tissues, organs, and people.

In a normally functioning physiological system, a balance exists between oxidant formation, antioxidant activity, and the various damage removal or repair mechanisms. During metabolism, a constant flux of free radicals and related oxidants is generated. The formation of free radicals has been described in a number of cellular subsystems, including mitochondria, microsomes, and peroxisomes. Additionally, isolated enzymes and certain enzymatic cascades can produce free radicals or oxidants: these include xanthine oxidase and the arachidonic acid degrading enzymes. On the other hand, the production of oxidant species is the normal function of certain cells, such as neutrophils and macrophages, and certain reactive oxygen and nitrogen species actually appear to be used as important mitogenic signals and/or second messengers (Davies, 1999). Because all of these processes continuously generate a flux of free radicals, most cells have to protect themselves from the damaging effects of these species. Primary antioxidant defense mechanisms evolved during evolution to scavenge many oxidizing species. Low-molecular-weight antioxidants like vitamins E and C, β-carotene, uric acid, and numerous other compounds act as free radical or oxidant scavenging substances. These scavengers are sacrificed (to oxidation) in order to protect vital cellular components. On the other hand, the superoxide dismutases, glutathione peroxidases, and catalases enable the cell to directly deactivate reactive oxygen species such as the superoxide radical and hydrogen peroxide. The glutathione/glutathione peroxidase system is also directed against the accumulation of organic hydroperoxides.

Although all of the primary antioxidant compounds and enzymes act very efficiently, oxidative modification of cellular structures and macromolecules still occurs. To prevent the accumulation of these, mostly non functional, oxidation products, cells developed a so-called secondary antioxidant defense system. This system is directed towards the repair and/or removal of damaged cellular components. The best characterized secondary antioxidant defenses are the DNA repair mechanisms. Other repair mechanisms, like protein repair enzymes and membrane repair pathways, also are known. On the other hand, several oxidatively modified macromolecules cannot be repaired. The bulk of oxidized proteins is actually degraded by an intracellular proteolytic system: the proteasome. A number of oxidation products formed exhibit various, mostly toxic, effects. Therefore, the accumulation of these secondary toxic oxidation products is prevented by enzymatic degradation, as shown for the degradation of lipid peroxidation products.

Cells are able to cope with a broad variety of oxidative stresses. On the other hand, one of the most fascinating properties of cells is their ability to adapt. A set of several dozen enzymes, including (but not limited to) both primary and secondary antioxidant defenses, is inducible. Adapted cells survive repeated low-dose exposures or acute oxidative stress much better than do naive cells.

It was postulated that radicals are one of the major factors responsible for the aging of cells. The "free radical theory of aging" was proposed 1956 by Denham Harman (1956). With increasing acceptance of the action of reactive oxygen species in many disease processes, the free radical theory of aging also has become further accepted and better developed (Beckman & Ames, 1998a,b; Harman, 1981; Pacifici & Davies, 1991). A number of investigations have demonstrated increasing formation of free radicals and other oxidants in aging biological systems (Desai et al., 1996a,b; Hagen et al., 1997; Muscari et al., 1990; Nohl et al., 1997; Shigenaga et al., 1994; Sohal & Sohal, 1991; Sohal et al., 1987). Increased formation of oxidants was also found in senescence-accelerated mice (Nakahara et al., 1998). In most of these studies, a leading role was suggested for mitochondria in the formation of oxidizing species (Sohal et al., 1990c). On the other hand, no consistent age-dependent changes in the functionality of antioxidant defenses were demonstrated (see Section VI). Therefore, the maximum life span of organisms often is negatively correlated with prooxidative capacity, but may not show any positive correlation with the activity of antioxidant defenses (Barja et al., 1994; Ku et al., 1993; Perez-Campo et al., 1998; Sohal & Brunk, 1992; Sohal et al., 1990b). It may also be that, because long-lived species have a relatively low oxidant producing activity, they only need a limited antioxidant defense and, therefore, the capacity of the antioxidant defenses in long-lived species is rather limited (Barja et al., 1994).

II. The Free Radical Theory of Aging

As previously mentioned, the "free radical theory of aging" was proposed in 1956 by Harman (1956). Since that time the theory has been revised and discussed many times (Beckman & Ames, 1998a,b; Harman 1981, 1988, 1991, 1992a,b, 1993; Pacifici & Davies, 1991). The idea proposed originally, that accumulating oxidative damage causes the senescence of cells and organisms (Ames & Shigenaga, 1992; Harman, 1956), is probably too simplistic because a multitude of other factors seem to be involved. Different (possibly causal) relationships seem to exist between oxidant production and maximum life span in mammals and insects (Fleming et al., 1992; Sohal & Orr, 1992). But in each case, mitochondria seem to play a major role (Fleming et al., 1982, 1992; Sohal & Orr, 1992; Yan & Sohal, 1998).

Beside the free radical theory of aging, several other radical-related or damage-accumulation-related theories of aging exist. The "network theory of aging" favors the enhanced accumulation of defective (oxidatively damaged?) mitochondria and increasing disturbance of cellular metabolism (Kirkwood & Kowald, 1997). The release of toxic quantities of nitric oxide due to recurrent infections over the life span is the basis of the "nitric oxide hypothesis of aging," which was proposed by McCann and co-workers (1998). All of these theories involve a change in cellular homeostasis, with a concomitant disruption in metabolism that would probably disturb both pro- and antioxidant processes (Martin et al., 1993). Because numerous questions about each of the various oxidation-based aging theories remain unanswered (Nohl, 1993), a great deal of work will have to be done in order to clarify the exact role of alterations in the equilibrium points of oxidation reactions and of antioxidant defenses during senescence.

III. Early Studies of Age-Related Oxidative Stress

It may be argued that studies on age-related oxidative stress actually began

with the discovery of age pigments by Hannover (1842). Hannover discovered the age pigments in human neuronal cells. An association between aging and the accumulation of this granulated pigment was proposed by Koneff (1886). In the 20th century, the accumulation of these pigments and their relationship to the aging process has been investigated intensively and controversially (Brizzee et al., 1974; Hammer & Braum, 1988; Hartroft & Porta, 1965; Tappel, 1975; Yin, 1996). Later this pigment was called lipofuscin. Age-related increases in tissue lipofuscin content were demonstrated in the 1970s by Strehler and co-workers (1959) in human myocardium and by Reichel et al., (1968) in rodent brain. Later, similar accumulations were demonstrated in flies (Miquel et al., 1974; Sheldal & Tappel, 1974; Sohal, 1973) and many other organisms. The effects of antioxidants on the formation of this pigment were investigated by Harman (1976) and by Harman and co-workers (1976a). This indicates the early understanding of the connection between pigment accumulation and oxidative processes. The similarities between the cross-linking effects of malonyldialdehyde on proteins and age-related changes were demonstrated in erythrocytes (Hochstein & Jain, 1981). After the discovery and description of the lipofuscin pigment, the investigation of oxidation reactions and of age-related changes in these oxidative processes largely focused on the effects of lipid peroxidation.

IV. Lipid Peroxidation and Cell Damage During Aging

Lipid peroxidation was one of the early oxidation processes investigated by many biochemists and cell physiologists. Many studies of lipid peroxidation during aging have produced contradictory results (Lippman, 1985; Rikans & Hornbrook, 1997; Sharma & Wadhwa, 1983). Both methodological difficulties and biological variability may have contributed to these apparent contradictions. Despite the fact that lipid peroxidation has been investigated for more than 40 years, no simple or readily standardized method exists to measure the absolute extent of lipid peroxidation. The most commonly used methods, such as the determination of malonyldialdehyde by thiobarbituric acid adduct formation, the measurements of conjugated dienes and various other peroxidation products are either nonspecific or highly complicated. Often other cellular components or oxidation products interfere with the method used. On the other hand, due to the aging process itself, cells or organs may change in composition. Similarly, the extracellular matrix and the cell-to-extracellular matrix ratio may change with age. Therefore, it is difficult to quantify lipid peroxidation in relation to number of cells, wet weight, protein amount, and so on. Different biological models may be a further reason for the contradictory results reported in age-related studies of lipid peroxidation. It was reported, for example, that birds have lower levels of polyunsaturated fatty acids— the substrates for a lipid peroxidation —in mitochondrial membranes than do mammals (Pamplona et al., 1996). Additionally, the content of hydroperoxides is species-dependent (Lippman, 1985).

A dramatic change in the membrane transition temperature of human (white matter) myelin was found in patients over the age of 50 (Chia et al., 1983), whereas no change in the transition temperature of rat cerebral microvessel membranes was found (Mooradian & Smith, 1992). An increase in lipid peroxidation in rat brain and liver homogenates (Sawada & Carlson, 1987) and in human plasma (Rodriguez-Martinez & Ruiz-Torres, 1992) was found. Because the brain is a rather complex organ with different metabolic changes in discrete regions,

several authors investigated lipid peroxidation in various brain regions. Zhang and co-workers (1994) found an age-dependent increase in the hydroperoxide level in the striatum of gerbils, but no parallel changes in the hippocampus or cortex. In contrast, Krisofikova and co-workers, (1995) found decreased levels of malonyldialdehyde in rat hippocampus. At the present time it is rather difficult to decide whether lipid peroxidation is an important component of normal aging.

The use of various oxidative stress challenge systems generally has produced more consistent results (than those mentioned previously) and has revealed, in most studies, an age-related increase in the oxidation of lipids following stress. For example, thiobarbituric acid reactive substances induced by diquat exposure were much higher in hepatocytes from old rats than from young controls (Rikans & Cai, 1992). Similarly, oxidative damage after reperfusion of cardiac tissue was higher in old rats than in young controls (Lucas & Szweda, 1998), and the accumulation of 4-hydroxynonenal-modified proteins after the administration of ferric nitriloacetate increased with the age of the rats (Iqbal et al., 1999). These changes can also occur as a result of age-related diseases, as shown by the more pronounced malonyldialdehyde formation in myocardium from spontaneously hypertensive rats in comparison to controls (Ito et al., 1992).

V. The Role of DNA Damage—Is Mitochondrial DNA Damage a Pacemaker of the Aging Process?

Genetic damage can be studied either by directly analyzing the DNA molecule or by investigating the amount of oxidatively modified bases excreted by an animal or human being. Both measurements will reflect aspects of the damaging effect of oxidants and the capacity of DNA repair mechanisms. The measurement of excreted oxidatively modified nucleosides and bases may be influenced further by the oxidation of low-molecular-weight compounds and by the ingestion of modified food components. Nevertheless, a correlation was found between the metabolic rate and the excretion of thymine and thymidine glycol and, therefore, an inverse correlation with the maximum life span (Adelman et al., 1988). More than 20 adducts were found from oxidized DNA (Ames, 1989), of which 8-hydroxydeoxyguanosine is one of the most intensively investigated. In particular, 8-hydroxydeoxyguanosine was found to be increased in mitochondrial DNA in comparison with the nuclear DNA, although both appear to accumulate with aging (Ames, 1989; Hayakawa et al., 1992, 1993). An especially high accumulation of 8-hydroxydeoxyguanosine was demonstrated in aging mitochondrial DNA (Ames, 1989; de la Ascunion Millan et al., 1996; Gupta et al., 1990; Hayakawa et al., 1992). The original estimates of 8-hydroxydeoxyguanosine in mitochondria appear to have been rather high due to technical difficulties (as discussed in more detail in Chapter 5 of this volume). Nevertheless, the concept that mitochondrial 8-hydroxydeoxyguanosine production or accumulation is higher than that seen in the nucleus does appear to hold true. This age-related increase in 8-hydroxydeoxyguanosine accumulation is tissue-specific (Sai et al., 1992). It was demonstrated that the age-dependent accumulation of 8-hydroxydeoxyguanosine was accompanied by increasing numbers of mitochondrial DNA deletions (Arnheim & Cotopassi, 1992; Fahn et al., 1996; Hayakawa et al., 1992, 1993). Senescence-accelerated mice also show these same changes at much younger chronological ages (Fujibayashi et al., 1998). The accumulation of various mitochondrial DNA deletions seems to be much more dramatic than the accumulation of oxidatively modified bases

(Arnheim & Cortopassi, 1992; Hayakawa et al., 1992) and also seems to be tissue-specific (Arnheim & Cortopassi, 1992; Kovalenko et al., 1998). A peak of mitochondrial DNA deletion levels was shown to occur in middle age in mice (Muscari et al., 1996). The rearrangement of mitochondrial DNA does not seem to be random, but 128 break points of human mitochondrial DNA have been described, with some regions acting as "hot spots" for DNA deletions (Hou & Wei, 1996). More than a dozen DNA deletions have been described in humans, with the 4977-bp deletion being the most abundant one (Wei, 1992; Wei et al., 1996). Several authors described an age-dependent fragmentation of mitochondrial DNA (Hayakawa et al., 1996; Higami et al., 1994a) measured by the migration of DNA in an electric field.

Obviously the DNA rearrangement, including various deletions, may produce a wide series of different metabolic effects due to compromised mitochondrial functions. A further problem may be a vicious cycle of enhanced production of oxidizing species, produced by compromised mitochondria, which may further accelerate the aging process (Cutler, 1992; Lu et al., 1999; Tengan et al., 1997; Wei, 1998; Wei et al., 1998). It has been proposed that these processes do not occur equally in all cells of a tissue, but that different subpopulations of cells may be more or less vulnerable to oxidative DNA damage (Higami et al., 1994b). The incidence of mitochondrial DNA alterations generally is much more pronounced in postmitotic tissues than in mitotic tissues; this issue is discussed in detail in Chapter 5 of this volume.

VI. Investigations of Age-Related Changes in Antioxidant Defenses

Most of the primary antioxidant defense systems have been investigated intensively in various aging models. The results of these investigations often have been quite confusing for both scientists and lay people to interpret. A series of studies was performed to investigate aging effects on the plasma and cellular concentrations of various low-molecular-weight antioxidants. It was found that vitamin E follows a biphasic concentration curve, with maximal concentrations occurring around the median life span for rats (Vericel et al., 1994). Similar results have been reported in studies of human plasma vitamin E levels (Vandewoude & Vandewoude, 1987). In contradiction to these results, the level of vitamin C in human plasma was reported to decrease gradually over time (Sasaki et al., 1983). Because high concentrations of vitamin C in people aged 65 or older are accompanied by a better memory performance (Perrig et al., 1997), these results are of some concern. On the other hand, the concentration of vitamins C and E in the serum does not always seem to reflect the actual tissue concentrations of these vitamins. In fact, an age-dependent decline in both vitamins C and E was reported to occur in the serum, but not in the liver, of rats (De & Darad, 1991). A decline in both antioxidants was also reported to occur in mouse epidermis (Lopez-Torres et al., 1994). The fact that rodents synthesize their own ascorbate, whereas humans require it as dietary vitamin C, may account for some (or many) of these differences.

Besides vitamins C and E, the concentration of a number of other antioxidants has been investigated during aging. Coenzyme Q (ubiquinone) was reported to show only slight age differences in brain mitochondria (Battino et al., 1995), but an age-dependent biphasic concentration curve was found in rat heart and kidney mitochondria (Beyer et al., 1985). Not all investigators view coenzyme Q as a true antioxidant, and the potential danger of coenzyme Q, due to its ability to act as a prooxidant in the mitochon-

dria, has been highlighted (Nohl et al., 1998). The hormone melatonin has been shown to have some antioxidant properties (although its tissue concentration may be too low for bulk antioxidant activity), and melatonin levels also undergo an age-related decline (Reiter, 1995a,b, 1998; Reiter et al., 1998). The potential loss of antioxidants and antioxidant capacity led several authors to conclude that antioxidant supplementation might actually be able to protect against certain age-related changes (Reiter, 1995a; Vina et al., 1992).

As discussed previously, low-molecular-weight antioxidants represent only a minor part of the antioxidant defense strategies of cells. Therefore, the vast majority of studies on age-related changes in pro- and antioxidant metabolism have investigated changes in the activities of the superoxide dismutases, catalases, and glutathione/glutathione peroxidase systems. The maximum life span potential of various mammalian species demonstrated a positive correlation with superoxide dismutase and catalase activities, a negative correlation with glutathione content, and a rather mixed pattern with glutathione peroxidase activity (Sohal et al., 1990b). On the other hand, the life span of erythrocytes of various mammals was found to correlate with their activities for superoxide dismutase and glutathione peroxidase and with their glutathione content (Kurata et al., 1993). The measurement of several parameters of antioxidant defense led Ito and co-workers (1998) to the conclusion that there is a significant age-related impairment of antioxidant defense mechanisms.

Several authors have also investigated age-related changes in antioxidant capacity in aging (or senescing) tissue cultures. In senescent WI-38 human lung fibroblasts, the catalase activity was elevated, whereas the glutathione peroxidase mRNA was decreased (Allen et al., 1999).

In apparent contradiction to these results, Caldini and co-workers (1998) found an increase in glutathione peroxidase in senescent MRC-5 cells, another human lung fibroblast cell line. The activities of both intracellular superoxide dismutases (the Cu/Zn and Mn superoxide dismutases) were found to be lower in primary cell lines established from fetal donors than from postnatal donors (Allen et al., 1995; Duncan et al., 1979). No effect of aging on the synthesis of superoxide dismutase was found in human T-cells (Grigolo et al., 1994) and/or erythrocytes (Stevens et al., 1975). Superoxide dismutase also did not show any age-related correlation in retinal pigment epithelium, whereas catalase was reported to decline with age (Liles et al., 1991).

Because human material for investigations often is very limited, the majority of studies have been performed with rodents. It was reported that catalase activity increases with age in mitochondria (Nohl et al., 1979), as does superoxide dismutase activity in rat skeletal muscle (Ji et al., 1990). Several groups have reported an increase in glutathione peroxidase activity with age in tissues ranging from rat skeletal muscle (Ji et al., 1990), to rat diaphragm (Powers et al., 1992), to mouse epidermis (Lopez-Torres et al., 1994) and brain (Hussain et al., 1995). On the other hand, glutathione peroxidase activity was unchanged in mitochondria (Nohl et al., 1979), rat lung (Perez et al., 1991), and liver and kidney (Barja de Quiroga et al., 1990). The same lack of age-related change was reported for glutathione reductase activity in rat lung and mouse epidermis (Perez et al., 1991; Lopez-Torres et al., 1994). No age-related changes were found for superoxide dismutase activities in rat liver, kidney, and serum (Barja de Quiroga et al., 1990; De & Darad, 1991), mitochondria (Nohl et al., 1979), and mouse epidermis (Lopez-Torres et al., 1994). Catalase activity also was unchanged in mouse epidermis and brain

(Hussain et al., 1995; Lopez-Torres et al., 1994), and rat lung, liver, and serum (De & Darad, 1991; Perez et al., 1991). In contradiction to these studies, an age-related decline in the activities of catalase in mouse and rat brains has been reported (Ghatak & Ho, 1996; Mo et al., 1995; Semsei et al., 1991). The same organs also were reported to exhibit diminished superoxide dismutase activities (de Haan et al., 1992; Mo et al., 1995; Semsei et al., 1991). Enzymatic components of the glutathione system in rat and mouse brains were reported to decrease during aging (Ghatak & Ho, 1996; Mo et al., 1995). There are also reports that the glutathione content of aged mouse lung and rat serum and liver is decreased (De & Darad, 1991; Teramoto et al., 1994). A decrease in glutathione concentration was demonstrated in senescence-accelerated mice (Liu & Mori, 1993).

Several authors have reported a mixed pattern of changes in antioxidant defenses (Ciriolo et al., 1991; Sohal et al., 1990a) or biphasic age-dependent activity profiles for superoxide dismutase, catalase, and glutathione peroxidase in rat cerebellum and hepatocytes (Sahoo & Chainy, 1997; Sanz et al., 1997). A constant ratio of hydrogen peroxide producing activity by superoxide dismutase to the hydrogen peroxide detoxification activities of catalase and glutathione peroxidase was reported in rat liver and kidney during aging (de Haan et al., 1995).

Despite the sometimes contradictory results presented earlier and the great variety of tissues investigated, it was concluded nevertheless that an age-dependent decline in antioxidant enzymes activities occurs in most rat tissues (Tian et al., 1998), and the same seems to be true for the glutathione content (Sastre et al., 1992). This decline appears to be especially dramatic in postmitotic tissues such as the brain.

If aging is associated with a decline in the effectiveness of antioxidant enzymes, it would be of great interest to test whether improved antioxidant capacity could delay aging. So far it has been reported that high activities of catalase (Orr & Sohal, 1992) and overexpression of superoxide dismutase (Orr & Sohal, 1993) do not affect the life spans of flies. On the other hand, transgenic flies with simultaneous overexpression of both Cu/Zn superoxide dismutase and catalase have a 30% extension in life span (Orr & Sohal, 1994). Somewhat in contrast with these results, Sun and Tower (1999) found that even overexpression of superoxide dismutase alone increased life span and that catalase overexpression had no additional effect, probably due to a preexisting excess of catalase. The differences between the results of Orr and Sohal (1994) and those of Sun and Tower (1999) may have a great deal to do with technical innovations that have occurred since the Orr and Sohal (1994) study. Whatever the reason(s) for the differences between these two important studies were, both clearly make the point that overexpression of at least one antioxidant enzyme can actually increase life span in *Drosophila*. Interestingly, Phillips *et al.* (1989) previously found that superoxide dismutase null mutations in *Drosophila* decreased life span. We are unaware of any mammalian antioxidant enzyme transgenic overexpression studies reporting an increased life span.

VII. Accumulation of Oxidized Proteins during Aging

A. Protein Oxidation

The oxidation of peptides and proteins, as well as the oxidation of free amino acids, has been studied by many laboratories (Davies, 1987; Davies & Delsignore, 1987; Davies *et al.*, 1987a,b; Dean *et al.*, 1997; Heinecke *et al.*, 1993; Stadtman, 1993). Readers are also directed to Chapter 3 of this volume, which

discusses this subject in detail. The degree of protein damage caused by a given oxidative stress depends on many factors, including the nature and relative location of the oxidant or free radical source, the proximity of the radical or oxidant to a protein target, and the nature and concentrations of available antioxidant enzymes and compounds. A number of derivatized amino acid side chains have been described in proteins (Dean *et al.*, 1997; Giulivi & Davies, 1993, 1994; Heinecke *et al.*, 1993; Stadtman, 1993). Examples include the oxidation of leucine, which results in the formation of various hydroxyleucines, tryptophan oxidation to form *N*-formylkynurenine, histidine oxidation to form aspartate or asparagine, and methionine oxidation to methionine sulfoxide (Stadtman, 1993). Furthermore, tyrosine oxidation can form 3,4-dihydroxyphenylalanine (DOPA) or dityrosine (Giulivi & Davies 1993, 1994). In addition to the modification of amino acid side chains, oxidation reactions can mediate the fragmentation of polypeptide chains and both intra- and intermolecular cross-linking of peptides and proteins (Davies, 1987; Davies & Delsignore, 1987; Davies *et al.*, 1987a,b; Stadtman, 1993; Dean *et al.*, 1997; Grune *et al.*, 1997).

A large body of literature exists on the measurement of protein oxidation during aging in different models. Most of these studies measured the formation of protein-bound carbonyls (Agarwal & Sohal, 1993; Agarwal & Sohal, 1996; Aksenova *et al.*, 1998; Banaclocha *et al.*, 1997; Bradley *et al.*, 1975; Butterfield *et al.*, 1997; Carney *et al.*, 1991; Chao *et al.*, 1997; Cini & Moretti, 1995; de la Cruz *et al.*, 1996; Dubey *et al.*, 1995, Dubey 1996; Forster *et al.*, 1996; Martinez *et al.*, 1996; Smith *et al.*, 1991; Sohal & Dubey, 1994; Sohal *et al.*, 1993, 1994, 1995; Stadtman *et al.*, 1992; Tian *et al.*, 1995; Youngman *et al.*, 1992), although this method has been seriously questioned (Cao & Cutler,

1995). Other authors suggested or used other amino acid modifications, including the tyrosine oxidation products dityrosine, o-tyrosine, and nitrotyrosine (Leuwenburgh et al., 1997, 1998; Meucci et al., 1991; Wells-Knecht et al., 1993, 1997), the formation of 5-hydroxy-2-aminovaleric acid (Ayala & Cutler, 1996), or the formation of methionine sulfoxide (Wells-Knecht et al., 1997). Changes in protein thiol content were taken as measures of age-related changes in protein structure (Agarwal & Sohal, 1994a,b). Additionally, measurements of changes in protein structure and aggregation have been used in attempts to demonstrate age-related changes in protein oxidation (Chao et al., 1997; Nakano et al., 1995; Porta et al., 1995; Yin, 1996).

It has been reported that protein carbonyl content increases with age in the brains of gerbils (Carney et al., 1991; Dubey et al., 1995), rats (Aksenova et al., 1998; Cini & Moretti, 1995; de la Cruz et al., 1996), mice (Dubey et al., 1996; Forster et al., 1996; Sohal et al., 1994), and humans (Smith et al., 1991). Other authors reported increased amounts of oxidized proteins in the liver, lens, lymphocytes, heart, skin, and skeletal muscles of various animal species (Agarwal & Sohal, 1996; Chao et al., 1997; Leuwenburgh et al., 1997; Sohal et al., 1994; Stadman et al., 1992; Tian et al., 1995; Wells-Knecht et al., 1993, 1997; Youngman et al., 1992). For various rodent and fly species, a correlation was found between life expectancy and protein oxidation (Agarwal & Sohal, 1996; Sohal et al., 1995).

A number of studies have investigated age-related changes in protein oxidation using flies (Agarwal & Sohal, 1993, 1994a,b; Sohal et al., 1993, 1994). Several authors emphasized the role of oxidative protein glycation and measured increased products from this process (Dunn et al., 1989; Hunt & Wolff, 1991; Wolff et al.,

1991). Because developments in the "free radical theory of aging" have emphasized the central role of mitochondria in oxidant generation, it is especially interesting to study age-related changes in mitochondrial protein oxidation. The level of oxidized proteins increases in fly muscle mitochondria (Agarwal & Sohal, 1995; Sohal & Dubey, 1994) and mice synaptic mitochondria (Martinez et al., 1996, 1997) during aging. It is interesting to note that the accumulation of oxidized proteins is not a completely random process, because certain oxidized proteins accumulate at higher rates than others during aging. Selective accumulation of oxidized high-molecular-weight (cross-linked) forms of certain mitochondrial proteins (Agarwal & Sohal, 1995), mitochondrial aconitase (Yan et al., 1997), mitochondrial adenine nucleotide translocase (Yan & Sohal, 1998), hemoglobin F (Advani et al., 1992), glyceraldehydr-3-phosphate dehydrogenase (Dulic & Gafni, 1987), and the cytosolic carbonic anhydrase III (Cabiscol & Levine, 1995), has been reported. Whether this accumulation is due to increased targeting of these proteins to oxidation, the result of a decline in the degradation of oxidized proteins, or a selective inability to degrade these particular oxidized proteins remains to be determined.

Decreases in the activity of numerous enzymes during aging have been described in various models. Such enzymes include glutamine synthetase (Agarwal & Sohal, 1993; Aksenova et al., 1998; Butterfield et al., 1997; Carney et al., 1991; Smith et al., 1991; Stadman et al., 1992), glucose-6-phosphate dehydrogenase (Stadman et al., 1992), tyrosine hydroxylase (de la Cruz et al., 1996), and various antioxidant defense enzymes (Beier et al., 1993; Gomi & Matsuo, 1998; Tian et al., 1998). An increase in ferritin was reported to be able to prevent the accumulation of free iron (Rikans et al., 1997). Because it remains unclear whether such changes in protein activity are the result of altered transcription, translation, or posttranslational modifications, the conclusions from these studies are rather limited.

It can be concluded from the studies reported here, performed in various models and using different methods, that oxidized proteins do accumulate to some extent in most organs and tissues during aging. Unfortunately, it is still unclear whether this is the result of increased oxidation of proteins or decreased repair and removal systems (or a combination of the two). Importantly, the accumulation of oxidized proteins seems to involve both a background random low level of oxidation and a specific oxidation of certain proteins.

B. Protein Oxidation and Removal of Oxidized Proteins

Mammalian cells contain major proteolytic systems, including the lysosomal cathepsins, the cytoskeletal calpains, and the 20S/26S proteasome system, which is located within the cytosol, nuclei, and endoplasmic reticulum of cells. It was demonstrated in a number of studies that the proteasome is able to recognize and selectively degrade oxidized proteins (Davies, 1987; Grune et al., 1995, 1996, 1997; Ullrich et al., 1999) and that this system is responsible for the degradation of most soluble intracellular proteins (Coux et al., 1996). Although it was demonstrated that the isolated "core" 20S proteasome is able to recognize and degrade oxidatively modified proteins, it is still unclear which role the core proteasome has in living cells (Coux et al., 1996; Grune et al., 1997; Shang & Taylor, 1995) because the proteasome activity in cells is dependent upon numerous regulator proteins (Coux et al., 1996), phosphorylation status (Mason et al., 1996), and subunit composition (Groettrup et al., 1996).

In in vitro systems it was shown that the surface hydrophobicity of oxidized proteins is the key factor in the recognition of proteasome substrates (Chao et al., 1997; Giulivi et al., 1994; Grune et al., 1998; Pacifici et al., 1993). With increasing oxidant modification of a substrate protein, degradation by the proteasome gradually increases. On the other hand, strongly oxidized proteins tend to aggregate and form covalent cross-links. These protein aggregates are poor proteasome substrates (Chao et al., 1997; Friguet et al., 1994; Friguet & Szweda, 1997; Giulivi et al., 1994; Grune et al., 1997, 1998; Pacifici et al., 1993). To prevent the formation of such protein aggregates, cells tend to degrade oxidized proteins rapidly. We were able to demonstrate enhanced protein degradation after oxidative stress in various cell lines (Grune et al., 1995, 1996; Sitte et al., 1998). This increase in protein turnover is accompanied by a decline in oxidized proteins, as demonstrated in MRC-5 fibroblasts (Sitte et al., 1998). On the other hand, cells do not have the ability to selectively degrade oxidized proteins without proteasome, as demonstrated by using antisense oligonucleotides directed against one of the essential proteasome subunits (Grune et al., 1995, 1996). Therefore, the removal of oxidized proteins seems to be one of the essential cellular functions of the proteasome.

Because the age-related accumulation of oxidized proteins may be the result of both increased protein oxidation and/or decreased protein breakdown, it is important to investigate the activity of intracellular proteolytic systems. This has proven to be difficult, because our knowledge about the function, regulation, and interaction of various proteolytic systems is still rather limited. Carney et al. (1991), Stadtman et al. (1992), and Starke-Reed and Oliver (1989) demonstrated that neutral alkaline protease activity (proteasome) declines in the brain and liver during aging. The decreased function of the major cytosolic proteolytic system has been discussed by various authors (Berlett & Stadtman, 1997; Grune et al., 1997). Some investigators reported no changes in proteasome activity during the aging of houseflies (Agarwal & Sohal, 1994a,b) or in livers of old rats (Sahakian et al., 1995). Because these experiments were performed under widely different conditions, it is difficult to directly compare or evaluate the results. On the other hand, investigations of proteolytic enzymes by using potentially natural substrates, such as oxidized proteins (Sahakian et al., 1995), may be a more reliable approach than the degradation of artificial fluorogenic peptide substrates, which are very common in proteolysis research today. The use of such artificial substrates was seriously questioned by Cao and Cutler (1995), although it can also be argued that the study of multiple fluorogenic peptide substrates can actually give the greatest insight into discrete changes in each of the catalytically active sites of the proteasome. In several such studies, it was reported that only the peptidyl glutamyl hydrolyzing activity of the proteasome was severely affected during aging (Anselmi et al., 1998; Conconi & Friguet, 1997; Conconi, et al., 1996). Although the trypsin-like activity also is oxidation-dependent, it seems to be protected during aging due to the interaction of the proteasome with HSP90 (Conconi & Friguet, 1997). In studies using an in vitro, "oxygen-accelerated," senescence model consisting of postmitotic human epithelial cells, we have found that proteasome activity is progressively inhibited by accumulating oxidized and cross-linked cellular proteins (Sitte et al., 2000). This result held true for both fluoropeptide substrates and oxidized proteins, although the peptidyl-glutamyl hydrolyzing activity certainly was the most affected of all proteasome properties studied.

The preceding investigations analyzed the activity of the 20S "core" proteasome, because it is assumed that this form of the proteasome is responsible for the degradation of oxidized proteins (Ullrich et al., 1999). On the other hand, we are unaware of any studies that have actually tested for a possible role for the ATP-stimulable 26S proteasome during aging, relative to the accumulation of oxidized proteins. Taylor and co-workers reported an elevation in ubiquitin–mRNA, high-molecular-weight ubiquitin aggregates, and an activation of the E1 and E2 ubiquitinylation enzymes in the livers of aged Emory mice (Mura et al., 1996; Scrofano et al., 1998). On the other hand, the same group also reported on the response of the ubiquitin system to oxidative stress in cultured lens cells (Shang & Taylor, 1995; Shang et al., 1997).

Although several studies have demonstrated that the proteasome is responsible for the degradation of the bulk of intracellular proteins (Coux et al., 1996), including oxidatively modified proteins (Chao et al., 1997; Grune et al., 1995, 1996, 1997, 1998), very little is known about the oxidation- and age-related changes of lysosomal proteolytic systems, which seem to remain constant (Benuck et al., 1992a,b; Porta et al., 1995). Other authors suggested an increase in cathepsin B, D, and E activities (Benuck et al., 1993; Sawada et al., 1993; Yamamoto et al., 1989).

C. Oxidized/Cross-Linked Proteins and AGE Pigment-Like Fluorophores

Besides the oxidation of amino acid side chains, the formation of protein aggregates also occurs during free radical reactions (Grune et al., 1997; Stadtman, 1993). A fairly broad spectrum of protein aggregates form not due to covalent cross-links but due to hydrophobic and electrostatic interactions (Davies, 1987; Grune et al., 1997; Stadtman, 1993; Sommerburg *et al.*, 1998). On the other hand, many covalent cross-links also are involved in protein aggregation. One of the most thoroughly investigated cross-links is the formation of a 2,2′-biphenyl cross-link by two tyrosyl radicals (Giulivi & Davies, 1993, 1994; Giulivi *et al.*, 1994; Heinecke *et al.*, 1993; Stadtman, 1993). The formation of S-S bonds due to free radical action also seems to be fairly common. In addition to those cross-links directly involving amino acids, numerous "natural" cross-linking reagents are formed as a result of oxidative stress. During the oxidation of lipids, for example, numerous lipid peroxidation products are formed, many of which can act as protein cross-linkers. Two of the most abundant lipid peroxidation products, malonyl-dialdehyde and 4-hydroxynonenal, have long been known as potent protein cross-linking reagents (Friguet *et al.*, 1994, 1997). Another group of potential protein cross-linking compounds are carbohydrates or oxidized carbohydrates, although these compounds have been less intensively investigated. One encouraging finding is an apparent reversal of cross-links formed by advanced glycation end products (AGEs) in canine myocardium by the experimental AGE cross-link breaker, phenyl-4, 5-dimethylthiazolium chloride (Asif *et al.*, 2000). Whether such thiazolium compounds may eventually lead to clinically useful drugs remains to be seen.

The final step in the process of protein cross-linking is the formation of an insoluble fluorescent material that can accumulate within cells. This material has been called various names by different authors, including lipofuscin, ceroid, or AGE pigment-like fluorophores, indicating the involvement of carbohydrates in final fluorophore formation (Yin, 1995, 1996). Several authors believe that all of these pigments have the same principal origin (Yin, 1996), although there might be tissue-specific, age-related, or disease-specific differences (Fearnley *et al.*, 1990; Hunt *et al.*, 1994; Jolly *et al.*, 1995; Katz *et al.*, 1994; Klikugawa *et al.*, 1995; Yin, 1996). The involvement of cross-linked protein oxidation products in lipofuscin was demonstrated by the immunohistochemical detection of dityrosine within the pigments (Kato *et al.*, 1998). It was shown by various authors that lipofuscin accumulates during aging in postmitotic cells (Brunk & Terman, 1998; Marzabadi *et al.*, 1992; Nakanq *et al.*, 1995). The involvement of free radicals as one of the initial steps in the formation of fluorescent oxidized/cross-linked aggregates was postulated (Aloj-Totaro *et al.*, 1986; Brunk *et al.*, 1992; Carpenter *et al.*, 1995; Nakano *et al.*, 1995; Yin, 1992; Sohal & Brunk, 1989; Zs.-Nagy *et al.*, 1995). The formation of AGE pigment-like fluorescent substances can be simulated *in vitro* by peroxidation of model membranes (Shimasaki *et al.*, 1984). The influence of vitamins E and C on lipofuscin formation was demonstrated by Blackett and Hall (1981) and Yin (1992). Additionally, the role of "catalytic iron" has been emphasized (Brunk & Terman, 1998; Zs. -Nagy *et al.*, 1995). Such catalytic iron might be released from autophagocytosed mitochondria, as postulated by Brunk and Terman (1998). Lipid peroxidation products also are involved in the cross-linking reactions of non-degraded material (Shimasaki *et al.*, 1995; Yin, 1995, 1996). Because large amounts of the fluorescent oxidized/cross-linked aggregates were found in lysosomes, age-dependent loss of lysosomal function, particularly the loss of lysosomal proteolytic capacities, has been proposed as a cause for lipofuscin formation (Brunk & Terman, 1998; Rattan, 1996; Terman, 1995). We have found that artificially generated lipofuscin-like or ceroid-like material, produced by extensive oxidation of mitochondrial proteins *in vitro*, is a very potent inhibitor of the proteasome and have proposed that lipofuscin/ceroid formation during aging may lead to progressive proteasome inactivation and further increases in lipofuscin/ceroid accumulation (Sitte *et al.*, 2000).

VIII. Adaptive Responses to Oxidative Stress and Regulation of Gene Expression

One of the most striking phenomena of the cellular response to oxidative stress is the process of adaptation. Very important early studies on transient adaptation to oxidative stress were performed by Spitz and co-workers (1987, 1990), and Laval (1988). After 4–6 hr of temporary growth arrest, many cells undergo further changes that can be characterized as transient adaptation to oxidative stress (Scheme 2). In mammalian fibroblasts, we (Crawford & Davies, 1997; Crawford *et al.*, 1994, 1996a–c, 1997; Leahy *et al.*, 1999; Wang *et al.*, 1996; Wiese *et al.*, 1995) and others (Laval, 1988; Spitz *et al.*, 1987) have studied maximal adaptation, which is seen approximately 18 hr after initial exposure to hydrogen peroxide, i.e., some 12–14 hr, after they exit temporary growth arrest. In bacteria such as *Escherichia Coli* and *Salmonella*, maximal adaptation is seen 20–30 min after oxidant exposure (Christman *et al.*, 1985; Crawford *et al.*, 1994; Demple & Halbrook, 1983), whereas yeast cells require some 45 min for maximal adaptation (Crawford *et al.*, 1994; Davies *et al.*, 1995).

In both prokaryotes and eukaryotes, transient adaptation to oxidative stress depends upon transcription and translation. A large number of genes undergo altered expression during the adaptive response. Some genes are up-regulated, some are down-regulated, and some are modulated early in the adaptation, whereas the expression of others is affected at later times. In mammalian fibroblasts, we observe three broad "waves" of altered gene expression during adaptation: one 0–4 hr following H_2O_2 exposure, one at 4–8 hr, and one at 8–12 hr. Inhibition of either transcription or translation during the adaptive response greatly limits the development of increased H_2O_2 resistance. If both transcription and translation are inhibited, little or no adaptation will occur. Therefore, the transient adaptive response to oxidative stress largely depends on altered gene expression, but also partly depends on increased translation of preexisting mRNAs. It further appears that message stabilization (for some mRNAs), increased message degradation (for other mRNAs), and altered precursor processing are all involved in altered translational responses (Crawford *et al.*, 1994, 1996a–c, 1997; Crawford & Davies, 1997; Davies, 1995; Davies *et al.*, 1995; Leahy *et al.*, 1999; Wang *et al.*, 1996; Wiese *et al.*, 1995).

Elegant studies in *E. coli* and *Salmonella* have shown that two particular regulons are responsible for many of the bacterial adaptive responses to oxidative stress: the oxyR regulon (Storz & Tartaglia, 1992) and the soxRS regulon (Greenberg *et al.*, 1990). In mammalian cells, no "master regulation molecules" have been found, but at least 40 gene products are involved in the adaptive response. Several of the mammalian adaptive genes are involved in antioxidant defenses, and others are damage removal or repair enzymes. Many classic shock or stress genes are involved very early in adaptive responses. As indicated in the preceding section, *gadd153*, *gadd45*, and *adapt15* play important roles in inducing temporary growth arrest, which is a very important early portion of the adaptive response to oxidative stress (Bartlett *et al.*, 1992; Crawford *et al.*, 1996a–c; Fornace *et al.*, 1989, 1992; Wiese *et al.*, 1995) The transcription factor, adapt66 (a *mafG* homologue) is probably responsible for inducing the expression of several other adaptive genes (Crawford *et al.*, 1996c). A number of other "adapt" genes has been discovered, but their functions are not yet clear. One of these genes is the calcium-dependent *adapt33* (Wang *et al.*, 1996) and another is *adapt73*, which appears to be homologous to a cardiogenic shock gene called *PigHep3* (Crawford & Davies, 1997). *adapt 78* has also been called *DSCR1* (Crawford *et al.*, 1997; Leahy *et al.*, 1999) and, in addition to its induction during oxidative stress adaptation, now appears to be involved in Down's syndrome, Parkinson's disease, and Alzheimer's disease.

Numerous other genes have been shown to be inducible in mammalian cell lines following exposure to the relatively mild level of hydrogen peroxide oxidative stress that we find will cause transient adaptation. These include the protooncogenes c-*fos* and c-*myc* (Crawford *et al.*, 1988), c-*jun*, *egr*, and JE (Muehlematter *et al.*, 1989; Nose *et al.*, 1991; Shibanuma *et al.*, 1988). Similar oncogene induction has also been reported following exposure to *t*-butyl hydroperoxide (Muehlematter *et al.*, 1989; Nose *et al.*, 1991). The induction of heme oxygenase by many oxidants, including mild peroxide stress, may have a strong protective effect, as proposed by Keyse and Tyrrell (1989). Other gene products that have been reported to be induced by relatively mild hydrogen peroxide stress in dividing mammalian cell cultures include the following: CL 100 phosphatase (Keyse & Emslie, 1992), interleukin-8 (DeForge *et al.*, 1993), catalase, glutathione peroxidase, and mitochondrial manganese superoxide dismutase (Shull *et al.*, 1991), natural killer-enhancing factor-B (Kim *et al.*, 1997), mitogen-activated protein kinase (Guyton *et al.*, 1996), and γ-glutamyl transpeptidase (Kugelman *et al.*, 1994). Relatively low levels of nitric oxide have also been shown to induce the expression of c-*jun* (Janssen *et al.*, 1997), c-*fos* (Janssen *et al.*, 1997; Morris, 1995),

and zif/268 (Morris, 1995). The list of oxidant-stress-inducible genes is much longer than the space limitations of this article will allow; apologies are extended to those investigators whose studies have not been cited here. It is, however, very important to note that many of the gene inductions reported in this paragraph have not actually been studied in an adaptive cell culture model. Thus, although many of the genes discussed in this paragraph appear to be excellent candidates for involvement in transient adaptation to oxidative stress, their actual importance remains to be tested.

Sohal (1988) reported that flies chronically exposed to hydrogen peroxide exhibited altered life spans. Interestingly, those flies exposed to a moderate concentration of hydrogen peroxide in their drinking water exhibited the longest life span, with no change in superoxide dismutase and catalase activities but associated with increased glutathione (GSH) levels. Several studies have been performed on adaptation and oxidative stress susceptibility in *in vitro* aging models. It has been reported that human fibroblasts in a replicative senescent stage showed increased susceptibility to oxidative stress (Yuan *et al.*, 1996). On the other hand, it was demonstrated that hydrogen peroxide is able to trigger senescence-like growth arrest in fibroblasts and, at higher concentrations, can cause apoptotic reactions (Bladier *et al.*, 1997; Davies, 1999; Gansauge *et al.*, 1997). Several of the adaptation-related regulatory factors like MAP kinases decline during the aging process (Guyton *et al.*, 1998).

Several studies have also been performed at an organismal level. For several strains of *Caenorhabditis elegans*, it was shown that longevity correlates with increased resistance to oxidative stress (Larsen, 1993). Hearts of old rats showed impairments in metabolic and functional tolerance to oxidative stress (Abete *et al.*, 1999). In senescent-accelerated mice, the induction of the heat-shock protein HSP70 and heme oxygenase-1 was found to be diminished (Nakanishi & Yasumoto, 1997). In apparent contradiction to these results, however, aged rats actually showed greater tolerance to hyperoxia, with delayed activation of various transcription factors (Choi et al., 1995). Furthermore, King and Tower (1999) have found a highly significant increase (up to 60-fold) in the expression of another heat-shock protein, HSP22, during normal aging in Drosophila.

In concluding this section, a note must be made of important studies involving permanent (or stable) oxidative stress resistance. Investigators have chronically exposed cell lines to various levels of oxidative stress over several generations and have selected for preexisting or mutant phenotypes that confer oxidative stress resistance. Several such studies have reported dramatic increases in catalase activity (relative to the parent population), such as the 20-fold higher levels reported by Spitz et al. (1990). Stable oxidative stress resistance may tell us a great deal about the importance of individual genes to overall cellular survival, and the value of such cell lines should not be underestimated. It should be clear, however, that transient adaptive responses in gene expression and stable stress resistance are quite different entities.

IX. Diminishing Oxidative Stress during Aging by Dietary Interventions

There are two major proposals to modify or prevent the age-related accumulation of oxidized materials. First, numerous antioxidants (both natural and synthetic) have been suggested as potentially effective dietary supplements to prevent the negative action of free radicals. Second, some investigators have felt it possible that restriction of the total dietary input

of calories and/or proteins might diminish the metabolic formation of free radicals.

Naturally occurring and synthetic antioxidants have been used in attempts to prevent age-related changes in antioxidant defenses. Possible prevention of age-related oxidative changes by the major lipophilic antioxidant vitamin E were proposed very early (Harman et al., 1976b). Later it was shown that vitamin E is able to prevent lipofuscin accumulation in mouse brain cells (Kan et al., 1991), lipid peroxidation in aged rat kidneys (Reckelhoff et al., 1998), and protein oxidation in brain cells and lymphocytes (Poulin et al., 1996). High doses of vitamin E seem to have an anti-immunosenescence effect in mice (Brohee & Neve, 1995) and protect blood vessels against vasoconstrictory changes during aging by an unknown mechanism (Guarnieri et al., 1996). Vitamin E also appears to stabilize various homeostatic functions in elderly individuals (Meydani, 1992).

In addition to vitamin E, "anti-aging effects" have been reported for vitamin C (Sharma et al., 1998). Lipoic acid (Hagen et al., 1999) has been reported to show beneficial effects on age-related changes in mitochondrial function; however, coenzyme Q apparently has no beneficial effect on life span or diminishing AGE pigment accumulation in rats (Lonnrot et al., 1995). Another potential antioxidant that exhibits anti-aging effects in some cases seems to be melatonin (Anisimov et al., 1997; Gonca-Akbulut et al., 1999), although it is not clear whether the proposed antioxidant properties of melatonin are as important as its role as a hormone.

In addition to classical antioxidants, a number of nutritional supplements have been reported to exert anti-aging properties. L-carnitine and acetyl-L-carnitine decrease the accumulation of single-strand breaks in DNA (Boerrigter et al., 1993). It was reported that acetyl-L-carnitine is even able to restore vital mito-chondrial functions (Hagen *et al.*, 1998a, b). The peptide carnosine also is reported to exhibit anti-aging properties (Hipkiss, 1998; Hipkiss *et al.*, 1998). L-Arginine is able to decrease the adverse accumulation of kidney collagen in aging mice (Lubec *et al.*, 1995), the sulfur-containing amino acid methionine increased life span in insects (Sharma *et al.*, 1995), and the amino acid derivative *n*-acetylcysteine improved the function of mitochondria (Miquel, *et al.*, 1995).

The substances discussed previously were all natural antioxidants or food supplements. Studies involving a number of synthetic antioxidants, such as the spin traps PBN and Tempol, have also been performed (Howard *et al.*, 1996). PBN was shown to reduce age-related oxidative damage in the central nervous system of gerbils (Carney & Floyd, 1991) and to improve the cognitive perfor-mance and survival of rats (Sack *et al.*, 1996). PBN is also able to reduce some age-related changes in senescence-accel-erated mice (Butterfield *et al.*, 1997; Edamatsu *et al.*, 1995). The age-associ-ated accumulation of protein carbonyls in rodents was prevented or reduced by PBN administration (Carney *et al.*, 1991; Dubey *et al.*, 1995; Stadtman, 1992; Stadtman *et al.*, 1992), as was the age-associated loss of glutamine synthase activity (Carney & Floyd, 1991; Stadtman *et al.*, 1992). There is not complete agreement on the effects of PBN, however, and whereas Stadtman *et al.* (1992) demonstrated a restoration of protease activity and decreased protein carbonyl accumulation after PBN treat-ment, Cao and Cutler (1995) found no such influence of PBN on either protein carbonyl content or protease activity. On the other hand, PBN does seem to be effective in protecting synaptosomal membrane proteins from oxidation, in senescence-accelerated mice (Butterfield *et al.*, 1997).

Other synthetic antioxidants have shown various degrees of promise as potential anti-aging supplements. For example, butylated hydroxytoluene is able to prolong the life span of *Drosophila* (Sharma & Wadhwa, 1983), 2-mercap-toethylamine enables WI-38 human fibroblasts to undergo more population doublings *in vitro* (Mori *et al.*, 1998), and thioproline improves the function of mouse lymphocytes (de la Fuente *et al.*, 1993). Several other substances with potential antioxidant properties have been studied (Carrillo *et al.*, 1994; Palmina *et al.*, 1979), including several plant prepartions like *Gingko biloba* extracts (EGb-761) (al Zuhair *et al.*, 1998; Sastre *et al.*, 1998), β-catechin (Kumari *et al.*, 1997), and various Asian herbs (Inada *et al.*, 1996; Ma *et al.*, 1997).

Various dietary regimes have been employed in attempts to reduce the meta-bolic production of free radicals. One such approach involves changing fatty acid intake to decrease the polyunsatu-rates available to undergo lipid peroxida-tion (Davis *et al.*, 1993; Eddy & Harman, 1977). The other major dietary approach is to reduce total caloric or protein intake, although it is not clear that dietary restriction can have any effect on metabolic rate or free radical production. Numerous studies have reported a stabi-lization of mitochondrial function and decreased generation of oxidants by mito-chondria due to overall caloric restriction (Desai *et al.*, 1996b; Feuers, 1998; Gabbita *et al.*, 1997; Kristal & Yu, 1998; Lass *et al.*, 1998; Sohal *et al.*, 1994). It has also been reported that dietary restriction can change the prooxidant–antioxidant balance to a lower value. The concentra-tion of lipid peroxidation products was reduced by caloric restriction (Chipalkatti *et al.*, 1983; Rao *et al.*, 1990), lipofuscin accumulation was diminished (Chipalkatti *et al.*, 1983; Rao *et al.*, 1990), and protein oxidation (as measured by dityrosine accumulation) was lower

(Leuwenburgh et al., 1997). Lower levels of protein carbonyls in diet-restricted animals (in comparison to controls) were found in rat livers, brains, and lymphocytes and in the hearts, brains, and kidneys of mice (Aksenova et al., 1998; Dubey et al., 1996; Sohal et al., 1994; Tian et al., 1995; Youngman et al., 1992). Additionally, a reduced accumulation of N-(carboxymethyl)lysine and pentosidine was demonstrated in the skin collagen of calorie-restricted rats (Cefalu et al., 1995), and lower levels of dityrosine were found in the hearts and skeletal muscles of calorie-restricted rodents (Aksenova et al., 1998). Dietary restriction also seems to prevent activation of the ubiquitinylation system in old mice (Mura et al., 1996; Scrofano et al., 1998) and to prevent the decline of the peptidyl glutamyl hydrolyzing activity of the proteasome (Anselmi et al., 1998). Additionally, the formation (or accumulation) of oxidatively modified DNA appears to be decreased by dietary restriction (Chung et al., 1992). Finally, tissue antioxidant enzyme activities may be significantly increased by dietary restriction (Dhahbi et al., 1998; Luhtala et al., 1994).

X. Future Developments

Numerous studies using both natural and synthetic nutritional supplements and dietary antioxidants as possible stabilizers for age-related changes are already underway, and even more studies are in the planning stages. Some of these investigations are large-scale population studies, whereas others are smaller, more mechanistic experiments. It appears highly likely that the next 10 years will see major advances in our understanding of the relationship between diet and age-related oxidative damage. It is also probable that we shall see many new (and hopefully effective) dietary supplements and dietary antioxidants, with both

derived from "natural" sources and synthetic products, in the marketplace.

The use of transgenic animals to study the importance of primary and secondary antioxidant enzymes, as well as the relative importance of various adaptive genes, will certainly increase over the next 10 years. As previously mentioned, some studies of transgenic animals have not shown significant effects on life span. For example, superoxide dismutase overexpression failed to affect life span (Seto et al., 1990), despite having at least some beneficial effect on diminishing protein and DNA oxidation (Cardozo-Pelaez et al., 1998). In contrast, other transgenic studies in Drosophila have reported clear life-extending effects of simultaneously co-overexpressing both superoxide dismutase and catalase (Orr & Sohal, 1994) or even overexpressing superoxide dismutase alone (Sun & Tower, 1999). In apparent agreement with the results of Sun and Tower (1999), Phillips et al. (1989) previously found that superoxide dismutase null mutations in Drosophila decreased life span. On the other hand, we are unaware of any transgenic studies in mammals that demonstrate increased life span with overexpression of either superoxide dismutase or catalase. Clearly transgenic studies in this area are still in their infancy, and we can certainly expect to see more sophisticated experiments in the future and, hopefully, better answers to basic questions.

The "status" of free radical reactions in general, and oxidation in particular, within the aging field has undergone a significant transformation during the past few years. Twenty years ago it would have been difficult to find a "serious" gerontologist who considered free radicals of importance to the aging process. Today it is not at all uncommon to hear respected scientists declare that the free radical theory of aging is the only aging theory to have stood the test of time. Research over the next several years hopefully will provide us with a quantitative estimate of the specific role(s) and extent of free radical involvement in aging.

Acknowledgments

The work of T.G. was supported by DFG and Stiftung "VerUm" and K.J.A.D. was generously supported by NIH/NIEHS Grant No. ES 03598 and NIH/NIA Grant No. AG 16256.

References

Abete, P., Napoli, C., Santoro, G., Ferrara, N., Tritto, I., Chiariello, M., Rengo, F., & Ambrosio, G. (1999). Age-related decrease in cardiac tolerance to oxidative stress. *Journal of Molecular and Cellular Cardiology, 31,* 227–236.

Adelman, R., Saul, R. L., & Ames, B. N. (1988). Oxidative damage to DNA: Relation to species metabolic rate and life span. *Proceedings of the National Academy of Sciences, USA, 85,* 2706–2708.

Advani, R., Mentzer, W., Andrews, D., & Schrier, S. (1992). Oxidation of hemoglobin F is associated with the aging process of neonatal red blood cells. *Pediatric Research, 32,* 165–168.

Agarwal, S., & Sohal, R. S. (1993). Relationship between aging and susceptibility to protein oxidative damage. *Biochemical and Biophysical Research Communications, 194,* 1203–1206.

Agarwal, S., & Sohal, R. S. (1994a). Aging and protein oxidative damage. *Mechanisms of Aging and Development, 75,* 11–19.

Agarwal, S., & Sohal, R. S. (1994b). Aging and proteolysis of oxidized proteins. *Archives of Biochemistry and Biophysics, 309,* 24–28.

Agarwal, S., & Sohal, R. S. (1995). Differential oxidative damage to mitochondrial proteins during aging. *Mechanisms of Aging and Development, 85,* 55–63.

Agarwal, S., & Sohal, R. S. (1996). Relationship between susceptibility to protein oxidation, aging, and maximum life span potential of different species. *Experimental Gerontology, 31/3,* 387–392.

Aksenova, M. V., Aksenova, M. Y., Carney, J. M., & Butterfield, D. A. (1998). Protein oxidation and enzyme activity decline in old brown Norway rats are reduced by dietary restriction. *Mechanisms of Aging and Development, 100,* 157–168.

Allen, R. G., Keogh, B. P., Gerhard, G. S., Pignolo, R., Horton, J., & Cristofalo, V. (1995). Expression and regulation of superoxide dismutase activity in human skin fibroblasts from donors of different ages. *Journal of Cell Physiology, 165,* 576–587.

Allen, R. G., Tresini, M., Keogh, B. P., Doggett, D. L., & Cristofalo, V. J. (1999). Differences in electron transport potential, antioxidant defenses, and oxidant generation in young and senescent fetal lung fibroblasts (WI-38). *Journal of Cell Physiology, 180,* 114–122.

Aloj-Totaro, E., Cuomo, V., & Pisanti, F. A. (1986). Influence of environmental stress on lipofuscin production. *Archives of Gerontology and Geriatrics, 5,* 343–349.

al Zuhair, H., Abd el Fattah, A., & el Sayed, M. I. (1998). The effect of meclofenoxate with *Ginkgo biloba* extract or zinc on lipid peroxide, some free radical scavengers and the cardiovascular system of aged rats. *Pharmacology Research, 38,* 65–72.

Ames, B. N. (1989). Endogenous DNA damage as related to cancer and aging. *Mutation Research, 214,* 41–46.

Ames, B. N., & Shigenaga, M. K. (1992). Oxidants are a major contributor to aging. *Annals of the New York Academy of Sciences, 663,* 85–96.

Anisimov, V. N., Mylnikov, S. V., Oparina, T. I., & Khavinson, V. K. (1997). Effect of melatonin and pineal peptide preparation epithalamin on life span and free radical oxidation in *Drosophila melanogaster*. *Mechanisms of Ageing and Development, 97,* 81–91.

Anselmi, B., Conconi, M., Veyrat-Durebex, C., Turlin, E., Biville, F., Alliot, J., & Friguet, B. (1998). Dietary self-selection can compensate an age-related decrease of rat liver 20S proteasome activity observed with standard diet. *Journal of Gerontology, 53,* B173–B179.

Arnheim, N., & Cortopassi, G. (1992). Deleterious mitochondrial DNA mutations accumulate in aging human tissues. *Mutation Research, 275*, 157–167.

Asif, M., Egan, J., Vasaqn, S., Jyothirmayi, G. N., Masurekar, M. R., Lopez, S., Williams, C., Torrez, R. L., Wagle, D., Ulrich, P., Cerami, A., Brines, M., & Regan, T. J. (2000) An advanced glycation end product cross-link breaker can reverse age-related increases in myocardial stiffness. *Proceedings of the National Academy of Sciences, USA, 97*, 2809–2813.

Ayala, A., & Cutler, R. G. (1996). The utilization of 5-hydroxyl-2-aminovaleric acid as a specific marker of oxidized arginine and proline residues in proteins. *Free Radical Biology & Medicine, 21*, 65–80.

Banaclocha, M., Hernandez, A. I., Martinez, N., & Ferrandiz, M. L. (1997). N-Acetylcysteine protects against age-related increase in oxidized proteins in mouse synaptic mitochondria. *Brain Research, 762*, 256–258.

Barja de Quiroga, G., Perez-Campo, R., & Lopez-Torres, M. (1990). Anti-oxidant defenses and peroxidation in liver and brain of aged rats. *Biochemical Journal, 272*, 247–250.

Barja, G., Cadenas, S., Rojas, C., Lopez-Torres, M., & Perez-Campo, R. (1994). A decrease of free radical production near critical targets as a cause of maximum longevity in animals. *Comparative Biochemistry and Physiolology, Biochemistry Molecular Biology, 108*, 501–512.

Bartlett, J. D., Luethy, J. D., Carlson, S. G., Sollott, S. J., & Holbrook, N. J. (1992) Calcium ionophore A23187 induces expression of the growth arrest and DNA damage inducible CCAAT/enhancer-binding protein (C/EBP)-related gene, gadd153. Ca^{2+} increases transcriptional activity and mRNA stability. *Journal of Biological Chemistry, 267*, 20465–20470.

Battino, M., Gorini, A., Villa, R. F., Genova, M. L., Bovina, C., Sassi, S., Littarru, G. P., & Lenaz, G. (1995). Coenzyme Q content in synaptic and non-synaptic mitochondria from different brain regions in the ageing rat. *Mechanisms of Ageing and Development, 78*, 173–187.

Beckman, K. B., & Ames, B. N. (1998a). Mitochondrial aging: Open questions. *Annals of the New York Academy of Sciences, 854*, 118–127.

Beckman, K. B., & Ames, B. N. (1998b). The free radical theory of aging matures. *Physiological Reviews, 78*, 547–581.

Beier, K., Völkl, A., & Fahimi, H. D. (1993). The impact of aging on enzyme proteins of rat liver peroxisomes: quantitative analysis by immunoblotting and immunoelectron microscopy. *Cell Pathology, 63*, 139–146.

Benuck, M., Banay-Schwartz, M., & Lajtha, A. (1992). Proteolytic activity is altered in brain tissue of rats upon chronic exposure to ozone. *Life Sciences, 52*, 877–881.

Benuck, M., Banay-Schwartz, M., & Lajtha, A. (1993). Proteolytic activity is altered in brain tissue of rats upon chronic exposure to ozone. *Life Sciences, 52*, 877–881.

Benuck, M., Banay-Schwartz, M., Ramacci, M. T., & Lajtha, A. (1992). Peroxidative stress effects on calpain activity in brain of young and adult rats. *Brain Research, 596*, 296–298.

Berlett, B. S., & Stadtman, E. R. (1997). Protein oxidation in aging, disease, and oxidative stress. *Journal of Biological Chemistry, 272*, 20313–20316.

Beyer, R. E., Burnett, B. A., Cartwright, K. J., Edington, D. W., Falzon, M. J., Kreitman, K. R., Kuhn, T. W., Ramp, B. J., Rhee, S. Y., & Rosenwasser, M. J. (1985). Tissue coenzyme Q (ubiquinone) and protein concentrations over the life span of the laboratory rat. *Mechanisms of Ageing and Development, 32*, 267–281.

Blackett, A. D., & Hall, D. A. (1981). Tissue vitamin E levels and lipofuscin accumulation with age in the mouse. *Journal of Gerontology, 36*, 529–533.

Bladier, C., Wolvetang, E. J., Hutchinson, P., de Haan, J. B., & Kola, I. (1997). Response of a primary human fibroblast cell line to H_2O_2: senescence-like growth arrest or apoptosis? *Cell Growth and Differentiation, 8*, 589–598.

Boerrigter, M. E., Franceschi, C., Arrigoni-Martelli, E., Wie, J. Y., & Vijg, J. (1993). The effect of L-carnitine and acetyl-L-carnitine on the disappearance of DNA single-strand breaks in human peripheral blood lymphocytes. *Carcinogenesis, 14*, 2131–2136.

Bradley, M. O., Dice, J. F., Hayflick, L., & Schimke, R. T. (1975). Protein alterations in aging W138 cells as determined by proteolytic susceptibility. *Experimental Cell Research, 96*, 103–112.

Brizzee K. R., Ordy, J. M., & Kaack, B. (1974) Early appearance and regional differences in intraneuronal and extraneuronal lipofuscin accumulation with age in the brain of a nonhuman primate (*Macaca mulatta*). *Journal of Gerontology, 29*, 366–381.

Brohee, D., & Neve, P. (1995). Effect of dietary high doses of vitamin E on the cell size of T and B lymphocyte subsets in young and old CBA mice. *Mechanisms of Ageing and Development, 85*, 147–159.

Brunk, U. T., & Terman, A. (1998). The mitochondrial–lysosomal axis theory of cellular aging. In E. Cadenas, L. Packer (Eds.), *Understanding the Process of Aging* (pp. 229–250). Basel, Switzerland: Marcel Dekker.

Brunk, U. T., Jones, C. B., & Sohal, R. S. (1992). A novel hypothesis of lipofuscinogenesis and cellular aging based on interactions between oxidative stress and autophagocytosis. *Mutation Research, 275*, 395–403.

Butterfield, D. A., Howard, B. J., Yatin, S., Allen, K. L., & Carney, J. (1997). Free radical oxidation of brain proteins in accelerated senescence and its modulation by *N-tert*-butyl-alpha-phenylnitrone. *Proceedings of the National Academy of Sciences, USA, 94*, 674–678.

Cabiscol, E., & Levine, R. L. (1995). Carbonic anhydrase III. *Journal of Biological Chemistry, 270*, 14742–14747.

Caldini, R., Chevanne, M., Mocali, A., Tombaccini, D., & Paoletti, F. (1998). Premature induction of aging in sublethally H_2O_2-treated young MRC5 fibroblasts correlates with increased glutathione peroxidase levels and resistance to DNA breakage. *Mechanisms of Ageing and Development, 105*, 137–150.

Cao, G., & Cutler, R. G. (1995). Protein oxidation and aging. I. Difficulties in measuring reactive protein carbonyls in tissues using 2,4-dinitrophenylhydrazine. *Archives of Biochemistry and Biophysics, 320*, 106–114.

Cao, G., & Cutler, R. G. (1996). Protein oxidation and aging. II. Difficulties in measuring alkaline protease activity in tissues using the fluorescamine procedure. *Archives of Biochemistry and Biophysics, 320*, 195–201.

Cardozo-Pelaez, F., Song, S., Parthasarathy, A., Epstein, C. J., & Sanchez-Ramos, J. (1998). Attenuation of age-dependent oxidative damage to DNA and protein in brainstem of Tg Cu/Zn SOD mice. *Neurobiology of Aging, 19*, 311–316.

Carney, J. M., & Floyd, R. A. (1991). Protection against oxidative damage to CNS by alpha-phenyl-*tert*-butylnitrone (PBN) and other spin-trapping agents: A novel series of nonlipid free radical scavengers. *Journal of Molecular Neurosciences, 3*, 47–57.

Carney, J. M., Starke-Reed, P. E., Oliver, C. N., Landum, R. W., Cheng, M. S., Wu, J. F., & Floyd, R. A. (1991). Reversal of age-related increase in brain protein oxidation, decrease in enzyme activity, and loss in temporal and spatial memory by chronic administration of the spin-trapping compound *N-tert*-butyl -α- phenylnitone. *Proceedings of the National Academy of Sciences, USA, 88*, 3633–3636.

Carpenter, K. L. H., van der Veen, C., Taylor, S. E., Hardwick, S. J., Clare, K., Hegyi, L., & Mitchinson, M. J. (1995). Macrophages, lipid oxidation, ceroid accumulation and alpha-tocopherol depletion in human atherosclerotic lesions. In K. Kitani, G. O. Ivy, H. Shimasaki (Eds.), *Lipofuscin and ceroid pigments* (pp. 53–64). Basel, Switzerland: S. Karger.

Carrillo, M. C., Kitani, K., Kanai, S., Sato, Y., Miyasaka, K., & Ivy, G. O. (1994). The effect of a long-term (6 months) treatment with (–)deprenyl on antioxidant enzyme activities in selective brain regions in old female Fischer 344 rats. *Biochemical Pharmacology, 47*, 1333–1338.

Cefalu, W. T., Bell-Farrow, A. D., Wang, Z. Q., Sonntag, W. E., Fu, M.-X., Baynes, J. W., & Thorpe, S. R. (1995). Caloric restriction decreases age-dependent accumulation of the glycoxidation products, N^{ε}-(carboxymethyl)lysine and pentosidine, in rat skin collagen. *Journal of Gerontology, 50*, B337–B341.

Chao, C.-C., Ma, Y.-S., & Stadtman, E. R. (1997). Modification of protein surface hydrophobicity and methionine oxidation by oxidative systems. *Proceedings of the*

National Academy of Science, USA, 94, 2969–2974.

Chia, L. S., Thompson, J. E., & Moscarello, M. A. (1983). Changes in lipid phase behaviour in human myelin during maturation and aging. Involvement of lipid peroxidation. *FEBS Letters, 157,* 155–158.

Chipalkatti, S., De, A. K., & Aiyar, A. S. (1983). Effect of diet restriction on some biochemical parameters related to aging in mice. *Journal of Nutrition, 113,* 944–950.

Choi, A. M., Sylvester, S., Otterbein, L., & Holbrook, N. J. (1995). Molecular responses to hyperoxia *in vivo:* Relationship to increased tolerance in aged rats. *American Journal of Respiratory Cell, and Molecular Biology, 13,* 74–82.

Christman, M. F., Morgan, R. W., Jacobson, F. S., & Ames, B. N. (1985) Positive control of a regulon for a defense against oxidative stress and heat-shock proteins in *Salmonella typhimurium. Cell, 41,* 753–762.

Chung, M. H., Kasai, H., Nishimura, S., & Yu, B. P. (1992). Protection of DNA damage by dietary restriction. *Free Radical Biology & Medicine, 12,* 523–525.

Cini, M., & Moretti, A. (1995). Studies on lipid peroxidation and protein oxidation in the aging brain. *Neurobiology of Aging, 16,* 53–57.

Ciriolo, M. R., Fiskin, K., De Martino, A., Corasaniti, M. T., Nistico, G., & Rotilio, G. (1991). Age-related changes in Cu,Zn superoxide dismutase, Se-dependent and -independent glutathione peroxidase and catalase activities in specific areas of rat brain. *Mechanisms of Ageing and Development, 61,* 287–297.

Conconi, M., & Friguet, B. (1997). Proteasome inactivation upon aging and on oxidation effect of HSP 90. *Molecular Biology Reports, 24,* 45–50.

Conconi, M., Szweda, L. I., Levine, R. L., Stadtman, E. R., & Friguet, B. (1996). Age-related decline of rat liver multicatalytic proteinase activity and protection from oxidative inactivation by heat-shock protein 90. *Archives of Biochemistry and Biophysics, 331,* 232–240.

Coux, O., Tanaka, K., & Goldberg, A. L. (1996). Structure and functions of the 20S and 26S proteasomes. *Annual Reviews of Biochemistry, 65,* 801–847.

Crawford, D. R. & Davies, K. J. A. (1997) Modulation of a cardiogenic shock inducible RNA by chemical stress: *adapt73*/PigHep3. *Surgery 121,* 581–587.

Crawford, D. R., Edbauer-Nechamen, C., Lowry, C. V., Salmon, S. L., Kim, Y. K., Davies, J. M. S., & Davies, K. J. A. (1994) Assessing gene expression during oxidative stress. *Methods in Enzymology: Oxygen Radicals in Biological Systems, Part D, 234,* 175–217.

Crawford, D. R., Leahy, K. P., Abramova, N., Lan, L., Wang, Y., & Davies, K. J. A. (1997) Hamster *adapt78,* mRNA is a Down Syndrome critical region homologue that is inducible by oxidative stress. *Archives of Biochemistry and Biophysics, 342,* 6–12.

Crawford, D. R., Leahy, K. P., Wang, Y., Schools, G. P., Kochheiser, J. C. & Davies, K. J. A. (1996c) Oxidative stress induces the levels of a *mafG* homolog in hamster HA–1 cells. *Free Radical Biology & Medicine, 21,* 521–525.

Crawford, D. R., Schools, G. P., & Davies, K. J. A. (1996b) Oxidant-inducible *adapt15* is associated with growth arrest and DNA damage-inducible *gadd153* and *gadd45. Archives of Biochemistry and Biophysics, 329,* 137–144.

Crawford, D. R., Schools, G. P., Salmon, S. L., & Davies, K. J. A. (1996a) Hydrogen peroxide induces the expression of *adapt15,* a novel RNA associated with polysomes in hamster HA–1 cells. *Archives of Biochemistry and Biophysics, 325,* 256–264.

Crawford, D., Zbinden, I., Amstad, P., & Cerutti, P. A. (1988) Oxidant stress induces the protooncogenes c-*fos* and c-*myc* in mouse epidermal cells. *Oncogene, 3,* 27–32.

Cutler, R. G. (1992). Genetic stability and oxidative stress: Common mechanisms in aging and cancer. *Experientia, 62,* 31–46.

Davies, K. J. A. (1987) Protein damage and degradation by oxygen radicals: I. General aspects. *Journal of Biological Chemistry, 262,* 9895–9901.

Davies, K. J. A. (1995) Oxidative Stress: The paradox of aerobic life. *Biochemical Society Symposium, 61,* 1–31.

Davies, K. J. A. (1999) The broad spectrum of responses to oxidants in proliferating cells: A new paradigm for oxidative stress. *IUBMB Life, 48,* 41–47.

Davies, K. J. A. & Delsignore, M. E. (1987) Protein damage and degradation by oxygen radicals: III. Modification of secondary and tertiary structure. *Journal of Biological Chemistry, 262,* 9908–9913.

Davies, K. J. A., Delsignore, M. E., & Lin, S. W. (1987) Protein damage and degradation by oxygen radicals: II. Modification of amino acids. *Journal of Biological Chemistry, 262,* 9902–9907.

Davies, K. J. A., Lin, S. W., & Pacifici, R. E. (1987c) Protein damage and degradation by oxygen radicals: IV. Degradation of denatured protein. *Journal of Biological Chemistry, 262,* 9914–9920.

Davies, J. M. S., Lowry, & and Davies, K. J. A. (1995) Transient adaptation to oxidative stress in yeast. *Archives of Biochemistry and Biophysics, 317,* 1–6.

Davis, L. J., Tadolini, B., Biagi, P. L., Walford, R., & Licastro, F. (1993). Effect of age and extent of dietary restriction on hepatic microsomal lipid peroxidation potential in mice. *Mechanisms of Ageing and Development, 72,* 155–163.

De, A. K., & Darad, R. (1991). Age-associated changes in antioxidants and antioxidant enzymes in rats. *Mechanisms of Ageing and Development, 59,* 123–128.

Dean, R. T., Fu, S., Stocker R., & Davies, M. (1997). Biochemistry and pathology of radical-mediated protein oxidation. *Biochemical Journal, 324,* 1–18.

DeForge, L. E., Preston, A. M., Takeuchi, E., Kenney, J., Boxer, L. A., & Remick, D. G. (1993) Regulation of interleukin 8 gene expression by oxidant stress. *Journal of Biological Chemistry, 268,* 25568–25576.

de Haan, J. B., Cristiano, F., Iannello, R. C., & Kola, I. (1995). Cu/Zn-superoxide dismutase and glutathione peroxidase during aging. *Biochemistry and Molecular Biology International, 35,* 1281–1297.

de Haan, J. B., Newman, J. D., & Kola, I. (1992). Cu/Zn superoxide dismutase mRNA and enzyme activity, and susceptibility to lipid peroxidation, increases with aging in murine brains. *Molecular Brain Research, 13,* 179–187.

de la Asuncion, J. G., Millan, A., Pla, R., Bruseghini, L., Esteras, A., Pallardo, F. V., Sastre, J., & Vina, J. (1996). Mitochondrial glutathione oxidation correlates with age-associated oxidative damage to mitochondrial DNA. *FASEB Journal, 10,* 333–338.

de la Cruz, C. P., Revilla, E., Venero J. L., Ayala, A., Cano, J., & Machado, A. (1996). Oxidative inactivation of tyrosine hydroxylase in substantia nigra of aged rat. *Free Radical Biology & Medicine, 20,* 53–61.

de la Fuente, M., Ferrandez, D., Munoz, F., de Juan, E., & Miquel, J. (1993). Stimulation by the antioxidant thioproline of the lymphocyte functions of old mice. *Mechanisms of Ageing and Development, 68,* 27–36.

Demple, B., & Halbrook, J. (1983) Inducible repair of oxidative DNA damage in *Escherichia coli. Nature, 304,* 466–468.

Desai, V. G., Feuers, R. J., Hart, R. W., & Ali, S. F. (1996). MPP(+)-induced neurotoxicity in mouse is age-dependent: Evidenced by the selective inhibition of complexes of electron transport. *Brain Research, 715,* 1–8.

Desai, V. G., Weindruch, R., Hart, R. W., & Feuers, R. J. (1996). Influences of age and dietary restriction on gastrocnemius electron transport system activities in mice. *Archives of Biochemistry and Biophysics, 333,* 145–151.

Dhahbi, J. M., Tillman, J. B., Cao, S., Mote, P. L., Walford, R. L., & Spindler, S. R. (1998). Caloric intake alters the efficiency of catalase mRNA translation in the liver of old female mice. *Journal of Gerontology 53,* B180–185.

Dubey, A., Forster, M. J., Lal, H., & Sohal, R. S. (1996). Effect of age and caloric intake on protein oxidation in different brain regions and on behavioral functions of the mouse. *Archives of Biochemistry and Biophysics, 333,* 189–197.

Dubey, A., Forster, M. J., & Sohal, R. S. (1995). Effect of the spin-trapping compound *N-tert*-butyl -α- phenylnitone on protein oxidation and life span. *Archives of Biochemistry and Biophysics, 324,* 249–254.

Dulic, V., & Gafni, A. (1987). Mechanism of aging of rat muscle glyceraldehyde-3-phosphate dehydrogenase studied by selective enzyme oxidation. *Mechanisms of Ageing and Development, 40,* 289–306.

Duncan, M. R., Dell'orco, R. T., & Kirk, K. D. (1979). Superoxide dismutase specific activities in cultured human diploid cells of various donor ages. *Journal of Cell Physiology, 98,* 437–441.

Dunn, J. A., Patrick, J. S., Thorpe, S. R., & Baynes, J. W. (1989). Oxidation of glycated proteins: Age-dependent accumulation of N^E-(carboxymethyl)lysine in lens proteins. *Biochemistry, 28,* 9464–9468.

Edamatsu, R., Mori, A., & Packer, L. (1995). The spin-trap N-tert-alpha-phenyl-butylnitrone prolongs the life span of the senescence accelerated mouse. *Biochemical and Biophysical Research Communications, 211,* 847–849.

Eddy, D. E., & Harman, D. (1977). Free radical theory of aging: Effect of age, sex and dietary precursors on rat-brain docosahexanoic acid. *Journal of the American Geriatrics Society, 25,* 220–229.

Fahn, H. J., Wang, L. S., Hsieh, R. H., Chang, S. C., Kao, S. H., Huang, M. H., & Wie, Y. H. (1996). Age-related 4,977 bp deletion in human lung mitochondrial DNA. *American Journal of Respiratory and Critical Care. Medicine, 154,* 1141–1145.

Fearnley, I. M., Walker, J. E., Martinus, R. D., Jolly, R. D., Kirkland, K. B., Shaw, G. J., & Palmer, D. N. (1990). The sequence of the major protein stored in ovine ceroid lipofuscinosis is identical with that of the dicyclohexylcarbodiimide-reactive proteolipid of mitochondrial ATP synthase. *Journal of Biochemistry, 268,* 751–758.

Feuers, R. J. (1998). The effects of dietary restriction on mitochondrial dysfunction in aging. *Annals of the New York Academy of Sciences, 854,* 192–201.

Fleming, J. E., Miquel, J., Cottrell, S. F., Yengoyan, L. S., & Economos, A. C. (1982). Is cell aging caused by respiration-dependent injury to the mitochondrial genome? *Gerontology, 28,* 44–53.

Fleming, J. E., Reveillaud, I., & Niedzwiecki, A. (1992). Role of oxidative stress in *Drosophila* aging. *Mutation Research, 275,* 267–279.

Fornace, A. J., Jr., Jackman, J., Hollander, M. C., Hoffman-Liebermann, B., & Liebermann, D. A. (1992) Genotoxic-stress-response genes and growth-arrest genes. *gadd, MyD,* and other genes induced by treatments eliciting growth arrest. *Annals of the New York Academy of Sciences, 663,* 139–153.

Fornace, A. J., Jr., Nebert, D. W., Hollander, M. C., Luethy, J. D., Papathanasiou, M., Fargnoli, J., & Holbrook, N. J. (1989) Mammalian genes coordinately regulated by growth arrest signals and DNA-damaging agents. *Molecular and Cellular Biology, 9,* 4196–4203.

Forster, M. J., Dubey, A., Dawson, K. M., Stutts, W. A., Lal, H., & Sohal, R. S. (1996). Age-related losses of cognitive function and motor skills in mice are associated with oxidative protein damage in the brain. *Proceedings of the National Academy of Sciences, USA, 93,* 4765–4769.

Friguet, B., & Szweda, L. I. (1997). Inhibition of the multicatalytic proteinase (proteasome) by 4-hydroxynonenal cross-linked protein. *FEBS Letters, 405,* 21–25.

Friguet, B., Stadtman, E. R., & Sweda, L. I. (1994). Modification of glucose–6-phosphate dehydrogenase by 4-hydroxynonenal. Formation of cross-linked protein that inhibits the multicatalytic protease. *Journal of Biological Chemistry, 269,* 21639–21643.

Fujibayashi, Y., Yamamoto, S., Waki, A., Konishi, J., & Yonekura, Y. (1998). Increased mitochondrial DNA deletion in the brain of SAMP8, a mouse model for spontaneous oxidative stress brain. *Neuroscience Letters, 254,* 109–112.

Gabbita, S. P., Butterfield, D. A., Hensley, K., Shaw, W., & Carney, J. M. (1997). Aging and caloric restriction affect mitochondrial respiration and lipid membrane status: An electron paramagnetic resonance investigation. *Free Radical Biology & Medicine, 23,* 191–201.

Gansauge, S., Gansauge, F., Gause, H., Poch, B., Schoenberg, M. H., & Beger, H. G. (1997). The induction of apoptosis in proliferating human fibroblasts by oxygen radicals is associated with a p53- and p21WAF1CIP1 induction. *FEBS Letters, 404,* 6–10.

Ghatak, S., & Ho, S. M. (1996). Age-related changes in the activities of antioxidant enzymes and lipid peroxidation status in ventral and dorsolateral prostate lobes of noble rats. *Biochemical and Biophysical Research Communications, 222,* 362–367.

Giulivi, C., & Davies, K. J. A. (1993) Dityrosine and tyrosine oxidation products are endogenous markers for the selective proteolysis of oxidatively modified red blood cell hemoglobin by the (19S) proteasome. *Journal of Biological Chemistry, 268*, 8752–8759.

Giulivi, C., & Davies, K. J. A. (1994) Dityrosine: A marker for oxidatively modified proteins and selective proteolysis. *Methods in Enzymology: Oxygen Radicals in Biological Systems, Part C, 233*, 363–371.

Giulivi, C., Pacifici, R. E., & Davies, K. J. A. (1994). Exposure of hydrophobic moieties promotes the selective degradation of hydrogen peroxide-modified hemoglobin by the multicatalytic proteinase complex, proteasome. *Archives of Biochemistry and Biophysics, 311*, 329–341.

Gomi, F., & Matsuo, M. (1998). Effects of aging and food restriction on the antioxidant enzyme activity of rat livers. *Journal of Gerontology, 53*, B161–167.

Gonca-Akbulut, K., Gonu, l.-B., & Akbulut, H. (1999). Differential effects of pharmacological doses of melatonin on malondialdehyde and glutathione levels in young and old rats. *Gerontology, 45*, 67–71.

Greenberg, J., Monach, P., Chou, J, Josephy, P. D., & Demple, B. (1990) Positive control of a global antioxidant defense regulon activated by superoxide-generating agents in *Escherichia coli. Proceedings of the National Academy of Sciences, USA, 87*, 6181–6185.

Grigolo, B., Borzi, R. M., Mariani, E., Monaco, M. C., Cattini, L., Porstmann, T., & Facchini, A. (1994). Intracellular Cu/Zn superoxide dismutase levels in T and non-T cells from normal aged subjects. *Mechanisms of Ageing and Development, 73*, 27–37.

Groettrup, M., Soza, A., Eggers, M., Kuehn, L., Dick, T. P., Schild, H., Rammensee, H.-G., Koszinowski, U. H., & Kloetzel, P. M. (1996). A role for the proteasome regulator PA28α in antigen presentation. *Nature, 381*, 166–168.

Grune, T., Blasig, I. E., Sitte, N., Roloff, B., Haseloff, R., & Davies, K. J. A. (1998). Peroxynitrite increases the degradation of aconitase and other cellular proteins by proteasome. *Journal of Biological Chemistry, 273*, 10857–10862.

Grune, T., Reinheckel, T., & Davies, K. J. A. (1996). Degradation of oxidized proteins in K562 human hematopoietic cells by proteasome. *Journal of Biological Chemistry, 271*, 15504–15509.

Grune, T., Reinheckel, T., & Davies, K. J. A. (1997). Degradation of oxidized proteins in mammalian cells. *FASEB Journal, 11*, 526–534.

Grune, T., Reinheckel, T., Joshi, M., & Davies, K. J. A. (1995). Protein degradation in cultured liver epithelial cells during oxidative stress. *Journal of Biological Chemistry, 270*, 2344–2351.

Guarnieri, C., Giordano, E., Muscari, C., Grossi, L., & Caldarera, C. M. (1996). Alpha-tocopherol pretreatment improves endothelium-dependent vasodilation in aortic strips of young and aging rats exposed to oxidative stress. *Molecular and Cellular Biochemistry, 157*, 223–228.

Gupta, K. P., van Golen, K. L., Randerath, E., & Randerath, K. (1990). Age-dependent covalent DNA alterations (I-compounds) in rat liver mitochondrial DNA. *Mutation Research, 237*, 17–27.

Guyton, K. Z., Gorospe, M., Wang, X., Mock, Y. D., Kokkonen, G. C., Liu, Y., Roth, G. S., & Holbrook, N. J. (1998). Age-related changes in activation of mitogen-activated protein kinase cascades by oxidative stress. *Journal of Investigative Dermatology Symposium Proceedings, 3*, 23–27.

Guyton, K. Z., Liu, Y., Gorospe, M., Xu, Q., & Holbrook, N. J. (1996) Activation of mitogen-activated protein kinase by H_2O_2. Role in cell survival following oxidant injury. *Journal of Biological Chemistry, 271*, 4138–4142.

Hagen, T. M., Ingersoll, R. T., Lykkesfeldt, J., Liu, J., Wehr, C. M., Vinarsky, V., Bartholomew, J. C., & Ames, A. B. (1999). (R)-alpha-lipoic acid-supplemented old rats have improved mitochondrial function, decreased oxidative damage, and increased metabolic rate. *FASEB Journal, 13*, 411–418.

Hagen, T. M., Ingersoll, R. T., Wehr, C. M., Lykkesfeldt, J., Vinarsky, V., Bartholomew, J. C., Song, M. H., & Ames, B. N. (1998). Acetyl-L-carnitine fed to old rats partially restores mitochondrial function and ambulatory activity. *Proceedings of the National Academy of Sciences, USA, 95*, 9562–9566.

Hagen, T. M., Wehr, C. M., & Ames, B. N. (1998). Mitochondrial decay in aging.

Reversal through supplementation of acetyl-L-carnitine and N-tert-butyl-alpha-phenyl-nitrone. *Annals of the New York Academy of Sciences, 854*, 214–223.

Hagen, T. M., Yowe, D. L., Bartholomew, J. C., Wehr, C. M., Do, K. L., Park, J. Y., & Ames, B. N. (1997). Mitochondrial decay in hepatocytes from old rats: membrane potential declines, heterogeneity and oxidants increase. *Proceedings of the National Academy of Sciences, USA, 94*, 3064–3069.

Hammer, C., & Braum, E. (1988) Quantification of age pigments (lipofuscin). *Comparative Biochemistry & Physiology B., 90*, 7–17.

Hannover, A. (1842) Mikroskopiske undersögelser af nervesystemet. *Kgl. Danske Videsk. Kabernes Selskobs Naturv. Math. Afh. (Copenhagen), 10*, 1–112.

Harman, D. (1956). Aging: A theory based on free radical and radiation chemistry. *Journal of Gerontology, 2*, 298–300.

Harman, D. (1976) The clinical gerontologist. *Journal of the American Geriatric Society, 24*, 452–453.

Harman, D. (1981). The aging process. *Proceedings of the National Academy of Sciences, USA, 78*, 7124–7128.

Harman, D. (1988). Free radicals in aging. *Molecular and Cellular Biochemistry, 84*, 155–161.

Harman, D. (1991). The aging process: major risk factor for disease and death. *Proceedings of the National Academy of Sciences, USA, 88*, 5360–5363.

Harman, D. (1992a). Free radical theory of aging. *Mutation Research, 275*, 257–266.

Harman, D. (1992b). Free radical theory of aging: History. *Experientia, 62*, 1–10.

Harman, D. (1993). Free radical involvement in aging. Pathophysiology and therapeutic implications. *Drugs and Aging, 3*, 60–80.

Harman, D., Eddy, D. E., & Noffsinger, J. (1976). Free radical theory of aging: Inhibition of amyloidosis in mice by antioxidants, possible mechanism. *Journal of the American Geriatric Society, 24*, 203–210.

Harman, D., Hendricks, S., Eddy, D. E., & Seibold, J. (1976). Free radical theory of aging: Effect of dietary fat on central nervous system function. *Journal of the American Geriatric Society, 24*, 301–307.

Hartroft, W. S., & Porta, E. A. (1965) Ceroid. *American Journal of Medical Sciences, 250*, 324–345.

Hayakawa, M., Hattori, K., Sugiyama, S., & Ozawa, T. (1992). Age-associated oxygen damage and mutations in mitochondrial DNA in human hearts. *Biochemical and Biophysical Research Communications, 189*, 979–985.

Hayakawa, M., Katsumata, K., Yoneda, M., Tanaka, M., Sugiyama, S., & Ozawa, T. (1996). Age-related extensive fragmentation of mitochondrial DNA into minicircles. *Biochemical and Biophysical Research Communications, 226*, 369–377. (Published erratum appears in *Biochemical and Biophysical Research Communications*, (1997), 232, 832).

Hayakawa, M., Sugiyama, S., Hattori, K., Takasawa, M., & Ozawa, T. (1993). Age-associated damage in mitochondrial DNA in human hearts. *Molecular and Cellular Biochemistry, 119*, 95–103.

Heinecke, J. W., Li, W., Daehnke, H. L., & Goldstein, J. A. (1993). Dityrosine, a specific marker of oxidation, is synthesized by the myeloperoxidase–hydrogen peroxide system of human neutrophiles and macrophages. *Journal of Biological Chemistry, 268*, 4069–4077.

Higami, Y., Shimokawa, I., Okimoto, T., & Ikeda, T. (1994a). An age-related increase in the basal level of DNA damage and DNA vulnerability to oxygen radicals in the individual hepatocytes of male F344 rats. *Mutation Research, 316*, 59–67.

Higami, Y., Shimokawa, I., Okimoto, T., & Ikeda, T. (1994b). Vulnerability to oxygen radicals is more important than impaired repair in hepatocytic deoxyribonucleic acid damage in aging. *Laboratory Investigation, 71*, 650–656.

Hipkiss, A. R. (1998). Carnosine, a protective, anti-ageing peptide? *International Journal of Biochemistry and Cell Biology, 30*, 863–868.

Hipkiss, A. R., Preston, J. E., Himsworth, D. T., Worthington, V. C., Keown, M., Michaelis, J., Lawrence, J., Mateen, A., Allende, L., Eagles, P. A., & Abbott, N. J. (1998). Pluripotent protective effects of carnosine, a naturally occurring dipeptide. *Annals of the New York Academy of Sciences, 854*, 37–53.

Hochstein, P., & Jain, S. K. (1981). Association of lipid peroxidation and polymerization of membrane proteins with erythrocyte aging. *Federation Proceedings, 40*, 183–188.

Hou, J. H., & Wei, Y. H. (1996). The unusual structures of the hot-regions flanking large-scale deletions in human mitochondrial DNA. *Biochemical Journal, 318*, 1065–1070.

Howard, B. J., Yatin, S., Hensley, K., Allen, K. L., Kelly, J. P., Carney, J., & Butterfield, D. A. (1996). Prevention of hyperoxia-induced alterations in synaptosomal membrane-associated proteins by N-tert-butyl-alpha-phenylnitrone and 4-hydroxy–2,2,6,6-tetramethylpiperidin–1-oxyl (Tempol). *Journal of Neurochemistry, 67*, 2045–2050.

Hunt, J. V., Bottoms, M. A., Clare, K., Skamarauskas, J. T., & Mitchinson, M. J. (1994). Glucose oxidation and low-density lipoprotein-induced macrophage ceroid accumulation: possible implications for diabetic atherosclerosis. *Journal of Biochemistry, 300*, 243–249.

Hunt, J. V., & Wolff, S. P. (1991). Oxidative glycation and free radical production: a causal mechanism of diabetic complications. *Free Radical Research Communications, 12–13 (Pt 1)*, 115–123.

Hussain, S., Slikker, W., Jr, & Ali, S. F. (1995). Age-related changes in antioxidant enzymes, superoxide dismutase, catalase, glutathione peroxidase and glutathione in different regions of mouse brain. *International Journal of Developmental Neuroscience, 13*, 811–817.

Inada, K., Yokoi, I., Kabuto, H., Habu, H., Mori, A., & Ogawa, N. (1996). Age-related increase in nitric oxide synthase activity in senescence accelerated mouse brain and the effect of long-term administration of superoxide radical scavenger. *Mechanisms of Ageing and Development, 89*, 95–102.

Iqbal, M., Giri, U., Giri, D. K., Alam, M. S., & Athar, M. (1999). Age-dependent renal accumulation of 4-hydroxy–2-nonenal (HNE)-modified proteins following parenteral administration of ferric nitrilotriacetate commensurate with its differential toxicity: Implications for the involvement of HNE-protein adducts in oxidative stress and carcinogenesis. *Archives of Biochemistry and Biophysics, 365*, 101–112.

Ito, Y., Kajkenova, O., Feuers, R. J., Udupa, K. B., Desai, V. G., Epstein, J., Hart, R. W., & Lipschitz, D. A. (1998). Impaired glutathione peroxidase activity accounts for the age-related accumulation of hydrogen peroxide in activated human neutrophils. *Journal of Gerontology A, 53*, M169–175.

Ito, H., Torii, M., & Suzuki, T. (1992). A comparative study on defense systems for lipid peroxidation by free radicals in spontaneously hypertensive and normotensive rat myocardium. *Comparative Biochemistry and Physiology B., 103*, 37–40.

Janssen, Y. M., Matalon, S., & Mossman, B. T., 1997, Differential induction of c-*fos*, c-*jun*, and apoptosis in lung epithelial cells exposed to ROS or RNS. *American Journal of Physiology, 273*, L789–L796.

Ji, L. L., Dillon, D., & Wu, E. (1990). Alteration of antioxidant enzymes with aging in rat skeletal muscle and liver. *American Journal of Physiology, 258(4 Pt 2)*, R918–923.

Jolly, R. D., Douglas, B. V., Davey, P. M., & Roiri, J. E. (1995). Lipofuscin in bovine muscle and brain: a model for studying age pigment. In K. Kitani, G. O. Ivy, H., & Shimasaki (Eds.), *Lipofuscin and Ceroid Pigments* (pp. 283–293). Basel, Switzerland: S. Karger.

Kan, S., Devi, S. A., & Kawashima, S. (1991). Effect of vitamin E on the accumulation of fluorescent material in cultured cerebral cortical cells of mice. *Experimental Gerontology, 26*, 365–374.

Kato, Y., Maruyama, W., Naoi, M., Hashizume, Y., & Osawa, T. (1998). Immunohistochemical detection of dityrosine in lipofuscin pigments in the aged human brain. *FEBS Letters, 439*, 231–234.

Katz, M. L., Christianson, J. S., Norbury, N. E., Gao, C.-L., & Koppang, N. (1994). Lysine methylation of mitochondrial ATP synthase subunit c stored in tissues of dogs with hereditary ceroid lipofuscinosis. *Journal of Biological Chemistry, 269*, 9906–9911.

Keyse, S. M., & Emslie, E. A. (1992) Oxidative stress and heat shock induce a human gene encoding a protein-tyrosine phosphatase, *Nature, 359*, 644–647.

Keyse, S. M., & Tyrrell, R. M. (1989) Heme oxygenase is the major 32-kDa stress protein induced in human skin fibroblasts by UVA radiation, hydrogen peroxide, and sodium arsenite. *Proceedings of the National Academy of Sciences, USA, 86,* 99–103.

Kim, A. T., Sarafian, T. A., & Shau, H. (1997) Characterization of antioxidant properties of natural killer-enhancing factor-B and induction of its expressionby hydrogen peroxide. *Toxicology and Applied Pharmacology, 147,* 135–142.

King, V., & Tower, J. (1999) Aging-specific expression of *Drosophila hsp22. Developmental Biology, 207,* 107–118.

Kirkwood, T. B., & Kowald, A. (1997). Network theory of aging. *Experimental Gerontology, 32,* 395–399.

Klikugawa, K., Beppu, M., & Sato, A.. (1995). Extraction and purification of yellow-fluorescent lipofuscin in rat kidney. In K. Kitani, G. O. Ivy, H. Shimasaki (Eds.), *Lipofuscin and Ceroid Pigments* (pp. 1–12). Basel, Switzerland: S. Karger.

Koneff, J. H. (1886) Beiträge zur Kenntnis der Nervenzellen der peripheren Ganglien. *Mitt. Naturforsch. Gesellsch. Bern, 44,* 13–14.

Kovalenko, S. A., Kopsidas, G., Kelso, J., Rosenfeldt, F., & Linnane, A. W. (1998). Tissue-specific distribution of multiple mitochondrial DNA rearrangements during human aging. *Annals of the New York Academy of Sciences, 854,* 171–181.

Kristal, B. S., & Yu, B. P. (1998). Dietary restriction augments protection against induction of the mitochondrial permeability transition. *Free Radicals in Biology and Medicine, 24,* 1269–1277.

Kristofikova, Z., Klaschka, J., & Tejkalova, H. (1995). Effect of aging on lipid peroxide levels induced by L-glutamic acid and estimated by means of a thiobarbituric acid test in rat brain tissue. *Experimental Gerontology, 30,* 645–657.

Ku, H. H., Brunk, U. T., & Sohal, R. S. (1993). Relationship between mitochondrial superoxide and hydrogen peroxide production and longevity of mammalian species. *Free Radical Biology & Medicine, 15,* 621–627.

Kugelman, A., Choy, H. A., Liu, R., Shi, M. M., Gozal, E.; & Forman, H. J. (1994) gamma-Glutamyl transpeptidase is increased by oxidative stress in rat alveolar L2 epithelial cells. *American Journal of Respiratory and Cell Molecular Biology, 11,* 586–592.

Kumari, M. V., Yoneda, T., & Hiramatsu, M. (1997). Effect of "beta CATECHIN" on the life span of senescence accelerated mice (SAM-P8 strain). *Biochemistry and Molecular Biology International, 41,* 1005–1011.

Kurata, M., Suzuki, M., & Agar, N. S. (1993). Antioxidant systems and erythrocyte life-span in mammals. Comp. *Biochemistry and Physiology B., 106,* 477–487.

Larsen, P. L. (1993). Aging and resistance to oxidative damage in *Caenorhabditis elegans. Proceedings of the National Academy of Sciences, USA, 90,* 8905–8909.

Lass, A., Sohal, B. H., Weindruch, R., Forster, M. J., & Sohal, R. S. (1998). Caloric restriction prevents age-associated accrual of oxidative damage to mouse skeletal muscle mitochondria. *Free Radical Biology & Medicine, 25,* 1089–1097.

Laval, F. (1988) Pretreatment with oxygen species increases the resistance to hydrogen peroxide in Chinese hamster fibroblasts. *Journal of Cell Physiology, 201,* 73–79.

Leahy, K. P., Davies, K. J. A., Dull, M., Kort, J. J., Lawrence, K. W., & Crawford, D. A. (1999) *Adapt78,* a stress-inducible mRNA, is related to the glucose-regulated family of genes. *Archives of Biochemistry and Biophysics, 368,* 67–74.

Leuwenburgh, C., Wagner, P., Holloszy, J. O., Sohal, R. S., & Heinecke, J. W. (1997). Caloric restriction attenuates dityrosine cross-linking of cardiac and skeletal muscle proteins in aging mice. *Archives of Biochemistry and Biophysics, 346,* 74–80.

Leuwenburgh, C., Hansen, P., Shaish, A., Holloszy, J. O., & Heinecke, J. W. (1998). Markers of protein oxidation by hydroxyl radical and reactive nitrogen species in tissues of aging rats. *American Journal of Physiology, 274,* R453–R461.

Liles, M. R., Newsome, D. A., & Oliver, P. D. (1991). Antioxidant enzymes in the aging human retinal pigment epithelium. *Archives of Ophthalmology, 109,* 1285–1288.

Lippman, R. D. (1985). Rapid in vivo quantification and comparison of hydroperoxides and oxidized collagen in aging mice, rabbits and man. *Experimental Gerontology, 20,* 1–5.

Liu, J., Mori, A. (1993). Age-associated changes in superoxide dismutase activity, thiobarbituric acid reactivity and reduced glutathione level in the brain and liver in senescence accelerated mice (SAM): a comparison with ddY mice. *Mechanisms of Ageing and Development, 71,* 23–30.

Lonnrot, K., Metsa-Ketela, T., & Alho, H. (1995). The role of coenzyme Q–10 in aging: A follow-up study on life-long oral supplementation Q–10 in rats. *Gerontology., 41 (Suppl 2),* 109–120.

Lopez-Torres, M., Shindo, Y., & Packer, L. (1994). Effect of age on antioxidants and molecular markers of oxidative damage in murine epidermis and dermis. *Journal of Investigative Dermatology, 102,* 476–480.

Lu, C. Y., Lee, H. C., Fahn, H. J., & Wei, Y. H. (1999). Oxidative damage elicited by imbalance of free radical scavenging enzymes is associated with large-scale mtDNA deletions in aging human skin. *Mutation Research, 423,* 11–21.

Lubec, B., Golej, J., Marx, M., Weninger, M., & Hoeger, H. (1995). L-arginine reduces kidney lipid peroxidation, glycoxidation and collagen accumulation in the aging NMRI mouse. *Renal Physiology and Biochemistry, 18,* 97–102.

Lucas, D. T., & Szweda, L. I. (1998). Cardiac reperfusion injury: Aging, lipid peroxidation, and mitochondrial dysfunction. *Proceedings of the National Academy of Sciences, USA, 95,* 510–514.

Luhtala, T. A., Roecker, E. B., Pugh, T., Feuers, R. J., & Weindruch, R. (1994). Dietary restriction attenuates age-related increases in rat skeletal muscle antioxidant enzyme activities. *Journal of Gerontology, 49,* B231–238.

Ma, Y. X., Zhu, Y., Wang, C. F., Wang, Z. S., Chen, S. Y., Shen, M. H., Gan, J. M., Zhang, J. G., Gu, Q., & He, L. (1997). The aging retarding effect of "Long-Life CiLi". *Mechanisms of Ageing and Development, 96,* 171–180.

Martin, G. R., Danner, D. B., & Holbrook, N. J. (1993). Aging—causes and defenses. *Annual Review of Medicine, 44,* 419–429.

Martinez, M., Hernandez, A. I., Martinez, N., & Ferrandiz, M. L. (1996). Age-related increase in oxidized proteins in mouse synaptic mitochondria. *Brain Research, 731,* 246–248.

Marzabadi, M. R., Yin, D., & Brunk, U. T. (1992). Lipofuscinogenesis in a model system of cultured cardiac myocytes. *EXS, 62,* 78–88.

Mason, G. G. F., Hendil, K. B., & Rivett, A. J. (1996). Phosphorylation of proteasomes in mammalian cells. *European Journal of Biochemistry, 238,* 453–462.

McCann, S. M., Licinio, J., Wong, M. L., Yu, W. H., Karanth, S., & Rettorri, V. (1998). The nitric oxide hypothesis of aging. *Experimental Gerontology, 33,* 813–826.

Meucci, E., Mordente, A., & Martorana, G. E. (1991). Metal-catalyzed oxidation of human serum albumin: conformational and functional changes. *Journal of Biological Chemistry, 266,* 4692–4699.

Meydani, M. (1992). Vitamin E requirement in relation to dietary fish oil and oxidative stress in the elderly. *Experientia., 62,* 411–418.

Miquel, J., Ferrandiz, M. L., De Juan, E., Sevila, I., & Martinez, M. (1995). N-Acetylcysteine protects against age-related decline of oxidative phosphorylation in liver mitochondria. *European Journal of Pharmacology, 292,* 333–335.

Miquel, J., Tappel, A. L., Dillard C. J., Herman, M. M., Bensch, K. G. (1974) Fluorescent products and lysosomal components in aging Drosophila melanogaster. *Journal of Gerontology, 29,* 622–637.

Mo, J. Q., Hom, D. G., & Andersen, J. K. (1995). Decreases in protective enzymes correlates with increased oxidative damage in the aging mouse brain. *Mechanisms of Ageing and Development, 81,* 73–82.

Mooradian, A. D., & Smith, T. L. (1992). The effect of age on lipid composition and order of rat cerebral microvessels. *Neurochemistry Research, 17,* 233–237.

Mori, A., Utsumi, K., Liu, J., & Hosokawa, M. (1998). Oxidative damage in the senescence-accelerated mouse. *Annals of the New York Academy of Sciences, 854,* 239–250.

Morris, B. J. (1995). Stimulation of immediate early gene expression in striatal neurons by nitric oxide. *Journal of Biological Chemistry, 270,* 24740–24744.

Muehlematter, D., Ochi, T., & Cerutti, P. (1989) Effects of tert-butyl hydroperoxide on promotable and non-promotable JB6 mouse epidermal cells. *Chemical and Biological Interactions, 71*, 339–352.

Mura, C. V., Gong, X., Taylor, A., Villalobos-Molina, R., & Scrofano, M. M. (1996). Effects of calorie restriction and aging on the expression of antioxidant enzymes and ubiquitin in the liver of Emory mice. *Mechanisms of Aging and Development, 91*, 115–129.

Muscari, C., Frascaro, M., Guarnieri, C., & Caldarera, C. M. (1990). Mitochondrial function and superoxide generation from submitochondrial particles of aged rat hearts. *Biochimica et Biophysica Acta, 1015*, 200–204.

Muscari, C., Giaccari, A., Stefanelli, C., Viticchi, C., Giordano, E., Guarnieri, C., & Caldarera, C. M. (1996). Presence of a DNA–4236 bp deletion and 8-hydroxy-deoxyguanosine in mouse cardiac mitochondrial DNA during aging. *Aging Milano, 8*, 429–433.

Nakahara, H., Kanno, T., Inai, Y., Utsumi, K., Hiramatsu, M., Mori, A., & Packer, L. (1998). Mitochondrial dysfunction in the senescence accelerated mouse (SAM). *Free Radical Biology & Medicine, 24*, 85–92.

Nakanishi, Y., & Yasumoto, K. (1997). Induction after administering paraquat of heme oxygenase-1 and heat shock protein 70 in the liver of senescence-accelerated mice. *Bioscience Biotechnology and. Biochemistry, 61*, 1302–1306.

Nakano, M., Oenzil, F., Mizuno, T., & Gotoh, S. (1995). Age-related changes in the lipofuscin accumulation of brain and heart. In K. Kitani, G. O. Ivy, & H. Shimasaki (Eds.), *Lipofuscin and Ceroid Pigments* (pp. 69–77). Basel, Switzerland: S. Karger.

Nohl, H. (1993). Involvement of free radicals in ageing: A consequence or cause of senescence. *British Medical Bulletin, 49*, 653–667.

Nohl, H., Gille, L., & Staniek, K. (1998). The biochemical, pathophysiological, and medical aspects of ubiquinone function. *Annals of the New York Academy of Sciences, 854*, 394–409.

Nohl, H., Hegner, D., & Summer, K. H. (1979). Responses of mitochondrial superoxide dismutase, catalase and glutathione peroxidase activities to aging. *Mechanisms of Ageing and Development, 11*, 145–151.

Nohl, H., Staniek, K., & Gille, L. (1997). Imbalance of oxygen activation and energy metabolism as a consequence or mediator of aging. *Experimental Gerontology, 32*, 485–500.

Nose, K., Shibanuma, M., Kikuchi, K., Kageyama, H., Sakiyama, S., & Kuroki, T. (1991) Transcriptional activation of early-response genes by hydrogen peroxide in a mouse osteoblastic cell line. *European Journal of Biochemistry, 201*, 99–106.

Orr, W. C., & Sohal, R. S. (1992). The effects of catalase gene overexpression on life span and resistance to oxidative stress in transgenic Drosophila melanogaster. *Archives of Biochemistry and Biophysics, 297*, 35–41.

Orr, W. C., & Sohal, R. S. (1993). Effects of Cu-Zn superoxide dismutase overexpression of life span and resistance to oxidative stress in transgenic Drosophila melanogaster. *Archives of Biochemistry and Biophysics, 301*, 781–783.

Orr, W. C., & Sohal, R. S. (1994). Extension of life-span by overexpression of superoxide dismutase and catalase in Drosophila melanogaster. *Science., 263*, 1128–1130.

Pacifici, R. E., & Davies, K. J. A. (1991) Protein, lipid, and DNA repair systems in oxidative stress: The free radical theory of aging revisited. *Gerontology, 37*, 166–180.

Pacifici, R. E., Kono, Y., & Davies, K. J. A. (1993). Hydrophobicity as the signal for selective degradation of hydroxyl radical modified hemoglobin by the multicatalytic proteinase complex, proteasome. *Journal of Biological Chemistry, 268*, 15405–15411.

Palmina, N. P., Obukhova, L. K., Bunto, T. V., & Smirnov, L. D. (1979). Antioxidant activity of lipids in mice during aging and administration of an antioxidant with gerontological protective action. *Biology Bulletin of the Academy of Science, USSR., 6*, 243–246.

Pamplona, R., Prat, J., Cadenas, S., Rojas, C., Perez-Campo, R., Lopez-Torres, M., & Barja, G. (1996). Low fatty acid unsaturation protects against lipid peroxidation in liver mitochondria from long-lived species: The pigeon and human case. *Mechanisms of Ageing and Development, 86*, 53–66.

Perez, R., Lopez, M., & Barja de Quiroga, G. (1991). Aging and lung antioxidant enzymes, glutathione, and lipid peroxidation in the rat. *Free Radical Biology & Medicine*, 10, 35–39.

Perez-Campo, R., Lopez-Torres, M., Cadenas, S., Rojas, C., & Barja, G. (1998). The rate of free radical production as a determinant of the rate of aging: evidence from the comparative approach. *Journal of Comparative Physiology B.*, 168, 149–158.

Perrig, W. J., Perrig, P., & Stahelin, H. B. (1997). The relation between antioxidants and memory performance in the old and very old. *Journal of the American Geriatric Society*, 45, 718–724.

Phillips, J. P., Campbell, S. D., Michaud, D., Charbonneau, M., & Hilliker, A. J. (1989) Null mutation of copper/zinc superoxide dismutase in *Drosophila* confers hypersensitivity to paraquat and reduced longevity. *Proceedings of the National Academy of Sciences, USA*, 86, 2761–2765.

Porta, E. A., & Hartroft, W. S. (1969) Lipid pigments in relation to aging and dietary factors (lipofuscins). In M. Wolman (Ed.), *Pigments in Pathology* (pp. 191–235). New York: Academic Press.

Porta, E. A., Llesuy, S., Monserrat, A. J., Benavides, S., & Travacio, M. (1995). Changes in cathepsin B and lipofuscin during development and aging in rat brain and heart. In K. Kitani, G. O. Ivy, & H. Shimasaki (Eds.), *Lipofuscin and Ceroid Pigments* (pp. 81–89). Basel, Switzerland: S. Karger.

Poulin, J. E., Cover, C., Gustafson, M. R., & Kay, M. B. (1996). Vitamin E prevents oxidative modification of brain and lymphocyte band 3 proteins during aging. *Proceedings of the National Academy of Sciences, USA*, 93, 5600–5603.

Powers, S. K., Lawler, J., Criswell, D., Lieu, F. K., & Dodd, S. (1992). Alterations in diaphragmatic oxidative and antioxidant enzymes in the senescent Fischer 344 rat. *Journal of Applied Physiology*, 72, 2317–2321.

Rao, G., Xia, E., Nadakavukaren, M. J., & Richardson, A. (1990). Effect of dietary restriction on the age-dependent changes in the expression of antioxidant enzymes in rat liver. *Journal of Nutrition*, 120, 602–609.

Rattan, S. I. S. (1996). Synthesis, modifications, and turnover of proteins during aging. *Experimental Gerontology*, 31, 33–47.

Reckelhoff, J. F., Kanji, V., Racusen, L. C., Schmidt, A. M., Yan, S. D., Marrow, J., Roberts, L. J.-2nd, & Salahudeen, A. K. (1998). Vitamin E ameliorates enhanced renal lipid peroxidation and accumulation of F2-isoprostanes in aging kidneys. *American Journal of Physiology*, 274(3 Pt 2), R767–774.

Reichel, E., Holander, J., Clark, H. J., & Strehler, B. L. (1968) Lipofuscin pigment accumulation as a function of age and distribution in rodent brain. *Journal of Gerontology*, 23, 71–78.

Reiter, R. J. (1995a). Oxidative processes and antioxidant defense mechanisms in the aging brain. *FASEB Journal*, 9, 526–533.

Reiter, R. J. (1995b). Oxygen radical detoxification processes during aging: the functional importance of melatonin. *Aging Milano*, 7, 340–351.

Reiter, R. J. (1998). Cytoprotective properties of melatonin: presumed association with oxidative damage and aging [see comments]. *Nutrition.*, 14, 691–696.

Reiter, R. J., Guerrero, J. M., Garcia, J. J., & Acuna-Castroviejo, D. (1998). Reactive oxygen intermediates, molecular damage, and aging. Relation to melatonin. *Annals of the New York Academy of Scences.*, 854, 410–424.

Rikans, L. E., & Cai, Y. (1992). Age-associated enhancement of diquat-induced lipid peroxidation and cytotoxicity in isolated rat hepatocytes. *Journal of Pharmacology and Experimental Therapeutics*, 262, 271–278.

Rikans, L. E., & Hornbrook, K. R. (1997). Lipid peroxidation, antioxidant protection and aging. *Biochimica et Biophysica Acta.*, 1362, 116–127.

Rikans, L. E., Ardinska, V., & Hornbrook, K. R. (1997). Age-associated increase in ferritin content of male rat liver: Implication for diquat-mediated oxidative injury. *Archives of Biochemistry and Biophysics*, 344, 85–93.

Rodriguez-Martinez, M. A., & Ruiz-Torres, A. (1992). Homeostasis between lipid peroxidation and antioxidant enzyme activities in healthy human aging. *Mechanisms of Ageing and Development*, 66, 213–222.

Sack, C. A., Socci, D. J., Crandall, B. M., & Arendash, G. W. (1996). Antioxidant treatment with phenyl-alpha-tert-butyl nitrone (PBN) improves the cognitive performance and survival of aging rats. *Neuroscience Letters, 205*, 181–184.

Sahakian, J. A., Szweda, L. I., Friguet, B., Kitani, K., & Levine, R. L. (1995). Aging of the liver: Proteolysis of oxidatively modified glutamine synthetase. *Archives of Biochemistry and Biophysics, 318*, 411–417.

Sahoo, A., & Chainy, G. B. (1997). Alterations in the activities of cerebral antioxidant enzymes of rat are related to aging. *International Journal of Developmental Neuroscience, 15*, 939–948.

Sai, K., Takagi, A., Umemura, T., Hasegawa, R., & Kurokawa, Y. (1992). Changes of 8-hydroxydeoxyguanosine levels in rat organ DNA during the aging process. *Journal of Environmental Pathology, Toxicology and Oncology, 11*, 139–143.

Sanz, N., Diez-Fernandez, C., Alvarez, A., & Cascales, M. (1997). Age-dependent modifications in rat hepatocyte antioxidant defense systems. *Journal of Hepatology, 27*, 525–534.

Sasaki, R., Kurokawa, T., & Tero-Kubota, S. (1983). Ascorbate radical and ascorbic acid level in human serum and age. *Journal of Gerontology, 38*, 26–30.

Sastre, J., Millan, A., Garcia de la Asuncion, J., Pla, R., Juan, G., Pallardo, O'Connor, E., Martin, J. A., Droy-Lefaix, M. T., & Vina, J. (1998). A Ginkgo biloba extract (EGb 761) prevents mitochondrial aging by protecting against oxidative stress. *Free Radical. Biology & Medicine, 24*, 298–304.

Sastre, J., Rodriguez, J. V., Pallardo, F. V., Gasco, E., Asensi, M., Ferrer, J. V., Miquel, J., & Vina, J. (1992). Effect of aging on metabolic zonation in rat liver: acinar distribution of GSH metabolism. *Mechanisms of Ageing and Development, 62*, 181–190.

Sawada, M., & Carlson, J. C. (1987). Changes in superoxide radical and lipid peroxide formation in the brain, heart and liver during the lifetime of the rat. *Mechanisms of Ageing and Development, 41*, 125–137.

Sawada, M., Sester, U., & Carlson, J. C. (1993). Changes in superoxide radical formation, lipid peroxidation, membrane fluidity and cathepsin B activity in aging and spawning male Chinook salmon (Oncorhynchus tschawytscha). *Mechanisms of Ageing and Development, 69*, 137–147.

Scrofano, M. M., Shang, F., Nowell, T. R., Jr., Gong, X., Smith, D. E., Kelliher, M., Dunning, D. E., Mura, C. V., & Taylor, A. (1998). Aging, calorie restriction and ubiquitin-dependent proteolysis in the livers of Emory mice. *Mechanisms of Ageing and Development, 101*, 277–296.

Semsei, I., Rao, G., & Richardson, A. (1991). Expression of superoxide dismutase and catalase in rat brain as a function of age. *Mechanisms of Ageing and Development, 58*, 13–19.

Seto, N. O., Hayashi, S., & Tener, G. M. (1990). Overexpression of Cu-Zn superoxide dismutase in Drosophila does not affect life-span. *Proceedings of the National Academy of Sciences, USA, 87*, 4270–4274.

Shang, F., Gong, X., & Taylor, A. (1997). Activity of ubiquitin-dependent pathway in response to oxidative stress. *Journal of Biological Chemistry, 272*, 23086–23093.

Shang, F., & Taylor, A. (1995). Oxidative stress and recovery from oxidative stress are associated with altered ubiquitin conjugating and proteolytic activities in bovine lens epithelial cells. *Biochemical Journal, 307*, 297–303.

Sharma, S. P., & Wadhwa, R. (1983). Effect of butylated hydroxytoluene on the life span of *Drosophila* bipectinata. *Mechanisms of Ageing and Development, 23*, 67–71.

Sharma, S. P., Sharma, M., & Kakkar, R. (1995). Methionine-induced alterations in the life span, antioxidant enzymes, and peroxide levels in aging *Zaprionus paravittiger* (Diptera). *Gerontology., 41*, 86–93.

Sharma, P., Rupar, C. A., & Rip, J. W. (1998). Consequences of aging on mitochondrial respiratory chain enzymes in cultured human fibroblasts treated with ascorbate. *Gerontology, 44*, 78–84.

Sheldal, J. A., Tappel, A. L. (1974) Fluorescent products from aging *Drosophila melanogaster*: An indicator of free radical lipid peroxidation damage. *Experimental Gerontology, 9*, 33–41.

Shibanuma, M., Kuroki, T., & Nose, K. (1988) Induction of DNA replication and expression of proto-oncogene c-*myc* and c-*fos* in quiescent Balb/3T3 cells by xanthine/ xanthine oxidase. *Oncogene 3*, 17–21.

Shigenaga, M. K., Hagen, T. M., & Ames, B. N. (1994). Oxidative damage and mitochondrial decay in aging. *Proceedings of the National Academy of Sciences, USA, 91*, 10771–10778.

Shimasaki, H., Ueta, N., Mowri, H. O., & Inoue, K. (1984). Formation of AGE pigment-like fluorescent substances during peroxidation of lipids in model membranes. *Biochimica et Biophysica Acta., 792*, 123–129.

Shimasaki, H., Maeba, R., Tachibana, R., & Ueta, N. (1995). Lipid peroxidation and ceroid accumulation in macrophages cultured with oxidized low density lipoprotein. In K. Kitani, G. O. Ivy, & H. Shimasaki (Eds.), *Lipofuscin and Ceroid Pigments* (pp. 39–48). Basel, Switzerland: S. Karger.

Shull, S., Heintz, N. H., Periasamy, M., Manohar, M., Janssen, Y. M., Marsh, J. P., & Mossman, B. T. (1991) Differential regulation of antioxidant enzymes in response to oxidants. *Journal of Biological Chemistry, 266*, 24398–24403.

Sitte, N., Huber, M., Grune, T., Ladhoff, A., Doecke, W.-D., von Zglinicki, T., & Davies, K. J. A. (2000). Proteasome inhibition by lipofuscin/ceroid during postmitotic aging of fibroblasts. *FASEB Journal, 14*, (in press).

Sitte, N., Merker, K., & Grune, T. (1998). Proteasome-dependent degradation of oxidized proteins in MRC–5 fibroblasts. *FEBS Letters, 440*, 399–402.

Smith, C. D., Carney, J. M., Starke-Reed, P. E., Oliver, C. N., Stadtman, E. R., Floyd, R. A., & Markesbery, W. R. (1991). Excess brain protein oxidation and enzyme dysfunction in normal aging and in Alzheimer disease. *Proceedings of the National Academy of Sciences, USA, 88*, 10540–10543.

Sohal, R. S. (1973) Fine structural alterations with age in the fat body of the adult male housefly, Musca domestica. *Z. Zellforsch Mikroski Anatomy, 140*, 169–175.

Sohal, R. S. (1988). Effect of hydrogen peroxide administration on life span, superoxide dismutase, catalase and glutathione in the adult housefly, Musca domestica. *Experimental Gerontology, 23*, 211–216.

Sohal, R. S., & Brunk, U. T. (1989). Lipofuscin as an indicator of oxidative stress and aging. *Advances in Experimental Medicine and Biology, 266*, 17–26, discussion 27–29.

Sohal, R. S., & Brunk, U. T. (1992). Mitochondrial production of pro-oxidants and cellular senescence. *Mutation Research, 275*, 295–304.

Sohal, R. S., & Dubey, A. (1994). Mitochondrial oxidative damage, hydrogen peroxide release, and aging. *Free Radical Biology & Medicine, 16*, 612–626.

Sohal, R. S., & Orr, W. C. (1992). Relationship between antioxidants, prooxidants, and the aging process. *Annals of the New York Academy of Sciences, 663*, 74–84.

Sohal, R. S., & Sohal, B. H. (1991). Hydrogen peroxide release by mitochondria increases during aging. *Mechanisms of Ageing and Development, 57*, 187–202.

Sohal, S. R., Agarwal, S., Dubey, A., & Orr, W. C. (1993). Protein oxidative damage is associated with life expectancy of houseflies. *Proceedings of the National Academy of Sciences, USA, 90*, 7255–7259.

Sohal, R. S., Arnold, L. A., & Sohal, B. H. (1990). Age-related changes in antioxidant enzymes and prooxidant generation in tissues of the rat with special reference to parameters in two insect species. *Free Radical Biology & Medicine, 9*, 495–500.

Sohal, R. S., Ku, H. H., Agarwal, S., Forster, M. J., & Lal, H. (1994). Oxidative damage, mitochondrial oxidant generation and antioxidant defenses during aging and in response to food restriction in the mouse. *Mechanisms of Ageing and Development, 74*, 121–133.

Sohal, R. S., Sohal, B. H., & Brunk, U. T. (1990). Relationship between antioxidant defenses and longevity in different mammalian species. *Mechanisms of Ageing and Development, 53*, 217–227.

Sohal, R. S., Sohal, B. H., & Orr, W. C. (1995). Mitochondrial superoxide and hydrogen peroxide generation, protein oxidative damage, and longevity in different species of flies. *Free Radical Biology & Medicine, 19*, 499–504.

Sohal, R. S., Svensson, I., & Brunk, U. T. (1990). Hydrogen peroxide production by liver mitochondria in different species. *Mechanisms of Ageing and Development, 53*, 209–215.

Sohal, R. S., Toy, P. L., & Farmer, K. J. (1987). Age-related changes in the redox status of the housefly, *Musca domestica, Archives of Gerontology and Geriatrics, 6,* 95–100.

Sommerburg, O., Ullrich, O., Sitte, N., & von Zglinicki, D. (1998). Dose- and wavelength-dependent oxidation of crystallins by UV light–selective recognition and degradation by the 20S proteasome. *Free Radical Biology & Medicine, 24,* 1369–1374.

Spitz, D. R., Dewey, W. C., & Li, G. C. (1987) Hydrogen peroxide or heat shock induces resistance to hydrogen peroxide in Chinese hamster fibroblasts. *Journal of Cell Physiology, 131,* 364–373.

Spitz, D. R., Elwell, J. H., Sun, Y., Oberley, L. W., Oberley, T. D., Sullivan, S. J., & Roberts, R. J. (1990) Oxygen toxicity in control and hydrogen H_2O_2-resistant Chinese hamster fibroblast cell lines. *Archives of Biochemistry and Biophysics, 279,* 249–260.

Stadtman, E. R. (1992). Protein oxidation and aging. *Science., 257,* 1220–1224.

Stadtman, E. R. (1993). Oxidation of free amino acids and amino acid residues in proteins by radiolysis and by metal-catalyzed reactions. *Annual Reviews of Biochemistry, 62,* 797–821.

Stadtman, E. R., Starke-Reed, P. E., Oliver, C. N., Carney, J. M., & Floyd, R. A. (1992). Protein modification in aging. In I. Emerit & B. Chance (Eds.). *Free Radicals and Aging* (pp. 64–72). Basel, Switzerland: Birkhäuser Verlag.

Starke-Reed, P. E., & Oliver, C. N. (1989). Protein oxidation and proteolysis during aging and oxidative stress. *Archives of Biochemistry and Biophysics, 275,* 559–567.

Stevens, C., Goldblatt, M. J., & Freedman, J. C. (1975). Lack of erythrocyte superoxide dismutase change during human senescence. *Mechanisms of Ageing and Development, 4,* 415–421.

Storz, G. & Tartaglia, L. A. (1992). OxyR: a regulator of antioxidant genes. *Journal of Nutrition, 122,* 627–630.

Strehler, B. L., Mark, D. D., Mildvan, A. S., & Gee, M. V. (1959) Rate of magnitude of AGE pigment accumulation in the human myocardium. *Journal of Gerontology, 14,* 430–439.

Sun, J., & Tower, J. (1999) FLP Recombinase-mediated induction of Cu/Zn-superoxide dismutase transgene expression can extend the life span of adult *Drosophila melanogaster* flies. *Molecular and Cellular Biology, 19,* 216–228.

Tengan, C. H., Gabbai, A. A., Shanske, S., Zeviani, M., & Moraes, C. T. (1997). Oxidative phosphorylation dysfunction does not increase the rate of accumulation of age-related mtDNA deletions in skeletal muscle. *Mutation Research, 379,* 1–11.

Teramoto, S., Fukuchi, Y., Uejima, Y., Teramoto, K., Ito, H., & Orimo, H. (1994). Age-related changes in the antioxidant screen of the distal lung in mice. *Lung, 172,* 223–230.

Terman, A. (1995). The effect of age on formation and elimination of autophagic vacuoles in mouse hepatocytes. In K. Kitani, G. O. Ivy, & H. Shimasaki (Eds.), *Lipofuscin and Ceroid Pigments* (pp. 319–325). Basel, Switzerland: S. Karger.

Tian, L., Cai, Q., Bowen, R., & Wei, H. (1995). Effects of caloric restriction on age-related oxidative modifications of macromolecules and lymphocyte proliferation in rats. *Free Radical Biology & Medicine, 19,* 859–865.

Tian, L., Cai, Q., & Wei, H. (1998). Alterations of antioxidant enzymes and oxidative damage to macromolecules in different organs of rats during aging. *Free Radical Biology & Medicine, 24,* 1477–1484.

Ullrich, O., Reinheckel, T., Sitte, N., Hass, R., Grune, T., & Davies, K. J. A. (1999) Poly-ADP ribose polymerase activates nuclear proteasome to degrade oxidatively damaged histones. *Procedings of the National Academy of Sciences, USA, 96,* 6223–6228.

Vandewoude, M. F., Vandewoude, M. G. (1987). Vitamin E status in a normal population: The influence of age. *Journal of the American College of Nutrition, 6,* 307–311.

Vericel, E., Narce, M., Ulmann, L., Poisson, J. P., & Lagarde, M. (1994). Age-related changes in antioxidant defence mechanisms and peroxidation in isolated hepatocytes from spontaneously hypertensive and normotensive rats. *Molecular and Cellular Biochemistry, 132,* 25–29.

Vina, J., Sastre, J., Anton, V., Bruseghini, L., Esteras, A., & Asensi, M. (1992). Effect of aging on glutathione metabolism. Protection by antioxidants. *Experientia, 62,* 136–144.

Wang, Y., Crawford, D. R., & Davies, K. J. A. (1996) Adapt33, a novel oxidant-inducible RNA from Hamster HA-1 cells. *Archives of Biochemistry and Biophysics, 332,* 255–260.

Wei, Y. H. (1992). Mitochondrial DNA alterations as ageing-associated molecular events. *Mutation Research, 275(3–6),* 145–155.

Wei, Y. H. (1998). Oxidative stress and mitochondrial DNA mutations in human aging. *Proceedings of the Society of Experimental Biology and Medicine, 217,* 53–63.

Wei Y. H., Kao S. H., & Lee H. C. (1996). Simultaneous increase of mitochondrial DNA deletions and lipid peroxidation in human aging. *Annals of the New York Academy of Sciences, 786,* 24–43.

Wei, Y. H., Lu, C. Y., Lee, H. C., Pang, C. Y., & Ma, Y. S. (1998). Oxidative damage and mutation to mitochondrial DNA and age-dependent decline of mitochondrial respiratory function. *Annals of the New York Academy of Sciences, 854,* 155–170.

Wells-Knecht, M. C., Lyons, T. J., Mc Cance, D. R., Thorpe, S. R., & Baynes, J. W. (1997). Age-dependent increase in ortho-tyrosine and methionine sulfoxide in human skin collagen is accelerated in diabetes. *Journal of Clinical Investigation, 100,* 839–846.

Wells-Knecht, M. C., Huggins, T. G., Dyer, D. G., Thorpe, S. R., & Baynes, J. W. (1993). Oxidized amino acids in protein with age. *Journal of Biological Chemistry, 268,* 12348–12352.

Wiese, A. G., Pacifici, R. E. & Davies, K. J. A. (1995) Transient adaptation to oxidative stress in mammalian cells, *Archives of Biochemistry and Biophysics, 318,* 231–240.

Wolff, S. P., Jiang, Z. Y., & Hunt, J. V. (1991). Protein glycation and oxidative stress in diabetes mellitus and ageing. *Free Radical Biology & Medicine, 10,* 339–352.

Yamamoto, K., Yamada, M., & Kato, Y. (1989). Age-related and phenylhydrazine-induced activation of the membrane-associated cathepsin E in human erythrocytes. *Journal of Biochemistry, Tokyo., 105,* 114–119.

Yan, L.-J., Levine, R. L., & Sohal, R. S. (1997). Oxidative damage during aging targets mitochondrial aconitase. *Proceedings of the National Academy of Sciences, USA, 94,* 11168–11172.

Yan, L. J., & Sohal, R. S. (1998). Mitochondrial adenine nucleotide translocase is modified oxidatively during aging. *Proceedings of the National Academy of Sciences, USA, 95,* 12896–12901.

Yin, D. Z. (1992). Lipofuscin-like fluorophores can result from reactions between oxidized ascorbic acid and glutamine. Carbonyl-protein cross-linking may represent a common reaction in oxygen radical and glycosylation-related ageing processes. *Mechanisms of Ageing and Development, 62,* 35–45.

Yin, D. (1995). Studies on age pigments evolving into a new theory of biological aging. In K. Kitani, G. O. Ivy, & H. Shimasaki (Eds.), *Lipofuscin and Ceroid Pigments,* (pp.159–170). Basel, Switzerland: S. Karger.

Yin, D. (1996). Biochemical basis of lipofuscin, ceroid, and AGE pigment-like fluorophophores. *Free Radical Biology & Medicine, 21,* 871–888.

Youngman, L. D., Park, J.-Y. K., & Ames, B. N. (1992). Protein oxidation associated with aging is reduced by dietary restriction of protein or calories. *Proceedings of the National Academy of Sciences, USA, 89,* 9112–9116.

Yuan, H., Kaneko, T., & Matsuo, M. (1996). Increased susceptibility of late passage human diploid fibroblasts to oxidative stress. *Experimental Gerontology, 31,* 465–474.

Zhang, J. R., Andrus, P. K., & Hall, E. D. (1994). Age-related phospholipid hydroperoxide levels in gerbil brain measured by HPLC-chemiluminescence and their relation to hydroxyl radical stress. *Brain Research, 639,* 275–282.

Zs.-Nagy, I., Streiber, J., & Jeney, F. (1995). Induction of age pigment accumulation in the brain cells of young male rats through iron injection into the cerebrospinal fluid. In K. Kitani, G. O. Ivy, & H. Shimasaki (Eds.), *Lipofuscin and ceroid pigment* (pp. 145–156). Basel, Switzerland: S. Karger.

Three

Protein Structure and Turnover

Ari Gafni

I. Introduction

A basic tenet of contemporary biology is
that all instructions for the creation,
development, and sustenance of a living
organism are stored in its genome, where
they are encoded in the nucleotide
sequences of DNA. It is, however, the
translation of this archival information
into sequences of amino acids of specific
proteins that allows for all life processes
to take place. Proteins are highly modular
macromolecules that serve to execute,
regulate, and mediate nearly all activities
of a living organism. The complexity of
life requires that many thousands of
different proteins be present in each
living cell at any given moment, each
performing a specific task. To ensure that
only reactions beneficial to the organism
occur to any significant extent, cells need
to be able to produce, and degrade,
selected proteins upon demand, and the
protein molecules themselves, in addition, need to possess the ability to be
regulated by external stimuli (for example, by becoming phosphorylated in
response to signals from hormones) so
that their activities can be turned on or
off when needed. Indeed, at any given
moment, it is the combination of both
the relative quantities of different
proteins in the cell and their individual
levels of activity that determines the
cellular status, and it is easy to understand how changes in the levels and
biological activities of proteins have the
potential to affect cellular conditions and
to feature both in aging and disease. In
this context, the well-documented age-
related decline in the rates of both protein
synthesis and degradation (Rattan, 1996;
see Chapter 6 in this volume) is of great
interest. Not only can these reduce the
amount of proteins, but because slower
degradation results in longer dwell times
for proteins in old tissues, these may
allow for an increased level of damaging
postsynthetic modifications to occur.

A number of hypotheses to explain the
origin of biological aging and to provide
more mechanistic insight into the
process have been developed that lend
themselves to be tested by experiment.
These have been described in several
reviews and research publications
(Johnson et al., 1996; Martin et al., 1993;
1996; Masoro & Austad, 1996; Rose,
1991; Vijg & Wei, 1995). Notable among
these hypotheses have been the Error

Catastrophe and Free Radicals theories, in that they attempted to explain aging using specific molecular mechanisms that affect the functional properties of proteins.

The Error Catastrophe theory. The possibility that, in addition to age-related changes in the rate of protein synthesis, there may also occur alterations in the fidelity of this process, has received much attention and constituted the basis for Orgel's Error Catastrophe theory (Orgel, 1963, 1970). This theory proposed that the low level of errors introduced into protein sequences during normal synthesis tends to increase exponentially with advancing age because some of the erroneous proteins, which initially are created randomly, will be enzymes involved in protein synthesis. Defects in these proteins will result in an increased level of ill-produced new proteins, and this vicious cycle, where the errors are amplified in each consecutive generation of proteins, would lead to catastrophic conditions for the cell. Orgel's theory stimulated a burst of experimental work searching for modified proteins in aging cells, and many were discovered. Whereas evidence that increased fidelity of protein synthesis can enhance longevity has been presented (Silar & Picard, 1994), no clear evidence for error amplification during aging was found.

The Free Radicals theory. Oxidative free radicals are produced constantly in the cell as byproducts of normal metabolic processes. These highly reactive species can rapidly interact with, and damage, various cellular components (proteins, nucleic acids, lipids). Indeed, the existence of oxidative damage both in nuclear and in mitochondrial DNA has been well-documented, although the level of damage is still in dispute (Beckman & Ames, 1999). This topic is covered in more detail in Chapter 5 of this volume. The potential role that oxidative free radicals may play in both

aging and disease was recognized as early as 1956, when Harman proposed his "free radical theory of aging" (Harman, 1956, 1988). Although a large number of studies have addressed this issue since then (Agarwal & Sohal, 1995; Carney & Carney, 1994; Dean *et al.*, 1992; Smith *et al.*, 1992), our understanding of the role of oxidative stress in aging is still incomplete. It is, however, clear that some proteins are substantially modified by oxidation in old organisms. Support for this statement is provided both by the observation that proteins from old animals contain covalent modifications that clearly are the result of oxidation reactions and by the fact that it is possible to mimic the age-related modifications in proteins by exposure to oxidative conditions *in vitro* (Davies, 1993, 1995; Kritchevsky & Muldoon, 1996; Pacifici, & Davies, 1991; Stadtman, 1995a,b). Whereas cells possess defense mechanisms against free radical attack, this protection is not perfect and a low level of oxidation occurs continuously. Moreover, there is evidence that the efficiency of protection against free radical attack may decline with advancing age, leading to an increased rate of damage accumulation (Agarwal & Sohal, 1995). Indeed, because some of the enzymes involved in oxidative damage control may themselves be affected by free radical oxidation, and because the average dwell time of proteins in tissues increases with aging, one would expect the rate of damaging oxidative reactions to increase with age in a process conceptually akin to the one postulated by the Error Catastrophe theory. As will be discussed later, evidence for this type of behavior has indeed been found.

Both the Error Catastrophe and Free Radicals theories of aging have stimulated an active search for age-modified proteins in cells and tissues, resulting in the discovery of a large number of such examples, as covered in several reviews (Gafni, 1991, 1997; Rattan, 1996; Rothstein, 1985; Stadtman, 1988; Stadtman *et al.*, 1993). It is now well-established that the level of modified proteins in living organisms increases markedly toward the end of the life span and that this is at the origin of a number of age-associated diseases and pathologies. Detailed studies of the age-associated modifications revealed that these often involve the functional properties, stability, and structural integrity of the affected proteins. Old proteins (i.e., the modified forms found in tissues of old animals) often display a reduction in their biological activity (Gafni, 1985; Gershon & Gershon, 1970; Gordillo *et al.*, 1988), a modified heat-inactivation pattern, reflecting alterations in the stability of the folded state (Gafni, 1983; Reiss & Rothstein, 1974; Sharma *et al.*, 1980), or a modified affinity toward antibodies raised against the young form of the protein, a reflection of changes in structural integrity (Dovrat *et al.*, 1986; Reiss & Sacktor, 1983).

The observed increase in the level of modified proteins in tissues of old organisms has been found to be primarily due to an increase in the extent of a number of different postsynthetic modifications. These alterations and the mechanisms responsible for their appearance are the topic of the following discussion.

Because the age-related alterations are postsynthetic, it stands to reason that their level will increase if the dwell time in the cell of the protein being affected is prolonged. Indeed, a significant body of evidence has been accumulating that demonstrates that both protein synthesis and degradation rate decline during aging, resulting in a longer dwell time for the average protein in the cell. The role of changes in protein turnover in their modifications during aging thus is potentially of great significance and is discussed in this review.

II. Classification of Aging-Related Protein Modifications

Broadly defined, the observed age-related modifications in proteins fall into two categories: covalent and noncovalent. Both classes of modifications lead to structural changes and, as a rule, to alterations in the biological activity of a protein; however, there is an important distinction between them. The effects of noncovalent structural modifications are erased when the protein is unfolded, and modifications of this type therefore may be removed by subjecting the old protein to an unfolding–refolding protocol. In contrast, covalent modifications have a more permanent effect because they change the identity of the affected amino acids, causing the modified polypeptide sequence, as a rule, to refold into the altered structure. Both covalent and conformational alterations tend to predispose a protein to proteolysis, and the decline in the activity of proteolytic enzymes with aging may explain the observed increase in the level of modified proteins. The fact that the age-related modifications are postsynthetic explains why they usually are more prevalent in long-lived proteins relative to those with short dwell times in the tissue.

In the following discussion, we review several specific mechanisms that introduce aging-related covalent modifications into proteins. This section is followed by a discussion of the origin of noncovalent alterations in old forms of proteins, which can reflect either a failure to fold correctly due to modified conditions in the old cell or the development of conformational transitions subsequent to an initially correct folding.

A. Covalent Modifications

1. Oxidation

Proteins in living tissues are continuously subjected to modification by reactive chemical species, particularly reactive oxygen species (ROS). It has been well-documented that the level of oxidatively modified proteins increases sharply during aging, as well as under some pathological conditions (Stadtman & Berlett, 1998). Moreover, evidence has been presented that the life expectancy of houseflies is inversely correlated with the level of protein oxidative damage (Agarwal & Sohal, 1995; Sohal et al., 1993; Sohal & Dubey, 1994). The mechanisms responsible for the generation of ROS, as well as those involved in the modification of biomolecules by ROS, have been explored by a number of groups (Berlett & Stadtman, 1997; Conconi & Friguet, 1997; Lenaz, 1998; Schoneich, 1999; Stadtman & Berlett, 1998; see Chapter 2 in this volume) and, generally, can lead to protein backbone oxidation, polypeptide fragmentation, or oxidation of amino acid side chains.

Protein Backbone Cross-Linking and Cleavage. The metal-catalyzed cleavage of H_2O_2 (a byproduct of several biological oxidation reactions) creates hydroxyl radicals (OH), which, in turn, can abstract the α-hydrogen atom from an amino acid residue, generating a carbon-centered radical. Two such radicals can interact to generate cross-linked proteins. Alternately, the C- centered radical can react with molecular oxygen to form an alkylperoxyl radical, which, in turn, can lead to chain cleavage. This process has been described in detail by Berlett and Stadtman (1997).

Peptide bond cleavage also has been found to follow the oxidation of the side chains of some amino acid residues, i.e., glutamate, aspartate, and proline, by ROS (Berlett & Stadtman, 1997; Stadtman & Berlett, 1998).

Amino Acid Side Chain Oxidation. Whereas all amino acid residues can be oxidized by some ROS (particularly OH), the S-containing cysteine and methionine are the most susceptible to this reaction.

Cysteine residues are easily converted into disulfides, whereas methionine is converted to methionine sulfoxide. It is interesting to note that most living organisms have reductases, which are enzymes that can reduce the oxidized forms of cysteine and methionine back to the native amino acids, making these the only known oxidative modifications of proteins that are repaired in vivo. Stadtman and co-workers made the interesting observation that the oxidation of exposed methionine residues in some proteins has only a small effect on their biological activity and suggested that these residues may serve as an antioxidant defense mechanism that can scavenge ROS in the cell (Levine et al., 1996).

Another group of amino acids with a high sensitivity toward ROS is the aromatic residues. Thus, tryptophan is readily converted to formylkynurenine and kynurenine, whereas phenylalanine and tyrosine are converted into several hydroxy derivatives that are prone to cross-linking. Indeed, the formation of bityrosine cross-links has been documented in α-crystallin in old eye lenses and is an important contributor to age-related lens opacification and cataract formation (Fujimori, 1982). Histidine also is readily oxidized to form 2-oxohistidine, asparagine, or aspartate.

Generation of Carbonyl Derivatives. A prominent age-related oxidative modification in proteins is revealed through the increase in the content of carbonyl, a product of the oxidation of several amino acid side chains, including proline, arginine, and lysine, as well as of oxidation reactions that leads to the cleavage of peptide bonds (Berlett & Stadtman, 1997; Stadtman & Berlett, 1998; Stadtman, 1990). Carbonyl groups also are introduced into proteins by reactions with aldehydes, the latter being produced during lipid peroxidation (Berlett et al., 1996; Farber & Levine, 1996; Uchida, & Kawakishi, 1993), as well as by glycation and glycoxidation reactions (to be discussed later). Protein glycation thus adds to the pool of carbonyl-containing proteins in a way that is affected by disease (diabetes) and, probably, by aging.

In view of the preceding discussion it is not surprising that the carbonyl content of proteins in a number of different tissues, in whole body homogenates, as well as in mitochondria has been found to increase rapidly with age (Orr & Sohal, 1992; Sohal & Dubey, 1994; Stadtman, 1992) and that the level of carbonyls can be used as a marker of ROS-mediated protein oxidation (Berlett, & Stadtman, 1997; Carney et al., 1991; Garland et al., 1988; Oliver et al., 1987; Smith et al., 1991; Sohal et al., 1993; Starke-Reed & Oliver, 1989). It has been estimated that, in an old animal, about 30–50% of all cellular proteins may be affected by oxidation (Stadtman, 1995a), a range that is typical of the reduction in catalytic activity observed for many enzymes in old organisms. The accumulation of protein carbonyls (i.e., oxidative damage) has also been documented in several aging-associated diseases, including Alzheimer's disease, cataractogenesis, progeria, and Werner's syndrome.

Agarwal and Sohal (1995) have assessed the oxidative damage to mitochondrial proteins and found that this damage is not introduced randomly, but that high-molecular-weight proteins are more susceptible to oxidative modifications. Thus, the large protein complexes involved in mitochondrial electron transport appear to be particularly prone to oxidative damage.

A wealth of experimental evidence now points to protein oxidation as an important mechanism for protein modification during aging. The steady-state level of oxidized proteins in the cell is determined by a combination of the rate of oxidation, which may increase during aging, and the level of protection against oxidation, which likely decreases with advancing age. Because the appearance of oxidation-involving modifications in a protein marks this protein for degradation by a number of cellular proteinases (Conconi et al., 1996; Pacifici & Davies, 1990), the accumulation of oxidized proteins during aging is believed to be the result not only of the accelerated rate of oxidation but also, as importantly, of the age-related decline in the efficacy of these proteinases (Conconi et al., 1996; Tatsmo et al., 1992). The resulting increase in the level of oxidized proteins, in turn, is accompanied by a loss in biological activity and may, therefore, be at the origin of some of the functional deficits that characterize aging and some degenerative aging-associated diseases and pathologies.

Example of Postsynthetic Oxidative Modifications: The Sarcoplasmic Reticulum Calcium ATPase. The sarcoplasmic reticulum (SR) Ca-ATPase affects muscle relaxation by pumping intracellular calcium into the lumen of the SR, a process coupled to ATP hydrolysis. Both contraction and relaxation times of muscle become prolonged during aging (Larsson & Ansved, 1995), and a role for the SR-ATPase in this process has been suggested. An increase in the heat lability of the SR-ATPase during aging was reported by Gafni and Yuh (1989a), who suggested that the membrane environment of the protein was altered in SR vesicles obtained from old rats. Other studies focusing on the membrane composition of rat skeletal muscle SR were reported by Krainev and co-workers (1995); however, these compositional differences did not affect the physical properties of the bulk or protein-associated lipids or the rotational dynamics of the Ca-ATPase molecule. Evidence for heat-induced formation of Ca-ATPase aggregates has been provided (Viner et al., 1997), and it was found that preparations from old rats displayed a faster loss of protein mobility than those from young rats, as monitored by saturation transfer electron paramagnetic resonance (EPR) measurements of SR Ca-ATPase derivatized with a maleimide spin label (Ferrington et al., 1997).

Evidence for oxidation-induced damage to the SR-ATPase in slow-twitch muscle was provided by Narayanan and co-workers (1996), who reported that Ca^{2+} uptake was significantly reduced during aging in the SR of this muscle type, which is particularly susceptible to oxidative modification. Because the levels of antioxidant enzymes (superoxide dismutase, glutathione peroxidase and catalase) have been observed to increase with age (Oh-Ishi et al., 1995), the age-related changes in the slow-twitch muscle reveal either a disproportionate increase in the level of reactive oxygen species compared to that of the antioxidant enzymes or changes in the localization of reactive oxygen species relative to the antioxidant enzymes.

Recent studies from Bigelow's laboratory (Schoneich et al., 1999) focused on the chemical characterization of the age-related posttranslational modifications in rat skeletal muscle SR-ATPase isoforms SERCA1 and SERCA2a obtained from 5- and 28-month-old male Fischer 344 rats. Whereas the prevalent (90%) SERCA1 isoform displayed an age-dependent loss of cysteine and arginine, the minor isoform SERCA2a revealed, in addition to a loss of cysteine, a significant accumulation of 3-nitrotyrosine (a product of peroxynitrite oxidation of tyrosine). The in vitro exposure of SERCA1-rich SR vesicles from 5-month-old rats to low levels of peroxyl radicals yielded SR vesicles in which the Ca-ATPase appeared identical to that observed in preparations obtained from 28-month-old rats.

The peroxyl-radical-modified SR-ATPase revealed a loss of cysteine and arginine and, in addition, serine and methionine. This indicates that peroxyl radical, although a good model oxidant to generate "aged" SR vesicles, may not be the only oxidant responsible for the chemical modification of the SR Ca-ATPase in vivo. In fact, efficient thiol modification of the SERCA1 isoform was also observed upon exposure to peroxynitrite, an oxidant that selectively nitrated the tyrosine residues of the SERCA2a isoform even in the presence of an excess of SERCA1. It thus appears plausible that peroxynitrite may be responsible for the age- dependent modification of the SR-ATPase in vivo.

2. Protein Glycation and Glycoxidation

Glycation, the nonenzymatic glycosylation of proteins, is a complex reaction that begins when a carbonyl group of a reducing sugar reacts with an amino group on a protein (usually a lysine or the N-terminal amino group) to form a Schiff base. This derivative reacts further, by an Amadori rearrangement, to produce a ketoamine, which is subsequently cross-linked and converted by a series of reactions to advanced glycosylation end products (AGEs), the latter being fluorescent, brown pigments (Brownlee, 1995; Monnier et al., 1993). Oxidation by molecular oxygen has been found to play an important role in glycation and is involved in some of the steps leading to the formation of the AGEs (Knecht et al., 1992; Wells-Knecht et al., 1994). Moreover, oxidation of the participating sugar leads to the production of reactive dicarbonyls (such as glyoxal), and these rapidly interact with amino groups on the protein to ultimately produce N-carboxymethyl amino acid derivatives (most frequently from lysine) in a process termed glycoxidation (Wells-Knecht et al., 1995).

The time scales involved in protein glycation and glycoxidation have been studied both in vitro and in vivo. Whereas the formation of the Schiff base can occur rapidly under physiological conditions, the Amadori product typically develops over several days, and the AGEs are formed even more slowly, over a period of weeks to months (Lee & Cerami, 1992). It is important to realize that the reactions leading to the formation of both the Schiff base and the Amadori product are reversible, and these products thus are present at steady-state levels within tissues. In contrast, some of the reactions that give rise to the AGEs are irreversible, and these species tend to accumulate over time. For proteins that have a long dwell time in the tissue, the extent of glycation may become very significant. Because many glycation products accumulate over time, it is not surprising that the level of glycated proteins in tissues is significantly enhanced with aging and that this pathology is more pronounced in diabetic subjects whose glucose levels are elevated, thereby speeding up the process.

Glycation was found to be more prevalent in extracellular matrix proteins, and this is probably due to the fact that these proteins tend to be longer lived than their intracellular counterparts. Indeed, an aging-related increase in the level of glycated extracellular proteins has been observed in almost all species studied so far. For example, in the structural protein collagen, a buildup of glycated lysines with age has been documented in a number of studies (Garlick et al., 1988; Kohn et al., 1984; Mikski & Deyl, 1991; Oimomi et al., 1986). The glycation-induced cross-linking of collagen type I was shown to effect an expansion of the molecular packing (Tanaka et al., 1988) and to covalently cross-link this protein to soluble plasma proteins (Brownlee et al., 1983, 1985; Sensi et al., 1986), a reaction that may contribute to the narrowing of the vascular lumen. In both basement membrane collagen and laminin, the AGEs were found to interfere with normal associations and with the proper self-assembly of these proteins (Charonis, Reger, & Dege, 1990; Tsilbary, Charonis, & Reger, 1988). Glycation-induced abnormalities in the extracellular matrix were found to alter both the structure and the function of intact vessels, thereby implicating these reactions as a contributing factor in atherosclerosis (Hogan et al., 1992). In this context, it is interesting to note the study reporting that treatment of dogs for one month with the AGE cross-link breaker ALT–711 resulted in a significant reduction (40%) in the level of age-related left ventricular stiffness, which is characteristic of the old heart, with a concomitant improvement in cardiac function (Asif et al., 1999). An age-related increase in the level of glycation of the unusually long-lived eye lens protein α-crystallin has been reported to occur in bovine lenses (Harding et al., 1989), but surprisingly not in human or rat lenses (Patrick et al., 1990; Perry et al., 1987). Thus, the reaction may be species-dependent. It is interesting to note that α-crystallin has been shown to be a member of the family of small heat-shock proteins and was found to effectively protect a number of proteins against glycation in vitro (Ganea & Harding, 1994, 1995; Heath et al., 1996). Whether this protein affords similar protection to cellular proteins in vivo remains to be tested.

Whereas glycation is most prevalent in extracellular proteins, it is important to mention that some intracellular proteins, whose turnover rate is slow, also are susceptible to AGE formation. For example, red blood cell hemoglobin, whose dwell time in human erythrocytes is ca. 120 days, is measurably glycated. Indeed, in normal individuals glycated hemoglobin constitutes 3–5% of total hemoglobin, and the extent of modification increases significantly in diabetics, who may have levels as high as 15% (Trivelli et al., 1971). This large increase in the level of glycated hemoglobin can serve in the clinical identification of diabetic individuals. It is also pertinent to mention that, because the tetrameric hemoglobin displays strong cooperativity in oxygen binding and release, modification of any one of the subunits may affect the biological activity of the unaffected subunits in the same molecule and, therefore, the effect of glycation on biological activity may be significantly larger than the level of modification.

The relatively high turnover rate of most intracellular proteins makes them less likely to form AGEs; however, it is important to realize that these proteins can still react with sugars to produce significant amounts of the more rapidly forming Amadori product. Such modifications were indeed found to occur in liver alcohol dehydrogenase *in vivo* (Shilton & Walton, 1991). Several reports reveal that the glycolytic enzyme glyceraldehyde-3-phosphate dehydrogenase (GAPDH) isolated from rabbit muscle or from erythrocytes is also partially glycated (He *et al.*, 1995), and whereas the chemical identity of the product was not determined, clearly it must be quite stable because glycated GAPDH could be isolated and studied. It therefore appears likely that glycation went beyond the Amadori product. The activity of glycated GAPDH was found to be reduced relative to that of the native enzyme, and modifications to its tertiary (but not secondary) structure were found, which were assigned to the active site domain (He *et al.*, 1995).

3. Asparagine Modification

Asparagine residues in proteins may undergo deamidation to produce aspartate and ammonia. Because aspartate is ionized at physiologic pH, the deamidation reaction introduces a negative charge into a protein. In a number of studies, Gracy and co-workers have demonstrated that the extent of deamidation in several proteins increases with aging. They showed that in both triose-3-phosphate isomerase and glucose-6-phosphate isomerase the electrostatic repulsion among the negative charges introduced by deamidation destabilizes the enzymes, rendering them more susceptible to proteolysis (Cini & Gracy, 1986; Sun *et al.*, 1992a,b; 1995).

Two byproducts of asparagine deamidation in proteins are isoaspartate and D-aspartate. In the production of isoaspartate, the side chain carboxyl group becomes connected in the peptide bond, freeing the α-carboxyl. In contrast, the generation of D-aspartate is due to a racemization reaction where the native L-amino acid is converted into its optical antipode. A detailed model for asparagine deamidation, isomerization, and racemization was presented by Clarke and co-workers (Clarke, 1987; Geiger & Clarke, 1987), who reported that the rates of these reactions in a protein depend both on the amino acid that follows the asparagine residue in the sequence and on the three-dimensional structure of the protein, which imposes conformational restrictions on these reactions. It is pertinent to mention that the racemization of amino acids is a slow process under physiologic conditions. Indeed, aspartic acid, which is the most susceptible to racemization of all of the natural amino acids, only undergoes the transition at a rate of about 0.14% per year. Therefore, one may expect that even in old tissues only a relatively small fraction of aspartate residues will be modified, and it is not surprising that the accumulation of modified aspartate is only significant in long-lived proteins and has been documented in the eye lens, where protein turnover is almost nonexistent, and in red blood cells, where the dwell time of proteins is several months (Brunauer & Clarke, 1986; McFadden & Clarke, 1986; Ota *et al.*, 1987). Thus, whereas isomerization and racemization of asparagine can lead to protein modification, their contribution to the pool of altered proteins is relatively small and will not, as a rule, alter most cellular proteins, whose turnover rate is too high to be affected.

B. Noncovalent Modifications

1. Age-Related Conformational Alterations

The biological activity of a protein critically depends on its precise three-dimensional structure. It is, therefore, easy to understand why any structural alteration may have profound effects on the biological activity. The suggestion that the age-related declines in functional properties of some proteins are due to conformational modifications without accompanying covalent alterations was first made by Rothstein (1979, 1982, 1985), who proposed that this behavior may be due to a longer dwell time of proteins in the cells of old animals. Whereas experimental evidence for such longer dwell times in old tissues does exist, it is important to note that changes in the fidelity of structure evolution during folding can also produce misfolded protein species. Compelling evidence in support of conformational changes as the origin of the age- related modifications in a number of proteins was provided experimentally. Sharma and Rothstein (1978) demonstrated that the two distinct forms of the glycolytic enzyme enolase, isolated from young and old nematodes, respectively, display different activities but share the same amino acid sequence. When these two enzyme species were unfolded by guanidine hydrochloride (a strong denaturant of proteins) and then allowed to refold, they formed an identical structure that was, however, similar to that of old enolase. Although demonstrating that the young and old forms of enolase are conformational isomers, this experiment also revealed that the experimental conditions can determine which of the two conformations will be produced during folding. The presence of young enolase in tissues of young animals thus attests to the presence, in these tissues, of conditions that favor folding into this species.

Strong evidence also was found for conformational modifications as the origin of the observed aging effects in rat kidney maltase (Reiss & Sacktor, 1983) and in rat muscle GAPDH (Gafni, 1985). None of these studies, however, provided direct conclusive evidence that there were no other changes in the old forms of these proteins and, hence, that the alterations responsible for the effects seen were indeed purely conformational.

An Example of Age-Related Conformational Modifications: The Glycolytic Enzyme Phosphoglycerate Kinase (PGK). This enzyme was found to become modified during aging in a number of rat tissues. The most remarkable modification was a marked increase in the protein's heat stability, a property that was, therefore, used to assess the status of this enzyme (Gafni & Yuh, 1989b; Sharma et al., 1980; Sharma & Rothstein, 1984). In an effort to identify the origin of the age-related modifications in PGK, carboxymethylated samples of young and old PGK were treated with three different proteases, and the peptide fragments obtained from each sample were separated by HPLC. These fragments were found to be identical in young and old PGKs (Hardt & Rothstein, 1985), strongly indicating that the old form of PGK possesses no covalent modifications in its structure. In light of the previously discussed study, experiments to test for noncovalent structural changes were conducted. To this end, samples of both young and old PGK were unfolded extensively by guanidine hydrochloride, thereby erasing all differences between the folded structures of the two proteins. Upon refolding following denaturant removal, it was found that both proteins became identical and displayed the characteristics of young PGK (Yuh & Gafni, 1987; Zuniga & Gafni, 1988), as depicted in Fig. 1. This rejuvenation of old PGK by unfolding–refolding

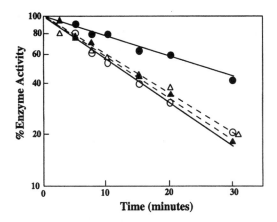

Figure 1. Heat inactivation kinetics of native and unfolded-refolded samples of young and old rat muscle PGKs incubated at 47°C in pH 7.3 buffer containing 10 mM 2-mercaptoethanol. Open symbols represent young enzyme, whereas solid symbols represent the old protein. ($\bigcirc$,$\bullet$), native proteins; ($\triangle$,$\blacktriangle$), unfolded-refolded proteins. (Adapted from Yuh and Gafni, 1987).

provides direct evidence that the aging-related modifications affect only the conformation of this protein.

The precise nature of the structural modifications in old PGK is still to be determined, however, experiments that simulated the aging process of this protein *in vitro* and that produced an enzyme species identical to that found in old tissues indicated that a temporary oxidation of two cysteine residues to form a disulfide bridge serves as an intermediate step in the process. This oxidized PGK intermediate is depicted in Fig. 2. This model gained strong support from the demonstration (Fig. 3) that young PGK in which one of these cysteines has been covalently blocked by methylation, becomes resistant to *in vitro* aging (Cook & Gafni, 1988).

Evidence that old PGK accumulates in aged tissues due to a slower protein turnover, giving the protein more time to undergo structural changes, was provided

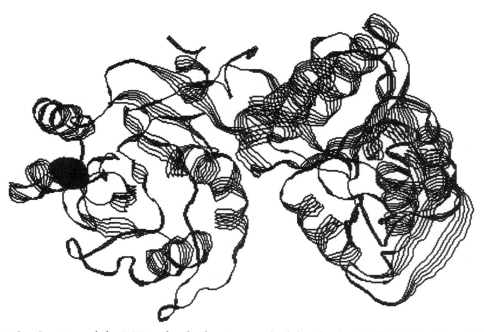

Figure 2. Structure of the PGK molecule showing, on the left side, the disulfide bridge formed by the oxidation of the two juxtaposed cysteine residues. Formation of the S-S bond introduces a conformational change in the protein producing the more stable old form.

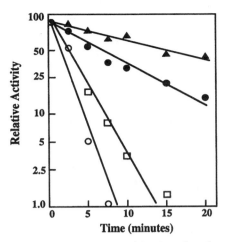

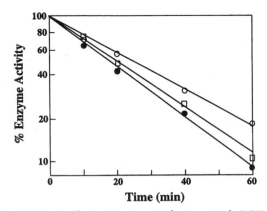

Figure 3. Heat inactivation kinetics of native and methylated PGKs at 47°C. Open circles represent native young PGK; filled triangles represent native young PGK aged *in vitro* by oxidation-reduction; open squares represent young PGK methylated prior to oxidation-reduction; and filled circles represent native old PGK. (Data adapted from Cook and Gafni, 1988).

Figure 4. The inactivation kinetics of PGK samples isolated from young (squares), sedentary old (open circles) and endurance-trained old (filled circles) rats. Young animals were 4.5 months old and old rats were 22 months old. Enzyme solutions in 70 mM Tris-acetate buffer (pH 8.0) containing 10 mM 2-mercaptoethanol were incubated at 45°C and their activities were assayed as a function of incubation time. The inactivation kinetics of the PGK from endurance-trained old rats clearly is much more similar to that of enzyme from young animals than to PGK from sedentary old rats. (Adapted from Zhou *et al.*, 1990).

by experiments with regenerating liver (Hiremath & Rothstein, 1982). Young and old rats were partially hepatectomized, and PGK from the regenerating tissues was purified at different times and tested. The results revealed no difference between freshly synthesized enzyme in young and old animals, whereas nine days into regeneration the enzyme in the old animals displayed the characteristics of old PGK. It was concluded that the old enzyme is derived from young enzyme by postsynthetic modifications.

Further support for the hypothesis that structural modifications develop in old PGK due to its longer dwell time in the tissue was lent by experiments with endurance-trained rats (Zhou *et al.*, 1990). Exercise-induced damage to muscle proteins triggers *de novo* protein synthesis and was, therefore, expected to increase the rate of turnover of proteins in these cells. Indeed, as shown in Fig. 4, when PGK samples from young, sedentary old, and endurance- trained old rats

were compared, the enzymes from the young and the trained-old rats were found to be similar and distinctly different from the old enzyme from sedentary old animals. Moreover, the old protein could be converted to its young counterpart by an unfolding–refolding protocol as described earlier.

The results of the previously described studies strongly support the notion that the age- related modifications observed in PGK are purely conformational. Moreover, the structural alterations develop after the protein has folded to its native state (as opposed to being the result of incorrect folding of the newly synthe- sized protein due, for example, to the lack of a chaperone protein in the old cells). These structural modifications occur slowly under reducing conditions but are greatly accelerated in a cysteine-oxidized protein (with the conformational alter- ation persisting after cysteine reduction).

Thus, covalent cysteine oxidation is likely to produce an intermediate in the aging reaction. The alterations found in PGK are prevalent in old tissues because the rate of turnover of the protein is reduced (under sedentary conditions, but can be enhanced by exercise), allowing the molecules more time to convert to the old form

2. Protein Aggregation and Amyloid Formation

In their native folded state, soluble globular proteins as a rule place hydrophobic amino acid residues in the interior and expose only polar residues to the aqueous solvent. Exposure of "sticky" domains, rich in hydrophobic amino acid residues, leads to protein aggregation and precipitation, a common fate of misfolded proteins. Not surprisingly, a number of age-associated diseases and pathologies are characterized by the tissue deposition of aggregates composed of conformationally modified proteins. In some cases, these precipitates are amorphous as, for example, the protein deposits responsible

for the age-related opacification of the mammalian eye lens, whereas in other cases the modified protein assembles into ordered, fibrillar structures termed amyloid. In amyloid fibrils the individual protein molecules assume a predominantly β-sheet-type secondary structure and assemble into a characteristic cross-β-structure, as shown in Fig. 5 (Kelly, 1996). These deposits are the major pathology in several devastating age-associated human diseases, including Alzheimer's disease and late-onset diabetes (Kelly & Lansbury, 1994).

The formation of amyloid is believed to follow a nucleation-dependent polymerization mechanism, though it is important to mention that this process still is not fully understood. About 20 proteins are known to possess a high propensity to form amyloid, and it is interesting to note that they display little sequence or structural homology (Kelly, 1996). The similarity among amyloidogenic proteins thus is not in their native folded structure (they are, in fact, not amyloidogenic in their normal state), but rather in their tendency to undergo a conformational

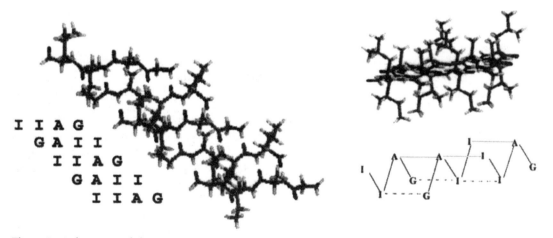

Figure 5. A depiction of the structure of a segment of the Aβ fibril modeled after the corresponding structure of the h-IAPP fibril derived from solid-state NMR (From Griffiths, *et al.*, 1995). The left panel shows a top view, whereas the right panel presents a side view. Each view is accompanied by a schematic depiction of the arrangement of the participating residues, GAII.

modification and to acquire amyloido-genicity. A comparison of the evolution of amyloid deposits in different diseases reveals that the process does not follow a uniform pathway, but rather is specific to the protein involved. Thus, the amyloido-genic species may be an erroneously produced fragment of a protein or a cleav-age peptide, which is part of the normal degradation process of the protein. In other cases, the amyloid is formed from the intact protein in a "spontaneous" process, whereas in yet other cases aggre-gation of the otherwise normal protein is triggered by infection with the diseased form of the protein. Examples of proteins in the first category include fibrinogen fragments, whose deposition is responsi-ble for hereditary renal amyloidosis (Uemichi et al., 1994), serum amyloid A, whose fragment is involved in secondary systemic amyloidosis (Cohen, 1994), and the amyloid precursor protein, whose cleavage product, β-amyloid, is deposited to form plaques in the brain of Alzheimer's disease patients (Kelly & Lansbury, 1994). Examples of proteins from the second category include the pancreatic hormone amylin, whose amyloid deposits are prevalent in non-insulin- dependent diabetes (Edwards & Morley, 1992; O'Brien et al., 1993), and transthyretin, which is featured in senile systemic amyloidosis (Kelly, 1996). Prominent in the class of infectious amyloidogenic proteins are the prion proteins which are deposited in the brain in a number of diseases including scrapie and Creutzfeldt-Jakob disease (Come & Lansbury, 1994; Nguyen et al., 1995; Zhang et al., 1995).

Some amyloid diseases display a pronounced age dependence, and their prevalence increases rapidly toward the end of the life span. Possibly the best known of these is Alzheimer's disease, which is characterized by the deposition of amyloid fibrils in the brain. As mentioned earlier, these fibrils are composed mostly of the β-amyloid peptide, a 40–43 amino acid fragment of the much larger amyloid precursor protein (APP). The conformational changes that convert the soluble peptide to its amyloidogenic form involve a trans-formation from a predominantly α-heli-cal structure, which is nonaggregatable, to a mostly β-sheet structure, which is highly aggregatable.

The deposition of amyloid composed of the 37-amino acid peptide amylin in the pancreas of patients with late-onset diabetes mellitus also involves the conversion of the peptide's secondary structure from a predominantly α-helical one to a β-sheet (Charge et al., 1995; Lorenzo et al., 1994). This system has not been studied in as much detail as the β-amyloid one, and our understanding of the changes in the cellular environment responsible for amylin aggregation, as well as the relevance of the amylin deposits in diabetes, is still sketchy.

The thyroxine transporter plasma protein transthyretin (TTR) can undergo conformational modifications that lead to its aggregation and deposition as amyloid in the heart and can cause congestive heart failure. This condition, termed senile systemic amyloidosis, is strongly age- dependent and usually develops around the age of 80. In its native state, TTR is a homotetrameric protein (Blake et al., 1978); however, upon dissociation into monomeric subunits, the protein undergoes a conformational change and becomes highly amyloidogenic (Colon & Kelly, 1992; Lai et al., 1996; McCutchen et al., 1993, 1995). Mutants of TTR isolated from individuals with the famil-ial form of the disease (which is much more aggressive and displays an early onset) were indeed found to form less stable protein tetramers and revealed a strong correlation between tetramer instability and amyloidogenicity, as discerned both from fibril formation in vitro and from the age of onset of the disease *in vivo* (Colon & Kelly, 1992). On the basis of these results, as well as extensive biophysical studies, Kelly and co-workers have proposed a structure for the amyloidogenic intermediate of TTR in which the tertiary structure is modified but the secondary structure remains native (Kelly, 1996). As in the other amyloidogenic diseases described previously, the structural and mechanistic studies of fibril formation, although very instructive, do not provide a clear answer to the question of why the process is so strongly age-related. Some possible reasons will be discussed next.

3. Origin of Age-Related Increase in Misfolded and Aggregated Proteins

The age-related modifications in proteins described in this section all involve the conversion of a correctly folded protein into a conformational isomer. In some cases, the altered protein remains monomeric and soluble, albeit with modified properties (for example, PGK), whereas in other cases the new structure has a high propensity to self-assemble into amyloid deposits. Several factors may account for the enhanced accumulation of these two types of conformationally modified proteins in old tissues.

1. The process of protein folding, as with any chemical reaction, is driven toward the lowest possible free energy, where the system reaches equilibrium and ceases to change. However, the biologically active (native) form of a protein may be associated with a metastable intermediate structure, which does not represent the equilibrium state. The protein in such cases therefore will continue to fold, given enough time, to more stable conformations. One example of this type of behavior, PGK, has been described earlier.

2. As discussed in previous sections, a large body of work exists that demonstrates a progressive increase, with aging, in the level of proteins that have been covalently modified by reactions such as glycation, oxidation, etc. The altered polypeptide chain, as a rule, encodes a different folded structure for the protein, which in the majority of cases will be functionally deficient. This altered conformation often may also expose "sticky" domains and thus promote aggregation. Such an increase with aging in the concentration of the amyloidogenic form of a protein may be responsible for the amyloid formation by the Alzheimer's peptide (Bhattacharya *et al.*, 1994; Hensley *et al.*, 1995), as well as by proteins involved in other amyloidogenic diseases.

3. A major tenet of modern biology is that all of the information needed for the correct folding of a protein is contained in its amino acid sequence. However, it has become evident that the folding of most proteins in the cell requires assistance from auxiliary proteins. Some of these helper proteins are enzymes, such as protein disulfide isomerase, which catalyzes the formation of the correct disulfide bonds within proteins, and peptidyl prolyl isomerase, which accelerates the cis–trans isomerization of prolyl peptide bonds (two intrinsically slow reactions that, when not accelerated, tend to clog the folding pathway). Another important group of folding assistants is the molecular chaperones, proteins that help direct folding along the correct pathway by inhibiting off-pathway processes and interactions (Hendrick & Hartl, 1993; Horwitz, 1992), that would otherwise lead to the accumulation of protein precipitates, called inclusion bodies, in the cell (Chrunyk *et al.*, 1993). A pronounced induction of chaperone protein production is a major organismal response to stressful conditions, which damage cellular proteins and trigger a burst of *de novo* protein synthesis. An age-related decline in the ability of cells to induce chaperone protein production in response to stress has been documented in a number of studies (Fargnoli

et al., 1990; Heydari *et al.*, 1994; Kregel *et al.*, 1995; Pahlavani *et al.*, 1995), and it therefore appears likely that the structural fidelity of cellular proteins may be affected, leading to the observed increase in the prevalence of amyloidogenic diseases with aging.

It is interesting to note that evidence has been presented demonstrating that chaperone proteins may also facilitate "misfolding" (i.e., folding into biologically pathological structures), if the fully folded state of the protein is not the active state but rather the pathological one. This idea has been suggested to explain the conversion, by chaperone proteins, of prion proteins to their diseased state (DebBurman *et al.*, 1997; Schirmer & Lindquist, 1997). Whether this activity of chaperone proteins also is featured in the production of the old forms of other cellular proteins remains to be tested.

III. Age-Related Changes in Protein Maturation and Turnover

In all living organisms, the rate of protein turnover is kept under tight control to ensure that the activities of these molecules are well-regulated at any point in time. Protein synthesis, folding, and post-translational processing, as well as protein degradation, are highly complex processes that use significant cellular energy. Changes during aging in any component of these processes thus are of great potential importance. Age-related changes in protein turnover have been reviewed in detail by Rattan (1996), and only a brief summary of current knowledge is presented here.

A. Changes in Protein Synthesis

Changes, during aging, in the accuracy and rate of protein synthesis or of their postsynthetic processing, as well as changes in the fidelity of protein folding, may result in a significant alteration in their observed activities, and all of these aspects have been studied. Whereas direct estimates of the age-related changes in the level of amino acid mis-incorporation into proteins have not been reported yet, a comparison of the charged state of proteins extracted from young and old cells, as well as from young and old specimens of *Caenorhabditis elegans*, by two-dimensional electrophresis revealed no differences (Harley *et al.*, 1980; Johnson & McCaffrey, 1985; Rattan, 1996). This shows that no mis-incorporation of charged amino acids has occurred. Another approach to probe the accuracy of protein synthesis during aging was used in studies that tested the capacity and accuracy of ribosomes in young and old cells to translate poly(U) in cell-free extracts (Filion & Laughrea, 1985; Laughrea & Latulippe, 1988). No significant age-related effects were found; however, the validity of these results is not clear because the error frequencies revealed in the essays were severalfold larger than the estimated frequencies of natural error (Holliday, 1995).

The presence of age-related changes in the accuracy of protein synthesis by mouse liver ribosomes in cell-free medium was also tested by measuring the incorporation of radioactive lysine during the translation of trout protamine mRNA, which does not have codons for lysine (Mori *et al.*, 1983). No aging-related changes were found. In contrast, a sevenfold increase in cysteine mis-incorporation during cellular aging was reported in experiments with cell extracts made from young and old human fibroblasts (Luce & Bunn, 1989). Addition of the antibiotic paromomycin, which is known to reduce ribosomal translation accuracy both *in vivo* and *in vitro*, to cell extracts prepared from senescent human fibroblasts was found to induce more errors in the translation of CcTMV coat protein mRNA than those induced in extracts from young cells (Luce & Bunn, 1989).

Clearly the protein synthetic machinary in old cells is more error-prone under this "antibiotic-induced stress" and potentially under other stressful conditions. Additional, though again indirect, evidence for the role that an increased level of error in protein synthesis may play in aging is provided by studies that demonstrate that mutants of *Podospora anserina* that possess a high fidelity of protein synthesis display increased longevity (Silar & Picard, 1994). It is pertinent to mention that this age-related decline in the fidelity of protein synthesis originates in the synthetic apparatus, not in gene mutation, and therefore does not involve the feedback mechanism that is at the basis of the "Error Catastrophe" theory.

B. Changes in Protein Folding

The successful synthesis of a protein's polypeptide chain is not sufficient to ensure the production of the corresponding biological activity. For the latter to develop, the polypeptide chain must assume a precise three-dimensional structure. This is achieved by a process termed protein folding, in which the information contained in the sequence of amino acids is translated into a biologically active structure. As mentioned earlier, the folding of most proteins *in vivo* relies on assistance from specific helper proteins. The levels of these chaperone proteins in the cell are highly elevated in response to exposure to a variety of stressful conditions to allow for the folding of the large amounts of proteins synthesized to replace damaged ones. One of the hallmarks of aging is the loss of the ability of the organism to respond effectively and rapidly to external stresses, and there is good evidence that the induction of the expression of HSP70, the most studied chaperone protein, in different tissues of rats in response to stress is greatly attenuated during aging

(Blake *et al.*, 1991; Moore *et al.*, 1998; Richardson & Holbrook 1996; see Chapter 6 in this volume). Richardson and co-workers have shown that the defect occurs at the level of transcription and that it strongly correlates with a decrease in the affinity of binding of the HSP transcription activator to the corresponding DNA sequence, known as the heat-shock element. Whereas reduction, during aging, in the quantity or activity of other chaperone proteins has not been studied, it appears likely that, when old cells are placed under stressful conditions and are forced to make a large amount of proteins, a lack of the chaperone proteins needed to assist these nascent proteins in folding may lead to the accumulation of misfolded, aberrant proteins. More studies should be done to test this possibility.

C. Changes in Protein Degradation

The degradation of cellular proteins is a highly regulated process that allows the living organism not only to remove damaged proteins but to turn off activities that are no longer needed. Indeed, in living tissues the rates of degradation of individual proteins vary by many orders of magnitude (from several minutes to many days). There is still no systematic documentation of the effects of aging on the rate of protein degradation; however, published work supports the notion that protein degradation slows down during the latter part of life. A comprehensive review of this topic has been presented (Van Remmen *et al.*, 1995). The reason proposed for this decline is a reduction in the proteolytic activities of both lysosomal and cytoplasmic proteases. This, in turn, may be due to a reduced rate of synthesis of these proteases, lowering their concentrations in the cell, postsynthetic modifications that lower their activities, or an aging-related increase in the levels of specific protease inhibitors in the tissue. For example, there is evidence that the levels of the tissue inhibitor of metalloproteinases (Wick *et al.*, 1994), as well as that of trypsin inhibitor (Hearn *et al.*, 1994), are increased during aging in human fibroblasts, leading to a decrease in the proteolytic activities of the corresponding proteases and to slower protein degradation.

The multicatalytic proteinase, termed proteasome, is the major proteolytic system responsible for the degradation of cellular proteins. Changes, with aging, in the proteolytic activities of proteasomes in a number of rat tissues have been addressed. Though not ubiquitous, significant declines in this activity were found to occur in old tissues (Conconi, & Friguet, 1997; Hayashi & Goto, 1998; Keller *et al.*, 2000) as well as in T-cells (Ponnappan *et al.*, 1999). It thus appears that decreased proteasome-mediated protein degradation may play an important role in the accumulation of altered proteins during aging and may be central to immune dysfunction in old age (Ponnappan *et al.*, 1999).

Our understanding of changes, with aging, in the rate of protein degradation or of the effects such changes have on the levels and activities of cellular proteins is still incomplete. This problem represents an important area for future research.

IV. Concluding Remarks and Future Prospects

More than 30 years have passed since Orgel proposed his Error Catastrophe theory in an attempt to provide a molecularly based explanation for aging. Though later withdrawn, this hypothesis prompted the search for age-modified proteins that led, several years later, to the discovery of the first example of such species (Gershon & Gershon, 1970). We now know that many, though not all, proteins are modified in the tissues of old animals. Whereas defects in protein synthesis may shorten cellular life span, the age-related protein modifications identified thus far are mostly introduced by postsynthetic events and usually are not the result of deficiencies in the protein-synthesizing machinery. A number of mechanisms that lead to protein modifications have been identified and studied, some introducing covalent alterations into the polypeptide chain and others affecting the fidelity of the folding pattern of the protein. A reduced ability of cells in old organisms to respond to stressful conditions by elevating the levels of chaperone proteins may be featured in this age-related accumulation of misfolded proteins. Whereas the question of whether modified proteins are at the origin of the aging process or its victims has not been answered, it is clear that their accumulation in old tissues can be highly detrimental. Indeed, an increasing number of devastating diseases has been linked to the presence of structurally modified, and functionally defective, proteins. Some of these diseases are strongly aging- associated and are characterized by the appearance of amyloid deposits composed of misfolded, aggregated proteins in the diseased tissue. A search for the molecular basis of these diseases and for successful intervention strategies is currently underway in a large number of laboratories. This is a timely effort because, with the projected increase in life expectancy, the number of people affected by diabetes, Alzheimer's disease, etc. is expected to increase rapidly, and the importance of strategies to treat or, better yet, inhibit these diseases cannot be overstated.

Acknowledgement

The preparation of this manuscript has been supported in part by a grant from the National Institute on Aging.

References

Agarwal, S., & Sohal, R. S. (1995). Differential oxidative damage to mitochondrial proteins during aging. *Mechanisms of Ageing and Development, 85*, 55–63.

Asif, M., Egan, J., Vasan, S., Jyothirmayi, G. N., Masurekar, M. R., Lopez, S., Williams, C., Torres, R. L., Wagle, D., Ulrich, P., Cerami, A., Brines, M., & Regan, T. J. (1999). An advanced glycation endproduct cross-link breaker can reverse age-related increases in myocardial stiffness. *Proceedings of the National Academy of Science, USA, 97*, 2809–2813.

Beckman, K. B., & Ames, B. N. (1999). Endogenous oxidative damage of mtDNA. *Mutation Research, 424*, 51–58.

Berlett, B. S., & Stadtman, E. R. (1997). Protein oxidation in aging, disease, and oxidative stress. *Journal of Biological Chemistry, 272*, 20313–20316.

Berlett, B. S., Levine, R. L., & Stadtman, E. R. (1996). A comparison of the effects of ozone on the modification of amino acid residues in glutamine synthetase and bovine serum albumin. *Journal of Biological Chemistry, 271*, 4177–4182.

Bhattacharya, K., Glendening, J. M., Stopa, E., Vlassara, H., Bucala, R., Manogue, K., & Cerami, A. (1994). Advanced glycation end products contribute to amyloidosis in Alzheimer disease. *Proceedings of the National Academy of Science, USA, 91*, 4766–4770.

Blake, C. C. F., Geisow, M. J., & Oatley, S. J. (1978). Structure of prealbumin (transthyretin): Secondary, tertiary and quaternary interactions determined by Fourier refinement at 1.8 Å. *Journal of Molecular Biology, 121*, 339–356.

Blake, M. J., Fargnoli, J., Gershon, D., & Holbrook, N. J. (1991). Concomitant decline in heat-induced hyperthermia and HSP70 mRNA expression in aged rats. *American Journal of Physiology, 260*, 663–667.

Brownlee, M. (1995). Advanced protein glycosylation in diabetes and aging. *Annual Reviews of Medicine, 46*, 223–234.

Brownlee, M., Pongor, S., & Cerami, A. (1983). Covalent attachment of soluble protein by nonenzymatically glycosylated collagen: Role in the *in situ* formation of immune complexes. *Journal of Experimental Medicine, 158*, 1739–1744.

Brownlee, M., Vlassara, H., & Cerami, A. (1985). Non-enzymatic glycosylation products of collagen covalently trap low-density lipo-protein. *Diabetes, 34*, 938–941.

Brunauer, L. S., & Clarke, S. (1986). Age-related accumulation of protein residues which can be hydrolyzed to D-aspartic acid in human erythrocytes. *Journal of Biological Chemistry, 261*, 12538–12543.

Carney, J. M., & Carney, A. M. (1994). Role of protein oxidation in aging and in age-associated neurodegenerative diseases. *Life Science, 55*, 2097–2103.

Carney, J. M., Starke-Reed, P. E., Oliver, C. N., Landum, R. W., Cheng, M. S., Wu, J. F., & Floyd, R. A. (1991). Reversal of age-related increase in brain protein oxidation, decrease in enzyme activity and loss in temporal and spatial memory by chronic administration of the spin-trapping compound *N-tert*-butyl-alpha-phenylnitrone. *Proceedings of the National Academy of Science, USA, 88*, 3633–3636.

Charge, S. B., de-Koning, E. J., & Clark, A. (1995). Effect of pH and insulin on fibrillogenesis of islet amyloid polypeptide *in vitro*. *Biochemistry, 34*, 14588–14593.

Charonis, A. S., Reger, L. A., Dege, J. E., Kouzi-Koliakos K., Furcht L. T., Wohlhueter R. M., & Tsilibary E. C. (1990). Laminin alterations after *in vitro* nonenzymatic glycosylaton. *Diabetes, 39*, 807–814.

Chrunyk, B. A., Evans, J., & Wetzel, R. (1993). Probing the role of protein folding in inclusion body formation. In (Cleland, J. L., Ed.), *Protein Folding: In Vivo and In Vitro* (pp. 46–58). Washington, DC: American Chemical Society.

Cini, J. K., & Gracy, R. W. (1986). Molecular basis of the isozymes of bovine glucose-6- phosphate isomerase. *Archives of Biochemistry and Biophysics, 249*, 500–505.

Clarke, S. (1987). Propensity for spontaneous succinimide formation from aspartyl and asparaginyl residues in cellular proteins. *International Journal of Peptide and Protein Research, 30*, 808–821.

Cohen, A. S. (1994). Proteins of the systemic amyloidoses. *Curreent Opinions in Rheumatology, 6,* 55–67.

Colon, W., & Kelly, J. W. (1992). Partial denaturation of transthyretin is sufficient for amyloid fibril formation *in vitro. Biochemistry, 31,* 8654–8660.

Come, J. H., & Lansbury, P. T., Jr. (1994). Predisposition of prion protein homozygotes to Creutzfeldt-Jakob disease can be explained by a nucleation-dependent polymerization mechanism. *Journal of the American Chemical Society, 116,* 4109–4110.

Conconi, M., & Friguet, B. (1997). Proteasome inactivation upon aging and on oxidation- effect of HSP 90. *Molecular Biology Reports, 24,* 45–50.

Conconi, M., Szweda, L. I., Levine, R. L., Stadtman, E. R., & Friguet, B. (1996). Age-related decline of rat liver multicatalytic proteinase activity and protection from oxidative inactivation by heat-shock protein 90. *Archives of Biochemistry and Biophysics, 331,* 232–240.

Cook, L. L., & Gafni, A. (1988). Protection of phosphoglycerate kinase against *in vitro* aging by selective cysteine methylation. *Journal of Biological Chemistry, 263,* 13991–13993.

Davies, K. J. (1993). Protein modification by oxidants and the role of proteolytic enzymes. *Biochemical Society Transactions, 21,* 346–353.

Davies, K. J. (1995). Oxidative stress: The paradox of aerobic life. *Biochemical Society Symposia, 61,* 1–31.

Dean, R. T., Gebicki, J., Gieseg, S., Grant, A. J., & Simpson, J. A. (1992). Hypothesis: A damaging role in aging for reactive protein oxidation products? *Mutations Research, 275,* 387–393.

DebBurman, S. K., Raymond, G. J., Caughey, B., & Lindquist, S. (1997). Chaperone-supervised conversion of prion protein to its protease-resistant form. *Proceedings of the National Academy of Science, USA, 94,* 13938–13943.

Dovrat A, Scharf J, Eisenbach L, & Gershon, D. (1986). Glucose–6-phosphate dehydrogenase molecules devoid of catalytic activity are present in the nucleus of the rat lens. *Experimental Eye Research, 42,* 489–496.

Edwards, J. A., & Morley, J. E. (1992). Amylin. *Life Science, 51,* 1899–1912.

Farber, J. M., & Levine, R. L. (1996). Sequence of a peptide susceptible to mixed-function oxidation: Probable cation binding site in glutamine synthetase. *Journal of Biological Chemistry, 261,* 4574–4578.

Fargnoli, J., Kunisada, T., Fornace, A. J., Schneider, E. L., & Holbrook, N. J. (1990). Decreased expression of heat shock protein 70 mRNA and protein after heat treatment in cells of aged rats. *Proceedings of the National Academy of Science, USA, 87,* 846–850.

Ferrington, D. A., Jones, T. E., Qin, Z., Miller-Schlyer, M., Squier, T. C., & Bigelow, D. J. (1997). Decreased conformational stability of the sarcoplasmic reticulum Ca-ATPase in aged skeletal muscle. *Biochimica et Biophysica Acta, 1330(2),* 223–47.

Filion, A. M., & Laughrea, M. (1985). Translation fidelity in the aging mammal. Studies with an accurate *in vitro* system on aged rats. *Mechanisms of Ageing and Development, 29,* 125–142.

Fujimori, E. (1982). Crosslinking and blue-fluorescence of photo-oxidized calf-lens alpha- crystallin. *Experimental Eye Research, 34,* 381–388.

Gafni, A. (1983). Molecular origin of the aging effects in glyceraldehyde–3-phosphate dehydrogenase. *Biochimica et Biophysica Acta, 742,* 91–99.

Gafni, A. (1985). Age-related modifications in a muscle enzyme. In *Modifications of Proteins During Aging* (pp. 19–39). New York: Alan R. Liss.

Gafni, A. (1991). Altered protein metabolism in aging. *Annual Reviews of Gerontology and Geriatrics, 10,* 117–131.

Gafni A. (1997) Structural modification in proteins during aging. *Journal of the American Geriatrics Society, 45,* 871–880.

Gafni, A., & Yuh, K. C. (1989a). A comparative study of the Ca^{2+}–Mg^{2+} dependent ATPase from skeletal muscles of young, adult and old rats. *Mechanisms of Ageing and Development, 49,* 105–117.

Gafni, A., & Yuh, K. C. M. (1989b). Age-related molecular changes in skeletal muscle. In (D. L. Snyder, Ed.), *Dietary Restriction and Aging* (pp. 277–282). New York: Alan R. Liss.

Ganea, E., & Harding, J. J. (1994). Inactivation of glucose–6-phosphate dehydrogenase by glycation. *Biochemical Society Transactions, 22,* 445S.

Ganea, E., & Harding, J. J. (1995). Molecular chaperones protect against glycation-induced inactivation of glucose-6-phosphate dehydrogenase. *Europian Journal of Biochemistry, 231,* 181–185.

Garland, D., Russell, P., & Zigler, J. S. (1988). *The Oxidative Modification of Lens Proteins* (pp. 347–353). New York: Plenum Press.

Garlick, R. L., Bunn, H. F., & Spiro, R. G. (1988). Nonenzymatic glycation of basement membranes from human glomeruli and bovine sources: Effect of diabetes and aging. *Diabetes, 37,* 1144–1155.

Geiger, T., & Clarke, S. (1987). Deamidation, isomerization and racemization at asparaginyl and aspartyl residues in proteins. *Journal of Biological Chemistry, 262,* 785–794.

Gershon, H., & Gershon, D. (1970). Detection of inactive enzyme molecules in aging organisms. *Nature, 227,* 1214–1218.

Gordillo, E., Ayala, A., F-Lobato, M., Bautista, J., & Machado, A. (1988). Possible involvement of histidine residues in the loss of enzymatic activity of rat liver malic enzyme during aging. *Journal of Biological Chemistry, 263,* 8053–8057.

Griffiths, J. M., Ashburn, T. T., Auger, M., Costa, P. R., Griffin, R. G., & Lansbury, P. T. Jr. (1995). Rotational resonance solid-state NMR elucidates a structural model of pancreatic amyloid. *Journal of the American Chemical Society, 117,* 3539–3546.

Harding, J. J., Beswick, H. T., Ajiboye, R., Huby, R., Blakytny, R., & Rixon, K. C. (1989). Non-enzymic post-translation modification of proteins in ageing. A review. *Mechanisms of Ageing and Development, 50,* 7–16.

Hardt, H., & Rothstein, M. (1985). Altered phosphoglycerate kinase form old rat muscle shows no change in primary structure. *Biochimica et Biophysica Acta, 831,* 13–21.

Harley, C. B., Pollard, J. W., Chamberlain, J. W., Stanners, C. P., & Goldstein, S. (1980). Protein synthetic errors do not increase during the aging of cultured human fibroblasts. *Proceedings of the National Academy of Science, USA, 77,* 1885–1889.

Harman, D. (1956). Aging: a theory based on free radical and radiation chemistry. *Journal of Gerontology, 11,* 298–300.

Harman, D. (1988). Free radicals in aging. *Molecular and Cellular Biochemistry, 84,* 155–161.

Hayashi, T., & Goto, S. (1998). Age-related changes in the 20S and 26S proteasome activities in the liver of male F344 rats. *Mechanisms of Ageing and Development, 102,* 55–66.

He, R. Q., Yang, M. D., Zheng, X., & Zhou, J. X. (1995). Isolation and some properties of glycated D-glyceraldehyde–3-phosphate dehydrogenase from rabbit muscle. *Biochemical Journal, 309,* 133–139.

Hearn, M. G. Edland, S. D., Ogburn, C. E., Smith, A. C., Bird, T. D., Martin, G. M., & Fukuchi, K. I. (1994). Trypsin inhibitor activities of fibroblasts increase with age of donor and are unaltered in familial Alzheimer's disease. *Experimental Gerontology, 29,* 611–623.

Heath, M. M., Rixon, K. C., & Harding, J. J. (1996). Glycation-induced inactivation of malate dehydrogenase protection by aspirin and a lens molecular chaperone, alpha-crystallin. *Biochimica et Biophysica Acta, 1315,* 176–184.

Hendrick, J. P., & Hartl, F. U. (1993). Molecular chaperone functions of heat shock proteins. *Annual Reviews of Biochemistry, 62,* 349–384.

Hensley, K., Butterfield, D. A., Mattson, M., Aksenova, M., Harris, M., Wu, J. F., Floyd, R., & Carney, J. (1995). A model for beta-amyloid aggregation and neurotoxicity based on the free radical generating capacity of the peptide: Implications of "molecular shrapnel" for Alzheimer's disease. *Proceedings of the Pharmacological Society, 38,* 113–120.

Heydari, A. R., Takahashi, R., Gutsmann, A., You, S., & Richardson, A. (1994). Hsp 70 and aging. *Experientia, 50,* 1092–1098.

Hiremath, L. S., & Rothstein, M. (1982) Regenerating liver in aged rats produces unaltered phosphoglycerate kinase. *Journal of Gerontology, 37,* 680–683.

Hogan, M., Cerami, A., & Bucala, R. (1992). Advanced glycosylation end products block the antiproliferative effect of nitric oxide. *Journal of Clinical Investigations, 90,* 1110–1115.

Holliday, R. (1995). *Understanding Ageing.* Cambridge, England: Cambridge University Press.

Horwitz, J., (1992). Alpha crystallin can function as a molecular chaperone. *Proceedings of the National Academy of Science, USA, 89,* 10449–10453.

Johnson, T. E., & McCaffrey, G. (1985). Programmed aging or error catastrophe: An examination by two-dimensional polyacrylamide gel electrophoresis. *Mechanisms of Ageing and Development, 30,* 285–287.

Johnson, T. E., Lithgow, G. J., & Murakami, S. (1996). Hypothesis: interventions that increase the response to stress offer the potential for effective life prolongation and increased health. *Journal of Gerontology Biological Sciences, 51A,* B392-B395.

Keller, J. N., Hanni, K. B., and Markesbery, W. R. (2000). Possible involvement of proteasome inhibition in aging: Implications for oxidative stress. *Mechanisms of Ageing and Development, 113,* 61–70.

Kelly, J. W. (1996). Alternative conformations of amyloidogenic proteins govern their behavior. *Current Opinions in Structural Biology, 6,* 11–17.

Kelly, J. W., & Lansbury, P. T. (1994). A chemical approach to elucidate the mechanism of transthyretin and beta-protein amyloid fibril formation. *Amyloid, 1,* 186–205.

Knecht, K. J., Thorpe, S. R., & Baynes, J. W. (1992). Role of oxygen in cross-linking and chemical modification of collagen by glucose. *Diabetes, 41,* 42–48.

Kohn, R. R., Cerami, A., & Monnier, V. M. (1984). Collagen aging in vitro by nonenzymatic glycosylation and browning. *Diabetes, 33,* 57–59.

Krainev, A. G., Ferrington, D. A., Williams, T. D., Squier, T. C., & Bigelow, D. J. (1995). Adaptive changes in lipid composition of skeletal sarcoplasmic reticulum membranes associated with aging. *Biochimica et Biophysica Acta, 1235,* 406–18.

Kregel, K. C., Moseley, P. L., Skidmore, R., Gutierrez, J. A., & Guerriero, V., Jr. (1995). Hsp 70 accumulation in tissues of heat-stressed rats is blunted with advancing age. *Journal of Applied Physiology, 79,* 1673–1678.

Kritchevsky, S. B., & Muldoon, M. F. (1996). Oxidative stress and aging: still a hypothesis. *Journal of the American Geriatrics Society, 44,* 873–875.

Lai, Z., Colon, W., & Kelly, J. W. (1996). The acid-mediated denaturation of transthyretin proceeds through an intermediate that partitions into amyloid. *Biochemistry, 35,* 6470–6482.

Larsson, L., & Ansved, T. (1995). Effects of ageing on the motor unit. *Progress in Neurobiology, 45,* 397–458.

Laughrea, M., & Latulippe, J. (1988). The poly(U) translation capacity of Fischer 344 rat liver does not deteriorate with age and is not affected by dietary regime. *Mechanisms of Ageing and Development, 45,* 137–143.

Lee, A. T., & Cerami, A. (1992). Role of glycation in aging. *Annals of the New York Academy of Science, 663,* 63–70.

Lenaz, G. (1998). Role of mitochondria in oxidative stress and ageing. *Biochimica et Biophysica Acta, 1366,* 53–67.

Levine, R. L., Mosoni, L., Berlett, B. S., & Stadtman, E. R. (1996). Methionine residues as endogenous antioxidants in proteins. *Proceedings of the National Academy of Sciences USA, 93,* 15036–40.

Lorenzo, A., Razzaboni, B., Weir, G. C., & Yankner, B. A. (1994). Pancreatic islet cell toxicity of amylin associated with type-2 diabetes mellitus. *Nature, 368,* 756–760.

Luce, M. C., & Bunn, C. L. (1989). Decreased accuracy of protein synthesis in extracts from aging human diploid fibroblasts. *Experimental Gerontology, 24,* 113–125.

Martin, G. R., Austad, S. N., & Johnson, T. E. (1996). Genetic analysis of aging: Role of oxidative damage and environmental stresses. *Nature Genetics, 13,* 25–34.

Martin, G. R., Danner, D. B., & Holbrook, N. J. (1993). Aging—causes and defenses. *Annual Reviews of Medicine, 44,* 419–429.

Masoro, E. J., & Austed, S. N. (1996). The evolution of the anti aging action of dietary restriction. *Journal of Gerontology Biological Sciences, 51A,* B387-B391.

McCutchen, S. L., Colon, W., & Kelly, J. W. (1993). Transthyretin mutation Leu-55-Pro significantly alters tetramer stability and increases amyloidogenicity. *Biochemistry, 32*, 12119–12127.

McCutchen, S. L., Lai, Z., Miroy, G., Kelly, J. W., & Colon, W. (1995). Comparison of lethal and non-lethal transthyretin variants and their relationship to amyloid disease. *Biochemistry, 34*, 13527–13536.

Mcfadden, P. N., & Clarke, S. (1986). Protein carboxyl methyltransferase and methyl, acceptor proteins in aging and cataractous tissue of the human eye lens. *Mechanisms of Ageing and Development, 34*, 91–105.

Mikski, I., & Deyl, Z. (1991). Change in the amount of epsilon-hexosyllysine UV absorbance and fluorescence of collagen with age in different animal species. *Journal of Gerontology Biological sciences, 46*, B111-B116.

Monnier, V. M., Sell, D. R., Miyata, S., & Nagara, R. H. (1993). The Maillard reaction as a basis for a theory of aging. In P. A. Finot, (Ed.), *Proceedings of the 4th International Symposium on the Maillard Reaction* (pp. 393–515). Basel: Birkhausert-Verlag.

Moore, S. A., Lopez, A., Richardson, A., & Pahlavani, M. A. (1998). Effect of age and dietary restriction on expression of heat shock protein 70 in rat alveolar macrophages. *Mechanisms of Ageing and Development, 104*, 59–73.

Mori, N., Hiruta, K., Funatsu, Y., & Goto, S. (1983). Codon recognition fidelity of ribosomes at the first and second position does not decrease during aging. *Mechanisms of Ageing and Development, 22*, 1–10.

Narayanan, N., Jones, D. L., Xu, A., & Yu, J. C. (1996). Effects of aging on sarcoplasmic reticulum function and contraction duration in skeletal muscles of the rat. *American Journal of Physiology, 271*, C1032–40.

Nguyen, J., Baldwin, M. A., Cohen, F. E., & Prusiner, S. B. (1995). Prion protein peptides induce alpha-helix to beta sheet conformational transitions. *Biochemistry, 34*, 4186–4192.

O'Brien, T. D., Butler, P. C., Westermark, P., & Johnson, K. H. (1993). Islet amyloid polypeptide: A review of its biology and potential roles in the pathogenesis of diabetes mellitus. *Veterinary Pathology, 30*, 317–332.

Oh-Ishi, S., Kizaki, T., Yamashita, H., Nagata, N., Suzuki, K, Taniguchi, N., & Ohno, H. (1995). Alterations of superoxide dismutase iso-enzyme activity, content, and mRNA expression with aging in rat skeletal muscle. *Mechanisms of Ageing and Development, 84(1)*, 65–76.

Oimomi, M., Kitamura, Y., Nishimoto, S., Matsamuro, S., Hatanaka, H., & Bada, S. (1986). Age-related acceleration of glycation of tissue proteins in rats. *Journal of Gerontology, 41*, 695–698.

Oliver, C. N., Ahn, B. W., Moerman, E. J., Goldstein, S., & Stadtman, E. R. (1987). Age- related changes in oxidized proteins. *Journal of Biological Chemistry, 262*, 5488–5491.

Orgel, L. E. (1963). The maintenance of the accuracy of protein synthesis and its relevance to aging. *Proceedings of the National Academy of Science, USA, 49*, 517–521.

Orgel, L. E. (1970). The maintenance of the accuracy of protein synthesis and its relevance to ageing: A correction. *Proceedings of the National Academy of Science, USA, 67*, 1476.

Orr, W. C., & Sohal, R. S. (1992). Relationship between antioxidants, prooxidants, and the aging process. *Annals of the New York Academy of Science, 663*, 71–73.

Ota, IM, Ding, L., & Clarke, S. (1987). Methylation at specific altered aspartyl and asparaginyl residues in glucagon by the erythrocyte protein carboxyl methyltransferase. *Journal of Biological Chemistry, 262*, 8522–8531.

Pacifici, R. E., & Davies, K. J. (1990). Protein degradation as an index of oxidative stress. *Methods in Enzymology, 186*, 485–502.

Pacifici, R. E., & Davies, K. J. (1991). Protein, lipid and DNA repair systems in oxidative stress: The free-radical theory of aging revisited. *Gerontology, 37*, 166–180.

Pahlavani, M. A., Harris, M. D., Moore, S. A., Weindruch, R., & Richardson, A. (1995). The expression of heat shock protein 70 decreases with age in lymphocytes from rats and rhesus monkeys. *Experimental Cell Research, 218,* 310–318.

Patrick, J. S., Thorpe, S. R., & Baynes, J. W. (1990). Nonenzymatic glycosylation of protein does not increase with age in human lenses. *Journal of Gerontology Biological Sciences, 45,* B18–B23.

Perry, R. E., Swamy, M. S., & Abraham, E. C. (1987). Progressive changes in lens crystallin glycation and high-molecular weight aggregate formation leading to a cataract development in streptozotocin-diabetes. *Experimental Eye Research, 44,* 269–282.

Ponnappan, U., Zhong, M., & Trebilcock, G. U. (1999). Decreased proteasome-mediated degradation in T cells from the elderly: A role in immune senescence. *Cellular Immunology, 192(2),* 167–174.

Rattan, S. I. S. (1996). Synthesis, modifications, and turnover of proteins during aging. *Experimental Gerontology, 31,* 33–47.

Reiss, U., & Rothstein, M. (1974). Heat labile isozymws of isocitrate lyase from aging *Turbatrix aceti. Biochemical and Biophysical Research Communications, 61,* 1012–1016.

Reiss, U., & Sacktor, B. (1983). Monoclonal antibodies to renal brush border membrane maltase: Age-related antigenic alterations. *Proceedings of the National Academy of Science, USA, 80,* 3255–3260.

Richardson, A., & Holbrook, N. J. (1996). Aging and the cellular response to stress: Reduction in the heat shock response. In N. J., Holbrook, G. R., Martin, and R. A., Lockshine, (Eds.), *Cellular Aging and Cell Death* (pp. 67–80). New York: Wiley-Liss.

Rose, M. R. (1991). *Evolutionary Biology of Aging.* New York: Oxford University Press.

Rothstein, M. (1979). The formation of altered enzymes in aging animals. *Mechanisms of Ageing and Development, 9,* 197–202.

Rothstein, M. (1982). *Biochemical Approaches to Aging* (pp. 213–255). New York: Academic Press.

Rothstein, M. (1985). Age-related changes in enzyme levels and enzyme properties. *Reviews of Biological Research on Aging, 2,* 421–433.

Schirmer, E. C., & Lindquist, S. (1997). Interactions of the chaperone hsp104 with yeast sup35 and mammalian prp. *Proceedings of the National Academy of Science, USA, 94,* 13932–13937.

Schoneich, C. (1999). Reactive oxygen species and biological aging: A mechanistic approach. *Experimental Gerontology, 34,* 19–34.

Schoneich, C., Viner, R. I., Ferrington, D. A., & Bigelow, D. J. (1999) Age-related chemical modification of the skeletal muscle sarcoplasmic reticulum Ca-ATPase of the rat. *Mechanisms of Ageing and Development, 107(3),* 221–31.

Sensi, M., Tanzi, B., Bruno, R. M., Pozzilli, P., Mancuso, M., Gambardella, S,. & Di Mario, U. (1986). Human glomerular basement membrane: Altered binding characteristics following *in vitro* non-enzymatic glycosylation. *Annals of the New York Academy of Science, 488,* 549–552.

Sharma, H. K., & Rothstein, M. (1978). Age-related changes in the properties of enolase from *Turbatrix aceti. Biochemistry, 17,* 2869–2876.

Sharma, H. K., & Rothstein, M. (1984). Altered brain phosphoglycerate kinase from aging rats. *Mechanisms of Ageing and Development, 25,* 285–296.

Sharma, H. K., Prasanna, H. R., & Rothstein, M. (1980). Altered phosphoglycerate kinase in aging rats. *Journal of Biological Chemistry, 255,* 5043–5050.

Shilton, B. H., & Walton, D. J. (1991). Sites of glycation of human and horse liver alcohol dehydrogenase *in vivo. Journal of Biological Chemistry, 266,* 5587–5592.

Silar, P., & Picard, M. (1994). Increased longevity of EF–1α high-fidelity mutants in *Podospora anserina. Journal of Molecular Biology, 235,* 231–236.

Smith, C. D., Carney, J. M., Starke-Reed, P. E., Oliver, C. N., Stadtman, E. R., & Floyd, R. A. (1991). Excess brain protein oxidation and enzyme dysfunction in normal aging and in Alzheimer's disease. *Proceedings of the National Academy of Science, USA, 88,* 10540–10543.

Smith, C. D., Carney, J. M, Tatsumo, T., Stadtman, E. R., Floyd, R. A., & Markesbery, W. R. (1992). Protein oxidation in aging brain. *Annals of the New York Academy of Science, 663,* 110–119.

Sohal, R. S., & Dubey, A. (1994). Mitochondrial oxidative damage, hydrogen peroxide release and aging. *Free Radicals in Biology and Medicine, 16,* 621–626.

Sohal, R. S., Agarwal, S., Dubey, A., & Orr, W. C. (1993). Protein oxidative damage is associated with life expectancy of house flies. *Proceedings of the National Academy of Science, USA, 90,* 7255–7259.

Stadtman, E. R. (1988). Protein modification in aging. *Journal of Gerontology Biological Sciences, 43,* B112–B120.

Stadtman, E. R. (1990). Metal-ion catalyzed oxidation of proteins: biochemical mechanism and biological consequences. *Free Radicals in Biology and Medicine, 9,* 315–325.

Stadtman, E. R. (1992). Protein oxidation and aging. *Science, 257,* 1220–1224.

Stadtman, E. R. (1995a). Role of oxidized amino acids in protein breakdown and stability. *Methods in Enzymology, 258,* 379–393.

Stadtman, E. R. (1995b). The status of oxidatively modified proteins as a marker of aging. In (K. Esser, & G. M. Martin, (Eds.). *Molecular Aspects of Aging* (pp. 129–143). New York: John Wiley & Sons Ltd.

Stadtman, E. R., & Berlett, B. S. (1998). Reactive oxygen-mediated protein oxidation in aging and disease. *Drug Metabolism Reviews 30,* 225–43.

Stadtman, E. R., Oliver, C. N., Starke-Reed, P. E., & Rhee, S. G. (1993). Age-related oxidation reaction in proteins. *Toxicology and Industrial Health, 9,* 187–196.

Starke-Reed, P. E., & Oliver, C. N. (1989). Protein oxidation and proteolysis during aging and oxidative stress. *Archives of Biochemistry and Biophysics, 275,* 559–567.

Sun, A. Q., Yuksel, K. U., & Gracy, R. W. (1992). Relationship between the catalytic center and the primary degradation site of triosephosphate isomerase: effects of active site modification and deamidation. *Archives of Biochemistry and Biophysics, 293,* 382–390.

Sun, A. Q., Yuksel, K. U., & Gracy, R. W. (1995). Terminal marking of triosephosphate isomerase: Consequences of deamidation. *Archives of Biochemistry and Biophysics, 322,* 361–368.

Sun, A. Q., Yuksel, K. U., Rao, G. S., & Gracy, R. W. (1992). Effects of active site modification and reversible dissociation on the secondary structure of triosephosphate isomerase. *Archives of Biochemistry and Biophysics, 295,* 421–428.

Tanaka, S., Avigad, G., Brodsky, B., & Eikenberry, E. F. (1988). Glycation induces expansion of the molecular packing of collagen. *Journal of Molecular Biology, 203,* 495–505.

Tatsmo, T., Stadtman, E. R., Floyd, R. A., & Markesbery, W. R. (1992). Protein oxidation in aging brain. *Annals of the New York Academy of Science, 663,* 110–119.

Trivelli, L. A., Ranney, H. M., & Lai, H. T. (1971). Hemoglobin components in patients with diabetes mellitus. *New England Journal of Medicine, 284,* 353–357.

Tsilbary, E. C., Charonis, A. S., Reger, L. A., Wohlhueter, R. M., & Furcht, L. T. (1988). The effect of nonenzymatic glycosylation on the binding of the main noncollagenous NCI domain to type IV collagen. *Journal of Biological Chemistry, 263,* 4302–4308.

Uchida, K., & Kawakishi, S. (1993). 2-Oxohistidine as a novel biological marker for oxidatively modified proteins. *FEBS Letters, 332,* 208–210.

Uemichi, T., Liepnieks, J. J., & Benson, M. D. (1994). Hereditary renal amyloidosis with a novel variant fibrinogen. *Journal of Clinical Investigations, 93,* 731–736.

Van Remmen, H., Ward, W. F., Sabia, R. V., & Richardson, A. (1995). A gene expression and protein degradation. In E. Masoro, (Ed.). *Handbook of Physiology: Aging* (pp. 171–234). New York: Oxford University Press.

Vijg, J., & Wei, Y. (1995). Understanding the biology of aging: the key to prevention and therapy. *Journal of the American Geriatrics Society, 43,* 426–434.

Viner, R. I., Ferrington, D. A., Aced, G. I., Miller-Schlyer, M., Bigelow, D. J., & Schoneich, C. (1997). *In vivo* aging of rat skeletal muscle sarcoplasmic reticulum Ca-ATPase. Chemical analysis and quantitative simulation by exposure to low levels of peroxyl radicals. *Biochimica et Biophysica Acta, 1329(2)*, 321–35.

Wells-Knecht, K. J., Blackledge, J. A., Lyons, T. J., Thorpe, S. R., & Baynes, J. W. (1994). Glycation, glycoxidation, and cross-linking of collagen by glucose. Kinetics, mechanisms, and inhibition of late stages of the Maillard reaction. *Diabetes, 43*, 676–683.

Wells-Knecht, K. J., Zyzak, D. V., Litchfield, J. E., Thorpe, S. R., & Baynes, J. W. (1995). Mechanism of autoxidative glycosylation: Identification of glyoxal and arabinose as intermediates in the autoxidative modification of proteins by glucose. *Biochemistry, 34*, 3702–3709.

Wick, M., Burger, C., Brusselbach, S., Lucibello, F.C., & Muller R. (1994). A novel member of human tissue inhibitor of metalloproteinases (TIMP) gene family is regulated during GI progression, mitogenic stimulation, differentiation, and senescence. *Journal of Biological Chemistry, 269*, 18953–18960

Yuh, K. C. M., & Gafni, A. (1987). Reversal of age-related effects in rat muscle phosphoglycerate kinase. *Proceedings of the National Academy of Science, USA, 84*, 7458–7462.

Zhang, H., Kaneko, K., Nguyen, J. T., Livshits, T. L., Baldwin, M. L., Cohen, F. E., James, T. L., & Prusiner, S. B. (1995). Conformational transitions in peptides containing two putative a-helices of the prion protein. *Journal of Molecular Biology, 250*, 514–526.

Zhou, J. Q., White, T. P., & Gafni, A. (1990). Endurance-training induced changes in skeletal muscle phosphoglycerate kinase of old wistar rats. *Mechanisms of Ageing and Development, 58*, 163–175.

Zuniga, A. & Gafni, A. (1988). Age-related modifications in rat cardiac phosphoglycerate kinase. Rejuvenation of the old enzyme by unfolding-refolding. *Biochimica et Biophysica Acta, 955*, 50–57.

Four

Instability of the Nuclear Genome and the Role of DNA Repair

Jan Vijg and Martijn E. T. Dollé

I. Definitions and Historical Background

Instability of the nuclear genome is a broad concept. For the purpose of this chapter, distinctions are made between DNA damage, DNA mutations, and epigenetic DNA alterations. DNA damage includes chemical alterations in DNA structure, leading to a noninformative template, i.e., a structure that can no longer serve as a substrate for faithful replication or transcription. As a consequence of DNA damage, for example, by mishandling of the damage by repair processes, mutations can be introduced. DNA mutations are heritable changes in the sequence of an organism's genome that are transmitted to daughter cells or to offspring (when they occur in germ cells). Mutations can vary from point mutations, involving single or very few base pairs to large deletions, insertions, duplications, and inversions. In organisms with multiple chromosomes, DNA from one chromosome can be joined to another, and the actual chromosome number can be affected. Epigenetic DNA alterations are changes in heritable patterns of DNA modification, such as methylation, that influence patterns of gene expression without altering the sequence of base pairs.

Spontaneous instability of the nuclear genome of somatic cells has been considered a possible explanation for aging since irradiation damage in animals, like generalized atrophy and neoplasia, was found to resemble premature aging in the late 1940s (Henshaw, *et al.*, 1947). Because radiation was known to induce mutations, it was proposed that aging could be the result of life-long exposure to low, natural levels of background radiation and other environmental agents capable of inflicting damage to DNA (Failla, 1958; Szilard, 1959). Indeed, a general accumulation of somatic DNA mutations could explain, to some extent, the exponential increase in cancer incidence with age. This increase in cancer risk is dependent on biological rather than chronological age. Whereas, for example, in the mouse cancer is very frequent at 2–3 years, in humans the peak seems to occur no earlier than 60–90 years. This difference is associated with an approximately 30-fold difference in life span and could very well be due to more sophisticated genome stability systems (such as DNA

Handbook of the Biology of Aging, Fifth Edition

repair) in the longer lived species (Hart *et al.*, 1979; Martin, 1991). Because there is no evidence for a much higher mutation frequency in cells from young rodents than from young humans (see following discussion), it is conceivable that species differences in the proficiency of genome stability systems are responsible for a more rapid mutation accumulation in the rodent somatic DNA. Interestingly, the observed individual variation in life span, which appears to correlate with the rate of occurrence of multiple pathological lesions in rodents, including tumors, (Burek, 1978), suggests that also within a species cancer risk depends first and foremost on biological and not chronological age.

In the past, a number of objections have been raised against nuclear genome alterations as a possible cause of aging. The most important of these objections reflected the consideration that the spontaneous somatic mutation rate *in vivo* (the rate at which new mutations arise over time) would be far too low to explain any of the observed aging-related changes, except cancer (Maynard Smith, 1959). Reasonably accurate measurements of the rate of mutation in organs and tissues of higher organisms are now possible (Gossen *et al.*, 1989; see the following discussion). The mutation rate in *Escherichia coli* is 10^{-6}–10^{-5} per locus per generation (Luria & Delbrück, 1943). On the basis of an estimated mutation rate of about 2×10^{-7} mutations per locus per cell division in cultured human cells, it has been concluded that a typical mammalian cell would not accumulate more than a few mutations in a lifetime (Jackson & Loeb, 1998). Indeed, such an *in vivo* somatic mutation rate has even been considered to be too low to account for tumorigenesis and the large numbers of mutations present in a tumor. Hence the proposal of a mutator phenotype, which, due to the accidental mutational inactivation of a genome stability gene,

would raise mutation rates and thereby increase the chance of generating a malignant tumor phenotype (Loeb, 1991). Such mutator phenotypes have been demonstrated to exist, but may not be necessary to explain all cancers. Indeed, estimates of mutation rates, expressed per unit of time rather than cell division (Morley, 1996), suggest a mutation rate of 73×10^{-4}, or almost 1 in 1000, over a 100-year life span. On the basis of an estimated total of about 100,000 genes per human genome, this figure would correspond to almost 100 mutant genes per cell at old age. In this respect, it has been proposed that age-related accumulation of somatic mutations could substitute for a mutator phenotype, at least for sporadic cancers that increase as a function of age (Turker, 1998). The preceding estimate of 73×10^{-4} per life span is not too far from what has been determined empirically in cells or tissues from old humans or rodents using current methods for mutation frequency determinations *in vivo* (see the following discussion). However, its potential impact is higher than the number suggests because it assumes one mutation per gene and does not account for large mutations affecting multiple genes or for gene–gene interactions.

This chapter critically reviews the evolutionary logic for genome instability as a cause of aging and the experimental evidence that DNA alterations accumulate with age. Two possible strategies to test the functional impact of genome instability are discussed: (1) manipulating various DNA processing pathways in the mouse and assessing its effects on genome stability, aging and life span, and (2) screening human elderly populations for associations between functional variants of genes involved in genome stability and aging-related phenotypes, such as extremely short or long life spans with different aging-related phenotypes, such as extreme longevity.

II. Evolutionary Logic of Genome Instability

Apart from adaptive mutagenesis, mutations can be expected to be almost always deleterious, except for the rare few that offer some selective advantage. It is because of these rare few that mutations are essential as the ultimate source of genetic variation upon which evolution depends. Too many mutations, however, will reduce fitness and can lead to population extinction. Relatively small asexual populations will tend to lose mutation-free genomes (due to genetic drift) and inevitably suffer from loss of viability (Muller, 1964). Experimental evidence for this phenomenon has been obtained in lower organisms, such as E. coli. For example, Kibota and Lynch (1996) demonstrated that deleterious mutations of small effect escaped selection in E. coli lines with repeated population bottlenecks, resulting in decreased fitness. Elena and Lenski (1997), also in E. coli, demonstrated that randomly introduced mutations interact to negatively affect fitness, i.e., the relationship between mutation number and decreased fitness was nearly log-linear.

In a somewhat simplistic manner, one could argue that the decreased fitness observed in these small populations of unicellular organisms resembles some early form of senescence caused by mutation accumulation. There is also evidence for a role of genome repair to maintain cellular vigor. Indeed, in small populations, recombination processes associated with sexual reproduction appear to reduce mutational loads and promote the accumulation of advantageous mutations (Muller, 1964; Andersson & Hughes, 1996). Interestingly, senescence-like phenomena attributed to the accumulation of deleterious mutations have been observed in Protozoa, but only in asexually propagated lineages (Bell, 1988).

Hence, DNA mutations are a double-edged sword. The spontaneous mutation rate is selected by evolution within specific boundaries: too few mutations would not permit natural selection to operate, whereas too many mutations would lead to population extinction. With the emergence of multicellular organisms, the cells set apart to form the body proper are unlikely to have a mutation rate lower than strictly necessary to reach the age of first reproduction. This is followed logically from the concept that aging ultimately is due to the loss of efficacy of natural selection, i.e., novel gene variants with beneficial effects at an early age are positively selected in contrast to late-acting traits, which escape natural selection (Rose, 1991). Hence, although novel gene variants encoding more efficient genome stability systems are expected to appear, maximization of genome maintenance beyond the first age of reproduction is not predicted by evolutionary theory (Kirkwood, 1989).

III. Origin of Mutations: DNA Damage

The ultimate source of somatic mutations, apart from replication errors per se, is the continuous introduction of chemical lesions in the DNA by a variety of environmental and endogenous physical, chemical, and biological agents. Breaks in the sugar phosphate backbone are induced spontaneously, e.g., under the influence of body heat, apurinic and apyrimidinic sites arise as a consequence of DNA hydrolysis, and naturally present methyl donors cause nonenzymatic methylation (Lindahl, 1993). A major source of age-associated endogenous DNA damage could be oxygen free radicals, which are byproducts of oxidative phosphorylation and several other biological and physiological processes (Harman, 1956; Ames et al., 1993; Martin, et al.,

1996a). In addition, a variety of exogenous agents, such as ultraviolet light, ionizing radiation, and a range of chemicals in food, can induce DNA damages in their target tissues, e.g., inter- and intrachromosomal cross-links, DNA single- and double-strand breaks, bulky adducts, and smaller adducts.

In spite of a wealth of methods to detect specific DNA lesions, it has been difficult to accurately assess spontaneous DNA damage loads *in vivo* in various organs and tissues during aging and rule out artifacts due to sample manipulation as the source of damage (Collins, 1999). It seems likely that under normal circumstances the steady-state level of spontaneous DNA lesions is very low. For example, Le *et al.*, (1998) reported less than 4.3 thymine glycols per 10^9 bases of DNA in cultured cells. At such low frequency, it would be unlikely for a lesion to occur within a gene or one of its regulatory regions, especially since it is realized that most of the lesions are not permanent but part of a steady-state situation. That is, lesions are removed continuously through DNA repair pathways and re-introduced. Thus, it seems unlikely that spontaneous DNA damage has any direct effect under normal circumstances, in terms of impaired transcription. It could, however, increase the level of spontaneous mutagenesis through errors in DNA damage processing. The resulting DNA sequence alterations can vary from large chromosomal alterations to point mutations. Such changes are irreversible except through cell elimination "repair." Indeed, cell death, including programmed cell death in response to severe molecular damage, is considered a major end point of the aging process (Warner *et al.*, 1995). Other end points are neoplastic transformation (Martin, 1991) and replicative senescence (Campisi, 1996).

Large genome rearrangements, especially those involving millions of base pairs of DNA, could seriously affect normal patterns of gene regulation, i.e., through gene dosage or position effects (Vijg, 2000). Large DNA mutations could also induce DNA conformational changes, which in turn could affect gene regulation. These changes could be subtle and not result in any drastic changes, such as cell death or neoplastic transformation. They may, however, lead to small individual declines in cellular functions, which could lead to reduced capacity of the organ or tissue as a whole and increased chance of disease. A hypothetical sequence of events for how DNA damage induction through DNA processing, mutation, and its various cellular end points can lead to organismal aging is depicted schematically in Fig 1. The different components of genome instability and the evidence for increased DNA alterations with age will be reviewed next.

IV. DNA Alterations with Age

A. Cytogenetic Changes

Due to a lack of methods to quantify and characterize mutation loads *in vivo*, i.e., in different organs and tissues, it has proved difficult to test the premise that mutations accumulate during the aging of mammals in a sufficiently high number to cause some of the pathophysiological symptoms of aging. Curtis and Crowley (1963) were the first to provide evidence for an increasing level of mutations during aging. They looked at mouse liver parenchymal cell metaphase plates after partial hepatectomy and found considerably higher numbers of cells with abnormal chromosomes in old as compared to young animals (i.e., from about 10% of the cells in 4 to 5 month-old mice to 75% in mice older than 12 months). Later, such large structural changes in DNA, i.e., aneuploidy, translocations, and dicentrics, were observed to increase with donor age in the white blood cells of human individuals, i.e., from about 2–4%

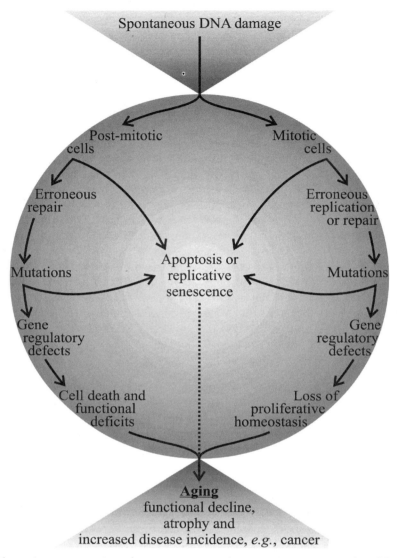

Figure 1. Schematic representation of mutation accumulation in postmitotic and proliferative cells *in vivo*, leading to functional decline, atrophy, and neoplasms.

of the cells with a chromosomal aberration in young individuals to about 6 times higher in the elderly. It is conceivable that these chromosomal changes reflect changes in the hematopoietic stem cells. The use of more advanced methods, such as chromosome painting, has amply confirmed the increase in cytogenetic damage with age in both humans (Ramsey *et al.*, 1995) and mice (Tucker *et al.*, 1999). In both humans and mice, the increase in chromosome aberrations appeared to be exponential, which is interesting in view of the fact that the mortality rate also increases exponentially in human and mouse populations (Finch *et al.*, 1990).

B. Gene Mutations

With the development of tests based on selectable endogenous target genes, it became possible to assess the mutant frequency at these loci among T-cells from human and animal donors. By using the hypoxanthine phosphoribosyl transferase (*HPRT*) locus test (Albertini *et al.*, 1993), different investigators have now shown that mutation frequencies at this locus increase with donor age. For example, results obtained with this assay suggest that mutation frequencies in humans (expressed as the number of mutated cells versus the total number of cells, corrected for the plating efficiency) increase with age from about 2×10^{-6} in young individuals to about 1×10^{-5} in middle-aged and old individuals (Jones *et al.*, 1995). In mice, mutation frequencies have been reported from about 5×10^{-6} in young animals to about 3×10^{-5} in middle-aged mice (Dempsey *et al.*, 1993a). However, in both mice and humans, these values could be underestimates. Indeed, results from Grist and co-workers (1992), who assayed the *HLA* locus (using immunoselection for the mutationally lost HLA antigen) in human lymphocytes, indicate 2–3 times higher mutant frequencies. Values higher than *HPRT* also were found with other assays involving selectable target genes, and the discrepancy has been explained in terms of the inability of the *HPRT* test to detect mitotic recombination events (*HPRT* is X-linked) and a relatively strong *in vivo* selection against *HPRT* mutants (Grist *et al.*, 1992). Indeed, *HPRT* mutant frequencies have been found to decrease with time following exposure to mutagenic agents, such as ethylnitrosourea and radiation (Da Cruz *et al.*, 1996). Another, more general, reason why observed mutation frequencies at selectable target loci are underestimates is that large genome rearrangement events could affect not only the target gene but also neighboring genes essential for the survival of the cell.

In mice subjected to caloric restriction, the only intervention demonstrated to increase life span in mammals (Masoro, 1993), *HPRT* mutation frequencies were found to increase with age at a significantly slower rate than in the *ad libitum* fed animals (Dempsey *et al.*, 1993b). These results were confirmed independently in rats by Aidoo and co-workers (1999) and suggest that the level of accumulated somatic mutations reflects biological rather than chronological age. This conclusion was further strengthened by Odagiri and co-workers (1998), who demonstrated accelerated accumulation of *HPRT* mutations in peripheral blood lymphocytes of so-called senescence-accelerated mice (SAM). Although the SAM model is not generally accepted as a mouse model of accelerated aging, these findings nevertheless demonstrate a link between somatic mutation rate and physiological decline.

Interestingly, the *HPRT* test has been used on tubular epithelial cells of kidney tissue from 2- to 94-year-old human donors. The mutation frequencies found were much higher than the previously mentioned values for blood lymphocytes and also were increasing with age, from about 5×10^{-5} to about 2.5×10^{-4} (Martin *et al.*, 1996b). The high mutation frequency in the kidney cells could reflect a relatively slow turnover compared to T-cells.

With the development of transgenic mouse models harboring chromosomally integrated reporter genes, it became possible to directly test the hypothesis that somatic mutations in a neutral gene accumulate with age in different organs and tissues (Gossen *et al.*, 1989). By using one of these models, harboring the *lacI* gene as a target, Lee and co-workers (1994) were the first to demonstrate an age-related increase in mutant frequency (expressed as the number of mutant reporter genes versus the total number of recovered reporter genes) in spleen, from about 3×10^{-5} in mice of a few weeks old to $1–2 \times 10^{-4}$ in 24-month-old animals. Subsequent results from other laboratories indicated age-related increases in mutation frequency in some, but not all, organs. Dollé, and co-workers (1997), for example, demonstrated that mutation frequencies at a *lacZ* transgene increase with age in the liver from about 4×10^{-5} in the young adults to about 15×10^{-5} in old animals (about 30 months), whereas such an increase was virtually absent in the brain. The increased susceptibility to spontaneous mutagenesis of the liver versus the brain corresponds with the observed higher frequency of focal pathological lesions in the mouse liver compared to brain (Bronson & Lipman, 1991). The pattern of organ specificity in age-related mutation accumulation has been expanded with the observation of age-related increases in mutation frequencies in spleen, heart, and small intestine, but not in testes (Dollé, *et al.*, 2000 and unpublished results).

Essentially the same results as those obtained by Dollé *et al.* (1997) were found by Ono and co-workers (2000). These investigators used the original CD2 (rather than C57Bl/6) mouse model made by Gossen *et al.* (1989), harboring the same *lacZ* transgene. They also observed an age-related increase in *lacZ* mutation frequency in liver, heart, and spleen, but virtually no increase in brain and testes. There are multiple explanations for the organ specificity of mutation frequencies as they develop with age. The most logical one is that the mutation frequency is simply a function of organ-specific proliferative activity. Indeed, it is reasonable to assume that with higher proliferative activity there is a higher chance of replication errors, one of the major mechanisms of mutation generation (see preceding discussion). This could explain the relatively high mutation frequency in small intestine, which increases approximately fivefold during aging (Dollé *et al.*, 2000). It does not explain, however, the relatively low age-related increase in spleen and the absence of an increase in testes; both of these organs should contain plenty of actively proliferating cells. Other

factors, possibly closely related to the function of each particular organ, its DNA repair status, etc., almost certainly play a role.

Dollé *et al.* (1997) also observed striking organ specificity with respect to the mutational spectrum of the old animals. Whereas in small intestine and brain almost only point mutations accumulated (the small increase in this latter organ was almost totally due to point mutations), in the liver and especially the heart, large deletion mutations were a prominent part of the spectrum (Dollé *et al.*, 1997, 2000).

In interpreting these data, it should be noted that the observed increases were modest (varying from less than twofold to little more than fourfold) and appeared to level off at middle age (Lee *et al.*, 1994; Dollé *et al.*, 1997). The relatively small age-related increase in mutant frequencies can be interpreted as evidence against a major role for somatic mutations in aging (Warner & Johnson, 1997). However, although transgenic reporter genes do not suffer from a selection bias (as is the case with most selectable endogenous targets like the *HPRT* gene), it still provides an underestimate of the real mutation load and its adverse effects. Homologous (mitotic) recombination, for example, leading to the deletion of entire reporter gene copies (loss of heterozygosity), is a frequent mutational event and goes undetected in the transgenic assays. Most of the transgenic models also do not account for mutational hot spots (see the following discussion), and important functional end points such as cell death are missed. Indeed, to put the results on mutant frequencies of different organs and tissues at various age levels into context, it will be necessary also to assess cell proliferation and cell death. Most importantly, it will be necessary at some point to determine the critical level of cellular mutation loads in terms of physiological consequences.

C. Mutational Hot Spots

At some loci or regions of the genome, the spontaneous mutation frequencies are higher than average. For example, Gossen and co-workers (1991) studied a *lacZ* transgenic line with the reporter integrated near the pseudo-autosomal region of the X chromosome and found spontaneous somatic and germ line mutation frequencies that were up to 100 times higher than for all other lines tested. Recognized mutational hot spots are the families of repeat elements that are a major component of the mammalian genome. Evidence is accumulating that, rather than being "junk" DNA, such repeat elements may have some functional relevance, for example, as transcription factor binding sites (Krontiris, 1995). The two major families, termed L1 and Alu elements in humans, are considered to be retrotransposable. Although the capability of such elements to retrotranspose has been demonstrated in human cell lines (Kimberland *et al.*, 1999), there is no unambiguous evidence yet that they contribute much to somatic instability. For other repeat element loci, such as minisatellites, mutation frequencies as high as $10^{-2}-10^{-1}$ have been found (Jeffreys *et al.*, 1990; Dubrova *et al.*, 1993). Related forms of genetic instability are triplet repeat expansion and telomere shortening. Triplet repeat expansion is associated with human genetic diseases and increases with age (Wong *et al.*, 1995). Telomere shortening is discussed extensively elsewhere, but can be considered as a form of genomic instability in its own right with apparent signaling to enter stages of apoptosis or replicative senescence (Chapter 8 of this volume).

D. Mutations in Germ Cells

Other evidence for increased genome deterioration with age involves germ cells. It is generally assumed that an age-related increase in chromosomal abnormalities and other types of mutations in parental germ cells is responsible for the increased risk of offspring with a genetic defect, such as Down's syndrome (Evans, 1996). Indeed, chromosomal abnormalities, including aneuploidy and chromosome structural rearrangements, occur in 10–20% of spermatozoa and oocytes (Kamiguchi *et al.*, 1994). At least 15% of all recognized human pregnancies abort, most likely as a consequence of chromosomal mutations (Plachot *et al.*, 1987). In fact, 50% of all spontaneous abortions contain a gross chromosomal mutation. The picture that emerges of the germ line, therefore, is that of an effective sieve that allows most mutations to be lost by negative selection, i.e., through the death of germ cells or early embryos. In aging tissues, such a sieve as a mechanism to select against cells rendered dysfunctional by mutations could also be present, but it is destined to be less effective because cell death is itself a major end point of the aging process, which can lead to functional decline. Interestingly, with the possibility of cloning mammals by transferring nuclei from adult somatic cells into enucleated oocytes, the functional consequences of genome deterioration with age can be investigated directly. Indeed, the success rate of cloning animals from the somatic cells of old individuals should be markedly lower. Although the results obtained thus far with cloned sheep and mice suggest that cloning is less efficient from cells of adult animals than from fetal or embryonal cells, the numbers still are too low to draw conclusions (Wilmut *et al.*, 1997; Wakayama *et al.*, 1998).

E. Changes in DNA Modification and Conformation

Most attention in the study of somatic DNA alterations in aging has been focused on genotypic alteration, that is, irreversible changes in DNA sequence information resulting from error-prone processing of DNA damage (see preceding discussion). Another type of DNA alteration involves changes in DNA modification and conformation. This kind of epigenetic variation can involve protein–DNA complexes as well as chemical modification of the DNA molecule per se. The best-known example of the latter is DNA methylation. Heritable changes in the DNA methylation profile are called epimutations (Holliday, 1991). In mammals, methylation involves transfer of the methyl group from S-adenosyl-methionine to the CpG acceptor site. Generally, hypermethylation has been found to be associated with transcriptional silence and vice versa. Changes in methylation can be caused by DNA damage, including oxidative damage, for example, by interference with the ability of DNA to serve as a substrate for the DNA-methyltransferase (Wachsman, 1997). Methylated CpG sites strongly contribute to spontaneous mutagenesis, e.g., deamination of 5-methylcytosine yields thymine, which generates T:A transition mutations from C:G base pairs. There is evidence that methylation plays an important role in developmental processes, such as imprinting (Li et al., 1993) and X-inactivation (Migeon, 1990), as well as in cancer. With respect to cancer, both hypermethylation (in silencing tumor suppressor genes) and hypomethylation (to facilitate genomic instability) could be important (Jones & Gonzalgo, 1997). For aging, the situation is much less clear. Although there is some evidence for a general demethylation in aging, as well as numerous reports on changes in the methylation status of individual genes during aging (Van Remmen et al., 1995), the functional relevance of these changes is unknown. There is also very little information on the possible repair of epigenetic mistakes of this kind, although the enzyme responsible for

methylation, DNA-methyltransferase, is known (Bestor et al., 1988) and a protein with demethylase activity also has been identified (Bhattacharya et al., 1999).

In view of the relationship between chromatin structure and gene expression, it is of interest to know the possible conformational changes that may occur in the DNA of the genome during the aging process. For example, changes in the stability of nucleosomes, the fundamental unit of chromatin structure, could lead to repression or de-repression of gene expression. There also are a number of DNA conformers, such as Z-DNA, triplex DNA, and cruciform DNA, that can be formed under physiological conditions (Van Holde & Zlatanova, 1994). Little is known about the frequency of such DNA structures and how they influence nucleosomal positioning and gene expression. Because the local structure of DNA is nucleotide sequence dependent, mutations can be expected to influence the chromatin, thereby causing gene expression changes. The same is true for DNA damage, which has been demonstrated to influence changes in nucleosome positioning (Mann et al., 1997). A number of age-related DNA conformational changes have been reported, suggesting increases in nucleosome spacing with age and a lower sensitivity to nucleases (Kanungo, 1994). It is possible that these changes are caused by changes in the primary structure of DNA (DNA damage, mutations, and/or methylation changes) or by modifications of histones and non-histone proteins, such as phosphorylation, acetylation, and methylation.

DNA methylation and DNA–protein interactions together are thought to organize the genome into transcriptionally active and inactive zones. It is important to realize that both DNA damage and mutations can disturb this pattern of regulation, thereby causing normally silenced alleles to be expressed and vice versa. Age-related changes in DNA methylation patterns and DNA–protein interactions therefore are likely to be secondary rather than primary events in the aging process.

V. *In Vivo* End Points of Nuclear Genome Instability

Of the three categories of DNA alterations defined at the beginning of this chapter, it has been fairly well established by now that mutations accumulate with age. This is summarized in Table I. (For reasons explained in the text, the situation is less clear for DNA damage and epigenetic changes.) On the basis of the data from our laboratory (which do not appear to deviate significantly from other estimates; Table I), the average number of mutations accumulated in an old cell was estimated (Table II). Of the different types

Table 1

Spontaneous Age-Related Mutagenic Events Obtained by Different *in Vivo* Mammalian Mutation Detection Models

Assay	Locus	Species	Tissue	Mutagenic frequency (Age)[a]	Units	Reference
Cytogenetic						
Chromosome aberrations	Micronuclei	Human	Lymphocytes	0.9 (20y)–2.6 (80y)	Per 100 cells	Peace & Succop, 1999
		Mouse	Reticulocytes	0.2 (1.5m)–0.33 (23m)	Per 100 cells	Dass *et al.*, 1997
		Mouse	Spermatids	0.04 (2.4m)–0.2 (28m)	Per 100 cells	Lowe *et al.*, 1995
	Painting	Human	Lymphocytes	0.36 (0y)–2.9 (>49y)	Per 100 cells[b]	Ramsey *et al.*, 1995
		Mouse	Lymphocytes	0.3 (2.5m)–1.9 (20m)	Per 100 cells	Tucker *et al.*, 1999
Specific locus						
Endogenous	*Dlb-1*	Mouse	Small intestine	0.5 (0.8m)–6.8 (6.5m)	Ribbons/10⁴ villi	Winton *et al.*, 1998
	HPRT	Human	Lymphocytes	0.1 (3y)–0.25 (25y)	Per 10^5 loci	Finette *et al.*, 1994
		Human	Lymphocytes	0.67 (30y)	Per 10^5 loci	Hakoda *et al.*, 1990
		Human	Lymphocytes	0.37 (20y)–0.87 (50y)	Per 10^5 loci	Jones *et al.*, 1995
		Human	Lymphocytes	0.47 (30y)–1.1 (80y)	Per 10^5 loci	Akiyama *et al.*, 1995
		Human	Kidney fibroblasts	5 (5y)–25 (80y)	Per 10^5 loci	Martin *et al.*, 1996a,b
	Hprt	Mouse	Lymphocytes	0.67 (1m)–3.0 (12m)	Per 10^5 loci	Dempsey *et al.*, 1993a
		Mouse	Lymphocytes	1.0 (3m)–1.5 (30m)	Per 10^5 loci	Inamizu *et al.*, 1986
		Mouse	Lymphocytes	0.08 (4m)	Per 10^5 loci	Van Sloun *et al.*, 1998
	APRT	Human	Lymphocytes	13 (30y)	Per 10^5 loci	Hakoda *et al.*, 1990
	Aprt	Mouse	Lymphocytes	0.87 (3.8m)	Per 10^5 loci	Van Sloun *et al.*, 1998
		Mouse	Kidney fibroblasts	9 (3–6m)	Per 10^5 loci	Turker *et al.*, 1999
		Mouse	Ear fibroblasts	11 (3–6m)	Per 10^5 loci	Turker *et al.*, 1999
		Mouse	Ear fibroblasts	12 (3m)	Per 10^5 loci	Shao *et al.*, 1999
		Mouse	Skin fibroblasts	17 (3–5m)	Per 10^5 loci	Stambrook *et al.*, 1996
	HLA-A	Human	Lymphocytes	0.71 (0y)–6.5 (78y)	Per 10^5 loci	Grist *et al.*, 1992
	H-2	Mouse	Lymphocytes	24.2 (3–6m)	Per 10^5 loci	Dempsey *et al.*, 1993b
Transgenic	*lacI-λ*	Mouse	Spleen	3.5 (0m)–15 (24m)	Per 10^5 loci	Lee *et al.*, 1994
		Mouse	Spermatozoa	0.8 (2m)–4.9 (28m)	Per 10^5 loci	Walter *et al.*, 1998
	lacZ-λ	Mouse	Brain	5.5 (0m)–9.5 (23m)	Per 10^5 loci	Ono *et al.*, 2000
		Mouse	Liver	6.0 (0m)–14 (23m)	Per 10^5 loci	Ono *et al.*, 2000
		Mouse	Heart	5.5 (0m)–14 (23m)	Per 10^5 loci	Ono *et al.*, 2000
		Mouse	Spleen	5.0 (0m)–13 (23m)	Per 10^5 loci	Ono *et al.*, 2000
		Mouse	Skin	5.5 (0m)–8.5 (23m)	Per 10^5 loci	Ono *et al.*, 2000
		Mouse	Testis	7.0 (2m)–9.0 (23m)	Per 10^5 loci	Ono *et al.*, 2000
	lacZ-plasmid	Mouse	Brain	2.8 (0m)–5.0(m)	Per 10^5 loci	Dollé *et al.*, 1997
		Mouse	Liver	3.9 (0m)–12 (30m)	Per 10^5 loci	Dollé *et al.*, 1997
		Mouse	Heart	5.6 (5m)–13 (31m)	Per 10^5 loci	Dollé *et al.*, 2000
		Mouse	Small intestine	11 (5m)–26 (31m)	Per 10^5 loci	Dollé *et al.*, 2000

[a] Age expressed in years (y) for human samples and in months (m) for mouse samples.
[b] For chromosomes 1, 2, and 4.

of mutations found to accumulate, large genome rearrangements especially could explain some aspects of age-related cellular degeneration and death. However, direct evidence that associates increased rates of mutation accumulation *in vivo* with accelerated senescence is lacking thus far. Defects in the critical determinants of mutation accumulation, i.e., genome stability systems, would be expected to accelerate both aging and

mutation accumulation. Most of the knowledge on repair pathways and other genome stability systems has been obtained from unicellular organisms, such as *E. coli* and yeast, or from human and animal cell cultures. Hence the possibility that our current knowledge of repair pathways and mutagenesis is biased toward actively proliferating cells in culture. In the various organs and tissues of mammals, highly proliferating cell populations are nonexistent or rare. Therefore, to assess the consequences of imperfect repair leading to mutation accumulation, *in vivo* model systems are needed. Newly generated animal models deficient in specific genome stability pathways could be useful tools to gain more insight into the effects of imperfect cellular maintenance and repair on the status of organs and tissues in intact animals over their life span. Such insight also would greatly facilitate human population studies in which polymorphic variations at critical loci are assessed in relation to aging-related phenotypes, e.g., longevity and preservation of organ function. Next, we will first review the situation with respect to current mouse models with defects in genome stability genes. All genes discussed are listed in Table III with their corresponding

Table II

Categorized Mutation Frequencies per Organ in Young and Old Mice

Organ	Age (months)	*LacZ* mutant frequency ($\times 10^{-5}$) (Mutations/cell[a])	
		Point mutations[b]	Size changes[b]
Brain	4	2.5 (50)	0.6 (11)
	30	3.7 (74)	0.4 (9)
Liver	4	2.0 (39)	1.1 (22)
	30	5.6 (113)	4.3 (86)
Heart	3	1.8 (37)	2.2 (45)
	33	5.1 (103)	5.0 (99)
Small intestine	3	4.5 (89)	1.7 (34)
	33	16.6 (332)	2.9 (58)

[a] Mutational events per diploid genome, based on a 3000-bp target locus and a (6×10^9)-bp diploid genome.
[b] Classification based on restriction fragment analysis on agarose gels. Due to resolution limits of this method, the point mutation group may contain small deletions or insertions of up to 50 bp.

Table III

Major Mammalian Genome Stability Pathways with Some Selected Genes

Pathway	Gene[a]	Protein	Function (if known in some detail; actual function might be broader than described here)
Cell cycle control	*Trp53*	p53	Cell cycle arrest and apoptosis control (tumor suppressor gene)
	Atm	Atm	Protein kinase, capable of phosphorylating p53 and Brca1
Mismatch repair	*Mlh1*	Mlh1	Mediates cross-talk between Msh2 and other members of the repair complex
(MMR)	*Msh2*	Msh2	Mismatch recognition
	Pms1	Pms1	Associates with Mlh 1
	Pms2	Pms2	Associates with Mlh 1
Base excision repair[b]	*Oggl*[c]	8-Oxoguanine DNA-glycosylase 1	Hydrolytic cleavage of the base–deoxyribose glycosyl bond of 8-oxoguanidine.
(BER)	*Apex*	Apurinic/apyrimidinic endonuclease	Makes the first single-stranded nick 5′ of the removed base

(continues)

Table III   *(Cont'd)*

Pathway	Gene[a]	Protein	Function (if known in some detail; actual function might be broader than described here)
	Polb	DNA polymerase β	Fills the DNA gap resulting from exonuclease activity
	Lig1	DNA ligase 1	Seals the newly synthesized fragment to the repaired strand
Nucleotide excision repair (NER)	*Xpc*	Xpc	Damage recognition in combination with Hr23b for global genome repair
	Hr23b	Hr23b	Damage recognition in combination with Xpc for global genome repair
	Csa	Csa	Dissociates stalled RNA polymerase in combination with Csb for transcription-coupled repair
	Ercc6	Csb	Dissociates stalled RNA polymerase in combination with Csa for transcription-coupled repair
	Xpa	Xpa	Damage recognition and anchor for NER machinery
	Rpa	Rpa	Associated with Xpa
	Erccl	Erccl	5′ endonuclease in combination with Xpf
	Ercc4	Xpf	5′ endonuclease in combination with Erccl
	Ercc5	Xpg	3′ endonuclease
	Ercc2	Xpd	5′→3′ helicase subunit of transcription factor IIH
	Ercc3	Xpb	3′→5′ helicase subunit of transcription factor IIH
	Ttda	Ttda	Subunit of transcription factor IIH
	Xpe	Xpe	DNA binding protein
Nonhomologous end-joining (NHEJ)	*Xrcc5*	PK regulatory subunit Ku80	Protein kinase subunit (forms heterodimer with Ku70), binds to (stabilizes) DNA ends
	Xrcc6	PK regulatory subunit Ku70	Protein kinase subunit (forms heterodimer with Ku80), binds to (stabilizes) DNA ends
	Xrcc7	PK catalitic subunit	Protein kinase subunit
	Xrcc4	Xrcc4	Associates with (or possibly recruits/activates) DNA ligase IV
	Lig4	DNA ligase IV	Connects loose DNA ends
Recombinational repair	*Atm*	Atm	Protein kinase, capable of phosphorylating p53 and Brca 1
	Brca1	Brca1	Activates DNA repair through association with Brca2 and Rad51
	Brca2	Brca2	Associates with Rad51
	Rad51	Rad51	recA homologue (*E. coli*), mediates DNA strand pairing and exchange
	Rad52	Rad52	ssDNA annealing, stimulates DNA strand pairing and exchange
	Rad54	Rad54	DNA-dependent ATPase, involved in DNA strand pairing
	Ercc1	Ercc1	Errcc1–Xpf complex cleaves protruding single strands during single-strand annealing
Telomere maintenance	*Tert*	Telomerase	Reverse transcriptase, maintenance, and/or extension of telomeres
	Terc		Telomerase RNA component
	Xrcc5	PK regulatory subunit Ku80	Protein kinase subunit (forms heterodimer with Ku70), binds to (stabilizes) DNA ends
	Xrcc6	PK regulatory subunit Ku70	Protein kinase subunit (forms heterodimer with Ku80), binds to (stabilizes) DNA ends
RecQ helicase family	*RecQ1*	RecQ1	DNA helicase
	Blm	Blm	DNA helicase
	Wrn	Wrn	Recombination suppressor with DNA helicase and exonuclease function
	RecQ4	Rts	DNA helicase
	RecQ5	RecQ5	DNA helicase

[a]Mouse gene nomenclature is used.
[b]Enzymes involved in "short-patch" or single-nucleotide replacement BER ("long-patch" or several nucleotide replacement also exists).
[c]A number of damage-specific glycosylases exist, but only one example is given.

genome stability pathway. Then, attention will be focused on the prospects of using the rapid advances in human genomic research to start searching for individual heritable variation in genome stability genes and its possible association with aging-related phenotypes, such as extreme longevity.

A. Transgenic Mouse Modeling

To test the hypothesis that accelerated mutation accumulation is associated with the early appearance of some features of aging, genetic defects in genome stability systems can be modeled in the mouse, e.g., by mutational inactivation of the relevant gene in the germ line. Mutant mouse models affected in some of the major genome stability pathways will be discussed.

1. The Trp53 Tumor Suppressor Gene

The p53 tumor suppressor protein is a transcription factor that is activated in response to a variety of DNA-damaging agents, leading to cell cycle arrest at the G1/S boundary or the induction of apoptosis. Mutations in the TP53 gene, disrupting these pathways, are the most common genetic alterations in human cancers, occurring in a wide variety of tissues [for a review, see Levine (1997)]. To study the role of p53 in mammalian development and tumor formation, Trp53 knockout mice have been generated (Donehower et al., 1992; Jacks et al., 1994). Approximately 8–16% of mice lacking the TP53 tumor suppressor gene suffer from neural tube closure defects during embryonic development that are incompatible with postnatal survival (Sah et al., 1995). However, most p53-deficient mice develop normally and are indistinguishable from their wild-type littermates at young age. At a later age, i.e., between 2 and 7 months, they develop cancer and die (Donehower et al., 1992; Jacks et al., 1994).

To investigate the effect of p53 deficiency on genome stability, crosses have been made between transgenic reporter mice and a Trp53 knockout mouse (Nishino et al., 1995; Sands et al., 1995; our laboratory, unpublished results). At an early age, around 2 months, mutation frequencies in the liver and spleen of homozygous Trp53 knockout mice were not different from the heterozygous mutants or the wild-type control animals (Nishino et al., 1995; Sands et al., 1995). Indeed, after treatment with 100 mg/kg bodyweight of the powerful mutagen ethyl nitrosourea, equal amounts of mutations were induced in these young Trp53$^{-/-}$ mice and the controls (our laboratory, unpublished results). However, at a somewhat older age, up to 7 months, spontaneous mutation frequencies in the Trp53$^{-/-}$ animals rapidly increased with a high individual variation. The mutation frequency increase was statistically significant for the spleen, but not for the liver, and appeared to be a characteristic of the normal tissues, because histopathological analysis indicated no sign of tumors in the organ samples taken for mutant frequency determinations (results not shown).

In some of the tumors also analyzed (mainly in thymus and lymph node), slightly higher mutation frequencies than those found in the normal tissues were observed. Further characterization showed that in most cases these mutations involved point mutations. In this respect, it should be noted that tumor genomes from Trp53$^{-/-}$ mice are cytogenetically highly unstable and are characterized by excessive aneuploidy and other chromosomal aberrations (Smith & Fornace, 1995). Thus, whereas p53 is important in maintaining chromosomal stability, apparently it is much less important in maintaining stability at the nucleotide level.

On the basis of the results thus far, p53 does not seem to play the major role in mutation induction that its function as "guardian of the genome" might have suggested. This is in spite of its important role in carcinogenesis. This seeming discrepancy can be explained by the assumption that p53's early role as a cell cycle checkpoint and in the apoptosis of cells with severe DNA damage can be taken over by alternative pathways. At later ages, however, mutations are accumulating at an accelerated pace compared to the normal aging process. This is accompanied by an increased predisposition to tumor formation. Apparently, at this adult stage the role of p53 in apoptosis is important in preventing the accumulation of mutated and tumorigenic cells.

2. Mismatch Repair Mutants

One step away from DNA damage control through cell cycle shutdown or apoptosis is DNA repair, the many different pathways of which can act in both mitotic and postmitotic cells. A major repair pathway with a number of possible roles in the cell is DNA mismatch repair (MMR). The major function of MMR probably is to monitor the newly synthesized DNA strand for incorrect or mismatched bases, which are removed and replaced by the correct equivalents (Modrich, 1994). MMR overlaps with other repair pathways, in that it is also involved in the repair of chemical damage to DNA and the processing of recombination intermediates (Modrich, 1994). Kolodner and co-workers were the first to identify and clone human homologs of bacterial and yeast DNA mismatch repair genes (Fishel et al., 1993). As it turned out, germ line mutations in a number of these genes, e.g., MLH1, MSH2, PMS1, and PMS2, have been associated with hereditary nonpolyposis colorectal cancer in humans (Fishel et al., 1993; Nicolaides et al., 1994). Tumor cells from these patients (homozygously mutated) demon-strate accelerated mutation of simple repeat sequences (microsatellites) in the genome (Perucho, 1996).

Mice that are deficient in DNA mismatch repair genes have been generated at several laboratories (De Wind et al., 1998). Msh2-deficient mice succumb within 1 year to lymphomas, a common cause of death also in normally aged mice (Reitmair et al., 1996). Within the first year, no difference was observed between wild-type mice and the Msh2 heterozygotes. To investigate the spontaneous mutation frequencies in various organs and tissues in these animals, Msh2- and Pms2-deficient mice were crossed with transgenic mutation reporter mice. The results indicated greatly elevated spontaneous mutation frequencies in several organs and tissues of up to 15-fold (Andrew et al., 1997) or even up to 100-fold (Narayanan et al., 1997). Virtually all of these mutations were point mutations, which could reflect the transgenic mutation systems used (based on bacteriophage λ vectors, which lack the capability to recover large deletions) or the genome stability pathway involved (DNA mismatch repair deficiency appears to be associated with small insertions/deletions in small mononucleotide repeat runs). Interestingly, these data immediately refute the possibility that high levels of random mutations (that is, point mutations) are incompatible with normal development. However, at this stage nothing is known about the situation at later ages because complete life span studies on these mice have not yet been performed. The possibility should be taken into account that smaller mutations, i.e., point mutations and small deletions or insertions, are less important in creating a general spectrum of age-related degeneration than large rearrangement mutations. Indeed, as suggested by the high level of DNA rearrangement mutations observed in the lymphocytes of Werner syndrome patients (see the following discussion), large DNA rearrangements could be key DNA mutations in explaining adverse effects at old age.

3. Base and Nucleotide Excision Repair Mutants

Nucleotide excision repair and its sister pathway, base excision repair (BER), are considered to be the most important pathways to remove a large variety of structural lesions from DNA. Complete inactivation of the BER pathway, for example through the inactivation of polymerase β, is lethal (Sobol et al., 1996). However, in BER, release of altered bases is initiated by glycosylases, of which there are many (Lindahl & Wood, 1999). Some glycosylases have been inactivated in the mouse germ line, and the resulting mice were viable. Another example is the inactivation of the DNA glycosylase specific for the excison of 8-oxoG from DNA. This is a major oxidative lesion and, in the absence of its DNA glycosylase encoded by the gene OGG1, it was found to accumulate in the genome of these animals (Klungland et al., 1999). However, the animals were viable and only a moderately increased mutation frequency was found in nonproliferative tissues, which was explained in part by the action of nucleotide excision repair acting as a backup system.

Nucleotide excison repair (NER) entails multiple steps that employ a number of proteins to eliminate a broad spectrum of structurally unrelated, helix-distorting lesions, such as UV-induced photoproducts, chemical adducts, intrastrand cross-links, and some forms of oxidative damage. Deficiency in NER has been shown to be associated with human inheritable disorders, such as xeroderma pigmentosum (XP), Cockayne's syndrome (CS), and trichothiodystrophy (TTD) (Bootsma et al., 1998). XP patients can be

classified into at least seven complementation groups (XPA–XPG), XPA being the most frequent. XPA deficiency inactivates both subpathways of NER, i.e., global and transcription-coupled NER, and causes severe symptoms, the most prominent of which are a >2000-fold increased frequency of UVB-induced skin cancer and accelerated neurodegeneration (Bootsma et al., 1998). The XPA protein, in combination with replication protein A, has been proposed to be involved in DNA damage recognition, i.e., a preincision step (Sugasawa et al., 1998). Hence, in contrast to BER, NER is not dependent on an arsenal of different lesion-specific glycosylases, but acts in a more general way.

Mice deficient in NER have been generated by the mutational inactivation of the gene Xpa and appeared to mimic the phenotype of humans with xeroderma pigmentosum, that is, increased sensitivity to UVB-induced skin cancer (De Vries et al., 1995). However, at early age, NER-deficient mice do not show spontaneous abnormalities. These mice develop normally and are indistinguishable from wild-type mice. At older ages, i.e., from about 15 months onward, $Xpa^{-/-}$ mice show an increased frequency of hepatocellular adenomas (De Vries et al., 1997), which in normal mice is a common pathological lesion only at old age (Bronson & Lipman, 1991). The lack of spontaneous abnormalities in young mice might be due to the fact that, under normal conditions, mice have only limited exposure to sources of NER-processed DNA damage. Hence, at early ages NER appears to be dispensable, which is in contrast to BER, the complete inactivation of which is lethal (see preceding discussion). In order to test the hypothesis that loss of NER causes accelerated mutation accumulation, preceding the onset of accelerated tumor formation and aging, Xpa-deficient mice were crossed with transgenic mutation reporter gene mice. In the liver, but not in the brain of the hybrids, mutation frequencies showed an accelerated age-related increase from about 4 months onward (Giese et al., 1999). After 9–12 months, mutation frequencies were in the range of the maximum level reported earlier for 25 to 34-month-old lacZ control mice, with a similar high individual variation (Giese et al., 1999).

The absence of a severe spontaneous phenotype in the NER-deficient animals (at least until middle age) is in striking contrast to the corresponding human syndrome, xeroderma pigmentosum. Humans with XP rarely survive beyond the third decade of life, a consequence of the dramatic increase in sunlight-induced skin cancer (Cleaver & Kraemer, 1995). Skin cancer does not occur in rodents, which have fur that cannot be penetrated by UV rays and also are kept under conditions not permitting exposure to sunlight. This explains the lack of a phenotype of the Xpa mutation at early ages. In the young animals, NER could be essentially redundant, but become increasingly important at later ages. Indeed, it has been argued repeatedly that the loss of redundancy in, e.g., cell number, gene copy number, and functional pathways could be responsible for the gradual loss of individual stability and increased incidence of disease associated with aging (Strehler & Freeman, 1980). Complete life span studies of the NER-deficient animals ultimately will reveal whether a late-age phenotype and shortened life span are associated with the observed accelerated mutation accumulation.

Another NER gene defect that has been modeled in the mouse involves the homologue of the gene that is defective in the human genetic disorder, Cockayne syndrome (CS). In cells from such patients, only transcription-coupled NER is absent. However, the A and B proteins

of CS play a role not only in NER but also in transcription (Van Gool et al., 1997). For CS, both Csb and Csa knockout mice have been made. In the Csb mouse mutant, initially a less severe phenotype than that from the human disorder was found (Van der Horst et al., 1997). However, after crossing with the NER-deficient XPA knockout mouse, a very severe CS phenotype was observed (J. H. Hoeijmakers, personal communication). This underscores the notion that the inactivation of multiple functions in DNA transactions is more likely to cause severe senescence-related phenotypes than single defects. Indeed, the fact that the Xpa-deficient animals alone show normal development and, in the absence of mutagenic treatments, virtually no symptoms of accelerated aging, at least until middle age, suggests that the main problem in CS as a progeroid syndrome is not mutation avoidance but a transcription defect. This could, of course, also result in cell death and cell senescence (which would explain the symptoms of senescence) but probably not cell transformation, which could account for the fact that CS patients are not cancer-prone.

4. Double-Strand Break Repair Mutant Mice

Double-strand-break repair (DSBR) consists of two different pathways, nonhomologous end-joining (NHEJ) and homologous recombination. Double-strand breaks arise from somatic recombination, extensive overlapping excision repair tracts, ionizing radiation, oxidative insults, and interstrand cross-linking agents. Because double-strand breaks block replication and transcription and exposed ends are susceptible to further genetic loss by nuclease activity, efficient repair is necessary for local and overall genomic integrity and the maintenance of gene expression.

Mice defective in several different enzymes involved in NHEJ have been constructed. Knockout mice for DNA ligase IV and *Xrcc4* (which act in a complex to carry out the final steps of DSBR) are embryonically lethal (Barnes *et al.*, 1998; Gao *et al.*, 1998a). However, mice deficient in one of the three DNA-dependent protein kinase (DNA-PK) subunits are viable (Nussenzweig *et al.*, 1996; Gu *et al.*, 1997; Vogel *et al.*, 1999; Taccioli *et al.*, 1998; Gao *et al.*, 1998b). DNA-PK is a trimeric complex of the Ku70/86 (also termed Ku70 and Ku80) heterodimer and a catalytic subunit. The targeted 450-kDa catalytic subunit null mice appeared to have the same defect as the longer known severe combined immunodeficiency (SCID) mice (Kirchgessner *et al.*, 1995). All of these (viable) mouse models share severe immune deficiencies resulting from defective V(D)J recombination, which uses the same proteins as those involved in NHEJ. Cell lines deficient in any of these proteins show an increased sensitivity to ionizing radiation, indicating a poor repair capacity for double-strand breaks, and undergo premature replicative senescence (Kirchgessner *et al.*, 1995; Barnes *et al.*, 1998; Taccioli *et al.*, 1998; Vogel *et al.*, 1999). In contrast to DNA-PK catalytic subunit null mice, which exhibit no growth retardation (Gao *et al.*, 1998b), Ku80- and Ku70-deficient mice are about 50% of the size of littermate controls (Nussenzweig *et al.*, 1996; Li *et al.*, 1998). In addition, the knockout models for either Ku subunit show a shortened life span, with an early onset of senescence (Li *et al.*, 1998, Vogel *et al.*, 1999). The more severe senescent-like phenotype of the Ku-deficient mice compared to DNA-PK catalytic subunit null mice indicates another cellular function for the Ku proteins besides V(D)J recombination and NHEJ. Indeed, similar to its function in yeast, the Ku heterodimer in mammals seems to play a role in telomere maintenance, which is not dependent on the DNA-PK catalytic subunit (Hsu *et al.*, 1999).

Knockout mice also have been made for enzymes involved in recombinational repair. Recombinational repair is carried out by a pathway involving many members, including the products of the Rad52 epistasis group. Inactivation of a key gene in this pathway, i.e., *Rad51*, has been shown to be embryonically lethal (Lim & Hasty, 1996). Inactivation of the *Rad54* gene resulted in viable mice that were found to be sensitive to ionizing radiation, mitomycin C, and methyl methanesulfonate, but not to ultraviolet light (Essers *et al.*, 1997). Interestingly, the product of the *Rad51* gene has been demonstrated to interact with the Brca1 and -2 proteins (Scully *et al.*, 1997; Mizuta *et al.*, 1997), which brings these breast cancer susceptibility genes originally designated as tumor suppressor genes into the fold of DNA repair. Inactivation of *Brca1* or *Brca2* in cultured cells resulted in high levels of chromosomal abnormalities, as well as signs that pointed to accelerated replicative senescence (Patel *et al.*, 1998; Xu *et al.*, 1999). This is remarkably similar to some of the previously described NHEJ mouse mutants and what has been found after disrupting the gene *Ercc1*, which is involved in both NER and a mitotic recombination pathway (Weeda *et al.*, 1997). A direct molecular link between the Rad52 pathway and ATM, the mutational defect responsible for the human progeroid syndrome ataxia telangiectasia, has been established. It is assumed that BRCA1 is phosphorylated by the ATM protein kinase in response to DNA damage. The product of the *ATM* gene was first identified as a cell cycle checkpoint, functioning in the same pathway as p53 (Rotman & Shiloh, 1997). Chromosomal instability is also one of the hallmarks of ataxia telangiectasia.

5. Telomerase Mouse Mutants

The potential importance of large genome rearrangements for the aging phenotype is illustrated by results obtained with telomerase null mice. This is reviewed extensively elsewhere (Chapter 8 of this volume). Suffice to say that adverse effects, including a shortened life span, hematopoietic ablation, reduced capacity to respond to stresses, as well as increased incidence of spontaneous malignancies and genetic instability, were noted during a 2.5-year study of an aging cohort of mice from the third generation onward (Rudolph et al., 1999). These demonstrated effects of telomere instability and the accompanying genetic instability underscore the fact that loss of genome integrity in vivo can lead to the loss of proliferative homeostasis, as predicted by Martin (1991).

6. The RecQ Helicase Superfamily

The RecQ helicase superfamily has been implicated in DNA repair and recombination. Thus far, a total of five human helicases have been identified that belong to this family: RECQ1, BLM, WRN, RTS, and RECQ5β (Shimamoto et al., 2000; Lindor et al., 2000). Of the five RECQ genes, three are associated with diseases involving genomic instability and cancer when they are defective, i.e., BLM with Bloom syndrome, WRN with Werner syndrome, and RTS with Rothmund–Thomson syndrome. In spite of the similarities between the three genes in terms of several characteristics of the diseases they cause, most notably genomic instability and cancer, these genes are not the same and most likely have distinct roles in processes of DNA repair and recombination. For example, on the basis of a computer search, an exonuclease activity, in addition to the common helicase activity, was predicted for the wrn protein, a prediction that was confirmed after purification of the recombinant wild-type wrn protein by the demonstration of a 3′ → 5′ exonuclease activity in the N-terminal region (Huang et al., 1998). This exonuclease activity points toward a role of the WRN gene product in DNA repair, possibly in addition to other DNA transactions, and could explain the differences between Bloom and Werner syndromes.

Successful attempts have been made to genetically inactivate the homologs of two human RECQ genes in the mouse. Blm homozygous knockout mice die in utero by embryonic day 13.5, possibly due to massive apoptosis (Chester et al., 1998). Like in human Bloom syndrome patients, high numbers of sister chromatid exchanges (SCEs) were observed in cultured fibroblasts of these mice. In this respect, it is conceivable that human cells have more extensive possibilities to compensate for the loss of this particular RECQ genome stability gene, i.e., by a backup or redundant activity. Indeed, this could be an example of the previously mentioned evolvement of a more sophisticated genome stability system in long-lived humans.

The WRN gene is thought to play a role in suppressing genomic instability (Yamagata et al., 1998). Wrn knockout mice have been generated at different laboratories. The results were disappointing in the sense that, apart from increased sensitivity to topoisomerase inhibitors of the ES cells, no phenotype of these mice resembling the symptoms of Werner syndrome patients was observed during their first year of life (Lebel & Leder, 1998). In this respect, it is possible that the WRN gene in humans is more important than it is in the mouse, possibly because human WRN may have evolved differently over time.

7. Mouse Modeling: Future Prospects

On the basis of the ample symptoms of accelerated senescence observed in mice with defects in genome stability systems suppressing large DNA sequence changes, (e.g., DSBR, telomerase) it is tempting to speculate that genome rearrangements and chromosomal aberrations are of critical importance to aging. Interestingly, most human progeroid syndromes, including Werner syndrome, are associated with genome rearrangements in their white blood cells. This strongly suggests that, of all genome stability pathways, those involved in suppressing large genome rearrangements are the most likely candidates to further explore with respect to a potential impact on aging and longevity. However, it should be realized that the use of transgenic modeling as a tool for studying the relevance of genome stability systems in aging has just begun. Thus far, very few if any life span studies on these models have been completed, and those limited studies that have been done have not always been done with the necessary care with respect to sample sizes and specific pathogen-free colony maintenance that are now considered essential in the science of aging. In addition, a confounding factor is genetic background, which can have a major effect on the gene defects studied. Therefore, only the early effects of the introduced mutations and/or transgenes have been assessed. Moreover, very few combinations of genome stability mutations have been studied, and information on the effects of (combinations of) less severe mutations is absent. To study the effect of subtle mutations in a variety of genes on phenotypes related to aging, genetically heterogeneous human populations might be more suitable than mouse models. This relatively new area of study will be discussed next.

B. Genetic Epidemiology of Aging and Genome Stability

The potential impact of loss of genome integrity on the aging phenotype is underscored by the so-called segmental progeroid syndromes, which are characterized by the accelerated occurrence of certain aspects of the senescent phenotype (Turker & Martin, 1999). (There also are unimodal progeroid syndromes, in which only one aspect of aging is accelerated, e.g., Alzheimer's disease.) Most of these syndromes are caused by heritable mutations in genes involved in DNA processing, including DNA repair. There is no single hereditary disorder that mimics all symptoms of human aging, which by itself is subject to individual variations. However, this is not to be expected if the products of multiple genes play a role in the process. Nevertheless, the fact that, in these disorders, accelerated aging can be recognized as such suggests that one or a few molecular pathways, such as those involved in suppressing chromosomal instability, play a major role. The Werner syndrome in particular has received ample attention after the relevant gene was identified as a member of the RECQ-like DNA helicases (Yu et al., 1996). Werner patients show increased risk for atherosclerosis, cancer, osteoporosis, and type 2 diabetes as well as early hair loss, graying of the hair, atrophy of the skin, and cataracts. These symptoms might be caused by a defect in chromosome maintenance, although the exact mechanism of action of the WRN gene as yet is unknown (see preceding discussion). Indeed, cultured somatic cells from patients with Werner syndrome display an increased rate of somatic mutations and a variety of cytogenetic abnormalities, such as deletions and translocations (Fukuchi et al., 1989). This high level of genomic instability could be the cause of the severe limitation of in vitro life span demonstrated in Werner cells (Martin, 1977). (Heritable mutations in other members of the RECQ family also have been demonstrated to cause genome instability and symptoms of accelerated aging; see preceding discussion.)

To demonstrate that allelic variations at loci controlling genome stability pathways are associated with aging-related phenotypic end points, such as extreme longevity, a molecular epidemiologic approach appears to be most promising. Indeed, with the rapid emergence of complete sequence information for all human genes, it is possible theoretically to scrutinize all genes or families of genes suspected to be involved in the suppression of genome instability during aging for polymorphic variation. If genome stability is a determinant of the rate of aging, one would expect allelic variation at the many loci harboring genome stability genes to contribute to the observed variations in life span, functional preservation, and disease risk.

One of the most obvious candidate genome stability genes to study for polymorphic variation is the *WRN* gene. To study the potential role of this gene in normal aging, Castro and co-workers (1999) compared a group of Finnish centenarians with newborns for differences in the frequency of a polymorphic variant (1367 Cys/Arg). No such differences were found. This study is illustrative for the single most important problem that presently is encountered in such studies. No cost-effective technology is available to study all possible gene variants rather than single polymorphisms. This is especially true for large genes such as *WRN*.

As a first step in providing a basis for more comprehensive molecular epidemiology studies to relate genetic variation at specific DNA repair genes to reduced DNA repair capacity and increased cancer susceptibility, Mohrenweiser and Jones (1998) resequenced the exons of 9 genes involved in different repair pathways. They identified 15 different amino acid substitution variants in these 9 genes and determined their frequencies in a small sample of individuals. Familial aggregation of cancer has been described

extensively, and there is increased interest in weakly predisposing alleles as risk factors (White, 1998). To conduct such studies by nucleotide sequencing, however, is extremely expensive, in spite of progress in automation.

In a recent study, Cargill and co-workers (1999) systematically surveyed the coding regions of 106 genes relevant to cardiovascular disease, endocrinology, and neuropsychiatry for all possible variants in a sample of mixed ethnic groups. For this purpose, they used a combination of oligonucleotide chip array hybridization and DHPLC (HPLC of DNA fragments in a temperature gradient). In these 106 genes, a total of 560 single-nucleotide polymorphisms (SNPs) were discovered. To identify potentially functional SNPs involved in blood pressure homeostasis and hypertension, Halushka and co-workers (1999), also using DNA chips, assayed 75 candidate genes in a sample of 74 ethnically heterogeneous individuals with a range of hypertension phenotype diversity. A total of 387 SNPs were detected in gene-coding sequences, 54% of which were predicted to lead to altered protein. In neither of these studies had actual association studies been done. However, they demonstrated that it is possible to find an informative set of common gene-based SNPs with direct functional relevance to a complex phenotype. With the genome program drawing to a close in the next few years, it is reasonable to expect that complete sequence information and pathway assignments for most, if not all, human genes will become available. However, a potential limitation to screen directly for functional polymorphic variants determining a complex trait involves the technology to screen multiple genes in large numbers of individuals for all possible sequence variations, which is still in its infancy. Most technology is limited in this respect by the need to PCR amplify each individual target sequence for mutational scanning (Eng & Vijg, 1997). Moreover, the most advanced methods, such as the DNA chips used in the two studies described previously, involve relatively expensive technology that has not been completely validated (a significant number of variants are missed).

Hence, the search for functional polymorphisms in multiple, often large, genes is not trivial. As an alternative, we have developed a gene-scanning platform based on a combination of extensive multiplex PCR amplification and two-dimensional electrophoresis of DNA fragments in denaturing gradient gels. The procedure, termed two-dimensional gene scanning (TDGS), has been automated and is now used in a routine setting to analyze genes involved in genome stability, aging, and cancer (Van Orsouw et al., 1996, 1999). By using this method, population-based studies have been initiated on mutations and polymorphisms in the breast cancer susceptibility gene BRCA1. This gene is thought to play an important role in recombinational repair together with a number of other genes (see previous discussion). Comparisons were made between sporadic breast cancer patients and centenarians (who have a very low risk of breast cancer) and their control groups. Preliminary results indicate significant differences in the frequencies of haplotypes of functional polymorphisms in BRCA1 between centenarians and control groups. These results point to the possibility to extend health span, i.e., cancer- and disease-free survival, by the early detection of individuals with suboptimal allelic variants of genome stability genes and, ultimately, the manipulation of the relevant pathways to decrease risk. This line of research will be strengthened greatly by the further development of protein bioinformatics methods that can help analyze the sequence and structural variations and provide insight into function.

VI. Conclusions

Since the original papers on the subject, in the 1940s and 1950s, the study of DNA alterations as a possible cause of aging has come a long way. Not only have we managed to develop a variety of methods to quantify and characterize DNA damage and mutations in cells and tissues taken from the in vivo situation, but it is now possible to link the patterns of genome deterioration that are beginning to emerge to the many interconnected pathways of DNA maintenance and repair in whole animals. We also are witnessing the beginning of a whole new area of research in which it will be possible to directly link variations in gene sequence and expression to phenotypic hallmarks of aging, i.e., functional decline and disease. The evidence that has emerged thus far strongly suggests that instability of the nuclear genome, in conjunction with alterations in the mitochondrial genome (Chapter 5 in this volume), plays some role in the etiology of aging. This is demonstrated most clearly in the human genome instability syndromes, most of which mimic some aspects of accelerated aging, and is confirmed in many of the corresponding mouse models. However, the major question that remains involves the mechanisms by which predominantly random DNA alterations can lead to the spectrum of age-related defects that are observed.

One obvious possibility is through interference with gene transcription. It has already been argued that, on the basis of the very low steady-state levels of spontaneous DNA lesions, it is unlikely that they would have any effect at all, except under extremely high levels of genotoxic stress. Changes in DNA modification, such as methylation, or DNA conformation certainly could lead to interference with normal patterns of gene expression. Unfortunately, such changes are not easy to detect in whole organs or tissues, and thus far there is little concrete evidence that they occur and have functional consequences. However, it is quite possible that changes in DNA conformation are one of the consequences of increased levels of DNA damage or mutations.

As described, the strongest evidence for an effect of DNA alterations in relation to aging is for large DNA mutations, i.e., at the genomic or chromosomal level. This would make sense in view of the relatively low frequency of spontaneous mutation. As indicated in Table II, there are probably no more than about 100 random mutations per cell in most aged tissues. If these are all point mutations it is unlikely to have a major effect on cell functioning. Indeed, cellular systems are robust and insensitive to many mutations. However, as many as 100 genome rearrangements, some involving millions of base pairs of DNA, could seriously affect normal regulation of gene expression, i.e., through gene dosage or position effects (Rasnick & Duesberg, 1999). In actively proliferating cell compartments, one of the highly visible effects of genome instability would be the loss of proliferative homeostasis, i.e., hyperplasia, neoplasia, and tissue atrophy. Less visibly, in postmitotic cells a variety of functional pathways could be affected, leading to a mosaic of cells at different stages on a trajectory that would finally lead to cell death. Interestingly, if DNA damage and/or methylation changes play a major role in aging, they also are most likely to act by affecting DNA conformation.

The major problem in directly testing increased genomic DNA mutations and their hypothetical consequences in terms of an altered gene expression pattern is the current lack of single-cell methods sensitive enough to detect subtle changes. However, this situation is now changing rapidly, and methods are emerging that, for example, allow in situ studies to assess transcriptional control at the single-cell level (Gribnau et al., 1998) and

to make entire cDNA libraries from single cells (Kacharmina et al., 1999). It is, therefore, conceivable that in the next decades detailed maps of specific alterations in single cells will emerge, revealing aged tissues as mosaics of random molecular alterations. On the other hand, increased deterioration of the nuclear genome is expected to induce a set of consistent gene expressional changes in the form of various stress responses. Evidence using microarray-based gene expression profiling suggests that this is indeed the case (Lee et al., 1999).

Acknowledgments

We thank Ms. Julia Perkins for her help with the preparation of the manuscript and Drs. Heidi Giese and Nathalie van Orsouw for sharing their unpublished data with us. This work was supported by NIH Grants PO1 1801 AG10829–01, 1 P30 AG13319–05, and 1 RO1 ES/CA 08797–01.

References

Aidoo, A., Mittelstaedt, R. A., Lyn-Cook, L. E., Duffy, P. H., & Heflich, R. H. (1999). Effect of dietary restriction on lymphocyte Hprt mutant frequency in aging rats. *Journal of Environmental Molecular Mutagenetics, 33*, 5.

Akiyama, M., Kyoizumi, S., Hirai, Y., Kusunoki, Y., Iwamoto, K. S., & Nakamura, N. (1995). Mutation frequency in human blood cells increases with age. *Mutation Research, 338(1–6)*, 141–149.

Albertini, R. J., Nicklas, J. A., Fuscoe, J. C., Skopek, Th. R., Branda, R. F., & O'Neill, J. P. (1993). *In vivo* mutations in human blood cells: biomarkers for molecular epidemiology. *Environmental Health Perspectives, 99*, 135–141.

Ames, B. N., Shigenaga, M. K., & Hagen, T. M. (1993). Oxidants, antioxidants, and the degenerative diseases of aging. *Proceedings of the National Academy of Sciences of the United States of America, 90*, 7915–7922.

Andersson, D. I., & Hughes, D. D. (1996). Muller's ratchet decreases fitness of a

DNA-based microbe. *Proceedings of the National Academy of Sciences of the United States of America, 93*, 906–907.

Andrew, S. E., Reitmair, A. H., Fox, J., Hsiao, L., Francis, A., McKinnon, M., Mak, T. W., & Jirik, F. R. (1997). Base transitions dominate the mutational spectrum of a transgenic reporter gene in MSH2 deficient mice. *Oncogene, 15*, 123–129.

Barnes, D. E., Stamp, G., Rosewell, I., Denzel, A., & Lindahl, T. (1998). Targeted disruption of the gene encoding DNA ligase IV leads to lethality in embryonic mice. *Current Biology, 8(25)*, 1395–1398.

Bell, G. (1988). *Sex and Death in Protozoa*, Cambridge, UK: Cambridge University Press.

Bestor, T., Laudano, A., Mattaliano, R., & Ingram, V. (1988). Cloning and sequencing of a cDNA encoding DNA methyltransferase of mouse cells. The carboxyl-terminal domain of the mammalian enzymes is related to bacterial restriction methyltransferases. *Journal of Molecular Biology, 203*, 971–983.

Bhattacharya, S. K., Ramchandani, S., Cervoni, N., & Szyf, M. (1999). A mammalian protein with specific demethylase activity for mCpG DNA. *Nature, 397*, 579–583.

Bootsma, D., Kraemer, K. H., Cleaver, J., & Hoeijmakers, J. H. J. (1998). Nucleotide excision repair syndromes: Xeroderma pigmentosum, Cockayne syndrome and trichothiodystrophy. In B. Vogelstein & K. W. Kinzler (Eds.), *Genetic Basis of Human Cancer, Chapter 13*, (pp. 245–274), New York: McGraw-Hill.

Bronson, R. T., & Lipman, R. D. (1991). Reduction in rate of occurrence of age-related lesions in dietary restricted laboratory mice. *Growth, Development & Aging, 55*, 169–184.

Burek, J. D. (1978) *Pathology of Aging Rats*, Boca Raton, FL: CRC Press.

Campisi, J. (1996). Replicative senescence: an old lives' tale? *Cell, 84*, 497–500.

Cargill, M., Altshuler, D., Ireland, J., Sklar, P., Ardlie, K., Patil, N., Lane, C. R., Lim, E. P., Kalyanaraman, N., Nemesh, J., Ziaugra, L., Friedland, L., Rolfe, A., Warrington, J., Lipshutz, R., Daley, G. Q., & Lander, E. S. (1999). Characterization of single-nucleotide polymorphisms in coding regions of human genes. *Nature Genetics, 22*, 231–238.

Castro, E., Ogburn, C. E., Hunt, K. E., Tilvis, R., Louhija, J., Penttinen, R., Erkkola, R., Panduro, A., Riestra, R., Piussan, C., Deeb, S. S., Wang, L., Edland, S. D., Martin, G. M., & Oshima, J. (1999). Polymorphisms at the Werner locus: I. Newly identified polymorphisms, ethnic variability of 1367Cy/Arg, and its stability in a population of Finnish centenarians. *American Journal of Medical Genetics, 82*, 399–403

Cleaver, J. E., & Kraemer, K. H. (1995). In C. R., Scriver, A. L., Beaudet, W. S., Sly, and D. Valle (Eds.), *The Metabolic and Molecular Bases of Inherited Disease. 7th Ed., Vol.III*, (pp. 4393–4419). New York: McGraw-Hill.

Chester, N., Kuo, F., Kozak, C., O'Hara, C. D., & Leder, P. (1998) Stage-specific apoptosis, developmental delay, and embryonic lethality in mice homozygous for a targeted disruption in the murine Bloom's syndrome gene. *Genes Development, 12*, 3382–3393.

Collins, A. R. (1999). Oxidative DNA damage, antioxidants, and cancer, *BioEssays, 21*, 238–246.

Curtis, H. & Crowley, C. (1963). Chromosome aberrations in liver cells in relation to the somatic mutation theory of aging. *Radiation Research, 19*, 337–344.

Da Cruz, A. D., Curry, J., Curado, M. P., & Glickman, B. (1996). Monitoring hprt mutant frequency over time in T-lymphocytes of people accidentally exposed to high doses of ionizing radiation. *Environmental Molecular Mutagenesis, 27*, 165–175.

Dass, S. B., Ali, S. F., Heflich, R. H., & Casciano, D. A. (1997). Frequency of spontaneous and induced micronuclei in the peripheral blood of aging mice. *Mutation Research, 381(1)*, 105–110.

De Vries, A., van Oostrom, C. T. M., Dortant, P. M., Beems, R. B., van Kreijl, C. F., Capel, P. J. A., & van Steeg, H. (1997). Spontaneous liver tumours and Benzo[a]pyrene-induced lymphomas in XPA-deficient mice. *Molecular Carcinogenesis 19*, 46–53.

De Vries, A., van Oostrom, C. T. M., Hofhuis, F. M. A., Dortant, P., Berg, R. J. W., de Gruijl, F. R., Wester, P. W., van Kriejl, C. F., Capel, P. J. A., van Steeg, H., & Verbeek, S. J. (1995). Increased susceptibility to ultraviolet-B and carcinogens of mice lacking the DNA excision repair gene XPA. *Nature, 377*, 169–173.

De Wind, N., Dekker, M., van Rossum, A., van der Valk, M., & te Riele, H. (1998). Mouse models for hereditary nonpolyposis colorectal cancer. *Cancer Research, 58(2)*, 248–255.

Dempsey, J. L., Pfeiffer, M., & Morley, A. A. (1993a). Effect of dietary restriction on *in vivo* somatic mutation in mice. *Mutation Research, 291*, 141–145.

Dempsey, J. L., Odagiri, Y., & Morley, A. A. (1993b). *In vivo* mutations at the H–2 locus in mouse lymphocytes. *Mutation Research, 285(1)*, 45–51.

Dollé, M. E. T., Giese, H., Hopkins, C. L., Martus, H.-J., Hausdorff, J. M., & Vijg, J. (1997). Rapid accumulation of genome rearrangements in liver but not in brain of old mice. *Nature Genetics, 17*, 431–434.

Dollé, M. E. T., Snyder, W. K., Gossen, J. A., Lohman, P. H. M., & Vijg, J. (2000) Distinct spectra of somatic mutations accumulated with age in mouse heart and small intestine. Proceedings of the National Academy of Sciences of the USA.

Donehower, L. A., Harvey, M., Slagle, B. L., McArthur, M. J., Montgomery, C. A., Jr, Butel, J. S., & Bradley, A. (1992). Mice deficient for p53 are developmentally normal but susceptible to spontaneous tumours. *Nature, 356(6366)*, 215–221.

Dubrova, Y. E., Jeffreys, A. J., & Malashenko, A. M. (1993). Mouse minisatellite mutations induced by ionizing radiation. *Nature Genetics, 5*, 92–94.

Elena, S. F., & Lenski, R. E. (1997). Test of synergistic interactions among deleterious mutations in bacteria. *Nature, 390*, 395–398.

Eng, C., & Vijg, J. (1997). Genetic testing: The problems and the promise. *Nature Biotechnology, 15*, 422–426.

Essers, J., Hendriks, R. W., Swagemakers, S. M. A., Troelstra, C., de Wit, J., Bootsma, D., Hoeijmakers, J. H. J., & Kanaar, R.

(1997). Disruption of mouse RAD54 reduces ionizing radiation resistance and homologous recombination. *Cell 89*, 195–204.

Evans, H. J. (1996). Mutation and mutagenesis in inherited and acquired human disease. *Mutation Research Forum 1*, 5–10.

Failla, G. (1958). The aging process and carcinogenesis. *Annals of the New York Academy of Science, 71*, 1124–1135.

Finch, C. E., Pike, M. C., & Witten, M. (1990) Slow mortality rate accelerations during aging in some animals approximate that of humans. *Science, 249*, 902–905.

Finette, B. A, Sullivan, L. M., O'Neill, J. P., Nicklas, J. A, Vacek, P. M., & Albertini, R. J. (1994). Determination of hprt mutant frequencies in T-lymphocytes from a healthy pediatric population: Statistical comparison between newborn, children and adult mutant frequencies, cloning efficiency and age. *Mutation Research, 308(2)*, 223–231.

Fishel, R., Lescoe, M. K., Rao, M. R. S., Copeland, N. G., Jenkins, N. A., Garber, J., Kane, M., & Kolodner, R. (1993). The human mutator gene homolog MSH2 and its association with hereditary nonpolyposis colon cancer. *Cell, 75*, 1027–1038.

Fukuchi, K., Martin, G. M., & Monnat, R. J., Jr. (1989). Mutator phenotype of Werner syndrome is characterized by extensive deletions. *Proceedings of the National Academy of Sciences of the USA, 86*, 5893–5897.

Gao, Y., Sun, Y., Frank, K. M., Dikkes, P., Fujiwara, Y., Seidl, K. J., Sekiguchi, J. M., Rathbun, G. A., Swat, W., Wang, J., Bronson, R. T., Malynn, B. A., Bryans, M., Zhu, C., Chaudhuri, J., Davidson, L., Ferrini, R., Stamato, T., Orkin, S. H., Greenberg, M. E., & Alt, F. W. (1998a). A critical role for DNA end-joining proteins in both lymphogenesis and neurogenesis. *Cell, 95(7)*, 891–902.

Gao, Y., Chaudhuri, J., Zhu, C., Davidson, L., Weaver, D. T., & Alt, F. W. (1998b). A targeted DNA-PKcs-null mutation reveals DNA-PK-independent functions for KU in V(D)J recombination. *Immunity, 9(3)*, 367–376.

Giese, H., Dollé, M. E. T., Hezel, A., van Steeg, H., & Vijg, J. (1999). Accelerated accumulation of somatic mutations in mice deficient in the nucleotide excision repair gene XPA. *Oncogene, 18*, 1257–1260.

Gossen, J. A., de Leeuw, W. J. F., Tan, C. H. T., Lohman, P. H. M., Berends, F., Knook, D. L., Zwarthoff, E. C., & Vijg, J. (1989). Efficient rescue of integrated shuttle vectors from transgenic mice: a model for studying gene mutations *in vivo*. *Proceedings of the National Academy of Sciences of the USA, 86*, 7971–7975.

Gossen, J. A., de Leeuw, W. J. F., Verwest, A., Lohman, P. H. M., & Vijg, J. (1991). High somatic mutation frequencies in a LacZ transgene integrated on the mouse X-chromosome, *Mutation Research, 250*, 423–429.

Gribnau, J, de Boer, E, Trimborn, T, Wijgerde, M, Milot, E, Grosveld, F, & Fraser, P. (1998). Chromatin interaction mechanism of transcriptional control *in vivo*. *EMBO Journal, 17(20)*, 6020–6027

Grist, S. A., McCarron, M., Kutlaca, A., Turner, D. R., & Morley, A. A. (1992). *In vivo* human somatic mutation: Frequency and spectrum with age. *Mutation Research, 266*, 189–196.

Gu, Y., Seidle, K. J., Rathbun, G. A., Zhu, C., Manis, J. P., van der Stoep, N., Davidson, L., Cheng, H. L., Sekiguchi, J. M., Frank, K., Stanhope-Baker, P., Schlissel, M. S., Roth, D. B., & Alt, F. W. (1997). Growth retardation and leaky SCID phenotype of Ku70-deficient mice. *Immunity, 7*, 653–665.

Hakoda, M., Nishioka, K., & Kamatani, N. (1990). Homozygous deficiency at autosomal locus aprt in human somatic cells *in vivo* induced by two different mechanisms. *Cancer Research, 50(6)*, 1738–1741.

Halushka, M. K., Fan, J-B., Bentley, K., Hsie, L., Shen, N., Weder, A., Cooper, R., Lipshutz, R., & Chakravarti, A. (1999). Patterns of single-nucleotide polymorphisms in candidate genes for blood-pressure homeostasis. *Nature Genetics, 22(3)*, 239–247.

Harman D. (1956). Aging: A theory based on free-radical and radiation chemistry. *Journal of Gerontology, 6*, 298–300.

Hart, R. W., D'Ambrosio, S. M., Ng., K. J., & Modak, S. P. (1979). Longevity, stability and DNA repair. *Mechanisms of Ageing and Development, 9*, 203–223.

Henshaw, P. S., Riley, E. F., & Stapleton, G. E. (1947). The biologic effects of pile radiations, *Radiology, 49*, 349–364.

Holliday, R. (1991). Mutations and epimutations in mammalian cells. *Mutation Research, 250*, 351–363.

Hsu, H. L., Gilley, D., Blackburn, E. H., & Chen, D. J. (1999). Ku is associated with the telomere in mammals. *Proceedings of the National Academy of Sciences of the USA, 96(22)*, 12454–12458.

Huang, S., Li, B., Gray, M. D., Oshima, J., Mian, I. S., & Campisi, J. (1998). The premature ageing syndrome protein, WRN, is a $3' \rightarrow 5'$ exonuclease. *Nature Genetics, 20*, 114–116.

Inamizu, T., Kinohara, N., Chang, M. P., & Makinodan, T. (1986). Frequency of 6-thioguanine-resistant T cells is inversely related to the declining T-cell activities in aging mice. *Proceedings of the National Academy of Science USA, 83(8)*, 2488–2491.

Jacks, T., Remington, L., Williams, B. O., Schmitt, E. M., Halachmi, S., Bronson, R. T., & Weinberg, R. A. (1994). Tumor spectrum analysis in p53-mutant mice. *Current Biology, 4(1)*, 1–7.

Jackson, A. L., & Loeb, L. A. (1998). The mutation rate and cancer. *Genetics, 148*, 1483–1490.

Jeffreys, A. J., Neumann, R., & Wilson, V. (1990). Repeat unit sequence variation in minisatellites: A novel source of DNA polymorphism for studying variation and mutation by single molecule analysis. *Cell, 60*, 476–485.

Jones, I. M., Thomas, C. B., Tucker, B., Thompson, C. L., Pleshanov, P., Vorobtsova, I., & Moore, D. H., II. (1995). Impact of age and environment on somatic mutation at the hprt gene of T lymphocytes in humans. *Mutation Research, 338*, 129–139.

Jones, P.A., & Gonzalgo, M. L. (1997). Altered DNA methylation and genome instability: A new pathway to cancer? *Proceedings of the National Academy of Sciences of the USA, 94*, 2103–2105.

Kacharmina, J. E., Crino, P. B., & Eberwine, J. (1999), Preparation of cDNA from single cells and subcellular regions. *Methods in Enzymology, 303*, 3–18.

Kamiguchi, Y., Tateno, H., & Mikamo K. (1994). Chromosomally abnormal gametes as a cause of congenital anomalies in humans. *Congenital Anomalies, 34*, 1–12.

Kanungo, M. S. (1994). *Genes and Aging.* New York: Cambridge University Press.

Kibota, T. T., & Lynch, M. (1996). Estimate of the genomic mutation rate deleterious to overall fitness in *E. coli. Nature, 381*, 694–696.

Kimberland, M. L., Divoky, V., Prchal, J., Schwahn, U., Berger, W., & Kazazian, H. H., Jr. (1999). Full-length human L1 insertions retain the capacity for high frequency retrotransposition in cultured cells. *Human Molecular Genetics, 8*, 1557–1560.

Kirchgessner, C. U., Patil, C. K., Evans, J. W., Cuomo, C. A., Fried, L. M., Carter, T., Oettinger, M. A., & Brown, J. M. (1995). DNA-dependent kinase (p350) as a candidate gene for the murine SCID defect. *Science, 267(5201)*, 1178–1183.

Kirkwood, T. B. L. (1989). DNA, mutations and aging. *Mutation Research, 219*, 1–7.

Klungland, A., Rosewell, I., Hollenbach, S., Larsen, E., Daly, G., Epe, B., Seeberg, E., Lindahl, T., & Barnes, D. E. (1999). Accumulation of premutagenic DNA lesions in mice defective in removal of oxidative base damage. *Proceedings of the National Academy of Sciences of the USA, 96 (23)*, 13300–13305.

Krontiris, T. G. (1995). Minisatellites and human disease. *Science, 269*, 1682–1683.

Le, X. C., Xing, J. Z., Lee, J., Leadon, S. A., & Weinfeld, M. (1998). Inducible repair of thymine glycol detected by an ultrasensitive assay for DNA damage. *Science, 280*, 1066–1069.

Lebel, M., & Leder, P. (1998) A deletion within the murine Werner syndrome helicase induces sensitivity to inhibitors of topoisomerase and loss of cellular proliferative capacity. *Proceedings of the National Academy of Sciences USA, 95*, 13097–13102.

Lee, A. T., DeSimone, C., Cerami, A., & Bucala, R. (1994). Comparative analysis of DNA mutations in *lacI* transgenic mice with age. *Federation of American Societies for Experimental Biology Journal, 8*, 545–550.

Lee, C. K., Klopp, R. G., Weindruch, R., & Prolla, T. A. (1999). Gene expression profile of aging and its retardation by caloric restriction. *Science, 285*, 1390– 1393.

Levine, A. J. (1997). p53, the cellular gatekeeper for growth and division. *Cell, 88*, 323–331.

Li, E., Beard, C., & Jaenisch, R. (1993). Role for DNA methylation in genomic imprinting. *Nature, 366*, 362–365.

Li, G. C., Ouyang, H., Li, X., Nagasawa, H., Little, J. B., Chen, D. J., Ling, C. C., Fuks, Z., & Cordon-Cardo, C. (1998). Ku70: a candidate tumor suppressor gene for murine T cell lymphoma. *Molecular Cell, 2(1)*, 1–8.

Lim, D. S., & Hasty, P. (1996). A mutation in mouse rad51 results in an early embryonic lethal that is suppressed by a mutation in p53. *Molecular and Cellular Biology 12*, 7133–7143.

Lindahl T. (1993) Instability and decay of the primary structure of DNA. *Nature, 362*, 709–715.

Lindahl, T., & Wood, R. D. (1999). Quality control by DNA repair. *Science, 286(5446)*, 1897–905

Lindor, N. M., Furuichi, Y., Kitao, S., Shimamoto, A., Arndt, C., & Jalal, S. (2000) Rothmund-Thomson syndrome due to RECQ4 helicase mutations: report and clinical and molecular comparisons with Bloom syndrome and Werner syndrome. *American Journal of Medical Genetics, 90*, 223–228.

Loeb, L. A. (1991). Mutator phenotype may be required for multistage carcinogenesis. *Cancer Research, 51*, 3075–3079.

Lowe, X., Collins, B., Allen, J., Titenko-Holland, N., Breneman, J., van Beek, M., Bishop, J., & Wyrobek, A. J. (1995). Aneuploidies and micronuclei in the germ cells of male mice of advanced age. *Mutation Research, 338(1–6)*, 59–76.

Luria, S. E., & Delbrück, M. (1943). Mutations of bacteria from virus sensitivity to virus resistance. *Genetics, 28*, 491–511.

Mann, D. B., Springer, D. L., & Smerdon, M. J. (1997). DNA damage can alter the stability of nucleosomes: Effects are dependent on damage type. *Proceedings of the National Academy of Sciences of the USA, 94,* 2215–2220.

Martin, G. M. (1977). Cellular Aging-Postreplicative cells. A review (Part II), *American Journal of Pathology, 89,* 513–530.

Martin, G. M. (1991). Genetic and environmental modulations of chromosomal stability: their roles in aging and oncogenesis. *Annals of the New York Academy of Science, 621,* 401–417.

Martin, G. M., Austad, S. N., & Johnson, T. E. (1996a). Genetic analysis of ageing: role of oxidative age and environmental stresses. *Nature Genetics, 13,* 25–34.

Martin, G. M., Ogburn, C. E., Colgin, L. M., Gown, A. M., Edland, S. D., & Monnat, R. J. Jr. (1996b). Somatic mutations are frequent and increase with age in human kidney epithelial cells. *Human Molecular Genetics, 5,* 215–221.

Masoro, E. J. (1993). Dietary restriction and aging. *Journal of the American Geratric Society, 41,* 994–999.

Maynard Smith, J. (1959). A theory of ageing. *Nature, 184,* 956–957.

Migeon, B. R. (1990). Insights into X chromosome inactivation from studies of species variation, DNA methylation and replication, and vice versa. *Genetic Research, 56,* 91–98.

Mizuta, R., LaSalle, J. M., Cheng, H. L., Shinohara, A., Ogawa, H., Copeland, N., Jenkins, N. A., Lalande, M., & Alt, F. W. (1997). RAB22 and RAB163/mouse BRCA2: proteins that specifically interact with the RAD51 protein. *Proceedings of the National Academy of Sciences of the USA, 94(13),* 6927–6932.

Modrich, P. (1994). Mismatch repair, genetic stability, and cancer. *Science, 266,* 1959–1960.

Mohrenweiser, H. W., & Jones, I. M. (1998). Variation in DNA repair is a factor in cancer susceptibility: a paradigm for the promises and perils of individual and population risk estimation? *Mutation Research, 400,* 15–24.

Morley, A. A. (1996). The estimation of *in vivo* mutation rate and frequency from samples of human lymphocytes. *Mutation Research, 357,* 167–176.

Muller, H. J. (1964). The relation of recombination to mutational advance. *Mutation Research, 1,* 2–9.

Narayanan, L., Fritzell, J. A., Baker, S. M., Liskay, R. M., & Glazer, P. M. (1997). Elevated levels of mutation in multiple tissues of mice deficient in the DNA mismatch repair gene Pms2. *Proceedings of the National Academy of Sciences of the USA, 94,* 3122–3127.

Nicolaides, N. C., Papadopoulos, N., Liu, B., Wei, Y-F., Carter, K. C., Ruben, S. M., Rosen, C. H., Haseltine, W. A., Gleischmann, R. D., Fraser, C. M., Adams, M. D., Venter, J. C., Dunlop, M. G., Hamilton, S. R., Petersen, G. M., de la Chapelle, A, Vogelstein, B., & Kinzler, K. W. (1994). Mutations of two PMS homologues in hereditary nonpolyposis colon cancer. *Nature, 371,* 75–80.

Nishino, H., Knoll, A., Buettner, V. L., Frisk, C. S., Maruta, Y., Haavik, J., & Sommer, S. S. (1995). p53 wild-type and p53 nullizygous Big Blue transgenic mice have similar frequencies and patterns of observed mutation in liver, spleen and brain. *Oncogene, 11(2),* 263–70.

Nussenzweig, A., Chen, C., da Costa Soares, V., Sanchez, M., Sokol, K., Nussenzweig, M. C., & Li, G. C. (1996). Requirement for Ku80 in growth and immunoglobulin V(D)J recombination. *Nature, 382(6591),* 551–555.

Odagiri, Y., Uchida, H., Hosokawa, M., Takemoto, K., Morley, A. A., & Takeda, T. (1998). Accelerated accumulation of somatic mutations in the senescence-accelerated mouse. *Nature Genetics, 19(2),* 116–117

Ono, T., Ikehata, H., Nakamura, S., Saito, Y., Hosoi, Y., Takai, Y., Yamada, S., Onodera, J., & Yamamoto, K. (2000). Age-associated increase of spontaneous mutant frequency and molecular nature of mutation in newborn and old *lacZ*-transgenic mouse. *Mutation Research, 447,* 165–177.

Patel, K. J., Yu, V. P. C. C., Lee, H., Corcoran, A., Thistlethwaite, F. C., Evans, M. J., Colledge, W. H., Friedman, L. S., Ponder, B. A. J., & Venkitaraman, A. R. (1998). Involvement of Brca2 in DNA repair. *Molecular Cell, 1,* 347–357.

Peace, B. E., & Succop, P. (1999). Spontaneous micronucleus frequency and age: what are normal values? *Mutation Research, 425(2)*, 225–230.

Perucho, M. (1996). Microsatellite instability: The mutator that mutates the other mutator. *Nature Medicine, 2*, 676–681.

Plachot, M., De Grouchi, J., Junca, A-M., Mandelbaum, J., Turleau, C., Couillin, P., Cohen, J., & Salat-Baroux, J. (1987). From oocyte to embryo: A model, deduced from in vitro fertilization, for natural selection against chromosome abnormalities. *Annals of Génétics, 30*, 22–32.

Ramsey, M. J., Moore, D. H. II, Briner, J. F., Lee, D. A., Olsen, L. A., Senft, J. R., & Tucker, J. D. (1995). The effects of age and lifestyle factors on the accumulation of cytogenetic damage as measured by chromosome painting. *Mutation Research, 338*, 95–106.

Rasnick, D., & Duesberg, P. H. (1999). How aneuploidy affects metabolic control and causes cancer. *Biochemical Journal 340*, 621–630.

Reitmair, A. H., Redston, M., Cai, J. C., Chuang, T. C., Bjerknes, M., Cheng, H., Hay, K., Gallinger, S., Bapat, B., & Mak, T. W. (1996). Spontaneous intestinal carcinomas and skin neoplasms in Msh2-deficient mice. *Cancer Research, 56*, 3842–3849.

Rose, M. R. (1991). *Evolutionary Biology of Aging.* Oxford University Press.

Rotman, G., & Shiloh, Y. (1997) The ATM gene and protein: possible roles in genome surveillance, checkpoint controls and cellular defence against oxidative stress. *Cancer Surveys, 29*, 285–304.

Rudolph, K. L., Chang, S., Lee, H. W., Blasco, M., Gottlieb, G. J., Greider, C., & DePinho, R. A. (1999). Longevity, stress response, and cancer in aging telomerase-deficient mice. *Cell, 96*, 701–712.

Sah, V. P., Attardi, L. D., Mulligan, G. J., Williams, B. O., Bronson, R. T., & Jacks, T. (1995). A subset of p53-deficient embryos exhibits exencephaly. *Nature Genetics, 10(2)*, 175–180.

Sands, A. T., Suraokar, M. B., Sanchez, A., Marth, J. E., Donehower, L. A., & Bradley, A. (1995). p53 deficiency does not affect the accumulation of point mutations in a transgene target. *Proceedings of the National Academy of Sciences of the USA, 92(18)*, 8517–8521.

Scully, R., Chen, J., Plug, A., Xiao, Y., Weaver, D., Feunteun, J., Ashley, T., & Livingston, D. M. (1997). Association of BRCA1 with Rad51 in mitotic and meiotic cells. *Cell, 88*, 265–275.

Shao, C., Deng, L., Henegariu, O., Liang, L., Raikwar, N., Sahota, A., Stambrook, P. J., & Tischfield, J. A. (1999). Mitotic recombination produces the majority of recessive fibroblast variants in heterozygous mice. *Proceedings of the National Academy of Science of the USA, 96(16)*, 9230–9235.

Shimamoto, A., Nishikawa, K., Kitao, S., & Furuichi, Y. (2000). Human RecQ5beta, a large isomer of RecQ5 DNA helicase, localizes in the nucleoplasm and interacts with topoisomerases 3alpha and 3beta. *Nucleic Acids Research, 28*, 1647–1655.

Smith, M. L., & Fornace, A. J., Jr. (1995). Genomic instability and the role of p53 mutations in cancer cells. *Current Opinions in Oncology, 7(1)*, 69–75.

Sobol, R. W., Horton, J. K., Kuhn, R., Gu, H., Singhal, R. K., Prasad, R., Klaus, R., & Wilson, S. H. (1996). Requirement of mammalian DNA polymerase-B in base-excision repair. *Nature, 379*, 183–186.

Stambrook, P. J., Shao, C., Stockelman, M., Boivin, G., Engle, S. J., & Tischfield, J. A. (1996). APRT: A versatile *in vivo* resident reporter of local mutation and loss of heterozygosity. *Environmental Molecular Mutagenetics, 28(4)*, 471–482.

Strehler, B. L., & Freeman, M. R. (1980). Randomness, redundancy and repair: roles and relevance to biological aging. *Mechanisms of Ageing and Development, 14(1–2)*, 15–38.

Sugasawa, K., Ng, J. M., Masutani, C., Iwai, S., van der Spek, P. J., Eker, A. P., Hanaoka, F., Bootsma, D., & Hoeijmakers, J. H. (1998). Xeroderma pigmentosum group C protein complex is the initiator of global genome nucleotide excision repair. *Molecular Cell, 2*, 223–232.

Szilard, L. (1959). On the nature of the aging process. *Proceedings of the National Academy of Sciences of the USA, 45*, 30–45.

Taccioli, G. E., Amatucci, A. G., Beamish, H. J., Gell, D., Xiang, X. H., Torres Arzayus, M. I., Priestley, A., Jackson, S. P., Marshak

Rothstein, A., Jeggo, P. A., & Herrera, V. L. (1998). Targeted disruption of the catalytic subunit of the DNA-PK gene in mice confers severe combined immunodeficiency and radiosensitivity. *Immunity*, 9(3), 355–366.

Tucker, J. D., Spruill, M. D., Ramsey, M. J., Director, A. D., & Nath, J. (1999). Frequency of spontaneous chromosome aberrations in mice: effects of age, *Mutation Research*, 425(1), 135–141.

Turker, M. S. (1998). Estimation of mutation frequencies in normal mammalian cells and the development of cancer. *Seminars in Cancer Biology*, 8, 407–419.

Turker, M. S., & Martin, G. M. (1999) Genetics of human disease, longevity and aging. In W. R. Hazzard, J. P. Blass, W. H. Ettinger, Jr., J. B. Halter, & J. G. Ouslander (Eds.), *Principles of Geriatric Medicine and Gerontology (4th Edition)* (pp. 21–44). New York: McGraw-Hill.

Turker, M. S., Gage, B. M., Rose, J. A., Ponomareva, O. N., Tischfield, J. A., Stambrook, P. J., Barlow, C., & Wynshaw-Boris, A. (1999). Solid tissues removed from ATM homozygous deficient mice do not exhibit a mutator phenotype for second-step autosomal mutations. *Cancer Research*, 59(19), 4781–4783.

Van der Horst, G. T., van Steeg, H., Berg, R. J., van Gool, A. J., de Wit, J., Weeda, G., Morreau, H., Beems, R. B., van Kreijl, C. F., de Gruijl, F. R., Bootsma, D., & Hoeijmakers, J. H. (1997). Defective transcription-coupled repair in Cockayne syndrome B mice is associated with skin cancer predisposition. *Cell*, 89(3), 425–435.

Van Gool, A. J., van der Horst, G. T. J., Citterio, E., & Hoeijmakers, J. H. J. (1997). Cockayne syndrome: defective repair of transcription? *EMBO Journal*, 16, 4155–4162.

Van Holde, K., & Zlatanova, J. (1994). Unusual DNA structures, chromatin and transcription. *Biological Essays*, 16, 59–68.

Van Orsouw, N. J., Dhanda, R. K., Elhaji, Y., Narod, S. A., Li, F. P, Eng, C., & Vijg, J. (1999) A highly accurate, low cost test for *BRCA1* mutations. *Journal of Medical Genetics*, 36, 747–753.

Van Orsouw, N. J., Li, D., van der Vlies, P., Scheffer, H., Eng, C., Buys, C. H., Li, F. P., & Vijg, J. (1996) Mutational scanning of large genes by extensive PCR multiplexing and two-dimensional electrophoresis: application to the RB1 gene. *Human Molecular Genetics, 1996* 5, 755–761.

Van Remmen, H, Ward, W. F., Sabia, R. V., & Richardson, A. (1995). Gene expression and protein degradation. In E. Masoro (Ed.), *Handbook of Physiology: Aging* (171–234). Bethesda, Maryland: American Physiological Society.

Van Sloun, P. P., Wijnhoven, S. W., Kool, H. J., Slater, R., Weeda, G., van Zeeland, A. A., Lohman, P. H., & Vrieling, H. (1998). Determination of spontaneous loss of heterozygosity mutations in Aprt heterozygous mice. *Nucleic Acids Research* 26(21), 4888–4894.

Vijg J. (2000). Somatic mutations and aging: a re-evaluation. *Mutation Research*, 447, 117–135.

Vogel, H., Lim, D. S., Karsenty, G., Finegold, M., & Hasty, P., (1999). Deletion of Ku86 causes early onset of senescence in mice. *Proceedings of the National Academy of Sciences of the USA*, 96(19), 10770–10775.

Wachsman, J. T. (1997). DNA methylation and the association between genetic and epigenetic changes: relation to carcinogenesis. *Mutation Research*, 375, 1–8.

Wakayama, T., Perry, A. C., Zuccotti, M., Johnson, K. R., & Yanagimachi, R. (1998). Full-term development of mice from enucleated oocytes injected with cumulus cell nuclei. *Nature, 394*, 369–374

Walter, C. A., Intano, G. W., McCarrey, J. R. McMahan, C. A., & Walter, R. B. (1998). Mutation frequency declines during spermatogenesis in young mice but increases in old mice. *Proceedings of the National Academy of Science of the USA*, 95(17), 10015–10019.

Warner, H. R., & Johnson, T. E. (1997). Parsing age, mutations and time. *Nature Genetics*, 17, 368–370

Warner, H. R., Fernandes, G., & Wang E. (1995). A unifying hypothesis to explain the retardation of aging and tumorigenesis by caloric restriction. *Journal of Gerontology*, 50A, B107-B109.

Weeda, G., Donker, I., de Wit, J., Morreau, H., Janssens, R., Vissers, C. J., Niff, A., van Steeg, H., Bootsma, D., & Hoeijmakers, J. H. J. (1997). Disruption of mouse ERCC1 results in a novel repair syndrome with growth failure, nuclear abnormalities and senescence. *Current Biology, 7*, 427–439.

White, R. L. (1998). Excess risk of colon cancer associated with a polymorphism of the APC gene, *Cancer Research, 58*, 4038–4039.

Wilmut, I., Schnieke, A. E., McWhir, J., Kind, A. J., & Campbell, K. H. S. (1997). Viable offspring derived from fetal and adult mammalian cells. *Nature, 385*, 810–813.

Winton, D. J., Blount, M. A., & Ponder, B. A. (1988). A clonal marker induced by mutation in mouse intestinal epithelium. *Nature, 333(6172)*, 463–466.

Wong, L.-J. C., Ashizawa, T., Monckton, D. G., Caskey, C. T., & Richards, C. S. (1995). Somatic heterogeneity of the CTG repeat in myotonic dystrophy is age and size dependent. *American Journal Human Genetics, 56*, 114–122.

Xu, X., Wagner, K.-U., Larson, D., Weaver, Z., Li, C., Ried, T., Henninghausen, L., Wynshaw-Boris, A., & Deng, C-X. (1999). Conditional mutation of *Brca1* in mammary epithelial cells results in blunted ductal morphogenesis and tumour formation. *Nature Genetics, 22*, 37–43.

Yamagata, K., Kato, J., Shimamoto, A., Goto, M., Furuichi, Y., & Ikeda, H. (1998) Bloom's and Werner's syndrome genes suppress hyperrecombination in yeast sgs1 mutant: implication for genomic instability in human diseases. *Proceedings of the National Academy of Sciences of the USA, 95*, 8733–8738.

Yu, C-E., Oshima, J., Fu, Y-H., Wijsman, E. M., Hisama, F., Alisch, R., Matthews, S., Nakura, J., Miki, T., Ouais, S., Martin, G. M., Mulligan, J., & Schellenberg, G. D. (1996). Positional cloning of the Werner's syndrome gene. *Science, 272*, 258–262.

Five

Alterations of the Mitochondrial Genome

Jonathan Wanagat, Marisol E. Lopez, and Judd M. Aiken

I. Introduction

The discovery of mitochondrial DNA (mtDNA) in 1924 (Bresslau & Scremin, 1924) and its isolation in the 1960s (Nass, 1969) sparked the subsequent flourish of hypotheses that have implicated this "other genome" in numerous human diseases [reviewed in Wallace (1999)] and aging [reviewed in Cortopassi and Wong 1999]. The aim of this review is to survey the evidence supporting a causal link between alterations of the mitochondrial genome and aging, a link that arises from the basic biological role of the mitochondrion itself. The mitochondrion's central role in cellular anabolic and catabolic pathways brings with it the consequences of being a life-long source and target of free radicals and reactive oxygen species (ROS) that, together with the unique characteristics of this organelle's genome, is hypothesized to result in age-associated damage. The end results of this damage are largely unknown, but much of the interest has focused on the possibility that chronic oxidative damage could have detrimental effects on a variety of mitochondrial functions. As the damage overwhelms protective and repair pathways within the mitochondrion, there may be secondary alterations to the primary nucleotide sequence of the mtDNA. These age-associated alterations include changes of individual nucleotides (i.e., point mutations) as well as duplications or deletions of mtDNA segments. A crucial area of contention and inquiry involves the possible biological impact of these mutations, which typically are calculated to occur at low levels in tissue homogenate studies and whose *in vivo* cellular impact or progression is difficult to assess. Some indication of the potential biological impact of these mutations is suggested by studies of inherited and sporadic mitochondrial myopathies and their associated clinical syndromes. In aging, the area of biological impact is being addressed by the development of animal and *in vitro* models, as well as *in situ* analyses of tissues from aged organisms. Studies of the mitochondrial genome's involvement in aging are also benefiting from the growing information regarding basic mitochondrial biology and the role of this organelle in critical processes such as cell death (i.e., apoptosis and necrosis) and cellular signaling pathways. The outcome of this work undoubtedly will shed additional light on the biological significance of these mutations and the likelihood that they contribute to age-related changes in physiology and structure, the readily apparent signs of aging.

II. Characteristics of the Mitochondrial Genome and Implications for Age-Related Alterations

Many of the mitochondrial genome's basic characteristics of overall structure and cellular localization have important effects on its stability with aging. Mammalian mtDNA is a double-stranded, closed-circular DNA molecule of approximately 16 kilobase pairs. The complementary strands are referred to separately as the heavy and light strands due to an asymmetrical distribution of cytosine and guanosine residues. mtDNA is located in the mitochondrial matrix (Clayton, 1982), a spatial arrangement with obvious implications for the exposure of mtDNA to free radicals produced as normal byproducts of the inner-membrane-embedded electron transport system (ETS). Thus, the ETS serves as a chronic, life-long source of potential damage to the adjacent mtDNA and may be the primary mechanism responsible for age-related alterations.

The mitochondrial genome lacks some of the protection and repair components of its nuclear counterpart. The repair pathways are discussed in Section III. There are no mitochondrial cognates of the nuclear histone proteins, so that the mitochondrial genome lacks this protection from oxidative and other damage, although the high protein concentration of the matrix and accessory proteins (e.g., mtTFA and single-stranded DNA binding proteins) may confer some protection. Studies of isolated nuclear DNA demonstrate that "histone-free" DNA is more susceptible to free radical-mediated damage. *In vitro* exposure of naked, supercoiled DNA to hydroxyl radical, an ROS generated by the reaction of Fe(II)-EDTA and ascorbic acid, led to 100 times more strand breaks than were found with similar exposure of "native" chromatin (Ljungman & Hanawalt, 1992). This observation suggests that mtDNA is more vulnerable to biochemical attack by reactive molecules in the mitochondrial matrix.

Replication of the mitochondrial genome bears little resemblance to nuclear DNA (nDNA) replication, because it occurs in an asynchronous, bidirectional manner from two replication origins, the heavy-strand origin and the light-strand origin (Clayton, 1982). These two origins are located approximately 9 kb apart on the human mitochondrial genome. Replication begins at the heavy-strand origin (O_H) and involves displacement of the parental heavy strand that then remains in a single-strand conformation until the light-strand origin (O_L) is revealed and replication of the light strand begins in the opposite direction. Importantly, the circular nature of vertebrate mtDNA circumvents the need for the telomeres and telomerase activity that are required for maintenance of the linear nuclear genome. Replication of the entire genome is completed in approximately 2 hr in mouse L-cells (Clayton, 1982). This replication mechanism has possible ramifications for the formation of deletion and duplication mutants, as will be discussed later. Studies of the effects of aging on mtDNA replication have been limited to investigations of mtDNA turnover (Huemer *et al.*, 1971) or mtDNA replication intermediates (Piko *et al.*, 1988) in rodents and humans. The half-life of radioactively labeled brain mtDNA was found to be approximately 2 weeks in both 6-week-old and 28-month-old female mice. Replicative intermediates in aged humans (i.e., 80–89 years old) and aged rodents (i.e., 28 to 29-month-old mice and rats), in general, did not reveal any changes in mtDNA replication, with the exception of an increased frequency of some replicative forms in senescent mouse liver that suggests a change in the mtDNA metabolism in this tissue.

The complete mitochondrial sequence is known for over 100 eukaryotic species (Kogelnik *et al.*, 1998). In mammals, mtDNA encodes 13 polypeptides of the ETS as well as two ribosomal RNAs and 22 transfer RNAs required for protein translation. There are no introns and few noncoding regions in the mitochondrial genome, suggesting that mutations are more likely to occur within genes or cis-elements important in replication, transcription, translation, or a combination of these. This is in stark contrast to the nuclear genome, which contains large regions of noncoding sequence. The most significant noncoding region of the mitochondrial genome is the displacement loop (D-loop), which is important in the replication and transcription of the mitochondrial genome. Additionally, mutations involving the ribosomal or transfer RNA genes may also have broad effects on mitochondrial protein translation. Such effects have been observed in trans-mitochondrial cell lines and are discussed later (Section VIC).

Due to the mtDNA contribution to the ETS and OXPHOS (Table I), alterations of the genome are most likely to exert their effects on these critical energy transduction pathways. Mutations of the mitochondrial genome would likely have the greatest influence on those complexes to which the genome makes its largest contributions, namely, complex I (NADH dehydrogenase) and complex IV (cytochrome *c* oxidase). Although 65 of the 78 known complex subunits are nuclear-encoded, the subunits critical for activity are encoded by the mtDNA, whereas the nuclear-encoded subunits are thought to play a regulatory role (Taanman, 1997). The efficient movement of electrons through the ETS and OXPHOS likely decreases ROS generation by preventing the "pooling" of reducing equivalents (Benzi *et al.*, 1992; Richter, 1997); therefore, mutations of mitochondrial-encoded subunits of the ETS and OXPHOS could adversely affect complex activities with a resulting increase in ROS production.

III. Age-Related Biochemical Damage to the Mitochondrial DNA

The peculiarities of mtDNA structure and localization set the stage for the biochemical damage thought to precede age-associated mutations of the genome. This damage may result from both exogenous and endogenous insults. Exogenous sources include a variety of toxins, pharmacological agents, and ultraviolet (UV) radiation [i.e., implicated in human skin

Table I
Contributions of the Mammalian Mitochondrial and Nuclear Genomes to the ETS and OXPHOS

Complex	I	II	III	IV	V
Name	NADH dehydrogenase	Succinate dehydrogenase	Ubiquinol-cytochrome *c* reductase	Cytochrome *c* oxidase	ATP synthetase
mtDNA[a]	7	0	1	3	2
nDNA[b]	32	4	9	10	10

[a]Number of polypeptide subunits encoded by the mitochondrial genome.
[b]Number of polypeptide subunits encoded by the nuclear genome.

photoaging (Berneburg et al., 1999)], whereas endogenous sources are primarily the biochemical processes taking place within cells and mitochondria (Weindruch & Sohal, 1997). Of these sources, those that occur chronically throughout an organism's lifetime, such as oxidative stress of mitochondrial origin, may be the most relevant in the formation of age-related mtDNA mutations.

A wide range of endogenously produced ROS have been found to inflict damage on cellular macromolecules. The generation of superoxide by the single-electron reduction of oxygen can occur as the result of aerobic metabolism, peroxisomal enzymes, oxidases, cyochrome P-450 enzymes, and inflammatory cell oxidative bursts [reviewed in Weindruch and Sohal (1997)]. Approximately 1–5% of the oxygen utilized by the ETS is converted to free radicals by single-electron addition to oxygen, yielding superoxide radical (Boveris et al., 1972). The rate of superoxide radical formation is proportional to the rate of ETS oxygen consumption (Boveris & Chance, 1973). Complexes I and III of the ETS and the partially reduced form of coenzyme Q (i.e., the semiquinone) are thought to be the primary sources of superoxide generated by the ETS (Chance et al., 1979; Li & Trush, 1998). The superoxide generated can be metabolized by enzymatic and nonenzymatic processes or contribute to the formation of other ROS such as hydroxyl radicals and peroxynitrite. These, in turn, can inflict damage on lipids, proteins, and nucleic acids.

Of the numerous oxidative lesions occurring in DNA, 8-hydroxylation of the guanine base (8-OHdG) is thought to be the most abundant (Ames, 1989), and well-described protocols are available for its detection (Shigenaga et al., 1990). Consequently, 8-OHdG is a commonly used marker for estimating ROS-induced DNA damage, particularly in mtDNA.

There is, however, contention regarding the accuracy of reported steady-state 8-OHdG levels (Beckman & Ames, 1999). Early studies of 8-OHdG levels showed a >10-fold higher frequency of 8-OHdG in mitochondrial DNA than in nuclear DNA (Richter et al., 1988). Such findings appeared to agree with data indicating a greater mutation rate in mtDNA than in nDNA (Brown et al., 1979) and greater susceptibility of the mitochondrial genome to oxidative damage. Subsequent studies in a variety of tissues and species have demonstrated a range of levels that span a difference of some 60,000-fold (Beckman & Ames, 1999). This disparity has been attributed to artifactual oxidation during the isolation and preparation of nucleic acid samples (Helbock et al., 1998), particularly of the mtDNA fraction (Beckman & Ames, 1999), and has led these investigators to state that it is "impossible to conclude [from the published findings] that mitochondrial DNA suffers greater oxidation than nuclear DNA" (Beckman & Ames, 1999). Regardless of the relative steady-state levels of 8-OHdG in mtDNA versus nDNA, measurements in a variety of human and rodent tissues point to age-associated increases in the steady-state levels of this adduct in total DNA and in the mitochondrial genome (Table II).

Studies of the effects of oxidative DNA damage on the action of the mitochondrial polymerase γ have shown that these lesions have mutagenic potential (Pinz et al., 1995). Synthetic nucleotides containing 8-OHdG were used as templates for polymerase reactions using DNA polymerase γ purified from Xenopus laevis ovary mitochondria. Although elongation by DNA polymerase γ was not hindered by the 8-OHdG residue, an adenine nucleotide was inserted opposite the adduct in 27% of the extension products. This misincorporation was due to a lack of specificity of the polymerase rather than a lack of proofreading capability and

Table II
Age-Associated Increases in 8-OHdG[a]

Reference	Species	Tissue	Age range	8-OHdG range Young	8-OHdG range Old
Hayakawa et al. (1991)	Human	Diaphragm	42–85 years	<0.020[h]	0.51[h]
Hayakawa et al. (1992)	Human	Heart	24–97 years	nd	1.5[i]
Hayakawa et al. (1993)	Human	Heart	24–97 years	nd	1.5[i]
Hayakawa et al. (1993)	Rat[b]	Heart	7–100 weeks	0.49[i]	2.19[i]
Mecocci et al. (1993)	Human	Brain	42–97 years	nd	850[f]
Sohal et al. (1994)	Mouse[c]	Brain	8–27 months	23[f]	45[f]
Sohal et al. (1994)	Mouse[c]	Heart	8–27 months	23[f]	40[f]
Sohal et al. (1994)	Mouse[c]	Skeletal muscle	8–27 months	42[f]	74[f]
Sohal et al. (1994)	Mouse[c]	Kidney	8–27 months	12[f]	16[f]
Sohal et al. (1994)	Mouse[c]	Liver	8–27 months	14[f]	20[f]
Sohal et al. (1994)	Rat[d]	Liver	3–27 months	75[f]	127[f]
Kaneko et al. (1996)	Rat[e]	Liver	2–30 months	0.77[g]	1.80[g]
Kaneko et al. (1996)	Rat[e]	Heart		1.01[h]	2.02[h]
Kaneko et al. (1996)	Rat[e]	Kidney		0.75[h]	1.79[h]
Kaneko et al. (1996)	Rat[e]	Brain		1.24[h]	2.05[h]
Lee et al. (1998b)	Human	Lung	16–85 years	1[h]	6[h]
Lu et al. (1999)	Human	Skin	10–88 years	nd	0.033[g]

[a]References in bold measured 8-OHdG in isolated mtDNA.
[b]Wistar rats.
[c]C57BL/6 mice.
[d]Sprague–Dawley rats.
[e]Fischer 344.
[f]fmol/µg DNA.
[g]8-OHdG/dG, %.
[h]Ratio of 8-OHdG/10^5 dG.
[i]Ratio of 8-OHdG/(dG + 8-OHdG), %.

represents a G to T transversion that does not account for many of the clinically relevant human mtDNA point mutations. Therefore, more information is needed regarding additional types of mtDNA damage and their mutagenic potential.

IV. DNA Repair Mechanisms in the Mitochondrion

Following oxidative or other DNA damage, there are a number of pathways that may lead to the repair of the damage. These include (1) direct restitution, (2) base excision repair, (3) nucleotide excision repair, and (4) recombinational repair [reviewed in Henle and Linn (1997)]. The actions of these pathways in mtDNA repair have been reviewed (Croteau & Bohr, 1999) and will be presented here briefly. Direct restitution of carbon-centered free radicals in the DNA backbone by sulfhydryls, as described by Henle and Linn (1997), has not been reported in mitochondria. There is evidence that mitochondrial glutathione, a sulfhydryl agent, may contribute to the oxidation of mtDNA by an unknown mechanism (Giulivi & Cadenas, 1998). Base excision repair activity is present in the mitochondrion and is primarily responsible for removing oxidative and small alkylation damage in the mtDNA. This is accomplished by the coordinated action of nuclear-encoded enzymes, including lesion-specific endonucleases, deoxyribosephosphodiesterase, mtDNA polymerase γ, and an mtDNA ligase (Pinz & Bogenhagen, 1998). Nucleotide excision repair activity has not been detected in mammalian mitochondria, as indicated by an inability to repair UV or bulky DNA damage such as large alkylation lesions and some types of strand cross-links [Clayton et al., 1974; reviewed in LeDoux et al., (1999)]. Recombinational repair activity has also been detected in mammalian mitochondria (Thyagarajan et al., 1996).

Although the effect of aging on in vivo mtDNA repair is not known, there is in vitro evidence that some mtDNA repair enzyme activities change with age (Souza-Pinto et al., 1999). Synthetic double-stranded oligonucleotides containing either 8-OHdG or a U:A mismatch were incubated with mitochondrial extracts from liver and heart tissue of Wistar rats ages 6, 12, or 23-months. Enzymatic cleavage of the 8-OHdG-containing oligonucleotide showed increased activity in the tissues of 12- and 23-month-old rats compared to the 6-month-old rats. Cleavage activity of the U:A mismatch also was detected in the mitochondrial extracts, but this only showed a small increase with age in the heart mitochondrial extracts. These observations suggest that, whereas general mtDNA repair is not increased, there is a compensatory increase in the repair of the 8-OHdG lesion, possibly in response to the age-associated increase in mitochondrial oxidative damage. Clearly, more work is required to uncover the age-associated changes and the mechanisms by which the nucleus controls mtDNA repair.

V. Age-Associated Mutations of the Mitochondrial Genome

A. Introduction

Age-associated mutations of the mitochondrial genome are organized into three categories: point mutations, duplication mutations, and deletion mutations. The convergence of mitochondrial theories of aging and seminal discoveries in the late 1980s linking mtDNA mutations to mitochondrial myopathies led to the implication of mtDNA mutations in aging and age-related diseases (Lee et al., 1997; Wallace, 1999). The study of mitochondrial myopathies provided detailed information regarding the range and features of mtDNA mutations. These clinical studies have focused primarily on point and deletion mutations and have yielded numerous techniques for their study. Studies of age-associated mutations built on these findings and, with the aid of PCR-based and other molecular biology methodologies, have expanded studies to a wide range of animal models, tissues, and specific cell types. Although many studies of mtDNA mutations have focused on an increased incidence with age, the accumulation of age-associated mtDNA mutations within tissues and individual cells is an active area of investigation and contention.

B. Age-Associated Point Mutations

The study of age-associated point mutations stemmed from the characterization of human inherited pathological mtDNA point mutations. Mitochondrial diseases caused by point mutations of the mtDNA include Leber's hereditary optic neuropathy (LHON), neuropathy, ataxia, and retinitis pigmentosa (NARP), myoclonus epilepsy with ragged red fibers (MERRF), and mitochondrial encephalomyopathy, lactic acidosis, and strokelike episodes (MELAS). The point mutations associated with these diseases have been found in genes that encode for proteins (LHON and NARP) or in tRNA genes (MERRF and MELAS). Mitochondrial diseases caused by point mutations usually are inherited, in contrast to those diseases caused by deletions that typically occur in a sporadic fashion [reviewed in Shoffner and Wallace (1994)]. The abundance of these myopathy-associated point mutations varies. In MELAS, a comparison of affected individuals revealed relative proportions of mutated mtDNA ranging from 30–80% (Enter et al., 1991). In NARP, the mutational load is approximately 70% but can reach 90%, where it may have a different clinical presentation (Simon & Johns, 1999).

Whether mtDNA point mutations accumulate with age is not entirely clear (Table III), with different studies showing increases, decreases, and no correlation. Clearly, these mutations are very low in abundance, necessitating a PCR-based approach for their detection. This detection typically involves oligonucleotide primers with a 3′-position specific to a particular mutation that selectively amplifies mutant templates. A primer with a 3′-mismatch to a particular template will have a disadvantage during the amplification process compared to the perfectly matched primer as the annealing temperature is increased beyond a critical value. By using this technique, the abundance of the A-to-G transition mutation at nt 8344 (characteristic of the MERRF disease) increases with age in muscle (Muenscher et al., 1993). Analysis of the A-to-G transition mutation at nt position 3243 (previously detected in MELAS patients) also increased with age in muscle, heart, brain, and kidney (Liu et al., 1998; Zhang et al., 1993, 1998). However, Palloti et al. (1996) did not find any correlation of this point mutation with age in muscle. In addition, the abundance of the T-to-G transition at nt 8993 (associated with

NARP disease) does not increase with age in muscle (Pallotti et al., 1996; Zhang et al., 1998). Three other point mutations studied (not associated with disease) either were not correlated (7029 C → T and 7920 A → G) or decreased (13167 A → G) in muscle with age (Zhang et al., 1998).

Point mutations are found at very low levels (0.04–2.2%; Table III) in aging individuals compared to myopathy patients (Muenscher et al. 1993). Muenscher et al. (1993) studied the abundance of the A-to-G transition mutation at nt 8344 in skeletal muscle and found deleted genomes up to levels of 2.4% in individuals ~80 years old, whereas a MERRF patient had 73.6% of its genomes affected.

One study used denaturant gradient gel electrophoresis to analyze the age-associated accumulation of point mutations in the mitochondrial D-loop region (Michikawa et al., 1999). These investigators reported high levels (i.e., up to 50% heteroplasmy) of a 414 T → G transversion mutation in fibroblasts from individuals over 65 years old and its absence in younger individuals. Longitudinal analyses of two sets of samples from these individuals taken ~17 years apart showed the first sample with absent or very low levels of the mutation, whereas, in the later samples, the point mutation is more abundant (23–50%). In a third subject, however, the levels of this mutation decreased between the first and second biopsies. Interestingly, the levels of mtDNA point mutations were well above levels detectable in primary, uncultured tissue samples from aged individuals (Table III).

The biological impact of mtDNA point mutations and their role in aging and age-related disease are unclear. More information is needed regarding the accumulation of point mutations with age in relevant postmitotic tissues, as well as the localization of these mutations within tissues.

Table III
Detection and Abundance of mtDNA Point Mutations in Humans

Point mutation	Tissue	Abundance	Age association	Reference
A→G nt 8344	Muscle	2.2%	Increase	Muenscher *et al.* (1993)
A→G nt 3243	Muscle, heart, brain	0.1%	Increase	Zhang *et al.* (1993)
A→G nt 3243	Muscle, heart, kidney	0.75%	Increase	Liu *et al.* (1998)
A→G nt 3243	Muscle	0.4%	Increase	Zhang *et al.* (1998)
T→G nt 8993	Muscle	0.05%	No correlation	Zhang *et al.* (1998)
C→T nt 7029	Muscle	0.5%	No correlation	Zhang *et al.* (1998)
A→G nt 7920	Muscle	0.25%	No correlation	Zhang *et al.* (1998)
A→G nt 13167	Muscle	1.0%	Decrease	Zhang *et al.* (1998)
T→G nt 8993	Muscle	0.04%	No correlation	Pallotti *et al.* (1996)
A→G nt 3243	Muscle	0.6%	No correlation	Pallotti *et al.* (1996)

C. Age-Associated Duplication Mutations

mtDNA duplications were the first observed mtDNA mutations [reviewed in Clayton (1982)]. These duplications were oligomeric mtDNAs arranged as head-to-tail, unicircular dimers and were seen in studies of mitochondrial replication intermediates (Clayton *et al.*, 1970). In some mouse L-cell-line strains, the entire mtDNA population consists of these dimers suggesting little impact on mtDNA replication or cell physiology (Clayton, 1982). Soon after the discovery of the first mtDNA deletions in mitochondrial myopathies, Poulton *et al.* (1989) discovered evidence for duplications of mtDNA in a mitochondrial myopathy. Brockington *et al.* (1993) also identified a region of ~260 bp that was duplicated in the D-loop region of human mtDNA from 31% of mitochondrial deletion myopathy patients and all of their unaffected mothers. By using PCR techniques, the incidence of this ~260-bp duplication and another ~200-bp duplication was found to increase with age in human muscle mtDNA (Lee *et al.*, 1994b), whereas Wei *et al.* (1996) identified a variety of duplications that increased in frequency and abundance with age. Similarly, long extension PCR (i.e., a means of amplifying very large segments of DNA) of human deltoid muscle DNA

showed increased amounts of "oversized" amplification products in older subjects (Kovalenko *et al.*, 1997). There is no apparent correlation between the levels of mtDNA deletions and duplications (Manfredi *et al.*, 1995; Wei *et al.*, 1996) as had been suggested by earlier work.

The mechanisms leading to the formation of mtDNA duplications in aging are unknown. Suggestions have included slippage mispairing, recombination, and errors during repair of single-strand breaks (Bouzidi *et al.*, 1998; Negrier *et al.*, 1998; Poulton *et al.*, 1989). Slippage mispairing may be the most likely mechanism, as studies have shown that the duplications often are inserted at polycytosine segments. The instability of the initial duplication may cause further rearrangement of mtDNA, giving rise to triplication events (Tengan & Moraes, 1998).

Despite the distinct age-associated increase in mtDNA duplications, there is a paucity of information regarding the contribution of these abnormalities to aging processes. Their low absolute abundance at any age and lack of cellular impact, as demonstrated by cybrid studies, argue against a biologically significant role.

D. Age-Associated mtDNA Deletion Mutations

Age-associated mtDNA deletion mutations have been studied in numerous tissues from species as diverse as humans, monkeys, rodents, fruit flies, and nematodes [reviewed in Lee et al. (1997)]. The primary focus has been on the characteristics of these deletions, such as size, flanking sequences, and abundance with age. mtDNA deletion mutations are broadly categorized as "common" deletions, which are identical deletion mutations detected in different tissues or different individuals, or "unique" deletions, which differ widely between tissues and individuals.

1. Detection and Abundance of the "Common Deletion"

Studies of age-associated mtDNA deletion mutations also followed from genetic studies of mitochondrial myopathies. Progressive external ophthalmoplegia (PEO) and Kearns–Sayre syndrome (KSS) are mitochondrial myopathies caused by mtDNA deletions (Holt et al., 1989a; Zeviani et al., 1988). The size and position of the deletion event varies among individuals (2000–8000 bp), but within a given individual it is the same, suggesting that the mutant genome arises as a clonal event in oogenesis or early embryological development (Moraes et al., 1989). The deletion break points in these myopathies often were shown to involve direct repeat sequences. This is illustrated in the so-called "common" deletion (mtDNA^{4977}) found to occur frequently in mitochondrial myopathies that has a deletion break point that is flanked by two 13-bp direct repeat sequences.

The "common" deletion has been studied extensively in aging humans [reviewed in Lee et al., (1997); Liu et al., 1998; Zhang et al., 1998]. In myopathy patients, mtDNA deletions are found at high abundance, which allows detection by Southern blot analysis. In aging individuals, however, the abundance is much lower and, thus, more sensitive techniques like PCR amplification of mtDNA

are required. The PCR assay for the mtDNA^{4977} deletion involves the use of two primers flanking the 13-bp repeats that are approximately 5 kb apart. The occurrence of a deletion event brings the primers in closer opposition and allows the efficient amplification of a product. Cortopassi and Arnheim detected this deletion in heart and brain from adult (21–58 years old) individuals but not in fetal tissue (Cortopassi et al., 1992), whereas Linnane et al. (1990), reported the presence of this deletion in a wide range of tissues from adult (46–87 years) but not infant tissue. Other investigators have reported an age association of mtDNA^{4977} in various human tissues, such as skeletal muscle, heart, liver, and testis nematodes [reviewed in Lee et al., (1997)]. The highest deletion levels are found in postmitotic tissues with high energy requirements, such as heart, skeletal muscle, and brain (Cortopassi et al., 1992; Lee et al., 1994c; Simonetti et al., 1992). Although there is an age association in the abundance of the "common deletion" (compared to WT genomes), it is very low (0.0001–0.3%).

Another "common" mtDNA deletion is a 7436 mtDNA deletion (position 8649 to position 16084) with a 12-bp direct repeat sequence flanking the deletion break point. This deletion accumulated with age (32–97 years old) in human cardiomyocytes and was not detected in people younger than 30 years old (Hattori et al., 1991). Sugiyama et al. (1991) found the abundance of the 7436 mtDNA deletion to be 3% and 9% in the heart of subjects age 80 and 90 years, respectively. Zhang et al. (1992) later identified this deletion and determined that it was found not only in heart but also in brain and skeletal muscle. Two common deletions have been identified in rhesus monkeys. The break points of both are flanked by direct repeat sequences, with the more prevalent deletion having the longer direct repeat sequence (Lee et al.,

1994a). In several rodent studies, a common deletion (mtDNA^{4834}) has been found in tissues from aged animals (Edris et al., 1994; Yowe & Ames, 1998; Zhang et al., 1997). This deletion is characterized by a 16-bp direct repeat flanking the deletion break points. Specific age-associated mtDNA deletions have been detected in rodent heart, skeletal muscle, brain, liver, and kidney (Brossas et al., 1994; Edris et al., 1994; Gadaleta et al., 1992; Yowe & Ames, 1998; Zhang et al., 1997). It clearly has been determined, therefore, that there is an age association in the abundance of specific or "common" deletions in a variety of species. Further, the presence of deletions common in different individuals suggests the presence of "hot spots" for deletion formation.

2. Detection and Abundance of Multiple Age-Associated mtDNA Deletions

After an age association of specific mtDNA deletions was found, and with the large number of direct repeats found in various mitochondrial genomes, other investigators began to look for a wider range of mtDNA deletions. To estimate total mutations, long extension PCR, in which an entire mitochondrial genome is amplified to visualize all deletions, or multiple sets of primers over the genome to sum the total deleted species are needed. Multiple age-associated deletions have been identified in many human tissues, such as heart, skeletal muscle, brain, and kidney (Kovalenko et al., 1997; Liu et al., 1998; Melov et al., 1995; Zhang et al., 1992, 1998). Studies performed in our laboratory have found that the abundance of multiple deletion products increases with age in mouse (Chung et al., 1994) and rhesus monkey (Lee et al., 1993) skeletal muscle. In the rhesus monkey, deletions common to all animals are characterized by large direct

repeats, whereas unique deletions are not (Lee et al., 1994a). These studies indicate that both multiple and "common" mtDNA deletions are present in animal tissues and that their abundance increases with age. The size of the deletion varies from 4–14 kb in length (Melov et al., 1995; Zhang et al., 1992). Interestingly, full-length mtDNA PCR products are very low in old compared to young individuals, suggesting that most of the mtDNA in these subjects represents some kind of rearrangement (Kovalenko et al., 1997; Melov et al., 1995). The presence of multiple mtDNA deletions within a tissue indicates that the detection of an individual deletion (e.g., mtDNA^{4977}) represents a portion of the many different rearrangements that may be occurring in the cells.

3. Possible Mechanisms of mtDNA Deletion Formation

Deletion break points in myopathy patients are characterized by the presence of large direct repeats (13 bp) that have led to the proposal of mechanisms such as slip replication (Holt et al., 1989b; Schon et al., 1989; Shoffner et al., 1989) and site-specific recombination (Degoul et al., 1991) for the formation of mtDNA deletions. In our studies in mice, however, we found that short direct repeats (2–4 nt) are more prevalent. The size of these repeats would not give rise to the formation of a stable looped intermediate structure that is required for the slip-replication model. Thus, we have proposed a "replication jumping" model for deletion formation (Chung et al., 1996). This model assumes that the polymerase will stutter when it encounters an oxidatively modified base. The nascent strand then anneals to a complementary downstream region, and replication continues after the removal of single-stranded "excess" DNA up to a double-stranded region, resulting in a mutant genome. Because not all deletion break points are characterized by the presence of direct repeats exactly at the break point, secondary structures formed by tRNAs (Mita *et al.*, 1990) or hairpin structures formed by palindromic sequences (Mita *et al.*, 1990) have also been proposed to be causes of deletion formation.

4. Abundance and Cellular Distribution of mtDNA Deletions

It is clear that there is an age-associated increase in the abundance of both "common" and multiple deletions. In humans, the abundance is higher in postmitotic tissues with high energy demands, such as heart, brain, and skeletal muscle. In contrast, the abundance of mtDNA deletions in rodents has been found to be higher in kidney (Zhang *et al.*, 1997) or liver (Yowe & Ames, 1998) than in heart, skeletal muscle, or brain. Even in these tissues, age-associated mtDNA deletions are detected at a very low steady-state levels. These studies assume, however, that mtDNA deletions are distributed equivalently among all cells. Two approaches, (1) examination of a defined number of individual cells or fibers and (2) histology, have demonstrated that mtDNA deletions focally accumulate to high levels in a subset of cells.

To determine the distribution of mtDNA deletions in skeletal muscle, we studied defined numbers of muscle fibers from rhesus monkeys (Schwarze *et al.*, 1995) and determined the abundance of individual deletion products in tissue homogenates and muscle fiber bundles containing 75, 50, and 10 fibers/bundle using primers to the major arc of the mitochondrial genome. We found that, as the number of fibers decreased, (1) the number of individual deletion products decreased and (2) the calculated abundance of individual deletion products increased. The abundance of individual deletion products was low in muscle homogenates (0.02–0.1%), higher when 75 fibers/bundle were analyzed (0.7–2.1%), and reached even higher levels as the number of fibers analyzed was decreased to 10 fibers/bundle (4.6–13.2%). These data demonstrate the focal accumulation of mtDNA deletions within individual muscle fibers.

Age-associated mtDNA deletions also have been shown to accumulate within individual human cardiomyocytes (Khrapko *et al.*, 1999). Long extension PCR was used to amplify mtDNA from individual cardiomyocytes isolated from autopsy samples of human left ventricle. Of 350 cardiomyocytes examined, 4% demonstrated the presence of deleted mtDNA. The cardiomyocytes harboring these deleted mtDNAs were found only in centenarian samples, in concordance with an age-associated increase. Additionally, the estimated fraction of deleted mtDNA within individual cardiomyocytes ranged between 5% and 64%, a range known to have physiological impact in mitochondrial myopathies and cybrid studies of mtDNA deletions (Section VI.C).

A different approach, *in situ* hybridizaton, has been used to determine the *in situ* distribution of mtDNA deletions and has identified high accumulations of deleted mitochondrial genomes localized to individual cells and in phase with histochemical ETS abnormalities (Mueller-Hoecker *et al.*, 1993). Together, the micro-dissection and *in situ* hybridization studies indicate that mtDNA deletions are not distributed equivalently in all cells, but focally accumulate to physiologically relevant levels in a subset of cells. Therefore, whereas tissue homogenate studies fail to suggest a biological impact of mtDNA deletions, methods that allow the study of individual cells may uncover the important biological impact of these deletions at their site of initial and greatest action, i.e., at the cellular level.

VI. Cellular and Tissue Impact of Age-Associated Mitochondrial Genetic Alterations

A. Introduction

In the field of mtDNA mutation and aging, a critically important question remains unanswered: what is the biological impact, if any, of age-related mtDNA mutations? The following sections focus on evidence that demonstrates an impact of mtDNA mutations on cellular and tissue physiology. A variety of approaches are being used to elucidate the cellular consequences of age-associated mtDNA mutations, including (1) studies of mitochondrial myopathies; (2) transgenic mouse models of mtDNA mutations; (3) *in vitro* models of mtDNA deletions, e.g., cybrid cell lines; and (4) *in situ* studies of age-associated mtDNA mutations.

B. Mitochondrial Myopathies Indicate Pathological Potential of Age-Associated mtDNA Mutations

Mitochondrial myopathies demonstrate the full pathological potential of mtDNA mutations. In these varied disorders, where the mutant mitochondrial genome may reach steady-state levels of greater than 90% in specific tissues, the tissue involvement and physiological impact are more evident than in aging, where mtDNA mutations occur at significantly lower steady-state levels. Parallels can be drawn between the clinical findings in myopathy-associated mtDNA mutations and the organ-specific degenerative changes seen with aging in which mtDNA mutations (i.e., primarily mtDNA deletions) have been implicated (Table IV). These organs and tissues are largely postmitotic, highly dependent on oxidative metabolism, and include the brain, sensorineural and cardiovascular systems, skeletal muscles, pancreas, and kidney.

Table IV

Possible Pathophysiological Similarities between Myopathy-Associated mtDNA Mutations and Age-Associated mtDNA Mutations

Myopathy-associated mtDNA mutations	Age-associated mtDNA mutations
Brain	
Seizures	Alzheimer's
Ataxia	Parkinson's
Strokelike symptoms	Huntington's
Dystonia	
Eye	
Ptosis	Retinopathy
Retinopathy	
Ophthalmoplegia	
Ear	
Sensorineural hearing loss	Presbycusis
Heart and vasculature	
Conduction defects	Atherosclerosis
Cardiomyopathy	Cardiomyocyte death
Skeletal muscles	
Myopathy	Sarcopenia
RRF	RRF
Apoptosis	Fiber atrophy
Gene expression changes	
Pancreas	
Diabetes mellitus	Adult-onset diabetes
Kidney	
Fanconi syndrome	None associated

The clinical signs of sporadic and inherited mtDNA mutations in the central nervous system (CNS) generally have been categorized as mitochondrial encephalomyopathies and cover a wide range of clinical presentations [reviewed in DiMauro et al. (1998)]. Afflicted individuals may display myoclonus, seizures, ataxia, strokelike episodes, migraines, dementia, developmental delay, and neuropathy [reviewed in DiMauro et al. (1998); Fitzsimons, 1981; Harding & Holt, 1989; Harding et al., 1988; Lamont et al., 1998; Nissenkorn et al., 1999; Simon & Johns, 1999). Similarly, age-associated mtDNA mutations have been implicated in age-related neurodegenerative processes, including Alzheimer's, Parkinson's, and Huntington's diseases [reviewed in Beal (1998)]. These disorders share some of the clinical features of the mitochondrial encephalomyopathies, similarities that suggest the biological potential of age-associated mtDNA mutations in the CNS and a common pathogenesis between the mitochondrial encephalomyopathies and age-associated mtDNA mutations. The pathogenetic involvement of mtDNA mutations in these disorders is not understood, but may include the impairment of mitochondrial protein synthesis, immune system involvement, effects on cellular ATP levels with resulting excitotoxicity, or mitochondrial triggering of cell death (i.e., apoptosis or necrosis) [reviewed in DiMauro et al., (1998)].

Mitochondrial encephalomyopathies also often present with sensory organ defects that are analogous to some age-related changes. Retinopathy, most commonly seen as changes to the pigment layer, is a common feature of many mitochondrial encephalomyopathies [reviewed in Fitzsimons (1981); Harding & Holt, 1989; Harding et al., 1988; Lamont et al., 1998; Nissenkorn et al., 1999; Simon & Johns, 1999]. The human mtDNA^{4977}, i.e., the common deletion, also has been found to increase in both the retinal pigment epithelium and neural retina with age and may contribute to functional changes in the retina with age (Barreau et al., 1996).

The cardiovascular system commonly is affected in mitochondrial encephalomyopathies. This is observed as cardiomyopathic changes in the heart as well as conduction system defects, which manifest clinically as arrhythmias or heart block [reviewed in Fitzsimons (1981); Harding & Holt, 1989; Harding et al., 1988; Lamont et al., 1998; Nissenkorn et al., 1999; Simon & Johns, 1999]. Accumulation of deletions within individual cardiomyocytes (Khrapko et al., 1999) could be a molecular mechanism that triggers apoptotic or necrotic cell death in cardiomyocytes with aging, thereby giving

rise to the analogous cardiomyopathy of aging (Olivetti et al., 1991).

Some of the most extensive contributions from the study of mitochondrial encephalomyopathies to the understanding of the cellular impact of age-associated mtDNA mutations come from studies of myopathic changes. Histological examination of skeletal muscle from many individuals with myopathy reveals the presence of fibers that react with Gomori trichrome stain in a distinct manner ("ragged red fibers" or RRFs). Ultrastructural studies have revealed that these fibers harbor a large accumulation of enlarged mitochondria (Mueller-Hoecker et al., 1983). Due to the increased mitochondrial content, these fibers stain hyperreactively for succinate dehydrogenase (SDH^{++}) and, in the majority of cases, they are negative for cytochrome c oxidase (COX$^-$) activity. RRFs are a hallmark of both mitochondrial myopathies and age-related mtDNA alterations in skeletal muscle. These abnormal fibers provide an opportunity to investigate cellular changes, in addition to the obvious ETS abnormalities, which may adversely affect muscle fiber function. Walker and Schon (1998) found increased steady-state neurotrophin–4 (a neuronal signaling molecule expressed by skeletal muscle fibers) levels in RRFs compared to surrounding normal fibers. Increases also have been found in the levels of neural adhesion molecule (NCAM) in RRFs, and this increase appeared to precede the development of the ETS histochemical abnormality (Heuss, et al., 1995). Altered gene expression of myoglobin (Kunishige et al., 1996), manganese superoxide dismutase (the mitochondrial superoxide dismutase isoform) (Ohkoshi et al., 1995) and α β-crystallin (a stress-induced, heat-shock-related protein) (Iwaki et al., 1993) has also been observed in myopathy-associated RRFs. No evidence is available regarding these proteins in aging-associated RRFs.

Cell death is a common feature of aging and age-related processes in many tissues and organs, including the heart (Anversa et al., 1990; Olivetti et al., 1991), brain (Morrison & Hof, 1997), and skeletal muscle [reviewed in Lexell (1995)], and may occur through necrotic and apoptotic pathways (Johnson, et al., 1999). The molecular mechanisms that initiate age-related cell death pathways are not known, but the growing evidence of the mitochondrion's role in apoptosis [reviewed in Green and Reed (1998)] suggests that age-related mtDNA mutations and their associated mitochondrial dysfunction are a potential trigger of this cell death. Although there is no evidence, to our knowledge, of apoptotic events occurring in age-associated RRFs, studies of mitochondrial myopathies have shown increased nuclear DNA fragmentation, a marker of apoptosis, in skeletal muscle fibers from afflicted individuals (DiMauro et al., 1998; Monici, 1998).

The myopathies clearly represent one end of the biological impact spectrum of mtDNA mutations. In these clinical disorders, the mutation load has reached a level that has a striking pathological impact. Despite differences from their age-related counterparts, studies of RRFs in mitochondrial myopathies provide a model for the elucidation of pathological processes and cellular pathways that may be triggered by age-associated mtDNA mutations.

C. In Vitro Models of Mitochondrial Abnormalities

In vitro models of cultured cells that harbor these mutations offer opportunities to study the cause and effect relationships of mtDNA mutations on cellular and organellar processes. Cell culture models of mtDNA mutations have focused almost exclusively on the mitochondrial myopathies. Cell lines have been established from cybrid fusion of enucleated cells harboring the mutant mtDNA with cells lacking mtDNA (Bentlage & Attardi, 1996; Dunbar et al., 1996; Hao & Moraes, 1997; Hayashi et al., 1991; Koga et al., 1995; Sancho et al., 1992; Trounce et al., 1994; van den Ouweland et al., 1999) and also have been established from primary cultures of patient fibroblasts (Antonicka et al., 1999; Cock et al., 1999; James et al., 1996; Matthews et al., 1995; Vazquez-Memije et al., 1998) and myoblasts (Rusanen et al., 2000). mtDNA point mutations, deletions, and duplications have been studied by these methods, and Table V summarizes the cellular impact of observed mtDNA mutations. The cellular impact, in these studies, typically was related to the degree of heteroplasmy in the cybrid clones. For example, heteroplasmy of mtDNA deletions did affect cell mitochondrial function until the deleted genome reached levels of 50–70% of the total mtDNA (Hayashi et al., 1991; Porteous et al., 1998; Sancho et al., 1992). This evidence points to an adverse effect on mitochondrial and cellular function in cells or regions of cells (i.e., in skeletal muscle fibers) that appear to be nearly homoplasmic for age-associated mtDNA deletions.

Only two studies, to our knowledge, have utilized in vitro cybrid methodologies to examine the mitochondrial genome's role in age-associated mitochondrial dysfunction. Hayashi et al. (1994a) measured a decrease in COX activity in human skin fibroblasts that correlated with subject age and not the in vitro age of the fibroblast cultures. The decrease in COX was not attributable to a decrease in mtDNA content between young and old fibroblasts, but did appear to correlate with a decrease in mitochondrial protein synthesis. They determined that the transfer of defective mitochondria to mtDNA-less HeLa cells or the transfer of HeLa cell nuclei to the dysfunctional fibroblasts resulted in

Table V
Summary of Cybrid Studies of mtDNA Mutations

Point Mutations[a–d,f,g,h,i,j]
  ↓ ETS and OXPHOS complex activities (activities disrupted may depend on
  position of mutation)
  ↓ Oxygen consumption
  ↓ Protein synthesis (seen mainly in tRNA mutations)
  ↓ Growth of cell line
Deletions[l,m]
  ↓ Growth of cell line
  ↓ Mitochondrial protein synthesis
  ↓ OXPHOS
  ↓ Complex IV activity
  ↓ Mitochondrial membrane potential
  ↓ Rate of ATP synthesis
  ↓ Cellular ATP/ADP ratio
Duplication[e]
  Normal oxygen consumption
  Normal growth of cell line
  Normal complex activities

---

[a]Bruno et al., 1999.
[b]van den Ouweland et al., 1999.
[c]Dunbar et al. 1996.
[d]Raha et al., 1999.
[e]Hao & Moraes, 1997.
[f]Koga et al., 1995.
[g] Trounce et al., 1994.
[h]Hayashi et al. 1994b.
[i]Mariotti et al., 1994.
[j]Hayashi et al., 1993.
[k]King et al., 1992.
[l]Hayashi et al., 1991.
[m]Porteous et al., 1998.

normalization of COX activity and protein synthesis. This suggested that a nuclear defect was responsible for the mitochondrial dysfunction. However, as noted by Laderman et al. (1996), the lack of selection against the parental fibroblasts could have resulted in an enrichment for respiratory-competent donor fibroblasts that had not been enucleated. Therefore, Laderman et al., (1996) attempted to refine these findings using a similar cybrid approach. Cybrids were constructed from fibroblasts from individuals ranging 39–103 years of age. Numerous clones were selected from each fusion experiment and expanded for analyses of oxygen consumption, mtDNA content, and growth rate. There was a decrease in growth rate, oxygen consumption, and mtDNA content that was directly proportional to cell donor age, suggesting that age-related mtDNA damage was responsible. Considerable variability existed in each parameter within clones from both young and old donors, and oxygen consumption was affected dramatically by the length of culture time.

There are numerous limitations of these cybrid analyses. The study of rapidly replicating mitotic cell lines is of limited use in determining the impact of mtDNA mutations on postmitotic cells. Cell density can have a significant impact on aerobic metabolism (Bereiter-Hahn et al., 1998), and the nuclear background has been shown to have a significant impact on the cellular phenotype of mutant mitochondrial genomes (Dunbar *et al.*, 1995). The common practice of culturing cells in a 20% oxygen environment is an additional caveat in these studies. As mentioned previously in Section VI.B, cell death may be an important pathway by which mtDNA mutations exert their effects, but there is no information regarding the susceptibility of these cybrid cell lines to apoptotic or necrotic cell death. In addition, the selection of cell lines that can be expanded to provide enough cells for analysis precludes any cell lines that harbor pathogenic mtDNA mutations.

D. Transgenic Models of mtDNA Mutations

Transgenic models of defined, pathological mtDNA mutations hold great promise in determining the biological relevance of age-related mitochondrial genetic alterations. These models would facilitate the development of therapeutic interventions that could be of benefit in lessening the impact of age-associated mtDNA mutations. The interaction of mtDNA mutations with other age-associated changes could also be investigated, for example, in crosses with transgenic mice that have alterations in antioxidant defenses or in DNA repair pathways. Additionally, these transgenic or "transmitochondrial" animals would reveal details of mutant mtDNA segregation and transmission and the role of heteroplasmy in the phenotypic expression of mtDNA mutations (Marchington *et al.*, 1999).

The first mouse model of a potentially pathogenic mtDNA point mutation was developed by Marchington *et al.* (1999) by generating a embryonic stem (ES) cell line that is heteroplasmic for wild-type and mutant mtDNA. The mutation, in this study, was an A-to-T transversion at nt 2379 (i.e., the mitochondrial 16S rRNA gene) that confers chloramphenicol resistance to mitochondria carrying this mutant mtDNA. Cells carrying mitochondria with this point mutation generate increased levels of lactate, and the ES cells displayed decreased cytochemical staining for COX activity. In the resulting transmitochondrial mice, the highest levels of the mutant mtDNA were found in the heart and diaphragm, with levels reaching ~6% of total mtDNA. The levels of mutant mtDNA, which had been greater than 90% in the ES cells, dropped to approximately 3% in the differentiated cells due to the lack of chloramphenicol selection. The transgenic mice did not display obvious phenotypic changes, and there were no histological changes seen in skeletal muscle. The mice did not undergo any exercise stress, and the ages of the mice in this study were not reported. There may be interesting late-life phenotypic effects of this mutation in response to exercise as well as effects on life span that may clarify the pathologic potential of such mtDNA point mutations with aging.

Another valuable model of mitochondrial disease, which may help determine factors involved in the generation of age-associated mtDNA mutations and their resulting biological impact, is the *Ant1* (the heart and skeletal muscle isoform of the adenine nucleotide translocator) knockout created by Graham *et al.* (1997). This model was developed to mimic the decreased energy production thought to be causally related to the pathological changes seen in the various mitochondrial myopathies. The presence of RRFs and mitochondrial cardiomyopathy in the Ant1 knockout mouse may facilitate the search for genes important in mitochondrial biogenesis and the pathological changes resulting from cellular energy deprivation.

E. *In Situ* Studies of Age-Associated mtDNA Mutations

The *in situ* analyses of age-associated mtDNA mutations and their associated biochemical abnormalities suggest that these alterations may have their greatest and initial impact at the level of individual cells in postmitotic tissues. Most of these studies have surveyed the presence of these age-associated mitochondrial abnormalities in a variety of tissues and animal species, as well as the increase in their abundance with age. These biochemical abnormalities and their associated mtDNA mutations, which are typically mtDNA deletions, have been found to increase with age in heart, skeletal muscle, parathyroid, liver, and diaphragm in rodents and humans [reviewed in Lee et al., (1997); Liu et al., 1998; Zhang et al., 1998]. Thus, histological analyses have demonstrated clearly an age-associated increase in the abundance of ETS abnormalities.

Because ETS abnormalities are segmental in nature (Yamamoto & Nonaka, 1988), that is, they are localized to certain regions within muscle fibers in myopathy patients and aging individuals, we have taken a longitudinal approach in which we analyze serial cross sections along the length of the muscle. We found that the abundance of fibers displaying ETS abnormalities increased from 0.05% in a single cross section to 0.31% (six-fold more) when the fibers from this animal were examined over a distance of 350 μm. This is a direct result of the fact that a two-dimensional probe of a given volume will encounter particles within the volume in proportion to their size. Thus, because age-associated ETS abnormal regions have a length that increases with age in monkeys (Lopez et al., 2000), we have employed exhaustive, serial sectioning to determine the number of ETS abnormal regions within a unit volume of muscle. By using this method of analysis, we estimate that ~60% of muscle fibers in a 34-year-old rhesus monkey vastus lateralis (Lopez et al., 2000) and ~15% of muscle fibers in the 38-month-old rat rectus femoris (Wanagat et al. in press)

harbor an ETS abnormal region. The magnitude of these estimations suggests an important biological role for these mtDNA mutation-related abnormalities in sarcopenia, the age-related loss of muscle mass.

In our histological analyses of rhesus monkey skeletal muscle, we examined sections within regions of ETS abnormalities by in situ hybridization and determined that ETS abnormalities are associated with deletions of the mitochondrial genome (Lee, et al., 1998a). Of the 26 fibers that we examined, 23 fibers (89%) contained deleted mitochondrial genomes. Deletions were scattered throughout the genome. Similar results have been found in muscle from patients with myopathy (Mita et al., 1989; Shoubridge et al., 1990) and aging individuals (Brierley, et al., 1998; Mueller-Hoecker et al., 1993). These data support the hypothesis that mtDNA deletions result in decreased ETS enzymatic activity with age. Deleted genomes or their transcripts are the most abundant species in affected muscle fibers (Moraes et al., 1992; Prelle et al., 1994; Sciacco et al., 1994). The predominance of deleted genomes suggests a process of accumulation of these smaller deleted genomes, probably due to a replicative advantage that these genomes may have over wild-type genomes.

In situ skeletal muscle studies of mtDNA deletions also have demonstrated an association of the abnormal region that harbors the deleted genomes and the presence of fiber atrophy (Lee et al., 1998a). Of the 90 fibers studied that harbored an ETS abnormal region that was in phase with mtDNA deletions, 13 fibers showed reductions in cross-sectional area (CSA) that ranged from 50–89% within the ETS abnormal region of the fiber. We have observed similar fibers in aging rat rectus femoris muscle (Wanagat et al., in press). These observations suggest that age-associated mtDNA deletions are associated with a severe derangement of skeletal muscle fiber morphology.

VII. Conclusion

The unique characteristics of mtDNA structure and function, together with its mitochondrial matrix localization, suggest increased susceptibility to many types of DNA damage. mtDNA may be particularly susceptible to oxidative damage secondary to normal, life-long, mitochondrial production of ROS, and this hypothesis is supported by measurements of mtDNA 8-OHdG content, which increases with age. The mitochondrion is equipped with a number of repair pathways, but little is known about the changes in these pathways with aging. Presumably, as these repair pathways are overcome, direct DNA damage induces mtDNA mutations including point, deletion, and duplication mutations. Deletion mutations are known to accumulate within tissues and individual cells in a broad range of species, whereas much less is known about duplication mutations and there is contradictory evidence regarding the accumulation of mtDNA point mutations with age. The mechanisms leading to mtDNA mutations largely are unknown. Point mutations may arise directly from oxidative damage, whereas deletions and duplications appear to involve some interaction of mtDNA structural elements, an interaction that may be promoted by oxidative damage.

The potential biological impact of age-associated mtDNA mutations is a critical and vexing question in mitochondrial biogerontology. Studies of mitochondrial myopathies, cybrid cell lines, and transgenic mouse models suggest that mtDNA mutations may result in severe pathological changes, but more information is needed in the context of the specific types and steady-state levels of mutations that are found in aged organisms. In situ studies of naturally occurring, age-associated mtDNA deletions and their corresponding histochemical abnormalities are revealing significant impacts on normal cellular morphology and suggest that these mitochondrial mutations may have their initial and most significant impact at the cellular level. The disruption of normal mitochondrial function suggests that mtDNA mutations may trigger or prime the inappropriate activation of cell death pathways. The progressive summation of the resulting cell loss and cellular dysfunction ultimately may contribute to the web of age-related physiological attrition and structural derangement.

References

Ames, B. N. (1989). Endogenous DNA damage as related to cancer and aging. *Mutation Research, 214*, 41–46.

Antonicka, H., Floryk, D., Klement, P., Stratilova, L., Hermanska, J., Houstkova, H., Kalous, M., Drahota, Z., Zeman, J., & Houstek, J. (1999). Defective kinetics of cytochrome c oxidase and alteration of mitochondrial membrane potential in fibroblasts and cytoplasmic hybrid cells with the mutation for myoclonus epilepsy with ragged-red fibres ("MERRF") at position 8344 nt. *Biochemical Journal, 342 Pt 3*, 537–44.

Anversa, P., Palackal, T., Sonnenblick, E. H., Olivetti, G., Meggs, L. G., & Capasso, J. M. (1990). Myocyte cell loss and myocyte cellular hyperplasia in the hypertrophied aging rat heart. *Circulation Research, 67*, 871–885.

Barreau, E., Brossas, J.-Y., Courtois, Y., & Treton, J. A. (1996). Accumulation of mitochondrial DNA deletions in human retina during aging. *Investigative Ophthalmology and Visual Science, 37*, 384–391.

Beal, M. F. (1998). Mitochondrial dysfunction in neurodegenerative diseases. *Biochimica et Biophysica Acta, 1366*, 211–23.

Beckman, K. B., & Ames, B. N. (1999). Endogenous oxidative damage of mtDNA. *Mutation Research, 424,* 51–58.

Bentlage, H. A., & Attardi, G. (1996). Relationship of genotype to phenotype in fibroblast-derived transmitochondrial cell lines carrying the 3243 mutation associated with the MELAS encephalomyopathy: Shift towards mutant genotype and role of mtDNA copy number. *Human Molecular Genetics, 5,* 197–205.

Benzi, G., Pastoris, O., Marzatico, F., Villa, R. F., Dagani, F., & Curti, D. (1992). The mitochondrial electron transfer alteration as a factor involved in the brain aging. *Neurobiology of Aging, 13,* 361–368.

Bereiter-Hahn, J., Munnich, A., & Woiteneck, P. (1998). Depedence of energy metabolism on the density of cells in culture. *Cell Structure and Function, 23,* 85–93.

Berneburg, M., Grether-Beck, S., Kurten, V., Ruzicka, T., Briviba, K., Sies, H., & Krutmann, J. (1999). Singlet oxygen mediates the UVA-induced generation of the photoaging-associated mitochondrial common deletion. *Journal of Biological Chemistry, 274,* 15345–15349.

Bouzidi, M. F., Poyau, A., & Godinot, C. (1998). Co-existence of high levels of a cytochrome b mutation and of a tandem 200 bp duplication in the D-loop of muscle human mitochondrial DNA. *Human Molecular Genetics, 7,* 385–391.

Boveris, A., & Chance, B. (1973). The mitochondrial generation of hydrogen peroxide. General properties and effect of hyperbaric oxygen. *Biochemical Journal, 134,* 707–716.

Boveris, A., Oshino, N., & Chance, B. (1972). The cellular production of hydrogen peroxide. *Biochemical Journal, 128,* 617–630.

Bresslau, E., & Scremin, L. (1924). Die kerne der trypanosomen und ihr verhalten zur nuclealreaktion. *Archiv für Protistenkunde, xlviii,* 509–515.

Brierley, E. J., Johnson, M. A., Lightowlers, R. N., James, O. F. W., & Turnbull, D. M. (1998). Role of mitochondrial DNA mutations in human aging: Implications for the central nervous system and muscle. *Annals of Neurology, 43,* 217–223.

Brockington, M., Sweeney, M. G., Hammans, S. R., Morgan-Hughes, J. A., & Harding, A. E. (1993). A tandem duplication in the D-loop of human mitochondrial DNA is associated with deletions in mitochondrial myopathies. *Nature Genetics, 4,* 67–71.

Brossas, J.-Y., Barreau, E., Courtois, Y., & Treton, J. (1994). Multiple deletions in mitochondrial DNA are present in senescent mouse brain. *Biochemical and Biophysical Research Communications, 202,* 654–659.

Brown, W. M., George, M. J., & Wilson, A. C. (1979). Rapid evolution of animal mitochondrial DNA. *Proceedings of the ·National Academy of Sciences of the USA, 76,* 1967–1971.

Bruno, C., Martinuzzi, A., Tang, Y., Andreu, A. L., Pallotti, R., Bonilla, E., Shanske, S., Fu, J., Sue, C. M., Angelini, C., DiMauro, S., & Manfredi, G. (1999). A stop-codon mutation in the human mtDNA cytochrome c oxidase I gene disrupts the functional structure of complex IV. *American Journal of Human Genetics, 65,* 611–20.

Chance, B., Sies, H., & Boveris, A. (1979). Hydroperoxide metabolism in mammalian organs. *Physiological Reviews, 59,* 527–605.

Chung, S. S., Eimon, P. M., Weindruch, R., & Aiken, J. M. (1996). Analysis of age-associated mitochondrial DNA deletion breakpoint regions from mice suggests a novel model of deletion formation. *Age, 19,* 117–128.

Chung, S. S., Weindruch, R., Schwarze, S. R., McKenzie, D. I., & Aiken, J. M. (1994). Multiple age-associated mitochondrial DNA deletions in skeletal muscle of mice. *Aging (Milano), 6,* 193–200.

Clayton, D. A. (1982). Replication of animal mitochondrial DNA. *Cell, 28,* 693–705.

Clayton, D. A., Davis, R. W., & Vinograd, J. (1970). Homology and structural relationships between the dimeric and monomeric circular forms of mitochondrial DNA from human leukemic leukocytes. *Journal of Molecular Biology, 47,* 137–153.

Clayton, D. A., Doda, J. N., & Friedberg, E. C. (1974). The absence of pyrimidine dimer repair mechanism in mammalian mitochondria. *Proceedings of the National Academy of Sciences of the USA, 71,* 2777–2781.

Cock, H. R., Cooper, J. M., & Schapira, A. H. (1999). Functional consequences of the 3460-bp mitochondrial DNA mutation associated with Leber's hereditary optic neuropathy. *Journal of the Neurological Sciences, 165,* 10–7.

Cortopassi, G. A., & Wong, A. (1999). Mitochondria in organismal aging and degeneration. *Biochimica et Biophysica Acta, 1410,* 182–193.

Cortopassi, G. A., Shibata, D., Soong, N.-W., & Arnheim, N. (1992). A pattern of accumulation of a somatic deletion of mitochondrial DNA in aging human tissues. *Proceedings of the National Academy of Sciences of the USA, 89,* 7370–7374.

Croteau, D. L., H., S. R., & Bohr, V. A. (1999). Mitochondrial DNA repair pathways. *Mutation Research, 434,* 137–148.

Degoul, F., Nelson, I., Amselem, S., Romero, N., Obermaier-Kusser, B., Ponsot, G., Marsac, C., & Lestienne, P. (1991). Different mechanisms inferred from sequences of human mitochondrial DNA deletions in ocular myopathies. *Nucleic Acids Research, 19,* 493–496.

DiMauro, S., Bonilla, E., Davidson, M., Hirano, M., & Schon, E. A. (1998). Mitochondria in neuromuscular disorders. *Biochimica et Biophysica Acta— Bioenergetics, 1366,* 199–210.

Dunbar, D. R., Moonie, P. A., Jacobs, H. T., & Holt, I. J. (1995). Different cellular backgrounds confer a marked advantage to either mutant or wild-type mitochondrial genomes. *Proceedings of the National Academy of Sciences of the USA, 92,* 6562–6566.

Dunbar, D. R., Moonie, P. A., Zeviani, M., & Holt, I. J. (1996). Complex I deficiency is associated with 3243G:C mitochondrial DNA in osteosarcoma cell cybrids. *Human Molecular Genetics, 5,* 123–129.

Edris, W. B., Stine, O. C., & Filburn, C. R. (1994). Detection and quantitation by competitive PCR of an age-associated increase in a 4.8 kb deletion in rat mitochondrial DNA. *Mutation Research, 316,* 69–78.

Enter, C., Mueller-Hoecker, J., Zierz, S., Kurlemann, G., Pongratz, D., Foerster, C., Obermaier-Kusser, B., & Gerbitz, K. (1991). A specific point mutation in the mitochondrial genome of Caucasians with MELAS. *Human Genetics, 88,* 233–236.

Fitzsimons, R. B. (1981). The mitochondrial myopathies: 9 case reports and a literature review. *Clinical and Experimental Neurology, 17,* 185–210.

Gadaleta, M. N., Rainaldi, G., Lezza, A. M. S., Milella, F., Fracasso, F., & Cantatore, P. (1992). Mitochondrial DNA copy number and mitochondrial DNA deletion in adult and senescent rats. *Mutation Research, 275,* 181–193.

Giulivi, C., & Cadenas, E. (1998). The role of mitochondrial glutathione in DNA base oxidation. *Biochimica et Biophysica Acta, 1366,* 265–274.

Graham, B. H., Waymire, K. G., Cottrell, B., Trounce, I. A., MacGregor, G. R., & Wallace, D. C. (1997). A mouse model for mitochondrial myopathy and cardiomyopathy resulting from a deficiency in the heart/muscle isoform of the adenine nucleotide translocator. *Nature Genetics, 16,* 226–234.

Green, D., & Reed, J. (1998). Mitochondria and apoptosis. *Science, 281,* 1309.

Hao, H., & Moraes, C. T. (1997). A disease-associated G5703A mutation in human mitochondrial DNA causes a conformational change and a marked decrease in steady-state levels of mitochondrial tRNA Asn. *Molecular and Cellular Biology, 17,* 6831–6837.

Hao, H., Manfredi, G., & Moraes, C. T. (1997). Functional and structural features of a tandem duplication of the human mtDNA promoter regions. *American Journal of Human Genetics, 60,* 1363–1372.

Harding, A. E., & Holt, I. J. (1989). Mitochondrial myopathies. *British Medical Journal, 45,* 760–771.

Harding, A. E., Petty, R. K. H., & Morgan-Hughes, J. A. (1988). Mitochondrial myopathy: a genetic study of 71 cases. *Journal of Medical Genetics, 25,* 528–535.

Hattori, K., Tanaka, M., Sugiyama, S., Obayashi, T., Ito, T., Satake, T., Hanaki, Y., Asai, J., Nagano, M., & Ozawa, T. (1991).

Age-dependent increase in deleted mitochondrial DNA in the human heart: Possible contributory factor to presbycardia. *American Heart Journal, 121,* 1735–1742.

Hayakawa, M., Hattori, K., Sugiyama, S., & Ozawa, T. (1992). Age-associated oxygen damage and mutations in mitochondrial DNA in human hearts. *Biochemical and Biophysical Research Communications, 189,* 979–985.

Hayakawa, M., Sugiyama, S., Hattori, K., Takasawa, M., & Ozawa, T. (1993). Age-associated damage in mitochondrial DNA in human hearts. *Molecular and Cellular Biochemistry, 119,* 95–103.

Hayakawa, M., Torii, K., Sugiyama, S., Tanaka, M., & Ozawa, T. (1991). Age-associated accumulation of 8-hydroxydeoxyguanosine in mitochondrial DNA of human diaphragm. *Biochemical and Biophysical Research Communications, 179,* 1023–1029.

Hayashi, J., Ohta, S., Kagawa, Y., Kondo, H., Kaneda, H., Yonekawa, H., Takai, D., & Miyabayashi, S. (1994a). Nuclear but not mitochondrial genome involvement in human age-related mitochondrial dysfunction. Functional integrity of mitochondrial DNA from aged subjects. *Journal of Biological Chemistry, 269,* 6878–6883.

Hayashi, J., Ohta, S., Kagawa, Y., Takai, D., Miyabayashi, S., Tada, K., Fukushima, H., Inui, K., Okada, S., & Goto, Y. (1994b). Functional and morphological abnormalities of mitochondria in human cells containing mitochondrial DNA with pathogenic point mutations in tRNA genes. *Journal of Biological Chemistry, 269,* 19060–19066.

Hayashi, J., Ohta, S., Kikuchi, A., Takemitsu, M., Goto, Y., & Nonaka, I. (1991). Introduction of disease-related mitochondrial DNA deletions into HeLa cells lacking mitochondrial DNA results in mitochondrial dysfunction. *Proceedings of the National Academy of Sciences of the USA, 88,* 10614–10618.

Hayashi, J., Ohta, S., Takai, D., Miyabayashi, S., Sakuta, R., Goto, Y., & Nonaka, I. (1993). Accumulation of mtDNA with a mutation at position 3271 in

tRNA(Leu)(UUR) gene introduced from a MELAS patient to HeLa cells lacking mtDNA results in progressive inhibition of mitochondrial respiratory function. *Biochemical and Biophysical Research Communications, 197,* 1049–1055.

Helbock, H. J., Beckman, K. B., Shigenaga, M. K., Wlater, P. B., Woodall, A. A., Yeo, H. C., & Ames, B. N. (1998). DNA oxidation matters: The HPLC-electrochemical detection assay of 8-oxo-deoxyguanosine and 8-oxoguanine. *Proceedings of the National Academy of Sciences of the USA, 95,* 288–293.

Henle, E. S., & Linn, S. (1997). Formation, prevention and repair of DNA damage by iron/hydrogen peroxide. *Journal of Biological Chemistry, 272,* 19095–19098.

Heuss, D., Engelhardt, A., Goebel, H., & Neundoerfer, B. (1995). Expression of NCAM (neural cell adhesion molecule) in mitochondrial myopathy. *Clinical Neuropathology, 14,* 331–336.

Holt, I. J., Harding, A. E., Cooper, J. M., Schapira, A. H. V., Toscano, A., Clark, J. B., & Morgan-Hughes, J. A. (1989a). Mitochondrial myopathies: Clinical and biochemical features of 30 patients with major deletions of muscle mitochondrial DNA. *Annals of Neurology, 26,* 699–708.

Holt, I. J., Harding, A. E., & Morgan-Hughes, J. A. (1989b). Deletions of muscle mitochondrial DNA in mitochondrial myopathies: Sequence analysis and possible mechanisms. *Nucleic Acids Research, 17,* 4465–4469.

Huemer, R. P., Lee, K. D., Reeves, A. E., & Bickert, C. (1971). Mitochondrial studies in senescent mice. II. Specific activity, buoyant density, and turnover of mitochondrial DNA. *Experimental Gerontology, 6,* 327–34.

Iwaki, T., Iwaki, A., & Goldman, J. E. (1993). Alpha B-crystallin in oxidative muscle fibers and its accumulation in ragged-red fibers: A comparative immunohistochemical and histochemical study in human skeletal muscle. *Acta Neuropathologica (Berlin), 85,* 475–480.

James, A. M., Wei, Y. H., Pang, C. Y., & Murphy, M. P. (1996). Altered mitochondrial function in fibroblasts containing MELAS or MERRF mitochondrial DNA mutations. *Biochemical Journal, 318*, 401–407.

Johnson, F. B., Sinclair, D. A., & Guarente, L. (1999). Molecular biology of aging. *Cell, 96*, 291–302.

Kaneko, T., Tahara, S., & Matsuo, M. (1996). Non-linear accumulation of 8-hydroxy-2'-deoxyguanosine, a marker of oxidized DNA damage, during aging. *Mutation Research, 316*, 277–285.

Khrapko, K., Bodyak, N., Thilly, W. G., van Orsouw, N. J., Zhang, X., Coller, H. A., Perls, T. T., Upton, M., Vijg, J., & Wei, J. Y. (1999). Cell-by-cell scanning of whole mitochondrial genomes in aged human heart reveals a significant fraction of myocytes with clonally expanded deletions. *Nucleic Acids Research, 27*, 2434–2441.

King, M. P., Koga, Y., Davidson, M., & Schon, E. A. (1992). Defects in mitochondrial protein synthesis and respiratory chain activity segregate with the tRNA(Leu(UUR)) mutation associated with mitochondrial myopathy, encephalopathy, lactic acidosis, and strokelike episodes. *Molecular and Cellular Biology, 12*, 480–490.

Koga, Y., Davidson, M., Schon, E. A., & King, M. P. (1995). Analysis of cybrids harboring MELAS mutations in the mitochondrial tRNA(Leu(UUR)) gene. *Muscle and Nerve, 3*, S119–23.

Kogelnik, A. M., Lott, M. T., Brown, M. D., Navathe, S. B., & Wallace, D. C. (1998). MITOMAP: a human mitochondrial genome database—1998 update. *Nucleic Acids Research, 26*, 112–115.

Kovalenko, S. A., Kopsidas, G., Kelso, J. M., & Linnane, A. W. (1997). Deltoid human muscle mtDNA is extensively rearranged in old age subjects. *Biochemical and Biophysical Research Communications, 232*, 147–152.

Kunishige, M., Mitsui, T., Akaike, M., Shono, M., Kawai, H., & Saito, S. (1996). Localization and amount of myoglobin and myoglobin mRNA in ragged-red fiber of patients with mitochondrial encephalomyopathy. *Muscle and Nerve, 19*, 175–182.

Laderman, K. A., Penny, J. R., Mazzucchelli, F., Bresolin, N., Scarlato, G., & Attardi, G.

(1996). Aging-dependent functional alterations of mitochondrial DNA (mtDNA) from human fibroblasts transferred into mtDNA-less cells. *The Journal of Biological Chemistry, 271*, 15891–15897.

Lamont, P. J., Surtees, R., Woodward, C. E., Leonard, J. V., Wood, N. W., & Harding, A. E. (1998). Clinical and laboratory findings in referrals for mitochondrial DNA analysis. *Archives of Disease in Childhood, 79*, 22–27.

Lee, C. M., Chung, S. S., J. M., K., Weindruch, R., & Aiken, J. M. (1993). Multiple mitochondrial DNA deletions associated with age in skeletal muscle of rhesus monkeys. *Journal of Gerontology Biological Sciences, 48*, B201–B205.

Lee, C. M., Eimon, P., Weindruch, R., & Aiken, J. M. (1994a). Direct repeat sequences are not required at the breakpoints of age-associated mitochondrial DNA deletions in rhesus monkeys. *Mechanisms of Ageing and Development, 75*, 69–79.

Lee, C. M., Lopez, M. E., Weindruch, R., & Aiken, J. M. (1998a). Association of age-related mitochondrial abnormalities with skeletal muscle fiber atrophy. *Free Radical Biology and Medicine, 25*, 964–972.

Lee, C. M., Weindruch, R., & Aiken, J. M. (1997a). Age-associated alterations of the mitochondrial genome. *Free Radical Biology and Medicine, 22*, 1259–1269.

Lee, C. M., Weindruch, R., & Aiken, J. M. (1997b). Age-associated alterations of the mitochondrial genome. *Free Radical Biology and Medicine, 22*, 1259–1269.

Lee, H.-C., Lu, C.-Y., Fahn, H.-J., & Wei, Y.-H. (1998b). Aging- and smoking associated alteration in the relative content of mitochondrial DNA in human lung. *FEBS Letters, 441*, 292–296.

Lee, H.-C., Pang, C.-Y., Hso, H.-S., & Wei, Y.-H. (1994b). Ageing-associated tandem duplications in the D-loop of mitochondrial DNA of human muscle. *FEBS Letters, 354*, 79–83.

Lee, H.-C., Pang, C.-Y., Hsu, H.-S., & Wei, Y.-H. (1994c). Differential accumulations of 4,977 bp deletion in mitochondrial DNA of various tissues in human ageing.

Biochimica et Biophysica Acta, 1226, 37–43.

Lexell, J. (1995). Human aging, musle mass, and fiber type composition. *Journal of Gerontology Series A, 50A,* 11–16.

Li, Y., & Trush, M. A. (1998). Diphenyleneiodonium, an NAD(P)H oxidase inhibitor, also potently inhibits mitochondrial reactive oxygen species production. *Biochemical and Biophysical Research Communications, 253,* 295–299.

Linnane, A. W., Baumer, A., Maxwell, R. J., Preston, H., Zhang, C., & Marzuki, S. (1990). Mitochondrial gene mutation: The ageing process and degenerative diseases. *Biochemistry International, 22,* 1067–1076.

Liu, V. W. S., Zhang, C., & Nagley, P. (1998). Mutations in mitochondrial DNA accumulate differentially in three different human tissues during ageing. *Nucleic Acids Research, 26,* 1268–1275.

Ljungman, M., & Hanawalt, P. C. (1992). Efficient protection against oxidative DNA damage in chromatin. *Molecular Carcinogenesis, 5,* 264–269.

Lopez, M. E., Van Zeeland, N.L., Dahl, D.B., Weindruch, R., & Aiken, J. M. (2000). Cellular phenotypes of age associated skeletal muscle mitochondrial abnormalities in rhesus monkeys. *Mutation Research, 452,* 123–138.

Lu, C.-Y., Lee, H.-C., Fahn, H.-J., & Wei, Y.-H. (1999). Oxidative damage elicited by imbalance of free radicals scavenging enzymes is associated with large-scale mtDNA deletions in aging human skin. *Mutation Research, 423,* 11–21.

Manfredi, G., Servidei, S., Bonilla, E., Shanske, S., Schon, E. A., DiMauro, S., & Moraes, C. T. (1995). High levels of mitochondrial DNA with an unstable 260-bp duplication in a patient with a mitochondrial myopathy. *Neurology, 45,* 762–768.

Marchington, D. R., Barlow, D., & Poulton, J. (1999). Transmitochondrial mice carrying resistance to chloramphenicol on mitochondrial DNA: Developing the first mouse model of mitochondrial DNA disease. *Nature Medicine, 5,* 957–960.

Matthews, P. M., Squier, M. V., Chalk, C., & Donaghy, M. (1995). Mitochondrial abnormalities are not invariably present in neurologic syndromes associated with multiple symmetric lipomatosis. *Neurology, 45,* 197–198.

Mecocci, P., MacGarvey, U., Kaufman, A. E., Koontz, D., Shoffner, J. M., Wallace, D. C., & Beal, M. F. (1993). Oxidative damage to mitochondrial DNA shows marked age-dependent increases in human brain. *Annals of Neurology, 34,* 609–616.

Melov, S., Shoffner, J. M., Kaufman, A., & Wallace, D. C. (1995). Marked increase in the number and variety of mitochondrial DNA rearrangements in aging human skeletal muscle. *Nucleic Acids Research, 23,* 4122–4126.

Michikawa, Y., Mazzucchelli, F., Bresolin, N., Scarlato, G., & Attardi, G. (1999). Aging-dependent large accumulation of point mutations in the human mtDNA control region for replication. *Science, 286,* 774–779.

Mita, S., Rizzuto, R., Moraes, C. T., Shanske, S., Arnaudo, E., Fabrizi, G. M., Koga, Y., DiMauro, S., & Schon, E. A. (1990). Recombination via flanking direct repeats is a major cause of large-scale deletions of human mitochondrial DNA. *Nucleic Acids Research, 18,* 561–567.

Mita, S., Schmidt, B., Schon, E. A., DiMauro, S., & Bonilla, E. (1989). Detection of "deleted" mitochondrial genomes in cytochrome-c oxidase-deficient muscle fibers of a patient with Kearns-Sayre syndrome. *Proceedings of the National Academy of Sciences of the USA, 86,* 9509–9513.

Monici, M. C. (1998). Apoptosis in metabolic myopathies. *Neuroreport, 9,* 2431–2435.

Moraes, C. T., DiMauro, S., Zeviani, M., Lombes, A., Shanske, S., Miranda, A. F., Nakase, H., Bonilla, E., Werneck, L. C., Servidei, S., Nonaka, I., Koga, Y., Spiro, A. J., Brownell, A. K. W., Schmidt, B., Schotland, D. L., Zupanc, M., DeVivo, D. C., Schon, E. A., & Rowland, L. P. (1989). Mitochondrial DNA deletions in progressive external ophthalmoplegia and Kearns-Sayre syndrome. *New England Journal of Medicine, 320,* 1293–1299.

Moraes, C. T., Ricci, E., Petruzzella, V., Shanske, S., DiMauro, S., Schon, E. A., & Bonilla, E. (1992). Molecular analysis of the muscle pathology associated with mitochondrial DNA deletions. *Nature Genetics, 1,* 359–367.

Morrison, J. H., & Hof, P. R. (1997). Life and death of neurons in the aging brain. *Science, 278,* 412–418.

Mueller-Hoecker, J., Pongratz, D., & Hubner, G. (1983). Focal deficiency of cytochrome-c-oxidase in skeletal muscle of patients with progressive external ophthalmoplegia. *Virchows Archiv, 402,* 61–71.

Mueller-Hoecker, J., Seibel, P., Schneiderbanger, K., & Kadenbach, B. (1993). Different *in situ* hybridization patterns of mitochondrial DNA in cytochrome c oxidase-deficient extraocular muscle fibers in the elderly. *Virchows Archiv, 422,* 7–15.

Muenscher, C., Rieger, T., Mueller-Hoecker, J., & Kadenbach, B. (1993). The point mutation of mitochondrial DNA characteristic for MERRF disease is found also in healthy people of different ages. *FEBS, 317,* 27–30.

Nass, M. M. K. (1969). Mitochondrial DNA II. Structure and physicochemical properties of isolated DNA. *Journal of Molecular Biology, 42,* 529–545.

Negrier, M. M., Coquet, M., Moretto, B., Lacut, J.-Y., Dupon, M., Bloch, B., Lestienne, P., & Vital, C. (1998). Partial triplications of mtDNA in maternally transmitted diabetes mellitus and deafness. *American Journal of Human Genetics, 63,* 1227–1232.

Nissenkorn, A., Zeharia, A., Lev, D., Fatal-Valevski, A., Barash, V., Gutman, A., Harel, S., & Lerman-Sagie, T. (1999). Multiple presentation of mitochondrial disorders. *Archives of Disease in Childhood, 81,* 209–215.

Ohkoshi, N., Mizusawa, H., Shiraiwa, N., Shoji, S., Harada, K., & Yoshizawa, K. (1995). Superoxide dismutases of muscle in mitochondrial encephalomyopathies. *Muscle and Nerve, 18,* 1265–1271.

Olivetti, G., Melissari, M., Capasso, J. M., & Anversa, P. (1991). Cardiomyopathy of the aging human heart. Myocyte loss and reactive cellular hypertrophy. *Circulation Research, 68,* 1560–1568.

Pallotti, F., Chen, X., Bonilla, E., & Schon, E. A. (1996). Evidence that specific mtDNA point mutations may not accumulate in skeletal muscle during normal human aging. *American Journal of Human Genetics, 59,* 591–602.

Piko, L., Hougham, A. J., & Bulpitt, K. J. (1988). Studies of sequence heterogeneity of mitochondrial DNA from rat and mouse tissues: Evidence for an increased frequency of deletions/additions with aging. *Mechanisms of Ageing and Development, 43,* 279–293.

Pinz, K., & Bogenhagen, D. F. (1998). Efficient repair of abasic sites in DNA by mitochondrial enzymes. *Molecular and Cellular Biology, 18,* 1257–1265.

Pinz, K., Shibutani, S., & Bogenhagen, D. F. (1995). Action of mitochondrial DNA polymerase gamma at sites of base loss or oxidative damage. *Journal of Biological Chemistry, 270,* 9202–9206.

Porteous, W. K., James, A. M., Sheard, P. W., Porteous, C. M., Packer, M. A., Hyslop, S. J., Melton, J. V., Pang, C. Y., Wei, Y. H., & Murphy, M. P. (1998). Bioenergetic consequences of accumulating the common 4977-bp mitochondrial DNA deletion. *European Journal of Biochemistry, 257,* 192–201.

Poulton, J., Deadman, M. E., & Gardiner, R. M. (1989). Duplications of mitochondrial DNA in mitochondrial myopathy. *Lancet, 1,* 961.

Prelle, A., Fagiolari, G., Checcarelli, N., Moggio, M., Battistel, A., Comi, G. P., Bazzi, P., Bordoni, A., Zeviani, M., & Scarlato, G. (1994). Mitochondrial myopathy: Correlation between oxidative defect and mitochondrial DNA deletions at single fiber level. *Acta Neuropathologica, 87,* 371–376.

Raha, S., Merante, F., Shoubridge, E., Myint, A. T., Tein, I., Benson, L., Johns, T., & Robinson, B. H. (1999). Repopulation of rho0 cells with mitochondria from a patient with a mitochondrial DNA point mutation in tRNA(Gly) results in respiratory chain dysfunction. *Human Mutation, 13,* 245–254.

Richter, C. (1997). Reactive oxygen and nitrogen species regulate mitochondrial Ca^{2+} homeostasis and respiration. *Bioscience Reports, 17,* 53–66.

Richter, C., Park, J. W., & Ames, B. N. (1988). Normal oxidative damage to mitochondrial and nuclear DNA is extensive. *Proceedings of the National Academy of Sciences of the USA, 85,* 6465–6467.

Rusanen, H., Majamaa, K., & Hassinen, I. E. (2000). Increased activities of antioxidant enzymes and decreased ATP concentration in cultured myoblasts with the 3243A→G mutation in mitochondrial DNA. *Biochimica et Biophysica Acta, 1500,* 10–16.

Sancho, S., Moraes, C. T., Tanji, K., & Miranda, A. F. (1992). Structural and functional mitochondrial abnormalities associated with high levels of paritally deleted mitochondrial DNAs in somatic cell hybrids. *Somatic Cell and Molecular Genetics, 18,* 431–442.

Schon, E. A., Rizzuto, R., Moraes, C. T., Nakase, H., Zeviani, M., & DiMauro, S. (1989). A direct repeat is a hotspot for large-scale deletion of human mitochondrial DNA. *Science, 244,* 346–349.

Schwarze, S. R., Lee, C. M., Chung, S. S., Roecker, E. B., Weindruch, R., & Aiken, J. M. (1995). High levels of mitochondrial DNA deletions in skeletal muscle of old rhesus monkeys. *Mechanisms of Ageing and Development, 83,* 91–101.

Sciacco, M., Bonilla, E., Schon, E. A., DiMauro, S., & Moraes, C. T. (1994). Distribution of wild-type and common deletion forms of mtDNA in normal and respiration-deficient muscle fibers from patients with mitochondrial myopathy. *Human Molecular Genetics, 3,* 13–19.

Shigenaga, M. K., Park, J. W., Cundy, K. C., Gimeno, C. J., & Ames, B. N. (1990). In vivo oxidative DNA damage: Measurement of 8-hydroxy-2'-deoxyguanosine in DNA and urine by high-performance liquid chromatography with electrochemical detection. *Methods in Enzymology, 186,* 521–530.

Shoffner, J. M., & Wallace, D. C. (1994). Oxidative phosphorylation diseases and mitochondrial DNA mutations: Diagnosis and treatment. *Annual Review of Nutrition, 14,* 535–568.

Shoffner, J. M., Lott, M. T., Voljavec, A. S., Soueidan, S. A., Costigan, D. A., & Wallace, D. C. (1989). Spontaneous Kearns-Sayre/chronic external ophthalmoplegia plus syndrome associated with a mitochondrial DNA deletion: A slip-replication model and metabolic therapy. *Proceedings of the National Academy of Sciences of the USA, 86,* 7952–7956.

Shoubridge, E. A., Karpati, G., & Hastings, K. E. M. (1990). Deletion mutants are functionally dominant over wild-type mitochondrial genomes in skeletal muscle fiber segments in mitochondrial disease. *Cell, 62,* 43–49.

Simon, D. K., & Johns, D. R. (1999). Mitochondrial disorders: Clinical and genetic features. *Annual Review of Medicine, 50,* 111–127.

Simonetti, S., Chen, X., DiMauro, S., & Schon, E. A. (1992). Accumulation of deletions in human mitochondrial DNA during normal aging: Analysis by quantitative PCR. *Biochimica et Biophysica Acta, 1180,* 113–122.

Sohal, R. S., Agarwal, S., Candas, M., Forster, M. J., & Lal, H. (1994). Effect of age and caloric restriction on DNA oxidative damage in different tissues of C57BL/6 mice. *Mechanisms of Ageing and Development, 76,* 215–224.

Souza-Pinto, N. C., Croteau, D. L., Hudson, E. K., Hansford, R. G., & Bohr, V. A. (1999). Age-associated increase in 8-oxodeoxyguanosine glycosylase/AP lyase activity in rat mitochondria. *Nucleic Acids Research, 27,* 1935–1942.

Sugiyama, S., Hattori, K., Hayakawa, M., & Ozawa, T. (1991). Quantitative analysis of age-associated accumulation of mitochondrial DNA with deletion in human hearts. *Biochemical and Biophysical Research Communications, 180,* 894–899.

Taanman, J. W. (1997). Human cytochrome c oxidase: structure, function, and deficiency. *Journal of Bioenergetics and Biomembranes, 29,* 151–163.

Tengan, C. H., & Moraes, C. T. (1998). Duplication and triplication with staggered breakpoints in human mitochondrial DNA. *Biochimica et Biophysica Acta, 1406,* 73–80.

Thyagarajan, B., Padua, R. A., & Campbell, C. (1996). Mammalian mitochondria possess homologous DNA recombination activity. *Journal of Biological Chemistry, 271,* 27536–27543.

Trounce, I., Neill, S., & Wallace, D. C. (1994). Cytoplasmic transfer of the mtDNA nt 8993 T→G (ATP6) point mutation associated with Leigh syndrome into mtDNA-less cells demonstrates cosegregation with a decrease in state III respiration and ADP/O ratio. *Proceedings of the National Academy of Sciences of the USA, 91,* 8334–8338.

van den Ouweland, J. M., Maechler, P., Wollheim, C. B., Attardi, G., & Maassen, J. A. (1999). Functional and morphological abnormalities of mitochondria harbouring the tRNA(Leu)(UUR) mutation in mitochondrial DNA derived from patients with maternally inherited diabetes and deafness (MIDD) and progressive kidney disease. *Diabetologia, 42,* 485–492.

Vazquez-Memije, M. E., Shanske, S., Santorelli, F. M., Kranz-Eble, P., DeVivo, D. C., & DiMauro, S. (1998). Comparative biochemical studies of ATPases in cells from patients with the T8993G or T8993C mitochondrial DNA mutations. *Journal of Inherited Metabolic Disease, 21,* 829–836.

Walker, U. A., & Schon, E. A. (1998). Neurotrophin–4 is up-regulated in ragged-red fibers associated with pathogenic mitochondrial DNA mutations. *Annals of Neurology, 43,* 536–540.

Wallace, D. C. (1999). Mitochondrial diseases in man and mouse. *Science, 283,* 1482–1488.

Wanagat, J., Cao, Z., Pathare, P., & Aiken, J. M. (2001). Mitochondiral DNA deletion mutations colocalize with segmental electron transport system abnormalities, muscle fiber atrophy, fiber splitting, and oxidative damage in sarcopenia, *FASEB Journal,* in press.

Wei, Y. H., Pang, C. Y., You, B. J., & Lee, H. C. (1996). Tandem duplications and large-scale deletions of mitochondrial DNA are early molecular events of human aging process. *Annals of the New York Academy of Sciences, 15,* 82–101.

Weindruch, R., & Sohal, R. S. (1997). Caloric intake and aging. *The New England Journal of Medicine, 337,* 986.

Yamamoto, M., & Nonaka, I. (1988). Skeletal muscle pathology in chronic progressive external ophthalmoplegia with ragged-red fibers. *Acta Neuropathologica, 76,* 558–563.

Yowe, D. L., & Ames, B. N. (1998). Quantitation of age-related mitochondrial DNA deletions in rat tissues shows that their pattern of accumulation differs from that in humans. *Gene, 209,* 23–30.

Zeviani, M., Moraes, C. T., DiMauro, S., Nakase, H., Bonilla, E., Schon, E. A., & Rowland, L. P. (1988). Deletions of mitochondrial DNA in Kearns Sayre syndrome. *Neurology, 38,* 1339–1346.

Zhang, C., Baumer, A., Maxwell, R. J., Linnane, A. W., & Nagley, P. (1992). Multiple mitochondrial DNA deletions in an elderly human individual. *FEBS, 297,* 34–38.

Zhang, C., Bills, M., Quigley, A., Maxwell, R. J., Linnane, A. W., & Nagley, P. (1997). Varied prevalence of age-associated mitochondrial DNA deletions in different species and tissues: A comparison between human and rat. *Biochemical and Biophysical Research Communications, 230,* 630–635.

Zhang, C., Linnane, A. W., & Nagley, P. (1993). Occurrence of a particular base substitution (3243 A to G) in mitochondrial DNA of tissues of ageing humans. *Biochemical and Biophysical Research Communications, 195,* 1104–1110.

Zhang, C., Liu, V. W. S., Addessi, C. L., Sheffield, D. A., Linnane, A. W., & Nagley, P. (1998). Differential occurrence of mutations in mitochondrial DNA of human skeletal muscle during aging. *Human Mutation, 11,* 360–371.

Six

Effect of Age on Gene Expression

Eun-Soo Han, Holly Van Remmen, Mark Steinhelper, Mohammad A. Pahlavani,
J. Randy Strong, and Arlan Richardson

I. Introduction

The regulation of cellular functions in all organisms occurs primarily through gene expression, i.e., the expression of genes coding for proteins that function as biological catalysts or components of cellular structure. Therefore, it is not surprising that the role of gene expression in aging has been studied extensively over the past three decades. These studies have been of two types: studies on the identification of genes that are associated with increased longevity and studies on the effect of aging on the process of gene expression. In this review, we will focus on those studies in which investigators have examined how aging alters the expression of genes. Specifically, we will describe how aging affects the transcription of genes and the synthesis of proteins. Davies and Grune (Chapter 2, this volume) and Gafni (Chapter 3, this volume) review the effect of aging on protein turnover/degradation in this volume. Over the past decade, a number of review articles have been published on aging and various aspects of gene

expression (Danner & Holbrook, 1990; Papaconstantinou et al., 1996; Levine & Stadtman, 1996; Johnson & Finch, 1996; Van Remmen et al., 1995). Therefore, we will not attempt a comprehensive review of all of the literature in this area. Rather, we will concentrate those areas of gene expression on which most of the research on aging has focused and in which there is agreement on how the processes are affected by aging.

II. Transcription

The initial studies on the effect of age on transcription in the 1960s and 1970s measured RNA synthesis in various tissues/cells from young and old organisms by the incorporation of radioactive precursors into RNA. However, it is not clear how accurately these studies measure RNA synthesis because of the problems in measuring RNA synthesis in whole cells or tissues (Van Remmen et al., 1995). The development of procedures for measuring RNA synthesis in isolated nuclei with radiolabeled nucleotide triphosphates gave investigators a system that they could use to compare accurately the transcriptional activity of tissues from young and old animals. Almost all studies using isolated nuclei have reported an age-related decrease in RNA synthesis of 25–85% (Van Remmen et al., 1995). Although these studies indicate that transcriptional activity decreases with age, the information gained from them is limited because investigators are measuring total RNA synthesis in this system, and rRNA makes up the majority of the RNA synthesized by isolated nuclei.

Interest in the effect of age on rRNA synthesis began in 1972 when Johnson and Strehler reported an age-related decrease in ribosomal genes in several tissues from dogs. They suggested that the decrease in rDNA reduced the synthesis of rRNA to a level that resulted in an insufficient number of ribosomes to support cellular functions. Subsequently, a number of investigators observed a decrease in rRNA synthesis in a variety of mammalian tissues (Richardson et al., 1983; Medvedev, 1986). For example, Richardson et al. (1982) reported that the rate of rRNA synthesis by isolated rat hepatocytes decreased by 40% between 12 and 30 months of age. Although rRNA synthesis appears to decrease with age, other studies indicate that ribosomal genes are not lost with increasing age (Peterson et al., 1984). Peterson et al. (1984) argue that the age-related decrease in rDNA observed in the earlier studies arose because of a reduced hybridization capacity of the DNA, which occurred because proteins were tightly bound to DNA isolated from the old animals. Improved DNA isolation procedures, which eliminated the problems of protein binding to DNA, show no age-related loss of rDNA (Medvedev, 1986). In addition, even though rRNA synthesis decreases with age, the number of ribosomes changes only slightly with age, and it

does not appear that the number of ribosomes is a rate-limiting factor in the age-related decline in protein synthesis (Van Remmen et al., 1995; Rattan, 1996). Therefore, the initial suggestion by Johnson and Strehler (1972) that a loss of ribosomal genes plays a role in aging in mammals is not supported by the current evidence. However, Sinclair and Guarente (1997) report that extrachromosomal rDNA circles accumulate in old yeast cells as a result of the fragmentation of the nucleolus. They propose that this accumulation of rDNA circles is a possible cause of aging in yeast.

It is also important to know how aging affects mRNA, because this macromolecule carries the genetic information from the nucleus to the site of protein synthesis in the cytoplasm. The first studies on the effect of aging on mRNA expression measured the ability of cells to synthesize poly(A) containing RNA. The few studies that have measured the effect of age on mRNA synthesis have reported an age-related decrease in poly(A)+RNA synthesis in the liver (Park & Buetow, 1990; Richardson et al., 1982) and brain (Semsei et al., 1982) of rats. However, the total level of poly(A)+RNA does not appear to change significantly with age (Van Remmen et al., 1995).

A. Effect of Age on mRNA Level

With the advent of DNA recombinant technology in the 1980s, investigators have been able to study how aging alters the levels of individual mRNA transcripts. With the use of probes to specific mRNAs, investigators have measured the levels of mRNA transcripts in tissues from young and old animals. Over the past 15 years, there has been an enormous explosion in the amount of data in this area, and these studies have been described comprehensively in previous reviews (Van Remmen et al., 1995; Danner & Holbrook, 1990;

Papaconstantinou *et al.*, 1996; Levine & Stadtman, 1996; Johnson & Finch, 1996). The data clearly demonstrate that the effect of aging on mRNA levels varies dramatically from transcript to transcript, e.g., some mRNA transcripts increase with age, some decrease, and some do not change significantly. In addition, the effect of age on a specific mRNA transcript may vary from tissue to tissue.

Because of the complexity of many mRNA transcripts within a cell, several approaches have been developed over the past decade to screen cells/tissues for differentially expressed genes, e.g., differential cDNA library screening (plus/minus screening) (Dworkin & David, 1980), subtractive cDNA library screening (Sargent, 1998), differential display by polymerase chain reaction (PCR) (Liang & Pardee, 1992), and serial analysis of gene expression (SAGE) (Velculescu *et al.*, 1995). Although these approaches have been able to detect major alterations in the expression of genes under certain conditions, there have been no published studies using these methods to identify genes that are expressed differentially in aging animals. This appears to be due to the limited sensitivity of these systems. For example, these methods are suitable for identifying five-fold or greater changes in gene expression, e.g., when genes are either turned off or on. However, these systems are inadequate for detecting subtle (e.g., 30–60%) changes in gene expression. The current data on the effect of age on specific mRNA transcripts demonstrate that over 90% of the mRNA transcripts show less than three-fold change with age (Van Remmen *et al.*, 1995; Pahlavani *et al.*, 1994).

With the sequencing of the genome and the advent of high-density array analyses, a powerful technology is now available for monitoring global gene expression: oligonucleotide or cDNA arrays (Ramsay, 1998). By using arrays, one can assess global gene expression in cells/tissues by a technique that is sensitive, quantitative, and rapid. For example, two-fold changes in the levels of mRNA transcripts can be detected, and hundreds, or even thousands, of genes can be screened simultaneously. In addition, the quantification of mRNA levels using cDNA arrays has been reported to be "better than obtained by Northern blotting" (Ramsay, 1998; Schena *et al.*, 1996). The array technology is extremely useful in studying a complex, multigenetic process like aging, where one needs to understand the interaction of a large number of genes. Arrays also allow investigators to study, in a systematic way, the behavior of large groups of functionally related genes as an organism ages. In addition, it will be possible to group genes on the basis of similarities in their expression patterns during aging. Lee *et al.* (1999) was the first group to use arrays to study the effect of aging on gene expression. They analyzed the gene expression profiles of gastrocnemius muscle from 5- and 30-month-old mice by using high-density oligonucleotide arrays containing 6347 genes. Of the genes screened, only 58 genes (0.9%) showed a greater than two-fold increase in expression levels as a function of age, and 55 genes (0.9%) displayed a greater than two-fold decrease in expression. Of the 58 genes that showed increased expression, 16% are involved in stress responses, including the heat-shock factors hsp71 and hsp27, protease Do, and the DNA damage-inducible gene GADD45. Of the 55 genes that displayed a greater than two-fold decrease in expression, 13% are involved in energy metabolism. Lee *et al.* (1999) also showed that most alterations in gene expression by aging were either completely or partially prevented by dietary restriction, an experimental intervention known to attenuate the aging process in laboratory rodents. This report reveals the exciting potential of the array technology; however, there are several limitations of this initial study using arrays to examine gene expression. First, no statistical analysis was performed on the data to demonstrate that the two-fold or greater changes in mRNA levels were significant. This is particularly important because it is well-recognized that the number of false positives increases in relation to the number of comparisons, which are very large in studies using arrays. One of the greatest challenges that investigators face in using arrays to study gene expression was stated aptly by DeRisi *et al.* (1997): "to develop efficient methods for organizing, distributing, interpreting and extracting insights from the large volumes of data these experiments will provide." Second, none of the changes in mRNA levels were validated by an independent method for assaying mRNA levels, e.g., Northern analysis. Whereas high-density arrays hold great promise for analyzing the effect of aging on gene expression at the level of mRNA transcripts, it will be important in the future to have widely accepted standards to guide the analysis and interpretation of the data obtained from arrays.

B. Physiological Importance of Altered mRNA Expression

For changes in the levels of mRNA transcripts to be important physiologically, the level of the protein product encoded by the transcript also must change. Investigators often assume that the changes they observed in an mRNA transcript will be paralleled by similar changes in the protein. Unfortunately, the majority of the studies in which investigators have measured the levels of a specific mRNA transcript have not measured the level (or enzymatic activity) of the protein product (Van Remmen *et al.*, 1995). Most of the studies in which both mRNA and protein expression have been measured show a good correlation between the changes in the two, i.e., the

changes in the mRNA transcripts are physiologically relevant. Examples of how aging alters the expression of four genes are given in Figs. 1–5. These genes were chosen as examples because (1) the effect of age on various steps of expression has been studied in these genes, (2) a number of investigators have studied these genes and there is agreement as to how aging alters the expression of these genes, and (3) dietary restriction alters the age-related changes in the expression of these genes (Pahlavani *et al.*, 1994).

Figure 1 shows the effect of aging on the expression of α_{2u}-globulin in rat liver. α_{2u}-Globulin is synthesized by hepatocytes, secreted into the blood stream, and excreted in the urine of male rats as one of the major urinary proteins. Several laboratories showed that the levels of α_{2u}-globulin mRNA decline dramatically with age (Richardson *et al.*, 1987; Chatterjee *et al.*, 1981, 1989). The data in Fig. 1 show that an excellent correlation is observed between the age-related decline in the level of α_{2u}-globulin mRNA in liver and the synthesis of α_{2u}-globulin by rat hepatocytes. The

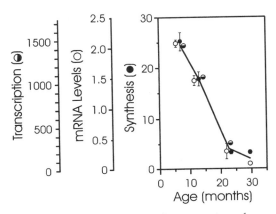

Figure 1. Effect of age on the expression of α_{2u}-globulin. The mRNA levels (O), synthesis (●), and nuclear transcription (◑) of α_{2u}-globulin were measured in hepatocytes isolated from rats of various ages. (Data obtained from Richardson *et al.* (1987). Figure reproduced from Van Remmen *et al.* (1995) with permission.)

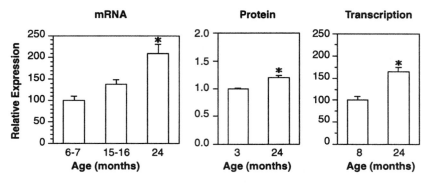

Figure 2. Effect of age on the expression of GFAP in rat brain. The GFAP mRNA levels, protein levels, and nuclear transcription were measured in hippocampus (mRNA and protein levels) and the outer molecular layer of the denate gyrus (nuclear transcription) of the brains of rats of various ages [data taken from Nichols *et al.* (1993), O'Callaghan and Miller (1991), and Yoshida *et al.* (1996)]. * The values for old rats are significantly different from values for young rats at the $p < 0.05$ level.

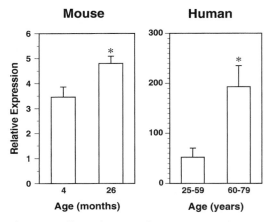

Figure 3. Effect of age on the expression of GFAP mRNA in mouse and human brain. GFAP mRNA levels were measured in the hippocampus from young and old mice and human subjects [data taken from Goss *et al.* (1991) for mice and Nichols *et al.* (1993) for humans]. *The values for the old animals are significantly different from values for young animals at the $p < 0.01$ level.

synthesis and mRNA levels of α_{2u}-globulin decrease by approximately 85% between 5 and 24 months of age (Richardson *et al.*, 1987).

Figures 2 and 3 show the effect of age on the expression of glial fibrillary acidic protein (GFAP) in brain tissue. GFAP is an astrocyte-specific intermediate filament protein that is recognized as a

biomarker of mammalian brain aging because an increase in GFAP has been observed in all species studied (Yoshida *et al.*, 1996; Nichols *et al.*, 1993; Goss *et al.*, 1991; O'Callaghan & Miller, 1991). This increase appears to be independent of pathological changes in the brain. Figures 2 and 3 show that the levels of GFAP mRNA increase by 1.4- to 3-fold in brain tissue from rats, mice, and humans. As Figure 2 shows, an increase in GFAP protein is also observed in the brains of rats.

Figure 4 shows the effect of age on the induction of heat-shock protein 70 (hsp70) expression. hsp70 belongs to the HSP70 class of heat-shock proteins. It is the most heat-inducible heat-shock protein and plays an important role in protecting cells/tissues from heat shock as well as other stresses. Research shows that a decrease in the induction of hsp70 expression by stress has been observed with age in all cells and tissues studied (Heydari *et al.*, 1994; Richardson & Holbrook, 1996). The data in Fig. 4 show that the decreased induction of hsp70 mRNA levels in hepatocytes or lymphocytes from rats is paralleled by a decrease in hsp70 synthesis or hsp70 protein levels. Thus, the age-related decrease in

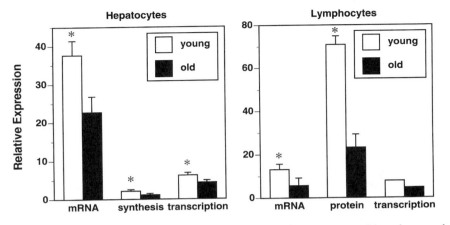

Figure 4. Effect of age on the induction of hsp70 expression in hepatocytes and lymphocytes from rats. Hepatocytes or splenic T-cells isolated from young (6 months) and old (24 months) rats were exposed to a heat shock (42.5°C for 30–60 min), and hsp70 mRNA levels, synthesis (hepatocytes), protein levels (lymphocytes), and nuclear transcription, were measured [data taken from Heydari *et al.* (1993) for hepatocytes and Pahlavani *et al.* (1995a) for lymphocytes]. *The values for old rats were significantly different from the values for the young rats at the $p < 0.05$ level.

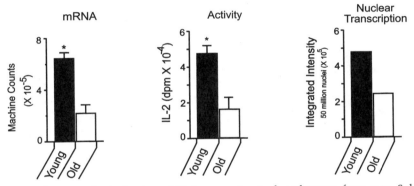

Figure 5. Effect of age on the induction of IL-2 expression in lymphocytes from rats. Splenic T-cells isolated from young (6 months) and old (24 months) rats were stimulated with concanavalin A, and IL-2 mRNA levels, activity, and nuclear transcription were measured [data taken from Pahlavani and Richardson (1996)]. *The values for old rats were significantly different from the values for the young rats at the $p < 0.001$ level.

the ability of cells to express hsp70 mRNA gives rise to less hsp70 protein produced by the cells. This age-related decline in hsp70 expression could be an important factor in aging, because it has become evident that experimental manipulations that lead to an increase in life span are associated with enhanced resistance to a variety of stresses in yeast (Jazwinski, 1999), *Caenorhabditis elegans* (Honda & Honda, 1999),

Drosophila (Lin *et al.*, 1998), rodents (Masoro, 1998), and birds (Masoro & Austad, 1996; Kapahi *et al.*, 1999).

Figure 5 shows data on the effect of age on the expression of interleukin-2 (IL-2). IL-2 is a cytokine that regulates the proliferation and function of various cells involved in cellular and humoral immunity. Almost all studies have reported an age-related decrease in the induction of IL-2 expression by T-cells, and these studies have been performed with cells isolated from rats, mice, and humans (Pahlavani & Richardson, 1996). Figure 5 shows that the mitogenic induction of IL-2 mRNA and IL-2 activity decreases by approximately 50% with age. Because IL-2 plays a critical role in the immune system, the decrease in IL-2 expression is believed to play an important role in the age-related decline in immune function, which is a universal characteristic of aging mammals (Pahlavani & Richardson, 1996).

Although most of the studies show a good correlation between the age-related changes in the levels of mRNA transcripts and their protein products, several studies have shown a discordance in mRNA and protein levels (Van Remmen *et al.*, 1995). Figure 6 shows three examples of such studies. Mooradian *et al.* (1998) observed a 3.5-fold increase in thyroid hormone responsive protein mRNA levels in the cerebral tissue of rats. However, thyroid hormone responsive protein levels decreased two-fold. In studying why thermogenic ability is impaired with age, Yamashita *et al.* (1994) observed that the level of the mRNA transcript for uncoupling protein

in brown adipose issue was 3.6-fold higher in old rats than in young rats. However, the uncoupling protein content in the mitochondria of brown adipose tissue was similar in young and old rats. In contrast, Sonntag *et al.* (1999) observed a decrease (36%) in the levels of insulin-like growth factor 1 (IGF-1) in the brains of rats with age, but no change in the levels of the mRNA transcript in 10- and 31-month-old rats. Thus, in spite of constant levels of IGF-1 mRNA, the cortical IGF-1 protein levels decreased significantly with age. The studies shown in Figure 6 clearly demonstrate that one can observe changes in an mRNA transcript without a similar change in the protein level, and, conversely, one can observe a change in the level of a protein without any change in the mRNA transcript coding for the protein. In other words, investigators cannot automatically assume that the changes they observe in an mRNA transcript with age will result in a similar change in the protein product. Therefore, it is necessary for investigators to measure both mRNA and protein levels to accurately assess the effect of age on the expression of a specific gene.

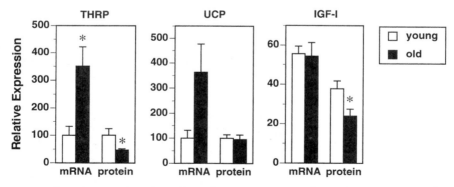

Figure 6. Examples of genes that show discordance in mRNA and protein expression with age. The mRNA and protein levels of thyroid hormone responsive protein (THRP) in the cerebral tissue of 4 and 24-month-old rats are shown [data taken from Mooradian *et al.* (1998)]. The mRNA and protein levels of the uncoupling protein (UCP) in the brown adipose tissue of 3 and 24-month-old rats are shown [data taken from Yamashita *et al.* (1994)]. The mRNA and protein levels of insulin-like growth factor-1 (IGF-1) in the cortex of 10- to 11- and 31- to 32-month-old rats are shown [data taken from Sonntag *et al.* (1999)]. *The values for old rats were significantly different from the values for the young rats at the $p < 0.05$ level.

C. Mechanism(s) for Age-Related Changes in mRNA Levels

The age-related changes in mRNA levels could arise at either the transcriptional or posttranscriptional level. In eukaryotes, mRNA transcripts are synthesized from the DNA template as much larger molecules, hnRNA, by RNA polymerase II. After the hnRNA transcripts are synthesized in the nucleus, they are processed through a series of posttranscriptional steps before mature mRNA appears in the cytoplasm as templates to direct the synthesis of proteins. Because mRNA transcripts are turning-over rapidly, mRNA levels can also be altered posttranscriptionally at the level of mRNA degradation.

1. Transcription of Specific mRNAs

Although there are a large number of studies comparing the levels of mRNA transcripts in young and old animals, only a few studies exist that have measured the effect of aging on both the levels and transcription of specific mRNAs. In an earlier edition of this volume, Danner and Holbrook (1990) concluded that "alterations in rates of transcription of specific mRNAs are not the basis for the observed age-related changes in mRNA levels." However, other reviews of the literature suggest that the age-related changes in the levels of most of the mRNA transcripts, in which transcription has also been measured, are due to an alteration in the transcription of the gene coding for the mRNA (Van Remmen *et al.*, 1995; Papaconstantinou *et al.*, 1996). For example, the changes in the mRNA levels of the four genes shown in Figs. 1–5 are correlated to changes in the rates of transcription, as measured by nuclear runoff assays or with an intronic probe. The level of α_{2u}-globulin mRNA in rat liver decreased by 85% between 5 and 24 months of age, whereas the transcription of α_{2u}-globulin decreased by 80% (Fig. 1). The nuclear transcription of GFAP increased with age in parallel with GFAP mRNA levels (Fig. 2), and the age-related decline in the induction of hsp70 mRNA levels by heat shock in both hepatocytes and lymphocytes from rats was due to a decrease in the transcription of the hsp70 gene (Fig. 4). The mitogenic induction of IL-2 mRNA and transcription was approximately 50% lower in spleen lymphocytes from 24-month-old rats than in 6-month-old rats. However, there are reports in which the levels of mRNA transcripts changed with age, but the nuclear transcription of the gene did not change (Van Remmen *et al.*, 1995; Pahlavani *et al.*, 1994). Because of the difficulty in measuring the transcription of specific genes using the nuclear runoff assay, investigators should be cautious in assuming that the age-related changes in mRNA arise posttranscriptionally unless they clearly demonstrate that either the posttranscriptional processing of hnRNA or mRNA degradation is actually altered.

One area of gene expression that often is ignored in aging studies is whether the age-related changes in the transcription of a gene are due to changes in the number of cells that are expressing the gene. Heydari *et al.* (1993) showed that the age-related decline in the induction of hsp70 was not due to the number of hepatocytes expressing hsp70. The same percentage of hepatocytes isolated from young and old rats expressed hsp70 after a heat shock, even though the expression of hsp70 decreased by over 50%. Therefore, hepatocytes isolated from old rats have a reduced ability to express hsp70. Tajuddin and Druse (1998) showed that aging was accompanied by a decrease in the expression of proenkephalin in the rostral striatum and the shell region of the nucleus accumbens of brains of rats. The decline in proenkephalin mRNA in these two brain regions was caused by a reduction in the number of cells that expressed proenkephalin mRNA. In addition, the percentage of proenkephalin mRNA-containing neurons that express a high amount of proenkephalin mRNA was lower in the rostral striatum of 24-month-old rats. Schiffmann and Vanderhaeghen (1993) studied the age-related decrease in the mRNA coding for adenosine A_2 receptor in the rat striatum. They found that the reduction of adenosine A_2 receptor mRNA mainly was due to neuronal loss. Thus, the decline in the expression of adenosine A_2 receptor in the striatum is not due to alterations in transcription but due to a loss of neuronal cells.

2. Posttranscriptional Processing of hnRNA

Although investigators have speculated that aging might alter the posttranscriptional processing of hnRNA, there are very little data on this area of aging. The effect of age on the posttranscriptional processing of hnRNA has been studied in only two genes: fibronectin and neural cell adhesion molecule (NCAM). By using a reverse transcription–PCR assay, Magnuson *et al.* (1991) initially reported significant changes (4–11%) in the levels of the alternatively spliced transcripts of fibronectin in the tissues of old rats. All three alternatively spliced exons were spliced out at a higher frequency in tissues of 30-month-old rats than 15-month-old rats. However, when Pagani *et al.* (1991, 1992) measured alternative splicing of the fibronectin transcript by the ribonuclease protection assay in various tissues of rats, they did not observe any consistent change in the relative amounts of the alternatively spliced transcripts. Data from Singh and Kanungo (1993) also indicate that posttranscriptional processing on fibronectin does not change with age in rat liver. Wagner *et al.* (1992) studied the posttranscriptional processing of the NCAM gene in the hippocampus and forebrain of rats. They

found that the NCAM mRNA isoforms (7.4, 6.7, 5.2, 4.3, and 2.9 kb) were regulated differentially during development and aging (E15 to 720 days of age). The 7.4- and 6.7-kb isoforms were reduced starting from day 21, and the 4.3-kb isoform, which is E15 and day 1 specific, is replaced with the 5.2-kb isoform starting at day 21. The 5.2-kb isoform remained constant throughout the life span of the rats. The 2.9-kb isoform, which was expressed abundantly at E15 and early postnatal stages, remained constant between 180 and 720 days. Thus, it does not appear that any major alterations occur with age in the integrity of the cellular machinery responsible for the posttranscriptional processing of hnRNA.

3. Degradation/Stability of mRNA

The early studies showing that poly(A)⁺RNA synthesis decreases with age in liver (Park & Buetow, 1990; Richardson *et al.*, 1982), whereas the levels of poly(A)⁺RNA do not change significantly (Birchenall-Sparks *et al.*, 1985; Horbach *et al.*, 1984; Moudgil *et al.*, 1979), suggested that the degradation of poly(A)⁺RNA declines with age. In 1980, Moore *et al.* measured the half-life of poly(A)⁺RNA in livers of 3- and 30-month-old rats. They observed an over four-fold increase in the half-life of poly(A)⁺RNA in the old rats. As investigators have begun to measure the degradation of specific mRNA transcripts, it has become evident that the half-life of an mRNA transcript varies considerably from transcript to transcript. It appears that both *cis*-acting elements in the 3′-untranslated region (UTR) of a number of mRNAs and *trans*-acting factors interact to regulate mRNA turnover. The first *cis*-acting sequence shown to impact message stability was the AU-rich element (ARE), which consists of multiple AUUA sequence motifs. It was found to be present in the 3′-UTR of a number of rapidly degraded transcripts coding for cytokines and protooncogenes, e.g., c-*fos* and granulocyte monophage colony-stimulating factor (Wilson & Brewer, 1999). Highly stable transcripts from a number of genes have been shown to contain a poly(C)-rich consensus sequence in the 3'-UTR, e.g., the tyrosine hydroxylase mRNA transcript (Czyzyk-Krzeska *et al.*, 1997). Exposure of PC12 cells, a cell line derived from the rat adrenal medulla, to reduced oxygen (hypoxia) has been shown to increase the half-life of tyrosine hydroxylase mRNA, and this increase was associated with increased binding of an RNA-binding protein to the 3'-UTR of the tyrosine hydroxylase message (Czyzyk-Krzeska & Beresh, 1996; Czyzyk-Krzeska *et al.*, 1994a, b, 1997). Mutations in 3'-UTR sequences blocked both the stabilizing effect of hypoxia on tyrosine hydroxylase mRNA and RNA–protein binding (Czyzyk-Krzeska *et al.*, 1997).

Heydari *et al.* (1993) measured the degradation/half-life of hsp70 mRNA by blocking RNA synthesis with actinomycin D. They reported a two-fold increase in the half-life of hsp70 mRNA in hepatocytes isolated from 25-month-old rats compared to those from 6-month old rats. By using actinomycin D, Pucci *et al.* (1998) measured the degradation of IL-2 mRNA in CD4+ T-cells from young (3 months) and old (19–20 months) mice. They reported that the IL-2 transcript was more stable in cells from young mice than from old mice.

At the present time, our greatest insight into how the aging process affects mRNA degradation comes from the tyrosine hydroxylase gene. Tyrosine hydroxylase is the rate-limiting enzyme in the catecholamine biosynthetic pathway. Circulating catecholamines play a major integrative role in maintaining physiological homeostasis. The principal source of circulating catecholamines is the adrenal medulla. Age-related increases in plasma catecholamine levels and turnover in

humans and laboratory animals have been reported consistently, both at rest and in response to stress (Fleg *et al.*, 1985; Esler *et al.*, 1981; Hoeldtke & Cilme, 1985; Morrow *et al.*, 1987; Veith *et al.*, 1986). Moreover, increased turnover of peripheral catecholamines has been implicated in the development and possible maintenance of hypertension in humans and in several experimental models (Ito *et al.*, 1986; Okamoto & Aoki, 1963; Westfall & Meldrum, 1985). Thus, the age-related increase in turnover of circulating catecholamines may contribute to the increased incidence of hypertension associated with aging (Tuck, 1989). Strong *et al.* (1990) showed that tyrosine hydroxylase mRNA increased linearly by three-fold in the adrenal medulla of rats between 2 and 24 months of age. This observation subsequently was confirmed by other laboratories (Kedzierski & Porter 1990; Kuchel *et al.*, 1997; Voogt *et al.*, 1990; Tumer *et al.*, 1992). As shown in Fig. 7, subsequent studies by Strong's group have shown that the increased tyrosine hydroxylase mRNA during aging was not associated with a significant increase in transcription; in fact, the transcription of the tyrosine hydroxylase gene decreased with age, as measured by nuclear run-on assays (Fernandez *et al.*, 1998). Other studies by Strong and his colleagues have shown that, during continuous stimulation of selected physiologically relevant receptors on adrenal chromaffin cells, the tyrosine hydroxylase message could be maintained for days in the absence of increased gene transcription, despite the fact that the half-life of the mRNA is only 3–6 hr (Corbitt *et al.*, 1998). Taken together, these data provide evidence that the tyrosine hydroxylase gene is regulated at the level of transcript degradation in a physiologically relevant context and suggest that the age-related increase in the tyrosine hydroxylase transcript is due to an alteration in the degradation/half-

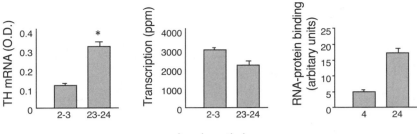

Age (months)

Figure 7. Effect of age on adrenal tyrosine hydroxylase mRNA content, gene transcription, and RNA-protein binding to the mRNA 3'-UTR. The levels of tyrosine hydroxylase mRNA were obtained from slot blots of at least four concentrations (0.06–4.0 mg) of total cellular RNA from each animal. The relative transcription rate of the gene for tyrosine hydroxylase was calculated from nuclear run-on assays as the difference in the radioactivity hybridized to filters with and without the tyrosine hydroxylase genomic probe. The amount of radioactivity bound to the filter was divided by the total amount of radioactivity added to the hybridization reaction (input cpm) and was expressed as parts per million (ppm). For the RNA–protein binding assay, cytoplasmic extracts of adrenal medullae from each animal were incubated with radiolabeled sequences of the 3'-UTR of tyrosine hydroxylase mRNA, incubated with RNAse T1 to digest unprotected RNA, and separated by polyacrylamide gel electrophoresis. Values for RNA–protein binding represent the volume density of bands corresponding to RNA–protein bound to 3'-UTR mRNA sequences. Each value represents the mean ± SEM of four animals.

life of the transcript. Strong's laboratory measured RNA–protein binding to radiolabelled transcripts of the 3'-untranslated region of the tyrosine hydroxylase mRNA using the mobility shift assay. They observed a three-fold increase in RNA–protein binding with age (Fig. 7). This increase in RNA–protein binding with age is identical to the three-fold increase in tyrosine hydroxylase mRNA levels observed in the adrenal glands of animals. Because RNA-protein binding has been shown to be related to tyrosine hydroxylase mRNA stability in a rat adrenal chromaffin cell line, it is reasonable to conclude that the increase in protein binding in the adrenal medulla of old rats is related to the increased tyrosine hydroxylase mRNA steady-state levels that are observed with age.

D. Mechanism(s) for the Age-Related Changes in Transcription

Transcription is regulated through the integrated interaction between *trans*-acting factors (polypeptides) and *cis*-

acting sequences in the promoter region of the gene and enhancer sequences, which are orientation-independent and can be located at significant distances from the gene. The regulation of gene transcription requires the recognition of specific DNA sequences by transcription factors that form a complex with RNA polymerase II to initiate the synthesis of RNA. RNA polymerase II cannot bind to the DNA directly and requires transcription factors to form a complex. The assembly of the transcription complex requires that the DNA in the chromatin be accessible to the transcription factors, RNA polymerase II, and the progression of the RNA polymerase II along the DNA. There is no evidence that RNA polymerase II activity changes with age (Van Remmen *et al.*, 1995). For example, an early study by Benson and Harker (1978) showed that the activities of purified RNA polymerase II from mouse liver and brain were similar for 18- and 31-month-old mice. Therefore, age-related changes in chromatin structure and transcription factors could be responsible for the alterations in transcription that are observed with increasing age.

1. Changes in Chromatin Structure

Chromatin consists of the DNA duplex wrapped around a series of histone octamers to form nucleosomes. Early studies on the effect of age on the histone content of DNA generally concluded that the content of the nucleosome core histones in chromatin did not change with age, although several reports indicate that the percentage of H1 histone, which is associated with the linker region of the nucleosome structure, changed with age (Rothstein & Seifert, 1981; Richardson et al., 1983; Medvedev, 1984). It is possible that modifications to the nucleosome such as histone acetylation might influence transcriptional activity. For example, acetylation of histones appears to be increased in regions of the DNA containing actively transcribed genes, and several studies in the 1970s indicated that histone acetylation decreases with age (Richardson et al., 1983). The age-related decline in histone acetylation might play a role in gene expression by reducing the binding of transcription factors to cis-acting sequences on genes. This is supported by the study of Lee et al. (1993), showing that acetylation of the N-terminal tails of the core histones facilitated the binding of the transcription factor TFIIIA to a model gene. Guarente's laboratory analysis of two mutations in the Sir2 gene suggests that nicotinamide adenine dinucleotide (NAD) histone deacetylase is involved in the extension of life span in yeast. The Sir2 genes encode NAD-dependent histone deacetylases that are components of heterochromatin, silence transcription at silent mating loci, telomeres, and rDNA, and suppress recombination in rDNA (Imai et al., 2000). Thus, histone acetylation might play an important role in aging; however, more defini-

tive studies are necessary to show that changes in histone acetylation are responsible for changes in gene expression or genome stability that could contribute to aging.

DNA transcription requires that the DNA to become unwound, allowing RNA polymerase II access to the transcription start site. The structure of actively transcribed genes therefore is relatively more exposed and can be measured by the increased susceptibility of chromatin to digestion with DNase I. The most sensitive regions of DNA to DNase I digestion represent hypersensitive sites in which the DNA is exposed and not organized in the regular nucleosome structure. The majority of chromatin is relatively resistant to DNase I and contains nonexpressed genes and other sequences not transcribed. Therefore, the sensitivity of chromatin to nuclease digestion is an indicator of actively expressed areas of the genome. Initial studies on the sensitivity of chromatin to nuclease digestion with age reported no age-related change in the sensitivity of liver chromatin from mice to digestion with either DNase I, DNase II, or micrococcal nuclease (Hill & Whelan, 1978; Gaubatz et al., 1979a, b). However, studies in liver and brain reported that chromatin from old mice was less susceptible to nuclease digestion than chromatin from young mice (Tas, et al., 1980; Tas & Walford, 1982; Berkowitz et al., 1983). However, chromatin from cerebral neuroglial cells showed no age-related change in sensitivity to nuclease digestion. The rate of DNase I digestion of chromatin from the cerebral hemispheres of rats has been shown to decrease with age (Chaturvedi & Kanungo, 1985). Singh et al. (1990) reported that the DNase I hypersensitive site in the albumin gene in liver becomes less sensitive to DNase I digestion with age. A decrease in the sensitivity of chromatin to nuclease digestion with age suggests that chromatin might become more condensed, which could alter the accessibility to the transcriptional apparatus.

DNA methylation (5-methylcytosine, 5mC) is another factor that has been proposed to play a role in the regulation of transcription (Cedar, 1988). The methyl group on cytosine is located in the DNA at a position that potentially can interact with other factors to regulate transcription. In certain genes, decreased methylation, or hypomethylation, has been correlated to increased gene expression, and increased methylation, or hypermethylation, has been correlated to decreased gene expression. Several studies have reported that global demethylation of DNA occurs with age in tissues from rats (Rath & Kanungo, 1989; Thakur & Kaur, 1992a), mice (Singhal *et al.*, 1987; Wilson *et al.*, 1987; Tawa *et al.*, 1992; Miyamura *et al.*, 1993), and humans (Drinkwater *et al.*, 1989; Wilson *et al.*, 1987; Tawa *et al.*, 1992). In addition, specific genes have also been reported to become demethylated with age, e.g., β-actin and c-*myc* (Slagboom *et al.*, 1990; Ono *et al.*, 1989). However, there is also evidence for hypermethylation with age in repetitive DNA sequences in rat brain (Rath & Kanungo, 1989) and in the c-*fos* gene in liver (Ono *et al.*, 1993). In addition, significant increases in promoter-associated CpG island methylation have been shown to occur with age (Issa *et al.*, 1994, 1996). Therefore, both methylation and demethylation have been reported with age; however, demethylation appears to be the predominant pattern.

Evidence for changes in DNA methylation playing a role in aging comes from studies on cellular senescence. Several studies have shown a progressive loss of 5mC residues from the genome of human fibroblasts with increasing passage number (Wilson & Jones, 1983). In contrast, incubation of human fibroblasts with 5-azacytidine, a compound that inhibits the methylation of cytosine in DNA and results in the hypomethylation of DNA, shortens the *in vitro* life span of human fibroblasts (Holliday, 1986; Fairweather *et al.*, 1987; Weller *et al.*, 1993). These results agree with the *in vivo* study of Wilson *et al.* (1987), which found that the rate of 5mC loss from DNA of the mucosa of the small intestine of mice (*Mus musculus*) was approximately twice as high as the rate of 5mC loss for DNA from the same cells of *Peromyscus leucopus*, which has a life span twice as long as *Mus musculus*, suggesting a correlation between the loss of 5mC residues from the genome and life span.

Although many studies have shown age-related changes in DNA methylation, the functional significance of these changes is not clear. A few studies have measured both methylation and gene expression to determine whether changes in methylation were functionally significant. For example, Singh *et al.* (1990) found an age-related increase in the methylation of the albumin gene in rat liver that was correlated to a decrease in the transcription of albumin. However, Horbach *et al.* (1984) did not observe any age-related changes in albumin transcription in rat liver. Swisshelm *et al.* (1990) found that the methylation of rRNA genes increased with age and was correlated to a decrease in the transcription of rRNA genes that could be reactivated after 5-azacytidine treatment. Slagboom *et al.* (1990) observed an age-related decrease in the methylation of the β-actin gene and an increase in β-actin expression in the spleen of rats. Whereas these studies would support the view that hypermethylation during aging results in reduced expression and that hypomethylation is correlated to an increased expression of genes, several other studies have found no correlation between age-related changes in methylation and gene expression (Slagboom *et al.*, 1990; Gaubatz *et al.*, 1991). Although it is possible that age-related changes in DNA methylation might alter the expression of specific genes, there is no evidence demonstrating that the age-related change in the transcription of a gene is due to alterations in DNA methylation.

2. Changes in Transcription Factors

The study of the role of transcription factors in the regulation of gene expression is one of the most actively studied areas of research in the field of aging. Over the past eight years, there have been a large number of studies in which age-related changes in a wide range of transcription factors have been studied, and these studies have been described comprehensively in previous reviews (Van Remmen et al., 1995; Papaconstantinou et al., 1996). In this review, we will focus on the most studied transcription factors (AP-1, NF-κB, and HSF1) and two transcription factors (NFAT and HSF1) that have been shown to play a fundamental role in the age-related changes in the expression of specific genes. Table I lists all of the reports in which the effect of age has been studied on these four transcription factors. The effect of aging on the DNA-binding activities of AP-1 and NF-κB varies considerably depending on the cell or tissue type. This is not unexpected because aging most likely affects diverse cells/tissues differently. On the other hand, the data on the effect of aging on HSF1 binding to DNA are sticking, in that all studies show a decrease in HSF1 binding activity with age; this has been observed in a wide variety of cells/tissues from rodents of different ages, as well as in cell cultures during cell senescence. In other words, the effect of aging on the DNA-binding activitiy of HSF1 appears to be universal.

a. Activator Protein-1 (AP-1). The AP-1 DNA-binding sequence was first identified in 1987, and it was found that members of the Fos and Jun families make up the proteins that bind to the AP-1 element (Papaconstantinou et al., 1996). The Jun family of polypeptides can form homo- or heterodimers that have AP-1 binding activity; however, the homodimers have a relatively low binding affinity. The Fos family of polypeptides cannot form homodimers, but can interact with the jun polypeptides to form heterodimers, which have high binding affinity for the AP-1 element. The fos and jun polypeptides (and, therefore, the AP-1 binding activity) are induced by a variety of agents, e.g., intrinsic factors such as polypeptide hormones, cytokines, growth factors, and neurotransmitters and extrinsic factors such as ultraviolet irradiation, DNA-damaging agents, phorbol esters, and oxidative stress. The signaling pathway that regulates AP-1 activity involves membrane-associated tyrosine kinases, protein kinase C, Ha-Ras, and the mitogen-activated kinases. Interest in AP-1 and aging was stimulated initially by the report of Seshadri and Campisi (1990), showing that the ability of late passage fibroblasts to induce fos expression was reduced dramatically compared to early passage fibroblasts. Table 1 lists all of the studies in which AP-1 binding activity has been measured as a function of age. All of the reports in which AP-1 binding activity has been studied during cellular senescence in human fibroblasts have reported a decrease in activity in late passage cells. However, during aging *in vivo*, the induction of AP-1 binding activity by serum addition was increased in fibroblasts from old humans compared to younger humans (Grassilli et al., 1996). Studies with lymphocytes from rats, mice, and humans have shown a significant age-related decrease in the mitogenic induction of AP-1 DNA binding activity. However, in other tissues of rodents, no clear trend is observed with respect to aging and AP-1 DNA binding activity. Pahlavani's laboratory (Pahlavani &

Table I.
Effect of Age on Transcription Factors

Tissue	Ages studied	Change with age	Reference
AP-1 Binding Activity			
Mice			
Splenocytes	3 and 18–20 months	Decrease (basal)	Sikora *et al.*, 1992
Splenocytes	3 and 18–20 months	Decrease (induced)	Sikora *et al.*, 1992
Heart	4 and 24 months	No change	Helenius *et al.*, 1996b
Rats			
Brain	4 and 30 months	No change	Ammendola *et al.*, 1992
Hippocampus (basal)	4 and 24 months	No change	Kaminska & Kaczmarek, 1993
Hippocampus (induced)	4 and 24 months	Increase	Kaminska & Kaczmarek, 1993
Frontal cortex and Hippocampus	3 and 24 months	Decrease	Asanuma *et al.*, 1995
Forebrain and Hippocampus	3, 18, and 30 months	Increase	Toliver-Kinsky *et al.*, 1997
Adrenal And hypothalamus	3 and 24 months	Decrease	Tumer *et al.*, 1997
Splenic T-cells	6 and 24 months	Decrease	Pahlavani *et al.*, 1997
Splenic T-cells	6 and 24 months	Decrease	Pahlavani *et al.*, 1998
Splenocytes	6 and 24 months	Decrease	Pahlavani *et al.*, 1996
Human			
Fibroblasts	Early/late passage	Decrease	Riabowol *et al.*, 1992
WI–38 lung fibroblasts	Early/late passage	Decrease	Dimri & Campisi., 1994
Fibroblasts	7–65 and 100+ years	Increase (induced)	Grassilli *et al.*, 1996
WI-38 fibroblasts	Late passage	Decrease	Helenius *et al.*, 1996b
WI-38 and IMR–90 Fibroblasts	Early/late passage	Decrease	Helenius *et al.*, 1999
Endothelial cells	Early/late passage	Decrease	Kumazaki & Mitsui, 1996
T-cells	37 and 72–87 years	Decrease	Whisler *et al.*, 1996
NF-κB Binding Activity			
Mice			
Splenic T-cells	2–4 and 18–24 months	Decrease (induced)	Trebilcock & Ponnappan, 1996
Splenocytes	2 and 15 months	Increase	Poynter & Daynes, 1998
Liver	4 and 24 months	Increase	Helenius *et al.*, 1996b
Rats			
Splenic T-cells	6 and 24 months	Decrease	Pahlavani *et al.*, 1998
Splenocytes	6 and 24 months	Decrease	Pahlavani *et al.*, 1996
Cerebellum and cortex	18 and 30 months	Increase	Korhonen *et al.*, 1997
Forebrain/hippocampus	3, 18, and 30 months	Increase	Toliver-Kinsky *et al.*, 1997
Heart, liver	7, 18, and 30 months	Increase	Helenius *et al.*, 1996b
Liver	3, 18, and 22 months	Increase	Supakar *et al.*, 1995; Roy, 1997
Liver	15 and 25 months	Increase	Walter & Sierra, 1998
Human			
WI–38 lung fibroblasts	Early/late passage	No change	Dimri & Campisi, 1994
WI–38 fibroblasts	Late passage	Decrease	Helenius *et al.*, 1996b
WI–38 and IMR–90 Fibroblasts	Early/late passage	Decrease after UVB	Helenius *et al.*, 1999
T-cells	21–30 and 65–80 years	Decrease (induced)	Trebilcock & Ponnappan, 1996, 1998
T-cells	37 and 72–87 years	Decrease	Whisler *et al.*, 1996
NFAT Binding Activity			
Rats			
Splenic T-cells	6 and 24 months	Decrease	Pahlavani *et al.*, 1995
Splenocytes	6 and 24 months	Decrease	Pahlavani *et al.*, 1996
Splenic T-cells	6 and 24 months	Decrease	Pahlavani *et al.*, 1998
Splenic T-cells	6 and 24 months	Decrease	Pahlavani *et al.*, 1997
Human			
Lymphocytes	24 and 82 years	Decrease	Whisler *et al.*, 1996

(continues)

Table I.   (Cont'd)

Tissue	Ages studied	Change with age	Reference
HSF1 Binding Activity			
Rats			
Splenocytes	4–5 and 24–26 months	Decrease	Pahlavani et al., 1995
Splenocytes	4–8 and 20–22 months	Decrease	Gutsmann-Conrad et al., 1999b
Adrenal gland	5–6 and 25–26 months	Decrease	Fawcett et al., 1995
Heart	6 and 22 months	Decrease	Locke & Tanguay, 1996
Hepatocytes	4–6 and 24–26 months	Decrease	Heydari et al., 1993
Hepatocytes	4–8 and 20–22 months	Decrease	Gutsmann-Conrad et al., 1999b
Human			
IMR–90 fibroblasts	Early/late passage	Decrease	Liu et al., 1989
IMR–90 fibroblasts	Early/late passage	Decrease	Gutsmann-Conrad et al., 1999a
Melanocytes	Early/late passage	Decrease	Gutsmann-Conrad et al., 1999a
Skin fibroblasts	Young/old donors	Decrease	Gutsmann-Conrad et al., 1999a
Lymphocytes	Young/old donors	Decrease	Jurivich et al., 1997

Harris, 1996; Pahlavani et al., 1998) reported that the age-related decline in the induction of AP-1 activity by mitogens in rat splenocytes was due to a decline in the induction of fos expression; no age-related change in jun expression was observed. Similar results have been reported for the decline in AP-1 binding activity during cellular senescence in human fibroblasts (Riabowol et al., 1992). Because many genes contain AP-1 binding sites in their promoters and are responsive to AP-1 activation, the age-related decline in AP-1 binding activity could be important physiologically. However, at the present time, there is no evidence showing that a particular gene or function is altered with age specifically because of the age-related decline in AP-1 binding activity. Nevertheless, it is inviting to speculate that the decline in cell proliferation that is observed in cellular senescence and the immune system in aging animals could be due, at least partially, to the transcription factor, AP-1.

b. Nuclear Factor Kappa Beta (NF-κB).
NF-κB is a multi-subunit transcription factor found in many different cell types and tissues. It appears that NF-κB plays a central role in the regulation of many genes involved in cellular defense. For example, a wide variety of agents activate NF-κB, including oxidative stress, pathogenic and immunologic insults, inflammatory cytokines, and cell adhesion molecules (Schreck et al., 1992; Baeuerle & Baltimore, 1991). The consensus sequence for NF-κB is present in the promoter regions of a wide variety of NF-κB-responsive genes. Under nonstress conditions, NF-κB is present in the cytoplasm as an inactive complex (i.e., no DNA binding activity) composed of three subunits: two DNA-binding proteins, p50 and p65 (also known as Rel A), and an inhibitory subunit (IκB) bound to p65 (Baeuerle & Baltimore, 1988a,b, 1989). Stimulatory signals induce IκB phosphorylation at two serine residues by a ubiquitin-dependent protein kinase. The phosphorylated IκB is then degraded by the proteosome.

Because NF-κB activation is a critical step in the cellular defense against a wide variety of stresses, it has been proposed that NF-κB may play a role in the compromised ability of cells to adapt to environmental challenges with age (Roy, 1997). The data in Table I show that all studies that have measured NF-κB DNA binding activity as a function of age have observed an alteration in NF-κB binding activity. However, both an increase and a decrease in NF-κB binding activity with age have been observed. For example, both basal NF-κB DNA binding activity

(Helenius *et al.*, 1996a; Dimri & Campisi, 1994) and the induction of NF-κB activation by UVB exposure are reduced significantly in late passage human fibroblasts (Helenius *et al.*, 1999). In addition, the mitogen induction of NF-κB DNA binding activity is reduced with age in lymphocytes from mice (Poynter & Daynes, 1998), rats (Pahlavani *et al.*, 1998; Pahlavani & Harris, 1996), and humans (Ponnappan *et al.*, 1999; Trebilcock & Ponnappan, 1996, 1998; Whisler *et al.*, 1996). It has been proposed that the age-related decline in NF-κB binding activity compromises the ability of cells from old animals to respond to stress or other signals in which NF-κB activation induces transcription of specific genes. However, the nuclear binding activity of NF-κB has been reported to be higher in several tissues from old mice and rats. An increase in NF-κB binding with age was observed in liver (Supakar *et al.*, 1995; Helenius *et al.*, 1996a), heart (Helenius *et al.*, 1996a), and various brain regions (Korhonen *et al.*, 1997; Toliver-Kinsky *et al.*, 1997) of rats and mice. It has been argued that the age-related increase in NF-κB DNA binding activity is a response to an increase in oxidative stress in the cells of the old animals. However, it is evident from the data in Table 1 that not all cells/tissues from old animals show increased NF-κB DNA binding. Therefore, it is unclear how important age-related changes in oxidative stress are in the DNA binding activity of NF-κB.

c. Nuclear Factor of Activated T-Cells (NFAT). NFAT is a transcription factor that is unique to T-cells and binds to the NFAT purine-rich sequence in the promoter of the IL-2 gene. Four other transcription factors also bind to distinct sequences within the 300-bp region of the IL-2 promoter: AP-1, AP-3, NF-κB, and OCT-1, which are ubiquitous transcription factors, i.e., they are involved in the regulation of a variety of genes in various tissues (Pahlavani & Richardson, 1996). NFAT appears to play the predominant role in the regulation of IL-2 transcription because 70–90% of the transcriptional activity of an IL-2 promoter–reporter gene construct is lost when the NFAT sequence is mutated or deleted. In contrast, deletion of the other *cis*-elements (e.g., NF-κB, AP-1, etc.) from the IL-2 promoter results in only a slight decrease (less than 20%) in transcription (Ullman *et al.*, 1990).

In 1995, Pahlavani *et al.* (1995b) reported that the age-related decrease in the induction of IL-2 transcription by mitogens in rat splenocytes (shown in Fig. 5) was paralleled by a similar decrease in the induction of NFAT DNA binding activity. Subsequently, Whisler *et al.* (1996) showed that the induction of NFAT binding activity by mitogens was reduced in lymphocytes from old human subjects. Pahlavani *et al.* (1997) also showed that dietary restriction increased mitogen induction of both IL-2 transcription and NFAT binding activity. Thus, data strongly suggest that the age-related decline in the mitogen induction of IL-2 expression arises because of alterations in the transcription factor NFAT.

NFAT is a complex consisting of cytoplasmic and nuclear components (Pahlavani & Richardson, 1996). The transcription of the IL-2 gene requires both components, as shown in Fig. 8. The nuclear component of the NFAT complex contains both constitutive and inducible polypeptides. The inducible polypeptides are fos and jun, and the constitutive polypeptide is a member of the Ets oncogene family, specifically, Elf-1. The fos and jun heterodimer is believed to interact with Elf-1 and facilitate the binding of Elf-1 to the purine-rich 5′-sequence of the NFAT element. The cytoplasmic component of NFAT (NFAT-c) is a protein with a molecular weight of 94–116 kDa. NFAT-c is found in a phosphorylated form in the cytoplasm of resting T-cells. Upon mitogen/antigen stimulation, NFAT-c is dephosphorylated rapidly and translocates into the nucleus, where it binds to the nuclear components of the NFAT complex. Pahlavani's laboratory (Pahlavani *et al.*, 1998; Pahlavani & Richardson, 1996) showed that the age-related decrease in NFAT binding activity arose from alterations in both the nuclear and cytoplasmic components of the NFAT complex. These defects appear to be the result of age-related alterations in the signal transduction pathway shown in Fig. 8 that regulates IL-2 expression. For example, data published by Pahlavani *et al.* (1998) suggest that the defects in the nuclear components of NFAT arise from a decrease in the induction of fos because of an alteration in the activation of the Ras/MAPK cascade. However, age-related changes in the dephosphorylation of NAFT-c also appear to occur because of alterations in calcineurin (Pahlavani & Vargas, 1999). Thus, the age-related decline in the induction of IL-2 transcription in T-cells appears to arise from alterations in the transcription factor, NFAT, because of defects in the signal transduction pathway that activates it.

d. Heat-Shock Transcription Factor (HSF). The transcription factor HSF plays a key role in the response of cells to hyperthermia and other stresses that induce the expression of heat-shock proteins. The induction of the transcription of heat-shock genes is mediated by the binding of HSF to a highly conserved DNA sequence known as the heat-shock element (HSE), which is found in the 5'-flanking sequence of all heat-shock genes. As shown in Fig. 9, HSF is maintained in an inactive form that does not bind DNA in the cytoplasm of nonstressed cells as a monomer complexed to a negative regulatory factor (Morimoto, 1993). An increase in temperature in mammalian cells results in the conversion of HSF from an inactive monomer to a trimer that translocates to the nucleus and binds the HSE, which activates the transcription of the hsp70 gene (Sorger, 1991).

Because it is generally believed that the age-related loss in the ability of an organism to respond to stress and maintain homeostasis is at least partially responsible for the increase in morbidity/mortality that is observed as an organism ages, many investigators have studied the effect of age on the ability of cells/tissues/whole animals to express heat-shock proteins, e.g., hsp70, as shown in Fig. 4. All of these studies have shown that the induction of hsp70 (and other heat-shock proteins) declines with increasing age in animals and during replicative senescence in human fibroblasts (Heydari *et al.*, 1994). Because the age-related decline in hsp70 induction occurs at the level of transcription and because HSF plays a central role in the transcription of hsp70 in response to heat stress, numerous studies have measured the induction of HSF DNA binding activity by heat shock in cells/tissues from young and old animals. These studies are listed in Table I. It is striking that all eight published studies in this area have observed an age-related decline in the induction of HSF DNA binding activity. This age-related decrease has been observed in a variety of tissues/cells (hepatocytes, adrenal gland, heart, and splenocytes) from rats. Heydari *et al.* (1993) also showed that dietary restriction reversed/retarded the age-related decrease in HSF DNA binding in hepatocytes from rats. The induction of HSF binding activity by heat shock also has been observed to be reduced in cells (lymphocytes and fibroblasts) isolated from old human subjects. In addition, a decline in the induction of HSF DNA binding activity has been observed in a variety of cells (fibroblasts and melanocytes) during replicative senescence. Thus, this is an

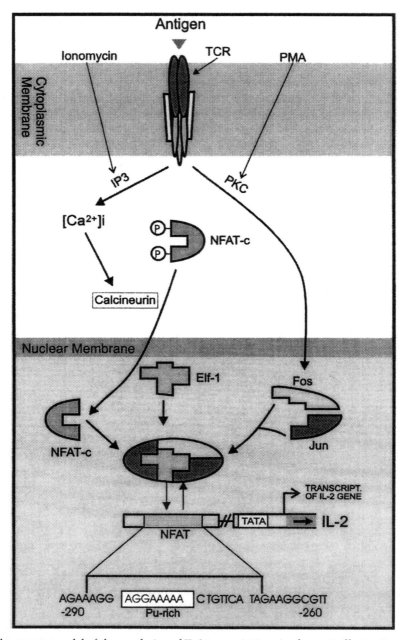

Figure 8. The current model of the regulation of IL-2 transcription. A schematic illustration of NFAT activation by T-cell receptor-mediated signal transduction pathways that lead to IL-2 transcription is presented. The stimulation of T-cells with an antigen/mitogen or phorbol ester induces the expression of the nuclear component of the NFAT complex, specifically fos and jun, through the PKC pathway. In addition, an antigen, mitogen, or calcium inophore stimulates the translocation of the NFAT-c from the cytoplasm into the nucleus through the inositol-1,4,5-triphosphate signal transduction pathway The cellular levels of calcium are elevated in the activated T-cells, and it is believed that the increased calcium levels activate the calcium-dependent phospatase activity of calcineurin, which dephosphorylates NFAT-c. The dephosphorylated NFAT-c then translocates into the nucleus and forms a complex with the nuclear components of the NFAT complex. Binding of the NFAT complex to the IL-2 promoter activates the transcription of the IL-2 gene. (Figure reproduced from Pahlavani and Richardson (1996) with permission.)

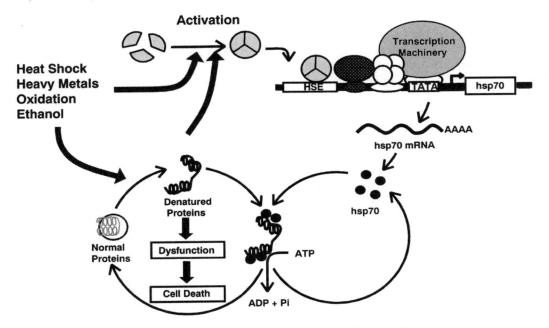

Figure 9. Model for the induction of hsp70 expression by HSF binding. hsp70 expression in response to stress is mediated by the binding of HSF to the highly conserved heat-shock element. HSF is converted from an inactive monomer to an active trimer in response to a variety of stresses, including abnormal proteins, heavy metals, oxidative stress, and ethanol, in addition to an increase in temperature. The active trimer binds to the HSE to induce transcription of the hsp70 mRNA. The mRNA produced directs the synthesis of hsp70, which accumulates and catalyzes the refolding of malfolded proteins that arise from the stress. The elimination of the malfolded proteins is believed to be an important factor in the ability of hsp70 to protect cells from the toxic effects of heat shock and other stresses.

example of a process in which the *in vitro* cellular senescence model reflects the changes that occur in hsp70 expression observed *in vivo*.

Multiple forms of HSFs have been found in mammals, and HSF1 is the transcription factor that is activated in response to stress and triggers hsp70 transcription (Baler *et al.*, 1993; Sarge *et al.*, 1993). By using super-shift experiments, in which HSF1 antiserum was added to the nuclear extracts before the gel-shift assay, several investigators have shown that the age-related decline in HSF binding activity is due to HSF1 in hepatocytes (Heydari *et al.*, 2000), adrenal gland (Fawcett *et al.*, 1995), and heart (Locke & Tanguay, 1996) of rats. In addition, Heydari *et al.* (1996) showed that the increase in HSF DNA binding observed with dietary restriction in rat hepatocytes

was due to HSF1. Thus, all of the current data clearly demonstrate that the age-related decline in the induction of hsp70 transcription is due to an alteration in the transcription factor HSF1.

Over the past five years, several investigators have studied the effect of age on HSF1. The levels of the mRNA transcript for HSF1 were found to be similar in hepatocytes and splenocytes from young and old rats (Gutsmann-Conrad *et al.*, 1999b; Heydari *et al.*, 2000). In addition, the level of HSF1 protein was observed to remain constant with age in the heart, adrenal gland, and splenocytes from rats (Fawcett *et al.*, 1995; Locke & Tanguay, 1996; Gutsmann-Conrad *et al.*, 1999b). Heydari *et al.* (1996) observed an age-related increase in HSF1 protein in rat hepatocytes that was reversed by dietary restriction. Thus, the studies with rats indicate that the age-related decline in HSF1 binding activity is not due to a decrease in HSF1 protein levels. Interestingly, an age-related decrease in HSF1 protein levels was observed in human fibroblasts during either replicative senescence (Liu *et al.*, 1989; Gutsmann-Conrad *et al.*, 1999a) or aging *in vivo* (Gutsmann-Conrad *et al.*, 1999a). Thus, the effect of age on HSF1 seems to be different in fibroblasts than in other cell types.

There is a substantial literature showing that abnormal or altered proteins accumulate with age, and this area is reviewed by Gafni (Chapter 3) in this volume. Observations by Heydari *et al.* (2000) show that HSF1 exhibits the two hallmark characteristics of altered proteins that accumulate with age: a decrease in activity per antigenic reactive material and altered thermosensitivity. Thus, they proposed that the age-related decline in the induction of hsp70 expression was due to the posttranslational alterations in HSF1 as shown in Fig. 10. Heydari *et al.* (2000) found that the degradation of the HSF1 polypeptide decreases

with age, resulting in an increase in the half-life of HSF1. The age-related decrease in HSF1 turnover leads to a longer dwell time for HSF1 in the cells/tissues of old animals than in young animals, increasing the probability that the HSF1 polypeptides will become posttranslationally altered and accumulate with age. On the basis of their data, Heydari *et al.* (2000) suggested that the hsp70 monomers that become altered with age can oligomerize and form trimers in response to heat shock. However, the DNA binding activity of the oligomers containing altered HSF1 monomers is reduced and shows reduced thermostability. All previous proteins that have been found to become altered with age have been structural proteins (e.g., collagen, α-crystalline, etc.) or proteins that function as classical enzymes, i.e., they catalyze specific metabolic reactions (Stadtman, 1992; Gafni & Yuh, 1989). This is the first report showing that a protein that functions as a transcription factor becomes altered with age. Heydari *et al.* (2000) proposed that posttranslational alterations in a transcription factor potentially

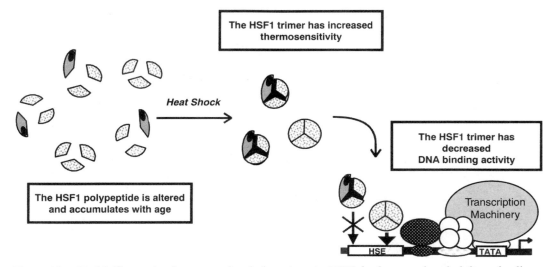

Figure 10. Model illustrating how age-related alterations in HSF1 lead to a reduced ability of cells to express hsp70 in response to heat shock and other stresses. The model shown in the figure is based on data published by Heydari *et al.* (2000).

could be important functionally because relatively small changes in the levels of the altered proteins could be amplified by oligomerization and protein–protein interactions, which are characteristic of transcription factors. They presented a model showing that a 40–55% accumulation of posttranslationally altered HSF1 monomers could result in the 80–90% decrease in the specific activity of HSF1 binding to DNA that was observed with age in rat hepatocytes.

III. Translation

Translation is the mechanism by which genetic information in the form of messenger RNA is used to order amino acids sequentially within a polypeptide chain. Eukaryotic protein synthesis requires over 200 macromolecules to translate one mRNA and is energetically expensive. Four high-energy phosphates are required to produce a single peptide bond. The translational macromolecules (rRNA, ribosomal proteins, tRNAs, aminoacyl-tRNA synthetases) are highly conserved across phyla. The ribosome, composed of two dissimilar subunits containing RNA and many proteins, is the site where two key substrates, mRNA and aminoacyl-tRNA, are positioned to determine which amino acid is inserted at a particular point on the nascent polypeptide chain. Because proteins are crucial to cellular function as biological catalysts and as essential components of cell structure, it is not surprising that the effect of aging on synthesis has been an area in which a great deal of information has been generated. Most of the early research on the effect of age on gene expression in the 1960s and 1970s focused on translation. Our knowledge of how aging affects gene expression at the level of translation has come from research published primarily in the 1970s and 1980s, and these studies have been described in detail in numerous reviews (Richardson & Ward, 1994; Van Remmen et al., 1995; Ward & Shibatani, 1994; Rattan & Clark, 1996; Rattan, 1996; Ward & Richardson, 2000).

A. Effect of Age on Protein Synthesis

1. Total Protein Synthesis

Over the past 30 years, numerous investigators have measured total or bulk protein synthesis as a function of age in various tissues and organisms. Most studies (18 of 21) of invertebrates showed an age-related decline in protein synthesis, and over 80% of the studies investigating the effect of age on protein synthesis in various tissues of rodents observed an age-associated decline that ranged from 20–75% (Van Remmen et al., 1995). A decline in protein synthesis has been observed in the liver, brain, heart, intestine, kidney, skeletal muscle, pancreas, and spleen of rats. In some instances, the decreased protein synthesis observed in organs such as thymus and uterus likely is secondary to developmental or endocrine changes and, thus, not primarily a consequence of aging (Azelis et al., 1982; Thakur & Kaur, 1992b). To a first approximation, the age-associated decrease in protein synthesis appears to be independent of cellular protein location. For example, the synthesis of mitochondria-specific proteins has been observed to decrease with age in *Drosophila* (Bailey & Webster, 1984), as well as in the liver (Bailey & Webster, 1984; Ibrahim et al., 1981; Marcus et al., 1982a,b), heart (Starnes et al., 1981), and kidney (van Bezooijen et al., 1976) of rodents. Taken together, these data suggest that further studies of bulk protein synthesis are unlikely to add significantly to our understanding of aging.

2. Synthesis of Individual Proteins

The application of high-throughput analytical technology to assess the entire complement of cellular proteins (proteomics) will allow future investigators to screen thousands of proteins simultaneously as a function of age. As shown in articles by Gygi's laboratory (Gygi *et al.*, 1999a–c), this technology will be essential in interpreting data from the cDNA arrays described in Section IIA. These investigators examined the relationship between mRNA levels (measured by serial analysis of gene expression, SAGE) and protein levels (measured by two-dimensional gel electrophoresis coupled with capillary liquid chromatography–tandem mass spectroscopy) in yeast growing at mid-log phase. They found that the correlation between protein and mRNA levels was insufficient to predict protein expression levels from quantitative mRNA data. For some genes, the mRNA levels did not change, whereas the corresponding protein levels varied by more than 20-fold. Conversely, invariant steady-state levels of certain proteins were observed, whereas the respective mRNA transcript levels varied by as much as 30-fold. These results clearly demonstrate the technical limitations of screening mRNA transcripts and relating these data to the steady-state levels of the protein products.

Several years ago, investigators began to screen the effect of aging on the synthesis of individual proteins using two-dimensional gel electrophoresis. The incorporation of radioactively labeled amino acids into hundreds of proteins was studied in nematodes (Johnson & McCaffrey, 1985), *Drosophila* (Fleming *et al.*, 1986a,b), and rat hepatocytes (Butler *et al.*, 1989). Figure 11 shows an example of the pattern of proteins synthesized by hepatocytes from young and old rats. Comparative analysis of young and old specimens revealed that the qualitative patterns of protein synthesis did not change substantively with increasing age. For example, few if any proteins either appeared or disappeared with age,

indicating that the spectra of proteins synthesized by old and young cells are virtually identical. Thus, aging does not appear to be a simple developmental continuum in which a different set of gene products is synthesized as an organism ages. Although few if any qualitative changes with age have been noted in these studies, it is apparent that quantitative changes in the synthesis of proteins do occur with age. Fleming *et al.* (1986a,b) noted significant age-related changes in 37 of 43 proteins studied in *Drosophila*. The vast majority (36) of the proteins showed reduced labeling, with only 1 showing an increase, albeit of over 200%. Butler *et al.* (1989) measured the synthesis of 36 randomly chosen proteins in rat hepatocytes isolated from 5- and 30-month-old rats. The synthesis of 35 of these proteins decreased with age by 15–60%. Although the decreases in protein synthesis with age do not appear to be uniform, with wide variation in rates of protein synthesis for individual proteins, it appears that the synthesis of most proteins does decrease with age (Van Remmen *et al.*, 1995). The variation suggests that the changes in the synthesis of individual proteins might be controlled at two or more levels. For example, as discussed earlier in Section IIB, one level could be the amount of the mRNA transcript coding for the protein. At this level, changes in the expression of individual proteins would be unique for each protein. A second level of control could be the translation of the mRNA transcripts. An age-related defect in the protein synthetic apparatus would give rise to a general decrease in the synthesis of all proteins. However, because of changes in the levels of the mRNA transcripts coding for individual proteins, the age-related decrease in the synthesis of proteins would not be uniform, and in some cases might actually increase because of a large increase in the level of an mRNA transcript.

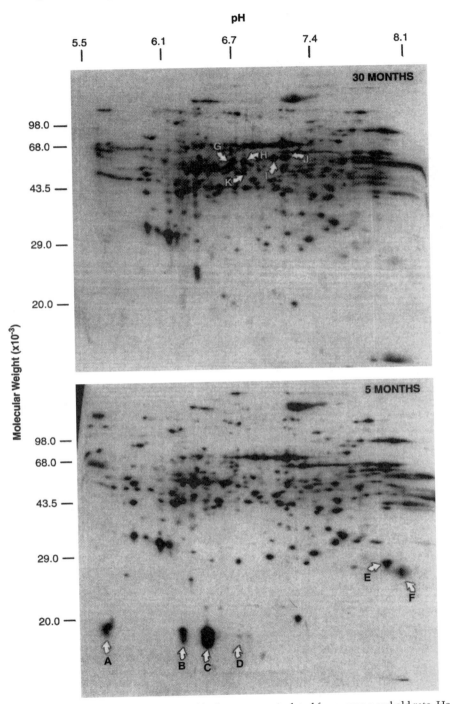

Figure 11. The pattern of proteins synthesized by hepatocytes isolated from young and old rats. Hepatocytes were isolated from 5- and 30-month-old rats, incubated with radiolabeled L-methionine, and subjected to two-dimensional gel electrophoresis and fluorography. The proteins that show changes are designated with letters. Proteins A–F disappeared with age, and proteins G–K increased or appeared with age. The autoradiographs of the gels are shown. [Figure reproduced from Butler *et al.*, (1989) with permission.]

B. Effect of Age on tRNA and tRNA Aminoacylation

Preparatory to addition to the polypeptide, each amino acid is attached to the 3′-end of a specific tRNA containing the anticodon corresponding to that particular amino acid. The aminoacyl-tRNA synthetases are a family of enzymes (one for each amino acid) that catalyze this reaction. The specificity of the aminoacyl-tRNA synthetases is dependent on extensive contacts they make with their respective tRNAs. In eukaryotes, tRNA transcription and maturation occur in the nucleus. In some instances, nuclear aminoacylation facilitates interactions with factors necessary for cytoplasmic export. In this way, the aminoacyl-tRNA synthetases ensure that mature, fully functional tRNAs (but not misfolded or unprocessed tRNAs) are exported to the cytoplasm. Some tRNAs are exported from the nucleus without prior aminoacylation. Their structural integrity is monitored by the RNA–GTPase exportint system prior to transport to the cytosol (Arts *et al.*, 1998).

It is essential for accurate translation that tRNAs are only coupled to amino acids corresponding to the RNA anticodon. This is largely, but not exclusively, achieved by the direct attachment of the appropriate amino acid to the 3′-end of the corresponding tRNA by the aminoacyl-tRNA synthetases. Extensive genetic, biochemical, and structural studies have shown that sequence-specific protein–RNA interactions facilitate accurate selection of the correct cognate tRNA and discrimination against other noncognate tRNAs. The structural diversity afforded by the various base combinations, both modified and unmodified, within tRNAs dictates that the cognate molecules can be specifically chosen by the cognate aminoacyl-tRNA synthetase.

The reactions leading to tRNA aminoacylation have been studied in detail to assess whether they may play a role in the age-related decrease in protein synthesis. Strehler *et al.* (1971) proposed the codon restriction theory of aging, which stated that a random loss of various isoaccepting tRNAs would progressively restrict the readability of codons and result in an age-related decrease in the efficiency and accuracy of protein synthesis. Although changes in some components of the tRNA aminoacylation system have been observed, there is no evidence that any of these changes are responsible for the decreased rate of protein synthesis observed with age [see reviews by Richardson and Birchenall-Sparks (1983), Richardson and Semsei (1987), and Van Remmen *et al.* (1995)].

There is good evidence that a shift in the pattern of isoaccepting tRNAs occurs during development and aging in some plants, nematodes, insects, and rat liver and skeletal muscle (Vinayak, 1987; Van Remmen *et al.*, 1995). A 30- to 60-fold increase in the amount of UAG suppressor tRNA has been reported in the brain, spleen, and liver of old mice and appears to be related to increased expression of Moloney murine leukemia virus (MO-MuLV) in fibroblasts (Schröder *et al.*, 1992). Other characteristics of tRNAs that have been studied with respect to aging include the rate of synthesis, total levels, aminoacylation capacity, and nucleoside composition. The aminoacylation capacity of different tRNAs varies to different extents during aging due to unknown reasons. The fidelity of aminoacylation does not differ significantly in cell-free extracts prepared from old and young rat livers. However, there is no generalized pattern that emerges from these studies, and the reported changes vary significantly between various species (Van Remmen *et al.*, 1995; Rattan *et al.*, 1992).

Variable changes in the specific activities of the aminoacyl-tRNA synthetases have been observed in various organs of aging mice without any discernible correlation with tissue or cell type and protein synthetic activity (Van Remmen et al., 1995). Interestingly, an increase in the proportion of the heat-labile fraction of several of these enzymes has been reported in certain tissues from aged rats (Takahashi & Goto, 1990). However, no widespread pattern is seen for the changes in activities of the various synthetases, and direct evidence for an age-related decrease in the efficiency of aminoacyl-tRNA synthetases is not available. The effects of age on aminoacyl-tRNA transport out of the nucleus have not been investigated. In general, defects in tRNA aminoacylation do not appear to be substantially responsible for the age-related decrease in protein synthesis.

C. Effect of Age on the Initiation of Protein Synthesis

The initiation of protein synthesis, where the complex of mRNA, Met-tRNA$_i^{Met}$, GTP, and the small ribosome subunit is formed, is a particularly important step because it is known that translation can be regulated at this point in protein synthesis. It is somewhat unclear what effect aging has on the initiation of protein synthesis because of the difficulty in accurately measuring this process. One repeatedly observed difference between aged and young animals is ribosome aggregation to mRNA. A decrease in polyribosomes and an increase in the 80S monomeric ribosomes that are not associated with mRNA have been observed in nematodes (Reznick & Gershon, 1979), Drosophila (Webster et al., 1981; Baker & Schmidt, 1976), and a variety of rodent tissues, e.g., liver (Layman et al., 1976; Claes-Reckinger et al., 1982; Vandenhaute et al., 1983; Makrides, 1983), skeletal muscle (Pluskal et al., 1984), and brain (Fando et al., 1980). A decrease in the number of ribosomes associated with mRNA and actively synthesizing protein would be expected to play an important role

in the age-related decline in protein synthesis.

It is logical to predict that the decline in ribosome aggregation arises because of a decrease in the attachment of the ribosomal subunits to the 5′-end of the mRNA, i.e., the formation of the initiation complex (mRNA, Met-tRNA$_i^{Met}$, GTP, and the small ribosome subunit). Of the various proteins/initiation factors involved in protein synthesis, eIF2 plays a central role in what is generally considered a major rate-limiting step in mRNA translation (Merrick, 1992). In this step, eIF2 binds GTP and Met-tRNA$_i^{Met}$ and transfers Met-tRNA$_i^{Met}$ to the 40S ribosomal subunit. At the end of the initiation process, GTP bound to eIF2 is hydrolyzed to GDP and the eIF2–GDP complex is released from the ribosome. The exchange of GDP bound to eIF2 for GTP is a prerequisite to binding Met-tRNA$_i^{Met}$ and is mediated by a second initiation factor, eIF2B. In what is probably the best characterized mechanism for the regulation of mRNA translation, phosphorylation of eIF2 on its smallest, or α, subunit (eIF2α) converts eIF2 from a substrate of eIF2B into a competitive inhibitor. Thus, phosphorylation of eIF2α effectively prevents formation of the eIF2–GTP–Met-tRNA$_i^{Met}$ complex and inhibits global protein synthesis. Phosphorylation of eIF2α has been shown to occur under a variety of conditions, e.g., viral infection, apoptosis, nutrient deprivation, heme deprivation, and certain stresses, through a double-stranded RNA-dependent protein kinase (PKB) (Brostrom, et al., 1996). However, there is only limited evidence to support a role for this process in aging. For example, a few studies suggest that the formation of the initiation complex in vitro may decrease with age (Webster et al., 1981; Nakazawa et al., 1984; Gabius et al., 1983; Blazejowski & Webster, 1984). Kimball et al. (1992) observed that the activity and protein levels of eIF-2 in various tissues of rats decreased between 1 and 10 months of age, and this decrease was correlated to a decrease in protein synthesis. Ladiges *et al.* (2000) measured the levels of eIF2α and PKB in most tissues of 2- and 20-month-old mice by Western blot analysis. In general, they observed an age-related decrease in eIF2α levels and an increase in PKB in all tissues studied. In addition, they showed, by isoelectric focusing, that the hyperphosphorylated form of eIF2α increased with age in liver and kidney tissues. This observation is consistent with the age-related decrease in ribosome aggregation to mRNA arising from a defect in the initiation of protein synthesis because of an increase in the phosphorylation of the eIF2α.

D. Effect of Age on Elongation of Protein Synthesis

After an aminoacyl-tRNA has been produced by its aminoacyl-tRNA synthetase, it must associate with elongation factor 1α (EF-1α) before participating in protein synthesis (Negrutskii & El'skaya, 1998; Clark *et al.*, 1999). The primary function of EF-1α is to transfer a broad range of aminoacyl-tRNAs to the ribosome. Consequently, EF-1α has wide substrate specificity. However, EF-1α is more than a simple docking molecule; it performs essential quality control steps. EF-1α helps maintain translational fidelity by excluding many tRNA species, such as uncharged tRNAs that lack an aminoacyl moiety. The aminoacyl-tRNA associates with EF-1α and GTP in a ternary complex that can then bind to the ribosome where anticodon:codon pairing occurs. The correct pairing of bases between the aminoacyl-tRNA and mRNA results in the hydrolysis of GTP and the release of EF-1α:GDP, and the aminoacyl-tRNA enters the ribosomal A site. The aminoacyl moiety then is transferred to the nascent polypeptide chain, forming a peptide bond in the growing polypeptide change. The final phase of

elongation is the translocation reaction, where the ribosome moves one codon down the mRNA transcript. EF-2 catalyzes this reaction using energy generated from GTP hydrolysis.

Several studies suggest that the elongation step of protein synthesis is altered with age (Van Remmen *et al.*, 1995). For example, Coniglio *et al.* (1979) observed that the ribosome half-transit time (the elongation time required for the synthesis of an average half-length of a nascent polypeptide chain) was 1.6-fold higher for hepatocytes isolated from old rats than for hepatocytes isolated from young rats. In addition, several investigators have reported an age-related decrease in EF-1α activity in cell extracts obtained from nematodes (Bolla & Brot, 1975), *Drosophila* (Webster & Webster, 1983; Webster, 1985), and a variety of rodent tissues (Rattan *et al.*, 1986, 1991; Gabius *et al.*, 1983; Cavallius *et al.*, 1989; Mohan & Radha, 1978). The data in Fig. 12 shows examples of three studies that have reported an age-related decline in EF-1α activity. EF-1α activity also has been observed to decrease significantly during

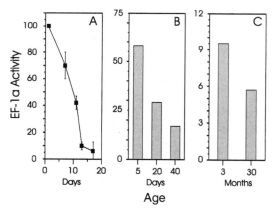

Figure 12. Effect of age on the activity of EF-1α. The activity of EF-1α is shown for *Drosophila* [A, data taken from Webster and Webster (1983)], nematodes [B, data taken from Bolla and Brot (1975)], and rat liver [C, data taken from Moldave *et al.* (1979)]. (Figure reproduced from Van Remmen *et al.* (1995) with permission).

replicative senescence (Cavallius, et al., 1986). However, Rattan et al. (1991) found that dietary restriction had little effect on elongation factor activity, which would suggest that the age-related decrease in EF-1α activity may not be important in aging because it is not altered by dietary restriction. Welle et al. (1997) measured the expression of EF-1α in dietary restriction and in muscle biopsies obtained from the vastus lateralis muscles of healthy young (22–31 years old) and old (61–74 years old) human subjects. Although they observed that the rate of myofibrillar protein synthesis was approximately 40% slower in the older muscle, no change was observed with age in either the mRNA or protein levels of EF-1α. Thus, it does not appear that the expression of EF-1α decreases in the muscle of humans as they age; however, this study cannot exclude the possibility that the activity of EF-1α declines because of posttranslational modifications.

In 1989, a great deal of interest in the role of elongation factors in aging was generated when transgenic Drosophila was produced by using a P-element vector containing a cDNA copy of the EF-1α gene under the control of the inducible hsp70 (70-kDa heat-shock protein) promoter. Shepherd et al. (1989) reported that the life span of the transgenic flies was greater than nontransgenic flies. This was the first report of a transgenic manipulation extending the life span of an organism and suggested that the age-related decline in EF-1α shown in Fig. 12 for Drosophila was important in aging. Unfortunately, later studies showed that these transgenic flies were not expressing more EF-1α mRNA or EF-1α protein, or exhibiting greater EF-1α activity (Shikama et al., 1994). Therefore, the longer life span of the transgenic Drosophila was not due to the overexpression of EF-1α but was due to a positional effect of where the transgene inserted into the genome (Kaiser et al., 1996). However, EF-1α mutants of Podospora anserina have an increased life span and show an increase in the fidelity of translation (Silar & Picard, 1994).

References

Ammendola, R., Mesuraca, M., Russo, T., & Cimino, F. (1992). Sp1 DNA binding efficiency is highly reduced in nuclear extracts from aged rat tissues. Journal of Biological Chemistry, 267, 17944–17948.

Arts, G. J., Kuersten, S., Romby, P., Ehresmann, B., & Mattaj, I. W. (1998). The role of exportin-t in selective nuclear export of mature tRNAs. EMBO Journal, 17, 7430–7441.

Asanuma, M., Kondo, Y., Nishibayashi, S., Iwata, E., Nakanishi, T., & Ogawa, N. (1995). Age-related changes in composition of transcription factor, AP–1 complex in the rat brain. Neuroscience Letters, 201, 127–130.

Azelis, A. E., McMullen, K. M., & Webster, G. C. (1982). Progressive reduction in protein synthesis during involution and aging of the mouse thymus. Mechanisms of Aging and Development, 20, 361–368.

Baeuerle, P. A., & Baltimore, D. (1988a). Activation of DNA-binding activity in the apparently cytoplasmic precursor of the NF kappa B transcription factor. Cell, 53, 211–217.

Baeuerle, P. A., & Baltimore, D. (1988b). I kappa B: a specific inhibitor of the nuclear factor kappa B transcription factor. Science, 242, 540–546.

Baeuerle, P. A., & Baltimore, D. (1989). A 65-kappa D subunit of active NF Kappa B is required for inhibition of NF Kappa B by I kappa B. Genes & Development, 3, 1689–1698.

Baeuerle, P. A., & Baltimore, D. (1991). Molecular aspects of cellular regulation. In P. Cohen, & J. G. Faulkes (Eds.), The Hormonal Control of Gene Transcription (pp. 409–432). Amsterdam: Elsevier, North Holland Biomedical Press.

Bailey, P. J., & Webster, G. C. (1984). Lowered rates of protein synthesis by mitochondria isolated from organisms of increasing age.

Mechanisms of Aging and Development, *24,* 233–241.

Baker, G. T., & Schmidt, T. (1976). Changes in 80S ribosomes from drosophila melanogaster with age. *Experientia, 32,* 1505–1506.

Baler, R., Dahl, G., & Voellmy, R. (1993). Activation of human heat shock genes is accompanied by oligomerization, modification, and rapid translocation of heat shock transcription factor HSF1. *Molecular and Cellular Biology, 13,* 2486–2496.

Benson, R. W., & Harker, C. W. (1978). RNA polymerase activities in liver and brain tissue of aging mice. *Journals of Gerontology, 33,* 323–328.

Berkowitz, E. M., Sanborn, A. C., & Vaughan, D. W. (1983). Chromatin structure in neuronal and neuroglial cell nuclei as a function of age. *Journal of Neurochemistry, 41,* 516–523.

Bick, M. D., & Strehler, B. L. (1971). Leucyl transfer RNA synthetase changes during soybean cotyledon senescence. *Proceedings of the National Academy of Science of the USA, 68,* 224–228.

Birchenall-Sparks, M. C., Roberts, M. S., Rutherford, M. S., & Richardson, A. (1985). The effect of aging on the structure and function of liver messenger RNA. *Mechanisms of Aging and Development, 32,* 99–111.

Blazejowski, C. A., & Webster, G. C. (1984). Effect of age on peptide chain initiation and elongation in preparations from brain, liver, kidney and skeletal muscle of the C57B/6J mouse. *Mechanisms of Aging and Development, 25,* 323–333.

Bolla, R., & Brot, N. (1975). Age dependent changes in enzymes involved in macromolecular synthesis in turbatrix aceti. *Archives of Biochemistry and Biophysics, 169,* 227–236.

Bolla, R. I., & Greenblatt, C. (1982). Age-related changes in rat liver total protein and tranferrin synthesis. *Age, 5,* 72–79.

Brostrom, C. O., Prostko, C. R., Kaufman, R. J., & Brostrom, M. A. (1996). Inhibition of translational initiation by activators of the glucose-regulated stress protein and heat shock protein stress response systems. Role of the interferon-inducible double-stranded RNA-activated eukaryotic initiation factor 2alpha kinase. *Journal of Biological Chemistry, 271,* 24995–25002.

Butler, J. A., Heydari, A. R., & Richardson, A. (1989). Analysis of effect of age on synthesis of specific proteins by hepatocytes. *Journal of Cellular Physiology, 141,* 400–409.

Cavallius, J., Rattan, S. I., & Clark, B. F. (1986). Changes in activity and amount of active elongation factor 1α in aging and immortal human fibroblast cultures. *Experimental Gerontology, 21,* 149–157.

Cavallius, J., Rattan, S. I., Riis, B., & Clark, B. F. (1989). A decrease in levels of mRNA for elongation factor–1α accompanies the decline in its activity and the amounts of active enzyme in rat livers during ageing. In K. W. Woodhouse, C. Yelland, & O. F. W. James (Eds.), *The Liver, Metabolism and Ageing* (pp. 125–132). Rijswijk, The Netherlands: INSERM-EURAGE/John Libbey Eurotext Ltd.

Cedar, H. (1988). DNA methylation and gene activity. *Cell, 53,* 3–4.

Chatterjee, B., Fernandes, G., Yu, B. P., Song, C., Kim, J. M., Demyan, W., & Roy, A. K. (1989). Calorie restriction delays age-dependent loss in androgen responsiveness of the rat liver. *FASEB J., 3,* 169–173.

Chatterjee, B., Nath, S. T., & Roy, A. K. (1981). Differential regulation of the messenger RNA for three major senescence maker proteins in male rat liver. *Journal of Biological Chemistry, 256,* 5939–5941.

Chaturvedi, M. M., & Kanungo, M. S. (1985). Analysis of conformation and function of the chromatin of the brain of young and old rats. *Molecular Biology of Reproduction, 10,* 215–219.

Cheung, H. T., Twu, J. S., & Richardson, A. (1983). Mechanism of the age-related decline in lymphocyte proliferation: role of IL–2 production and protein synthesis. *Experimental Gerontology, 18,* 451–460.

Claes-Reckinger, N., Vandenhaute, J., van Bezooijen, C. F., & Delcour, J. (1982). Functional properties of rat liver protein synthesizing machinery in relation to aging. *Experimental Gerontology, 17,* 281–286.

Clark B. F. Thirup S. Kjeldgaard M., & Nyborg J. (1999) Structural information for explaining the molecular mechanism of protein biosynthesis. *FEBS Letters. 452*, 41–46.

Coniglio, J. J., Liu, D. S., & Richardson, A. (1979). A comparison of protein synthesis by liver parenchymal cells isolated from Fischer F344 rats of various ages. *Mechanisms of Aging and Development, 11*, 77–90.

Corbitt, J., Vivekananda, J., Wang, S. S., & Strong, R. (1998). Transcriptional and post-transcriptional control of tyrosine hydroxylase gene expression during persistent stimulation of PACAP receptors on PC12 cells: regulation by PKA-dependent and PKA-independent pathways. *Journal of Neurochemistry, 71*, 478–486.

Czyzyk-Krzeska, M. F., & Beresh, J. E. (1996). Characterization of the hypoxia-inducible protein binding site within the pyrimidine-rich tract in the 3′-untranslated region of the tyrosine hydroxylase mRNA. *Journal of Biological Chemistry, 271*, 3293–3299.

Czyzyk-Krzeska, M. F., Dominski, Z., Kole, R., & Millhorn, D. E. (1994a). Hypoxia stimulates binding of a cytoplasmic protein to a pyrimidine-rich sequence in the 3-untranslated region of rat tyrosine hydroxylase mRNA. *Journal of Biological Chemistry, 269*, 9940–9945.

Czyzyk-Krzeska, M. F., Furnari, B. A., Lawson, E. E., & Millhorn, D. E. (1994b). Hypoxia increases rate of transcription and stability of tyrosine hydroxylase mRNA in pheochromocytoma (PC12) cells. *Journal of Biological Chemistry, 269*, 760–764.

Czyzyk-Krzeska, M. F., Paulding, W. R., Beresh, J. E., & Kroll, S. L. (1997). Post-transcriptional regulation of tyrosine hydroxylase gene expression by oxygen in PC12 cells. *Kidney International, 51*, 585–590.

Danner, D. B., & Holbrook, N. J. (1990). Alterations in gene expression with aging. In E. L. Schneider & J. W. Rowe (Eds.), *Handbook of the Biology of Aging 3 ed.*, (pp. 97–115). San Diego: Academic Press.

DeRisi, J. L., Iyer, V. R. & Brown, P. O. (1997). Exploring the metabolic and genetic control of gene expression on a genomic scale. *Science, 278*, 680–686.

Dimri, G. P., & Campisi, J. (1994). Altered profile of transcription factor-binding activities in senescent human fibroblasts. *Experimental Cell Research, 212*, 132–140.

Drinkwater, R. D., Blake, T. J., Morley, A. A., & Turner, D. R. (1989). Human lymphocytes aged in vivo have reduced levels of methylation in transcriptionally active and inactive DNA. *Mutation Research, 219*, 29–37.

Dworkin, M. B., & David, I. B. (1980). Use of a cloned library for the study of abundant poly(A)+ RNA during Xenopus laevis development. *Developmental Biology, 76*, 449–464.

Ekstrom, R., Liu, D. S., & Richardson, A. (1980). Changes in brain protein synthesis during the life span of male Fischer rats. *Gerontology, 26*, 121–128.

Esler, M., Skews, P., Leonard, G., Jackman, A., Bobik, A., & Korner, P. (1981). Age-dependence of noradrenaline kinetics in normal subjects. *Clinical Science, 60*, 217–219.

Fairweather, D. S., Fox, M., & Margison, G. P. (1987). The in vitro lifespan of MRC–5 cells in shortened by 5-azacytidine-induced demethylation. *Experimental Cell Research, 168*, 153–159.

Fando, J. L., Salinas, M., & Wasterlain, C. G. (1980). Age-dependent changes in brain protein synthesis in the rat. *Neurochemical Research, 5*, 373–383.

Fawcett, T. W., Sylvester, S. L., Sarge, K. D., Morimoto, R. I., & Holbrook, N. J. (1995). Effects of neurohormonal stress and aging on the activation of mammalian heat shock factor 1. *Journal of Biological Chemistry, 269*, 32272–32278.

Fernandez, E., Corbitt, J., Yu, R., & Strong, R. (1998). Role for the tyrosine hydroxylase RNA 3′untranslated region in the post-transcriptional regulation of rat adrenal tyrosine hydroxylase gene expression. *Physiologist 41*, 373.

Fleg, J. L., Tzankoff, S. P., & Lakatta, E. G. (1985). Age-related augmentation of plasma catecholamines during dynamic exercise in healthy males. *Journal of Applied Physiology, 59*, 1033–1039.

Fleming, J. E., Melnikoff, P. S., Latter, G. I., Chandra, D., & Bensch, K. G. (1986a). Age dependent changes in the expression of dropsophila mitochondrial proteins. *Mechanisms of Aging and Development, 34*, 63–72.

Fleming, J. E., Quattrocki, E., Latter, G., Miquel, J., Marcuson, R., Zuckerkandl, E., & Bensch, K. G. (1986b). Age-dependent changes in proteins of *Drosophila melanogaster. Science, 231*, 1157–1159.

Gabius, H. J., Engelhardt, R., Deerberg, F., & Cramer, F. (1983). Age-related changes in different steps of protein synthesis of liver and kidney of rats. *FEBS Letters, 160*, 115–118.

Gafni, A., & Yuh, K. M. (1989). A comparative study of the Ca^{2+}-Mg^{2+} dependent atpase from skeletal muscles of young, adult and old rats. *Mechanisms of Aging and Development, 49*, 105–117.

Gaubatz, J. W., Arcement, B., & Cutler, R. G. (1991). Gene expression of an endogenous retrovirus-like element during murine development and aging. *Mechanisms of Aging and Development, 57*, 71–85.

Gaubatz, J. W., Ellis, M., & Chalkley, R. (1979a). The structural organization of mouse chromatin as a function of age. *FASEB Journal, 38*, 1973–1978.

Gaubatz, J. W., Ellis, M., & Chalkley, R. (1979b). Nuclease digestion studies of mouse chromatin as a function of age. *Journal of Gerontology, 34*, 672–679.

Goss, J. R., Finch, C. E., & Morgan, D. G. (1991). Age-related changes in glial fibrillary acidic protein mRNA in the mouse brain. *Neurobiology of Aging, 12*, 165–170.

Grassilli, E., Bellesia, E., Salomoni, P., Croce, M. A., Sikora, E., Radziszewska, E., Tesco, G., Vergelli, M., Latorraca, S., Barbieri, D., Fagiolo, U., Santacaterina, S., Amaducci, L., Tiozzo, R., Sorbi, S., & Franceschi, C. (1996). c-fos/c-jun expression and AP–1 activation in skin fibroblasts from centenarians. *Biochemical Biophysical Research Communications, 226*, 517–523.

Gutsmann-Conrad, A., Heydari, A. R., You, S., & Richardson, A. (1999a). The expression of heat shock protein 70 decreases with cellular senescence in vitro and in cells derived from young and old human subjects. *Experimental Cell Research, 241*, 404–13.

Gutsmann-Conrad, A., Pahlavani, M. A., Heydari, A. R., & Richardson, A. (1999b). The expression of heat shock protein 70 decreases with age in hepatocytes and splenocytes from female rats. *Mechanisms of Aging and Development, 107*, 255–270.

Gygi, S. P., Han, D. K., Gingras, A. C., Sonenberg, N., & Aebersold, R. (1999a). Protein analysis by mass spectrometry and sequence database searching: tools for cancer research in the post-genomic era. *Electrophoresis, 20*, 310–319.

Gygi, S. P., Rist, B., Gerber, S. A., Turecek, F., Gelb, M. H., & Aebersold, R. (1999b). Quantitative analysis of complex protein mixtures using isotope-coded affinity tags. *Nature Biotechnology, 17*, 994–999.

Gygi, S. P., Rochon, Y., Franza, B. R., & Aebersold, R. (1999c). Correlation between protein and mRNA abundance in yeast. *Molecular and Cellular Biology, 19*, 1720–1730.

Hardwick, J., Hsieh, W. H., Liu, D. S., & Richardson, A. (1981). Cell-free protein synthesis by kidney from the aging female Fischer F344 rat. *Biochimica et Biophysica Acta, 652*, 204–217.

Helenius, M., Hanninen, M., Lehtinen, S. K., & Salminen, A. (1996a). Changes associated with aging and replicative senescence in the regulation of transcription factor nuclear factor-kB. *Biochemical Journal, 318*, 603–608.

Helenius, M., Hanninen, M., Lehtinen, S. K., & Salminen, A. (1996b). Aging-induced up-regulation of nuclear binding activities of oxidative stress responsive NK-κB transcription factor in mouse cardiac muscle. *Journal of Molecular and Cellular Cardiology, 28*, 487–498.

Helenius, M., Makelainen, L., & Salminen, A. (1999). Attenuation of NF-kB signaling response to UVB light during cellular senescence. *Experimental Cell Research, 248*, 194–202.

Heydari, A. R., Takahashi, Y., Gutsmann, S., You, S., & Richardson, A. (1994). HSP70 and aging. *Experientia, 50*, 1092–1098.

Heydari, A. R., Wu, B., Takahashi, R., Strong, R., & Richardson, A. (1993). Expression of heat shock protein 70 is altered by age and diet at the level of transcription. *Molecular and Cellular Biology, 13*, 2909–2918.

Heydari, A. R., You, S., Takahashi, R., Gutsmann, A., Sarge, K. D., & Richardson, A. (1996). Effect of caloric restriction on the expression of heat shock protein 70 and the activation of heat shock transcription factor 1. *Developmental Genetics, 18*, 114–124.

Heydari, A. R., You, S., Takahashi, R., Gutsmann-Conrad, A., Sarge, K. D., & Richardson, A. (2000). Age-Related Alterations in the Activation of Heat Shock Transcription Factor 1 in Rat Hepatocytes. *Experimental Cell Research, 256*, 83–93.

Hill, B. T., & Whelan, R. D. H. (1978). Studies of the degradation of ageing chromatin DNA by nuclear and cytoplasmic factors and deoxyribonucleases. *Gerontology, 24*, 326–336.

Hoeldtke, R. D., & Cilme, K. M. (1985). Effects of aging on catecholamine metabolism. *Journal of Clinical Endocrinology, 60*, 479–484.

Holliday, R. (1986). Strong effects of 5-azacytidine on the in vitro lifespan of human diploid fibroblasts. *Experimental Cell Research, 166*, 543–552.

Honda, Y., & Honda, N. S. (1999). The daf-2 gene network for longevity regulates oxidative stress resistance and Mn-superoxide dismutase gene expression in *Caenorhabditis* elegans. *FASEB Journal, 13*, 1385–1393.

Horbach, G. J., Princen, H. M. G., Van Der Kroef, M., van Bezooijen, C. F., & Yap, S. H. (1984). Changes in the sequence content of albumin mRNA and in its translational activity in the rat liver with age. *Biochimica et Biophysica Acta, 783*, 60–66.

Ibrahim, N. G., Marcus, K. L., & Freedman, M. L. (1981). Maintenance of cytochrome P_{450} content in old rat livers in spite of decreased mitochondrial protein synthesis. *Journal of Clinical and Experimental Gerontology, 3*, 327–337.

Imai, S., Armstrong, C. M., Kaeberlein, M., & Guarente, L. (2000). Transcriptional silencing and longevity protein Sir2 is an NAD-dependent histone deacetylase, *Nature, 403*, 795–99.

Issa, J.-P. J., Ottaviano, Y. L., Celano, P., Hamilton, S. R., Davidson, N. E., & Baylin, S. B. (1994). Methylation of the oestrogen receptor CpG island links ageing and neoplasia in human colon. *Nature Genetics, 7*, 536–540.

Issa, J.-P. J., Vertine, P. M., Boehm, C. D., Newsham, I. F., & Baylin, S. B. (1996). Switch from monoallelic to biallelic human IGF2 promoter methylation during aging and carcinogenesis. *Proceedings National Academy of Sciences, 93*, 11757–11762.

Ito, K., Sato, A., & Sato, Y. (1986). Increases in adrenal catecholamine secretion and adrenal sympathetic nerve unitary activities with aging in rats. *Neuroscience Letters, 69*, 263–268.

Jazwinski, S. M. (1999). Molecular mechanisms of yeast longevity. *Trends in Microbiology, 7*, 247–252.

Johnson, S. A., & Finch, C. E. (1996). Changes in gene expression during brain aging: A survey. In E. Schneider & J. W. Rowe (Eds.), *Handbook of the Biology of Aging, 4th ed.*, (pp. 300–327). San Diego: Academic Press.

Johnson, T. E., & McCaffrey, G. (1985). Programmed aging or error catastropheα? An ecanination by two dimensional polyacrylamide gel electrophoresis. *Mechanisms of Aging and Development, 30*, 285–297.

Johnson, R., & Strehler, B. (1972). Loss of genes coding for ribosomal RNAAA in aging brain cells. *Nature, 240*, 412–414.

Jurivich, D. A., Qiu, L., & Welk, J. F. (1997). Attenuated stress responses in young and old human lymphocytes. *Mechanisms of Aging and Development, 94*, 233–249.

Kaiser, M., Gasser, M., Ackermann, R., & Stearns, S. C. (1996). P-element inserts in transgenic flies: a cautionary tale. *Heredity, 78*, 1–11.

Kaminska, B., & Kaczmarek, L. (1993). Robust induction of AP–1 transcription factor DNA binding activity in the hippocampus of aged rats. *Neuroscience Letters, 153*, 189–191.

Kapahi, P., Boulton, M. E., & Kirkwood, T. B. (1999). Positive correlation between mammalian lifespan and cellular resistance to stress. *Free Radical Biology & Medicine, 26*, 495–500.

Kedzierski, W., & Porter, J. C. (1990). Quantitative study of tyrosine hydroxylase mRNA in catecholaminergic neurons and adrenals during development and aging. *Brain Research Molecular Brain Research*, 7, 45–51.

Kim, S. K., Weinhold, P. A., Calkins, D. W., & Hartog, V. W. (1981). Comparative studies of the age-related changes in protein synthesis in the rat pancreas and parotid gland. *Experimental Gerontology*, 16, 91–99.

Kim, S. K., Weinhold, P. A., Han, S. S., & Wagner, D. J. (1980). Age-related decline in protein synthesis in the rat parotid gland. *Experimental Gerontology*, 15, 77–85.

Kimball, S. R., Vary, T. C., & Jefferson, L. S. (1992). Age-dependent decrease in the amount of eukaryotic initiation factor 2 in various rat tissues. *Biochemical Journal*, 286, 263–268.

Korhonen, P., Helenius, M., & Salminen, A. (1997). Age-related changes in the regulation of transcription factor NF-κB in rat brain. *Neuroscience Letters*, 225, 61–64.

Kuchel, G. A., Rowe, W., Meaney, M. J., & Richard, C. (1997). Neurotrophin receptor and tyrosine hydroxylase gene expression in aged sympathetic neurons. *Neurobiology of Aging*, 18, 67–79.

Kumazaki, T., & Mitsui, Y. (1996). Alterations in transcription factor-binding activities to fibronectin promoter during aging of vascular endothelial cells. *Mechanisms of Aging and Development*, 88, 111–124.

Ladiges, W., Morton, J., Blakely, C., & Gale, M. (2000). Increased expression of PKR protein kinase in aging B6D2F1 mice. *Mechanisms of Aging and Development*, in press.

Layman, D. K., Ricca, G. A., & Richardson, A. (1976). The effect of age on protein synthesis and ribosome aggregation to messenger RNA in rat liver. *Archives of Biochemistry and Biophysics*, 173, 246–254.

Lee, C. K., Klopp, R. G., Weindruch, R., & Prolla, T. A. (1999). Gene expression profile of aging and its retardation by caloric restriction. *Science*, 285, 1390–1393.

Lee, D. Y., Hayes, J. J., Pruss, D., & Wolffe, A. P. (1993). A positive role for histone acetylation in transcription factor access to nucleosomal DNA. *Cell*, 72, 73–84.

Levine, R. L., & Stadtman, E. R. (1996). Protein modifications with aging. In E. Schneider & J. W. Rowe (Eds.), *Handbook of the Biology of Aging*, 4th ed., (pp. 184–197). San Diego: Academic Press.

Liang, P., & Pardee, A. B. (1992). Differential display of eukaryotic messenger RNA by means of the polymerase chain reaction. *Science*, 257, 967–971.

Lin, Y. J., Seroude, L., & Benzer, S. (1998). Extended lifespan and stress resistance in the *Drosophila* mutant methuselah. *Science*, 282, 943–946.

Liu, A. Y., Lin, Z., Choi, H., Sorhage, F., & Li, B. (1989). Attenuated induction of heat shock gene expression in aging diploid fibroblasts. *Journal of Biological Chemistry*, 264, 12037–12045.

Liu, D. S., Ekstrom, R., Spicer, J. W., & Richardson, A. (1978). Age-related changes in protein, RNA and DNA content and protein synthesis in rat testes. *Experimental Gerontology*, 13, 197–205.

Locke, M., & Tanguay, R. M. (1996). Diminished heat shock response in the aged myocardium. *Cell Stress Chaperones*, 1, 251–260.

Magnuson, V. L., Young, M., Schattenberg, D. G., Mancini, M. A., Chen, D., Steffensen, B., & Klebe, R. J. (1991). The alternative splicing of fibronectin pre-mRNA is altered during aging and in response to growth factors. *Journal of Biological Chemistry*, 266, 14654–14662.

Makrides, S. C. (1983). Protein synthesis and degradation during aging and senescence. *Biological Reviews Cambridge Philosophical Society*, 58, 343–422.

Marcus, D. L., Ibrahim, N. G., & Freedman, M. L. (1982a). Age-related decline in the biosynthesis of mitochondrial inner membrane proteins. *Experimental Gerontology*, 17, 333–341.

Marcus, D. L., Lew, G., Gruenspecht-Faham, N., & Freedman, M. L. (1982b). Effect of inhibitors and stimulators on isolated liver cell mitochondrial protein synthesis from young and old rats. *Experimental Gerontology*, 17, 429–435.

Masoro, E. J. (1998). Influence of caloric intake on aging on the response to stressors. *Journal of Toxicology and Environmental Health*, 1, 243–257.

Masoro, E. J., & Austad, S. N. (1996). The evolution of the antiaging action of dietary restriction: a hypothesis. *Journals of Gerontology, 51,* B387–B391.

Medvedev, Z. A. (1984). Age changes of chromatin. *Mechanisms of Aging and Development, 28,* 139–154.

Medvedev, Z. A. (1986). Age-related changes of transcription and RNA processing. In D. Platt (Ed.), *Drugs and Aging* (pp. 1–19). Berlin: Springer Verlag.

Merrick, W. C. (1992). Mechanism and regulation of eukaryotic protein synthesis. *Microbiology Reviews, 56,* 291–315.

Miyamura, Y., Tawa, R., Koizumi, A., Uehara, Y., Kurishita, A., Sakurai, H., Kamiyama, S., & Ono, T. (1993). Effects of energy restriction on age-associated changes of DNA methylation in mouse liver. *Mutation Research, 295,* 63–69.

Mohan, S., & Radha, E. (1978). Age related changes in muscle protein degradation. *Mechanisms of Aging and Development, 7,* 81–87.

Moldave, K., Harris, J., Sabo, W., & Sadnik, I. (1979). Protein synthesis and aging: studies with cell-free mammalian systems. *FASEB Journal, 38,* 1979–1983.

Mooradian, A. D., Li, J., & Shah, G. N. (1998). Age-related changes in thyroid hoemone responsive protein (THRP) expression in cerebral tissue of rats. *Brain Research, 793,* 302–304.

Moore, R. E., Goldsworthy, T. L., & Pitot, H. C. (1980). Turnover of 3'-polyadenylate-containing RNA in livers from aged, partially hepatectomized, neonatal, and Morris 5123C hepatoma-bearing rats. *Cancer Research, 40,* 1449–1457.

Morimoto, R. I. (1993). Cells in stress: Transcriptional activation of heat shock genes. *Science, 259,* 1409–1410.

Morrow, L. A., Linares, O. A., Hill, T. J., Sanfield, J. A., Supiano, M. A., Rosen, S. G., & Halter, J. B. (1987). Age differences in the plasma clearance mechanisms for epinephrine and norepinephrine in humans. *Journal of Clinical Endocrinology and Metabolism, 65,* 508–511.

Moudgil, P. G., Cook, J. R., & Buetow, D. E. (1979). The proportion of ribosomes active in protein synthesis and the content of polyribosomal poly(A)-containing RNA in adult and senescent rat livers. *Gerontology, 25,* 322–326.

Nakazawa, T., Mori, N., & Goto, S. (1984). Functional deterioration of mouse liver ribosomes during aging: Translational activity and activity for formation of the 47S initiation complex. *Mechanisms of Aging and Development, 26,* 241–251.

Negrutskii B. S. El'skaya A. V. (1998) Eukaryotic translation elongation factor 1 alpha: Structure, expression, functions, and possible role in aminoacyl-tRNA channeling. *Progress in Nucleic Acid Research and Molecular Biology 60,* 47–78.

Nichols, N. R., Day, J. R., Laping, N. J., Johnson, S. A., & Finch, C. E. (1993). GFAP mRNA increases with age in rat and human brain. *Neurobiology of Aging, 14,* 421–429.

O'Callaghan, J. P., & Miller, D. B. (1991). The concentration of glial fibrillary acidic protein increases with age in the mouse and rat brain. *Neurobiology of Aging, 12,* 171–174.

Okamoto, K., & Aoki, K. (1963). Development of a strain of spontaneously hypertensive rats. *Japanese Circulatory Journal, 27,* 282–293.

Ono, T., Takahashi, N., & Okada, S. (1989). Age-associated changes in DNA methylation and mRNA level of the c-myc gene in spleen and liver of mice. *Mutation Research, 219,* 39–50.

Ono, T., Uehara, Y., Kurishita, A., Tawa, R., & Sakurai, H. (1993). Biological significance of DNA methylation in the ageing process. *Age & Ageing, 22,* S 34-S 43.

Pagani, F., Zagato, L., Coviello, D., & Vergani, C. (1992). Alternative splicing of fibronectin pre-mRNA during aging. *Annals NY Academy of Sciences, 663,* 477–478.

Pagani, F., Zagato, L., Vergani, C., Casari, G., Sidoli, A., & Baralle, F. E. (1991). Tissue-specific splicing pattern of fibronectin messenger RNA precursor during development and aging in rat. *Journal of Cellular Biology, 113,* 1223–1230.

Pahlavani, M. A., & Harris, M. D. (1996). The age-related changes in DNA binding activity of AP–1, NF-κB, OCT–1 transcription factors in lymphocytes from rats. *Age, 19,* 45–54.

Pahlavani, M. A., & Harris, M. D. (1998). Effect of in vitro generation of oxygen free radicals on T cell function in young and old rats. *Free Radical Biology & Medicine, 25*, 903–913.

Pahlavani, M. A., & Richardson, A. (1996). The effect of age on the expression of interleukin–2. *Mechanisms of Aging and Development, 89*, 125–154.

Pahlavani, M. A., & Vargas, D. (1999). Age-related decline in activation of calcium/calmodulin-dependent phosphatase calcineurin and kinase CaMK-IV in rat T cells. *Mechanisms of Aging and Development, 112*, 57–74.

Pahlavani, M. A., Denny, M., Moore, S. A., Weindruch, R., & Richardson, A. (1995a). The expression of heat shock protein 70 decreases with age in lymphocytes from rats and rhesus monkeys. *Experimental Cell Research, 218*, 310–318.

Pahlavani, M. A., Haley-Zitlin, V., & Richardson, A. (1994). Influence of dietary restriction on gene expression: Changes in the transcription of specific genes. In B. P.Yu (Ed.), *Modulation of the aging process by dietary restriction* (pp. 143–156). Boca Raton, FL: CRC Press.

Pahlavani, M. A., Harris, M. D., & Richardson, A. (1995b). The age-related decline in the induction of IL–2 transcription is correlated to changes in the transcription factor NFAT. *Cellular Immunology, 165*, 84.

Pahlavani, M. A., Harris, M. D., & Richardson, A. (1997). The increase in the induction of IL–2 transcription with caloric restriction is correlated to changes in the transcription factor NFAT. *Cellular Immunology, 180*, 10–19.

Pahlavani, M. A., Harris, M. D., & Richardson, A. (1998). Activation of p21ras/MAPK signal transduction molecules decreases with age in mitogen-stimulated T cells from rats. *Cell Immunology, 185*, 39–48.

Papaconstantinou, J., Reisner, P. D., Liu, L., & Kuninger, D. T. (1996). Mechanisms of altered gene expression with aging. In E. Schneider & J. W. Rowe (Eds.), *Handbook of the Biology of Aging 4th ed.*, (pp. 150–183). San Diego: Academic Press.

Park, G. H., & Buetow, D. E. (1990). RNA synthesis by hepatocytes isolated from adult and senescent Wistar rat liver. *Gerontology, 36*, 76–83.

Peterson, R. P., Cryar, J. R., & Gaubatz, J. W. (1984). Constancy of ribosomal RNA genes during ageing of mouse heart cells and during serial passage of WI–38 cells. *Archives of Gerontology and Geriatrics, 3*, 115–125.

Pluskal, M. G., Moreyra, M., Burini, R. C., & Young, V. R. (1984). Protein synthesis studies in skeletal muscle of aging rats. I. Alterations in nitrogen composition and protein synthesis using a crude polyribosome and pH 5 enzyme system. *Journals of Gerontology, 39*, 385–391.

Ponnappan, U., Trebilcock, G. U., & Zheng, M. Z. (1999). Studies into the effect of tyrosine phosphatase inhibitor phenylarsine oxide on NFKB activation in T lymphocytes during aging: evidence for altered IKB phosphorylation and degradation. *Experimental Gerontology, 34*, 95–107.

Poynter, M. E., & Daynes, R. A. (1998). Peroxisome proliferator-activated receptor alpha activation modulates cellular redox status, represses nuclear factor-KB signaling, and reduces inflammatory cytokine production in aging. *Journal of Biological Chemistry, 273*, 32833–32841.

Pucci, S., Doris, G., Barile, S., Pioli, C., & Frasca, D. (1998). Inhibition of IL–2 production by Nil-2-a in murine T cells. *International Immunology, 10*, 1435–1440.

Ramsay, G. (1998). DNA chips: state-of-the art. *Nature Genetics, 16*, 40–44.

Rath, P. C., & Kanungo, M. S. (1989). Methylation of repetitive DNA sequences in the brain during aging of the rat. *FEBS Letters, 244*, 193–198.

Rattan, S. I. (1996). Synthesis, modifications, and turnover of proteins during aging. *Experimental Gerontology, 31*, 33–47.

Rattan, S. I., & Clark, B. F. C. (1996). Intracellular protein synthesis, modifications and aging. *Biochemical Society Transactions, 24*, 1043–1049.

Rattan, S. I., Cavallius, J., Hartvigsen, G. K., & Clark, B. F. (1986). Amounts of active elongation factor 1 and its activity in livers of mice during aging. In *Modern Trends in*

Aging Research, 147 ed., (pp. 135–147). Rijswijk, The Netherlands: INSERM-EURAGE/John Libbey Eurotext Ltd.

Rattan, S. I., Derventzi, A., & Clark, B. F. (1992). Protein synthesis, posttranslational modifications, and aging. *Annals of the New York Academy Sciences, 663,* 48–62.

Rattan, S. I., Ward, W. F., Glenting, M., Svendsen, L., Riis, B., & Clark, B. F. (1991). Dietary calorie restriction does not affect the levels of protein elongation factors in rat livers during ageing. *Mechanisms of Aging and Development, 58,* 85–91.

Reznick, A. Z., & Gershon, D. (1979). The effect of age on the protein degradation system in the nematode *Turbatrix aceti. Mechanisms of Aging and Development, 11,* 403–415.

Riabowol, K., Schiff, J., & Gilman, M. Z. (1992). Transcription factor AP–1 activity is required for initiation of DNA synthesis and is lost during cellular aging. *Proceedings of the National Academy of Science of the USA, 89,* 157–161.

Richardson, A., & Birchenall-Sparks, M. C. (1983). Age-related changes in protein synthesis. In M. Rothstein (Ed.), *Biological Research in Aging, First ed.*, (pp. 255–273). New York, New York: Alan R. Liss, Inc.

Richardson, A., & Holbrook, N. J. (1996). Aging and the cellular response to stress: reduction in the heat shock response. In N. J. Holbrook, G. R. Martin, & R. A. Lockshin (Eds.), *Cellular Aging and Cell Death* (pp. 67–80). New York: Wiley-Liss, Inc.

Richardson, A., & Myers, J. (1982). A comparison of the cell-free protein synthetic activities of testicular tissue obtained from rats and mice of various ages. *Comparative Biochemistry and Physiology, 71B,* 709–712.

Richardson, A., & Semsei, I. (1987). Effect of aging on translation and transcription. In M. Rothstein (Ed.), *Review of Biological Research in Aging, 3 ed.*, (pp. 467–483). New York: Alan R. Liss.

Richardson, A., & Ward, W. F. (1994). Changes in protein turnover as a function of age and nutritional status. In R. R. Watson (Ed.), *Handbook of Nutrition in the Aged, 2 ed.*, pp. 309–315). Boca Raton, Florida: CRC Press.

Richardson, A., Birchenall-Sparks, M. C., & Staecker, J. L. (1983). Aging and transcription. In M. Rothstein (Ed.), *Biological Research in Aging, First ed.*, (pp. 275–294). New York, New York: Alan R. Liss, Inc.

Richardson, A., Birchenall-Sparks, M. C., Staecker, J. L., Hardwick, J., & Liu, D. S. (1982). The transcription of various types of ribonucleic acid by hepatocytes isolated from rats of various ages. *Journal of Gerontology, 37,* 666–672.

Richardson, A., Butler, J. A., Rutherford, M. S., Semsei, I., Gu, M. Z., Fernandes, G., & Chiang, W. H. (1987). Effect of age and dietary restriction on the expression of α_{2u} globulin. *Journal of Biological Chemistry, 262,* 12821–12825.

Rothstein, M., & Seifert, S. C. (1981). RNA synthesis. In J. R. Florini (Ed.), *Handbook of Biochemistry in Aging* (pp. 51–63). Boca Raton, Florida: CRC Press.

Roy, A. K. (1997). Transcription factors and aging. *Molecular Medicine, 3,* 496–504.

Sarge, K. D., Murphy, S. P., & Morimoto, R. I. (1993). Activation of heat shock gene transcription by heat shock factor 1 involves oligomerization, acquisition of DNA-binding activity, and nuclear localization and can occur in the absence of stress. *Molecular and Cellular Biology, 13,* 1392–1407.

Sargent, T. D. (1998). Isolation of differentially expressed genes. *Methods in Enzymology, 152,* 423–432.

Schena, M., Shalon, D., Heller, R., Chai, A., Brown, P. O., & Davis, R. W. (1996). Parallel human genome analysis: microarray-based expression monitoring of 1000 genes. *Proceedings of the National Academy of Science of the USA, 93,* 10614–10619.

Schiffmann, S. N., & Vanderhaeghen, J.-J. (1993). Age-related loss of mRNA encoding adenosine A2 receptor in the rat striatum. *Neuroscience Letters, 158,* 121–124.

Schreck, R., Albermann, K., & Baeuerle, P. A. (1992). Nuclear factor κ B: An oxidative stress-responsive transcription factor of eukaryotic cells (a review). *Free Radical Research Communications, 17,* 221–237.

Schröder H. C., Ugarkovic D., Müller W. E. G., Mizushima, H., Nemoto, F., Kuchino, Y., (1992). Increased expression of UAG suppressor tRNA in aged mice: consequences for retroviral gene expression. *European Journal of Gerontology, 1,* 452–457.

Semsei, I., Szeszak, F., & Zs.-Nagy, I. (1982). In vivo studies on the age-dependent decrease of the rates of total and mRNA synthesis in the brain cortex of rats. *Archives of Gerontology Geriatrics, 1,* 29–42.

Seshadri, T., & Campisi, J. (1990). Repression of c-fos transcription and an altered genetic program in senescent human fibroblasts. *Science, 247,* 205–209.

Shepherd, J. C. W., Walldorf, U., Hug, P., & Gehring, W. J. (1989). Fruit flies with additional expression of elongation factor EF-1α live longer. *Proceedings of the National Academy of Science of the USA, 86,* 7520–7521.

Shikama, N., Ackermann, R., & Brack, C. (1994). Protein synthesis elongation factor EF-1α expression and longevity in *Drosophila melanogaster*. *Proceedings of the National Academy of Science of the USA, 91,* 4106–4109.

Sikora, E., Kaminska, B., Radziszewska, E., & Kaczmarek, L. (1992). Loss of transcription factor AP-1 DNA binding activity during lymphocyte aging in vivo. *FEBS Letters, 312,* 179–182.

Silar, P., & Picard, M. (1994). Increased longevity of EF-1 α high-fidelity mutants in Podospora anserina. *Journal of Molecular Biology, 235,* 231–236.

Sinclair, D. A., & Guarente L. (1997). Extrachromosomal rDNA circles—a cause of aging in yeast. *Cell, 91,* 1033–1042.

Singh, S., & Kanungo, M. S. (1993). Changes in expression and CRE binding proteins of the fibronectin gene during aging of the rat. *Biochemical Biophysical Research Communications, 193,* 440–445.

Singh, A., Singh, S., & Kanungo, M. S. (1990). Conformation and expression of the albumin gene of young and old rats. *Molecular Biology Reports, 14,* 251–254.

Singhal, R. P., Mays-Hoopes, L. L., & Eichhorn, G. L. (1987). DNA methylation in aging of mice. *Mechanisms of Aging and Development, 41,* 199–210.

Slagboom, P. E., De Leeuw, W. J., & Vijg, J. (1990). Messenger RNA levels and methylation patterns of GAPDH and α-actin genes in rat liver, spleen and brain in relation to aging. *Mechanisms of Aging and Development, 53,* 243–257.

Sonntag, W. E., Lynch, C. D., Bennett, S. A., Khan, A. S., Thornton, P. L., Cooney, P. T., Ingram, R. L., McShane, T., & Brunso-Bechtold, J. K. (1999). Alterations in insulin-like growth factor–1 gene and protein expression and type 1 insulin-like growth factor receptors in the brains of ageing rats. *Neuroscience, 88,* 269–279.

Sorger, P. K. (1991). Heat shock factor and the heat shock response. *Cell, 65,* 363–366.

Stadtman, E. R. (1992). Protein oxidation and aging. (Review). *Science, 257,* 1220–1224.

Starnes, J. W., Beyer, R. E., & Edington, D. W. (1981). Effects of age and cardiac work in vitro on mitochondrial oxidative phosphorilation and [$_3$H]-leucine incorporation. *Journals of Gerontology, 36,* 130–135.

Strehler, B. L., Hirsch, G., Gusseck, D., Johnson, R., Bick, M. (1971) Codon restriction theory of ageing and development. *Journal of Theoretical Biology. 33,* 429–474.

Strong, R., Moore, M. A., Hale, C., Wessels-Reiker, M., Armbrecht, H. J., & Richardson, A. (1990). Modulation of tyrosine hydroxylase gene expression in the rat adrenal gland by age and reserpine. *Brain Research, 525,* 126–132.

Supakar, P. C., Jung, M. H., Song, C. S., Chatterjee, B., & Roy, A. K. (1995). Nuclear factor κB functions as a negative regulator for the rat androgen receptor gene and NF-κB activity increases during the age-dependent desensitization of the liver. *Journal of Biological Chemistry, 270,* 842.

Swisshelm, K., Disteche, C. M., Thorvaldsen, J., Nelson, A., & Salk, D. (1990). Age-related increase in methylation of ribosomal genes and inactivation of chromosome-specific rRNA gene clusters in mouse. *Mutation Research, 237,* 131–146.

Tajuddin, N. F., & Druse, M. J. (1998). Effect of chronic ethanol consumption and aging on proenkephlin and neurotensin. *Alcoholism, Clinical and Experimental Research, 22,* 1152–1160.

Takahashi, R., & Goto, S. (1990). Alteration of aminoacyl-tRNA synthetase with age: heat-labilization of the enzyme by oxidative damage. *Archives of Biochemistry and Biophysics, 277,* 228–233.

Tas, S., & Walford, R. L. (1982). Influence of disulfide-reducing agents on fractionation of the chromatin complex by endogenous nucleases and deoxyribonuclease I in aging mice. *Journal of Gerontology, 37,* 673–679.

Tas, S., Tam, C. F., & Walford, R. L. (1980). Disulfide bonds and the structure of the chromatin complex in relation to aging. *Mechanisms of Aging and Development, 12,* 65–80.

Tawa, R., Ueno, S., Yamamoto, K., Yamamoto, Y., Sagisaka, K., Katakura, R., Kayama, T., Yoshimoto, T., Sakurai, H., & Ono, T. (1992). Methylated cytosine level in human liver DNA does not decline in aging process. *Mechanisms of Aging and Development, 62,* 255–261.

Thakur, M. K., & Kaur, J. (1992a). Methylation of DNA and its modulation by estrogen in the uterus of aging rats. *Cellular and Molecular Biology, 38,* 525–532.

Thakur, M. K., & Kaur, J. (1992b). Estrogen-induced synthesis of uterine proteins declines during aging. *Molecular Biology Reports, 17,* 29–34.

Toliver-Kinsky, T., Papaconstantinou, J., & Perez-Polo, J. R. (1997). Age-associated alterations in hippocampal and basal forebrain nuclear factor kappa B activity. *Journal of Neuroscience Research, 48,* 580–587.

Trebilcock, G. U., & Ponnappan, U. (1996). Induction and regulation of NFKB during aging: role of protein kinases. *Clinical Immunology and Immunopathology, 79,* 87–91.

Trebilcock, G. U., & Ponnappan, U. (1998). Nuclear factor-kappaB induction in CD45RO+ and CD45RA+ T cell subsets during aging. *Mechanisms of Aging and Development 102,* 149–163.

Tuck, M. L. (1989). Treatment of hypertension in the elderly. In J. A. Armbrecht, R. Coe, & N. Wongsurawat (Eds.), *Endocrinology of Aging* (pp. 147–160). New York: Springer.

Tumer, N., Hale, C., Lawler, J., & Strong, R. (1992). Modulation of tyrosine hydroxylase gene expression in the rat adrenal gland by exercise: effects of age. *Molecular Brain Research, 14,* 51–56.

Tumer, N., Scarpace, P. J., Baker, H. V., & LaRochelle, J. S. (1997). AP–1 transcription factor binding activity in rat adrenal medulla and hypothalamus with age and cold exposure. *Neuropharmacology, 36,* 1065–1069.

Ullman, K. S., Northrop, J. P., Verweij, C. L., & Crabtree, G. R. (1990). Transmission of signals from the T lymphocyte antigen receptor to the genes responsible for cell proliferation and immune function: The missing link. *Annual Review of Immunolgy, 8,* 421–452.

van Bezooijen, C. F., Grell, T., & Knook, D. (1976). Albumin synthesis by liver parenchymal cells isolated from young, adult, and old rats. *Biochemical and Biophysical Research Communication, 31,* 513–519.

Vandenhaute, J., Claes-Reckinger, N., & Delcour, J. (1983). Age-related functional alteration of mouse liver ribosomes. *Experimental Gerontology, 18,* 355–363.

Van Remmen, H., Ward, W., Sabia, R. V., & Richardson, A. (1995). Effect of age on gene expression and protein degradation. In E. J. Masoro (Ed.), *Handbook of Physiology, Volume on Aging* (pp. 171–234). New York: Oxford University Press.

Veith, R. C., Featherstone, J. A., Linares, O. A., & Halter, J. B. (1986). Age differences in plasma norepinephrine kinetics in humans. *Journals of Gerontology, 41,* 319–324.

Velculescu, V. E., Zhang, L., Vogelstein, B., & Kinzler, K. W. (1995). Serial analysis of gene expression. *Science, 270,* 484–487.

Vinayak, M. (1987). A comparison of tRNA populations of rat liver and skeletal muscle during aging. *Biochemistry International, 15,* 279–285.

Voogt, J. L., Arbogast, L. A., Quadri, S. K., & Andrews, G. (1990). Tyrosine hydroxylase messenger RNA in the hypothalamus, substantia nigra and adrenal medulla of old female rats. *Brain Research Molecular Brain Research, 8,* 55–62.

Wagner, A. P., Beck, K. D., & Reck, G. (1992). Neural cell adhesion molecule (NCAM) and N-cadherin mRNA during development and aging: Selective reduction in the 7.4-kb and 6.7-kb NCAM mRNA levels in the hippocampus of adult and old rats. *Mechanisms of Aging and Development, 62*, 201–208.

Walter, R., & Sierra, F. (1998). Changes in hepatic DNA binding proteins as a function of age in rats [published erratum appears in *Journals of Gerontology A: Biol. Sci. Med. Sci.* (1998) 53(3):B172]. *Journals of Gerontology, 53*, B102–B110.

Ward, W. F., & Richardson, A. (2000). Changes in protein turnover as a function of age and nutritional status. In *Handbook of Nutrition in the Aged* (in press). Boca Raton, Florida: CRC Press.

Ward, W. F., & Shibatani, T. (1994). Dietary modulation of protein turnover. In B. P. Yu (Ed.), *Handbook of Modulation of Aging Processes by Dietary Restriction* (pp. 121). Boca Raton, Florida: CRC Press.

Webster, G. C. (1985). Protein synthesis in aging organisms. In R. S. Sohal, L. S. Birnbaum, & R. G. Cutler (Eds.), *Molecular Biology of Aging: Gene Stability and Gene Expression, 29 ed.*, (pp. 263–290). New York: Raven Press.

Webster, G. C., & Webster, S. L. (1983). Decline in synthesis of elongation factor one (EF–1) precedes the decreased synthesis of total protein in aging Drosophila melanogaster. *Mechanisms of Aging and Development, 22*, 121–128.

Webster, G. C., Webster, S. L., & Landis, W. A. (1981). The effect of age on the initiation of protein synthesis in Drosophila melanogaster. *Mechanisms of Aging and Development, 16*, 71–79.

Welle, S., Thornton, C., Bhatt, K., & Krym, M. (1997). Expression of elongation factor–1 alpha and S1 in young and old human skeletal muscle. *Journals of Gerontology, 52*, B235–B239.

Weller, E. M., Poot, M., & Hoehn, H. (1993). Induction of replicative senescence by 5-azacytidine: Fundamental cell kinetic differences between human diploid fibroblasts and NIH-3T3 cells. *Cell Proliferation, 26*, 45–54.

Westfall, T. C., & Meldrum, M. J. (1985). Alterations in the release of norepinephrine at the vascular neuroeffector junction in hypertension. *Annual Review of Pharmacology, 25*, 621– 641.

Whisler, R. L., Beiqing, L., & Chen, M. (1996). Age-related decreases in IL–2 production by human T cells are associated with impaired activation of nuclear transcriptional factors AP–1 and NF-AT. *Cell Immunology, 169*, 185–195.

Wilson, G. M., & Brewer, G. (1999). The search for trans-acting factors controlling messenger RNA decay. *Progress in Nucleic Acid Research and Molecular Biology, 62*, 257–291.

Wilson, V. L., & Jones, P. A. (1983). DNA methylation decreased in aging but not in immortal cells. *Science, 220*, 1055–1057.

Wilson, V. L., Smith, R. A., Ma, S., & Cutler, R. G. (1987). Genomic 5-methyldeoxycytidine decreases with age. *Journal of Biological Chemistry, 262*, 9948–9951.

Yamashita, H., Yamamoto, M., Ookawara, T., Sato, Y., Ueno, N., & Ohno, H. (1994). Discordance between thermogenic activity and expression of uncoupling protein in brown adipose tissue of old rats. *Journals of Gerontology, 49*, B54–B59.

Yoshida, T., Goldsmith, S. K., Morgan, T. E., Stone, D. J., & Finch, C. E. (1996). Transcription supports age-related increases of GFAP gene expression in the male rat brain. *Neuroscience Letters, 215*, 107–110.

Seven

Mitogen-Activated Protein Kinase Signaling Pathways and Aging

Yusen Liu and Nikki J. Holbrook

I. Introduction

The accumulation of damage to cells and tissues resulting from life-long exposure to various stresses is believed by many to be a key factor in the development of age-related diseases and disabilities and may underlie the normal aging process itself. A variety of defense mechanisms have evolved to help cells, tissues, and whole organisms cope with environmental insults, acting either to reduce the level of damage incurred or to aid its repair. However, aging appears to be accompanied by a diminished ability to mount many of these defense responses, thus resulting in a reduced tolerance to environmental insults, which could further exacerbate age-related deficits in physiologic functions. Strong genetic links between longevity and stress resistance have been established in lower organisms, particularly in the nematode, *Caenorhabditis elegans* (Hekimi *et al.*, 1998; Johnson *et al.*, 1996; Lin *et al.*, 1998). Although fewer studies are available in mammalian species, there is evidence suggesting that longevity is correlated with altered sensitivity to stress in mice. For example, telomerase-deficient mice exhibit a short-

ened life span and enhanced sensitivity to certain stresses (Rudolph *et al.*, 1999). In a reverse situation, mice in which a signaling adaptor protein, p66[SHC], has been deleted show increased longevity associated with enhanced resistance to acute environmental stress (Migliaccio *et al.*, 1999).

Mammalian aging also is accompanied by a loss in proliferative homeostasis, a topic discussed in detail in Chapter 8 in this volume. Proliferation is a complex and highly regulated process that is key to normal growth and development of an organism. However, even postdevelopment, it plays a vital role in the maintenance of renewable tissues and the repair of damaged organs. Indeed, proliferation is induced as an important response to certain stresses. Perturbations in growth regulatory mechanisms can have dire consequences for mammalian organisms and, depending on the nature of the dysregulation in proliferation, can lead to opposing conditions of hyperplasia/neoplasia and atrophy/cell death.

That these two features of aging (loss of proliferative homeostasis and reduced tolerance to stress) are in fact intimately linked has only become apparent as the signaling pathways involved in regulating the processes have begun to be unraveled. At the cellular level, external signals are received, processed, and transmitted internally through a variety of signaling cascades that together serve to coordinate the response to a given stimulus. Among the major pathways and/or central mediators involved in regulating cellular responses to external stimuli are the mitogen-activated protein kinase (MAPK)[1] signaling cascades (Garrington & Johnson, 1999), the phosphoinositide 3-kinase (PI3-K)/Akt pathway (Marte & Downward, 1997), the Jak/STAT pathway (Ransohoff, 1998), the NF-κB signaling system (Mercurio & Manning, 1999), p53 activation (Levine, 1997), and the heat-shock

response (Morimoto, 1993). Knowledge of these signaling pathways has increased enormously over the past few years and along with it the realization that common pathways regulate responses to both proliferative and stressful stimuli. Hence, perturbations of these signaling pathways with age could have broad effects on physiological function. Although many of the pathways noted earlier have not yet been studied extensively in this regard, there is significant evidence suggesting that perturbations in at least three different signal transduction pathways do occur with aging and are likely to contribute to age-related deficits in physiological function. These include the MAPK signaling pathways, the heat-shock response, and the activation of NF-κB.

Realizing that an attempt to review all of the signaling pathways noted previously would be an impossible task, we have chosen to concentrate our efforts on MAPK signaling cascades. MAPK pathways are central to many regulatory processes in mammalian cells and as such have been the subject of intensive investigation over the past decade (Garrington & Johnson, 1999). The extracellular signal-regulated kinase (ERK) pathway in particular plays an important role in mediating responses to a variety of mitogenic and stress stimuli and, as will be discussed, has been shown to undergo age-related changes in activity in numerous model systems. The heat-shock response and activation of NF-κB will not be covered in detail as they are discussed in Chapter 6 in this volume.

---

[1] **Abbreviations** MAPK, mitogen-activated protein kinase; PI3-K, phosphoinositide 3-kinase; Jak, Janus kinase; STAT, signal transducers and activators of transcription; NF-κB, nuclear factor κB; ERK, extracellular signal-regulated kinase; JNK, c-Jun N-terminal kinase; SAPK, stress-activated protein kinase; MAPKK, MAPK kinase; MAPKKK, MAPK kinase kinase; SH2, Src homology 2; SH3, Src homology 3; PTB, phosphotyrosine-binding; Grb2, growth factor receptor-bound protein 2; Sos, son of sevenless; Shc, SH2-domain-containing transforming protein; EGFR, epidermal growth factor receptor; PDGFR, platelet-derived growth factor receptor; TCR, T-cell receptor complex; Trk, receptor for nerve growth factor; UVC, ultraviolet light C; SEK1, SAPK/ERK kinase; JNKK, JNK kinase; MEKK, MAPKKK; MLK, mixed-lineage kinase; TAK1, transforming growth factor-activated protein kinase-1; ASK1, apoptosis signal-regulating kinase; MTK, MAP 3-kinase; PAK, p21-activated protein kinase; TNF-α, tumor necrosis factor-α; IL-1, interleukin-1; MK-2, MAP kinase-activated protein kinase-2; TCF, ternary complex factor; EGR1, early growth response protein-1; AP-1, activating protein-1; SRE, serum response element; IGF-1, insulin-like growth factor-1; IGF-1R, insulin-like growth factor-1 receptor; FGF, fibroblast growth factor; FGFR, FGF receptor; HSP, heat-shock protein; CDK, cyclin-dependent kinase; MEK, MAPK/ERK kinase; ITAM, immunoreceptor tyrosine-based activation motif; IL-2, interleukin-2; PLC-γ1, phospholipase C-γ1; IP3, inositol 1,4,5-trisphosphate; DAG, diacylglycerol.

II. MAPK Signaling Pathways

MAPK comprises an expanding family of proline-directed serine/threonine kinases that are activated by dual phosphorylation on threonine and tyrosine residues in response to a wide array of extracellular stimuli (Garrington & Johnson, 1999). Grouped according to the tripeptide signature motif (Thr-Xaa-Tyr) specifying their phosphorylation, three subfamilies have been identified so far in mammalian cells: ERK (Xaa=Glu), c-Jun N-terminal kinases (JNK) (Xaa=Pro), and p38 kinases (Xaa=Gly). As summarized in Fig. 1, the initiating mechanisms leading to activation of the three cascades vary, as do the intermediates involved. However, the overall organization of the MAPK pathways is conserved, with each consisting of a MAPK that is activated through phosphorylation by a MAPK kinase (MAPKK), which is in turn activated by another kinase (MAPKKK).

A. The ERK Pathway

The ERK pathway is the best characterized of the MAPK signaling cascades. First described in 1987 (Ray & Sturgill, 1987), it lies at the center of many signal transduction processes in mammalian cells and plays a key role in regulating cell growth and differentiation (Davis, 1993). ERK1 and ERK2, the major isoforms

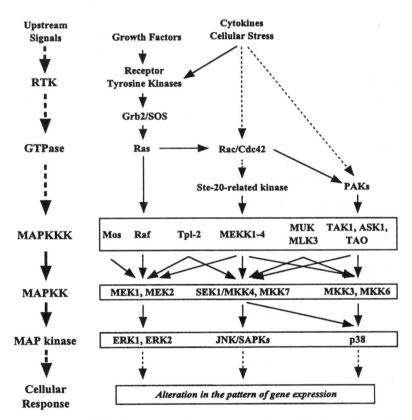

Figure 1. Schematic diagram of the three mammalian MAPK signal transduction pathways. The MAPKs are activated by MAPKKs, which in turn are activated by MAPKKKs. Both growth factors and cellular stress utilize receptor tyrosine kinases and Ras to activate the ERK pathway. Ras also plays a role in the activation of the JNK pathway in response to growth factors and cytokines. Crosstalk between the distinct pathways can occur at several levels. The ultimate outcome of the cellular response ranges from proliferation, differentiation, and growth arrest to apoptosis, depending on both the nature of the stimulus and the cell type involved. Bold arrows, direct activation of downstream components; dashed arrows, possible or indirect signaling routes.

representative of the ERK subfamily, are ubiquitously expressed, similarly regulated, and thus far functionally indistinct (Garrington & Johnson, 1999). Two additional ERK isoforms, ERK5 and ERK7, have been identified, but less is known concerning their regulation and functions (Abe *et al.*, 1999; Zhou *et al.*, 1995).

The ERK1/2 signaling pathway constitutes a major pathway through which growth factor receptors transduce proliferative signals to the nucleus (Davis, 1993, 1995; Treisman, 1996). In brief, ligand-mediated dimerization of growth factor receptors triggers the activation of the receptor-type tyrosine kinases, resulting in autophosphorylation of tyrosine residues (Schlessinger, 1993; Weiss & Schlessinger, 1998). These residues then serve as docking sites for the recruitment of downstream signaling mediators necessary for the activation of the membrane-localized small GTP-binding protein, Ras (Schlessinger, 1993). For example, the adaptor protein Grb2 binds to receptor phosphotyrosine residues through a Src homology 2 (SH2) domain to bring the Ras activator Son of Sevenless (Sos) from the cytoplasm to the vicinity of Ras. More often, however, the Grb2–Sos complexes are recruited to the phosphotyrosine sites through another adaptor protein, Shc, which binds to certain receptor phosphotyrosine sites through its phosphotyrosine-binding (PTB) domain. Shc then becomes tyrosine-phosphorylated, providing additional docking sites for Grb2 (Bonfini *et al.*, 1996). The ultimate outcome of these recruitments is the activation of Ras, which then initiates the phosphorylation cascade starting with the activation of the Raf protein kinases (A-Raf, B-Raf, or c-Raf) (Avruch *et al.*, 1994). Rafs are serine kinases that can phosphorylate and activate the MAPKK, MEK1, and MEK2, leading to activation of ERK1 and ERK2.

The ERK pathway initially was described as a pathway that was unrespon-sive to, or down-regulated by, stress stimuli (Kyriakis & Avruch, 1996). However, it has become apparent that certain stresses, most notably oxidant injury, lead to substantial activation of ERK and that growth factor receptors play an important role in mediating this effect. For example, many growth factor receptors, including epidermal growth factor receptor (EGFR), platelet-derived growth factor receptor (PDGFR), and the T-cell receptor complex (TCR), undergo phosphorylation in response to UVC irradiation (Huang *et al.*, 1996; Sachsenmaier *et al.*, 1994; Schieven *et al.*, 1994) or treatment with hydrogen peroxide or sodium arsenite (Chen *et al.*, 1998; Hardwick & Sefton, 1995). This results in Shc tyrosine phosphorylation and subsequent activation of the ERK1/2 cascade (Chen *et al.*, 1998; Huang *et al.*, 1996). In many cell types, treatments that prevent EGFR phosphorylation inhibit ERK activation in response to stress (Chen *et al.*, 1998; Guyton *et al.*, 1996; Sachsenmaier *et al.*, 1994), and cells expressing inactive mutant forms of the growth factor receptors show reduced activation of ERK by stress (Sachsenmaier *et al.*, 1994). Similarly, inhibition of TCR signaling prevents ERK activation in response to hydrogen peroxide or UVC irradiation in T-cells (Schieven *et al.*, 1994). Finally, elevated expression of certain growth factor receptors, such as the Trk receptor for nerve growth factor in rat PC12 cells, results in enhanced activation of ERK by hydrogen peroxide (Guyton *et al.*, 1998). The activation of ERK in response to such stresses generally is believed to deliver a prosurvival signal, as cell manipulations resulting in elevated ERK result in enhanced survival following exposure to hydrogen peroxide and other stresses, whereas manipulations or treatments that reduce ERK activation are correlated with reduced survival (Guyton *et al.*, 1996; Wang *et al.*, 1998).

G-protein-coupled receptors can also lead to the activation of ERK and, therefore, contribute to the regulation of gene expression in response to a variety of external stimuli, including neurotransmitters, hormones, and phospholipids (Gutkind, 1998). Like stress, G-protein-coupled receptors can stimulate EGFR tyrosine autophosphorylation and activate the ERK1/2 signaling pathway (Gutkind, 1998). Another mechanism leading to ERK1/2 MAP kinase activation involves down-regulation of the negative regulators that normally act to inhibit the pathway. It has been demonstrated that G-proteins can activate the ERK1/2 pathway by down-regulating the activity of Rap, a competitor of Ras (Mochizuki *et al.*, 1999b). Finally, because the activities of ERK1/2 are regulated through reversible phosphorylation, it is possible to elevate ERK1/2 activities by inhibiting the phosphatases responsible for their inactivation (Saxena *et al.*, 1999).

B. Stress-Activated Protein Kinase Pathways

The multimembered JNK and p38 MAPK subfamilies are also referred to as stress-activated protein kinases (Kyriakis & Avruch, 1996). They are potently activated by a diverse array of cellular stresses, including UVC irradiation, heat shock, inflammatory cytokines, and chemical and oxidative stresses, but are only weakly activated by growth factors (Kyriakis & Avruch, 1996). In the phosphorylation cascades leading to their activation, MKK4 (also known as SEK1 or JNKK) and MKK7 are the predominant MAPKKs responsible for JNK activation, whereas MKK3 and MKK6 are the major activators of p38. There is, however, considerable crosstalk between the JNK and p38 pathways at this level, such that in many cell types MKK4 can phosphorylate p38 (Garrington & Johnson, 1999). The identity of the specific MAPKKK involved in regulating the JNK and p38 pathways under physiologic conditions is less clear. More than 10 protein kinases have been shown to act at this level to trigger the activation of the JNK pathway in cotransfection experiments (Garrington & Johnson, 1999). These include several MKK kinases and "mixed-lineage" kinases (MLKs), transforming growth factor-activated protein kinase-1 (TAK1), the cellular homologue of the Tpl2 oncogene, apoptosis signal-regulating kinase (ASK1), and MTK1 [reviewed in Garrington and Johnson (1999)]. In the case of the JNK pathway, the complexity of the problem is further emphasized by the fact that the MAPKKs MKK4 and MKK7 are not always activated by the same signals. Thus, although MKK4 and MKK7 are both activated in response to stress stimuli, such as osmotic shock, UVC irradiation, and the protein synthesis inhibitor anisomycin, only MKK7 is activated after stimulation by the proinflammatory cytokines interleukin-1 and tumor necrosis factor in several cells and tissues (Garrington & Johnson, 1999).

As seen for Raf activation in the ERK pathway, activation of the MAPKKK involved in activating the JNK and p38 pathways likewise requires a small GTPase. Whereas activation of JNK by growth factors also is initiated by growth factor receptor tyrosine kinases and is mediated through Ras, other GTPases, including Rac, CDC42, and Rho, are involved in the activation of the JNK and p38 pathways by stress (Gutkind, 1998). The exact mechanism leading to activation of the JNK and p38 modules from these GTPases remains to be elucidated, but appears to involve an additional mediator linking them to MAPKKK activation (see Fig. 1).

Activation of JNK frequently is associated with apoptosis, and in many situations prevention of JNK activation leads to enhanced survival (Ichijo *et al.*, 1997; Wang *et al.*, 1998; Xia *et al.*, 1995). Such studies have implicated JNK and its downstream targets in mediating the cell death program. It should be emphasized, however, that in many of the reported studies JNK activation was not proven to be causative, but rather correlated with cell death, and there are also mounting studies that support a prosurvival function for JNK in other situations (Nishina et al., 1997; Potapova et al., 2000). Studies examining the influence of p38 activation are even more controversial. So far, the best characterized function of p38 is in regulating the production of inflammatory cytokines. Production of TNF-α and IL-1 in response to lipopolysaccharide is greatly attenuated by p38-specific inhibitors (Ono & Han, 2000). This action of p38 very likely is mediated by its downstream kinase, MAP kinase-activated protein kinase-2 (MK-2), because the disruption of MK-2 in transgenic mice also greatly reduces the production of inflammatory cytokines (Kotlyarov et al., 1999). In summary, depending on the cell type and/or conditions examined, the stress-activated kinases can be either proapoptotic (most instances), prosurvival, or exert no influence on survival. The basis for their differential influences is unclear.

C. Effects of MAPK on Gene Expression

Once activated, MAPK conveys extracellular signals to various downstream targets, leading to changes in gene expression, translation, cytoskeletal rearrangement, and morphology. A large number of proteins, including protein kinases, transcription factors, cytoskeletal proteins, and phospholipase, have been identified as substrates for MAPKs and, thus, constitute direct targets of the MAPK signaling pathways (Davis, 1993). Transcription factors comprise a particularly important group of MAPK targets. A representative listing of these is provided

in Table I. It is important to note that, in some cases, phosphorylation of the transcription factor is restricted to a specific kinase subfamily, whereas in other cases, the transcription factor can be phosphorylated by all three MAPKs. Interestingly, several of the transcription factors noted in the table have been shown to undergo alterations in their activities with aging (designated with an asterisk), which could reflect alterations in MAPK signaling. Particular genes whose expression is regulated by such transcription factors constitute secondary targets of these signaling pathways. Many such genes have been described [for a partial listing, the reader is referred to Liu et al. (1998a)]. Again, a number of these MAPK-regulated genes have been shown to undergo changes in expression with aging. Table II contains genes representative of this category. Interestingly, both the activity and expression of some transcription factors are dependent on MAPK, such as those seen for c-Fos and c-Jun (Treisman, 1996; Whitmarsh & Davis, 1996). For example, c-FOS transcription is regulated in large part through ERK-dependent phosphorylation of TCF, a component of the transcription factor complex that interacts with the serum response element in the c-FOS promoter (Treisman, 1996). Because TCF can also be phosphorylated by JNK and p38, this provides an additional mechanism for stress-induced c-FOS expression (Whitmarsh & Davis, 1996). This may explain the fact that serum-induced c-FOS expression is altered by aging (discussed in greater detail later), whereas stress-induced expression is not (Choi et al., 1995).

D. Age-Related Alterations in MAPK Signaling Pathways

As noted previously, two hallmarks of aging include a reduction in proliferative capacity and reduced tolerance to stress.

Table I
Transcription Factors That Have Been Demonstrated To Be Substrates of Members of the MAP Kinase Family

Transcription factor[a]	MAP kinase members shown to phosphorylate the transcription factor	References
ATF-1	p38	Iordanov et al., 1997
ATF-2	ERK, JNK, p38	Gupta et al., 1995
c-Fos*	ERK	Chen et al., 1993; Irving et al., 1992; Matsuda et al., 1992; Seshadri & Campisi, 1990
c-Jun*	JNK	Davis, 1995; Delpedro et al., 1998; Liu et al., 1996b
c-Myc*	ERK	Alvarez et al., 1991; Matsuda et al., 1992; Rittling et al., 1986
c-Myb	ERK	Vorbrueggen et al., 1996
CBP	ERK	Janknecht & Nordheim, 1996
C/EBP-β/NF-IL6*	ERK	Hsieh et al., 1998; Nakajima et al., 1993
CREB*	p38	Asanuma et al., 1996; Chin et al., 1996; Iordanov et al., 1997; Kumazaki & Mitsui, 1996
Erm	ERK	de Groot et al., 1993; Janknecht et al., 1996
Ets-1	ERK	Slupsky et al., 1998
Ets-2	ERK	Fowles et al., 1998
Fra-2	ERK	Gruda et al., 1994; Murakami et al., 1997
Gadd153/CHOP10	p38	Wang & Ron, 1996
Max	Mxi-2/p38	Zervos et al., 1995
MEF-2C	p38	Han et al., 1997
NF-ATc*	ERK, JNK, p38	Porter et al., 2000; Whisler et al., 1996a
NF-AT4*	JNK	Chow et al., 1997; Whisler et al., 1996a,b Atadja et al., 1994; Treisman, 1996;
p60^{TCF}/Elk1*	ERK, JNK, p38	Whitmarsh & Davis, 1996
p53*	ERK, JNK, p38	Atadja et al., 1995; Hu et al., 1997; Huang et al., 1999; Milne et al., 1994; Serrano et al., 1997
SAP-1a	ERK, JNK, p38	Janknecht & Hunter, 1997; Strahl et al., 1996; Whitmarsh et al., 1997
Stat1	ERK, p38	Goh et al., 1999
Stat3*	ERK, JNK	Jain et al., 1998; Sengupta et al., 1998; Xu & Sonntag, 1996
Stat5	ERK	Pircher et al., 1999
TAL1	ERK	Cheng et al., 1993
TFII-I	ERK	Kim & Cochran, 2000

[a]An asterisk indicate a transcription factor shown to undergo age-associated alteration in either expression (basal or induced) and/or activity in certain systems.

Because MAPK pathways play a critical role in regulating both of these processes, alterations in MAPK signaling pathways with aging provide a common link between these seemingly disparate features. In this section, we will review the literature indicating that MAPK signaling, and that of ERK in particular, is indeed altered with aging in a variety of different model systems.

1. Alterations in In Vitro Aged Human Diploid Fibroblasts

Normal human diploid fibroblasts undergo a limited number of cell divisions in culture before ceasing to replicate, a process referred to as *in vitro* senescence (Cristofalo & Pignolo, 1993; Hayflick, 1974). Limited *in vitro* life span is not restricted to fibroblasts but is also

Table II

Examples of Proliferation- or Stress-Associated Genes Whose Transcription Is Regulated by MAP Kinase
Pathways and Show Altered Expression with Age[a]

Gene	MAP kinase member involved in transcriptional regulation[b]	References
Angiotensin II type 1 receptors (AT1)	ERK	Heymes et al., 1998; Holzmeister et al., 1997
COX-2	ERK, JNK, p38	Chung et al., 1999; Guan et al., 1998; LaPointe & Isenovic, 1999; Ohzeki et al., 1999
c-FOS	ERK, JNK, p38	Irving et al., 1992; Matsuda et al., 1992; Seshadri & Campisi, 1990; Treisman, 1996; Whitmarsh & Davis, 1996
c-JUN	ERK, JNK, p38	Delpedro et al., 1998; Liu et al., 1996a,b; Rauscher et al., 1988; Whitmarsh & Davis, 1996
EGR-1	ERK	Cohen 1996; Meyyappan et al., 1996
Heme oxygenase-1 (HO-1)	ERK	Elbirt et al., 1998; Iijima et al., 1999; Nakanishi & Yasumoto, 1997
Interleukin-1 (IL-1)	ERK, JNK, p38	Kumar et al., 1992; Liao et al., 1993; Ono & Han, 2000; Shapiro & Dinarello, 1995; Shimizu et al., 1997; Srivastava et al., 1999
Interleukin-2 (IL-2)	ERK, JNK	Li et al., 1996; Liu et al., 1997; Pahlavani et al., 1997; Whisler et al., 1996
Matrix metalloproteinase-1 (MMP-1)	ERK, JNK, p38	Angel & Karin, 1991; Guo et al., 1999; Reed et al., 2000; Ricciarelli et al., 1999; Robert et al., 1997
Matrix metalloproteinase-9 (MMP-9)	ERK, JNK	Gum et al., 1997; Guo et al., 1999; Zeigler et al., 1999
MKP-1/CL100	ERK, JNK, p38	Bokemeyer et al., 1996; Cook et al., 1997; Liu et al., 1996b
p21/WAF1/CIP1/SDI1	ERK	Kitano et al., 1996; Liu et al., 1996a Noda et al., 1994; Smith et al., 1996
Tumor necrosis factor-α (TNF-α)	ERK, JNK, p38	Chang et al., 1996; Higashimoto et al., 1993; Ono & Han, 2000; Paganelli et al., 1994; Swantek et al., 1997; Tan et al., 1999
Urokinase plasminogen activator (uPA)	ERK, JNK, p38	Miralles et al., 1998; Miura et al., 2000; Mochizuki et al., 1999a

[a] Alteration could be either in basal levels or under conditions of induction. Both increases and decreases are included.
[b] MAP kinase members so far shown to be involved in the transcriptional regulation of the gene.

characteristic of other cells, including glial cells, keratinocytes, vascular smooth muscle cells, lens cells, endothelial cells, and lymphocytes (Cristofalo & Pignolo, 1993). Because in vivo aged cells also undergo a reduction in proliferative capacity, in vitro senescence has been used as a model for understanding basic mechanisms contributing to in vivo age-associated loss of proliferation. However, the relationship between in vitro senescence and in vivo aging is still unclear. The general topic of cellular senescence is covered in Chapter 8 in this volume. We will limit our discussion of this model system to studies examining changes in MAPK activities during in vitro aging.

Early studies examining in vitro senescence focused on the identification of genes whose expression was altered as a function of cell passage (Cristofalo et al., 1998; Seshadri & Campisi, 1990). Among the genes down-regulated in senescent cells are several that have been shown to a play a direct role in regulating cell proliferation and that are now known to be regulated, at least in part, through MAPK-dependent pathways.

These include the immediate early genes c-*FOS*, *EGR-1*, and c-*MYC* (in some cell types). c-*FOS* is of particular interest because c-Fos protein interacts with c-Jun to form AP-1 transcription factors (Angel & Karin, 1991); thus, its diminished induction during aging likely would affect the activity of the AP-1 transcription factor. Indeed, several studies have demonstrated a significant decrease in the amount and DNA binding activity of AP-1 in senescent cells (Choi *et al.*, 1995; Kumazaki & Mitsui, 1996; Liu *et al.*, 1996b; Riabowol *et al.*, 1992). Both the expression of *EGR-1* and its DNA binding activity are also reduced in senescent cells (Meyyappan *et al.*, 1996, 1999). Like c-*FOS* (discussed earlier), *EGR-1* transcription is regulated through a serum response element (SRE) in its promoter (Cohen, 1996). Because the transcription factors that interact with the SRE are known to be regulated by ERK, it is interesting to speculate that a defect in ERK signaling could account for the down-regulation of both genes (Treisman, 1996).

Despite the obvious links between MAPK signaling and genes whose expression is altered with *in vitro* aging, surprisingly few studies have actually examined MAPK activities in this model. Nonetheless, several interesting observations have been made. In examining the phosphorylation/activation of the ERK2 and ERK1 isoforms, Afshari *et al.* (1993) found that, in early passage fibroblasts, both isoforms become tyrosine-phosphorylated in response to serum stimulation, whereas in senescent cells only ERK1 becomes tyrosine-phosphorylated. Curiously, treatment of senescent cells with a protein phosphatase inhibitor rescues ERK2 phosphorylation and rejuvenates DNA synthesis (Afshari & Barrett, 1994). This abnormality of ERK activation in response to proliferative stimuli is not restricted to the human fibroblasts, because Medrano *et al.* (1994) observed a similar age-associated reduction in ERK2 activation/phosphorylation in aged melanocytes.

Because receptor tyrosine kinases play a key role in initiating the mitogenic response leading to ERK activation, alterations at the level of the growth factor receptor could explain the loss of ERK activation in response to proliferative stimuli. It appears that some late passage cells maintain receptor levels similar to those seen in early passage cells, whereas others display passage-related changes. In WI-38 cells, for example, the levels of receptors for epidermal growth factor (EGF), platelet-derived growth factor (PDGF), and insulin-like growth factor-1 (IGF-1) [EGF receptor (EGFR), PDGF receptor (PDGFR), and IGF-1 receptor (IGF-IR), respectively] all appear unaltered as a function of age (Cristofalo & Pignolo, 1993). Likewise, EGFR and PDGFR in aged cells appear to undergo autophosphorylation to an extent similar to that seen in young cells (Cristofalo & Pignolo, 1993). However, these findings do not rule out the possibility that subtle alterations in the functional properties of aged receptors exist, but have not been identified. In senescent humanomental microvascular endothelial cells, it has been reported that both the expression of EGFR mRNA and EGFR numbers are reduced significantly (Matsuda *et al.*, 1992). In human smooth muscle cells, at least PDGFR levels decrease with age (Aoyagi *et al.*, 1995). Finally, *in vitro* aging-related changes in the functional properties of receptor tyrosine kinases have been reported in several systems. In senescent human umbilical vein endothelial cells, treatment of cells with fibroblast growth factor (FGF) fails to induce tyrosine-phosphorylation of FGF receptor (FGFR) substrates such as Src (Garfinkel *et al.*, 1996).

Two studies have examined the activities of JNK in *in vitro* aged fibroblasts and they arrived at different conclusions.

Adler *et al.* (1996) reported that *in vitro* senescence is associated with reduced activation of JNK in response to both heat shock and UVC irradiation. In contrast, Volloch *et al.* (1998), reported that JNK activation in response to heat shock is elevated in late passage cells compared to their early passage counterparts. The cause for the discrepancies between these two studies is not clear. Volloch *et al.* (1998) have suggested that the increased JNK activity in old cells observed in their studies is due to the known impairment in HSP72 induction in aged cells. In other studies, they have provided evidence to suggest that HSP70 can interact directly with JNK to suppress its activation (Gabai *et al.*, 1997); hence, reduced HSP70 leads to elevated JNK. So far, no age-related changes in the activation of p38 pathways have been reported.

2. Alterations in In Vivo Aged Primary Hepatocytes

Unlike most other vital organs, the liver has a tremendous regenerative capacity (Michalopoulos & DeFrances, 1997). Regeneration is not dependent on stem or progenitor cells, as seen in other regenerative tissues such as bone marrow or skin, but instead is carried out by proliferation of existing mature cell populations comprising the intact organ (Diehl & Rai, 1996; Michalopoulos & DeFrances, 1997). Freshly isolated hepatocytes also are capable of undergoing one or two rounds of DNA synthesis in response to mitogenic stimuli. This property and the relative ease with which hepatocytes can be obtained from intact hosts have made this an attractive model for investigating mechanisms associated with age-related alterations in proliferation. Indeed, an age-related delay in DNA synthesis and a decline in proliferative capacity occur both in the livers of rats subjected to partial hepatectomy and in cultured hepatocytes stimulated with

growth factors (Ishigami *et al.*, 1993; Liu *et al.*, 1998b; Tsukamoto *et al.*, 1993).

In hepatocytes of Wistar rats, the age-related decline in EGF-stimulated DNA synthesis is correlated with lower activity of cyclin-dependent kinase 2 (CDK2) and a reduction in cyclin D1 expression (Liu *et al.*, 1998b). CDK2 and cyclin D1 are important mediators of cell cycle progression, because they are required for the movement of cells from the G1 phase into the S phase of the cell cycle. Comparison of ERK activation in young and aged hepatocytes in response to EGF stimulation revealed ~3-fold lower levels of ERK activity in aged cells (Liu *et al.*, 1996b, 1998b). The reduction in ERK activation likewise was associated with a reduction in the expression of the ERK-dependent genes c-*fos* and c-*jun*, and reduced AP-1 DNA binding activity (Liu *et al.*, 1996b). These findings were confirmed by Palmer *et al.* (1999) using young and aged hepatocytes derived from Fischer 344 rats.

In an attempt to identify the mechanisms responsible for the reduced ERK activity, the activities of upstream regulators of ERK, Ras, Raf1, and MEK have been examined. Although a previous study reported that MEK activity did not differ in young versus aged cells (Kitano *et al.*, 1998), by using a more specific assay, we have observed a significant reduction in MEK activity in aged cells consistent with the reduced activation of ERK (Hutter *et al.*, 2000). In addition, both Ras and Raf1 activities are reduced in the aged hepatocytes (Hutter *et al.*, 2000; Palmer *et al.*, 1999), suggesting that the basis for the defect in the aged cells resides at a level above Ras, i.e., at the level of the growth factor receptor.

By using classic receptor–ligand binding assays to characterize EGFR, Ishigami *et al.* (1993) reported that there was no difference in either the number or the affinity of EGFR in young versus aged rat hepatocytes. Direct comparison of the

EGFR protein content or its tyrosine phosphorylation in response to EGF stimulation also failed to detect any difference in the EGFR of young and aged hepatocytes (Hutter *et al.*, 2000; Palmer *et al.*, 1999). However, by investigating the interaction between EGFR and a crucial adaptor protein, Shc, we (Hutter *et al.*, 2000) and Palmer *et al.* (1999) independently observed that, in aged cells, Shc is unable to form stable complexes with EGFR following EGF treatment. In summary, as depicted in Fig. 2, a defect in retaining the Shc adaptor protein to the

EGFR appears to be a major contributor to the age-associated decline in EGF-stimulated ERK activation. The cause for the decreased EGFR–Shc interactions is unclear, but we offer several hypotheses here. First, aged hepatocytes may express a tyrosine phosphatase that specifically dephosphorylates the tyrosine residues responsible for interacting with Shc or, alternatively, aged hepatocytes might be dysfunctional in a mechanism that normally prevents dephosphorylation of EGFR by a tyrosine phosphatase. Such a change in phosphorylation would not be

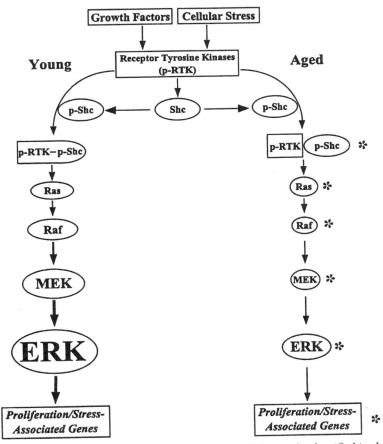

Figure 2. Schematic illustration of age-associated defects in the ERK cascade identified in the rat primary hepatocyte model. Aged hepatocytes are deficient in their ability to recruit and/or retain the adaptor protein Shc in receptor complexes, leading to reduced activities in all of the downstream steps of the pathway. Asterisks indicate where age-associated changes have been reported.

visible in the assays employed, which assess total EGFR phosphorylation. This hypothesis is supported by observations made by Palmer *et al.* (1999). By using a phosphospecific antibody that recognizes phosphotyrosine-1173 of the EGFR, they have examined its phosphorylation status. This site, which is known to be recognized by the Shc PTB domain, was found to be underphosphorylated in aged hepatocytes. Second, a post translational modification of either EGF receptor or Shc could result in the reduced interaction between these two molecules. Other investigators have provided evidence that aging is associated with increased oxidation of proteins (as discussed in Chapters 2, 3, and 6 in this volume). It is possible that such a modification could result in decreased interaction between Shc and EGFR. Finally, aged hepatocytes may express an inhibitory protein that physically disrupts this interaction

Certain stresses can also lead to the activation of ERK. By examining the response to heat stress as well as to hydrogen peroxide and the sulfhydral modifying agent sodium arsenite, we observed significantly lower activation of ERK in aged cells (Guyton *et al.*, 1998). Given that oxidants (at least hydrogen peroxide and sodium arsenite) appear to usurp the EGFR pathway to activate ERK (Chen *et al.*, 1998), it is likely that the same mechanism responsible for the decline in ERK activation in response to EGF applies to stress-induced activation of the kinase.

In contrast to the dramatic decrease in ERK activity seen in aged hepatocytes, we have not observed any changes in the activities of either JNK or p38 in these cells (Liu *et al.*, 1996b). It is worth pointing out that primary hepatocytes exhibit a very high basal level of JNK activity. It is possible that such a high basal activity may reflect a chronic state of stress in cells removed from the intact organ.

3. Alterations in T-Lymphocyte Signaling

It is well-established that aging is accompanied by a decline in immune responsiveness and, in particular, impairments in T-cell functions. Many of the defects in T-cell function are a reflection of reduced proliferation in response to antigenic or mitogenic stimuli. A number of reviews (Miller *et al.*, 1997) are available on this topic, and certain aspects of these defects are likewise discussed in Chapter 12 of this volume (Chakravarti & Abraham, 1999; Hirokawa, 1999). We will restrict our discussion to changes in immune function as they relate to the MAPK signaling pathways.

T-cell-dependent immune functions rely on the activation and clonal expansion of a small number of T-cells. There are two major routes of stimulation that result in proliferation and cytokine production in T-cells. One is mediated by the T-cell receptor (TCR) (Abraham *et al.*, 1992; Wange & Samelson, 1996), the other by cytokine receptors. TCR is composed of six different polypeptide chains thought to be organized into an eight-chain structure. These polypeptides include a ligand-binding heterodimer ($\alpha\beta$ or $\gamma\delta$) and the nonpolymorphic CD3ε, CD3γ, CD3δ, and TCRζ chains. The TCRζ and the CD3 chains all contain immunoreceptor tyrosine-based activation motifs (ITAMs) in their long cytoplasmic portions. Upon TCR activation, the tyrosine residues within the ITAMs become phosphorylated sequentially, giving rise to the activation of other tyrosine kinases associated with TCR complexes and CD4/8 molecules, such as Lck, Fyn, and ZAP-70 (Abraham *et al.*, 1992; Wange & Samelson, 1996). These tyrosine kinases are responsible for further transducing the signal initiated from the TCR to downstream signal signaling cascades, resulting in activation of the MAP kinase cascades, mobilization of intracellular Ca^{2+}, and enhanced expression of proliferative cytokines, most notably IL-2 (Abraham *et al.*, 1992; Wange & Samelson, 1996).

IL-2 production induced in response to TCR engagement is mediated mainly through a transcriptional mechanism, and ERK and JNK play important roles in this process through their stimulatory effect on AP-1 transcription factor complexes (Favero & Lafont, 1998; Pastor *et al.*, 1995). The mechanism through which Ca^{2+} exerts its effect on IL-2 induction is more complex, with both MAPK-independent and MAPK-dependent events being involved. Ca^{2+} can stimulate the activity of calcineurin, a Ca^{2+}/calmodulin-dependent protein phosphatase. Cacineurin in turn facilitates the nuclear translocation of NFAT, which is the critical transcription factor involved in IL-2 transcriptional regulation. Both ERK and JNK are important downstream effectors of the Ca^{2+} signal. Ca^{2+} can feed into the ERK pathway through activation of protein kinase C (PKC), which in turn activates Raf (and potentially Ras). The effect of Ca^{2+} on JNK activation has been demonstrated through the use of calcineurin inhibitors (Su *et al.*, 1994; Werlen *et al.*, 1998), but the mechanism involved in this regulation is still unclear. An age-related alteration occurring in any one of these signaling events could contribute to the decline in IL-2 production.

Numerous aged-related changes in T-cell signaling events have been documented (Chakravarti & Abraham, 1999; Hirokawa, 1999; Miller, 1991, 1994, 1996; Pawelec & Solana, 1997; Pawelec *et al.*, 1999; Solana & Pawelec, 1998). In human, rat, and mouse cells alike it has been found that mitogenic stimulation results in lower ERK activation in aged cells than in young cells (Gorgas *et al.*, 1997; Kirk & Miller, 1998; Liu *et al.*, 1997; Pahlavani & Vargas, 2000; Pahlavani *et al.*, 1998; Whisler *et al.*, 1996b). Importantly, caloric restriction, which leads to an extension in

the average life span of rats and attenuates other age-related declines in physiological function, significantly reduces the age-related loss in ERK activity (Pahlavani *et al.*, 1997; Pahlavani & Vargas, 2000).

Activation of JNK in response to mitogenic signals also appears to be lower in aged mouse and human cells (Kirk & Miller, 1999; Kirk *et al.*, 1999), but no loss in JNK activity was found in rat T-cells (Pahlavani *et al.*, 1998). Likewise, in mouse T-cells, JNK activation by several stresses, including hydrogen peroxide, ceramide, and osmotic stress, was not altered with age, whereas activation of the kinase in response to UVC irradiation and TCR stimulation was (Kirk & Miller, 1999). To our knowledge, no alterations in p38 signaling have yet been reported.

Examination of Ras and Raf activities has indicated that their mitogen-induced activation is also reduced in aged cells (Kirk & Miller, 1998; Pahlavani *et al.*, 1998; Pahlavani & Vargas, 2000). This suggests that, as seen for hepatocytes, the age-related decline in ERK (and possibly JNK) activation is likely to be due to alterations in the early signaling events of the pathway, occurring at or near the level of the TCR. The early signaling events surrounding TCR activation are highly complex, and a complete discussion of this process is beyond the scope of this review. In brief, however, a number of laboratories have provided evidence that the activities and/or phosphorylation patterns of several tyrosine kinases known to play a role in linking TCR activation to the MAPK pathways are altered in aged T-cells of humans and rodents. These include Fyn, ZAP-70, CD3ζ, and Lck (Guidi *et al.*, 1998; Hirokawa, 1999; Miller *et al.*, 1997; Pahlavani *et al.*, 1998; Whisler *et al.*, 1998, 1999). A reduction in the phosphorylation of Shc in response to anti-CD3 stimulation has also been reported (Ghosh & Miller, 1995).

In addition to the abnormalities detected in various tyrosine kinases, defects in other signaling molecules have been reported. Tyrosine phosphorylation of phospholipase C-γ1 (PLC-γ1) in response to TCR cross-linking was reported to be reduced in T-cells from aged mice (Grossmann *et al.*, 1995). Such a defect in PLC-γ1 regulation is consistent with reduced production of inositol 1,4,5-trisphosphate (IP3) and diacylglycerol (DAG) and reduced Ca^{2+} influx, ultimately leading to a deficiency in PKC

translocation and activation (Chakravarti & Abraham, 1999). As PKC can lead to activation of the ERK pathway through the activation of Raf, these events could contribute to reduced ERK activation.

In summary, age-related alterations have been reported at multiple levels of the signal transduction cascades in T-lymphocytes from human, rats, and mice. As illustrated in Fig. 3, any or all of these defects could contribute to the

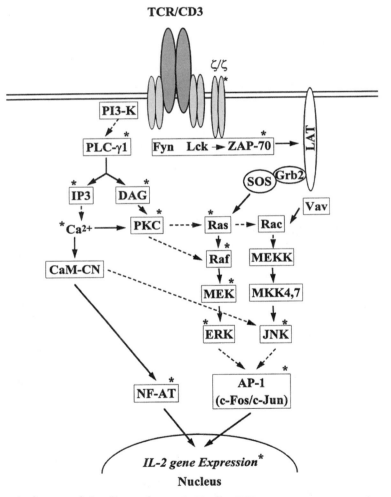

Figure 3. Schematic diagram of signaling pathways in T-cells. TCR engagement triggers the activation of a number of tyrosine kinases, leading to the activation of PLC-γ1 and the Ras/MAP kinase pathways. PLC-γ1 can mediate increases in DAG and intracellular free Ca^{2+}, resulting in the activation of protein kinase C (PKC) and the Ca^{2+}/calmodulin (CaM)-dependent protein phosphatase, calcineurin (CN). These pathways can crosstalk and merge at the promoter of the IL-2 gene. Asterisks indicate molecules showing age-related changes in one study or another.

age-related decline in MAP kinase activation.

4. Age-Related Impairment in MAP Kinase Pathways in Other In Vivo Systems

The commercial availability of a variety of high-quality antibodies for use in immunoprecipitation, immunohisto-chemical, and Western blot analyses, including phosphorylation-state-specific antibodies to the various MAPK subfamilies, has allowed the investigation of their expression and activities *in vivo*. Most studies examining age-related changes in MAPK activation so far have been performed with brain tissue.

Zhen *at al.* (1999) reported that levels of tyrosine-phosphorylated (activated) ERK1/ERK2 in the cerebral cortex of aged rats (24 months) were reduced by 40% compared to levels seen in young (6 months) or middle-aged (12 months) rats. ERK kinase activity likewise was about 50% lower in aged animal tissue. p38 kinase activity was decreased in the aged rat brains. These differences were not due to quantitative changes in the level of protein expression, because no age-related differences in the amounts of ERK or p38 proteins were observed. However, cytosolic ERK tended to aggregate in the neurons of aged rats. In addition to the decrease in basal ERK activity, cortical brain slices of 24-month-old rats displayed an attenuated ERK activation in response to EGF or PMA. This study also found that life-long caloric restriction completely prevented the age-related decrease in basal brain ERK activity and diminished the age-related reduction in p38 MAPK activity. Hu *et al.* (1998) also observed an age-related difference in the basal ERK activity in the cerebral cortex of rats, noting a significant reduction by 14 months of age. No difference in the activity of JNK was detected between young and middle-aged rats in the same study.

In addition to the alteration in ERK activity with normal brain aging, changes in the activity of this MAPK have been observed in pathological conditions of brain. Zitter rats contain a mutation that results in progressive neuronal degeneration and the development of spongiform encephalopathy (Rehm *et al.*, 1982). It was observed that brain-derived neurotrophic factor (BDNF) expression is reduced by about 50% in Zitter rats compared to age-matched littermates (Muto *et al.*, 1999). Because ERK is involved in regulating BDNF expression, these investigators also examined ERK activity in normal versus Zitter rat brain tissue. Consistent with the notion that BDNF is regulated by ERK, they observed a significant reduction in ERK activation in Zitter rats. It is possible that reduced ERK activity is responsible for the reduction in BDNF expression and contributes to the pathogenic process in Zitter rat brains.

MAPK signaling pathways have also been implicated in Alzheimer's disease pathology, but in this case (as opposed to what appears to be the case in normal aging) the kinase activities are increased. Pathological hallmarks of this disease include β-amyloid plaques, dystrophic neurites associated with plaques, and neurofibrillary tangles within nerve cell bodies. The neurofibrillary tangles primarily consist of aggregated paired helical filaments (PHFs) of hyperphosphorylated tau-protein. *In vitro*, tau can be phosphorylated by ERK, JNK, and p38 MAP kinases at the same sites found to be phosphorylated in neurofibrillary tangles. Likewise, Rapoport and Ferreira (2000) have demonstrated that the MEK-specific inhibitor PD98059 (which prevents ERK activaton) can inhibit the phosphorylation of tau at Ser199 and Ser202 (two of the major sites of abnormal phosphorylation) and partially prevent neurite degeneration. A study utilizing histochemical analysis to examine the activation state of

ERK in brains of Alzheimer's disease patients reported increased amounts of activated ERK in the same neurons displaying abnormal tau phosphorylation (Perry *et al.*, 1999). A second study reported that Alzheimer's brains showed increased levels of phosphorylated (active) p38 relative to age-matched normal brains (Hensley *et al.*, 1999). Intense phospho-p38 immuno-reactivity was associated with neuritic plaques, neuropil threads, and neurofibrillary tangle-bearing neurons. The antibody against phosphorylated p38 recognized many of the same structures as an antibody against aberrantly phosphorylated, paired helical filament tau, although PHF-positive tau did not cross-react with the phospho-p38 antibody.

The MAP kinase pathways have also been suggested to contribute to the pathogenic process of Alzheimer's disease through up-regulation of the β-amyloid protein precursor (APP) expression. The APP gene contains two AP-1 consensus elements, one of which has been shown to be involved in regulating APP promoter activity (Donnelly *et al.*, 1990; Yang *et al.*, 1998). The potential role of c-Jun and c-Fos in the pathogenic progress of Alzheimer's disease is consistent with the increased immuno-reactivity for these proteins in neurons with paired helical filament (Anderson *et al.*, 1994; Ferrer *et al.*, 1996). The mechanisms contributing to enhanced MAPK activity seen in Alzheimer's disease, as well as proof of their involvement in the neurodegenerative process, remain to be determined.

III. Summary, Conclusions, and Future Directions

Since the first description of ERK (Ray & Sturgill, 1987), the prototypical member of the MAPK family, a little more than a decade ago, our knowledge concerning the MAPK signaling pathways has increased enormously. Along with this has come an appreciation for the central role these kinases play in regulating growth differentiation and cellular homeostasis. Indeed, altered expression or regulation of these signaling pathways, and ERK in particular, offers an explanation for two important hallmarks of aging: loss in proliferative capacity and reduced stress tolerance. As we have summarized herein, activation of ERK has been found to be reduced with aging in a number of cell types and/or model systems. This, in turn, can be linked to the altered expression of certain MAPK-dependent transcription factors and the genes whose expression they regulate.

Given that the MAPK signaling cascades are regulated in part through reversible phosphorylation of MAPK, MAPKK, and MAPKKK, it is possible that changes in phosphatase could contribute to the reduced ERK activation seen with aging, and indeed we hypothesized such a mechanism to explain reduced activation of ERK in aged rat hepatocytes (Liu *et al.*, 1996b). However, other studies have not provided support for this hypothesis (Palmer *et al.*, 1999). Rather, the existing evidence suggests that the cause for reduced MAPK activation by growth factor signaling (and similarly stress) encompasses the very early events involved in initiating the response at or around the level of the growth factor receptor. If this is the case, then it would be anticipated that other signaling pathways that rely on early common signaling events likewise would be affected. One such pathway that is receiving a lot of attention is that leading to the activation of the serine/threonine kinase Akt. Also known as protein kinase B (PKB), Akt is activated via a PI3-K-dependent mechanism in response to growth factors, insulin, and other cytokines (Marte & Downward, 1997). It has received widespread attention as an important antiapoptotic protein through which various survival signals suppress cell death induced by growth factor withdrawal, cell cycle discordance, and detachment of cells from their extracellular matrix (Marte & Downward, 1997). We have demonstrated that Akt also is activated in response to oxidants and enhances the survival of hydrogen-peroxide-treated cells (Wang *et al.*, 2000). Like ERK activation discussed earlier, this activation relies on growth factor receptor signaling events. There are, as yet, no reports examining Akt activity as a function of aging in mammalian cells. It is interesting to note, however, that homologues of both Akt and PI3-K have been described in *Caenorhabditis elegans*. Curiously, and seemly paradoxically, alterations in these genes that disrupt their functions have been found to enhance stress tolerance and increase longevity in the nematode (Hekimi *et al.*, 1998; Johnson *et al.*, 1996).

It is important to emphasize that the various signal pathways activated in response to environmental signals do not act in isolation but rather in concert to coordinate the cellular response to stimuli. Not only can the responses between two pathways be additive or nullify one another, but in many situations they are interdependent. There are many points of intersection between MAPK and other signaling pathways. Two examples include the phosphorylation of p53 by both JNK and p38 MAPK, which significantly influences its proapoptotic functions (Fuchs *et al.*, 1998), and the ability of upstream mediators of the JNK pathway to influence the activation of NF-κB (Lee *et al.*, 1997). Hence, age-related effects on the MAPK pathway clearly could impact other signaling pathways.

Finally, in addition to the MAPK signaling pathway, an age-related decline has been observed in at least two other pathways: that leading to induction of the heat-shock proteins, thus referred to as the heat-shock response, and that culminating in the activation of NF-κB. These transcription factors, the basic mechanisms involved in their activation, and age-related alteration in their activation are covered in detail in Chapter 6 in this volume. Like ERK activation, these pathways also influence cell survival in certain conditions of stress. Thus, even though a decline in the function of a given pathway with age may seem small, if present in combination with another signaling defect, it could have devastating consequences. The aged hepatocyte serves as one example of such a situation, as a reduction in both ERK activation and heat-shock protein production in response to oxidant injury and heat stress is observed in aged cells. An increased understanding of the relevance of age-related alterations in signal transduction pathways to the aging phenotype should permit the development of strategies to prevent or delay their declines, thereby improving physiological function and enhancing quality of life in the aged.

References

Abe, M. K., Kuo, W. L., Hershenson, M. B., & Rosner, M. R. (1999). Extracellular signal-regulated kinase 7 (ERK7), a novel ERK with a C-terminal domain that regulates its activity, its cellular localization, and cell growth. *Molecular and Cellular Biology, 19*, 1301–1312.

Abraham, R. T., Karnitz, L. M., Secrist, J. P., & Leibson, P. J. (1992). Signal transduction through the T-cell antigen receptor. *Trends in Biochemical Sciences, 17*, 434–438.

Adler, V., Dolan, L. R., Kim, J., Pincus, M., Barrett, J. C., & Ronai, Z. (1996). Changes in jun N-terminal kinase activation by stress during aging of cultured normal human fibroblasts. *Molecular Carcinogenesis, 17*, 8–12.

Afshari, C. A., & Barrett, J. C. (1994). Disruption of G0–G1 arrest in quiescent and senescent cells treated with

phosphatase inhibitors. *Cancer Research,*
54, 2317–2321.

Afshari, C. A., Vojta, P. J., Annab, L. A.,
Futreal, P. A., Willard, T. B., & Barrett, J.
C. (1993). Investigation of the role of G1/S
cell cycle mediators in cellular senescence.
Experimental Cell Research, 209, 231–237.

Alvarez, E., Northwood, I. C., Gonzalez, F.
A., Latour, D. A., Seth, A., Abate, C.,
Curran, T., & Davis, R. J. (1991). Pro-Leu-
Ser/Thr-Pro is a consensus primary
sequence for substrate protein
phosphorylation. Characterization of the
phosphorylation of c-myc and c-jun
proteins by an epidermal growth factor
receptor threonine 669 protein kinase.
Journal of Biological Chemistry, 266,
15277–15285.

Anderson, A. J., Cummings, B. J., & Cotman,
C. W. (1994). Increased immunoreactivity
for Jun- and Fos-related proteins in
Alzheimer's disease: association with
pathology. *Experimental Neurology, 125,*
286–295.

Angel, P., & Karin, M. (1991). The role of Jun,
Fos and the AP-1 complex in cell-
proliferation and transformation.
Biochimica et Biophysica Acta, 1072,
129–157.

Aoyagi, M., Fukai, N., Ogami, K., Yamamoto,
M., & Yamamoto, K. (1995). Kinetics of
125I-PDGF binding and down-regulation of
PDGF receptor in human arterial smooth
muscle cell strains during cellular
senescence in vitro. *Journal of Cellular
Physiology, 164,* 376–384.

Asanuma, M., Nishibayashi, S., Iwata, E.,
Kondo, Y., Nakanishi, T., Vargas, M. G., &
Ogawa, N. (1996). Alterations of cAMP
response element-binding activity in the
aged rat brain in response to
administration of rolipram, a cAMP-
specific phosphodiesterase inhibitor. *Brain
Research.Molecular Brain Research, 41,*
210–215.

Atadja, P. W., Stringer, K. F., & Riabowol, K.
T. (1994). Loss of serum response element-
binding activity and hyperphosphorylation
of serum response factor during cellular
aging. *Molecular and Cellular Biology, 14,*
4991–4999.

Atadja, P., Wong, H., Garkavtsev, I., Veillette,
C., & Riabowol, K. (1995). Increased

activity of p53 in senescing fibroblasts.
*Proceedings of the National Academy of
Sciences of the USA, 92,* 8348–8352.

Avruch, J., Zhang, X. F., & Kyriakis, J. M.
(1994). Raf meets Ras: completing the
framework of a signal transduction
pathway. *Trends in Biochemical Sciences,
19,* 279–283.

Bokemeyer, D., Sorokin, A., Yan, M., Ahn, N.
G., Templeton, D. J., & Dunn, M. J. (1996).
Induction of mitogen-activated protein
kinase phosphatase 1 by the stress-
activated protein kinase signaling pathway
but not by extracellular signal-regulated
kinase in fibroblasts. *Journal of Biological
Chemistry, 271,* 639–642.

Bonfini, L., Migliaccio, E., Pelicci, G.,
Lanfrancone, L., & Pelicci, P. G. (1996).
Not all Shc's roads lead to Ras. *Trends in
Biochemical Sciences, 21,* 257–261.

Chakravarti, B. & Abraham, G. N. (1999).
Aging and T-cell-mediated immunity.
*Mechanisms of Ageing and Development,
108,* 183–206.

Chang, H. N., Wang, S. R., Chiang, S. C.,
Teng, W. J., Chen, M. L., Tsai, J. J.,
Huang, D. F., Lin, H. Y., & Tsai, Y. Y.
(1996). The relationship of aging to
endotoxin shock and to production of
TNF-α. *Journal of Gerontology: A
Biological Sciences Medical Sciences, 51,*
M220–M222.

Chen, R. H., Abate, C., & Blenis, J. (1993).
Phosphorylation of the c-Fos
transrepression domain by mitogen-
activated protein kinase and 90-kDa
ribosomal S6 kinase. *Proceedings of the
National Academy of Sciences of the USA,
90,* 10952–10956.

Chen, W., Martindale, J. L., Holbrook, N. J.,
& Liu, Y. (1998). Tumor promoter arsenite
activates extracellular signal-regulated
kinase through a signaling pathway
mediated by epidermal growth factor
receptor and Shc. *Molecular and Cellular
Biology, 18,* 5178–5188.

Cheng, J. T., Cobb, M. H., & Baer, R. (1993).
Phosphorylation of the TAL1 oncoprotein
by the extracellular-signal-regulated
protein kinase ERK1. *Molecular and
Cellular Biology, 13,* 801–808.

Chin, J. H., Okazaki, M., Frazier, J. S., Hu, Z.
W., & Hoffman, B. B. (1996). Impaired

cAMP-mediated gene expression and decreased cAMP response element binding protein in senescent cells. *American Journal of Physiology, 271,* C362–C371.

Choi, A. M., Pignolo, R. J., apRhys, C. M., Cristofalo, V. J., & Holbrook, N. J. (1995). Alterations in the molecular response to DNA damage during cellular aging of cultured fibroblasts: reduced AP-1 activation and collagenase gene expression. *Journal of Cellular Physiology, 164,* 65–73.

Chow, C. W., Rincon, M., Cavanagh, J., Dickens, M., & Davis, R. J. (1997). Nuclear accumulation of NFAT4 opposed by the JNK signal transduction pathway. *Science, 278,* 1638– 1641.

Chung, H. Y., Kim, H. J., Shim, K. H., & Kim, K. W. (1999). Dietary modulation of prostanoid synthesis in the aging process: Role of cyclooxygenase-2. *Mechanisms of Ageing and Development, 111,* 97–106.

Cohen, D. M. (1996). Urea-inducible Egr-1 transcription in renal inner medullary collecting duct (mIMCD3) cells is mediated by extracellular signal-regulated kinase activation. *Proceedings of the National Academy of Sciences of the USA, 93,* 11242–11247.

Cook, S. J., Beltman, J., Cadwallader, K. A., McMahon, M., & McCormick, F. (1997). Regulation of mitogen-activated protein kinase phosphatase-1 expression by extracellular signal-related kinase-dependent and Ca^{2+}-dependent signal pathways in Rat-1 cells. *Journal of Biological Chemistry, 272,* 13309–13319.

Cristofalo, V. J. & Pignolo, R. J. (1993). Replicative senescence of human fibroblast-like cells in culture. *Physiological Reviews, 73,* 617–638.

Cristofalo, V. J., Volker, C., Francis, M. K., & Tresini, M. (1998). Age-dependent modifications of gene expression in human fibroblasts. *Critical Reviews In Eukaryotic Gene Expression, 8,* 43–80.

Davis, R. J. (1993). The mitogen-activated protein kinase signal transduction pathway. *Journal of Biological Chemistry, 268,* 14553–14556.

Davis, R. J. (1995). Transcriptional regulation by MAP kinases. *Molecular Reproduction and Development, 42,* 459–467.

de Groot, R. P., den Hertog, J., Vandenheede, J. R., Goris, J., & Sassone-Corsi, P. (1993). Multiple and cooperative phosphorylation events regulate the CREM activator function. *EMBO Journal, 12,* 3903–3911.

Delpedro, A. D., Barjavel, M. J., Mamdouh, Z., Faure, S., & Bakouche, O. (1998). Signal transduction in LPS-activated aged and young monocytes. *Journal of Interferon Cytokine Research, 18,* 429–437.

Diehl, A. M. & Rai, R. M. (1996). Liver regeneration 3: Regulation of signal transduction during liver regeneration. *FASEB Journal, 10,* 215–227.

Donnelly, R. J., Friedhoff, A. J., Beer, B., Blume, A. J., & Vitek, M. P. (1990). Interleukin-1 stimulates the β-amyloid precursor protein promoter. *Cellular and Molecular Neurobiology, 10,* 485–495.

Elbirt, K. K., Whitmarsh, A. J., Davis, R. J., & Bonkovsky, H. L. (1998). Mechanism of sodium arsenite-mediated induction of heme oxygenase-1 in hepatoma cells. Role of mitogen-activated protein kinases. *Journal of Biological Chemistry, 273,* 8922–8931.

Favero, J., & Lafont, V. (1998). Effector pathways regulating T cell activation. *Biochemical Pharmacology, 56,* 1539–1547.

Ferrer, I., Segui, J., & Planas, A. M. (1996). Amyloid deposition is associated with c-Jun expression in Alzheimer's disease and amyloid angiopathy. *Neuropathology and Applied Neurobiology, 22,* 521–526.

Fowles, L. F., Martin, M. L., Nelsen, L., Stacey, K. J., Redd, D., Clark, Y. M., Nagamine, Y., McMahon, M., Hume, D. A., & Ostrowski, M. C. (1998). Persistent activation of mitogen-activated protein kinases p42 and p44 and ets-2 phosphorylation in response to colony-stimulating factor 1/c-fms signaling. *Molecular and Cellular Biology, 18,* 5148–5156.

Fuchs, S. Y., Adler, V., Pincus, M. R., & Ronai, Z. (1998). MEKK1/JNK signaling stabilizes and activates p53. *Proceedings of the National Academy of Sciences of the USA, 95,* 10541–10546.

Gabai, V. L., Meriin, A. B., Mosser, D. D., Caron, A. W., Rits, S., Shifrin, V. I., & Sherman, M. Y. (1997). Hsp70 prevents activation of stress kinases. A novel pathway of cellular thermotolerance. *Journal of Biological Chemistry, 272,* 18033–18037.

Garfinkel, S., Hu, X., Prudovsky, I. A., McMahon, G. A., Kapnik, E. M., McDowell, S. D., & Maciag, T. (1996). FGF-1-dependent proliferative and migratory responses are impaired in senescent human umbilical vein endothelial cells and correlate with the inability to signal tyrosine phosphorylation of fibroblast growth factor receptor-1 substrates. *Journal of Cell Biology, 134,* 783–791.

Garrington, T. P., & Johnson, G. L. (1999). Organization and regulation of mitogen-activated protein kinase signaling pathways. *Current Opinion In Cell Biology, 11,* 211–218.

Ghosh, J., & Miller, R. A. (1995). Rapid tyrosine phosphorylation of Grb2 and Shc in T cells exposed to anti-CD3, anti-CD4, and anti-CD45 stimuli: Differential effects of aging. *Mechanisms of Ageing and Development, 80,* 171–187.

Goh, K. C., Haque, S. J., & Williams, B. R. (1999). p38 MAP kinase is required for STAT1 serine phosphorylation and transcriptional activation induced by interferons. *EMBO Journal, 18,* 5601–5608.

Gorgas, G., Butch, E. R., Guan, K. L., & Miller, R. A. (1997). Diminished activation of the MAP kinase pathway in CD3-stimulated T lymphocytes from old mice. *Mechanisms of Ageing and Development, 94,* 71–83.

Grossmann, A., Rabinovitch, P. S., Kavanagh, T. J., Jinneman, J. C., Gilliland, L. K., Ledbetter, J. A., & Kanner, S. B. (1995). Activation of murine T-cells via phospholipase-C gamma 1-associated protein tyrosine phosphorylation is reduced with aging. *Journal of Gerontology: A Biological Sciences Medical Sciences, 50,* B205-B212.

Gruda, M. C., Kovary, K., Metz, R., & Bravo, R. (1994). Regulation of Fra-1 and Fra-2 phosphorylation differs during the cell cycle of fibroblasts and phosphorylation in vitro by MAP kinase affects DNA binding activity. *Oncogene, 9,* 2537–2547.

Guan, Z., Buckman, S. Y., Miller, B. W., Springer, L. D., & Morrison, A. R. (1998). Interleukin-1β-induced cyclooxygenase-2 expression requires activation of both c-Jun NH2-terminal kinase and p38 MAPK signal pathways in rat renal mesangial cells. *Journal of Biological Chemistry, 273,* 28670–28676.

Guidi, L., Antico, L., Bartoloni, C., Costanzo, M., Errani, A., Tricerri, A., Vangeli, M., Doria, G., Gatta, L., Goso, C., Mancino, L., & Frasca, D. (1998). Changes in the amount and level of phosphorylation of p56(lck) in PBL from aging humans. *Mechanisms of Ageing and Development, 102,* 177–186.

Gum, R., Wang, H., Lengyel, E., Juarez, J., & Boyd, D. (1997). Regulation of 92 kDa type IV collagenase expression by the jun aminoterminal kinase. *Oncogene, 14,* 1481–1493.

Guo, L., Hussain, A. A., Limb, G. A., & Marshall, J. (1999). Age-dependent variation in metalloproteinase activity of isolated human Bruch's membrane and choroid. *Investigative Ophthalmology and Visual Science, 40,* 2676–2682.

Gupta, S., Campbell, D., Derijard, B., & Davis, R. J. (1995). Transcription factor ATF2 regulation by the JNK signal transduction pathway. *Science, 267,* 389–393.

Gutkind, J. S. (1998). The pathways connecting G protein-coupled receptors to the nucleus through divergent mitogen-activated protein kinase cascades. *Journal of Biological Chemistry, 273,* 1839–1842.

Guyton, K. Z., Liu, Y., Gorospe, M., Xu, Q., & Holbrook, N. J. (1996). Activation of mitogen-activated protein kinase by H_2O_2. Role in cell survival following oxidant injury. *Journal of Biological Chemistry, 271,* 4138–4142.

Guyton, K. Z., Gorospe, M., Wang, X., Mock, Y. D., Kokkonen, G. C., Liu, Y., Roth, G. S., & Holbrook, N. J. (1998). Age-related changes in activation of mitogen-activated protein kinase cascades by oxidative stress. *Journal of Investigative Dermatology Symposium Proceedings, 3,* 23–27.

Han, J., Jiang, Y., Li, Z., Kravchenko, V. V., & Ulevitch, R. J. (1997). Activation of the transcription factor MEF2C by the MAP kinase p38 in inflammation. *Nature, 386,* 296–299.

Hardwick, J. S. & Sefton, B. M. (1995). Activation of the Lck tyrosine protein kinase by hydrogen peroxide requires the phosphorylation of Tyr-394. *Proceedings of the National Academy of Sciences of the USA, 92,* 4527–4531.

Hayflick, L. (1974). The longevity of cultured human cells. *Journal of the American Geriatrics Society, 22,* 1–12.

Hekimi, S., Lakowski, B., Barnes, T. M., & Ewbank, J. J. (1998). Molecular genetics of life span in C. elegans: how much does it teach us? *Trends in Genetics, 14,* 14–20.

Hensley, K., Floyd, R. A., Zheng, N. Y., Nael, R., Robinson, K. A., Nguyen, X., Pye, Q. N., Stewart, C. A., Geddes, J., Markesbery, W. R., Patel, E., Johnson, G. V., & Bing, G. (1999). p38 kinase is activated in the Alzheimer's disease brain. *Journal of Neurochemistry, 72,* 2053–2058.

Heymes, C., Silvestre, J. S., Llorens-Cortes, C., Chevalier, B., Marotte, F., Levy, B. I., Swynghedauw, B., & Samuel, J. L. (1998). Cardiac senescence is associated with enhanced expression of angiotensin II receptor subtypes. *Endocrinology, 139,* 2579–2587.

Higashimoto, Y., Fukuchi, Y., Shimada, Y., Ishida, K., Ohata, M., Furuse, T., Shu, C., Teramoto, S., Matsuse, T., & Sudo, E. (1993). The effects of aging on the function of alveolar macrophages in mice. *Mechanisms of Ageing and Development, 69,* 207–217.

Hirokawa, K. (1999). Age-related changes of signal transduction in T cells. *Experimental Gerontology, 34,* 7–18.

Holzmeister, J., Graf, K., Warnecke, C., Fleck, E., & Regitz-Zagrosek, V. (1997). Protein kinase C-dependent regulation of the human AT1 promoter in vascular smooth muscle cells. *American Journal of Physiology, 273,* H655–H664.

Hsieh, C. C., Xiong, W., Xie, Q., Rabek, J. P., Scott, S. G., An, M. R., Reisner, P. D., Kuninger, D. T., & Papaconstantinou, J. (1998). Effects of age on the posttranscriptional regulation of CCAAT/enhancer binding protein α and CCAAT/enhancer binding protein β isoform synthesis in control and LPS-treated livers. *Molecular Biology of the Cell, 9,* 1479–1494.

Hu, M. C., Qiu, W. R., & Wang, Y. P. (1997). JNK1, JNK2 and JNK3 are p53 N-terminal serine 34 kinases. *Oncogene, 15,* 2277–2287.

Hu, Y., Schett, G., Zou, Y., Dietrich, H., & Xu, Q. (1998). Abundance of platelet-derived growth factors (PDGFs), PDGF receptors and activation of mitogen-activated protein kinases in brain decline with age. *Brain Research. Molecular Brain Research, 53,* 252–259.

Huang, R. P., Wu, J. X., Fan, Y., & Adamson, E. D. (1996). UV activates growth factor receptors via reactive oxygen intermediates. *Journal of Cell Biology, 133,* 211–220.

Huang, C., Ma, W. Y., Maxiner, A., Sun, Y., & Dong, Z. (1999). p38 kinase mediates UV-induced phosphorylation of p53 protein at serine 389. *Journal of Biological Chemistry, 274,* 12229–12235.

Hutter, D., Yo, Y., Chen, W., Liu, P., Holbrook, N. J., Roth, G. S., & Liu, Y. (2000). Age- related decline in Ras/ERK mitogen-activated protein kinase cascade is linked to a reduced association between Shc and EGF receptor. *Journal of Gerontology: A Biological Sciences Medical Sciences, 55,* B125-B134.

Ichijo, H., Nishida, E., Irie, K., ten Dijke, P., Saitoh, M., Moriguchi, T., Takagi, M., Matsumoto, K., Miyazono, K., & Gotoh, Y. (1997). Induction of apoptosis by ASK1, a mammalian MAPKKK that activates SAPK/JNK and p38 signaling pathways. *Science, 275,* 90–94.

Iijima, N., Tamada, Y., Hayashi, S., Tanaka, M., Ishihara, A., Hasegawa, M., & Ibata, Y. (1999). Expanded expression of heme oxygenase-1 (HO–1) in the hypothalamic median eminence of aged as compared with young rats: an immunocytochemical study. *Neuroscience Letters, 271,* 113–116.

Iordanov, M., Bender, K., Ade, T., Schmid, W., Sachsenmaier, C., Engel, K., Gaestel, M., Rahmsdorf, H. J., & Herrlich, P. (1997). CREB is activated by UVC through a p38/HOG–1- dependent protein kinase. *EMBO Journal, 16,* 1009–1022.

Irving, J., Feng, J., Wistrom, C., Pikaart, M., & Villeponteau, B. (1992). An altered repertoire of fos/jun (AP-1) at the onset of replicative senescence. *Experimental Cell Research, 202,* 161–166.

Ishigami, A., Reed, T. D., & Roth, G. S. (1993). Effect of aging on EGF stimulated DNA synthesis and EGF receptor levels in primary cultured rat hepatocytes. *Biochemical and Biophysical Research Communications, 196,* 181–186.

Jain, N., Zhang, T., Fong, S. L., Lim, C. P., & Cao, X. (1998). Repression of Stat3 activity by activation of mitogen-activated protein kinase (MAPK). *Oncogene, 17,* 3157–3167.

Janknecht, R. & Hunter, T. (1997). Convergence of MAP kinase pathways on the ternary complex factor Sap–1a. *EMBO Journal, 16,* 1620–1627.

Janknecht, R., & Nordheim, A. (1996). MAP kinase-dependent transcriptional coactivation by Elk–1 and its cofactor CBP. *Biochemical and Biophysical Research Communications, 228,* 831–837.

Janknecht, R., Monte, D., Baert, J. L., & de Launoit, Y. (1996). The ETS-related transcription factor ERM is a nuclear target of signaling cascades involving MAPK and PKA. *Oncogene, 13,* 1745–1754.

Johnson, T. E., Lithgow, G. J., & Murakami, S. (1996). Hypothesis: interventions that increase the response to stress offer the potential for effective life prolongation and increased health. *Journal of Gerontology: A: Bological Sciences Medical Sciences, 51,* B392–B395.

Kim, D. W., & Cochran, B. H. (2000). Extracellular signal-regulated kinase binds to TFII-I and regulates its activation of the c-*fos* promoter. *Molecular and Cellular Biology, 20,* 1140–1148.

Kirk, C. J., & Miller, R. A. (1998). Analysis of Raf–1 activation in response to TCR activation and costimulation in murine T-lymphocytes: effect of age. *Cellular Immunology, 190,* 33–42.

Kirk, C. J., & Miller, R. A. (1999). Age-sensitive and -insensitive pathways leading to JNK activation in mouse CD4(+) T-cells. *Cellular Immunology, 197,* 83–90.

Kirk, C. J., Freilich, A. M., & Miller, R. A. (1999). Age-related decline in activation of JNK by TCR- and CD28-mediated signals in murine T-lymphocytes. *Cellular Immunology, 197,* 75–82.

Kitano, S., Fawcett, T. W., Yo, Y., & Roth, G. S. (1998). Molecular mechanisms of impaired stimulation of DNA synthesis in cultured hepatocytes of aged rats. *American Journal of Physiology, 275,* C146–C154.

Kitano, S., Venable, S., Smith, J. R., Reed, T. D., & Roth, G. S. (1996). Effect of aging on regulation of sdi-1 in rat hepatocytes. *Biochemical and Biophysical Research Communications, 225,* 122–127.

Kotlyarov, A., Neininger, A., Schubert, C., Eckert, R., Birchmeier, C., Volk, H. D., & Gaestel, M. (1999). MAPKAP kinase 2 is essential for LPS-induced TNF-α biosynthesis. *Nature Cell Biology, 1,* 94–97.

Kumar, S., Millis, A. J., & Baglioni, C. (1992). Expression of interleukin 1-inducible genes and production of interleukin 1 by aging human fibroblasts. *Proceedings of the National Academy of Sciences of the USA, 89,* 4683–4687.

Kumazaki, T., & Mitsui, Y. (1996). Alterations in transcription factor-binding activities to fibronectin promoter during aging of vascular endothelial cells. *Mechanisms of Ageing and Development, 88,* 111–124.

Kyriakis, J. M., & Avruch, J. (1996). Protein kinase cascades activated by stress and inflammatory cytokines. *Bioessays, 18,* 567–577.

LaPointe, M. C., & Isenovic, E. (1999). Interleukin-1β regulation of inducible nitric oxide synthase and cyclooxygenase-2 involves the p42/44 and p38 MAPK signaling pathways in cardiac myocytes. *Hypertension, 33,* 276–282.

Lee, F. S., Hagler, J., Chen, Z. J., & Maniatis, T. (1997). Activation of the IκBα kinase complex by MEKK1, a kinase of the JNK pathway. *Cell, 88,* 213–222.

Levine, A. J. (1997). p53, the cellular gatekeeper for growth and division. *Cell, 88,* 323–331.

Li, W., Whaley, C. D., Mondino, A., & Mueller, D. L. (1996). Blocked signal transduction to the ERK and JNK protein kinases in anergic CD4+ T cells. *Science, 271,* 1272–1276.

Liao, Z., Tu, J. H., Small, C. B., Schnipper, S. M., & Rosenstreich, D. L. (1993). Increased urine interleukin-1 levels in aging. *Gerontology, 39*, 19–27.

Lin, Y. J., Seroude, L., & Benzer, S. (1998). Extended life-span and stress resistance in the Drosophila mutant methuselah. *Science, 282*, 943–946.

Liu, B., Carle, K. W., & Whisler, R. L. (1997). Reductions in the activation of ERK and JNK are associated with decreased IL-2 production in T cells from elderly humans stimulated by the TCR/CD3 complex and costimulatory signals. *Cellular Immunology, 182*, 79–88.

Liu, Y., Gorospe, M., Holbrook, N. J., & Anderson, C. (1998a). Post-translational mechanisms leading to mammalian gene activation in response to genotoxic stress. In M. F. Hoekstra & J. A. Nickoloff (Ed.) *DNA Damage and Repair, Vol. 2: DNA Repair in Higher Eukaryotes.* (pp. 263–298). Totowa, NJ: Humana Press.

Liu, Y., Martindale, J. L., Gorospe, M., & Holbrook, N. J. (1996a). Regulation of p21[WAF1/CIP1] expression through mitogen-activated protein kinase signaling pathway. *Cancer Research, 56*, 31–35.

Liu, Y., Guyton, K. Z., Gorospe, M., Xu, Q., Kokkonen, G. C., Mock, Y. D., Roth, G. S., & Holbrook, N. J. (1996b). Age-related decline in mitogen-activated protein kinase activity in epidermal growth factor-stimulated rat hepatocytes. *Journal of Biological Chemistry, 271*, 3604–3607.

Liu, Y., Gorospe, M., Kokkonen, G. C., Boluyt, M. O., Younes, A., Mock, Y. D., Wang, X., Roth, G. S., & Holbrook, N. J. (1998b). Impairments in both p70 S6 kinase and extracellular signal-regulated kinase signaling pathways contribute to the decline in proliferative capacity of aged hepatocytes. *Experimental Cell Research, 240*, 40–48.

Marte, B. M., & Downward, J. (1997). PKB/Akt: connecting phosphoinositide 3-kinase to cell survival and beyond. *Trends in Biochemical Sciences, 22*, 355–358.

Matsuda, T., Okamura, K., Sato, Y., Morimoto, A., Ono, M., Kohno, K., & Kuwano, M. (1992). Decreased response to epidermal growth factor during cellular senescence in cultured human microvascular endothelial cells. *Journal of Cellular Physiology, 150*, 510–516.

Medrano, E. E., Yang, F., Boissy, R., Farooqui, J., Shah, V., Matsumoto, K., Nordlund, J. J., & Park, H. Y. (1994). Terminal differentiation and senescence in the human melanocyte: repression of tyrosine-phosphorylation of the extracellular signal-regulated kinase 2 selectively defines the two phenotypes. *Molecular Biology of the Cell, 5*, 497–509.

Mercurio, F., & Manning, A. M. (1999). NF-κB as a primary regulator of the stress response. *Oncogene, 18*, 6163–6171.

Meyyappan, M., Atadja, P. W., & Riabowol, K. T. (1996). Regulation of gene expression and transcription factor binding activity during cellular aging. *Biological Signals, 5*, 130–138.

Meyyappan, M., Wheaton, K., & Riabowol, K. T. (1999). Decreased expression and activity of the immediate-early growth response (Egr-1) gene product during cellular senescence. *Journal of Cellular Physiology, 179*, 29–39.

Michalopoulos, G. K., & DeFrances, M. C. (1997). Liver regeneration. *Science, 276*, 60–66.

Migliaccio, E., Giorgio, M., Mele, S., Pelicci, G., Reboldi, P., Pandolfi, P. P., Lanfrancone, L., & Pelicci, P. G. (1999). The p66shc adaptor protein controls oxidative stress response and life span in mammals. *Nature, 402*, 309–313.

Miller, R. A. (1991). Aging and immune function. *International Review of Cytology, 124*, 187–215.

Miller, R. A. (1994). Nathan Shock Memorial Lecture 1992. Aging and immune function: cellular and biochemical analyses. *Experimental Gerontology, 29*, 21–35.

Miller, R. A. (1996). The aging immune system: primer and prospectus. *Science, 273*, 70–74.

Miller, R. A., Garcia, G., Kirk, C. J., & Witkowski, J. M. (1997). Early activation defects in T lymphocytes from aged mice. *Immunological Reviews, 160*, 79–90.

Milne, D. M., Campbell, D. G., Caudwell, F. B., & Meek, D. W. (1994). Phosphorylation of the tumor suppressor protein p53 by mitogen-activated protein kinases. *Journal of Biological Chemistry, 269*, 9253–9260.

Miralles, F., Parra, M., Caelles, C., Nagamine, Y., Felez, J., & Munoz-Canoves, P. (1998).

UV irradiation induces the murine urokinase-type plasminogen activator gene via the c-Jun N- terminal kinase signaling pathway: Requirement of an AP1 enhancer element. *Molecular and Cellular Biology, 18*, 4537–4547.

Miura, S., Yamaguchi, M., Shimizu, N., & Abiko, Y. (2000). Mechanical stress enhances expression and production of plasminogen activator in aging human periodontal ligament cells. *Mechanisms of Ageing and Development, 112*, 217–231.

Mochizuki, K., Yamaguchi, M., & Abiko, Y. (1999). Enhancement of LPS-stimulated plasminogen activator production in aged gingival fibroblasts. *Journal of Periodontal Research, 34*, 251–260.

Mochizuki, N., Ohba, Y., Kiyokawa, E., Kurata, T., Murakami, T., Ozaki, T., Kitabatake, A., Nagashima, K., & Matsuda, M. (1999). Activation of the ERK/MAPK pathway by an isoform of rap1GAP associated with Gα(i). *Nature, 400*, 891–894.

Morimoto, R. I. (1993). Cells in stress: transcriptional activation of heat shock genes. *Science, 259*, 1409–1410.

Murakami, M., Sonobe, M. H., Ui, M., Kabuyama, Y., Watanabe, H., Wada, T., Handa, H., & Iba, H. (1997). Phosphorylation and high level expression of Fra–2 in v-src transformed cells: a pathway of activation of endogenous AP-1. *Oncogene, 14*, 2435–2444.

Muto, Y., Hayashi, T., Higashi, Y., Endo, T., Yamamoto, T., & Sato, K. (1999). Age-related decrease in brain-derived neurotrophic factor gene expression in the brain of the zitter rat with genetic spongiform encephalopathy. *Neuroscience Letters, 271*, 69–72.

Nakajima, T., Kinoshita, S., Sasagawa, T., Sasaki, K., Naruto, M., Kishimoto, T., & Akira, S. (1993). Phosphorylation at threonine-235 by a ras-dependent mitogen-activated protein kinase cascade is essential for transcription factor NF-IL6. *Proceedings of the National Academy of Sciences of the USA, 90*, 2207–2211.

Nakanishi, Y., & Yasumoto, K. (1997). Induction after administering paraquat of heme oxygenase-1 and heat shock protein 70 in the liver of senescence-accelerated mice. *Bioscience, Biotechnology, and Biochemistry, 61*, 1302–1306.

Nishina, H., Fischer, K. D., Radvanyi, L., Shahinian, A., Hakem, R., Rubie, E. A., Bernstein, A., Mak, T. W., Woodgett, J. R., & Penninger, J. M. (1997). Stress-signalling kinase Sek 1 protects thymocytes from apoptosis mediated by CD95 and CD3. *Nature, 385*, 350–353.

Noda, A., Ning, Y., Venable, S. F., Pereira-Smith, O. M., & Smith, J. R. (1994). Cloning of senescent cell-derived inhibitors of DNA synthesis using an expression screen. *Experimental Cell Research, 211*, 90–98.

Ohzeki, K., Yamaguchi, M., Shimizu, N., & Abiko, Y. (1999). Effect of cellular aging on the induction of cyclooxygenase-2 by mechanical stress in human periodontal ligament cells. *Mechanisms of Ageing and Development, 108*, 151–163.

Ono, K. & Han, J. (2000). The p38 signal transduction pathway: activation and function. *Cellular Signalling, 12*, 1–13.

Paganelli, R., Scala, E., Quinti, I., & Ansotegui, I. J. (1994). Humoral immunity in aging. *Aging (Milano.), 6*, 143–150.

Pahlavani, M. A., Harris, M. D., & Richardson, A. (1997). The increase in the induction of IL-2 expression with caloric restriction is correlated to changes in the transcription factor NFAT. *Cellular Immunology, 180*, 10–19.

Pahlavani, M. A., Harris, M. D., & Richardson, A. (1998). Activation of p21ras/MAPK signal transduction molecules decreases with age in mitogen-stimulated T cells from rats. *Cellular Immunology, 185*, 39–48.

Pahlavani, M. A., & Vargas, D. M. (2000). Influence of aging and caloric restriction on activation of Ras/MAPK, calcineurin, and CaMK-IV activities in rat T cells. *Proceedings of the Society for Experimental Biology and Medicine, 223*, 163–169.

Palmer, H. J., Tuzon, C. T., & Paulson, K. E. (1999). Age-dependent decline in mitogenic stimulation of hepatocytes. Reduced association between Shc and the epidermal growth factor receptor is coupled to decreased activation of Raf and extracellular signal- regulated kinases.

Journal of Biological Chemistry, 274, 11424–11430.

Pastor, M. I., Woodrow, M., & Cantrell, D. (1995). Regulation and function of p21ras in T lymphocytes. *Cancer Surveys, 22,* 75–83.

Pawelec, G., & Solana, R. (1997). Immunosenescence. *Immunology Today, 18,* 514–516.

Pawelec, G., Wagner, W., Adibzadeh, M., & Engel, A. (1999). T cell immunosenescence in vitro and in vivo. *Experimental Gerontology, 34,* 419–429.

Perry, G., Roder, H., Nunomura, A., Takeda, A., Friedlich, A. L., Zhu, X., Raina, A. K., Holbrook, N., Siedlak, S. L., Harris, P. L., & Smith, M. A. (1999). Activation of neuronal extracellular receptor kinase (ERK) in Alzheimer disease links oxidative stress to abnormal phosphorylation. *Neuroreport, 10,* 2411–2415.

Pircher, T. J., Petersen, H., Gustafsson, J. A., & Haldosen, L. A. (1999). Extracellular signal-regulated kinase (ERK) interacts with signal transducer and activator of transcription (STAT) 5a. *Molecular Endocrinology, 13,* 555–565.

Porter, C. M., Havens, M. A., & Clipstone, N. A. (2000). Identification of amino acid residues and protein kinases involved in the regulation of NF-ATc subcellular localization. *Journal of Biological Chemistry, 275,* 3543–3551.

Potapova, O., Gorospe, M., Dougherty, R. H., Dean, N. M., Gaarde, W. A., & Holbrook, N. J. (2000). Inhibition of c-Jun N-terminal kinase 2 expression suppresses growth and induces apoptosis of human tumor cells in a p53-dependent manner. *Molecular and Cellular Biology, 20,* 1713–1722.

Ransohoff, R. M. (1998). Cellular responses to interferons and other cytokines: The JAK–STAT paradigm. *New England Journal of Medicine, 338,* 616–618.

Rapoport, M., & Ferreira, A. (2000). PD98059 prevents neurite degeneration induced by fibrillar β-amyloid in mature hippocampal neurons. *Journal of Neurochemistry, 74,* 125–133.

Rauscher, F. J., III, Cohen, D. R., Curran, T., Bos, T. J., Vogt, P. K., Bohmann, D., Tjian, R., & Franza, B. R., Jr. (1988). Fos-associated protein p39 is the product of the *jun* proto-oncogene. *Science, 240,* 1010–1016.

Ray, L. B., & Sturgill, T. W. (1987). Rapid stimulation by insulin of a serine/threonine kinase in 3T3-L1 adipocytes that phosphorylates microtubule-associated protein 2 *in vitro. Proceedings of the National Academy of Sciences of the USA, 84,* 1502–1506.

Reed, M. J., Corsa, A. C., Kudravi, S. A., McCormick, R. S., & Arthur, W. T. (2000). A deficit in collagenase activity contributes to impaired migration of aged microvascular endothelial cells. *Journal of Cellular Biochemistry, 77,* 116–126.

Rehm, S., Mehraein, P., Anzil, A. P., & Deerberg, F. (1982). A new rat mutant with defective overhairs and spongy degeneration of the central nervous system: Clinical and pathologic studies. *Laboratory Animal Science, 32,* 70–73.

Riabowol, K., Schiff, J., & Gilman, M. Z. (1992). Transcription factor AP-1 activity is required for initiation of DNA synthesis and is lost during cellular aging. *Proceedings of the National Academy of Sciences of the USA, 89,* 157–161.

Ricciarelli, R., Maroni, P., Ozer, N., Zingg, J. M., & Azzi, A. (1999). Age-dependent increase of collagenase expression can be reduced by α-tocopherol via protein kinase C inhibition. *Free Radical Biology and Medicine, 27,* 729–737.

Rittling, S. R., Brooks, K. M., Cristofalo, V. J., & Baserga, R. (1986). Expression of cell cycle-dependent genes in young and senescent WI-38 fibroblasts. *Proceedings of the National Academy of Sciences of the USA, 83,* 3316–3320.

Robert, V., Besse, S., Sabri, A., Silvestre, J. S., Assayag, P., Nguyen, V. T., Swynghedauw, B., & Delcayre, C. (1997). Differential regulation of matrix metalloproteinases associated with aging and hypertension in the rat heart. *Laboratory Investigation, 76,* 729–738.

Rudolph, K. L., Chang, S., Lee, H. W., Blasco, M., Gottlieb, G. J., Greider, C., & DePinho, R. A. (1999). Longevity, stress response, and cancer in aging telomerase-deficient mice. *Cell, 96,* 701–712.

Sachsenmaier, C., Radler-Pohl, A., Zinck, R., Nordheim, A., Herrlich, P., & Rahmsdorf,

H. J. (1994). Involvement of growth factor receptors in the mammalian UVC response. *Cell, 78,* 963–972.

Saxena, M., Williams, S., Tasken, K., & Mustelin, T. (1999). Crosstalk between cAMP- dependent kinase and MAP kinase through a protein tyrosine phosphatase. *Nature Cell Biology, 1,* 305–311.

Schieven, G. L., Mittler, R. S., Nadler, S. G., Kirihara, J. M., Bolen, J. B., Kanner, S. B., & Ledbetter, J. A. (1994). ZAP-70 tyrosine kinase, CD45, and T cell receptor involvement in UV-and H_2O_2-induced T cell signal transduction. *Journal of Biological Chemistry, 269,* 20718–20726.

Schlessinger, J. (1993). How receptor tyrosine kinases activate Ras. *Trends in Biochemical Sciences, 18,* 273–275.

Sengupta, T. K., Talbot, E. S., Scherle, P. A., & Ivashkiv, L. B. (1998). Rapid inhibition of interleukin–6 signaling and Stat3 activation mediated by mitogen-activated protein kinases. *Proceedings of the National Academy of Sciences of the USA, 95,* 11107–11112.

Serrano, M., Lin, A. W., McCurrach, M. E., Beach, D., & Lowe, S. W. (1997). Oncogenic ras provokes premature cell senescence associated with accumulation of p53 and p16^{INK4a}. *Cell, 88,* 593–602.

Seshadri, T., & Campisi, J. (1990). Repression of c-fos transcription and an altered genetic program in senescent human fibroblasts. *Science, 247,* 205–209.

Shapiro, L., & Dinarello, C. A. (1995). Osmotic regulation of cytokine synthesis in vitro. *Proceedings of the National Academy of Sciences of the USA, 92,* 12230–12234.

Shimizu, N., Goseki, T., Yamaguchi, M., Iwasawa, T., Takiguchi, H., & Abiko, Y. (1997). In vitro cellular aging stimulates interleukin-1β production in stretched human periodontal-ligament-derived cells. *Journal of Dental Research, 76,* 1367–1375.

Slupsky, C. M., Gentile, L. N., Donaldson, L. W., Mackereth, C. D., Seidel, J. J., Graves, B. J., & McIntosh, L. P. (1998). Structure of the Ets-1 pointed domain and mitogen-activated protein kinase phosphorylation site. *Proceedings of the National Academy of Sciences of the USA, 95,* 12129–12134.

Smith, J. R., Nakanishi, M., Robetorye, R. S., Venable, S. F., & Pereira-Smith, O. M. (1996). Studies demonstrating the complexity of regulation and action of the growth inhibitory gene SDI1. *Experimental Gerontology, 31,* 327–335.

Solana, R., & Pawelec, G. (1998). Molecular and cellular basis of immunosenescence. *Mechanisms of Ageing and Development, 102,* 115–129.

Srivastava, S., Weitzmann, M. N., Cenci, S., Ross, F. P., Adler, S., & Pacifici, R. (1999). Estrogen decreases TNF gene expression by blocking JNK activity and the resulting production of c-Jun and JunD. *Journal of Clinical Investigation, 104,* 503–513.

Strahl, T., Gille, H., & Shaw, P. E. (1996). Selective response of ternary complex factor Sap 1a to different mitogen-activated protein kinase subgroups. *Proceedings of the National Academy of Sciences of the USA, 93,* 11563–11568.

Su, B., Jacinto, E., Hibi, M., Kallunki, T., Karin, M., & Ben Neriah, Y. (1994). JNK is involved in signal integration during costimulation of T lymphocytes. *Cell, 77,* 727–736.

Swantek, J. L., Cobb, M. H., & Geppert, T. D. (1997). Jun N-terminal kinase/stress-activated protein kinase (JNK/SAPK) is required for lipopolysaccharide stimulation of tumor necrosis factorα (TNF-α) translation: Glucocorticoids inhibit TNF-α translation by blocking JNK/SAPK. *Molecular and Cellular Biology, 17,* 6274–6282.

Tan, J., Town, T., Saxe, M., Paris, D., Wu, Y., & Mullan, M. (1999). Ligation of microglial CD40 results in p44/42 mitogen-activated protein kinase-dependent TNF-α production that is opposed by TGF-β1 and IL–10. *Journal of Immunology, 163,* 6614–6621.

Treisman, R. (1996). Regulation of transcription by MAP kinase cascades. *Current Opinion In Cell Biology, 8,* 205–215.

Tsukamoto, I., Nakata, R., & Kojo, S. (1993). Effect of ageing on rat liver regeneration after partial hepatectomy. *Biochemistry and Molecular Biology International, 30,* 773–778.

Volloch, V., Mosser, D. D., Massie, B., & Sherman, M. Y. (1998). Reduced thermotolerance in aged cells results from a loss of an hsp72- mediated control of JNK signaling pathway. *Cell Stress & Chaperones*, 3, 265–271.

Vorbrueggen, G., Lovric, J., & Moelling, K. (1996). Functional analysis of phosphorylation at serine 532 of human c-Myb by MAP kinase. *Biological Chemistry*, 377, 721–730.

Wang, X. Z., & Ron, D. (1996). Stress-induced phosphorylation and activation of the transcription factor CHOP (GADD153) by p38 MAP kinase. *Science, 272,* 1347–1349.

Wang, X., Martindale, J. L., Liu, Y., & Holbrook, N. J. (1998). The cellular response to oxidative stress: influences of mitogen- activated protein kinase signalling pathways on cell survival. *Biochemical Journal, 333 (Pt 2)*, 291–300.

Wang, X., McCullough, K. D., Franke, T. F., & Holbrook, N. J. (2000). Epidermal growth factor receptor-dependent akt activation by oxidative stress enhances cell survival. *Journal of Biological Chemistry, 275*, 14624–14631.

Wange, R. L., & Samelson, L. E. (1996). Complex complexes: Signaling at the TCR. *Immunity, 5*, 197–205.

Weiss, A., & Schlessinger, J. (1998). Switching signals on or off by receptor dimerization. *Cell, 94*, 277–280.

Werlen, G., Jacinto, E., Xia, Y., & Karin, M. (1998). Calcineurin preferentially synergizes with PKC-theta to activate JNK and IL–2 promoter in T lymphocytes. *EMBO Journal, 17*, 3101–3111.

Whisler, R. L., Beiqing, L., & Chen, M. (1996a). Age-related decreases in IL-2 production by human T cells are associated with impaired activation of nuclear transcriptional factors AP-1 and NF-AT. *Cellular Immunology, 169*, 185–195.

Whisler, R. L., Chen, M., Liu, B., & Newhouse, Y. G. (1999). Age-related impairments in TCR/CD3 activation of ZAP-70 are associated with reduced tyrosine phosphorylations of zeta-chains and p59[fyn]/p56[lck] in human T cells. *Mechanisms of Ageing and Development, 111*, 49–66.

Whisler, R. L., Newhouse, Y. G., & Bagenstose, S. E. (1996b). Age-related reductions in the activation of mitogen-activated protein kinases p44[mapk]/ERK1 and p42[mapk]/ERK2 in human T cells stimulated via ligation of the T cell receptor complex. *Cellular Immunology, 168*, 201–210.

Whisler, R. L., Karanfilov, C. I., Newhouse, Y. G., Fox, C. C., Lakshmanan, R. R., & Liu, B. (1998). Phosphorylation and coupling of zeta-chains to activated T-cell receptor (TCR)/CD3 complexes from peripheral blood T-cells of elderly humans. *Mechanisms of Ageing and Development, 105*, 115–135.

Whitmarsh, A. J., & Davis, R. J. (1996). Transcription factor AP–1 regulation by mitogen- activated protein kinase signal transduction pathways. *Journal of Molecular Medicine, 74*, 589–607.

Whitmarsh, A. J., Yang, S. H., Su, M. S., Sharrocks, A. D., & Davis, R. J. (1997). Role of p38 and JNK mitogen-activated protein kinases in the activation of ternary complex factors. *Molecular and Cellular Biology, 17*, 2360–2371.

Xia, Z., Dickens, M., Raingeaud, J., Davis, R. J., & Greenberg, M. E. (1995). Opposing effects of ERK and JNK-p38 MAP kinases on apoptosis. *Science, 270*, 1326–1331.

Xu, X., & Sonntag, W. E. (1996). Growth hormone-induced nuclear translocation of Stat–3 decreases with age: Modulation by caloric restriction. *American Journal of Physiology, 271*, E903-E909.

Yang, Y., Quitschke, W. W., & Brewer, G. J. (1998). Upregulation of amyloid precursor protein gene promoter in rat primary hippocampal neurons by phorbol ester, IL-1 and retinoic acid, but not by reactive oxygen species. *Brain Research Molecular Brain Research, 60*, 40–49.

Zeigler, M. E., Chi, Y., Schmidt, T., & Varani, J. (1999). Role of ERK and JNK pathways in regulating cell motility and matrix metalloproteinase 9 production in growth factor-stimulated human epidermal keratinocytes. *Journal of Cellular Physiology, 180*, 271–284.

Zervos, A. S., Faccio, L., Gatto, J. P., Kyriakis, J. M., & Brent, R. (1995). Mxi2, a mitogen-activated protein kinase that recognizes and phosphorylates Max protein. *Proceedings of the National Academy of Sciences of the USA, 92,* 10531–10534.

Zhen, X., Uryu, K., Cai, G., Johnson, G. P., & Friedman, E. (1999). Age-associated impairment in brain MAPK signal pathways and the effect of caloric restriction in Fischer 344 rats. *Journal of Gerontology: A Biological Sciences Medical Sciences, 54,* B539-B548.

Zhou, G., Bao, Z. Q., & Dixon, J. E. (1995). Components of a new human protein kinase signal transduction pathway. *Journal of Biological Chemistry, 270,* 12665–12669.

Eight

Cell Proliferation in Mammalian Aging

Peter J. Hornsby

I. The Maintenance of Organ Size: Atrophy and Hypertrophy in Aging

Although there are changes in cell proliferation during aging, as reviewed here, the more remarkable fact is that organ and tissue size do not change greatly with aging beyond the point of maturity of the body. This fact is inherent in the life history of most animals, although some continue to grow throughout their life span and have no fixed body size (Finch, 1991). In most species, including all mammals, a fixed body size is achieved at maturity and changes are relatively minor beyond that point. Of course, there are some easily recognized exceptions. Fat deposits change in distribution, and some organs, such as muscle and the dermis of the skin, show some degree of atrophy. Although histological structure may change during aging (see later discussion), most organs and tissues are unchanged in size from maturity to old age. It is easy to overlook the significance of this fact; it is nontrivial and requires explanation, although knowledge of how tissue and organ size are regulated is mostly lacking

(Tanner, 1999). Of course for some cell types, such as neurons and muscle fibers, the number of cells is relatively fixed, but even in these cases there is the possibility of replacement from stem cell compartments throughout life (Flax et al., 1998; Carpenter et al., 1999), and other cells in the nervous system and in muscles are not postmitotic. In most tissues there is constant cell turnover throughout life, even though it may be quite slow compared to embryonic growth. In some tissues, such as the skin epidermis, the gut epithelium, and the hematopoietic system, there is relatively rapid cell proliferation occurring throughout the life span. The healthy function of these tissues is dependent on regulated cell proliferation. In these tissues with rapid cell turnover, organ size is determined mainly by the architecture of the tissue: separation of the stem cell compartment from the rest of the tissue and localized loss of cells from another compartment (the surface of the skin, the lining of the gut, or the removal of old red cells from circulation). In other organs, such as the liver and most endocrine organs, total organ size remains constant despite cell proliferation occurring within the tissue,

Handbook of the Biology of Aging, Fifth Edition

and there is not a clear architectural separation of the stem cell compartment. The constancy implies feedback mechanisms that monitor total organ size, presumably by the level of function of the tissue, but these mechanisms are poorly understood.

There are some few exceptions to the general rule of constant organ size. A notorious example is the prostate gland in humans. Beyond the age of about 50 the prostate increases in size, a process termed benign prostatic hyperplasia (Oesterling et al., 1993), which may result from defective apoptosis (Kyprianou et al., 1996). Although this might be viewed as a specific pathological process, i.e., a disease rather than aging, it becomes symptomatic in almost all individuals by the age of about 90, and there is little reason not to consider it part of normal aging, with the extent of the phenomenon and the age of onset of symptoms being quite variable (Oesterling et al., 1993). This example of continued growth highlights by comparison how successful size maintenance is for other organs. Even in the case of the prostate gland, although there must be an excess of proliferation over cell death, the excess is very small or else the gland would expand rapidly like a growing tumor. Therefore, there is only a minimal perturbation in the normal control of organ size, but unfortunately for male human health the control is not perfect.

We need to distinguish these postmaturity changes from changes in tissues that are essentially developmental. This is the case for the involution of the thymus. Because this involution starts well before maturity and is more or less complete before the end of the reproductive period, it should not be considered as an aging process. This is not simply a semantic question, because any process that begins well before reproductive age must be under strong evolutionary selective pressure, whereas those processes that either do not start until after reproductive age or

have slight effects before reproductive age may escape the force of natural selection (Lithgow & Kirkwood, 1996). Therefore, mechanisms for pre-maturity and post-maturity changes may be quite different. The changes in the prostate are manifest only well after maturity and have escaped the force of natural selection. A possible example of true involution of a tissue during aging is the decrease in size and function of the zona reticularis of the human adrenal cortex, the zone of the cortex that secretes dehydroepiandrosterone (DHEA) (Hornsby, 1995). It is likely that these cells disappear during aging, whereas the cortisol-secreting zone, the zona fasciculata, is maintained by feedback mechanisms that apparently are lacking for the maintenance of the zona reticularis (Hornsby, 1995).

Questions about changes in cell proliferation in aging must be posed in terms of the overall maintenance of organ size. If there are changes in proliferation, they are compensated for primarily by changes in the rate of cell death. Alternatively, and possibly more likely, changes in cell death rates during aging are compensated for by changes in cell proliferation, so as to maintain constant organ size.

Another consequence of the argument presented previously is that it seems very unlikely that in aging there is simply a cessation of cell proliferation in any tissue that shows some cell turnover over most of the life span. Basic data on cell proliferation rates have come from cell labeling studies in vivo. [³H]Thymidine or bromodeoxyuridine (BrdU) is administered to an animal, and the incorporation of these nucleotides into DNA is assessed by autoradiography of tissue sections or by immunohistochemistry. In situations where the administration of precursors is not possible or practical, e.g., for human surgical specimens, direct counting of mitotic figures can be done, but this requires very large numbers of sections.

Surrogate markers for cell proliferation can be useful, such as immunohistochemistry for Ki–67 antigen or proliferating cell nuclear antigen (PCNA). More indirect measures are of enzymes that are required for DNA synthesis or of proteins that increase when cells are stimulated by mitogens, such as c-Myc (Majumdar *et al.*, 1989). Direct measurements of cell proliferation rates confirm that, in tissues with continuously dividing cells, proliferation continues throughout life (reviewed later).

However, raw data on changes in cell proliferation in aging are not necessarily very useful. For each tissue or organ being studied, it is important to understand the specific way in which cell division is regulated, particularly with respect to the stem cell compartment if there are stem cells in the tissue. As emphasized earlier, because most organs maintain a constant size in old age, if there are decreases or increases in the proliferation rate, they must be compensated for by changes in the rate of cell loss by apoptosis or other means.

For each of the tissues and organs where cell proliferation occurs throughout life, the questions that need to be addressed are as follows: (a) whether there are any age-related changes in cell proliferation under normal conditions, and if there are changes, whether these changes result from intrinsic changes in cell proliferation capacity or whether they are secondary to the environment of the cell (exposure of the cell to hormones, cytokines, changes in extracellular matrix, or alterations in the blood supply); (b) whether there are changes that are only apparent when the reserve capacity of the tissue is challenged, e.g., by injury or stresses such as blood loss; and (c) whether changes in cell proliferation have indirect effects, i.e., effects of the presence of cells within the tissue that have lost the ability to divide. The data that are reviewed here show that great progress has been made in answering these questions in some organ systems, but that in others many fundamental questions have yet to be addressed.

II. Principles of Growth Control

A. Cell Proliferation in Culture versus *In Vivo*

There is a very practical reason why the control of tissue and organ size is much less well understood than the basic control of the cell cycle: most of our knowledge of cell cycle regulation comes from experiments initially performed on cells in culture. Studies in knockout mice have complemented the cell culture studies, but it is the rule rather than the exception that basic knowledge of the regulation of cell proliferation has been obtained first in cultured cells and only afterward applied to whole animal systems. Obviously, one must be very careful in applying the knowledge of the regulation of cell proliferation obtained from cell culture to the *in vivo* situation. The problem is that cell culture gives us a rather one-sided view of proliferation control. In culture, proliferation is driven by the availability of mitogens and by the fact that the cells are attached to a surface that is permissive for cell division. Provided the cells do not become too crowded, a parameter that is under the control of the experimenter, proliferation is driven purely by mitogen concentrations. *In vivo*, the situation is much more complex, and we must apply our knowledge of control of the cell cycle to the mechanism by which tissue size is regulated.

B. Role of Angiogenesis

One very important aspect of the regulation of tissue size is the regulation of angiogenesis in tissues. This was first recognized from studies of malignant tumors that require new angiogenesis to grow beyond a very small size (Hanahan & Folkman, 1996). Angiogenesis also is likely to regulate and limit the growth of normal tissues (Risau, 1997). The sprouting of capillaries, proliferation of endothelial cells, and maturation of new capillaries are tightly linked to proliferation of the other cells in the tissue. This lock-step system is much more suited to fine-tuning of tissue and organ size than simple mitogen availability, as in cell culture. Moreover, the model naturally accommodates normal cell turnover: as cells die, they are replaced by cell division according to the capacity of the vascular system to support a specific mass of cells.

III. Replicative Senescence and Immortalization

A. Human Cells

It has been known since the pioneering experiments of Leonard Hayflick in the 1960s that the limited replicative capacity of human cells in culture is very unlikely to be a experimental artifact, but is a reproducible biological phenomenon (Hayflick, 1980). However, it was not until it was discovered that the limitation of replicative capacity directly correlates with telomere shortening that the notion that it might be a culture artifact was finally laid to rest (Harley et al., 1990; Allsopp et al., 1992). Telomeres shorten in most dividing human somatic cells because of the lack of telomerase activity that is required for telomere maintenance (Greider, 1990; Harley, 1991). The lack of telomerase activity results from the absence of expression of the reverse transcriptase subunit (TERT) of the telomerase ribonucleoprotein complex (Lingner et al., 1997; Meyerson et al., 1997). When cells divide in the absence of telomerase activity, about 40–100 bp of the terminal telomeric repeat DNA are

not replicated (Greider, 1990; Harley, 1991). This amount is a constant for various types of human cells, thus providing a kind of mitotic counter (Greider, 1990; Harley, 1991).

After a normal human cell has divided a certain number of times, that number varying with the specific cell type and culture conditions, the telomeres become so short that they trigger a cell cycle checkpoint that puts the cell into a terminally nondividing state. This state commonly has been termed "cellular senescence" or "replicative senescence," the implication of these terms being that it is a form of aging. In this chapter, the phenomenon is termed replicative senescence, but that term is used without the intention of implying that it is necessarily a manifestation of aging at the cellular level. The block to proliferation in replicative senescence is similar to that caused by double-strand breaks in cellular DNA (Harley, 1991), although whether this is actually the mechanism by which short telomeres are recognized is not clear. Further cell division then is blocked by inhibitors of cell proliferation, such as $p21^{SDI1/WAF1/CIP1}$ and $p16^{INK4A}$ (Noda et al., 1994; Smith & Pereira-Smith, 1996). When this checkpoint is abrogated by oncoproteins, such as SV40 T-antigen, this first checkpoint (sometimes termed M1) is bypassed and cells eventually enter a second state, termed crisis or M2 (Holt et al., 1996). In this state, the much shorter telomeres undergo end-to-end fusions resulting in chromosomal breakage—fusion cycles that cause the cells to undergo apoptosis. There is massive loss of cells from the culture, whereas in replicative senescence (M1) cells do not die but enter a permanently nonreplicating state (Smith & Pereira-Smith, 1996). In this state cells are more resistant to apoptosis (Wang, 1995).

The term replicative senescence therefore encompasses two different phenomena: one is the process of telomere shortening, resulting from the lack of expression of TERT, and the second is the process by which telomere shortening shuts off further cell division. It is important to distinguish these two processes because they may have quite different implications for aging *in vivo*.

Most cancer cells that can be grown in culture do not show limits on replication and can divide indefinitely; they are said to be immortalized, and again this term is used here without implying reversal of an aging process. In the absence of genetic changes like the introduction of SV40 T-antigen, most human cells have an unmeasurably low rate of spontaneous immortalization, whereas when SV40 T-antigen is present, rare cells escape from crisis and become immortalized by reexpression of TERT or by other mechanisms (Shay & Wright, 1989; Ray & Kraemer, 1993; Shay et al., 1993; Cheng et al., 1997; Xia et al., 1997; Shammas et al., 1997). The mechanisms by which cancer cells reactivate the expression of TERT or activate alternate mechanisms for avoiding telomere shortening are largely unknown. There appear to be several pathways by which these processes can occur: however, that there are at least four is shown by the fact that immortal human cells may be divided into four complementation groups (Smith & Pereira-Smith, 1996). Within each complementation group, fusion of a cell from one line with a cell from the same or another line produces hybrid cells with indefinite replicative capapcity, whereas fusions of cells from different complementation groups result in hybrid cells that enter the replicative senescent state after a limited number of divisions. The genes involved in these effects have been located to specific chromosomes, and the effects of fusion of two nuclei can be duplicated by the introduction of single chromosomes or chromosome fragments into a cell (Bertram et al., 1999; Cuthbert et al., 1999).

The phenomenon of telomere shortening clearly is the result of the lack of expression of TERT in many normal human somatic cells. At first this was described simply as the absence of telomerase activity in most normal human somatic cells and the presence of telomerase activity in the germ line and in cancer cells. Subsequently, it has become clear that many normal human cells, including many stem cells and other cells that are required to undergo repeated replications, do express TERT, but that expression is tightly regulated by processes not yet well-understood (Belair et al., 1997; Ramakrishnan et al., 1998; Wu et al., 1999; Hodes, 1999). In some cell types, telomerase activity is induced when cells are first isolated from the body and stimulated to divide in culture (Yasumoto et al., 1996; Hsiao et al., 1997; Kunimura et al., 1998). Curiously, however, longer term proliferation is associated with a decline in telomerase activity, sometimes very rapid, so that few long-term cultures of any normal human cells have shown both telomerase activity and telomere maintenance sufficient for immortalization. However, there is at least one and possibly other important exceptions to this generalization. Embryonic stem cells have been isolated and placed in culture at a stage of embryogenesis before TERT expression is down-regulated (Thomson et al., 1998). If they are grown under conditions that prevent differentiation from occurring, telomerase activity is maintained at a level sufficient for indefinite growth. Mesenchymal stem cells show telomerase activity even after extensive growth in culture (Pittenger et al., 1999), but it is not known whether they can grow indefinitely. Additionally, human neural stem cells can be grown for long periods in culture, but their potential for indefinite growth is unknown (Flax et al., 1998; Carpenter et al., 1999).

Proof that the limitation on indefinite cell division in most human cells results from lack of expression of TERT was obtained by showing that forced expression of TERT is sufficient to immortalize normal human fibroblasts and retinal pigmented epithelial cells and is required (although not sufficient by itself) to immortalize keratinocytes and mammary epithelial cells (Bodnar et al., 1998; Kiyono et al., 1998). Immortalization was accompanied by increased or stabilized telomere length, but cells retain a normal karyotype (Jiang et al., 1999; Morales, 1999). Conversely, immortalized cells suffer telomere shortening and the eventual cessation of growth when telomerase is inhibited (Hahn et al., 1999b; Zhang et al., 1999; Shammas et al., 1999).

The second part of the phenomenon of replicative senescence is the state that cells enter when shortening of telomeres has occurred. This state is characterized by high levels of expression of cell cycle inhibitors, principally p21[SDI1/WAF1/CIP1] and p16[INK4A] (Noda et al., 1994; Smith & Pereira-Smith, 1996). A useful biochemical marker, although one of unknown biological sigificance, is the high level of β-galactosidase enzymatic activity with a pH optimum of 6.0, termed senescence-associated β-galactosidase (SA-βgal) (Dimri et al., 1995). The same biochemical pathway and molecular markers can occur under circumstances that do not involve telomere shortening; it is possible to drive cells into this state by mechanisms that do not involve cell division at all, such as oxidative stress, radiation, and the ectopic expression of some signal transduction molecules and cyclin-dependent kinase inhibitors (Robles & Adami, 1998; Serrano et al., 1997; Zhu et al., 1998). Interestingly, many of these interventions potentially are oncogenic. There are indications that some human cell types enter replicative senescence by a replication-dependent process that does not involve telomere shortening, but the

mechanisms are not well-understood (Wynford-Thomas, 1999).

Patterns of gene expression in replicative senescent cells clearly differ from those of cells in the nonsenescent state. In fibroblasts, the pattern resembles that of fibroblasts in inflammation (Shelton et al., 1999). Of particular significance is the production of proteases that may erode the surrounding extracellular matrix and the production of cytokines that could have effects on neighboring cells (Sottile et al., 1989; West, et al., 1989; Kumar et al., 1992; Millis et al., 1992). Interestingly, other cell types (retinal pigmented epithelial cells and endothelial cells) show different patterns of alteration of gene expression when they reach replicative senescence (Shelton et al., 1999). The data are consistent with the hypothesis that the triggering of the block to DNA synthesis that is characteristic of replicative senescence is accompanied by dysregulation of the expression of various other genes and that the pattern of dysregulation will be cell-type-specific.

Therefore, the replicative senescent state appears to be a universal process that is a reaction of mammalian cells to certain kinds of damage. The process presents a puzzle in terms evolutionary biology. The kinds of damage that cause cells to enter this state are very similar to those kinds of damage that cause other cells to enter apoptosis. From the point of view of the organism and the genome, making cells undergo apoptosis makes sense because the damaged cell and its progeny, carrying potentially damaged copies of the genome, are removed from the body. One may consider cells to be very cheap in terms of the overall economy of the body—millions of cells are born and die every day, and there would seem to be no reason why cells should be preserved via the "replicative senescence" process rather than killed off via apoptosis. It is possible that the process is related to the mechanisms whereby fine control is exerted over tissue growth and organ size (Martin, 1993), but there is no completely convincing explanation.

B. Important Differences Between Human and Mouse Cells

A recurring theme in this chapter will be to emphasize differences in the changes in proliferation during aging in humans and other primates versus mice and other rodents. There is an emphasis on contrasting human cell properties with those of mouse cells because of the extraordinary value of the experimental ability to make germ-line genetic changes in mice. To summarize the argument made here, although there are changes in cell proliferation observed in mice and rats with age, these changes do not necessarily have the same significance as changes in cell proliferation in humans. Human cells have relatively short telomeres compared to those of mice and rats (although not all rodents have long telomeres) (Blasco et al., 1997; Coviello-McLaughlin & Prowse, 1997). Whereas most somatic human tissues and cells are telomerase-negative, many mouse and rat tissues and cells are telomerase-positive (Prowse & Greider, 1995). It is interesting that both human and rodent cells have a limited replicative capacity in culture. Moreover, some of the biochemical features of the nonreplicating state that the cells enter appear to be common between human and mouse cells. However, the mechanism by which cells enter replicative senescence in culture clearly has been shown to result from telomere shortening in human cells, but this cannot be the case for mouse cells. Mouse cells undergo 10–20 divisions in culture before replicative arrest and arrest without significant telomere shortening. Cells isolated from mice in which the gene for the telomerase RNA component has been inactivated (TR$^{-/-}$ mice), which have shorter telomeres than wild-type

cells, also undergo 10–20 doublings in culture before growth arrest (Blasco et al., 1997). Moreover, mouse cells bypass the replicative senescent state and undergo spontaneous immortalization at a very high rate; no specific experimental interventions are required to obtain immortalized cell lines (Wright & Shay, 2000). Immortalization occurs in 100% of cells from p19$^{ARF-/-}$ or p53$^{-/-}$ mice (Harvey et al., 1993; Kamijo et al., 1997). Immortalized mouse cells are almost always aneuploid (Worton & Duff, 1979), but the genetic changes that have taken place to bypass the initial step in replication are not known.

However, the mouse cell "replicative arrest" in culture and human cell "replicative senescence" have some biochemical similarities (Wright & Shay, 2000). The function of p53, although not pRb, is required in mouse cells; the arrest is maintained by high levels of cell cycle inhibitory proteins, and SA-βgal is induced. Mouse cells enter replicative arrest after exposure to the same agents that induce replicative senescence in human cells. A reasonable hypothesis is that replicative arrest in mouse cells is a direct result of the transition from the *in vivo* to the cell culture environment, because of DNA damage or other factors (Wright & Shay, 2000).

Considering the differences between the species, there is a much greater possibility that there could be exhaustion of cellular proliferation in humans than in mice. Consider also that the task of human stem cells is to repopulate and to supply a much larger number of cells over a much longer period than is the case for the mouse. For example, in the hematopoietic system, stem cells in humans have to supply red blood cells for a blood volume that is about 4000 times larger than that of the mouse over a time period that is about 30 times longer than the 3-year maximum life span of the mouse.

Unfortunately, the possibility that human and mouse cellular aging might differ means that data from proliferation during the aging of mice with various genetic changes or experimental manipulations must be evaluated carefully in relation to its potential relevance to aging in humans. The same genetic and other interventions usually are not possible in humans, and available data are restricted to clinical observations and experiments on cells isolated and studied in culture.

Mice with an inactivated telomerase RNA gene (TR$^{-/-}$ mice), whose cells lack telomerase activity, suffer telomere shortening (Blasco et al., 1997). Could the TR$^{-/-}$ mouse provide a more "humanized" rodent model for aging? The data are very interesting, but not conclusive, at the time of writing this chapter (Rudolph et al., 1999; Herrera et al., 1999; Kipling & Faragher, 1999). After three generations, the normally long mouse telomeres have shortened in the TR$^{-/-}$ animals, and these mice present a picture of a "segmental progeroid syndrome," i.e., some aspects of the phenotype resemble accelerated aging. They have premature graying and loss of hair, poor wound healing, increased cancer incidence, gastrointestinal defects, infertility, decreased adipose tissue, and a shortened life span. Clearly, each of these phenotypic effects must be caused by the lack of telomerase activity (i.e., shortening of telomeres) in some cell type or other, but a problem for interpretation is that short telomeres in these animals might not necessarily induce the same cellular state that has been characterized as replicative senescence in human cells. TR$^{-/-}$ mice are viable to the sixth generation. Well before this point, increased numbers of end-to-end chromosome fusions are observed (0 in metaphase in wild type; 0.26 in generation 2; 0.56 in generation 4; and 1.93 in generation 6) (Blasco et al., 1997). Regeneration of the liver is impaired in sixth-generation mice, but cells do not arrest at G1/S, as expected if the short telomeres trigger replicative senescence, but instead hepatocytes have impaired progress through mitosis and show many aberrant mitotic figures (Rudolph et al., 2000). Although there are karyotypic abnormalities in human cells nearing senescence (Chen & Ruddle, 1974), most cells appear to stop dividing with a normal karyotype. Bovine cells also senesce as a result of telomere shortening; the fact that animals can be cloned from the nuclei of bovine cells close to senescence also shows that replicative senescence is not associated with chromosomal abnormalities, at least not those that would prevent the formation of a viable organism (Lanza et al., 2000).

The human genetic disease X-linked dyskeratosis congenita was identified as a disease of impaired telomerase activity and shortened telomeres (Mitchell et al., 1999). The protein product of the gene that is defective in DKC, dyskerin, is required for proper RNA processing, including the RNA of the telomerase ribonucleoprotein complex. In this syndrome, there are proliferative defects in tissues known to have telomerase-positive stem cells (hematopoietic system and skin). DKC patients have very short telomeres in fibroblasts and white blood cells. They usually die of bone marrow failure at a young age. However, the disease is also associated with chromosomal abnormalities and early death from some malignancies. Therefore, there are similarities between telomerase-deficient mice and telomerase-deficient humans. In both, chromosomal aberrations may cause defective proliferation. Whether replicative senescence accounts for some of the pathology in dyskeratosis congenita is unknown, but the evidence could also be interpreted as indicating that shortening of telomeres in human tissues in vivo might lead to crisis rather than replicative senescence.

C. Repression of TERT Expression as an Anti-cancer Mechanism

Because TERT appears to be reexpressed in the great majority of human cancers, it has been hypothesized that the process by which TERT is repressed in most somatic cells is an anticancer mechanism. It may contribute to the large difference in susceptibility to cancer (calculated on a per cell basis) between mice and humans. Suppose that mice and humans have the same risk of dying of cancer over their life spans [approximately true at least for some strains of mice (Peto et al., 1985)]. However, a human being is about 3000 times heavier than a 25-g mouse and lives about 30 times as long. Consider also that cells are about the same size in mice as in humans and that cell turnover occurs at about same rate. All of these assumptions may not be entirely correct but this does not substantially affect the basic validity of this argument. It then is evident that human cells are approximately 90,000 times more resistant to tumorigenic conversion per unit of time than are mouse cells. Presumably, as part of the evolution of the life history of the human species, anticancer mechanisms evolved that were not present in short-lived ancestors. In this case, the anticancer process may provide an example of antagonistic pleiotropy, the genetic event (repression of TERT) having beneficial effects early in the life span and possibly negative effects late in the life span (Williams, 1957; Campisi, 1997). The best evidence that TERT repression is indeed an anticancer mechanism in human cells comes from data showing that the well-known oncoproteins Ras and SV40 T-antigen cannot transform a normal human cell into a tumor cell unless they are also expressed together with TERT (Hahn et al., 1999a). Presumably, the reason that TERT can cooperate with other oncogenes is that, during the process by which a normal cell becomes a fully malignant tumor cell, many cell divisions must take place and telomeres would become critically short unless the cell activates telomerase or other mechanisms to prevent telomere shortening. In mice, such anticancer strategies are unnecessary for their life history. Their small size and short life span mean that they are not more likely than humans to die of cancer before being able to reproduce. Thus, there has not been an evolutionary selective pressure to repress TERT expression in this species (and presumably in other similar small, short-lived mammals, although this has not yet been well-studied). Presumably there are similar arguments that can be made in terms of trade-offs between the advantages and disadvantages of long and short telomeres (Wright & Shay, 2000). Evidently, however, an organism that adopts TERT repression as an evolutionary anticancer strategy must also have short telomeres, or TERT repression becomes irrelevant to the suppression of malignant transformation.

D. Replicative Senescence: Summary and Conclusions

Data on the limited replicative capacity of cultured cells isolated from humans and mice of different ages and genotypes must be interpreted carefully in view of the likely different mechanisms by which terminally nondividing states are achieved in human and mouse cells. In humans, there is substantial evidence that telomere shortening occurs in vivo, as reviewed later, thus linking in vivo aging to the cell culture phenomenon of replicative senescence. When human cells without TERT or with low levels of TERT divide, they suffer telomere shortening, and this occurs whether they are dividing in vivo or in culture. However, in the absence of knowing precisely what limits mouse cell growth in culture, it is not possible to state that the process by which mouse cells exhibit a limited replicative capacity in culture does or does not occur *in vivo*.

IV. Methods for Studying Cell Proliferation in Aging

Experimental transplantation of cells and tissues has been very useful in addressing basic questions of whether there are intrinsic limits on the proliferation of cells *in vivo* and whether those limits are reached during aging. One protocol is to transplant cells or tissues to a recipient animal from which the corresponding endogenous tissue has been removed. For example, this can be done by irradiation in the case of the hematopoietic system or by "clearing" the mammary fat pad in the case of the mammary gland (see later discussion). After the transferred tissue has engrafted and expanded to its maximum size in the host, it is removed and the procedure is repeated with a second recipient animal. The transfer is repeated to successive recipients to test whether there is a point when reconstitution of the recipient fails. Unfortunately, there are a variety of technical obstacles in such transplantation experiments; in stem cell systems, repeated transplantation may fail after some number of passages, not because of an intrinsic limitation on stem cell proliferation but because the handling of the cells during the cell transplantation procedures causes the cells to lose their pluripotent characteristics or because of a failure to transfer a constant number of stem cells each time (see Section VIII on stem cells). The application of cell transplantation techniques to study human aging has been very limited, but these methods could play an important role. It is important to recognize that cell transplantation can provide both an experimental system for studying fundamental aspects of aging processes as well as potential therapies

(Hornsby, 1999). An approach taken in the author's research is to find out how aging affects the ability of human adrenocortical cells to form a functional, vascularized adrenal tissue structure after transplantation into *scid* mice (Hornsby *et al.*, 1998). By transplanting adrenocortical cells into a neutral environment (the young *scid* mouse), we can test how cellular behavior and patterns of gene expression change as a function of population doubling level in culture and as a function of the age of the donor. Cell transplantation experiments can help to elucidate both universal cellular aging processes, the changes that affect all cells in aging, as well as the unique aging processes that occur in specific cell types.

In experimental animals, one can study the effects of interventions that affect life span, such as dietary restriction. Animals under caloric restriction have been reported to show lower cell proliferation rates (Heller *et al.*, 1990; Lok *et al.*, 1990; Hursting *et al.*, 1994; Wolf *et al.*, 1995), but the significance of this observation for the life-prolonging effect is unknown. Genetic effects that affect life span, such as perturbations of growth hormone status, have provided provocative data. Stimulation of growth of the organism as a whole was associated with shortened life span and decreased proliferative potential of isolated cells, whereas genetic defects of growth hormone increase life span (Pendergrass *et al.*, 1993; Brown-Borg *et al.*, 1996).

V. Telomere Shortening and Replicative Senescence *In Vivo*

Human cell proliferation in aging can also be investigated by making primary cultures of cells from donors of different ages and studying their proliferation in culture. In some cases, the complete replicative potential of such cells has been studied, i.e., the cells have been grown until they reached replicative senescence. In others, colony-forming efficiency has been studied in the primary culture, as a surrogate measure for total replicative capacity (Smith et al., 1978).

Much attention has been paid to the observation originally made in the 1970s that the replicative capacity of human fibroblasts in culture decreases as a function of donor age (Martin et al., 1970). It was well-known even at the time of these initial observations that there was much variation within each decade of age in the maximal and minimal proliferative capacity of the different cell samples. Subsequently, the generality of the observation was challenged by finding that the decrease as a function of donor age applied only to fibroblasts isolated from diabetic and "prediabetic" patients (Goldstein et al., 1978) and was not evident in fibroblasts obtained from non-sun-exposed skin (Gilchrest, 1980; Cristofalo et al., 1998). However, other sets of data have upheld the original observations (Allsopp et al., 1992). Fibroblasts from older donors also showed a higher level of expression of collagenase, which is characteristic of replicative senescent cells (Burke et al., 1994). Additionally, cells from patients with Werner syndrome, a segmental progeroid syndrome, have decreased replicative potential and accelerated telomere shortening (Salk, 1985; Schulz et al., 1996). Fibroblasts are cultured readily, and most cell culture data on the molecular basis for replicative senescence have come from studies on fibroblasts. Unfortunately, fibroblasts as a cell type are not ideal for these kinds of studies. First, the cell population that is isolated is hard to standardize. When fibroblasts are isolated by allowing cells to migrate out from an explant, there is a great deal of selection for which cells form the "starting" culture population (designated as population doubling level zero). Some of the lack of agreement among investiga-

tors could result from different isolation techniques, which have provided differing degrees of initial selection. Second, the biology of fibroblasts undoubtedly differs from one organ to another, and even from one part of the skin to another, but these distinctions have not always been considered. Third, most fibroblasts probably are proliferatively quiescent in vivo after maturity and undergo very low rates of cell division. Therefore, it would not be surprising if little or no exhaustion of proliferative capacity were observed.

It would be much better to study the effects of donor age on replicative capacity in those cell types where pure populations can be isolated reproducibly from defined sites in the body and where some cell turnover occurs throughout life. In such cell populations there would be at least the potential for exhaustion of proliferative capacity. Such studies become more powerful when there is an ability to correlate the donor age cell culture data with direct in vivo data on replicative potential, although obviously this is difficult in humans when such data are from clinical observations rather than from direct experimental intervention.

Studies that have been done on nonfibroblast cell populations have shown much larger decreases in proliferative capacity than was observed as a function of donor age in fibroblasts. In some nonfibroblast cell types, many cells in the population isolated from older donors have very limited or no proliferative capacity. Some examples are age-related decrements in proliferative potential in lens epithelial cells (Tassin et al., 1979; Power et al., 1993), retinal pigmented epithelial cells (Flood et al., 1980), smooth muscle cells (Bierman, 1978; Start et al., 1991; Ruiz-Torres et al., 1999), and osteoblasts (Koshihara et al., 1991; Kassem et al., 1997; D'Ippolito et al., 1999) (Figs. 1 and 2).

Proliferative capacity is closely related to telomere length in endothelial cells

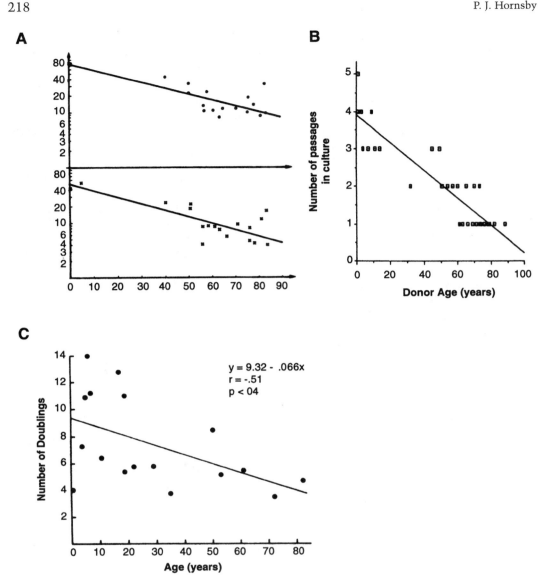

Figure 1. Age-related decline in proliferative potential in human lens epithelial cells and human smooth muscle cells. (A) Labeling index ([³H]thymidine autoradiography) plotted against donor age for primary cultures of lens epithelial cells: top, labeling for 48 hr; bottom, labeling for 24 hr. Reproduced with permission from Tassin *et al.* (1979). (B) Maximum number of passages in culture for lens epithelial cells as a function of donor age. Reproduced with kind permission from Kluwer Academic Publishers from Power *et al.* (1993). (C) Cumulative population doublings for arterial smooth muscle cells as a function of donor age. From Bierman (1978), copyright 1978 by the Society for In Vitro Biology (formerly the Tissue Culture Association). Reproduced with permission of the copyright owner.

(Fig. 2A). Telomere lengths in endothelial cells decreased as a function of donor age, with a greater decline being observed in cells isolated from the iliac artery compared to cells from the thoracic artery (Chang & Harley, 1995) (Fig. 2B). The greater decline in telomere length was observed in the cells that had likely undergone more proliferation *in vivo*, because they resided in a part of the

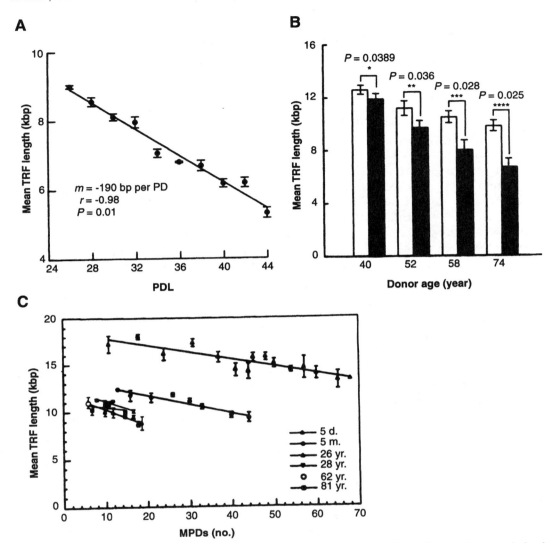

Figure 2. Telomere length and proliferative potential in human endothelial cells and human skeletal muscle satellite cells. (A) Relationship between telomere length (TRF = telomere restriction fragment) in the primary culture and the population doubling level at replicative senescence in umbilical vein endothelial cells (various donors). (B) Decrease in TRF in primary endothelial cells as a function of donor age: open bars, thoracic artery endothelial cells; solid bars, iliac artery endothelial cells. Panels A and B from Chang and Harley (1995), copyright 1995 National Academy of Sciences, USA. (C) Telomere length and population doublings (MPDs) in satellite cells from donors of various ages. Reproduced with permission from Decary et al. (1997).

vascular system where blood flow might cause the most chronic damage to the endothelium. Unfortunately, because the data are from human specimens, it is difficult to test this hypothesis directly. Skeletal muscle satellite cells can be isolated from human muscle samples and exhibit a limited replicative potential in culture. They show decreasing proliferative potential as a function of donor age and decreased telomere length (Fig. 2C), but muscle fiber nuclei showed stable telomere length (Decary *et al.*, 1997). In the author's laboratory, studies on the effects of age on the proliferation of adrenocortical cells from donors show a great decrease in proliferative capacity, and this has also been shown to be associated with short telomeres in cells from older donors (Hornsby *et al.*, 1992; W. Wright & P. Hornsby, unpublished observations).

These examples are consistent with the hypotheses that cell proliferation occurring over the life span of the donor causes telomere shortening and that cell cultures then are initiated with cells that have a lowered remaining proliferative potential because continued cell division in culture shortens telomeres to a point where replicative senescence occcurs.

VI. Diminution of Reserve Capacity

No data show a complete loss of cell proliferative potential in any human organ as a function of age, and it is unlikely that the day-to-day functions of tissues are compromised by changes in replicative potential. However, tissues may suffer a loss of ability to repair damage efficiently or to restore sudden losses of cells during aging. The proliferative reserve capacity of the tissue is impaired, even if the replication capacity that they need for normal maintenance and cell turnover is always adequate. This concept is in agreement with other measurements in aging that show that the gradual decline in organ function, resulting from a large variety of aging processes, has its biggest impact on the loss of the reserve capacity of the organism to react to events that injure the tissue or require its function at a level greater than that normally required. Age-related disease processes may be exacerbated by, or actually caused by, this loss of reserve capacity.

Under conditions where there is a chronic stimulus to divide, there is evidence, albeit limited, that cells can reach replicative senescence under *in vivo* conditions. In patients with chronic ulcers, fibroblasts were observed to have decreased proliferative capacity and increased senescence markers (Raffetto *et al.*, 1999; Agren *et al.*, 1999). These effects were more pronounced in ulcers that had been present for >3 years (Raffetto *et al.*, 1999). In conditions of muscle fiber death and excessive cell turnover in the muscle, such as Duchenne muscular dystrophy, satellite cells show a short replicative potential even when isolated from young donors, and this becomes worse over time (Blau *et al.*, 1983). More examples are found in the hematopoietic system and the liver, as discussed later.

Whether these cells have truly reached the end of their proliferation *in vivo* before isolation is difficult to assess. An unanswered question is whether the short-telomere signal for replicative senescence can be modulated by factors in the environment of the cell. Because a state resembling replicative senescence can be triggered by many manipulations other than telomere shortening, there is the possibility that some factor in the cell culture environment (e.g., some degree of DNA damage by exposure to oxygen and light), which by itself does not cause replicative senescence, can synergize with the short-telomere signal. Thus, although donor age effects clearly indicate the potential for exhaustion of replicative capacity, the imperfect cell culture environment might amplify the effect. On the other hand, telomere shortening can be accelerated in cell culture by DNA damage (Petersen *et al.*, 1998), indicating the possibility that cells isolated from tissues may not always have acquired their short-telomere state by repeated cell division.

VII. Possible Occurrence of Cells with Characteristics of Replicative Senescence in Tissues

Tissue function may be affected by the presence of replicative senescent cells, even if the cell population as a whole retains replicative capacity. Such senescent cells may have been formed by telomere shortening or by one of the numerous other processes that have been shown to place cells in the same state. The presence of cells that have senescence-associated β-galactosidase (SA-βgal) was reported first for human skin (Dimri *et al.*, 1995) and subsequently was shown in the rhesus monkey in retinal pigmented epithelium (Mishima *et al.*, 1999) and in the epidermis (Pendergrass *et al.*, 1999). In all three studies, the number of SA-βgal-positive cells increased as a function of donor age. These intriguing observations require much more study. First, there is an obvious need to study the mechanism by which such cells are formed. Whether SA-βgal positive cells *in vivo* result from telomere shortening is not known. The suspicion that they might not exists for RPE cells, because these cells are mostly postmitotic in adult life (Hjelmeland, 1999). Second, whether such cells *in vivo* actually have the same range of changes in gene expression observed in replicative senescent cells in culture is also unknown. This is important because it has been speculated that these changes may result in a procarcinogenic state in tissues that could aid the growth of premalignant cells and provide a permissive environment for tumor progression (Campisi, 1997; Dunsmuir *et al.*, 1998). At the moment that hypothesis lacks direct experimental confirmation, but deserves full consideration. Many properties of aging tissues might result from the presence of relatively small numbers of replicative senescent cells.

The fact that both human and mouse cells can become SA-βgal-positive by various forms of damage unfortunately leaves us without good *in situ* assays that unambiguously indicate that cells have exhausted their replicative capacity *in vivo* by telomere shortening.

Independent of the question of whether replicative senescent cells affect tissue function, it is clear that telomere shortening does occur in human tissues *in vivo*, potentially putting cells ever closer to replicative senescence. It is important to distinguish the phenomenon of telomere shortening from its significance. The significance is still under debate, but the fact that it does indeed occur should not be considered controversial.

VIII. Stem Cells

An important subject is how aging affects the properties and numbers of stem cells in continuously proliferating tissues. Critical questions for stem cells are the following: (a) is there an age-dependent (i.e., time-dependent) change in the number of stem cells and/or an age-dependent change in their properties; and (b) do stem cells have a finite proliferative potential (or are immortal in terms of cell division) and does repeated cell division change their properties. These two questions must be separated because the most pluripotent stem cells divide only rarely *in vivo* (Morrison, *et al.*, 1997). Most cell division is done by the more committed progenitor cells and by differentiating cells.

In any organ system where cell proliferation is critical to function, such as the hematopoietic system, it would be anticipated that any intrinsic changes in cell proliferation would be compensated via feedback to maintain overall function at the appropriate level. As discussed previously, it might be expected that deficits in aging would become apparent when the system is stressed by the increased demand for cell proliferation. Various experimental protocols have been devised to search for such deficits. Additionally, experimental systems have been set up to address the questions of whether there are ultimate limits to proliferation and whether such eventual limits may be reached normally. If an organ system does have intrinsic limits on cell proliferation, this should be taken into account in any study of age-related diseases in that organ. It is possible that proliferative limits are reached under at least some set of conditions during aging.

IX. Age-Related Changes in Cell Proliferation

Major organ systems that have been studied for changes in cell proliferation during aging include the hematopoietic system, liver, mammary glands, skin, and gastrointestinal system.

A. Hematopoietic System

When hematopoietic stem cells divide, they regenerate either two new stem cells (equivalent to the parent cell, i.e., a process of self-renewal) or one stem cell and one cell that is more committed to differentiation; the latter gives rise to the various specific cell types of the hematopoietic system. Because methods for characterizing hematopoietic stem cells are complex and have been subject to refinement over time, the nomenclature used by the authors of the various studies discussed has been retained.

1. Mouse

The mouse has been studied extensively as an experimental animal with respect to aging and the hematopoietic system. There are no changes in the ability to maintain normal numbers of red blood cells in old mice except when the animals are stressed by crowding (Williams et al., 1986). Under stressed conditions there were declines in hematocrit, CFU-E (colony-forming units erythroid), BFU-E (burst-forming units erythroid), and CFU-C (colony-forming units culture). On the other hand, measurements of stem cell numbers in mice during aging have shown great variations depending on the strain of animals studied. In the DBA strain, the number of stem cells (cobblestone-area-forming cells, CAFC) decreased markedly between 12 and 20 months of age, but in B6 mice this population increased at a constant rate from late gestation to 20 months (de Haan & Van Zant, 1999). Variable increases in stem cell number were observed in several other strains (Harrison et al., 1989; Morrison et al., 1996; de Haan et al., 1997). In BXD recombinant inbred strains, differences in CAFC numbers from 2 to 20 months ranged from a ~10-fold decrease to a ~10-fold increase. Several genomic loci were found to contribute to these differences (de Haan & Van Zant, 1999).

There is some decline in the repopulating capacity of mouse hematopoietic stem cells with age. In one study, stem cells from old mice were ~25% as efficient as those from young animals in homing and engraftment in the bone marrow of recipients (Morrison et al., 1996). In another study, fetal stem cells had 1.6–3.0 times the functional capacity of young adult stem cells; young adult (3 months) cells had 1.6–2.0 times the functional capacity of old (25–28 months) mice (Chen et al., 1999). It is not clear whether these data indicate true replicative senescence of stem cells or whether this represents an age-dependent shift in the relative populations of pluripotent and more committed cells. There is a decreased replicative capacity in mouse hematopoietic stromal cells (Jiang et al., 1992) and a reduced frequency of stromal cell precursors in primary cultures of bone marrow cells from old mice (Globerson, 1999). Aging effects on stromal cells may indirectly affect stem cell function.

In any case, the available data show relatively mild effects of aging on overall hematopoietic system function in the mouse, despite the changes in absolute numbers of stem cells. Presumably, homeostatic mechanisms increase the stem cell pool to compensate for age-associated decreases in stem cell function; but the situation in those strains that show decreases in stem cell number in aging is unexplained.

Measurements of stem cell proliferation in mice (long-term self-renewing hematopoietic stem cells, LT-HSC) showed that stem cells divide every 57 days on average (Cheshier et al., 1999). This means that a stem cell would divide about 6 times per year or 18 times over a 3-year mouse life span. Serial cell transplantation experiments have been performed on the hematopoietic system in rodents as a means of attempting to exhaust the proliferative potential of stem cells. Such experiments are important and have had a major impact on the concept of the possibility of age-related exhaustion of cell proliferation. The progeny of a single stem cell can maintain hematopoiesis over the life span of an animal receiving a transplant (Jordan & Lemischka, 1990). However, there are limitations on the interpretation of serial cell transplantation experiments that should be considered carefully. Because of the continuous increase in our knowledge of stem cells, not all experiments in the past have been performed with ideal protocols. The best method would seem to be to isolate highly defined stem cells (at either the most primitive or the more committed stages) and to transplant a constant number of such cells to the recipient (a lethally irradiated or other suitable recipient, such as the anemic

mouse mutant W; Harrison & Astle, 1991). At the end of the reconstitution process in the recipient, the isolation procedure would be repeated and the transplantation continued in a second recipient, and so on. Unfortunately for aging research, knowledge of how to isolate and handle such stem cells still is not perfect. The methods for isolating and growing highly defined stem cells in culture are still being refined. When they are out of the body, they must not be inadvertently stimulated to enter a more committed state. Even when these technical problems are solved, an unavoidable problem is that the most primitive stem cells may undergo a relatively small number of divisions in each transplant generation, and it is difficult to measure this number. Therefore, the question of whether such stem cells have a finite proliferative capacity or are "immortal" is intrinsically difficult to assess by serial transplantation.

Early serial transplantation experiments in mice suggested a limit to the number of times stem cells could be transferred to successive recipient animals and still successfully reconstitute the hematopoietic system of the recipients, but it was later recognized that this failure likely is technical in nature (Harrison, 1985; Harrison et al., 1988). Subsequent experiments used a strategy of measuring the number of stem cells (long-term reconstituting cells, LTRCs) at each transfer to ensure that similar numbers are transferred. When the number of LTRCs was taken into account, no change in repopulating capacity was observed over four transplant generations (Iscove & Nawa, 1997). It was calculated that there was an expansion of 8400-fold in the stem cell number relative to the original input population. This represents a minimum of ~13 doublings of the stem cells (not taking into account those doublings that produce one stem cell and one committed cell). Thus, it is clear that a large number of transplant generations would be required before stem cell exhaustion might be anticipated. If the measurement of stem cell proliferation in humans is correct (see later discussion), 13 doublings represent only a small fraction of the total proliferation of a stem cell over the human life span.

An alternative to serial transplantation as a means to study the total replicative potential of stem cells is to repeatedly stimulate stem cell proliferation *in vivo* in a single experimental animal. When such experiments were performed by repeated treatment with hydroxyurea (Ross *et al.*, 1982) or repeated irradiation (Harrison *et al.*, 1984), there was no exhaustion of hematopoietic potential. However, it is not known how many times the stem cells actually divide in these experiments. The problem here is to stimulate the proliferation of the most pluripotent cells rather than more committed successors. Mice with targeted disruption of the p21[SDI1/WAF1/CIP1] gene exhibit more stem cell cycling and impaired self-renewal of primitive cells in serial transplantation (Cheng *et al.*, 2000). This type of genetic approach to stem cell senescence is very promising. Unfortunately, it is difficult to distinguish whether the genetic intervention (in this case the lack of p21) causes true senescence of stem cells (i.e., causes pluripotent stem cells to divide so many times that they eventually have impaired cell division capability) or in fact changes the probability of the commitment of primitive stem cells to more differentiated cells, resulting in stem cell exhaustion.

Another method for studying the total replicative potential of stem cells is to grow them in culture, followed by the reconstitution of recipient animals after different numbers of cell generations. As in serial cell transplantation experiments, a problem is to keep the cells in their uncommitted state in culture. That such

problems essentially are technical is shown by the fact that mouse embryonic stem cells can be grown under special conditions in which differentiation is prevented.

The preceding discussion of the available evidence on hematopoietic stem cells in the mouse suggests that effects of aging on the function of the hematopoietic system are small under normal conditions. The maximum proliferative potential of mouse stem cells is unknown, but evidently it is sufficient to supply the need for cells well past the normal life span. Because of the different characteristics of mouse and human cells with respect to telomerase and telomere regulation emphasized earlier and in view of the fact that human stem cells must supply a much larger population over a much longer time period, it would be unwise to apply these findings uncritically to human biology.

2. Human

Most of the data available on hematopoietic stem cells in human aging are from clinical measurements and cell culture data. Strategies that have been valuable for investigating rodent stem cells in aging would need to be modified to study human stem cells. A reconstitution assay is available for human cells in the form of the *scid-hu* mouse, in which mice with the *scid* (severe combined immunodeficiency) mutation that lack functional T- and B-cells are irradiated and rescued with human bone marrow or peripheral blood stem cells (Dao & Nolta, 1999). Mice with the *scid* mutation plus other mutations that enable the xenotransplantation of human cells may also be used (Dao & Nolta, 1999). Studies of donor age effects and replicative potential in serial cell transplantation in this model should be very valuable.

In the absence of disease, the supply of red blood cells to the body in elderly humans still is efficient. However, anemia is common in older humans (Zauber & Zauber, 1987; Izaks et al., 1999), but is not considered to be a part of normal aging. In most individuals, there is only a slight change in hematocrit as a function of age. There are many causes of anemia (Zauber & Zauber, 1987; Izaks et al., 1999); true age-related changes in cell proliferation, as opposed to disease-related causes, are unlikely. In normal subjects the number of CD34$^+$ bone marrow cells did not change in 70- to 80-year-olds versus 20- to 30-year-olds, although there was a decline in the proliferative response of the cells to G-CSF (granulocyte colony-stimulating factor) (Chatta et al., 1993). In a study of 88-year-old subjects compared to subjects 21–57 years of age, there were no changes in CFU-E or BFU-E, but there was a decrease in CFU-GM (Nilsson-Ehle et al., 1995).

Circulating peripheral blood stem cells (CD34$^+$) and PB-CFU-GM (peripheral blood colony-forming unit granulocyte/macrophage) decreased with age in the range of 20–90 years (Egusa et al., 1998). When peripheral blood CD34$^+$ stem cells are mobilized by the administration of G-CSF, there is a small decline in the number of cells that can be mobilized in donors more than 60 years of age (Anderlini et al., 1997). However, in healthy (nonanemic) donors, the decrease was mild and did not prevent the harvesting of sufficient numbers of these stem cells for transplantation.

These data are in agreement with those in mice, that aging has rather little effect on normal hematopoiesis. However, there is ample evidence, reviewed next, that the reserve capacity of the proliferative potential of the hematopoietic system in humans is much less than in mice. In many pathological conditions the system approaches exhaustion.

There are indications that stem cell number may fall to very low levels in older humans. In many elderly women there is a skewed X-chromosome inactivation pattern in white blood cells, indicating that the number of stem cells giving rise to the peripheral circulating cells has greatly decreased (Champion et al., 1997; Gale et al., 1997). A possible alternate explanation for the observed age-dependent skewing is that there is a selective survival or proliferation advantage for cells expressing a particular allele of a gene on the X-chromosome (Abkowitz et al., 1998).

Telomere length is very valuable in the analysis of cell proliferation in the human hematpoietic system. A major question is whether the level of telomerase activity in human hematopoietic stem cells is sufficient to prevent telomere shortening and thereby to prevent eventual replicative senescence. Cell populations enriched in stem cells have telomerase activity (Yui, et al., 1998).

Telomere shortening is observed in bone marrow cells from adult humans compared to fetal liver and umbilical cord blood cells (Vaziri et al., 1994). A population enriched in stem cells (CD34$^+$ CD38$^-$) also had shorter telomeres in adults (Vaziri et al., 1994). Lymphocytes show a continuous decline in telomere length with age, consistent with a continuous decline in telomere length in stem cells (Hastie et al., 1990; Vaziri et al., 1993). The loss of telomere DNA has been measured by a fluorescence technique in lymphocytes and granulocytes from a large number of human donors in the range of 0–90 years of age. There was a very striking continuous decline in telomere length, which fits a pattern of somewhat greater loss of telomere DNA up to the age of about 1 year followed by a constant linear rate of loss up to the oldest ages studied (Frenck et al., 1998; Rufer et al., 1999) (Fig. 3A). These data all suggest that telomerase in hematopoietic stem cells is insufficient to mantain telomere length. Direct data for this is difficult to obtain because of the fact that

A

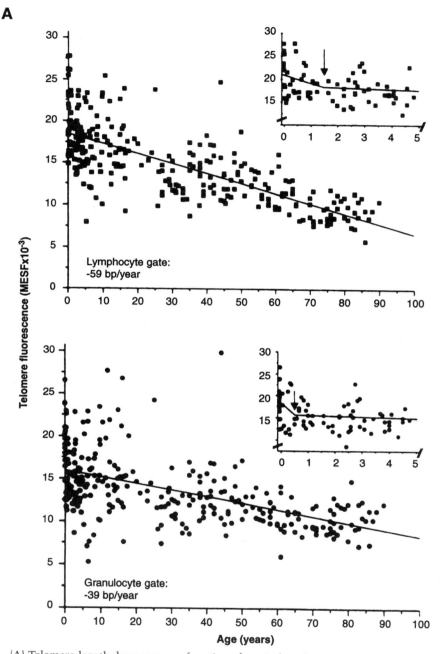

Figure 3. (A) Telomere length decreases as a function of age in lymphocytes and granulocytes. Telomere length was measured by flow FISH (fluorescent *in situ* hybridization). Insets show the results of bisegmented fit analysis. Arrows indicate the optimal intersection of calculated regression lines. Reproduced from Rufer *et al.* (1999) by copyright permission of The Rockefeller Press. (B) Telomere shortening after bone marrow transplantation. DNA was extracted from neutrophils. TRFs were measured using a probe specific for the subtelomeric region of chromosome 7q. Measurements were performed on the donors and on the recipients at a median of 23 months following transplantation. The data also are plotted as a scattergram, the horizontal dotted line indicating the threshold of background in the method used. Additionally, the decrease in telomere length is plotted against the number of infused cells. From Notaro *et al.* (1997),

B

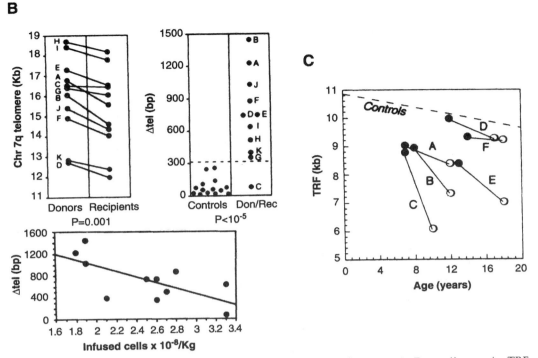

copyright 1997 National Academy of Sciences, USA. (C) Telomere shortening in Fanconi's anemia. TRFs were measured in DNA extracted from mononuclear cells isolated at the indicated ages. Patients A–C suffered an increase in the severity of their symptoms over the period between the two samples. Reproduced with permission from Leteurtre *et al.* (1999).

it is now understood that telomerase in many cell types is regulated, as discussed earlier. This fact means that very quiescent stem cells that are not stimulated to divide in culture might be capable of telomerase induction, but this cannot be proved until culture conditions are found that cause them to proliferate and retain stem cell properties (Yui *et al.*, 1998; Glimm & Eaves, 1999).

If it is assumed that the level of telomerase activity in stem cells does not prevent telomere loss at all, the data from peripheral white blood cells suggest that human stem cells undergo 15–30 divisions in the first half-year of life, followed by less than one division per year thereafter (Rufer *et al.*, 1999). Such a model requires regulated asymmetric division so that the most primitive stem cells divide

far fewer times than more committed descendents (Brummendorf *et al.*, 1998). However, the rate of division could be much higher if telomerase partially, but not completely, prevents telomere shortening in stem cells.

Following the transplantation of bone marrow cells in humans, telomere length in the transplanted cells decreases dramatically, by about 1–2 kb, compared to the length in the donor (Notaro *et al.*, 1997; Wynn *et al.*, 1998; Lee *et al.*, 1999) (Fig. 3B). Thus, during the transplantation procedure, the rate of cell division exceeds the ability of the telomerase activity in the repopulating cells to maintain telomere length. In auto-PBSCT (peripheral blood stem cell transplantation), telomere length decreased by 2.36 kb, which was calculated to be equivalent to 61.5 years of normal aging (Lee *et al.*, 1999). In contrast, peripheral blood progenitor cells (PBPC) were mobilized with G-CSF in mice and transplanted into lethally irradiated recipients; after one year, PBPC could be remobilized and used to reconstitute the hematopoietic system of a second recipient (Yan *et al.*, 1998). This suggests a much greater capacity for long-term growth of these cells in mice than in humans. The consequence of these observations for aging in human bone marrow recipients is not yet known.

Patients with syndromes of increased replication of hematopoietic cells, such as aplastic anemia, including Fanconi's anemia, show variable increases in the rate of telomere shortening and sometimes are elevated quite dramatically (Ball *et al.*, 1998; Leteurtre *et al.*, 1999) (Fig. 3C). Another situation of increased replication is in patients undergoing cancer chemotherapy. The greater bone marrow toxicity in the elderly suggests a decreased capacity for adapting to the need for increased hematopoietic stem cell function.

It has been pointed out that telomere lengths in differentiated human white blood cells are not as short as might be expected on the basis of the usual concepts of cell turnover in continuously proliferating human tissues (Morris, 1999). This observation suggested the important concept that control of the hierarchy of stem cells in humans and other long-lived species may differ from that in rodents (Morris, 1999). Although this concept deserves thorough experimental investigation, it does not take into account the fact that many stem cell types have some telomerase activity resulting from regulated expression of TERT. This may be sufficient to slow down the rate of telomere shortening in stem cells, making it difficult to calculate the number of cell generations based only on final telomere length.

In summary, direct measures of the proliferative potential of human hematopoietic stem cells await the development of appropriate methods for directly studying this question. The human hematopoietic system begins life with shorter telomeres than in mice, and the level of telomerase does not prevent telomere shortening from occurring in the entire system throughout the life span. The data are consistent with the hypothesis that the stem cell proliferative potential is adequate for the supply of the system over a normal human life span, but has a limited excess capacity that is significant in very old age or under pathological conditions. The limitation of replicative capacity, by the suppression of TERT in most of the system, can be viewed as as an evolutionary trade-off. In a system that is so dependent on cell proliferation for normal function, the opportunity for neoplastic transformation over the life span is very large. Suppression of TERT may prevent many abnormal preneoplastic clones of cells from evolving into lethal cancers, but this evolutionary strategy may leave the system vulnerable to exhaustion in old age.

B. T-Cells

T-cells exhibit a limited proliferative potential in culture, resulting from telomere shortening, like other normal human cell types (Effros & Pawelec, 1997). Senescent T-cells lack expression of CD28 (Effros *et al.*, 1994). In aging, the proportion of CD28⁻ T-cells increases, and in the elderly such cells may comprise more than 50% of the T-cell subset that controls viral infections (killer, or cytotoxic, T-cells) (Boucher *et al.*, 1998). In HIV infection, more than 65% of cytotoxic T-cells may be CD28⁻ and have telomere lengths of 5–7 kb, a size consistent with replicative senescence (Effros *et al.*, 1996). Thus, T-cells provide an important and clear example of the occurrence of replicative senescence *in vivo*. Other aspects of immune senescence are discussed in Chapter 12 of this volume.

C. Liver

There are two cell populations in adult mammalian liver that behave as stem cells. First, the mature differentiated hepatocytes behave functionally as stem cells (Alison, 1998). The liver normally is a mitotically quiescent organ, but it can regenerate efficiently after damage. Liver regeneration can be observed in experimental animals after the removal of two-thirds of the liver. In this experimental protocol, the restoration of the organ normally is dependent on hepatocytes, which clearly are capable of self-renewal like stem cells. Under specific circumstances, however, the liver can be rescued through proliferation of bile-duct-derived cells termed oval cells (Alison, 1998). Oval cells can differentiate into hepatocytes; they appear after parenchymal damage when regeneration by surviving hepatocytes is compromised. Both oval cells and hepatocytes can be transplanted into the liver. Thus, both cell types have stem-cell-like properties, but the available data on cell proliferation in the aging of the liver is for hepatocytes rather than for oval cells.

Following partial hepatectomy, the restoration of liver size occurs through the proliferation of almost all of the hepatocytes, together with biliary epithelial cells, endothelial cells, Kupffer cells and cells of Ito (Michalopoulos & DeFrances, 1997). The restoration of liver size is brought about by coordinated proliferation of these cell types over a 10-day period. In old animals the liver still regenerates after partial hepatectomy, but there are changes in kinetics (Finch, 1991). Regeneration becomes progressively slower as a function of age (Bucher & Glinos, 1950; Bourliere & Molimard, 1957), and the onset of DNA synthesis is

delayed (Bucher *et al.*, 1964; Stocker & Heine, 1971; Schapiro *et al.*, 1982). Additionally, although >95% of hepatocytes undergo DNA synthesis in young animals, only about 75% do so in very old animals (Stocker & Heine, 1971).

The age-related changes in regeneration following partial hepatectomy must originate in changes in the microenvironment of the hepatocytes or in the hormonal control of hepatocyte proliferation; they are unlikely to result from any intrinsic changes in the proliferative potential of hepatocytes. Over the life span of the animal, hepatocytes divide relatively infrequently, and the liver can regenerate after at least 12 successive partial hepatectomies (Ingle & Baker, 1957). Serial cell transplantation experiments show a much greater proliferative potential. To perform serial transplantation experiments on hepatocytes, methods have been devised to transplant cells into the livers of recipient animals in which the native hepatocytes have a high rate of cell death, thus providing the transplanted cells with a competitive advantage in colonizing the organ. One system used mice with a plasminogen activator transgene driven by the albumin promoter (Rhim *et al.*, 1994), and another used mice with a lethal type of hereditary tyrosinemia type 1 (Overturf *et al.*, 1997). By using hepatocytes marked with a *lacZ* transgene, it was possible to follow the repopulation of the recipient liver by the transplanted cells. When this was performed through multiple successive recipients, mouse hepatocytes were found to be capable of doubling between 69 and 86 times without a loss of repopulating capacity (Overturf *et al.*, 1997).

Clearly, the vast proliferative potential of rodent hepatocytes means that it would be difficult to reach any limit on proliferative capacity over a normal life span. Comparable data for human hepatocytes are limited. Normal human hepatocytes lack telomerase activity; telomere shortening has been detected in normal aging and in chronic diseases of the liver, such as hepatitis and cirrhosis, where there is continuous cell turnover (Urabe et al., 1996; Takubo et al., 2000). Indeed, it has been suggested that the cause of cirrhosis of the liver is the ultimate failure of hepatocytes to proliferate, following chronic increased cell death and consequent continuous proliferation of cells, resulting in telomere shortening (Rudolph et al., 2000). Like most cancers, established hepatocellular carcinomas (HCCs) are telomerase-positive. Interestingly, in moderately differentiated HCCs, there is a decrease in telomere length until the HCC reaches about 5 cm in diameter and an increase thereafter, suggesting that the late activation of telomerase allows the continued growth of these cancers (Urabe et al., 1996).

D. Mammary Gland

Experiments on serial transplantation of mouse mammary tissue have been influential in supporting the concept that normal cells can reach a limit of proliferation in vivo. In the mouse, mammary tissue can be transplanted into the "cleared" mammary fat pad (a mammary fat pad from which the endogenous epithelium has been removed, surgically or chemically). The tissue grows to fill the fat pad and produces an almost complete mammary gland, with the normal ductal and alveolar structures. Serial transplants of epithelial ductal fragments were made into successive nulliparous hosts until they lost the ability to undergo branching morphogenesis (Daniel & Young, 1971). If fragments from these ducts were then transplanted again, they could not produce branching ducts; however, they could develop secretory lobules in a pregnant host or following the administration of cholera toxin, showing that the cells did not absolutely lose the ability for cell proliferation (Daniel et al., 1984). The rate

at which fragments of mammary epithelium reached this stage was greater when transplants were made from the periphery versus the center of previously transplanted tissue (Daniel & Young, 1971). On the other hand, some lines of mouse mammary cells that have undergone spontaneous immortalization in culture, which form ductal outgrowths in the mammary fat pad, can be transplanted indefinitely (Medina & Kittrell, 1993). Taken together, these observations suggest that mammary epithelial cells in the mouse are not capable of indefinite division, unless they undergo genetic changes that permit immortalization. However, in the absence of biochemical data to act as a marker for replicative senescence (such as telomere length or SA-βgal, although neither of these is necessarily useful in this particular case), it is difficult to know whether the limitation of mouse mammary cell proliferation is really a phenomenon of replicative senescence or is a reflection of the loss of pluripotent stem cells during the experimental procedure. This question has been subjected to much more extensive analysis in the hematopoietic system, as discussed earlier, and the lesson from that system is that more definitive interpretation of the data was possible only when certain key features of the cell transplantation were understood—markers for stem cells and knowledge of how many stem cells were transferred to each successive recipient. There is increasing understanding of the biology of mammary epithelial stem cells (Chepko & Smith, 1999), and future experiments on serial transplantation of mammary epithelial cells should be able to take advantage of this progress.

E. Gastrointestinal System

In the aging rat gastrointestinal system, there is hyperproliferation in epithelial cells of the stomach, small intestine, and colon. In the gastric mucosa of the rat, there is an increase in cell proliferation with aging (Majumdar *et al.*, 1988; 1989; 1990). This is accompanied by a diminished cell proliferation reponse to injury, perhaps as a result of an already maximally stimulated level of cell division that cannot be increased further (Majumdar *et al.*, 1988, 1989, 1990).

Although earlier work suggested that cell proliferation in the small intestine was reduced as a function of age, careful studies later showed that there is an increase in proliferation with aging when care is taken to avoid handling effects on the animals and when animals in ill health are excluded (Atillasoy & Holt, 1993). In the duodenum and jejunum of Fischer 344 rats, the number of villus-absorbing cells was unchanged in 25- to 27-month-old animals compared to 4- to 5-month-old animals (Holt *et al.*, 1984). However, crypt cell numbers were greater in the older animals and the crypt cell production rate increased by about one-third (Holt & Yeh, 1989). In 28- to 30-month-old ICRFa mice there was an increase in the number of clonogenic cells in small intestine crypts compared to 6- to 7-month-old animals (Martin *et al.*, 1998). Aging animals show a dramatic change in the distribution of proliferating cells in crypts. There was an increase in the crypt proliferative zone in all parts of the small intestine under fed, starved, and refed conditions (Holt & Yeh, 1989). Similarly, crypt hyperplasia, an increased rate of proliferation, and a broadened proliferative zone were observed in the colon of 26- to 28-month-old Fischer 344 rats compared to 3- to 4-month-old animals (Holt & Yeh, 1988). In 24- to 26-month-old Fischer 344 rats there was an increase in metaphase chromosome aberrations in jejunal crypts compared to 3- to 7-month-old animals (Ellsworth & Schimke, 1990). In rectal biopsies from elderly human subjects without adenomatous polyps, there is also an increase in proliferating cells in the upper 40% of the crypt (Paganelli *et al.*, 1990; Corazza *et al.*, 1998). This change is a type of proliferative lesion associated in young individuals with many premalignant conditions throughout the gastrointestinal tract, including Barrett's epithelium, chronic gastritis, inflammatory bowel disease, and colonic polyps, and is induced by carcinogens in rodents (Eastwood, 1995).

Food intake normally controls the intestinal cell proliferation rate (Johnson, 1987). Caloric restriction decreases the rate of cell turnover in rodents (Lok *et al.*, 1988; Albanes *et al.*, 1990) and in obese humans (Steinbach *et al.*, 1994). Rectal biopsies from calorically restricted human subjects showed a 39% reduction in the whole-crypt labeling index and a 57% reduction in the upper-crypt labeling index, suggesting a normalization of the abnormal proliferating cell distribution. The changes in distribution of proliferating cells in the aging rat intestine are hypothesized to reflect a failure of the normal control of cell production in response to variations in food intake (Atillasoy & Holt, 1993). In aging, there is a delay in differentiation as the cells move from the crypt to the tip of the villus. Caloric restriction did not alter small intestine villus architecture, but prevented age-associated crypt hyperplasia in the rat (Heller *et al.*, 1990). Additionally, in gnotobiotic rats, which have a much lower intestinal proliferation rate because of the absence of bacteria in the gut, there was no change in proliferation in aging (Ecknauer *et al.*, 1982).

In humans, the lower one-third of the intestinal crypt is telomerase-positive, but interestingly, intestinal cell telomeres are shorter in adults than in children (Hiyama *et al.*, 1996). This suggests that regulation of TERT expression in this system is adequate to provide for continued cell proliferation over the life span, yet not high enough to prevent developmental changes in telomere length. Moreover, in ulcerative colitis telomeres were shorter than in controls (Kinouchi et al., 1998), suggesting that the telomerase level also does not maintain telomere length under conditions of excessive cell proliferation.

Thus, in the gastrointestinal system, the changes in cell proliferation in aging do not seem to impair the function of the organs. Rather, as in some rodent models of hematopoietic stem cell function, it may be that unknown changes in stem cell function in aging are compensated for by changes in the numbers of clonogenic cells and changes in the distribution of proliferating cells. These changes could predispose the colon to tumorigenesis and might be involved in the increased rate of colon cancer in aging (Eastwood, 1995).

F. Skin

Like the gastrointestinal system, the epidermis of the skin is dependent on continuous proliferation for its function. A population of keratinocytes in the basal layer of human skin has the property of stem cells and is telomerase-positive (Harlebachor & Boukamp, 1996; Yasumoto et al., 1996; Li et al., 1998). The progeny of these stem cells appear to be telomerase-negative. In culture, even though biochemically identified stem cells are present in the starting cell population, the culture becomes telomerase-negative. The cells continue to proliferate and eventually undergo replicative senescence, a process that can be bypassed by TERT in cooperation with oncoproteins that abrogate pRb function (Kiyono et al., 1998). Thus, telomerase activity (i.e., expression of TERT) is closely regulated in keratinocytes, as in other normal human cells. Telomerase activity in stem cells in the basal layer may be required to permit the continued proliferation of cells over the life span.

Although there are well-known changes in human skin structure and function in aging, changes in keratinocyte proliferation in the epidermis are slight. In one study, it was observed that 8% of cells in the epidermis are cycling in the young (20- to 35-year-old donors), as evidenced by immunohistochemistry with the Ki-S3 marker. The value was 5.8% in older donors (>60 years of age), but in biopsies of areas of dry skin (xerosis), the values were slightly higher and were almost identical in young and old skin (Engelke et al., 1997).

Skin wound healing is slower in the elderly (Grove, 1982; Reed et al., 1996). Wound healing is complex, dependending on the interplay of a variety of processes, not only cell division, and there is little evidence for age-related intrinsic changes in cell proliferation (as opposed to changes in the microenvironment of the cells that might change their behavior) that affect wound healing (Ashcroft et al., 1995). The dermis, in contrast to the epidermis, is a proliferatively quiescent tissue, and exhaustion of proliferative capacity would seem unlikely; the need for increased cell proliferation may occur in one specific location in the body only once in a lifetime. This applies to the normal healing of a clean wound, as opposed to chronic conditions like ulcers (see previous discussion). There is a decrease in blood vessel density in the skin in aging, yet hyperemic responses measured by laser–Doppler are more rapid (Kelly et al., 1995). In older animals, there is evidence for delayed angiogenesis in wound healing, but whether this might involve an intrinsic proliferative defect is not clear (Arthur et al., 1998; Reed et al., 1998).

G. Changes in Proliferation Resulting from Endocrine Changes

It is widely assumed that the well-documented changes in the endocrine system in aging, such as the decline in growth hormone secretion, affect proliferation *in vivo*, but there is little direct evidence for this. Some intriguing data have been obtained on the replicative potential of rat hepatocytes. There is a donor-age-dependent diminution of proliferation in primary culture in response to β-adrenergic hormones; this could be restored by prior transplantation of the animal with thymus from a young animal (Basso *et al.*, 1998). This presumably reflects an endocrine effect of the thymus on the age-related changes in hepatocyte proliferation, but this is unexplained. It was suggested that the life-extending effects of caloric restriction in rodents might be exerted by decreasing insulin concentrations and a consequent reduction in the rate of cell proliferation (Lev-Ran, 1998), but this has yet to be demonstrated directly.

X. Changes in Tissue Structure Resulting from Changes in Proliferation

There are significant changes in histological structure in many organs, which have been suggested to result from focal hyperplasias of various cells (Martin, 1987, 1993). An important concept is that, in these organs, gradual exhaustion of the proliferative potential of some of the cells within the organ increases the proliferation of others within the tissue that have a higher remaining proliferative potential. This is hypothesized to result from feedback control of proliferation—hormonal, paracrine, or some other form of proliferative homeostasis. A range of pathologies observed in aging could result from this process (Martin, 1987, 1993). Of course, these disturbances of tissue structure in turn may result in further changes in cell proliferation.

One example of this is in the aging human adrenal cortex. In aging, the human adrenal cortex becomes somewhat atrophic in comparison with the tissue in the young adult, yet simultaneously accumulates small, presumably clonal, groups of cells termed nodules (Dobbie, 1969; Neville, 1978; Neville & O'Hare, 1982, 1985). Some individuals show minimal detectable histological changes, whereas others have markedly nodular adrenals in old age. With the increased use of CAT and MRI scanning, adrenal nodules became a common incidental finding (Ross & Aron, 1990), and it has become apparent that such nodules represent one end of the spectrum of "normal" aging and are not in themselves of pathological significance. Although nodules are hypothesized to be hyperplasias, they do not necessarily show continued growth; they may remain at the same size over many years. Only very rarely may they undergo neoplastic transformation (Neville & O'Hare, 1982, 1985).

XI. Neoplastic Changes as a Function of Age

The question of the relationship of cancer and aging is complex and has been the subject of much debate (Miller, 1991; Ershler & Longo, 1997). The issue is whether the well-known increases in cancer in aging is the result of fundamental age-related changes in cell properties, rendering them more susceptible to neoplastic transformation, or whether it results simply from the passage of time, enabling cells to accumulate the number of genetic hits that are needed to escape normal growth controls and grow into a malignant tumor. Human fibroblasts or kidney epithelial cells infected with retroviruses encoding TERT, SV40 T-antigen, and oncogenic H-ras become tumorigenic (Hahn *et al.*, 1999a). Therefore, the minimum number of molecular processes in a human cell that must be targeted to achieve full tumorigenicity is at least three, but perhaps as many as five or six (Hahn et al., 1999a; Weitzman & Yaniv, 1999). The uncertainty arises because proteins like SV40 T-antigen and Ras might affect multiple targets.

The data from the various organ systems reviewed here support a true age-related increase in susceptibility to neoplasia only in the gastrointestinal tract, where the shift in the proliferative zone resembles a preneoplastic lesion known to have the propensity to progress to cancer. However, interpretation of this observation should be cautious, because all individuals show these changes, but most of them will not show a progression to cancer over their entire life span. This lack of progression is made more significant by the fact that, in the colon, the sequence of progression from normal epithelium to cancer is well-described (Lengauer et al., 1998). Additionally, the data on the effects of caloric restriction in the gastrointestinal tract suggest that the proliferative changes might be reversible—if so, they certainly could not be termed intrinsic cellular changes.

It is important to distinguish the intrinsic susceptibility of cells to tumorigenesis from influences on tumorigenesis extrinsic to the cell. For example, tumor angiogenesis is impaired in older host animals (Pili et al., 1994). The more speculative concept that the presence of replicative senescent cells within tissues increases the likelihood of malignant conversion of other cells in the tissue, as discussed earlier, requires a thorough investigation. If this suggestion is correct, it supports the concept that intrinsic cell changes during aging affect tumorigenesis in other cells, but not in the cell undergoing senescent changes. If the age-dependent cancer incidence were the result of intrinsic changes in the cells giving rise to the tumor, we would observe a more ready conversion of replicative senescent cells (or cells close to senescence) to

neoplasia. It is difficult to reconcile this concept with the idea that TERT repression, leading to telomere shortening and replicative senescence, is an anticancer mechanism. The absence of in vivo evidence that there is an effect of aging on the intrinsic susceptibility of cells to tumorigenic conversion resulted in the famous cynical statement of Richard Peto that "there is no such thing as aging and cancer is not related to it" (Peto et al., 1985).

XII. Conclusions and Summary

Data on rodents show little evidence for intrinsic changes in cell proliferation that might limit the proliferative capacity of tissues in aging, with the important exception of mammary epithelial cells. Apart from that exception, many mouse organs (e.g., hematopoietic system, liver, gut) appear to contain cells that are functionally immortal, although the proof that such cells really have no proliferative limitation will be hard to come by. Under normal conditions, changes in cell proliferation in aging are relatively slight, suggesting that intrinsic changes in proliferative capacity (if any) and changes in the microenvironment of the cells are compensated. For example, in the hematopoietic system, there may be changes in the populations of stem cells, but the overall function of the system is little affected.

As a species, mice and other rodents have a life history in which maximal suppression of cancer timing and incidence is not as important as in long-lived species such as humans. The evolution of anticancer strategies at the cellular level is an essential part of the life history of the human species. Repression of TERT and short telomeres in human cells together form an anticancer mechanism. Telomerase activity is regulated and/or negligible in most cell types, leading to telomere shortening and replicative senescence. Remarkably, although this process occurs *in vivo*, organ systems seem to be endowed with just enough total replicative capacity for even the extremes of human longevity, if the reserve capacity of the systems is not excessively challenged.

Acknowledgments

Research mentioned in this chapter from the author's laboratory was supported by the National Institute on Aging and the Breast Cancer Research Program of the Army Materiel and Medical Command. I am very grateful to suggestions made by readers of an earlier draft of the text, especially Judith Campisi, George M. Martin, James R. Smith, Rita Effros, and Robert J. S. Reis.

References

Abkowitz, J. L., Taboada, M., Shelton, G. H., Catlin, S. N., Guttorp, P., & Kiklevich, J. V. (1998). An X chromosome gene regulates hematopoietic stem cell kinetics. *Proceedings of the National Academy of Sciences of the USA, 95,* 3862–3866.

Agren, M. S., Steenfos, H. H., Dabelsteen, S., Hansen, J. B., & Dabelsteen, E. (1999). Proliferation and mitogenic response to PDGF-BB of fibroblasts isolated from chronic venous leg ulcers is ulcer-age dependent. *Journal of Investigative Dermatology, 112,* 463–469.

Albanes, D., Salbe, A. D., Levander, O. A., Taylor, P. R., Nixon, D. W., & Winick, M. (1990). The effect of early caloric restriction on colonic cellular growth in rats. *Nutrition and Cancer, 13,* 73–80.

Alison, M. (1998). Liver stem cells: A two compartment system. *Current Opinion in Cell Biology, 10,* 710–715.

Allsopp, R. C., Vaziri, H., Patterson, C., Goldstein, S., Younglai, E. V., Futcher, A. B., Greider, C. W., & Harley, C. B. (1992). Telomere length predicts replicative capacity of human fibroblasts. *Proceedings of the National Academy of Sciences of the USA, 89,* 10114–10118.

Anderlini, P., Przepiorka, D., Lauppe, J., Seong, D., Giralt, S., Champlin, R., & Korbling, M. (1997). Collection of peripheral blood stem cells from normal donors 60 years of age or older. *British Journal of Haematology, 97,* 485–487.

Arthur, W. T., Vernon, R. B., Sage, E. H., & Reed, M. J. (1998). Growth factors reverse the impaired sprouting of microvessels from aged mice. *Microvascular Research, 55,* 260–270.

Ashcroft, G. S., Horan, M. A., & Ferguson, M. W. J. (1995). The effects of ageing on cutaneous wound healing in mammals. *Journal of Anatomy, 187,* 1–26.

Atillasoy, E., & Holt, P. R. (1993). Gastrointestinal proliferation and aging. *Journal of Gerontology, 48,* B43–49.

Ball, S. E., Gibson, F. M., Rizzo, S., Tooze, J. A., Marsh, J. C., & Gordon-Smith, E. C. (1998). Progressive telomere shortening in aplastic anemia. *Blood, 91,* 3582–3592.

Basso, A., Piantanelli, L., Rossolini, G., & Roth, G. S. (1998). Reduced DNA synthesis in primary cultures of hepatocytes from old mice is restored by thymus grafts. *Journal of Gerontology, 53A,* B111–116.

Belair, C. D., Yeager, T. R., Lopez, P. M., & Reznikoff, C. A. (1997). Telomerase activity: a biomarker of cell proliferation, not malignant transformation. *Proceedings of the National Academy of Sciences of the USA, 94,* 13677–13682.

Bertram, M. J., Berube, N. G., Hang-Swanson, X., Ran, Q., Leung, J. K., Bryce, S., Spurgers, K., Bick, R. J., Baldini, A., Ning, Y., Clark, L. J., Parkinson, E. K., Barrett, J. C., Smith, J. R., & Pereira-Smith, O. M. (1999). Identification of a gene that reverses the immortal phenotype of a subset of cells and is a member of a novel family of transcription factor-like genes. *Molecular and Cellular Biology, 19,* 1479–1485.

Bierman, E. L. (1978). The effect of donor age on the in vitro life span of cultured human arterial smooth-muscle cells. *In Vitro, 14,* 951–955.

Blasco, M. A., Lee, H. W., Hande, M. P., Samper, E., Lansdorp, P. M., DePinho, R. A., & Greider, C. W. (1997). Telomere shortening and tumor formation by mouse cells lacking telomerase RNA. *Cell, 91,* 25–34.

Blau, H. M., Webster, C., & Pavlath, G. K. (1983). Defective myoblasts identified in Duchenne muscular dystrophy. *Proceedings of the National Academy of Sciences of the USA, 80,* 4856–4860.

Bodnar, A. G., Ouellette, M., Frolkis, M., Holt, S. E., Chiu, C. P., Morin, G. B., Harley, C. B., Shay, J. W., Lichtsteiner, S., & Wright, W. E. (1998). Extension of lifespan by introduction of telomerase into normal human cells. *Science, 279,* 349–352.

Boucher, N., Dufeu-Duchesne, T., Vicaut, E., Farge, D., Effros, R. B., & Schachter, F. (1998). CD28 expression in T cell aging and human longevity. *Experimental Gerontology, 33,* 267–282.

Bourliere, F., & Molimard, R. (1957). L'action de l'age sur la regeneration du foie chez le rat. *Comptes Rendues de la Societe de Biologie (Paris), 151,* 1345–1348.

Brown-Borg, H. M., Borg, K. E., Meliska, C. J., & Bartke, A. (1996). Dwarf mice and the ageing process. *Nature 384, 33.*

Brummendorf, T. H., Dragowska, W., Zijlmans, J. M. J. M., Thornbury, G., & Lansdorp, P. M. (1998). Asymmetric cell divisions sustain long-term hematopoiesis from single-sorted human fetal liver cells. *Journal of Experimental Medicine, 188,* 1117–1124.

Bucher, N. L. R., & Glinos, A. D. (1950). The effect of age on the regeneration of rat liver. *Cancer Research, 10,* 324–332.

Bucher, N. L. R., Swaffield, M. N., & DiTroia, J. F. (1964). The influence of age upon the incorporation of thymidine–2–14C into the DNA of regenerating rat liver. *Cancer Research, 24,* 509–512.

Burke, E. M., Horton, W. E., Pearson, J. D., Crow, M. T., & Martin, G. R. (1994). Altered transcriptional regulation of human interstitial collagenase in cultured skin fibroblasts from older donors. *Experimental Gerontology, 29,* 37–53.

Campisi, J. (1997). Aging and cancer: The double-edged sword of replicative senescence. *Journal of the American Geriatrics Society, 45,* 482–488.

Carpenter, M. K., Cui, X., Hu, Z. Y., Jackson, J., Sherman, S., Seiger, A., and Wahlberg, L.

U. (1999). In vitro expansion of a multipotent population of human neural progenitor cells. *Experimental Neurology, 158,* 265–278.

Champion, K. M., Gilbert, J. G., Asimakopoulos, F. A., Hinshelwood, S., & Green, A. R. (1997). Clonal haemopoiesis in normal elderly women: Implications for the myeloproliferative disorders and myelodysplastic syndromes. *British Journal of Haematology, 97,* 920–926.

Chang, E., & Harley, C. B. (1995). Telomere length and replicative aging in human vascular tissues. *Proceedings of the National Academy of Sciences of the USA, 92,* 11190–11194.

Chatta, G. S., Andrews, R. G., Rodger, E., Schrag, M., Hammond, W. P., & Dale, D. C. (1993). Hematopoietic progenitors and aging: Alterations in granulocytic precursors and responsiveness to recombinant human G-CSF, GM-CSF, and IL–3. *Journal of Gerontology, 48,* M207–212.

Chen, T. R., & Ruddle, F. H. (1974). Chromosome changes revealed by the Q-band staining method during cell senescence of WI-38. *Proceedings of the Society for Experimental Biology and Medicine, 147,* 533–536.

Chen, J., Astle, C. M., & Harrison, D. E. (1999). Development and aging of primitive hematopoietic stem cells in BALB/cBy mice. *Experimental Hematology, 27,* 928–935.

Cheng, R. Z., Shammas, M. A., Li, J., & Shmookler Reis, R. J. (1997). Expression of SV40 large T antigen stimulates reversion of a chromosomal gene duplication in human cells. *Experimental Cell Research, 234,* 300–312.

Cheng, T., Rodrigues, N., Shen, H., Yang, Y.-G., Dombkowski, D., Sykes, M., & Scadden, D. T. (2000). Hematopoietic stem cell quiescence maintained by p21[cip1/wafl]. *Science, 287,* 1804–1808.

Chepko, G., & Smith, G. H. (1999). Mammary epithelial stem cells: Our current understanding. *Journal of Mammary Gland Biology and Neoplasia, 4,* 35–52.

Cheshier, S. H., Morrison, S. J., Liao, X., & Weissman, I. L. (1999). In vivo proliferation and cell cycle kinetics of long-term self-renewing hematopoietic stem cells. *Proceedings of the National Academy of Sciences of the USA, 96,* 3120–3125.

Corazza, G. R., Ginaldi, L., Quaglione, G., Ponzielli, F., Vecchio, L., Biagi, F., & Quaglino, D. (1998). Proliferating cell nuclear antigen expression is increased in small bowel epithelium in the elderly. *Mechanisms of Ageing and Development, 104,* 1–9.

Coviello-McLaughlin, G. M., & Prowse, K. R. (1997). Telomere length regulation during postnatal development and ageing in Mus spretus. *Nucleic Acids Research, 25,* 3051–3058.

Cristofalo, V. J., Allen, R. G., Pignolo, R. J., Martin, B. G., & Beck, J. C. (1998). Relationship between donor age and the replicative lifespan of human cells in culture: A reevaluation. *Proceeding of the National Academy of Sciences of the USA, 95,* 10614–10619.

Cuthbert, A. P., Bond, J., Trott, D. A., Gill, S., Broni, J., Marriott, A., Khoudoli, G., Parkinson, E. K., Cooper, C. S., & Newbold, R. F. (1999). Telomerase repressor sequences on chromosome 3 and induction of permanent growth arrest in human breast cancer cells. *Journal of the National Cancer Institute, 91,* 37–45.

Daniel, C. W., & Young, L. J. (1971). Influence of cell division on an aging process. Life span of mouse mammary epithelium during serial propagation in vivo. *Experimental Cell Research, 65,* 27–32.

Daniel, C. W., Silberstein, G. B., & Strickland, P. (1984). Reinitiation of growth in senescent mouse mammary epithelium in response to cholera toxin. *Science, 224,* 1245–1247.

Dao, M. A., & Nolta, J. A. (1999). Immunodeficient mice as models of human hematopoietic stem cell engraftment. *Current Opinion in Immunology, 11,* 532–537.

Decary, S., Mouly, V., Hamida, C. B., Sautet, A., Barbet, J. P., & Butler-Browne, G. S. (1997). Replicative potential and telomere length in human skeletal muscle: Implications for satellite cell-mediated gene therapy. *Human Gene Therapy, 8,* 1429–1438.

de Haan, G., & Van Zant, G. (1999). Dynamic changes in mouse hematopoietic stem cell numbers during aging. *Blood, 93,* 3294–3301.

de Haan, G., Nijhof, W., & Van Zant, G. (1997). Mouse strain-dependent changes in frequency and proliferation of hematopoietic stem cells during aging: Correlation between lifespan and cycling activity. *Blood, 89,* 1543–1550.

Dimri, G. P., Lee, X. H., Basile, G., Acosta, M., Scott, C., Roskelley, C., Medrano, E. E., Linskens, M., Rubelj, I., Pereira-Smith, O. M., Peacocke, M., & Campisi, J. (1995). A biomarker that identifies senescent human cells in culture and in aging skin in vivo. *Proceedings of the National Academy of Sciences of the USA, 92,* 9363–9367.

D'Ippolito, G., Schiller, P. C., Ricordi, C., Roos, B. A., & Howard, G. A. (1999). Age-related osteogenic potential of mesenchymal stromal stem cells from human vertebral bone marrow. *Journal of Bone and Mineral Research, 14,* 1115–1122.

Dobbie, J. W. (1969). Adrenocortical nodular hyperplasia: The ageing adrenal. *Journal of Pathology, 99,* 1–18.

Dunsmuir, W. D., Hrouda, D., & Kirby, R. S. (1998). Malignant changes in the prostate with ageing. *British Journal of Urology, 82,* 47–58.

Eastwood, G. L. (1995). A review of gastrointestinal epithelial renewal and its relevance to the development of adenocarcinomas of the gastrointestinal tract. *Journal of Clinical Gastroenterology, 21,* S1–11.

Ecknauer, R., Vadakel, T., & Wepler, R. (1982). Intestinal morphology and cell production rate in aging rats. *Journal of Gerontology, 37,* 151–155.

Effros, R. B., & Pawelec, G. (1997). Replicative senescence of T cells: Does the Hayflick limit lead to immune exhaustion? *Immunology Today, 18,* 450–454.

Effros, R. B., Zhu, X., & Walford, R. L. (1994). Stress response of senescent T lymphocytes: Reduced hsp70 is independent of the proliferative block. *Journal of Gerontology, 49,* B65–B70.

Effros, R. B., Allsopp, R., Chiu, C. P., Hausner, M. A., Hirji, K., Wang, L. L., Harley, C. B., Villeponteau, B., West, M. D., & Giorgi, J. V. (1996). Shortened telomeres in the expanded CD28⁻ CD8⁺ cell subset in HIV disease implicate replicative senescence in HIV pathogenesis. *AIDS*, 10, F17–F22.

Egusa, Y., Fujiwara, Y., Syahruddin, E., Isobe, T., & Yamakido, M. (1998). Effect of age on human peripheral blood stem cells. *Oncology Reports*, 5, 397–400.

Ellsworth, J. L., & Schimke, R. T. (1990). On the frequency of metaphase chromosome aberrations in the small intestine of aged rats. *Journal of Gerontology*, 45, B94–B100.

Engelke, M., Jensen, J. M., Ekanayake-Mudiyanselage, S., & Proksch, E. (1997). Effects of xerosis and ageing on epidermal proliferation and differentiation. *British Journal of Dermatology*, 137, 219–225.

Ershler, W. B., & Longo, D. L. (1997). Aging and cancer: Issues of basic and clinical science. *Journal of the National Cancer Institute*, 89, 1489–1497.

Finch, C. E. (1991). *Longevity, Senescence, and the Genome*. Chicago: University of Chicago Press.

Flax, J. D., Aurora, S., Yang, C., Simonin, C., Wills, A. M., Billinghurst, L. L., Jendoubi, M., Sidman, R. L., Wolfe, J. H., Kim, S. U., & Snyder, E. Y. (1998). Engraftable human neural stem cells respond to developmental cues, replace neurons, and express foreign genes. *Nature Biotechnology*, 16, 1033–1039.

Flood, M. T., Gouras, P., & Kjeldbye, H. (1980). Growth characteristics and ultrastructure of human retinal pigment epithelium in vitro. *Investigative Ophthalmology and Visual Science*, 19, 1309–1320.

Frenck, R. W., Jr., Blackburn, E. H., & Shannon, K. M. (1998). The rate of telomere sequence loss in human leukocytes varies with age. *Proceedings of the National Academy of Sciences of the USA*, 95, 5607–5610.

Gale, R. E., Fielding, A. K., Harrison, C. N., & Linch, D. C. (1997). Acquired skewing of X-chromosome inactivation patterns in myeloid cells of the elderly suggests stochastic clonal loss with age. *British Journal of Haematology*, 98, 512–519.

Gilchrest, B. A. (1980). Prior chronic sun exposure decreases the lifespan of human skin fibroblasts in vitro. *Journal of Gerontology*, 35, 537–541.

Glimm, H., & Eaves, C. J. (1999). Direct evidence for multiple self-renewal divisions of human in vivo repopulating hematopoietic cells in short-term culture. *Blood*, 94, 2161–2168.

Globerson, A. (1999). Hematopoietic stem cells and aging. *Experimental Gerontology*, 34, 137–146.

Goldstein, S., Moerman, E. J., Soeldner, J. S., Gleason, R. E., & Barnett, D. M. (1978). Chronologic and physiologic age affect replicative life-span of fibroblasts from diabetic, prediabetic, and normal donors. *Science*, 199, 781–782.

Greider, C. W. (1990). Telomeres, telomerase and senescence. *Bioessays*, 12, 363–369.

Grove, G. L. (1982). Age-related differences in healing of superficial skin wounds in humans. *Archives of Dermatological Research*, 272, 381–385.

Hahn, W. C., Counter, C. M., Lundberg, A. S., Beijersbergen, R. L., Brooks, M. W., & Weinberg, R. A. (1999a). Creation of human tumour cells with defined genetic elements. *Nature*, 400, 464–468.

Hahn, W. C., Stewart, S. A., Brooks, M. W., York, S. G., Eaton, E., Kurachi, A., Beijersbergen, R. L., Knoll, J. H., Meyerson, M., & Weinberg, R. A. (1999b). Inhibition of telomerase limits the growth of human cancer cells. *Nature Medicine*, 5, 164–170.

Hanahan, D., & Folkman, J. (1996). Patterns and emerging mechanisms of the angiogenic switch during tumorigenesis. *Cell*, 86, 353–364.

Harlebachor, C., & Boukamp, P. (1996). Telomerase activity in the regenerative basal layer of the epidermis in human skin and in immortal and carcinoma-derived skin keratinocytes. *Proceedings of the National Academy of Sciences of the USA*, 93, 6476–6481.

Harley, C. B. (1991). Telomere loss: Mitotic clock or genetic time bomb? *Mutation Research*, 256, 271–282.

Harley, C. B., Futcher, A. B., & Greider, C. W. (1990). Telomeres shorten during ageing of human fibroblasts. *Nature, 345,* 458–460.

Harrison, D. E. (1985). Cell and tissue transplantation: A means of studying the aging process. In C. E. Finch, and E. L. Schneider (Eds.), *Handbook of the Biology of Aging, Second Edition* (pp. 322–356). New York: Van Nostrand Reinhold.

Harrison, D. E., & Astle, C. M. (1991). Lymphoid and erythroid repopulation in B6 W-anemic mice: A new unirradiated recipient. *Experimental Hematology, 19,* 374–377.

Harrison, D. E., Astle, C. M., & Lerner, C. (1984). Ultimate erythropoietic repopulating abilities of fetal, young adult, and old adult cells compared using repeated irradiation. *Journal of Experimental Medicine, 160,* 759–771.

Harrison, D. E., Astle, C. M., & DeLaittre, J. (1988). Effects of transplantation and age on immunohemopoietic cell growth in the splenic microenvironment. *Experimental Hematology, 16,* 213–216.

Harrison, D. E., Astle, C. M., & Stone, M. (1989). Numbers and functions of transplantable primitive immunohemopoietic stem cells. Effects of age. *Journal of Immunology, 142,* 3833–3840.

Harvey, M., Sands, A. T., Weiss, R. S., Hegi, M. E., Wiseman, R. W., Pantazis, P., Giovanella, B. C., Tainsky, M. A., Bradley, A., & Donehower, L. A. (1993). In vitro growth characteristics of embryo fibroblasts isolated from p53-deficient mice. *Oncogene, 8,* 2457–2467.

Hastie, N. D., Dempster, M., Dunlop, M. G., Thompson, A. M., Green, D. K., & Allshire, R. C. (1990). Telomere reduction in human colorectal carcinoma and with ageing. *Nature, 346,* 866–868.

Hayflick, L. (1980). Cell aging. *Annual Review of Gerontology and Geriatrics, 1,* 26–67.

Heller, T. D., Holt, P. R., & Richardson, A. (1990). Food restriction retards age-related histological changes in rat small intestine. *Gastroenterology, 98,* 387–391.

Herrera, E., Samper, E., Martin-Caballero, J., Flores, J. M., Lee, H. W., & Blasco, M. A. (1999). Disease states associated with

telomerase deficiency appear earlier in mice with short telomeres. *EMBO Journal, 18,* 2950–2960.

Hiyama, E., Tatsumoto, N., Kodama, T., Hiyama, K., Shay, J. W., & Yokoyama, T. (1996). Telomerase activity in human intestine. *International Journal of Oncology, 9,* 453–458.

Hjelmeland, L. M. (1999). Senescence of the retinal pigmented epithelium. *Investigative Ophthalmology and Visual Science, 40,* 1–2.

Hodes, R. J. (1999). Telomere length, aging, and somatic cell turnover. *Journal of Experimental Medicine, 190,* 153–156.

Holt, P. R., & Yeh, K. Y. (1988). Colonic proliferation is increased in senescent rats. *Gastroenterology, 95,* 1556–1563.

Holt, P. R., & Yeh, K. Y. (1989). Small intestinal crypt cell proliferation rates are increased in senescent rats. *Journal of Gerontology, 44,* B9–14.

Holt, P. R., Pascal, R. R., & Kotler, D. P. (1984). Effect of aging upon small intestinal structure in the Fischer rat. *Journal of Gerontology, 39,* 642–647.

Holt, S. E., Shay, J. W., & Wright, W. E. (1996). Refining the telomere-telomerase hypothesis of aging and cancer. *Nature Biotechnology, 14,* 836–839.

Hornsby, P. J. (1995). Biosynthesis of DHEAS by the human adrenal cortex and its age-related decline. *Annals of the New York Academy of Sciences, 774,* 29–46.

Hornsby, P. J. (1999). The new science and medicine of cell transplantation. *A. S. M. (American Society for Experimental Microbiology) News, 65,* 208–214.

Hornsby, P. J., Cheng, C. Y., Lala, D. S., Maghsoudlou, S. S., Raju, S. G., & Yang, L. (1992). Changes in gene expression during senescence of adrenocortical cells in culture. *Journal of Steroid Biochemistry and Molecular Biology, 43,* 385–395.

Hornsby, P. J., Thomas, M., Northrup, S. R., Popnikolov, N. P., Wang, X., Tunstead, J. R., & Zheng, J. (1998). Cell transplantation: A tool to study adrenocortical cell biology, physiology, and senescence. *Endocrine Research, 24,* 909–918.

Hsiao, R., Sharma, H. W., Ramakrishnan, S., Keith, E., & Narayanan, R. (1997). Telomerase activity in normal human

240   P. J. Hornsby

endothelial cells. *Anticancer Research, 17,* 827–32.

Hursting, S. D., Perkins, S. N., & Phang, J. M. (1994). Calorie restriction delays spontaneous tumorigenesis in p53-knockout transgenic mice. *Proceedings of the National Academy of Sciences of the USA, 91,* 7036–7040.

Ingle, D. J., & Baker, B. L. (1957). Histology and regenerative capacity of liver following multiple partial hepatectomies. *Proceedings of the Society for Experimental Biology and Medicine, 95,* 813–815.

Iscove, N. N., & Nawa, K. (1997). Hematopoietic stem cells expand during serial transplantation in vivo without apparent exhaustion. *Current Biology, 7,* 805–808.

Izaks, G. J., Westendorp, R. G., & Knook, D. L. (1999). The definition of anemia in older persons. *JAMA, 281,* 1714–1717.

Jiang, D., Fei, R. G., Pendergrass, W. R., & Wolf, N. S. (1992). An age-related reduction in the replicative capacity of two murine hematopoietic stroma cell types. *Experimental Hematology, 20,* 1216–12122.

Jiang, X. R., Jimenez, G., Chang, E., Frolkis, M., Kusler, B., Sage, M., Beeche, M., Bodnar, A. G., Wahl, G. M., Tlsty, T. D., & Chiu, C. P. (1999). Telomerase expression in human somatic cells does not induce changes associated with a transformed phenotype. *Nature Genetics, 21,* 111–114.

Johnson, L. R. (1987). Regulation of gastrointestinal growth. In L. R. Johnson (Ed.), *Physiology of the Gastrointestinal Tract, Vol. 1* (pp 310–333). New York: Raven Press.

Jordan, C. T., & Lemischka, I. R. (1990). Clonal and systemic analysis of long-term hematopoiesis in the mouse. *Genes and Development, 4,* 220–232.

Kamijo, T., Zindy, F., Roussel, M. F., Quelle, D. E., Downing, J. R., Ashmun, R. A., Grosveld, G., & Sherr, C. J. (1997). Tumor suppression at the mouse INK4A locus mediated by the alternative reading frame product p19[ARF]. *Cell, 91,* 649–659.

Kassem, M., Ankersen, L., Eriksen, E. F., Clark, B. F. C., & Rattan, S. I. S. (1997). Demonstration of cellular aging and senescence in serially passaged long-term cultures of human trabecular osteoblasts. *Osteoporosis International, 7,* 514–524.

Kelly, R. I., Pearse, R., Bull, R. H., Leveque, J. L., de Rigal, J., & Mortimer, P. S. (1995). The effects of aging on the cutaneous microvasculature. *Journal of the American Academy of Dermatology, 33,* 749–756.

Kinouchi, Y., Hiwatashi, N., Chida, M., Nagashima, F., Takagi, S., Maekawa, H., & Toyota, T. (1998). Telomere shortening in the colonic mucosa of patients with ulcerative colitis. *Journal of Gastroenterology, 33,* 343–348.

Kipling, D., & Faragher, R. G. (1999). Telomeres. Ageing hard or hardly ageing? *Nature, 398,* 191.

Kiyono, T., Foster, S. A., Koop, J. I., McDougall, J. K., Galloway, D. A., & Klingelhutz, A. J. (1998). Both Rb/p16[INK4A] inactivation and telomerase activity are required to immortalize human epithelial cells. *Nature, 396,* 84–88.

Koshihara, Y., Hirano, M., Kawamura, M., Oda, H., & Higaki, S. (1991). Mineralization ability of cultured human osteoblast-like periosteal cells does not decline with aging. *Journal of Gerontology, 46,* B201–B206.

Kumar, S., Millis, A. J. T., & Baglioni, C. (1992). Expression of interleukin 1-inducible genes and production of interleukin 1 by aging human fibroblasts. *Proceedings of the National Academy of Sciences of the USA, 89,* 4683–4687.

Kunimura, C., Kikuchi, K., Ahmed, N., Shimizu, A., & Yasumoto, S. (1998). Telomerase activity in a specific cell subset co-expressing integrin β1/EGFR but not p75NGFR/bcl2/integrin β4 in normal human epithelial cells. *Oncogene, 17,* 187–197.

Kyprianou, N., Tu, H., & Jacobs, S. C. (1996). Apoptotic versus proliferative activities in human benign prostatic hyperplasia. *Human Pathology, 27,* 668–675.

Lanza, R. P., Cibelli, J. B., Blackwell, C., Cristofalo, V. J., Francis, M. K., Baerlocher, G. M., Mak, J., Schertzer, M., Chavez, E. A., Sawyer, N., Lansdorp, P. M., & West, M. D. (2000). Extension of cell life-span and telomere length in animals cloned from senescent somatic cells. *Science, 288,* 665–669.

Lee, J., Kook, H., Chung, I., Kim, H., Park, M., Kim, C., Nah, J., & Hwang, T. (1999). Telomere length changes in patients undergoing hematopoietic stem cell transplantation. *Bone Marrow Transplantation, 24,* 411–415.

Lengauer, C., Kinzler, K. W., & Vogelstein, B. (1998). Genetic instabilities in human cancers. *Nature, 396,* 643–649.

Leteurtre, F., Li, X., Guardiola, P., Le Roux, G., Sergere, J. C., Richard, P., Carosella, E. D., & Gluckman, E. (1999). Accelerated telomere shortening and telomerase activation in Fanconi's anaemia. *British Journal of Haematology, 105,* 883–893.

Lev-Ran, A. (1998). Mitogenic factors accelerate later-age diseases: Insulin as a paradigm. *Mechanisms of Ageing and Development, 102,* 95–113.

Li, A., Simmons, P. J., & Kaur, P. (1998). Identification and isolation of candidate human keratinocyte stem cells based on cell surface phenotype. *Proceedings of the National Academy of Sciences of the USA, 95,* 3902–3907.

Lingner, J., Hughes, T. R., Shevchenko, A., Mann, M., Lundblad, V., & Cech, T. R. (1997). Reverse transcriptase motifs in the catalytic subunit of telomerase. *Science, 276,* 561–567.

Lithgow, G. J., & Kirkwood, T. B. L. (1996). Mechanisms and evolution of aging. *Science, 273,* 80.

Lok, E., Nera, E. A., Iverson, F., Scott, F., So, Y., & Clayson, D. B. (1988). Dietary restriction, cell proliferation and carcinogenesis: A preliminary study. *Cancer Letters, 38,* 249–255.

Lok, E., Scott, F. W., Mongeau, R., Nera, E. A., Malcolm, S., & Clayson, D. B. (1990). Calorie restriction and cellular proliferation in various tissues of the female Swiss Webster mouse. *Cancer Letters, 51,* 67–73.

Majumdar, A. P., Edgerton, E. A., & Arlow, F. L. (1988). Gastric mucosal tyrosine kinase activity during aging and its relationship to cell proliferation in rats. *Biochimica et Biophysica Acta, 965,* 97–105.

Majumdar, A. P., Moshier, J. A., Arlow, F. L., & Luk, G. D. (1989). Biochemical changes in the gastric mucosa after injury in young and aged rats. *Biochimica et Biophysica Acta, 992,* 35–40.

Majumdar, A. P., Jasti, S., Hatfield, J. S., Tureaud, J., & Fligiel, S. E. (1990). Morphological and biochemical changes in gastric mucosa of aging rats. *Digestive Diseases Science, 35,* 1364–1370.

Martin, G. M. (1987). Interactions of aging and environmental agents: The gerontological perspective. In S. R. Baker, & M. Rogul (Eds.), *Environmental Toxicity and the Aging Processes* (pp. 25–80). New York: Alan R. Liss.

Martin, G. M. (1993). Clonal attenuation: Causes and consequences. *Journal of Gerontology, 48,* B171–B172.

Martin, G. M., Sprague, C. A., & Epstein, C. A. (1970). Replicative life-span of cultivated human cells: Effects of donor's age, tissue and genotype. *Laboratory Investigation, 23,* 86–92.

Martin, K., Potten, C. S., Roberts, S. A., & Kirkwood, T. B. (1998). Altered stem cell regeneration in irradiated intestinal crypts of senescent mice. *Journal of Cell Science, 111,* 2297–2303.

Medina, D., & Kittrell, F. S. (1993). Immortalization phenotype dissociated from the preneoplastic phenotype in mouse mammary epithelial outgrowths in vivo. *Carcinogenesis, 14,* 25–28.

Meyerson, M., Counter, C. M., Eaton, E. N., Ellisen, L. W., Steiner, P., Caddle, S. D., Ziaugra, L., Beijersbergen, R. L., Davidoff, M. J., Liu, Q., Bacchetti, S., Haber, D. A., & Weinberg, R. A. (1997). hEST2, the putative human telomerase catalytic subunit gene, is up-regulated in tumor cells and during immortalization. *Cell, 90,* 785–795.

Michalopoulos, G. K., & DeFrances, M. C. (1997). Liver regeneration. *Science, 276,* 60–66.

Miller, R. A. (1991). Gerontology as oncology. Research on aging as the key to the understanding of cancer. *Cancer, 68 Suppl.,* 2496–2501.

Millis, A. J., Hoyle, M., McCue, H. M., & Martini, H. (1992). Differential expression of metalloproteinase and tissue inhibitor of metalloproteinase genes in aged human fibroblasts. *Experimental Cell Research*, 201, 373–379.

Mishima, K., Handa, J. T., Aotaki-Keen, A., Lutty, G. A., Morse, L. S., & Hjelmeland, L. M. (1999). Senescence-associated β-galactosidase histochemistry for the primate eye. *Investigative Ophthalmology and Visual Science*, 40, 1590–1593.

Mitchell, J. R., Wood, E., & Collins, K. (1999). A telomerase component is defective in the human disease dyskeratosis congenita. *Nature*, 402, 551–555.

Morales, C. P., Holt, S. E., Ouellette, M., Kaur, K. J., Yan, Y., Wilson, K. S., White, M. A., Wright, W. E., & Shay, J. W. (1999). Absence of cancer-associated changes in human fibroblasts immortalized with telomerase. *Nature Genetics*, 21, 115–118.

Morris, J. A. (1999). The kinetics of epithelial cell generation: Its relevance to cancer and ageing. *Journal of Theoretical Biology*, 199, 87–95.

Morrison, S. J., Wandycz, A. M., Akashi, K., Globerson, A., & Weissman, I. L. (1996). The aging of hematopoietic stem cells. *Nature Medicine*, 2, 1011–1016.

Morrison, S. J., Shah, N. M., & Anderson, D. J. (1997). Regulatory mechanisms in stem cell biology. *Cell*, 88, 287–298.

Neville, A. M. (1978). The nodular adrenal. *Investigative Cell Pathology*, 1, 99–111.

Neville, A. M., & O'Hare, M. J. (1982). *The Human Adrenal Cortex. Pathology and Biology—An Integrated Approach*. Berlin: Springer-Verlag.

Neville, A. M., & O'Hare, M. J. (1985). Histopathology of the human adrenal cortex. *Clinical Endocrinology and Metabolism*, 14, 791–820.

Nilsson-Ehle, H., Swolin, B., & Westin, J. (1995). Bone marrow progenitor cell growth and karyotype changes in healthy 88-year-old subjects. *European Journal of Haematology*, 55, 14–18.

Noda, A., Ning, Y., Venable, S. F., Pereira-Smith, O. M., & Smith, J. R. (1994). Cloning of senescent cell-derived inhibitors of DNA synthesis using an expression screen. *Experimental Cell Research*, 211, 90–98.

Notaro, R., Cimmino, A., Tabarini, D., Rotoli, B., & Luzzatto, L. (1997). In vivo telomere dynamics of human

hematopoietic stem cells. *Proceedings of the National Academy of Sciences of the USA*, 94, 13782–13785.

Oesterling, J. E., Jacobsen, S. J., Chute, C. G., Guess, H. A., Girman, C. J., Panser, L. A., & Lieber, M. M. (1993). Serum prostate-specific antigen in a community-based population of healthy men. Establishment of age-specific reference ranges. *JAMA*, 270, 860–864.

Overturf, K., al-Dhalimy, M., Ou, C. N., Finegold, M., & Grompe, M. (1997). Serial transplantation reveals the stem-cell-like regenerative potential of adult mouse hepatocytes. *American Journal of Pathology*, 151, 1273–1280.

Paganelli, G. M., Santucci, R., Biasco, G., Miglioli, M., & Barbara, L. (1990). Effect of sex and age on rectal cell renewal in humans. *Cancer Letters*, 53, 117–121.

Pendergrass, W. R., Li, Y., Jiang, D.-Z., & Wolf, N. S. (1993). Decrease in cellular replicative potential in "giant" mice transfected with the bovine growth hormone gene correlates to shortened life span. *Journal of Cellular Physiology*, 156, 96–103.

Pendergrass, W. R., Lane, M. A., Bodkin, N. L., Hansen, B. C., Ingram, D. K., Roth, G. S., Yi, L., Bin, H., & Wolf, N. S. (1999). Cellular proliferation potential during aging and caloric restriction in rhesus monkeys (Macaca mulatta). *Journal of Cellular Physiology*, 180, 123–130.

Petersen, S., Saretzki, G., & von Zglinicki, T. (1998). Preferential accumulation of single-stranded regions in telomeres of human fibroblasts. *Experimental Cell Research*, 239, 152–160.

Peto, R., Parish, S. E., & Gray, R. G. (1985). There is no such thing as ageing and cancer is not related to it. In A. Likhachev, V. N. Anisimov, & R. Montesano (Eds.), *Age-Related Factors in Carcinogenesis* (pp. 43–53). Lyon: International Agency for Research on Cancer.

Pili, R., Guo, Y., Chang, J., Nakanishi, H., Martin, G. R., & Passaniti, A. (1994). Altered angiogenesis underlying age-dependent changes in tumor growth. *Journal of the National Cancer* Institute, 86, 1303–1314.

Pittenger, M. F., Mackay, A. M., Beck, S. C., Jaiswal, R. K., Douglas, R., Mosca, J. D., Moorman, M. A., Simonetti, D. W., Craig, S., & Marshak, D. R. (1999). Multilineage potential of adult human mesenchymal stem cells. *Science, 284,* 143–147.

Power, W., Neylan, D., & Collum, L. (1993). Growth characteristics of human lens epithelial cells in culture. Effect of media and donor age. *Documenta Ophthalmologica, 84,* 365–372.

Prowse, K. R., & Greider, C. W. (1995). Developmental and tissue-specific regulation of mouse telomerase and telomere length. *Proceedings of the National Academy of Sciences of the USA, 92,* 4818–1422.

Raffetto, J. D., Mendez, M. V., Phillips, T. J., Park, H. Y., & Menzoian, J. O. (1999). The effect of passage number on fibroblast cellular senescence in patients with chronic venous insufficiency with and without ulcer. *American Journal of Surgery, 178,* 107–112.

Ramakrishnan, S., Eppenberger, U., Mueller, H., Shinkai, Y., & Narayanan, R. (1998). Expression profile of the putative catalytic subunit of the telomerase gene. *Cancer Research, 58,* 622–625.

Ray, F. A., & Kraemer, P. M. (1993). Iterative chromosome mutation and selection as a mechanism of complete transformation of human diploid fibroblasts by SV40 T antigen. *Carcinogenesis, 14,* 1511–156.

Reed, M. J., Penn, P. E., Li, Y., Birnbaum, R., Vernon, R. B., Johnson, T. S., Pendergrass, W. R., Sage, E. H., Abrass, I. B., & Wolf, N. S. (1996). Enhanced cell proliferation and biosynthesis mediate improved wound repair in refed, caloric-restricted mice. *Mechanisms of Ageing and Development, 89,* 21–43.

Reed, M. J., Corsa, A., Pendergrass, W., Penn, P., Sage, E. H., & Abrass, I. B. (1998). Neovascularization in aged mice: Delayed angiogenesis is coincident with decreased levels of transforming growth factor β1 and type I collagen. *American Journal of Pathology, 152,* 113–123.

Rhim, J. A., Sandgren, E. P., Degen, J. L., Palmiter, R. D., & Brinster, R. L. (1994). Replacement of diseased mouse liver by hepatic cell transplantation. *Science, 263,* 1149–1152.

Risau, W. (1997). Mechanisms of angiogenesis. *Nature, 386,* 671–674.

Robles, S. J., & Adami, G. R. (1998). Agents that cause DNA double strand breaks lead to p16^{INK4A} enrichment and the premature senescence of normal fibrolasts. *Oncogene, 16,* 1113–1123.

Ross, N. S., & Aron, D. C. (1990). Hormonal evaluation of the patient with an incidentally discovered adrenal mass. *New England Journal of Medicine, 323,* 1401–1405.

Ross, E. A., Anderson, N., & Micklem, H. S. (1982). Serial depletion and regeneration of the murine hematopoietic system. Implications for hematopoietic organization and the study of cellular aging. *Journal of Experimental Medicine, 155,* 432–444.

Rudolph, K. L., Chang, S., Lee, H. W., Blasco, M., Gottlieb, G. J., Greider, C., & DePinho, R. A. (1999). Longevity, stress response, and cancer in aging telomerase-deficient mice. *Cell, 96,* 701–712.

Rudolph, K. L., Chang, S., Millard, M., Schreiber-Agus, N., & DePinho, R. A. (2000). Inhibition of experimental liver cirrhosis in mice by telomerase gene delivery. *Science, 287,* 1253–1258.

Rufer, N., Brummendorf, T. H., Kolvraa, S., Bischoff, C., Christensen, K., Wadsworth, L., Schulzer, M., & Lansdorp, P. M. (1999). Telomere fluorescence measurements in granulocytes and T lymphocyte subsets point to a high turnover of hematopoietic stem cells and memory T cells in early childhood. *Journal of Experimental Medicine, 190,* 157–167.

Ruiz-Torres, A., Gimeno, A., Melon, J., Mendez, L., Munoz, F. J., & Macia, M. (1999). Age-related loss of proliferative activity of human vascular smooth muscle cells in culture. *Mechanisms of Ageing and Development, 110,* 49–55.

Salk, D. (1985). Werner syndrome: A review of recent research with an analysis of connective tissue metabolism, growth control of cultured cells, and chromosomal aberrations. In D. Salk, Y. Fujiwara, & G. M. Martin (Eds.), *Werner's Syndrome and Human Aging* (pp. 121–160). New York: Plenum Press.

Schapiro, H., Hotta, S. S., Outten, W. E., & Klein, A. W. (1982). The effect of aging on rat liver regeneration. *Experientia, 38,* 1075–1076.

Schulz, V. P., Zakian, V. A., Ogburn, C. E., Mckay, J., Jarzebowicz, A. A., Edland, S. D., & Martin, G. M. (1996). Accelerated loss of telomeric repeats may not explain accelerated replicative decline of Werner syndrome cells. *Human Genetics, 97,* 750–754.

Serrano, M., Lin, A. W., Mccurrach, M. E., Beach, D., & Lowe, S. W. (1997). Oncogenic ras provokes premature cell senescence associated with accumulation of p53 and p16^{INK4A}. *Cell, 88,* 593–602.

Shammas, M. A., Xia, S. J. J., & Shmookler Reis, R. J. (1997). Induction of duplication reversion in human fibroblasts, by wild-type and mutated SV40 T antigen, covaries with the ability to induce host DNA synthesis. *Genetics, 146,* 1417–1428.

Shammas, M. A., Simmons, C. G., Corey, D. R., & Shmookler Reis, R. J. (1999). Telomerase inhibition by peptide nucleic acids reverses "immortality" of transformed human cells. *Oncogene, 18,* 6191–6200.

Shay, J. W., & Wright, W. E. (1989). Quantitation of the frequency of immortalization of normal human diploid fibroblasts by SV40 large T-antigen. *Experimental Cell Research, 184,* 109–118.

Shay, J. W., Van der Haegen, B. A., Ying, Y., & Wright, W. E. (1993). The frequency of immortalization of human fibroblasts and mammary epithelial cells transfected with SV40 large T-antigen. *Experimental Cell Research, 209,* 45–52.

Shelton, D. N., Chang, E., Whittier, P. S., Choi, D., & Funk, W. D. (1999). Microarray analysis of replicative senescence. *Current Biology, 9,* 939–945.

Smith, J. R., & Pereira-Smith, O. M. (1996). Replicative senescence: Implications for in vivo aging and tumor suppression. *Science, 273,* 63–67.

Smith, J. R., Pereira-Smith, O. M., & Schneider, E. L. (1978). Colony size distributions as a measure of in vivo and in vitro aging. *Proceedings of the National Academy of Sciences of the USA, 75,* 1353–1356.

Sottile, J., Mann, D. M., Diemer, V., & Millis, A. J. (1989). Regulation of collagenase and collagenase mRNA production in early-and late-passage human diploid fibroblasts. *Journal of Cellular Physiology, 138,* 281–290.

Start, R. D., Loomes, R. S., & Shortland, J. R. (1991). The relationship between donor age and the growth characteristics of human smooth muscle cultures of aorta and stomach. *International Journal of Experimental Pathology, 72,* 647–654.

Steinbach, G., Heymsfield, S., Olansen, N. E., Tighe, A., & Holt, P. R. (1994). Effect of caloric restriction on colonic proliferation in obese persons: Implications for colon cancer prevention. *Cancer Research, 54,* 1194–1197.

Stocker, E., & Heine, W. D. (1971). Regeneration of liver parenchyma under normal and pathological conditions. *Beitrage zur Pathologie, 144,* 400–408.

Takubo, K., Nakamura, K., Izumiyama, N., Furugori, E., Sawabe, M., Arai, T., Esaki, Y., Mafune, K., Kammori, M., Fujiwara, M., Kato, M., Oshimura, M., & Sasajima, K. (2000). Telomere shortening with aging in human liver. *Journal of Gerontology, 55,* B533–B536.

Tanner, J. M. (1999). The growth process. In J. L. Kostyo (Ed.), *Handbook of Physiology, Section 7: The Endocrine System, Vol. 5* (pp. 1–36). New York: Oxford University Press.

Tassin, J., Malaise, E., & Courtois, Y. (1979). Human lens cells have an in vitro proliferative capacity inversely proportional to the donor age. *Experimental Cell Research, 123,* 388–392.

Thomson, J. A., Itskovitz-Eldor, J., Shapiro, S. S., Waknitz, M. A., Swiergiel, J. J., Marshall, V. S., & Jones, J. M. (1998). Embryonic stem cell lines derived from human blastocysts. *Science, 282,* 1145–1147.

Urabe, Y., Nouso, K., Higashi, T., Nakatsukasa, H., Hino, N., Ashida, K., Kinugasa, N., Yoshida, K., Uematsu, S., & Tsuji, T. (1996). Telomere length in human liver diseases. *Liver, 16,* 293–297.

Vaziri, H., Schachter, F., Uchida, I., Wei, L., Zhu, X., Effros, R., Cohen, D., & Harley, C.

B. (1993). Loss of telomeric DNA during aging of normal and trisomy 21 human lymphocytes. *American Journal of Human Genetics, 52,* 661–667.

Vaziri, H., Dragowska, W., Allsopp, R. C., Thomas, T. E., Harley, C. B., & Lansdorp, P. M. (1994). Evidence for a mitotic clock in human hematopoietic stem cells: Loss of telomeric DNA with age. *Proceedings of the National Academy of Sciences of the USA, 91,* 9857–9860.

Wang, E. (1995). Senescent human fibroblasts resist programmed cell death, and failure to suppress bcl2 is involved. *Cancer Research, 55,* 2284–2292.

Weitzman, J. B., & Yaniv, M. (1999). Rebuilding the road to cancer. *Nature, 400,* 401–402.

West, M. D., Pereira-Smith, O. M., & Smith, J. R. (1989). Replicative senescence of human skin fibroblasts correlates with a loss of regulation and overexpression of collagenase activity. *Experimental Cell Research, 184,* 138–147.

Williams, G. C. (1957). Pleiotropy, natural selection, and the evolution of senescence. *Evolution, 11,* 389–411.

Williams, L. H., Udupa, K. B., & Lipshitz, D. A. (1986). Evaluation of the effect of age on hematopoiesis in the C57BL/6 mouse. *Experimental Hematology, 14,* 827–832.

Wolf, N. S., Penn, P. E., Jiang, D., Fei, R. G., & Pendergrass, W. R. (1995). Caloric restriction: conservation of in vivo cellular replicative capacity accompanies life-span extension in mice. *Experimental Cell Research, 217,* 317–323.

Worton, R. G., & Duff, C. (1979). Karyotyping. *Methods in Enzymology, 58,* 322–344.

Wright, W. E., & Shay, J.W. (2000). Telomere dynamics in cancer progression and prevention: Fundamental differences in human and mouse telomere biology. *Nature Medicine, 6,* 849–851.

Wu, K.-J., Grandori, C., Amacker, M., Simon-Vermot, N., Polack, A., Lingner, J., & Dalla-Favera, R. (1999). Direct activation of TERT transcription by c-MYC. *Nature Genetics, 21,* 220–224.

Wynford-Thomas, D. (1999). Cellular senescence and cancer. *Journal of Pathology, 187,* 100–111.

Wynn, R. F., Cross, M. A., & Testa, N. G. (1998). Telomeres and haematopoiesis. *British Journal of Haematology, 103,* 591–593.

Xia, S. J. J., Shammas, M. A., & Shmookler Reis, R. J. (1997). Elevated recombination in immortal human cells is mediated by hsRad51 recombinase. *Molecular and Cellular Biology, 17,* 7151–7158.

Yan, X. Q., Chen, Y., Hartley, C., McElroy, P., Fletcher, F., & McNiece, I. K. (1998). Marrow repopulating cells in mobilized PBPC can be serially transplanted for up to five generations or be remobilized in PBPC reconstituted mice. *Bone Marrow Transplantation, 21,* 975–81.

Yasumoto, S., Kunimura, C., Kikuchi, K., Tahara, H., Ohji, H., Yamamoto, H., Ide, T., & Utakoji, T. (1996). Telomerase activity in normal human epithelial cells. *Oncogene, 13,* 433–439.

Yui, J., Chiu, C. P., & Lansdorp, P. M. (1998). Telomerase activity in candidate stem cells from fetal liver and adult bone marrow. *Blood, 91,* 3255–3262.

Zauber, N. P., & Zauber, A. G. (1987). Hematologic data of healthy very old people. *JAMA, 257,* 2181–2184.

Zhang, X., Mar, V., Zhou, W., Harrington, L., & Robinson, M. O. (1999). Telomere shortening and apoptosis in telomerase-inhibited human tumor cells. *Genes and Development, 13,* 2388–2399.

Zhu, J., Woods, D., McMahon, M., & Bishop, J. M. (1998). Senescence of human fibroblasts induced by oncogenic Raf. *Genes and Development, 12,* 2997–3007.

Nine

Apoptosis and Aging

Eugenia Wang, Chantal Autexier, and Edwin Chen

I. Introduction

Since its initial discovery by Kerr *et al.* (1972) as a mechanism of cell death distinct from necrosis, the process of "apoptosis" has been the subject of intense scientific interest, and deregulation of apoptosis has been implicated as a fundamental pathogenic mechanism in a myriad of aging-related human diseases. For example, inefficient elimination of malignant or autoreactive cells can result in the development of cancer or autoimmune diseases. On the other hand, excessive apoptotic cell death may result in aberrant cell loss and organ atrophy, pathological events that underlie neurodegenerative diseases, cardiovascular dysfunction, muscle atrophy, intestinal disorders, and kidney disease. Indeed, the numerous and wide-ranging manifestations associated with dysregulation of apoptosis reflect the complexity of apoptotic signaling and the importance of its role in organismic homeostasis.

Unlike necrosis, which usually results from severe trauma to the cell and is manifested by an uncontrolled breakdown of cellular and organelle structure, cell lysis, and an inflammatory response, apoptosis can be induced by mild signals and occurs through an ATP-dependent, gene-driven, non-inflammatory process (Majno & Joris, 1995). Morphologically, necrosis exhibits cell swelling and loss of membrane integrity, whereas apoptosis is characterized by cell shrinkage, formation of membrane-enclosed bodies, preservation of organelles, and maintenance of membrane integrity. Phagocytosis of the apoptotic bodies by macrophages prevents an inflammatory response. Apoptosis is also characterized by chromatin condensation and margination and by fragmentation of the nuclear DNA into integer multiples of the internucleosomal length (approximately 180 bp) (Wyllie, 1980). Biochemically, apoptosis is accompanied by the *de novo* expression of a spectrum of genes that facilitate the execution of the cellular suicide program and/or the processing of preexisting gene/protein entities (such as caspase) into functional mode.

Apoptosis is necessary during development when excess cells need to be removed, for example, during organ morphogenesis. However, with age, the exquisite control of gene expression for apoptotic events may not be finely tuned, resulting in either retaining cells that should be eliminated or losing cells that should be retained. We hypothesize here that cells that inappropriately fail to die (apoptosis-resistant cells) and cells inappropriately prone to apoptotic death (apoptosis-susceptible cells) are dangerous to the tissues in which they reside. The former cells may act as seeds for transformation and neoplastic growth, whereas the absence of the latter may compromise tissue function. The activation or repression of "killer" or "survival" factors that modulate the regularity of apoptotic activity may be crucial to understanding the etiology of some age-dependent debility. Investigation of the molecular mechanisms leading to dysregulated apoptosis may provide tools necessary to the prognosis, diagnosis, and eventual treatment of age-related diseases such as cancer, Alzheimer's disease, and cardiovascular degeneration.

The past decade has seen an explosion of research into the biochemical signaling pathways of apoptosis. In this review, we provide an overview outlining important findings in the molecular mechanisms of apoptosis in general. We further discuss how these pathways may be initiated or circumvented in cells that exhibit apoptotic sensitivity or resistance, respectively, and the relevance of these phenotypes to aging and aging-associated diseases.

II. General Molecular Mechanism of Apoptosis

A. Caspases

A common end event in the execution of apoptotic cell death is the activation of a family of proteases called caspases [reviewed in Cohen (1997)], a family of cysteine proteases that mediate proteolysis of a variety of intracellular proteins at specific aspartate residues. Among the many caspase substrates that have been identified are poly(ADP-ribose) polymerase (PARP) (Lazebnik et al., 1994), lamin A (Orth et al., 1996), U1 70-kDa small nuclear ribonucleoprotein (Casciola-Rosen et al., 1996), actin (Mashima et al., 1995), fodrin (Martin et al., 1995), and the retinoblastoma tumor suppressor Rb (Janicke et al., 1996). The first mammalian caspase to be described, a protein previously known as interleukin–1β converting enzyme (ICE, now designated caspase 1), was identified as playing a role in apoptosis by virtue of its homology with the proapoptotic Caenorhabditis elegans protein, ced-3 (Yuan et al., 1993). Ten caspase family members have since been identified; caspases 3 and 7 are the key effector caspases upon which divergent apoptotic signaling pathways appear to converge. Overexpression of caspase 1 or 3 is sufficient to trigger apoptosis (Miura et al., 1993), and caspase 3 knockout mice exhibit an embryonic lethal phenotype due to abnormal brain formation caused by the inability to diminish neuronal numbers during development (Kuida et al., 1996).

Caspases are synthesized as proenzymes with variable prodomains and an enzymatic domain. Activation occurs by posttranslational cleavage within the enzymatic domain at specific aspartate residues, yielding large and small subunits; two large and two small subunits subsequently associate into an active heterotetrameric complex. Removal of the prodomain is not necessary for proteolytic activation, nor is its presence necessary for enzymatic activity (Salvesen & Dixit, 1997; Villa et al., 1997). Because activation requires cleavage at specific aspartate residues, an ability unique to the caspase family, activation can only be mediated through autoactivation or by another caspase.

Once the activation of caspases is effected, cell death appears to be inevitable. Therefore, researchers have turned to studying the upstream mechanisms that initiate the activation of caspases. A plethora of data now suggests that activation of caspases can be mediated through proapoptotic receptor signaling complexes at the cell surface, by mitochondrion-dependent processes within the cytosol, or by p53-dependent processes originating in the nucleus (Fig. 1).

B. Receptor-Dependent Caspase Activation

Proapoptotic signals can be transmitted from the extracellular milieu by associating extracellular death signal ligands with their respective receptors on the cell surface. Among the best characterized of the cell-surface-initiated apoptotic pathways is that initiated by the tumor necrosis factor receptor family, of which five members have been identified. These receptors include Fas, TNFR1, DR3, DR4,

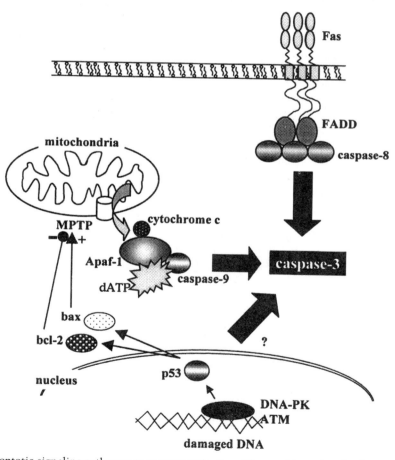

Figure 1. Apoptotic signaling pathways to caspase activation. The machinery involved in the induction of apoptotic signals and the activation of apoptotic effectors, such as caspases, is complex. Three well-studied mechanisms capable of leading to the apoptosis of cells include (i) mitochondrion-dependent pathways, (ii) Fas(receptor)-dependent pathways, and (iii) p53-dependent pathways. The pathways are not completely distinct, but exhibit a limited capacity of crosstalk. See text for details.

and DR5 [reviewed by Haunstetter and Izumo, (1998)]. These death receptors share a motif termed the "death domain," an approximately 80-amino acid stretch that resides in the cytoplasmic domain of these receptors and is necessary for their proapoptotic function. Signal transduction through these receptors requires binding of the appropriate ligand, such as Fas ligand (FasL), which associates with the Fas receptor, TNF-α, which binds to TNFR1, and Apo–3L, which interacts with DR3. The TRAIL ligand has been shown to interact with both DR4 and DR5. Receptor–ligand interaction results in the formation of a homotrimeric complex, facilitating the recruitment to the "death domain" of an intracellular adaptor protein by protein–protein interactions. In the case of TNFR1 and DR3, this adaptor protein is the TNFR-associated death domain protein (TRADD), whereas Fas and DR4 recruit the Fas-associated death domain protein, FADD. The adaptor protein involved in DR5 signaling remains unknown, suggesting the existence of hitherto undiscovered adaptor proteins.

FADD has been shown to interact directly with caspase 8, leading to its autoactivation (Boldin et al., 1996; Muzio et al., 1996), which is followed by the activation of caspase 3 and apoptosis (Fernandes-Alnemri et al., 1996).

C. Mitochondrion-Dependent Caspase Activation

Another potential mechanism by which apoptosis is initiated and caspases are activated is through mitochondrion-dependent pathways. Some apoptotic stimuli evidence a cascade of events that occur at the mitochondria and lead to cell death. These events include (i) opening of the mitochondrial permeability transition pore (MPTP) and (ii) release of cytochrome c from the intermitochondrial matrix, which induces (iii) the activation of caspases (Cai et al., 1998; Gross et al., 1999; Halestrap et al., 1998; Zoratti & Szabò, 1995).

The mitochondrial permeability transition pore (MPTP) is a proteinacous megachannel complex that spans the intermitochondrial matrix. It consists of several inner and outer mitochondrial membrane proteins, including the adenine nucleotide translocator (ANT), the voltage-dependent anion channel (VDAC), the peripheral benzodiazepine receptor (PBR), cyclophilin D, hexokinase, creatine kinase, and perhaps other unidentified components (Zoratti & Szabò, 1995). The MPTP functions primarily to control the efflux of mitochondrial matrix solutes with molecular masses <1500 Da from the mitochondria to the cytoplasm, thereby maintaining a mitochondrial matrix environment distinct from that of the cytoplasm (Zamzami et al., 1998). One of the first steps in the apoptotic process is the opening of the MPTP (Kroemer et al., 1997), followed by mitochondrial depolarization, organelle swelling, and uncoupling of oxidative phosphorylation.

Opening of the MPTP provides a channel for expulsion of key components of the mitochondrial electron transport chain, which is necessary for the activation of several downstream apoptotic executors. In particular, the intermitochondrial matrix protein cytochrome c is released from mitochondria following the initiation of apoptosis (Liu et al., 1996) and functions in the formation of an "apoptosome," a complex that also contains apoptosis protease activation factor 1 (Apaf-1) and procaspase 9. This complex subsequently catalyzes the autoactivation of caspase 9 by a dATP- or ATP-dependent mechanism (Li et al., 1997). Active caspase 9 subsequently activates caspase 3, precipitating cell death.

D. p53-Dependent Caspase Activation

Tumor suppressor p53 is a key "guardian of the genome," maintaining genomic stability after DNA damage [reviewed by Yonish-Rouach (1996)]. p53 is a nuclear-localized, sequence-specific transcriptional activator. The amino terminus of p53 functions as the transactivation domain, and the DNA binding domain interacts directly with DNA containing the sequence 5'-PuPuPuC(A/T) (T/A)GPyPyPy–3' (El-Deiry *et al.*, 1992; Kern *et al.*, 1991). The carboxy terminus is responsible for recognizing damaged DNA. Ordinarily, p53 exhibits a short half-life *in vivo*; in the presence of damaged DNA, however, p53 protein levels are increased by the stabilization of preexisting p53 protein and up-regulation of p53 transcription (Kastan *et al.*, 1991).

The first functional role to be ascribed to p53 was the induction of growth arrest at a restriction point in the G_1 phase of the cell cycle to allow the cell sufficient time to repair DNA damage (Diller *et al.*, 1990). Induction of cell cycle arrest involves the activation of transcription of several growth-arrest-associated proteins, such as p21, Gadd45, and cyclin G (El-Deiry *et al.*, 1993; Fornace *et al.*, 1989; Xiong *et al.*, 1993). Alternatively, in the presence of irreparable DNA damage, p53 functions as a proapoptotic factor and induces programmed cell death. Guillouf and co-workers (1995) demonstrated that the introduction of p53 into p53-deficient cells is sufficient to induce apoptosis and that p53 also activates growth arrest genes, suggesting that apoptosis may result from a conflict between signals stimulating and arresting cell growth. This hypothesis was later corroborated by the ability of p21-null cells to undergo p53-dependent apoptosis (Deng *et al.*, 1995), suggesting a distinction between the growth arrest and proapoptotic functions of p53.

The mechanism of p53-induced caspase activation and apoptosis remains poorly understood. Conflicting data have been reported regarding the dependence upon p53-mediated transcriptional activation in the execution of apoptosis. Cells can undergo apoptosis in the absence of p53-induced transcriptional transactivation (Caelles *et al.*, 1994). Indeed, Haupt and co-workers (1995) reported that p53 lacking the transactivation domain induces apoptosis in HeLa cells. However, other groups have reported the ability of p53 to activate the transcription of key proapoptotic genes. Miyashita and Reed (1995) demonstrated that p53 functions to up-regulate levels of Bax, a proapoptotic Bcl-2 homologue. Moreover, p53 down-regulates levels of the antiapoptotic protein, Bcl-2 (Hadler *et al.*, 1994). Bcl-2 has been shown to interact directly with components of the MPTP, specifically VDAC and ANT, in order to regulate the release of cytochrome *c* (Marzo *et al.*, 1998; Shimizu *et al.*, 1996). Overexpression of Bcl-2 is associated with decreased cytochrome *c* efflux, whereas increased Bax expression is associated with increased cytochrome *c* efflux. Given the opposing actions of Bax and Bcl-2 in caspase activation, it has been suggested that initiation of apoptosis by p53 may be controlled by its ability to alter the Bax–Bcl-2 equilibrium (Miyashita *et al.*, 1994).

III. Apoptotic Susceptibility in Aging

Untimely loss of irreplaceable cells in certain tissues is one mechanism by which deregulated apoptosis can exert a detrimental effect during the aging of an organism. One of the classical examples of an age-related phenomenon associated with an undesired diminution in cell number is cardiovascular dysfunction. Most cardiovascular dysfunction-associated fatalities are caused by a process referred to as "ischemic heart disease." The pathology of ischemic heart disease is initiated by thrombosis of a coronary artery, creating an occlusion of blood flow to the myocardium. Coronary blockage results in reduced oxygen supply to the heart, which, if sufficiently prolonged and severe, can induce membrane damage, necrosis, and cell loss. Paradoxically, whereas rapid reoxygenation and reestablishment of blood flow to the ischemic myocardium is critical in preventing excessive hypoxia-induced damage, the reperfusion event itself can exacerbate the damage to the myocardium. The additional injury inflicted upon the myocardium, independent of the ischemic event, is referred to as "reperfusion injury" (Hearse, 1977).

Reperfusion-associated cell death in the myocardium has long been associated with necrosis, because the rapid and early membrane damage and diminished ATP pool associated with hypoxia often leads to a generalized breakdown of cellular structure. For this reason, it was believed for many years that necrosis was the principal mechanism by which cardiac cell death was achieved (Katz, 1992). However, in a landmark study, Gottlieb and co-workers demonstrated that cardiomyocytes undergo cell death via two distinct mechanisms, depending on the insult: ischemia alone induces death in rabbit cardiomyocytes by necrosis, whereas reperfusion initiates cell death by apoptosis (Gottlieb et al., 1994). Kajstura et al. (1995) also revealed that post-reperfusion rat hearts contain both apoptotic and necrotic cells, but the abundance of the latter is sixfold greater than that of the former. Several independent studies have confirmed these findings, although some report the presence of apoptotic as well as necrotic cells with hypoxia. The death of irreplaceable, long-lived, terminally differentiated

cardiomyocytes results in fibroblast infiltration into the infarct zone, creating scar tissue; accumulation of scars ultimately results in heart failure.

The precise mechanism by which cell loss is initiated during reperfusion remains controversial. The favored hypothesis is the "free radical theory of reperfusion injury," which claims that a rapid burst of toxic reactive oxygen species (ROS) mediates cytotoxicity. Indeed, ROS are implicated in all three well-characterized pathways to caspase activation described earlier. In the case of receptor-dependent processes, incubation with ROS, such as H_2O_2 or the semiquinone menadione, is associated with increased expression of the Fas receptor and up-regulation of Fas ligand mRNA levels (Caricchio et al., 1999). At the mitochondria, ROS promote opening of the MPTP by causing thiol modification of the MPTP component, ANT, enhancing its ability to undergo a calcium-dependent conformational change and resulting in the formation a channel (Halestrap et al., 1998). Moreover, Stridh et al., (1998) and Kluck et al., (1997) demonstrated that H_2O_2 is capable of inducing translocation of cytochrome c from the mitochondria to the cytoplasm following 2 hr of oxidative stress in Jurkat and CEM T-lymphoblastoid cells. In both studies, cytochrome c release was followed by caspase 3 activation. Direct administration of prooxidants to cytoplasmic extracts that do not contain mitochondria, however, does not result in caspase activation, suggesting that the activation of caspases and the consequent induction of apoptosis induced by free radicals occurs through mitochondria-dependent (and, most likely, cytochrome c-dependent) mechanisms (Hampton et al., 1998). Finally, given that ROS are potent inducers of DNA damage and can cause single-stranded DNA breaks, chromosome deletions, dicentrics, and sister chromatid exchanges, it is not surprising that some investigators have demonstrated that p53-null fibroblasts are more resistant to apoptosis induced by ROS (Yin *et al.*, 1998).

What is puzzling, however, is why these irreplaceable postmitotic cells retain the ability to undergo apoptosis following oxidant damage at all. At first glance, it would seem advantageous for such cells to be impaired in their ability to execute apoptosis. After all, in the presence of overwhelming injury, cell number would be diminished by necrosis. Why would cardiomyocytes respond to a less-than-overwhelming insult, as is often the case with reperfusion, by programmed cell death? Heintz suggests that apoptotic pathways may persist in irreplaceable cells in order to guard against reentry into the cell cycle, which may lead to malignant transformation (Heintz, 1993). Given that one of the primary intracellular targets of oxidants is DNA, in the event of DNA-damage-induced oncogene activation or tumor suppressor inactivation, the survival of an organism may be better served if the potentially dangerous cell is deleted, despite the irreplaceability of the cell. In support of this hypothesis, ectopic expression of oncogenes in terminally differentiated cell types leads to cell death rather than cell proliferation. This "better dead than sick" principle may be the fundamental explanation for the existence of apoptotic mechanisms in cardiomyocytes and other irreplaceable cells (Barr & Tomei, 1994). In the end, the finding that apoptosis also occurs in the myocardium during heart disease will fuel the development of therapies for cardiovascular dysfunction geared toward preventing apoptosis.

IV. Apoptotic Resistance in Aging

One of the best studied models for human aging is the replicative senescence of human diploid fibroblasts. Hayflick (1965) first showed that fibroblasts possess a limited life span in *in vitro* cell culture, ultimately culminating in a loss of replicative capacity and the development of a flattened, enlarged morphology. Senescent cells are not dead, but rather, if provided regular replenishment of medium and serum, can exist in culture indefinitely (Campisi, 1996). The presence of senescent cells has also been detected *in vivo* in the skin (Dimri *et al.*, 1995). Moreover, senescence may be enhanced by mild oxidative stress. Two teams (Chen & Ames, 1994; de Haan *et al.*, 1995) have shown that administration of H_2O_2 to early passage human diploid fibroblast cultures induces a premature senescence phenotype.

Senescent cells are resistant to serum-deprivation-induced apoptosis, a phenotype that is, in part, attributed to an inability to down-regulate levels of the antiapoptotic Bcl-2 protein (Wang, 1995). In addition, heightened resistance may be due to the inability of the cells to traverse the cell cycle. In this regard, failure to replicate and failure to die may be regulated by the same molecular mechanism, because the activation of apoptosis in quiescent cells requires many of the same G_1 events as replication, and the triage point between life and death may reside at or near the G_1/S boundary. Thus, failure to express key G_1 genes, such as c-*fos* repression, seems to be a double-edged sword, blocking senescent human fibroblasts from both death and replication. Furthermore, this death resistance also may be due to an inability to respond to apoptosis signals.

Our studies have shown that, subsequent to the G_1/S checkpoint, serum-deprived cells are committed to eventual death. They cannot be rescued from death by returning them to serum-containing medium; this commitment point is marked by the proteolysis of a protein, terminin, from a precursor form, Tp90, to the final product form, Tp30. Therefore, Tp30 can be used as a biochemical marker for the irreversible commitment to apoptotic death. The cleavage of Tp90 to Tp30 closely resembles the noted apoptosis-dependent proteolysis of pro-ICE to ICE and, therefore, suggests key proteolytic steps as the half-way point directing the final apoptotic death.

As described earlier, immediately preceding the commitment to apoptosis marked by the proteolytic production of Tp30, an entire repertoire of immediate early genes is expressed. We and others have noted that there is even an attempt at low level, but significant DNA synthesis in some cells. Ultimately, upon prolonged serum deprivation, cells follow the path leading to DNA replication, though abortive in nature. Perhaps the signals for apoptosis also trigger the machinery preparing for DNA replication; however, in the milieu of a negative environment such as the absence of a functional "anti-death" factor, the enterprise for replicating DNA is aborted, which then sends the alternate signal to commit to death.

Thus, the antiapoptotic state in replicatively senescent human fibroblasts is a unique status marked by the lack of (1) down-regulation of survival factors, such as Bcl-2, (2) key proteolysis of terminin protein to Tp30, its death-specific form, and (3) DNA synthesis activity. This last feature distinguishes senescent fibroblasts from other apoptosis-resistant states, such as rapidly growing cancer cells, that escape the apoptotic fate by continuous proliferation.

Apoptosis-resistant cells, as described previously, provide many tissues with sufficient cellular building blocks. However, the accumulation of these death-refractile cells may be deleterious to the well-being of their host tissue; when dysfunctional cells fail to be eliminated, they may become a "hot-bed" for further insults and, thus, a platform leading to dysplasia. The presence of damaged neurons in the brain, or functionally impaired cardiomyocytes in the heart, may become weak spots that compromise organ function. Dysfunctional cells may either cause further damage when additional insults occur or by themselves prevent the whole tissue from functioning to its maximal capacity. Therefore, the accumulation of senescent cells during aging may contribute to increased loss of the function of organs, and the inability of an organism to delete these deleterious cells by apoptotic mechanisms may exacerbate this condition (Warner et al., 1995). This is consistent with a theory suggested by Franceschi et al., 1992), who assert that apoptosis can serve as an important cellular defense mechanism by deleting genetically unstable cells and that the oldest-old centenarian populations have attained such long life spans by their body's ability to effect apoptosis more efficiently. Also consistent with this theory are reports that calorically restricted rodents (which exhibit greater life spans than littermates fed ad libitum) display increased apoptotic incidence, which functions to remove potentially neoplastic cells (Grasl-Kraupp et al., 1994; James & Muskhelishvili, 1994). Warner et al. (1997) have proposed that the increased apoptosis in calorically restricted mice may also function to counteract the accumulation of otherwise apoptosis-resistant senescent cells, as another mechanism for extending life span. Thus, caloric restriction appears to increase the apoptotic capabilities of organisms to combat the age-dependent accumulation of defective apoptosis-resistant cells. How then to reactivate the apoptosis program to get rid of these dysfunctional cells is an avenue of future work, possibly employing gene therapy.

V. Telomerase, Telomeres, and Apoptosis

A. The Telomere Hypothesis

Telomeres, the ends of linear eukaryotic chromosomes, consist of short repeats and specialized proteins (Pardue & DeBaryshe, 1999; Wellinger & Sen, 1997). Telomeres and their associated proteins are essential for maintaining chromosomal stability (Price, 1999). Without telomeres, eukaryotic chromosomes undergo end-to-end fusions and rearrangements. The action of telomerase is one mechanism that organisms use to maintain telomeres (Nugent & Lundblad, 1998).

Human telomerase activity was first identified in 1989 in HeLa cells (Morin, 1989). Subsequent studies surveying telomerase activity in various human cell types found that telomerase activity is absent from most primary human cells, but is active in germ line cells and 85% of immortalized and tumor cells (Autexier & Greider, 1996; Shay & Bacchetti, 1997). In most human primary somatic cells, telomeres shorten with each round of cellular division due to the incomplete replication of linear chromosomes, as well as the absence of a compensatory telomere maintenance mechanism (Greider, 1996; Colgin & Reddel, 1999; Pardue & DeBaryshe, 1999). By contrast, in germ line cells and telomerase-positive immortal and tumor cells, telomere length is maintained. The correlation between telomere maintenance and telomerase activity serves as a foundation for the telomere hypothesis, first proposed by Calvin Harley (Autexier & Greider, 1996; Harley, 1991). This model postulates that, in cells lacking a telomere length maintenance mechanism, telomeres act as a "mitotic clock." After a certain number of doublings, when the telomeres become "critically short," a signal is transmitted, perhaps via a DNA damage checkpoint mechanism, and the cell exits the cell cycle and enters replicative senescence (Vaziri & Benchimol, 1996). The telomere hypothesis also proposes that telomerase activation may be one step in immortalization and/or tumorigenesis, making telomerase an attractive target for anticancer therapy.

B. Telomerase, Telomere Maintenance, Cell Growth, and Cancer

Human telomerase is a ribonucleoprotein consisting minimally of a catalytic reverse transcriptase protein subunit (hTERT) and an integral RNA component (hTR) that contains a short template region complementary to the telomeric $d(TTAGGG)_n$ repeats at the ends of vertebrate chromosomes (Nugent & Lundblad, 1998; Weinrich *et al.*, 1997; Beattie *et al.*, 1998). Telomerase activity correlates best with the expression of hTERT, whereas hTR is commonly expressed in both telomerase-positive and telomerase-negative cell lines, tumors, and tissues (Autexier, 1999; Price, 1999).

The identification of the hTERT gene permitted direct testing of the prediction that telomere length acts as a "mitotic clock." The first experimental evidence establishing a causal relationship between telomere shortening and replicative senescence came from the overexpression of hTERT in certain telomerase-negative primary cells (Bodnar *et al.*, 1998; Counter *et al.*, 1998; Vaziri & Benchimol, 1998). hTERT-transfected cells become telomerase-positive, exhibit increased or stabilized telomere lengths, and are able to divide beyond their "Hayflick limit" number of population doublings. Such extended life span cells do not display a transformed phenotype, as indicated by their inability to form foci in soft agar, normal cell cycle checkpoints and karyotypic stability, and inability to generate tumors *in vivo* (Jiang *et al.*, 1999; Morales *et al.*, 1999;

Vaziri *et al.*, 1999). The cells in these studies are defined as immortal because they more than double their maximum replicative life spans in culture. However, certain primary cells are not immortalized by the overexpression of hTERT alone, but also require the inactivation of the Rb/p16 pathway (Kiyono *et al.*, 1998).

Another prediction of the telomere hypothesis is that telomerase activation may be an essential step in tumorigenesis. Experiments to test this prediction indicate that the expression of the catalytic subunit of telomerase, in conjunction with alterations in p53, Rb, and *ras*, converts some, but not all, primary cells into tumorigenic cells (Hahn *et al.*, 1999a; Morales *et al.*, 1999). In one study, transfection of human fibroblasts with hTERT and *ras* (H-*ras*V12) combined with the human papillomavirus-16 E6/E7 viral oncoproteins (to inactivate Rb and p53) failed to stimulate transformation (Morales *et al.*, 1999). In a second study, transformation of fibroblasts and epithelial cells is possible by transfecting first SV40 large T-protein (to inactivate Rb and p53) and subsequently hTERT and *ras* (H-*ras*V12) (Hahn *et al.*, 1999a). The order in which the genes are introduced, and/or whether SV–40 large-T perturbs additional cellular functions, may explain the different results (Weitzman & Yaniv, 1999). These data indicate that telomerase activation may be one step toward immortalization and tumorigenesis for certain cell types. However, 15% of immortal and tumor cells utilize an alternative mechanism for telomere maintenance (ALT), suggesting that telomerase itself is not essential for immortalization and tumorigenesis. Furthermore, ALT cells invariably have long heterogeneous telomeres, indicating that telomere length maintenance clearly is essential for unlimited cell proliferation (Colgin & Reddel, 1999).

C. Telomerase, Telomere Maintenance, and Cellular Resistance to Apoptosis

The association of chromosomes through their telomeres (end-to-end fusions) is an early manifestation of programmed cell death, both *in vivo* and *in vitro*, and can be induced in normal fibroblasts and some tumor cell lines (Pathak *et al.*, 1994a,b). Penclomedine, a synthetic compound under evaluation in clinical trials as an anticancer agent, induces chromosome associations in HeLa cells and normal human fibroblasts (Pandita *et al.*, 1997). Penclomedine-induced chromosome end associations are significantly higher in telomerase-positive cells, suggesting that the effects of penclomedine on telomere maintenance may be telomerase-mediated. Indeed, penclomedine treatment elicits a decrease in the level of telomerase activity in HeLa cells (Pandita *et al.*, 1997). Cells with mutant p53 are more sensitive to penclomedine than cells with wild-type p53, as measured by cell viability assays, indicating that the absence of a p53 DNA-damage checkpoint and growth arrest may play a role in penclomedine-mediated cell death (Pandita *et al.*, 1997). In another study, the p53-negative non-small-cell lung cancer cell line H1299 shows reduced telomeric signals (shortened telomeres) and increased telomeric associations upon p53-mediated apoptosis; this occurs prior to nuclear fragmentation, indicating a role for p53 in telomere shortening (Mukhopadhyay *et al.*, 1998). Treatment of HeLa cells with the apoptosis-inducing anticancer drug cisplatin results in markedly shortened telomeres prior to the onset of apoptosis (Ishibashi & Lippard, 1998). These studies indicate that the induction of telomeric associations as a consequence of telomere shortening appears to be a common step preceding apoptosis in different cell types.

Chromosome end (telomeric) associations may also occur as a result of

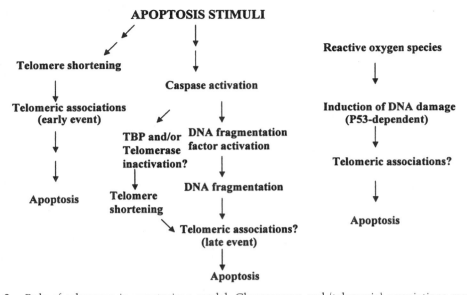

Figure 2. Role of telomeres in apoptosis: a model. Chromosome end (telomeric) associations resulting from telomere shortening appear to be an early event preceding apoptosis in different cell types. Telomeric associations may also occur as a result of DNA fragmentation and/or inactivation of telomere-binding proteins (TBP) and/or telomerase by caspase cleavage. Such associations presumably are late events. Telomeric associations may also result from the induction of DNA damage by reactive oxygen species.

telomere loss due to DNA fragmentation (Fig. 2). The DNA fragmentation factor (DFF), which mediates DNA fragmentation during apoptosis, is activated by caspase 3 (Liu *et al.*, 1997). The potential loss of telomeres during DNA fragmentation may result in telomeric associations; however, in this case, telomeric associations would be a late event in apoptosis. p53-dependent telomeric associations may also result from DNA damage caused by ROS; however, this hypothesis remains to be tested. Telomerase or telomere-binding proteins that regulate telomere length also may be specific substrates for cleavage by caspases (Holt *et al.*, 1999). Potential caspase sites are present in the human telomerase reverse transcriptase component (Holt *et al.*, 1999; Nakamura *et al.*, 1997). The inactivation of telomere-binding proteins, such as TRF2 (telomere repeat binding factor 2) (Karlseder *et al.*, 1999) and/or telomerase

(Hahn *et al.*, 1999b; Zhang *et al.*, 1999), results in telomere loss and apoptosis.

The induction of apoptosis in immortal human cells may or may not be mediated by the down-regulation of telomerase activity. Several studies have indicated decreases in telomerase activity upon the treatment of cells with apotosis-inducing agents. In some reports, telomerase activity is down-regulated prior to apoptosis, whereas in one report, telomerase activity appears to be down-regulated as a consequence of apoptosis. In pheochromocytoma (PC12) cells, a reduction in telomerase activity occurs prior to the detection of apoptotic nuclei following treatment with staurosporine, amyloid B-peptide, or Fe^{2+} (Fu *et al.*, 1999). Similarly, in the cytotoxic T-cell line, CTLL-2, down-regulation of telomerase activity is detected 8 hr after IL-2 deprivation before G_0/G_1 cell cycle arrest and/or apoptosis become evident at 24 hr (Mandal &

Kumar, 1997). However, exposure of leukemic U937 cells to etoposide reveals that decreases in telomerase activity occur only in late stage apoptotic or necrotic cells; these findings indicate that telomerase down-regulation is a consequence of apoptosis or necrosis (Akiyama et al., 1999). There also have been a few reports indicating no change in telomerase activity upon the treatment of cancer cells with apoptosis-inducing agents. Treatment of a metastatic murine melanoma cell line with paclitaxel induces apoptosis and telomeric associations, but no decrease in telomerase activity (Multani et al., 1999). Similarly, telomerase activity in the immortalized endothelial cell line ECV–304 is unaffected by the overexpression of p53 and apoptosis (Maxwell et al., 1997), indicating possible cell-type-specific differences in the interactions between cell cycle regulators, apoptotic signals, and telomerase regulation.

Inactivation of human telomerase and the subsequent induction of apoptosis may be an effective cancer treatment strategy (Autexier, 1999). In this appoach, the potential role of telomere length and telomerase activity in providing resistance to apoptosis is an important experimental parameter. However, the apoptosis resistance and potential risk of cancer that may be conferred by telomerase could be a concern in the use of telomerase in cell replacement therapy (Bodnar et al., 1998). Fu et al. (1999) demonstrated that PC12 cells overexpressing Bcl-2 have increased levels of telomerase activity and increased resistance to apoptosis. Moreover, upon differentiation of PC12 cells, levels of telomerase activity decrease and the cells exhibit increased sensitivity to apoptosis (Fu et al., 1999). Decreasing telomerase activity in PC12 cells through the use of telomerase inhibitors is also associated with increased vulnerability to apoptotic stimuli (Fu et al., 1999).

In addition, telomerase-negative normal human cells that have short telomeres are more susceptible to apoptosis than telomerase-negative normal human cells with longer telomeres (Holt et al., 1999). Telomerase-negative foreskin fibroblasts transfected with hTERT and with telomere lengths of 8.1–14 kb are more resistant to apoptosis than untransfected cells with telomere lengths of 6.6 kb (7.5–13% apoptosis versus 20%) (Holt et al., 1999). Moreover, telomerase-positive immortal SW39 cells exhibit greater survival and resistance to apoptosis than their telomerase-negative counterparts, SW13 and SW26 (Holt et al., 1999). Experimental elongation of the telomeres in telomerase-positive cells such as IDH4 (a line of T-antigen-immortalized human lung fibroblasts) or DU145 (a colon adenocarcinoma cell line) results in resistance to apoptosis and greater survival than in isogenic parental cells with shorter telomeres (Wright et al., 1996; Holt et al., 1999). The increased resistance of these cells to apoptosis appears to be associated with defects in two major apoptosis execution mechanisms: the induction of nuclear calcium-dependent endonucleases and the activation of caspases (Holt et al., 1999). These results clearly suggest a link between telomerase activity, telomere maintenance, and cellular resistance to apoptosis.

D. Roles of Bcl-2 and c-myc in Telomerase Regulation

The regulation of apoptosis involves a number of gene products, including the antiapoptotic factor Bcl-2. Interestingly, overexpression of Bcl-2 in HeLa cells is accompanied by increased levels of telomerase activity; moreover, downregulation of Bcl-2 in the cytotoxic T-cell line, CTLL-2, inhibits telomerase activity with no detectable apoptosis (Mandal & Kumar, 1997). Similarly, in PC12 cells overexpressing Bcl-2, levels of telomerase activity are increased by twofold (Fu *et al.*, 1999). However, in Jurkat T-cells, Bcl-2 has no effect on telomerase activity or telomere length (Johnson *et al.*, 1999). These apparently contradictory results indicate that it will be necessary to evaluate the link between Bcl-2 and telomerase regulation along with the regulation of other cell cycle and apoptosis factors in different human cancer cells.

c-myc is a key regulator of both cell proliferation and apoptosis in normal and cancer cells. Overexpression of c-myc in normal human mammary epithelial cells lacking telomerase activity results in the induction of hTERT mRNA and the stimulation of telomerase activity (Wang *et al.*, 1998). This stimulation of hTERT expression is due to transcriptional activation of the hTERT gene, whose promoter contains a number of conserved MYC-binding sequences (Cong *et al.*, 1999; Greenberg *et al.*, 1999; Horikawa *et al.*, 1999; Takakura *et al.*, 1999; Wu *et al.*, 1999). It is tempting to speculate that the elevated expression of MYC in numerous tumors may be responsible for the telomerase activity in these tumors (Greider, 1999). The link between MYC and telomerase is supported by studies in which the inhibition of MYC expression in leukemic cell lines inhibits telomerase activity (Fujimoto & Takahashi, 1997). However, the role of MYC in cellular immortalization is not simply a consequence of its effect on telomerase activation. In culture, rat embryonic fibroblasts are transformed efficiently by the cooperation of immortalizing proteins such as MYC and activated RAS (H-RAS^{G12V}). The substitution of MYC by mTERT (mouse TERT) in such a cooperation assay is not sufficient to immortalize primary rat cells, indicating that TERT is not equivalent to MYC in cellular immortalization (Greenberg *et al.*, 1999).

The regulation of apoptosis is complex and involves a number of survival genes, like Bcl-2, as well as killer genes, such as interleukin-1β-converting enzyme (ICE) and other key cellular proteases, the caspases (Adams & Cory, 1998; Thornberry & Lazebnik, 1998; Wang, 1995). In addition, genes such as p53, Rb, p21, and c-myc, which control cell cycle progression and checkpoints, often are up-regulated in cells undergoing apoptosis (Duttaroy *et al.*, 1997; Evan & Littlewood, 1998; Pandey & Wang, 1995; Wang, 1997). It will be important to delineate the role of telomerase and telomere maintenance in cellular resistance to apoptosis in various cell types. The next step will be to evaluate the molecular mechanisms of resistance, through analysis of the expression and activity of Bcl-2, ICE and other caspases, p53, Rb, p21, c-myc, and other genes.

VI. Potential Use of Telomerase Inhibition and Induction of Apoptosis as an Effective Anticancer Therapy

Studies with immortal human cells indicate that the expression of antisense telomerase RNA leads to telomere shortening and cell death (Feng *et al.*, 1995). A study reveals that antisense telomerase treatment of U251-MG human glioma cells induces two distinct responses: apoptosis and differentiation (Kondo *et al.*, 1998b). The U251-MG transfectants that apoptose express a high level of ICE. In a similar report, an antisense directed against telomerase RNA inhibits telomerase activity and induces apoptosis in human glioma cells in culture and *in vivo* in nude mice (Kondo *et al.*, 1998a). In further support of a link between telomerase activity and apoptosis, treatment of the cisplatin-resistant U251- MG human glioblastoma cell line with an antisense telomerase expression vector decreases telomerase activity and increases susceptibility to cisplatin-induced apoptotic cell death (Kondo *et al.*, Kondo, Tanaka, Haqqi, Barna, & Cowell, 1998c). These studies indicate that telomere integrity is compromised during apoptosis and that inhibition of telomerase may sensitize cells resistant to anticancer agents such as cisplatin. In addition, late generation mice in which telomerase RNA is inactivated genetically exhibit defective spermatogenesis, with increased programmed cell death (Lee *et al.*, 1998). These studies indicate that cells defective in telomerase, due to germ line targeting of the telomerase RNA component, can die by apoptosis.

Telomerase inhibitors that target hTERT have been reported (Hahn *et al.*, 1999b; Zhang *et al.*, 1999). The effects of inhibiting hTERT in various human cancer cell lines by the expression of dominant negative mutants include inhibition of telomerase activity, telomere loss, chromosome damage, apoptosis, and cell death. Apoptosis of cells with initially shorter telomeres (2–3 versus 3–5 kb) occurs more rapidly (Hahn *et al.*, 1999b; Zhang *et al.*, 1999). Although telomerase inhibition in cells with long telomeres (10–12 kb) results in telomere shortening, no apoptosis occurs (Zhang *et al.*, 1999). When the telomere length in these cells approaches 4 kb, the dominant-negative protein is lost, with the subsequent reactivation of telomerase activity and maintenance of telomere length. Interestingly, all the cell lines examined in these studies are p53-defective, indicating that the apoptosis that occurs is p53-independent. These studies convincingly indicate that p53-deficient cells in which telomerase is inhibited can die by apoptosis and suggest that tumors with short telomeres may be effectively and rapidly killed by inhibitors of telomerase. Moreover, there are a number of issues to consider in the development of telomerase inhibitors (Autexier,

1999). For instance, induction of the ALT pathway for telomere maintenance in cancer cells undergoing antitelomerase therapy could lead to resistance to telomerase inhibitors.

The evidence indicating a role for telomeres and telomerase in cellular resistance to apoptosis, as well as data showing that inhibition of telomerase can result in apoptosis, suggests an intimate link between telomeres, telomerase, and apoptosis. However, studies indicate a complex relationship between cell cycle, apoptosis, and telomerase regulation. The challenge of future experimentation will be to address and understand this complexity. Only then will it be possible to evaluate the consequences of antitelomerase therapies in various cell types.

VII. Concluding Remarks

The notion that a gene-directed program has evolved to remove extra cells during development, in order to optimize the pattern and shape of each organ, may seem counter-intuitive. However, this process of creating more cells than necessary at the start and then getting rid of them later offers precise control. Now, over a quarter century since the initial discovery of apoptosis, a plethora of information from our own and other laboratories suggests that apoptosis is regulated by the interplay of two opposing "Yin–Yang" families of genes. Members of families that function to tilt the balance toward killing are termed "death" genes, whereas those that promote survival are termed "antideath" genes. The final cell demise may be the result of up-regulation of "death" gene expression and/or down-regulation of "anti-death" gene expression. In certain cases, a lack of key proapoptotic gene expression results in resistance to apoptosis (as seen in senescent fibroblasts). Cells with defective cell cycle checkpoints and/or resistance to apoptosis can undergo unchecked proliferation. The accumulation of dysfunctional or potentially neoplastic cells within a tissue ultimately can compromise organ function or result in oncogenesis. On the other hand, excessive apoptosis is undesirable as well; examples include massive cell depletion of neurons, cardiomyocytes, or skeletal myotubes during neurodegenerative diseases, cardiac abnormalities, or muscle atrophy.

In this respect, then, it is important to understand that apoptosis itself is neither "good" nor "bad" for the aging individual, but that it must be regulated and balanced. The health of tissues, and indeed of organisms, thus depends upon the balance between controlled expression of both "death" and "anti-death" genes. This balance must be integrated with the many other signals that operate to accomplish normal cellular function. The balance of signaling pathways for cellular maintenance, replication, and apoptosis will be the focus of future research, which must also explain why, during aging, the apoptotic program is dysregulated and how this dysregulation precipitates the disability and degeneration associated with the aging process.

Acknowledgments

The authors thank Mr. Alan N. Bloch for proofreading this manuscript. The work is supported by grants to Eugenia Wang from the National Institute on Aging of the National Institutes of Health (R01AG09278) and to Dr. Chantal Autexier from the Medical Research Council of Canada (MT14026).

References

Adams, J. M., & Cory, S. (1998). The Bcl-2 protein family: arbiters of cell survival. *Science, 281*, 1322–1326.

Akiyama, M., Horiguchi-Yamada, J., Saito, S., Hoshi, Y., Yamada, O., Mizoguchi, H., & Yamada, H. (1999). Cytostatic concentrations of anticancer agents do not affect telomerase activity of leukaemic cells *in vitro*. *European Journal of Cancer, 35*, 309–315.

Autexier, C. (1999). Telomerase as a possible target for anticancer therapy. *Chemistry and Biology, 6*, R299–R303.

Autexier, C., & Greider, C. W. (1996). Telomerase and cancer: revisiting the telomere hypothesis. *Trends in Biochemical Science, 21*, 387–391.

Barr, P. J., & Tomei, L. D. (1994). Apoptosis and its role in human disease. *Biotechnology, 12*, 487–493.

Beattie, T. L., Zhou, W., Robinson, M. O., & Harrington, L. (1998). Reconstitution of human telomerase activity *in vitro*. *Current Biology, 8*, 177–180.

Bodnar, A. G., Ouellette, M., Frolkis, M., Holt, S. E., Chiu, C.-P., Morin, G. B., Harley, C. B., Shay, J. W., Lichtensteiner, S., & Wright, W. E. (1998). Extension of life-span by introduction of telomerase into normal human cells. *Science, 279*, 349–352.

Boldin, M. P., Goncharov, T. M., Goltsev, Y. V., & Wallach, D. (1996). Involvement of MACH, a novel MORT1/FADD-interacting protease, in Fas/APO–1-and TNF receptor-induced cell death. *Cell, 85*, 803–815.

Caelles, C., Helmberg, A., & Karin, M. (1994). p53-dependent apoptosis in the absence of transcriptioinal activation. *Nature, 370*, 220–223.

Cai, Y., Yang, J., & Jones, D. P. (1998). Mitochondrial control of apoptosis: the role of cytochrome c. *Biochimica et Biophysica Acta, 1366*, 139–149.

Campisi, J. (1996). Replicative senescence: an old lives tale? *Cell, 84*, 497–500.

Carrichio, R., Kovalenko, D., Kaufmann, W. K., & Cohen, P. L. (1999). Apoptosis provoked by the oxidative stress inducer menadione (Vitamin K(3)) is mediated by the Fas/Fas ligand system. *Clinical Immunology, 93*, 65–74.

Casciola-Rosen, L., Nicholson, D. W., Chong, T., Rowan, K. R., Thornberry, N. A., Miller, D. K., & Rosen, A. (1996). Apopain/CPP32 cleaves proteins that are essential for cellular repair: a fundamental principle of apoptotic death. *Journal of Experimental Medicine, 183,* 1957–1964.

Chen, Q., & Ames, B. N. (1994). Senescence-like growth arrest induced by hydrogen peroxide in human diploid fibroblast F65 cells. *Proceedings of the National Academy of Sciences of the USA, 91,* 4130–4134.

Cohen, G. M. (1997). Caspases: The executioners of apoptosis. *Biochemical Journal, 326,* 1–16.

Colgin, L. M., & Reddel, R. R. (1999). Telomere maintenance mechanisms and cellular immortalisation. *Current Opinion in Genetics and Development, 9,* 97–103.

Cong, Y.-S., Wen, J., & Bacchetti, S. (1999). The human telomerase catalytic subunit hTERT: organization of the gene and characterization of the promoter. *Human Molecular Genetics, 8,* 137–142.

Counter, C. M., Meyerson, M., Eaton, E. N., Ellisen, L. W., Dickinson Caddle, S., Haber, D. A., & Weinberg, R. A. (1998). Telomerase activity is restored in human cells by ectopic expression of hTERT (hEST2), the catalytic subunit of telomerase. *Oncogene, 16,* 1217–1222.

de Haan, J. B., Cristiano, F., Iannello, R., Bladler, C., Kelner, M., & Kola, I. (1995). Elevation in the ratio of Cu/Zn-superoxide dismutase to glutathione peroxidase activity induces features of cellular senescence, and this effect is mediated by hydrogen peroxide. *Human Molecular Genetics, 5,* 283–292.

Deng, C., Zhang, P., Harper, J. W., Elledge, S. J., & Leder, P. (1995). Mice lacking p21/PCII/WAF1 undergo normal development, but are defective in G1 checkpoint control. *Cell, 82,* 675–684.

Diller, L., Kassel, J., Nelson, C. E., Gryka, M. A., Litwak, G., Gebhardt, M., Bressac, B., Ozturk, M., Baker, S. J., Vogelstein, B., & Friend, S. H. (1990). p53 functions as a cell cycle control protein in osteosarcomas. *Molecular and Cellular Biology, 10,* 5772–5781.

Dimri, G. P., Lee, X., Basile, G., Acosta, M., Scott, G., Roskelley, C., Medrano, E. E., Linskens, M., Rubelj, I., Pereira-Smith, O., Peacocke, M., & Campisi, J. (1995). A biomarker that identifies senescent human cells in culture and in aging skin *in vivo*. *Proceedings of the National Academy of Sciences of the USA, 92,* 9363–9367.

Duttaroy, A., Qian, J.-F., Smith, J. S., & Wang, E. (1997). Up-regulated P21^{CIP1} expression is part of the regulation quantitatively controlling serum deprivation-induced apoptosis. *Journal of Cellular Biochemistry, 64,* 434–446.

El-Deiry, W. S., Kern, S. E., Pietenpol, J. A., Kinzler, K. W., & Vogelstein, B. (1992). Definition of a consensus binding site for p53. *Nature Genetics, 1,* 45–49.

El-Deiry, W. S., Tokino, T., Velculencu, V. E., Levy, D. B., Parsons, R., Trent, J. M., Lin, D., Mercer, E. W., Kinzler, K. W., & Vogelstein, B. (1993). WAF1, a potential mediator of p53 tumour suppression. *Cell, 71,* 817–825.

Evan, G., & Littlewood, T. (1998). A matter of life and cell death. *Science, 281,* 1317–1322.

Feng, J., Funk, W. D., Wang, S.-S., Weinrich, S. L., Avilion, A. A., Chiu, C.-P., Adams, R. R., Chang, E., Allsopp, R. C., Yu, J., Le, S., West, M. D., Harley, C. B., Andrews, W. H., Greider, C. W., & Villeponteau, B. (1995). The human telomerase RNA component. *Science, 269,* 1236–1241.

Fernandes-Alnemri, T., Armstrong, R. C., Krebs, J., Srinivasula, S. M., Wang, L., Bullrich, F., Fritz, L. C., Trapani, J. A., Tomaselli, K. J., Litwack, G., & Alnemri, E. S. (1996). *In vitro* activation of CPP32 and Mch3 by Mch4, a novel human apoptotic cysteine protease containing two FADD-like domains. *Proceedings of the National Academy of Sciences of the USA, 93,* 7464–7469.

Fornace, A. J., Nebert, D. W., Hollander, M. C., Luethy, J. D., Papathanasiou, M., Fargnoli, J., & Holbrook, N. J. (1989). Mammalian genes coordinately regulated by growth arrest signals and DNA-damaging agents. *Molecular and Cellular Biology, 9,* 4196–4203.

Franceschi, C., Monti, D., & Scarfi, M. R. (1992). Genomic instability and aging. *Annals of the New York Academy of Sciences, 663,* 4–16.

Fu, W., Begley, J. G., Killen, M. W., & Mattson, M. P. (1999). Anti-apoptotic role of telomerase in pheochromocytoma cells.

Journal of Biological Chemistry, 274, 7264–7271.

Fujimoto, K., & Takahashi, M. (1997). Telomerase activity in human leukemic cell lines is inhibited by antisense pentadecadeoxynucleotides targeted against c-myc mRNA. *Biochemical and Biophysical Research Communications, 241,* 775–781.

Gottlieb, R. A., Burleson, K. O., Kloner, R. A., Babior, B. M., & Engler, R. L. (1994). Reperfusion injury induces apoptosis in rabbit cardiomyocytes. *Journal of Clinical Investigation, 94,* 1621–1628.

Grasl-Kraupp, B., Bursh, W., & Ruttkay-Nedecky, B. (1994). Food restriction eliminates preneoplastic cells through apoptosis and antagonizes carcinogenesis in rat liver. *Proceedings of the National Academy of Sciences of the USA, 91,* 9995–9999.

Greenberg, R. A., O'Hagan, R. C., Deng, H., Xiao, Q., Hann, S. R., Adams, R. R., Lichtensteiner, S., Chin, L., Morin, G. B., & DePinho, R. A. (1999). Telomerase reverse transcriptase gene is a direct target of c-Myc but is not functionally equivalent in cellular transformation. *Oncogene, 18,* 1219–1226.

Greider, C. W. (1996). Telomere length regulation. *Annual Review of Biochemistry, 65,* 337–365.

Greider, C. W. (1999). Telomerase activation: one step on the road to cancer. *Trends in Genetics, 15,* 109–112.

Gross, A., McDonnell, J. M., & Korsmeyer, S. J. (1999). BCL-2 family members and the mitochondria in apoptosis. *Genes and Development, 13,* 1899–1911.

Guillouf, A., Grana, X., Selvakumaran, M., De Luca, X. A., Giordano, A., Hoffman, B., & Liebermann, D. A. (1995). Dissection of the genetic programs of p53-mediated G1 growth arrest and apoptosis: blocking p53-induced apoptosis unmasks G1 arrest. *Blood, 85,* 2691–2698.

Hadler, S., Negrini, M., Monne, M., Sabbioni, S., & Croce, C. M. (1994). Down regulation of bcl-2 by p53 in breast cancer cells. *Cancer Research, 54,* 2095–2097.

Hahn, W. C., Counter, C. M., Lundberg, A. S., Beijersbergen, R. L., Brooks, M. W., & Weinberg, R. A. (1999a). Creation of human tumour cells with defined genetic elements. *Nature, 400,* 464–468.

Hahn, W. C., Stewart, S. A., Brooks, M. W., York, S. G., Eaton, E., Kurachi, A., Beijersbergen, R. L., Knoll, J. H. M., Meyerson, M., & Weinberg, R. A. (1999b). Inhibition of telomerase limits the growth of human cancer cells. *Nature Medicine, 5,* 1164–1170.

Halestrap, A. P., Kerr, P. M., Javadov, S., & Woodfield, K. Y. (1998). Elucidating the molecular mechanism of the permeability transition pore and its role in reperfusion injury in the heart. *Biochimica et Biophysica Acta, 1366,* 79–94.

Hampton, M. B., Fadeel, B., & Orrenius, S. (1998). Redox regulation of the caspases during apoptosis. *Annals of the New York Academy of Sciences, 854,* 328–335.

Harley, C. B. (1991). Telomere loss: mitotic clock or genetic time bomb? *Mutation Research, 256,* 271–282.

Haunstetter, A., & Izumo, S. (1998). Apopsosis: basic mechanisms and implications for cardiovascular disease. *Circulation Research, 82,* 1111–1129.

Haupt, Y., Rowan, S., Shaulian, E., Vousden, K. H., & Oren, M. (1995). Induction of apoptosis in HeLa cells by trans-activation with deficient p53. *Genes and Development, 8,* 2170–2183.

Hayflick, L. (1965). The limited *in vitro* lifetime of human diploid cell strains. *Experimental Cell Research, 37,* 614–636.

Hearse, D. J. (1977). Reperfusion of ischaemic myocardium. *Journal of Molecular and Cellular Cardiology, 9,* 607–616.

Heintz, N. (1993). Cell death and the cell cycle: a relationship between transformation and neurodegeneration? *Trends in Biochemical Sciences, 18,* 157–159.

Holt, S. E., Glinsky, V. V., Ivanova, A. B., & Glinsky, G. V. (1999). Resistance to apoptosis in human cells conferred by telomerase function and telomere stability. *Molecular Carcinogenesis, 25,* 241–248.

Horikawa, I., Cable, P. L., Afshari, C., & Barrett, J. C. (1999). Cloning and characterization of the promoter region of *human telomerase reverse transcriptase gene.* Cancer Research, 59, 826–830.

Ishibashi, T., & Lippard, S. (1998). Telomere loss in cells treated with cisplatin. *Proceedings of the National Academy of Science of the USA, 95*, 4219–4223.

James, S. J., & Muskhelishvili, L. (1994). Rates of apoptosis and proliferation vary with caloric intake, and may influence incidence of spontaneous hepatoma in C57B/6 x C3HF1 mice. *Cancer Research, 65*, 5508–5510.

Janicke, R. U., Walker, P. A., Lin, X. Y., & Porter, A. G. (1996). Specific cleavage of the retinoblastoma protein by an ICE-like protease in apoptosis. *EMBO Journal, 15*, 6969–6978.

Jiang, X.-R., Jimenez, G., Chang, E., Frolkis, M., Kusler, B., Sage, M., Beeche, M., Bodnar, A. G., Wahl, G. M., Tisty, T. D., & Chiu, C.-P. (1999). Telomerase expression in human somatic cells does not induce changes associated with a transformed phenotype. *Nature Genetics, 21*, 111–114.

Johnson, V. L., Cooper, I. R., Jenkins, J. R., & Chow, S. C. (1999). Effects of differential overexpression of Bcl-2 on apoptosis, proliferation, and telomerase activity in Jurkat T cells. *Experimental Cell Research, 251*, 175–184.

Kajstura, J., Cheng, W., Reiss, K., Sonnenblick, E. H., Olivetti, G., & Anversa, P. (1995). Apoptotic and necrotic myocyte cell death are independent contributing variables of infarct size in rats. *Circulation, 92*, 772–777.

Karlseder, J., Broccoli, D., Dai, Y., Hardy, S., & de Lange, T. (1999). P53- and ATM-dependent apoptosis induced by telomeres lacking TRF2. *Science, 283*, 1321–1325.

Kastan, M. B., Onyekwere, O., Sidransky, D., Vogelstein, B., & Craig, R. W. (1991). Participation of p53 protein in the cellular response to DNA damage. *Cancer Research, 51*, 6304–6311.

Katz, A. D. (Ed.) (1992). *Physiology of the heart* (2nd ed.). New York: McGraw-Hill.

Kern, S. E., Kinzler, K. W., Bruskin, A., Jarosz, D., Friedman, P., Prives, C., & Vogelstein, B. (1991). Identification of p53 as a sequence-specific DNA binding protein. *Science, 252*, 1708–1711.

Kerr, J. F., Wyllie, A. H., & Currie, A. R. (1972). Apoptosis: a basic biological phenomenon with wide-ranging implications in tissue kinetics. *British Journal of Cancer, 26*, 239–257.

Kiyono, T., Foster, S. A., Koop, J. I., McDougall, J. K., Galloway, D. A., & Klingelhutz, A. J. (1998). Both Rb/p16[INK4a] inactivation and telomerase activity are required to immortalize human epithelial cells. *Nature, 396*, 84–88.

Kluck, R. M., Bossy-Wetzel, E., Green, D. R., & Newmeyer, D. D. (1997). The release of cytochrome c from mitochondria: a primary site for Bcl-2 regulation of apoptosis. *Science, 275*, 1132–1136.

Kondo, S., Kondo, Y., Li, G., Silverman, R. H., & Cowell, J. K. (1998a). Targeted therapy of human malignant glioma in a mouse model by 2–5A antisense directed against telomerase RNA. *Oncogene, 16*, 3323–3330.

Kondo, S., Tanaka, Y., Kondo, Y., Hitomi, M., Barnett, G. H., Ishizaka, Y., Liu, J., Haqqi, T., Nishiyama, A., Villeponteau, B., Cowell, J. K., & Barna, B. P. (1998). Antisense telomerase treatment: induction of two distinct pathways, apoptosis and differentiation. *FASEB Journal, 12*, 801–811.

Kondo, Y., Kondo, S., Tanaka, Y., Haqqi, T., Barna, B. P., & Cowell, J. K. (1998). Inhibition of telomerase increases the susceptibility of human malignant glioblastoma cells to cisplatin-induced apoptosis. *Oncogene, 16*, 2243–2248.

Kroemer, G., Zamzami, N., & Susin, S. A. (1997). Mitochondrial control of apoptosis. *Immunology Today, 18*, 45–51.

Kuida, K., Zheng, T. S., Na, S., Kuan, C., Yang, D., Karasuyama, H., Rakic, P., & Flavell, R. A. (1996). Decreased apoptosis in the brain and premature lethality in CPP32-deficient mice. *Nature, 384*, 368–372.

Lazebnik, Y. A., Kaufmann, S. H., Desnoyers, S., Poirier, G. G., & Earnshaw, W. C. (1994). Cleavage of poly(ADP-ribose) polymerase by a proteinase with properties like ICE. *Nature, 371*, 346–347.

Lee, H.-W., Blasco, M. A., Gottlieb, G. J., Horner, J. W., Greider, C. W., & DePinho, R. A. (1998). Essential role of mouse telomerase in highly proliferative organs. *Nature, 392*, 569–574.

Li, P., Nijhawan, D., Budihardjo, I., Srinivasula, S. M., Ahmad, M., Alnemri, E. S., & Wang, X. (1997). Cytochrome c and ATP-dependent formation of Apaf–1/Caspase–9 complex initiates an apoptotic protease cascade. *Cell*, *91*, 479–489.

Liu, X., Kim, C. N., Yang, J., Jemmerson, R., & Wang, X. (1996). Induction of apoptotic program in cell-free extracts: requirement for dATP and cytochrome c. *Cell*, *86*, 147–157.

Liu, X., Zou, H., Slaughter, C., & Wang, X. (1997). DFF, a heterodimeric protein that functions downstream of caspase–3 to trigger DNA fragmentation during apoptosis. *Cell*, *89*, 175–184.

Majno, G., & Joris, I. (1995). Apoptosis, oncosis, and necrosis: an overview of cell death. *American Journal of Pathology*, *146*, 3–15.

Mandal, M., & Kumar, R. (1997). Bcl-2 modulates telomerase activity. *Journal of Biological Chemistry*, *272*, 14183–14187.

Martin, S. J., O'Brien, G. A., Nishioka, W. J., McGahon, A. J., Mahboubi, A., Saido, T. C., & Green, D. R. (1995). Proteolysis of fodrin (non-erythroid spectrin) during apoptosis. *Journal of Biological Chemistry*, *270*, 6425–6428.

Marzo, I., Brenner, C., Zamzami, N., Jurgensmeier, J. M., Susin, S. A., Vieira, H. L. A., Prevost, M. C., Xie, Z., Matsuyama, S., Reed, J. C., & Kroemer, G. (1998). Bax and adenine nucleotide translocator cooperate in the mitochondrial control of apoptosis. *Science*, *281*, 2027–2031.

Mashima, T., Naito, M., Fujita, N., Noguchi, K., & Tsuruo, T. (1995). Identification of actin as a substrate of ICE and an ICE-like protease, and involvement of an ICE-like protease but not ICE in VP-16-induced U937 apoptosis. *Biochemical and Biophysical Research Communications*, *217*, 1185–1192.

Maxwell, S. A., Capp, D., & Acosta, S. A. (1997). Telomerase activity in immortalized endothelial cells undergoing p53-mediated apoptosis. *Biochemical and Biophysical Research Communications*, *241*, 642–645.

Miura, M., Zhu, H., Rotello, R., Hartwieg, E. A., & Yuan, J. (1993). Induction of apoptosis in fibroblasts by IL-1 beta-converting enyzme, a mammalian homolog of the *C. elegans cell death gene*, *ced-3*. *Cell*, *75*, 653–660.

Miyashita, T., Krajewski, S., Krajewska, M., Wang, H. G., Lin, H. K., Hoffman, B., Lieberman, D., & Reed, J. C. (1994). Tumour suppressor p53 is a regulator of bcl-2 and bax gene expression *in vitro* and *in vivo*. *Oncogene*, *9*, 1799–1805.

Miyashita, T., & Reed, J. C. (1995). Tumor suppressor p53 is a direct transcriptional activator of the human bax gene. *Cell*, *80*, 293–299.

Morales, C. P., Holt, S. E., Ouellette, M., Kaur, K. J., Yan, Y., Wilson, K. S., White, M. A., Wright, W. E., & Shay, J. W. (1999). Absence of cancer-associated changes in human fibroblasts immortalized with telomerase. *Nature Genetics*, *21*, 115–118.

Morin, G. B. (1989). The human telomere terminal transferase enzyme is a ribonucleoprotein that synthesizes TTAGGG repeats. *Cell*, *59*, 521–529.

Mukhopadhyay, T., Multani, A. S., Roth, J. A., & Pathak, S. (1998). Reduced telomeric signals and increased telomeric associations in human lung cancer cell lines undergoing p53-mediated apoptosis. *Oncogene*, *17*, 901–906.

Multani, A. S., Chun, L., Ozen, M., Imam, A. S., Wallace, S., & Pathak, S. (1999). Cell-killing by paclitaxel in a metastatic murine melanoma cell line is mediated by extensive telomere erosion with no decrease in telomerase activity. *Oncology Reports*, *6*, 39–44.

Muzio, M., Chinnaiyan, A. M., Kischkel, F. C., O'Rourke, K., Shevchenko, A., Ni, J., Scaffidi, C., Bretz, J. D., Zhang, M., Gentz, R., Mann, M., Krammer, P. H., Peter, M. E., & Dixit, V. M. (1996). FLICE, a novel FADD-homologous ICE/CED-3-like protease, is recruited to the CD96 (Fas/APO-1) death-inducing signaling complex. *Cell*, *85*, 817–827.

Nakamura, T. M., Morin, G. B., Chapman, K. B., Weinrich, S. L., Andrews, W. H., Lingner, J., Harley, C. B., & Cech, T. R. (1997). Telomerase catalytic subunit homologs from fission: yeast and human. *Science*, *277*, 955–959.

Nugent, C. I., & Lundblad, V. (1998). The telomerase reverse transcriptase: components and regulation. *Genes and Development, 12,* 1073–1085.

Orth, K., Chinnaiyan, A. M., Garg, M., Froelich, C. J., & Dixit, V. M. (1996). The CED-3/ICE-like protease Mch2 is activated during apoptosis, and cleaves the death substrate lamin A. *Journal of Biological Chemistry, 271,* 16443–16446.

Pandey, S., & Wang, E. (1995). Cells *en route* to apoptosis are characterized by the upregulation of c-fos, c-myc, c-jun, cdc2, and RB phosphorylation, resembling events of early cell-cycle traverse. *Journal of Cellular Biochemistry, 58,* 135–150.

Pandita, T. K., Benvenuto, J. A., Shay, J. W., Pandita, R. K., Rakovitch, E., Geard, C. R., Antman, K. H., & Newman, R. A. (1997). Effect of penclomedine (NSC-338720) on telomere fusions, chromatin blebbing, and cell viability with and without telomerase activity and abrogated p53 function. *Biochemical Pharmacology, 53,* 409–415.

Pardue, M.-L., & DeBaryshe, P. G. (1999). Telomeres and telomerase: more than the end of the line. *Chromosoma, 108,* 73–82.

Pathak, S., Dave, B. J., & Gagos, S. (1994a). Chromosome alterations in cancer development and apoptosis. *In Vivo, 8,* 843–850.

Pathak, S., Risin, S., Brown, N., & Berry, K. (1994b). Telomeric association of chromosomes is an early manifestation of programmed cell death. *International Journal of Oncology, 4,* 323–328.

Price, C. M. (1999). Telomeres and telomerase: broad effects on cell growth. *Current Opinion in Genetics and Development, 9,* 218–224.

Salvesen, G. S., & Dixit, V. M. (1997). Caspases: intracellular signaling by proteolysis. *Cell, 91,* 443–446.

Shay, J. W., & Bacchetti, S. (1997). A survey of telomerase activity in human cancer. *European Journal of Cancer, 33,* 787–791.

Shimizu, S., Eguchi, Y., Kamiike, W., Matsuda, H., & Tsujimoto, Y. (1996). Bcl-2 expression prevents activation of the ICE protease cascade. *Oncogene, 12,* 2251–2257.

Stridh, H., Kimland, M., Jones, D. P., Orrenius, S., & Hampton, M. B. (1998). Cytochrome c release and caspase activation in hydrogen peroxide- and tributylin-induced apoptosis. *FEBS Letters, 429,* 351–355.

Takakura, M., Kyo, S., Kanaya, T., Hirano, H., Takeda, J., Yutsudo, M., & Inoue, M. (1999). Cloning of human telomerase catalytic subunit (hTERT) gene promoter and identification of proximal core promoter sequences essential for transcriptional activation in immortalized and cancer cells. *Cancer Research, 59,* 551–557.

Thornberry, N. A., & Lazebnik, Y. (1998). Caspases: enemies within. *Science, 281,* 1312–1316.

Vaziri, H., & Benchimol, S. (1996). From telomere loss to p53 induction and activation of a DNA-damage pathway at senescence: the telomere loss/DNA damage model of cell aging. *Experimental Gerontology, 31,* 295–301.

Vaziri, H., & Benchimol, S. (1998). Reconstitution of telomerase activity in normal human cells leads to elongation of telomeres and extended replicative life span. *Current Biology, 8,* 279–282.

Vaziri, H., Squire, J. A., Pandita, T. K., Bradley, G., Kuba, R. M., Zhang, H., Gulyas, S., Hill, R. P., Nolan, G. P., & Benchimol, S. (1999). Analysis of genomic integrity and p53-dependent G_1 checkpoint in telomerase-induced extended-life-span human fibroblasts. *Molecular and Cell Biology, 19,* 2373–2379.

Villa, P., Kaufmann, S. H., & Earnshaw, W. C. (1997). Caspases and caspase inhibitors. *Trends in Biochemical Science, 22,* 388–393.

Wang, E. (1995). Senescent human fibroblasts resist programmed cell death, and failure to suppress *bcl-2* is involved. *Cancer Research, 55,* 2284–2292.

Wang, E. (1997). Regulation of apoptosis resistance and ontogeny of age-dependent diseases. *Experimental Gerontology, 32,* 471–484.

Wang, J., Xie, L. Y., Allan, S., Beach, D., & Hannon, G. J. (1998). Myc activates telomerase. *Genes and Development, 12,* 1769–1774.

Warner, H. R., Fernandes, G., & Wang, E. (1995). A unifying hypothesis to explain the retardation of aging and tumorigenesis by caloric restriction. *Journal of Gerontology, 50A*, B107–109.

Warner, H. R., Hodes, R. J., & Pocinki, K. (1997). What does cell death have to do with aging? *Journal of the American Geriatrics Society, 45*, 1140–1146.

Weinrich, S. L., Pruzan, R., Ma, L., Ouellette, M., Tesmer, V. M., Holt, S. E., Bodnar, A. G., Lichtensteiner, S., Kim, N. W., Trager, J. B., Taylor, R. D., Carlos, R., Andrews, W. H., Wright, W. E., Shay, J. W., Harley, C. B., & Morin, G. B. (1997). Reconstitution of human telomerase with the template RNA component hTR and the catalytic protein subunit hTRT. *Nature Genetics, 17*, 498–502.

Weitzman, J. B., & Yaniv, M. (1999). Rebuilding the road to cancer. *Nature, 400*, 401–402.

Wellinger, R. J., & Sen, D. (1997). The DNA structures at the ends of eukaryotic chromosomes. *European Journal of Cancer, 33*, 735–749.

Wright, W. E., Brasiskyte, D., Piatyszek, M. A., & Shay, J. W. (1996). Experimental elongation of telomeres in immortal human cells extends the lifespan of immortal x normal cell hybrids. *EMBO Journal, 15*, 1734–1741.

Wu, K.-J., Grandori, C., Amacker, M., Simon-Vermot, N., Polack, A., Lingner, J., & Dalla-Favera, R. (1999). Direct activation of *TERT* transcription by c-MYC. *Nature Genetics, 21*, 220–224.

Wyllie, A. H. (1980). Glucocorticoid-induced thymocyte apoptosis is associated with endogenous endonuclease activation. *Nature, 284*, 555–556.

Xiong, Y., Hannon, G. J., Zhang, H., Casso, D., Kobayashi, R., & Beach, D. (1993). p21 is a universal inhibitor of cyclin kinases. *Nature, 366*, 701–704.

Yin, Y., Terauchi, Y., Solomon, G. G., Aizawa, S., Rangarajan, P. N., Yazaki, Y., Kadowaki, T., & Barrett, J. C. (1998). Involvement of p85 in p53-dependent apoptotic response to oxidative stress. *Nature, 391*, 707–710.

Yonish-Rouach, E. (1996). The p53 tumour suppressor gene: a mediator of G_1 growth arrest and of apoptosis. *Experientia, 52*, 1001–1007.

Yuan, J., Shaham, S., Ledoux, S., Ellis, H. M., & Horvitz, H. R. (1993). The *C. elegans cell death gene* ced-3 encodes a protein similar to mammalian interleukin-1 beta-converting enzyme. *Cell, 75*, 653–660.

Zamzami, N., Brenner, C., Marzo, I., Susin, S. A., & Kroemer, G. (1998). Subcellular and submitochondrial mode of action of Bcl-2-like oncoproteins. *Oncogene, 16*, 2265–2282.

Zhang, X., Mar, V., Harrington, L., & Robinson, M. O. (1999). Telomere shortening and apoptosis in telomerase-inhibited human tumor cells. *Genes and Development, 13*, 2388–2399.

Zoratti, M., & Szabò, I. (1995). The mitochondrial permeability transition. *Biochimica et Biophysica Acta, 1241*, 139–176.

Part Three

Systemic Factors Influencing Organismic Aging

Edited by
Charles V. Mobbs

Ten

Effects of Aging on the Sympathoadrenal System

James B. Young

I. Introduction

Homeostatic regulation changes as a function of age. Because the sympathetic nervous system (SNS) plays a critically important role in the maintenance of homeostasis, age-related changes also must be taking place in the functioning of this portion of the nervous system. In his classic monograph *The Wisdom of the Body*, Cannon discussed the evidence available at that time for altered regulation of body temperature, blood sugar, and acid–base balance in elderly individuals (Cannon, 1939). Since then, the contributions of catecholamines, in general, and the SNS and adrenal medulla, in particular, to homeostatic regulation are better understood and more widely appreciated (Young & Landsberg, 1998).

Nevertheless, the impact of age on SNS and adrenal medullary function is not completely understood, having been variously attributed to changes in central nervous system regulation, the anatomy or function of the peripheral nerves themselves, or end-organ responses to catecholamines or other neurotransmitters.

Whereas studies in animals tend to emphasize morphological changes in the SNS with age, those in human subjects focus upon changes in the functional state of sympathetic nerves. Because the structure and function of the SNS in adult life is dependent, in part, upon how the SNS developed at the beginning, increasing evidence points to the lasting effects of intrauterine and neonatal events in the formation of the SNS in individual animals. Finally, evidence of age-related differences in the sympathetic innervation of the heart and sweat glands will be considered in detail.

II. Overview of the Sympathoadrenal System

A. Structure and Organization of the Sympathoadrenal System

The adrenal medulla and the SNS make up an anatomical and physiological unit that is often referred to as the *sympathoadrenal system*. The central neural connections involved in regulating sympathoadrenal outflow are complex and only partially characterized. Preganglionic neurons located in four topographically distinct nuclei within the intermediate spinal gray matter, including the intermediolateral cell column, ultimately innervate the postganglionic sympathetic neurons in the paravertebral and preaortic sympathetic ganglia (Cabot, 1990). These neurons receive inputs directly from several regions of the central nervous system (CNS), including the rostral ventrolateral medulla, the caudal raphe nuclei, and the hypothalamus, particularly the paraventricular nucleus and the lateral hypothalamic area (Guyenet, 1990). The various brain stem centers that innervate the sympathetic preganglionic neurons are, furthermore, interconnected. The precise anatomical pathways involved and the functional role of these brain stem centers and neurotransmitters have not been elucidated. Spinal inputs also connect directly to the sympathetic preganglionic nuclei.

The axons of preganglionic neurons, which originate principally between T–1 and L–2, either synapse with postganglionic sympathetic neurons in the paravertebral sympathetic ganglia, pass through the ganglia of T–5 through L–2 and form the splanchnic nerves that innervate the adrenal medulla, or synapse with postganglionic sympathetic neurons in the preaortic plexuses such as the celiac and superior mesenteric. The preganglionic sympathetic neurons are cholinergic; the receptors on the postganglionic sympathetic neurons predominantly are nicotinic. The postganglionic sympathetic fibers are distributed widely to blood vessels and viscera.

The topography of sympathetic outflow illustrates the phenomena of divergence and convergence at the level of the paravertebral ganglia. Each preganglionic nerve innervates several postganglionic neurons, including neurons above and below the level of the preganglionic cell (divergence). Moreover, each postganglionic cell, in turn, receives input from multiple preganglionic neurons (convergence). Because the number of postganglionic neurons in a sympathetic ganglion, such as the superior cervical ganglion, is not proportional to body size among mammalian species (Purves et al., 1988), large mammals, such as humans, offset the lower ratio of postganglionic neurons to body size by forming a greater number of neuronal connections between pre- and postganglionic nerve cells than do smaller animals, such as mice or rats. Electrical activity of individual ganglion cells likewise is higher in larger animals (Ivanov & Purves, 1989). This difference in the complexity of neuronal connection among mammalian species has implications for aging research and will be discussed subsequently.

As mentioned previously, the sympathoadrenal system generally is considered to be a single neuroendocrine unit within the autonomic nervous system as a whole. Although the early, classical studies in this area contrasted the seemingly more generalized responses of the sympathetic nervous system with the more discrete responses of the parasympathetic nervous system (Cannon, 1939), later work has emphasized the presence of numerous function-specific subunits within the SNS (Jänig & McLachlan, 1992a). These subunits (listed in Table I) are independently, though coordinately, regulated. Moreover, the neurochemical and electrophysiological characteristics of the neurons within the various subunits may differ (Jänig et al., 1992a, b). For example, whereas norepinephrine is the principal neurotransmitter in sympathetic nerves in general, acetylcholine serves this role in the postganglionic sudomotor fibers. Furthermore, the distribution of neuropeptides is not uniform within the SNS (Morris & Gibbins, 1992); neuropeptide Y (NPY), for example, is

Table I
Functional Subdivisions of the Sympathetic Nervous System[a]

Major subdivision	Target organ	Target tissue
Cardiovascular	Heart	Atrium, ventricle
Vasoconstrictor	Skeletal muscle	Resistance vessels (+)[b]
	Cutaneous	Resistance vessels (+)
	Visceral	Resistance vessels (+)
Vasodilator	Skeletal muscle	Resistance vessels (−)[b]
	Cutaneous	Resistance vessels (−)
Metabolic	Adipose tissue	Interstitial space
(nonvascular)	Brown fat	Adipocytes
	Liver	Hepatocytes
	Skeletal muscle	Interstitial space
Motility regulating	GI and urinary tracts	Visceral smooth muscle (+, −)
	Reproductive organs	Visceral smooth muscle
Endocrine	Pancreatic islets	α, β, and δ-cells
(nonvascular)	Kidney	Juxtaglomerular apparatus
		Peritubular cells
	Thyroid gland	Thyroid follicles
		Thyroid "C"-cells
	Parathyroid glands	Chief cells
	Gastric antrum and duodenum	Mucosa and submucosa
	Adrenal cortex	Zona fasciculata
		Zona glomerulosa
	Ovary	Granulosa cells of corpus luteum
		Theca cells
	Testis	Leydig cells
	Pineal	
Immunologic	Lymph nodes, spleen	
Inspiratory	Airways	Nasal mucosal vessels
Pilomotor	Hair follicles	Piloerector muscles
Blepharomotor	Eyelid	Superior tarsal muscle
Pupillomotor	Iris	Dilator pupillae muscle
Sudomotor	Skin	Sweat glands

[a] Modified from Jänig and McLachlan (1992a) and Young and Landsberg (1998).
[b] + and − refer to increased and decreased vasomotor tone, respectively.

distributed principally in sympathetic fibers innervating vascular structures.

The central nuclei that initiate descending impulse traffic within the different subunits are subject to regulatory influences by pathways from centers in the hypothalamus, limbic system, and cortex, as well as from a vast array of afferent impulses that initiate reflex changes in sympathetic outflow at the level of the brain stem. The composition of the extracellular fluid, including tonicity and the concentration of various substrates, hormones, and ions, also influences sympathoadrenal outflow via effects on the regulatory brain stem nuclei.

B. Development of the Sympathoadrenal System

Sympathetic neurons and chromaffin cells that form the adrenal medulla arise from a population of sympathoadrenal progenitor cells within the embryonic neural crest. In the presence of neurotrophic substances, such as basic fibroblast growth factor (bFGF) and nerve growth factor (NGF), and in the relative absence of glucocorticoids, these cells differentiate into sympathetic neurons (Anderson, 1993). Like nerve cells within the CNS, protoadrenergic neurons are produced in abundance, and estimates are that only one in four or five eventually becomes a terminally differentiated sympathetic neuron (Oppenheim, 1985); the others undergo apoptosis, the process of programmed cell death. What prevents apoptosis in all precursor cells is the presence of specific neuron survival factors that are synthesized and released by peripheral target cells. Neurotrophins are the best known of these survival factors and represent a family of highly homologous proteins produced by the innervated tissue that act in a paracrine manner to prevent apoptosis in the adrenergic neurons (Korsching, 1993). Of the known members of this family, only NGF and neurotrophin–3 (NT–3) have been specifically linked to the preservation of sympathetic innervation *in vivo* (Crowley *et al.*, 1994; Ernfors *et al.*, 1994; Fariñas *et al.*, 1994).

Neurotrophins exert several other effects on adrenergic nerves in addition to the suppression of apoptosis. During fetal development, these factors, along with other growth factors like bFGF, insulin, and IGF-I, promote the proliferation of adrenergic neurons (Black *et al.*, 1990; Anderson, 1993), though the preservation of neuronal cell populations in sympathetic ganglia during postnatal life results more from a reduction in cell loss than from an increase in neuronal division (Hendry & Campbell, 1976; Hendry, 1977). In mature neurons, the neurotrophins induce sprouting of dendrites and increased arborization of the network of sympathetic fibers in innervated tissues (Black *et al.*, 1990; Campenot, 1994). Consequently, the density of sympathetic innervation,

reflected in tissue norepinephrine (NE) levels, correlates positively with NGF gene expression in peripheral tissues (Korsching & Thoenen, 1983; Shelton & Reichardt, 1984). Even in adult animals the preservation of sympathetic neurons remains dependent upon continued exposure to NGF and NT–3 (Gorin & Johnson, 1980; Ruit *et al.*, 1990; Rush *et al.*, 1997).

SNS development, thus, may be divided into four periods. The initial period of neuronal proliferation occurs during fetal life and ends shortly after birth (Hendry, 1977; Rubin, 1985). This is succeeded by a second period in which the majority of sympathetic nerve cells undergo apoptosis, except for those protected by exposure to neurotrophins (Hendry, 1977). The third period involves the growth and expansion of axons and nerve endings from existing sympathetic neurons to keep pace with somatic growth of the innervated tissues (Purves *et al.*, 1988). A final phase represents preservation of the mature sympathetic innervation throughout the adult life of the individual. This last period is more dynamic than is usually appreciated, as evidenced by the remodeling of synapses over a 3-month interval that are observed in postganglionic neurons within the superior cervical ganglion of mice (Purves *et al.*, 1986).

Like that in other parts of the nervous system, this developmental program for the SNS is susceptible to modification by sensory experience or environmental exposures. For example, tissue content of NE, a measure of the density of innervation, is reduced in tissues of adult animals as a consequence of growth retardation during intrauterine life (Young & Morrison, 1998), implying that sympathetic development is affected along with somatic growth. On the other hand, environmental temperature during the postnatal period influences the development of brown fat sympathetic nerves and the regulation of sudomotor function (Bertin *et al.*, 1990; Diamond, 1991). The distinct and diverse effects of environmental factors suggest that each of the many functional subunits of the SNS may be susceptible to a different set of modifying factors during early life. If so, then the structure and function of the SNS in adults would be the net result of the environmental factors to which the individuals were exposed during intrauterine and early postnatal life. Although the long-term effects of these early life exposures have not been examined carefully, the differences in tissue NE levels persist well into adulthood. A further implication of these findings is that a deficit in sympathetic neuron number may occur secondary to either decreased cell proliferation (period 1) or increased neuronal apoptosis (period 2), though the long-term consequences of any alterations in SNS development are not known.

III. Effect of Age on the Sympathetic Innervation of Peripheral Tissues

A characteristic feature of the SNS in aged animals is a decrease in postganglionic sympathetic innervation in many peripheral tissues. Initial evidence for this age-related reduction in sympathetic innervation arose largely from biochemical analysis of tissue NE content and fluorescence histochemistry of tissue sections. These findings, however, have been confirmed in studies employing morphological techniques not dependent upon the presence of neuronal NE stores. Available data are summarized in Table II. Although interlaboratory variation may contribute to minor inconsistencies among reports of age-related differences in sympathetic innervation, the findings clearly document a decrease

Table II
Age-Related Differences in Sympathetic Innervation of Peripheral Tissues

Species (strain)	Innervation	Tissue	References
Rats (F344)	Decreased	Brown fat, female	McDonald *et al.*, 1993
		Caudal artery	Dawson & Meldrum, 1992
		Heart	Roberts & Goldberg, 1976; Mazzeo *et al.*, 1986; Mazzeo & Horvath, 1987; Dawson & Meldrum, 1992; McLean *et al.*, 1983; Kregel, 1994
		Kidney	Mazzeo *et al.*, 1986; Mazzeo & Horvath, 1987
		Liver	Mazzeo & Horvath, 1987; Mazzeo *et al.*, 1986; Mazzeo & Grantham, 1989; Kregel, 1994
		Lymph nodes	Madden *et al.*, 1995
		Spleen	Madden *et al.*, 1995; Bellinger *et al.*, 1992
		Superior mesenteric ganglion	Warburton & Santer, 1993
	Unchanged	Adrenal Epi	Mazzeo & Grantham, 1989; Martinez *et al.*, 1981; Schmidt *et al.*, 1992; Mazzeo *et al.*, 1986
		Adrenal NE	Mazzeo & Horvath, 1987; Martinez *et al.*, 1981; Kregel, 1994; Schmidt *et al.*, 1992; Mazzeo *et al.*, 1986
		Brown fat, male	McDonald *et al.*, 1993
		Heart	Martinez *et al.*, 1981; Avakian & Horvath, 1982; Mazzeo & Grantham, 1989
		Kidney	Martinez *et al.*, 1981; Kregel, 1994
		Portal vein	Dawson & Meldrum, 1992
		Renal artery	Dawson & Meldrum, 1992
		Soleus muscle	Mazzeo & Grantham, 1989

(continues)

Table II *(Cont'd)*

Species (strain)	Innervation	Tissue	References
		Spleen	Martinez et al., 1981
	Increased	Adrenal Epi	Mazzeo & Horvath, 1987
		Thymus	Madden et al., 1995
Rats (Sprague–Dawley)	Decreased	Brown fat	a
		Heart	a
		Kidney	Vega et al., 1990
		Pineal	Reuss et al., 1990
		Sweat glands	Abdel-Rahman & Cowen, 1993
	Unchanged	Iris	(Gavazzi et al., 1996b)
		Spleen	Avakian & Horvath, 1982
	Increased	Dorsal root ganglion	Ramer & Bisby, 1998
		Ductus deferens	Pellegrini et al., 1990
Rats (Wistar)	Decreased	Aorta	Santer, 1982
		Carotid artery	Santer, 1982
		Celiac–superior mesenteric ganglion	Santer et al., 1980
		Cerebrovascular arteries	Mione et al., 1988a
		Heart	Gey et al., 1965; Sirviö et al., 1994
		Hypogastric ganglion	Dering et al., 1996; Warburton & Santer, 1995
		Intestine	Santer & Baker, 1988; Baker et al., 1991
		Ovary	Ferrante et al., 1990
		Pelvic nerves	Dering et al., 1998
		SNS	Dering et al., 1998; Warburton & Santer, 1994
	Unchanged	Cervical SNS	Santer, 1993
		Heart	Santer, 1982
		Iris	Santer, 1991
		Pancreas	Santer, 1982
		Renal vein	Mione et al., 1988b
		Spinal arteries	Amenta et al., 1990
		Submandibular gland	Santer, 1991
		Superior mesenteric vein	Mione et al., 1988b
	Increased	Aorta	Pellegrini et al., 1994
		Heart	Pellegrini et al., 1994
		Portal vein	Mione et al., 1988b
		Renal artery	Mione et al., 1988b
		Superior mesenteric artery	Mione et al., 1988b
		Vasa nervorum	Mione et al., 1987
Mice	Decreased	Thyroid	Melander et al., 1975
	Unchanged	Brown fat	a
		Heart	a
Guinea pigs	Decreased	Femoral artery	Dhall et al., 1986
		Renal artery	Dhall et al., 1986
	Increased	Carotid artery	Dhall et al., 1986
		Mesenteric artery	Dhall et al., 1986
Rabbits	Decreased	Aorta	Shibata et al., 1971
		Carotid artery	Cowen et al., 1982
		Renal artery	Cowen et al., 1982
	Unchanged	Basilar artery	Cowen et al., 1982
		Femoral artery	Cowen et al., 1982
		Mesenteric artery	Cowen et al., 1982
Human	Decreased	Arteries of pia mater	Pigolkin et al., 1985
		Gingival vessels	Waterson et al., 1974
		Heart	Shvalev et al., 1986
		Superior mesenteric ganglion	Schmidt et al., 1993
		Sweat glands	Abdel-Rahman et al., 1992
	Unchanged	Superior cervical ganglion	Schmidt et al., 1993

a J. B., Young, unpublished observations.

in sympathetic innervation in old animals. This effect is not global, as some tissues are affected more than others, and tissues in some animals are affected more than the same tissues in other animals. In some tissues, older animals may even display an increased density of sympathetic fibers. For example, in vessels of guinea pigs and rats exhibiting an age-related decrease in perivascular noradrenergic innervation, perivascular neuropeptidergic nerves that mediate vasodilation actually increase (Dhall *et al.*, 1986; Mione *et al.*, 1988a). Studies of neural architecture in sympathetic ganglia suggest that the innervation of postganglionic sympathetic fibers by preganglionic nerves may also decrease with age in abdominal and pelvic, but not cervical, ganglia (Warburton & Santer, 1993; 1995; Santer *et al.*, 1980; Dering *et al.*, 1996, 1998; Schmidt *et al.*, 1993; Santer, 1993). Thus, aging appears to be associated with selective denervation affecting pre- and postganglionic neurons in the efferent sympathetic pathways.

A loss in sympathetic innervation may reflect a reduction in the number of pre- or postganglionic neurons or the number of nerve terminals per neuron. Although early in life neuronal loss secondary to apoptosis is widespread, in adult animals available evidence indicates that the rate of loss of pre- and postganglionic neurons is probably low. Studies of sympathetic ganglia indicate that cell numbers are well-maintained during adulthood (Baker & Santer, 1988; Santer, 1991; Cowen, 1993; Schmidt *et al.*, 1995). Thus, in those tissues exhibiting reduced sympathetic innervation in aged animals, the differences more likely are attributable to a reduction in the number of nerve terminals per neuron rather than to loss of nerve cells. Because of the greater dependence of human sympathetic nerves on increased connectivity between pre- and postganglionic nerves and between postganglionic nerves and the innervated tissue, as mentioned previously, age-related effects may be more prominent in humans than in smaller animals.

These differences in sympathetic innervation with age must be viewed in the context of ongoing neural remodeling, which is observed in adult animals (Purves *et al.*, 1987; Purves & Hadley, 1985) and presumably continues throughout life (Cowen & Gavazzi, 1998). Although the factors responsible for these changes are not well-understood, sympathetic neurons in adult animals require neurotrophin support, particularly NGF and NT–3 synthesized by innervated tissues, as do neonatal animals (Gorin & Johnson, 1980; Johnson *et al.*, 1982; Ruit *et al.*, 1990; Thrasivoulou & Cowen, 1995; Rush *et al.*, 1997; Zhou *et al.*, 1997). Molecules comprising the extracellular matrix, such as laminin, also influence sympathetic neuron growth and the density of innervation (Gavazzi *et al.*, 1996a), though their relation to the effects of aging is unclear (Cowen & Gavazzi, 1998). In young animals, development of neurons is also affected by the activity of the neural pathway of which they are a part (so-called activity-dependent regulation). Whether the activity of sympathetic neurons protects against or reverses processes leading to sympathetic denervation in aged animals is not known, though it is likely.

The relative importance of environmental exposures or the presence of disease for the age-related loss of sympathetic innervation of aging per se is not clear. The findings summarized in Table II are all from cross-sectional studies and, thus, differences in development may have contributed to the observed variations. Among potential environmental contributors, ethanol exposure induces sympathotoxic effects that are more pronounced in older than in younger rats (Jaatinen & Hervonen, 1994). Also, pathological conditions, such as diabetes mellitus and congestive heart failure, are associated with morphological changes in the SNS. Denervation of the heart, particularly the left ventricle, occurs in experimental as well as human cardiomyopathy (Daly & Sole, 1990; Pierpont et al., 1992; Hajjar et al., 1993; Oki et al., 1994). Whereas autonomic dysfunction is a common complication of diabetes mellitus, subtle changes in the morphology of neurons innervating the superior mesenteric, but not the superior cervical, ganglion are seen in diabetic individuals (Schmidt et al., 1993). These pathological findings are similar to those noted in older subjects without diabetes, but they occur earlier in the diabetics (Schmidt et al., 1993). Although age-related diseases may contribute to the morphological changes in sympathetic ganglia, the only factors associated statistically with the presence of dystrophic changes in the preganglionic axons are age and male gender (Schmidt et al., 1990). Thus, whereas other factors may contribute to the development of neuropathic changes in the SNS, their importance has not been established.

IV. Effect of Age on the Activity of the Peripheral Sympathetic Nervous System

Although comparative studies of sympathetic function in young and old subjects were reported in the early decades of the twentieth century (Cannon, 1939), current understanding of the impact of age on SNS activity dates from the 1970s with the advent of analytical methods sufficiently sensitive to measure catecholamines in plasma and neurophysiological techniques to monitor electrical activity in peripheral sympathetic nerves. Shortly after their development, both methods were employed in comparative studies of SNS activity in the young and old (Christensen, 1973; Sundlöf & Wallin, 1978). Despite more than two decades of

effort, there remains considerable uncertainty about the precise nature of the effects of aging and the factors responsible for them. Moreover, there is little appreciation of how the changes with age in SNS anatomy may affect sympathetic functions. Achieving a consensus regarding the impact of age on the SNS is made more difficult, in part, because of the absence of a "gold standard" for assessing SNS activity, especially in human subjects (Grassi & Esler, 1999).

For the purposes of this discussion, sympathetic nervous system activity is defined as the rate of neurotransmitter release at the neuroeffector junction, because that is the site where the efferent electrical impulses are converted into the chemical signals that trigger responses in the innervated tissue. By this definition, all techniques for assessing SNS activity, particularly those available for use in human subjects, are indirect and provide only an indirect estimate of neurotransmitter release. Although sympathetic nerves release multiple neurotransmitter substances, NE is the principal one throughout the SNS and will be the main focus of this review. Adrenal medullary activity, on the other hand, is synonymous with epinephrine (Epi) secretion and entry into the circulation.

A. Plasma and Urinary Levels of Norepinephrine

Because NE is a neurotransmitter, not a circulating hormone, the plasma pool of NE is derived from the small portion of neurotransmitter that escapes local reuptake and metabolism at adrenergic synapses throughout the body. This situation is reflected in the fact that, under most circumstances, plasma concentrations of NE are below the threshold for stimulation of adrenergic receptors (Silverberg et al., 1978). Moreover, the increment in circulating NE level required to stimulate sympathetically mediated processes greatly exceeds the plasma NE level that occurs during physiological sympathetic stimulation of the same processes. Concomitant increases in NE clearance from plasma may accompany changes in sympathetic activity, thereby lessening the impact of the change in sympathetic activity on the plasma NE level. Because the adrenal medulla secretes NE as well as Epi, increases in plasma NE concentration do not always reflect the activity of sympathetic nerves. Venous NE concentrations, moreover, represent the net result of processes in innervated tissues that extract NE from arterial plasma and add NE to the venous drainage. Despite these limitations, however, antecubital venous plasma NE levels can provide a useful estimate of sympathetic activity in humans.

Similar considerations apply to urinary NE excretion. Although a portion of NE in the urine originates from renal sympathetic nerves, the major fraction reflects the NE concentration in arterial blood. The principal disadvantage in the use of urinary NE excretion as an index of global SNS function is its lesser sensitivity than plasma levels to acute changes in SNS activity. Nonetheless, this approach provides a reasonable estimate of plasma NE concentrations integrated over time and is the only method that permits the assessment of sympathetic function in a subject's natural environment. As a result, it is the most appropriate means for assessing SNS activity in epidemiological studies.

Effect of aging: In cross-sectional studies of human subjects, plasma NE levels increase with advancing age under resting conditions in forearm, as well as renal, venous plasma (Christensen, 1973; Pedersen & Christensen, 1975; Ziegler et al., 1976; Kjeldsen et al., 1982; Messerli et al., 1981; Pfeifer et al., 1983). In addition to this age-related difference at baseline, plasma NE levels in the elderly are greater than in the young in response to

standing, isometric exercise, the cold pressor test, oral glucose ingestion, or mental stress (Ziegler et al., 1976; Palmer et al., 1978; Young et al., 1980; Barnes et al., 1982). Moreover, in several of these studies, values in the elderly remain elevated above those in young controls following removal of the stressor (Young et al., 1980; Barnes et al., 1982). By contrast, the increment in NE levels during aerobic exercise is less in the elderly than in young subjects (Jensen et al., 1994).

Comparisons of plasma NE in rats following prior insertion of a catheter for blood sampling yield variable results. Baseline levels tend to be elevated in aged rats (Chiueh et al., 1980; Irwin et al., 1992; Milakofsky et al., 1993; Kiritsy-Roy et al., 1992), though values in both young and old animals may be quite high due to the test procedure rendering interpretation of the results problematic (McCarty, 1985; Mabry et al., 1995; Cizza et al., 1995). Responses to stimulation also are quite variable.

Urinary NE excretion correlates positively with advancing age in some, but not all, studies conducted in ambulatory subjects (Weidmann et al., 1977; Jenner et al., 1987; Olsson et al., 1991; Moyer et al., 1979; Gerlo et al., 1991; Young et al., 1992). In one study performed in Fischer 344 rats, urinary NE excretion was higher in relation to body weight in 24-month-old than in 3-month-old animals both before and after a 2-week period of cold exposure (4°C) (J. B. Young, unpublished observations). Thus, NE levels in plasma or urine generally are higher in older than in younger individuals.

Demonstration of the age-related increase in plasma NE levels in human subjects raises the question of the extent to which this represents an increase in entry into or a decrease in removal of NE from the circulation. Although a number of early reports demonstrated no difference in plasma clearance between young and old subjects, thereby implying that the age-related difference in plasma NE was due exclusively to increased NE appearance, other studies provided clear evidence of diminished NE removal from plasma in elderly individuals (Esler *et al.*, 1981; Veith *et al.*, 1986; Poehlman *et al.*, 1990). Subsequent work by Esler and colleagues indicates that, whereas NE appearance is increased and NE clearance decreased in older men, the increase in NE appearance is not uniformly present in all peripheral tissues (Esler *et al.*, 1995c). NE spillover, an estimate of the net contribution of sympathetic nerves in one organ to NE appearance in the circulation, is elevated from the heart, but not kidney, in elderly men (Esler *et al.*, 1995c) whereas NE spillover from the hepatomesenteric bed may or may not be increased in old men (Vaz *et al.*, 1996; Mazzeo *et al.*, 1997). These data imply that differences in SNS activity as a function of age arise variably in individual organs, perhaps reflecting variable effects of aging within subdivisions of the SNS.

B. Plasma and Urinary Levels of Epinephrine

Epi is the principal catecholamine secreted by the adrenal medulla. Because the threshold level of Epi required to elicit metabolic and hemodynamic responses is within the range of circulating concentrations under normal conditions (Clutter *et al.*, 1980), plasma measurements reflect the adrenal medullary contribution to physiological regulation. Because Epi is extracted during passage through peripheral capillary beds and is also synthesized in peripheral tissues, such as heart, as well as in the adrenal medulla (Elayan *et al.*, 1990; Huang *et al.*, 1996), measurements of Epi in arterial plasma are a more sensitive index of adrenal medullary secretion than are venous Epi levels (Hjemdahl *et al.*, 1984). Like NE, Epi measured in urine

is a suitable index of adrenal medullary secretion integrated over time and correlates well with plasma levels during periods of adrenal medullary stimulation (Åkerstedt *et al.*, 1983).

Effect of aging In contrast to the age-related increase in plasma NE levels in human subjects, plasma Epi concentrations do not differ (Pfeifer *et al.*, 1983; Barnes *et al.*, 1982; Meneilly *et al.*, 1985, 1994) or are slightly lower in older individuals (Franco-Morselli *et al.*, 1977; Kjeldsen *et al.*, 1982; Messerli *et al.*, 1981). In situations of adrenal medullary stimulation, Epi levels do not differ in young and old in response to mental stress (Barnes *et al.*, 1982), but they are lower in the elderly in response to exercise or hypoglycemia (Jensen *et al.*, 1994; Meneilly *et al.*, 1994). Urinary Epi excretion correlates negatively with advancing age in some (Gerlo *et al.*, 1991; Young *et al.*, 1992), but not all, studies conducted in ambulatory subjects (Weidmann *et al.*, 1977; Jenner *et al.*, 1987; Moyer *et al.*, 1979). [Because women display lower Epi levels in plasma or urine than men (Gerlo *et al.*, 1991; Amiel *et al.*, 1993), studies of Epi as a function of age must control for gender.] Although an initial report noted no difference in Epi clearance in the elderly (Morrow *et al.*, 1987), later evidence suggests that Epi clearance is reduced in older men (Esler *et al.*, 1995a; Mazzeo *et al.*, 1997). Whether Epi entry into plasma is also lower in the elderly is unclear (Morrow *et al.*, 1987; Esler *et al.*, 1995a). These data suggest that one factor contributing to no difference in circulating Epi between the young and old may be an age-related reduction in the removal of Epi from the circulation.

Animal studies indicate that Epi secretion increases with age in anesthetized rats (Ito *et al.*, 1986) and that increments in urinary Epi during a 2-week exposure to cold (4°C) are proportionally greater in 24-month-old than in 3-month-old animals (+460% above ambient temperature baseline vs +210%; J. B. Young, unpublished observations). Although basal levels of Epi in plasma obtained from unanesthetized rats are high and show no difference between young and old animals, increments in Epi levels are greater in the old animals in response to stresses of cold, immobilization, swimming, and administration of the nonmetabolizable glucose analogue 2-deoxyglucose (McCarty, 1984, 1985; Mabry et al., 1995; Cizza et al., 1995). Thus, Epi levels in plasma or urine generally are less responsive to stimulation in older human subjects, though the reverse may be obtained in laboratory animals.

C. Norepinephrine Turnover in Experimental Animals

One approach to measuring SNS activity in the peripheral tissues of experimental animals is that of NE turnover. NE turnover refers to a set of kinetic techniques that assess the dynamic behavior of NE contained in storage granules of innervated tissues and is, thus, roughly analogous to the measurements of regional NE spillover obtained in human subjects. The principal methods for estimating NE turnover monitor the rate of fall in tissue NE levels following inhibition of tyrosine hydroxylase, the rate-limiting enzyme in NE biosynthesis, usually with α-methyl-p-tyrosine or the rate of disappearance of [^{3}H]NE from tissues following intravenous injection of tracer. Because the release of labeled or unlabeled NE in such experiments is dependent upon efferent nerve impulses, a higher rate of NE turnover signifies an increase in SNS activity and a lower rate signifies a decrease in SNS activity.

Comparisons of NE turnover rates have been carried out in Fischer 344 and Sprague-Dawley rats (Rappaport et al., 1980; Avakian & Horvath, 1982; Mazzeo & Horvath, 1987; Mazzeo & Grantham, 1989; Kregel, 1994; McDonald et al.,

1993) and in C57Bl/6J mice (J. B. Young, unpublished observations). Although baseline rates of NE turnover were lower in old animals in one report (Mazzeo & Horvath, 1987), this difference was not observed in the other studies. In the C57Bl/6J mice, [^{3}H]NE turnover rates in both heart and brown fat rose slightly, though not significantly, from 3- to 12- to 24-month-old animals at room temperature. Moreover, tissue NE levels in the mice did not differ among the age groups, whereas it was lower in heart and liver in the study reporting the age-related decrease in NE turnover (Mazzeo & Harvath, 1987). In support of a connection between NE turnover and tissue NE levels, a comparison of NE turnover responses to cold in male and female Fischer 344 rats showed decreased NE turnover and NE levels in brown fat in aged females, but an increase in NE turnover in the oldest males that also showed no reduction in tissue NE content (McDonald et al., 1993). Despite the heightened sympathetic output to brown fat, tissue responses were blunted in the old male rats (Gabaldón et al., 1995), implying diminished end-organ responsiveness in these animals. Sympathetic responses to cold and to dietary manipulations in other tissues were similar in young and old male Fischer rats (Rappaport et al., 1980; Avakian & Horvath, 1982), but were increased in old animals with exercise or nonexertional heating (Mazzeo & Grantham, 1989; Kregel, 1994). Consequently, these studies provide no evidence for a generalized increase in SNS activity in old animals. The possibility exists, however, that an increase in body heat load may activate portions of the SNS to a greater extent in older than in younger rats.

D. Microneurography

An alternate approach to assessing SNS activity that has attracted considerable interest involves the direct recording of impulse traffic from peripheral sympathetic nerves (termed microneurography). Whereas nerve recording techniques have been used in animals for many years, their use in humans is comparatively recent (Vallbo *et al.*, 1979). Recording electrodes are placed transcutaneously, usually into the peroneal nerve in the lower extremity, and thereby assess nerve impulse traffic in sympathetic fibers innervating skeletal muscle. These techniques are invasive, technically demanding, and feasible only for short-term studies, but have yielded much useful information regarding the regulation of sympathetic activity in this tissue. Because the sympathetic innervation in skeletal muscle is largely restricted to blood vessels, measurements of impulse traffic to muscle (often referred to as muscle sympathetic nerve activity or MSNA) provide information regarding vasoconstrictor tone in muscle. The relationship between MSNA and the activity of sympathetic nerves to other regions of the body, or in other subdivisions of the SNS, is conjectural.

Although nerve impulse recordings frequently are referred to as a "direct" measure of sympathetic activity, this is correct only in the limited sense that nerve impulses per se are an index of sympathetic activity. Moreover, several factors confound the use of electrical impulses as a surrogate for neurotransmitter release. Because high levels of impulse traffic facilitate neurotransmitter release, NE release at the sympathetic nerve ending is nonlinearly related to impulse traffic (Brock & Cunnane, 1993). Also, various factors acting on the presynaptic nerve cell membrane modify transmitter release by an incoming impulse (Young & Landsberg, 1998). Finally, the density of sympathetic innervation in peripheral tissues may differ among groups of individuals. Consequently, the relation between nerve impulse traffic

and NE release may differ from one individual to another or between groups of subjects, complicating the facile assumption that MSNA is synonymous with neurotransmitter release.

Effect of aging: Since it was first described over 20 years ago (Sundlöf & Wallin, 1978), MSNA has been shown repeatedly to be higher in older than in younger healthy subjects at rest (Yamada *et al.*, 1989; Iwase *et al.*, 1991; Ebert *et al.*, 1992; Ng *et al.*, 1993; Scherrer *et al.*, 1994; Kingwell *et al.*, 1994; Hausberg *et al.*, 1997). Moreover, resting MSNA correlates positively with antecubital venous NE levels (Wallin *et al.*, 1981; Scherrer *et al.*, 1994; Ng *et al.*, 1993) and also with cardiac NE spillover (Kingwell *et al.*, 1994). Intraindividual resting measurements of MSNA appear relatively stable over time (Wallin *et al.*, 1981; Fagius & Wallin, 1993). Values for MSNA were slightly higher when measured a second time in the same subjects after an average interval of 12 years, though the difference in measurements was of borderline statistical significance (Fagius & Wallin, 1993). Thus, available data clearly provide evidence of an age-related difference, possibly even an age-related change over time within the same individuals, in resting MSNA.

Despite elevations in MSNA at baseline, sympathetic responses to a variety of stressors are not increased and may even be attenuated in elderly subjects. Attempts to compare baroreflex responsiveness in MSNA between the young and old have employed postural change (including head-down as well as head-up tilting), immersion to the neck in thermoneutral water, Valsalva maneuver, and infusions of phenylephrine or nitroglycerin (Iwase *et al.*, 1991; Ng *et al.*, 1995; Tanaka *et al.*, 1999; Miwa *et al.*, 1996; Matsukawa *et al.*, 1996, 1998; Ebert *et al.*, 1992; Davy *et al.*, 1998). Due to the high levels of MSNA at baseline, proportional changes in MSNA with baroreflex stimulation or inhibition are less in the old, though the absolute changes in nerve impulse traffic frequently are similar in the young and old. Increased age does not affect the response of MSNA during the cold pressor test, isometric handgrip or hypoxia (Ebert *et al.*, 1992; Ng *et al.*, 1994; Davy *et al.*, 1997), though it slightly reduces the increment with euglycemic hyperinsulinemia (Hausberg *et al.*, 1997). The conclusion drawn from these studies is that the age-related difference in MSNA is greatest at baseline and either the same or less with sympathetic stimulation.

Comparative data regarding an effect of age are also available from animal experiments involving measurements of impulse traffic in sympathetic nerves. Because the studies require anesthesia and involve nerves innervating kidney, brown fat, and adrenal gland (but not skeletal muscle), the results may not be precisely comparable with the human data. Nonetheless, an increase in baseline SNA with older animals is observed in the renal nerves of beagles (Hajduczok *et al.*, 1991b), brown fat nerves of mice (Kawate *et al.*, 1993), and adrenal nerves of Wistar rats (Ito *et al.*, 1986). Other studies, however, show either diminished or slightly, but not significantly, increased renal SNA in older rats (Huang & Leenen, 1992; Stauss *et al.*, 1996; Kohata *et al.*, 1997). Whatever the baseline difference, however, the renal sympathetic response to a reduction in blood pressure or a low-sodium diet is attenuated in old animals (Hajduczok *et al.*, 1991b; Huang & Leenen, 1992; Kohata *et al.*, 1997). By contrast, sympathetic nerves to brown fat are always more active in old than in young mice (Talan *et al.*, 1996). Whereas the adrenal nerve response to baroreflex suppression is intact in aged rats (Kurosawa *et al.*, 1987), excitation by hypoxia is reduced (Sato & Trzebski, 1993). Thus, the presence or absence of age-related differences in sympathetic activation appears to be dependent upon both the stimulus presented and the particular sympathetic nerve chosen for study.

E. Spectral Analysis of Heart Rate and Blood Pressure

Another method for assessing sympathetic activity that has gained popularity in human studies because of its relative ease of application is the spectral analysis of heart rate. This method is based upon mathematical analysis of spontaneous fluctuations in heart rate and transformation of heart rate data from the time domain to the frequency domain (Pomeranz *et al.*, 1985; Malliani *et al.*, 1991). One component of the power spectrum, the so-called low-frequency band, purportedly represents sympathetic input to the heart (or a combination of sympathetic and parasympathetic inputs), whereas the high-frequency component represents parasympathetic input (Pomeranz *et al.*, 1985; Malliani *et al.*, 1991). Studies in adult human subjects consistently show reduced low-frequency power with increasing age (Kingwell *et al.*, 1994; Fluckiger *et al.*, 1999). The appropriateness of this approach to quantifying autonomic inputs to the heart, however, remains controversial (Eckberg, 1997; Malliani *et al.*, 1998). The major shortcoming of this method for studies of sympathetic activity in aging is that the chronotropic response of the heart to catecholamines is lower in older individuals (Cleaveland *et al.*, 1972). Consequently, measures of heart rate variability are confounded by age-related changes in end-organ response, which probably explains why estimates of cardiac SNS activity derived from heart rate analysis do not correlate with other measures of SNS activity, such as MSNA or cardiac NE spillover (Saul *et al.*, 1990; Kingwell *et al.*, 1994). Whatever the origins of the cardiac rhythms represented in the heart rate spectrum, this approach is not an acceptable measure of cardiac sympathetic activity, especially in studies of aging, when SNS activity is defined, as it is here, in terms of neurotransmitter release.

V. Potential Mechanisms Underlying the Effect of Age on SNS Activity

Are these age-related differences in SNS activity a consequence of aging per se, or do they represent characteristics that an individual acquires during his or her lifetime? Although no definitive answer can be provided for this question at present, indices of increased SNS activity are not universally present in elderly subjects, raising the possibility that heightened SNS activity is an acquired trait. Several factors have been suggested, and because they are not mutually exclusive, each may play a contributory role in individual subjects. First, among Danish men, the age-related increase in NE in venous plasma in both supine and upright positions occurs in long-term male smokers, but not in male nonsmokers (Jensen et al., 1993). Smoking, however, cannot be the sole explanation for the findings discussed previously, because evidence of an age-related increase in SNS activity is found in studies from which smokers were specifically excluded (Schwartz et al., 1987). Second, because body fat increases in many individuals during adulthood and correlates with various indices of SNS activity, several groups suggest that the age-related elevation in SNS activity is related to increasing adiposity (Schwartz et al., 1987; Poehlman et al., 1995; Scherrer et al., 1994; Jones et al., 1997). Moreover, after statistical adjustment of NE appearance rates for waist circumference, the age-related difference in whole body NE

appearance is no longer apparent (Poehlman et al., 1995). Also, older obese men who lose weight (–19% in body fat) manifest lower NE levels in venous plasma (Pratley et al., 1995). The underlying physiological changes with age reflected in these associations between body fat and SNS activity are unclear, however.

A third possibility is that the indices of increased SNS activity in aged animals or human subjects are, in some way, related to the decrease in sympathetic innervation with age. This explanation is easy to appreciate with respect to measurements of nerve impulse traffic because the increase in nerve impulses may represent a reflex attempt to compensate for the reduction in nerve endings per neuron. As noted earlier, the underlying causes for selective sympathetic denervation or the neuroaxonal dystrophy noted in the sympathetic ganglia of elderly men and women are not known (Schmidt et al., 1990). Nonetheless, the available data, especially those obtained in heart and sweat glands (discussed later), are compatible with a model of end-organ denervation. Further work will be needed to assess the contribution of sympathetic denervation in aging subjects, though its principal impact may be to confound measures of SNS activity, as discussed previously.

Finally, if SNS activity is truly increased in elderly individuals, then the possibility exists that such a change may arise as a consequence of an age-related decline in end-organ responsiveness to adrenergic stimulation. Decreased responsiveness is observed, for example, in the chronotropic response to β-adrenergic agonists (Cleaveland et al., 1972), vasoconstrictive response to an increase in MSNA (Sugiyama et al., 1996), and thermogenic response to β_3-adrenergic stimulation in rats (Scarpace et al., 1992). Because conditioning may restore deficient responsiveness (Scarpace et al.,

1996), diminished end-organ responses may reflect environmental factors more than aging per se.

VI. Effect of Age on Cardiovascular Regulation

A. Cardiac Sympathetic Nervous System Activity

A preponderance of data from animal and human studies, summarized in Table 10.2, is consistent with a decrease in cardiac innervation with aging. Support for this thesis includes decreased myocardial content of NE in most, though not all, studies (Gey et al., 1965; Roberts & Goldberg, 1976; Mazzeo et al., 1986; Mazzeo & Horvath, 1987; Dawson & Meldrum, 1992; Kregel, 1994; Sirviö et al., 1994), histological evidence of axonal degeneration in rats (McLean et al., 1983), and decreased adrenergic innervation in the hearts of accident victims, especially those above 60 years of age (Shvalev et al., 1992). In addition, cardiac imaging studies using [^{123}I]-miodobenzylguanidine ([^{123}I]MIBG), a radiopharmaceutical that is a substrate for the neuronal norepinephrine uptake mechanism, show reduced counts in older than in younger subjects following injection of [^{123}I]MIBG (Gill et al., 1993; Tsuchimochi et al., 1995). Whereas this difference may merely reflect decreased neuronal uptake per se, it is also consistent with loss of adrenergic innervation, as diminished [^{123}I]MIBG uptake is seen in patients with cardiac denervation due to autonomic failure, transplantation, or diabetes mellitus (Grassi & Esler, 1999; Guertner et al., 1995; Mäntysaari et al., 1992; Kreiner et al., 1995).

NE kinetics across the hearts in human subjects also indicates decreased neuronal uptake of NE in the elderly. The increase in NE spillover in old relative to young men is due entirely to reduced NE re-uptake not to any difference in NE appearance (Esler et al., 1995c). In the heart, uptake of NE occurs predominantly via neuronal uptake (so-called uptake$_1$), which is dependent upon the activity of the norepinephrine transporter (Goldstein et al., 1988). The age-related decrease noted in cardiac NE re-uptake, therefore, must represent either selective loss of transporter function or a reduction in the neuronal sites at which re-uptake occurs (i.e., nerve endings). Because in heart the quantity of NE that "spills over" into the circulation represents a much smaller fraction of estimated NE release (~5%) than in kidney (34%) (Kopin et al., 1998), a decrease in NE re-uptake in heart would produce a greater proportional increase in cardiac NE spillover than a similar change in re-uptake in kidney. This difference in regional NE kinetics may explain why the cardiac NE spillover data so clearly show an age-related change in NE re-uptake and not in NE release. Additional studies will be required to determine the relation, if any, of the age-related decrease in neuronal NE uptake to cardiac denervation. A decrease in NE re-uptake without a change in NE release would be expected to lead to an elevation in extracellular NE levels that, if sustained over time, might affect cardiac function. Thus, the available data raise the possibilities that cardiac innervation declines as a function of age and that denervation contributes to the observed alterations in cardiac NE spillover in the elderly.

B. Baroreflex Function

Aging alters reflex control of cardiovascular function. Nearly 30 years ago, Gribbin et al. demonstrated an inverse relation between an individual's age and the bradycardic response to an elevation in arterial pressure (Gribbin et al., 1971). Subsequent studies have confirmed and extended this observation by showing that the increase in heart rate due to a fall in blood pressure is also diminished in older subjects (Ferrari *et al.*, 1989). Whereas cardiac denervation may contribute to these phenomena of aging, available evidence indicates that cardiac SNS responses to various stressors are the same, if not greater, in elderly than in younger men (Esler *et al.*, 1995b). Despite the increase in cardiac NE spillover in older subjects (due to diminished re-uptake not enhanced release), heart rate responses to these stressors do not differ in the old and young (Esler *et al.*, 1995b). Thus, the principal factor underlying the age-related difference in baroreflex regulation of heart rate appears to be diminished chronotropic responsiveness of the heart to cholinergic and adrenergic stimulation. Whether chronic exposure of aged hearts to higher local NE concentrations (secondary to decreased re-uptake) contributes to the decrease in cardiac responsiveness is likely, though unproved.

In contrast to the decline in baroreflex control of heart rate, baroreflex control of sympathetic nerve activity is less clearly affected by age. Whereas inhibition of sympathetic activity in splanchnic and renal nerves with blood pressure elevation is impaired in older rats and dogs (Tanabe & Buñag, 1989; Hajduczok *et al.*, 1991a,b), a corresponding decrease in baroreflex sensitivity is not seen in humans before the eighth decade of life (Ebert *et al.*, 1992; Matsukawa *et al.*, 1996, 1998; Davy *et al.*, 1998; Tanaka *et al.*, 1999). Both animal and human studies, however, are complicated by the higher level of sympathetic activity noted in older subjects at baseline and in response to changes in blood pressure. Elderly men show alterations in vasomotor responses to sympathetic stimulation (Sugiyama *et al.*, 1996), suggesting that changes in end-organ responsiveness also may contribute to age-related alterations in vasomotor regulation, as they do with respect to heart rate.

VII. Effect of Age on Regulation of Sudomotor Function

Another portion of the SNS that exhibits degenerative changes with aging is the sudomotor system. This subdivision of the SNS employs acetylcholine as its principal neurotransmitter; the nerves initially are adrenergic, as in other subdivisions of the SNS, but convert to a cholinergic phenotype following exposure to an unknown factor released from sweat glands in response to adrenergic stimulation (Habecker & Landis, 1994). In both humans and rats, morphological studies demonstrate the loss of sympathetic nerve endings to sweat glands with concomitant degeneration of the sudomotor apparatus in skin (Abdel-Rahman *et al.*, 1992, 1993). Although an explanation for the loss of sudomotor innervation with age is not available, a change in behavior of the innervated tissue is likely because sweat glands from mature and aged donors transplanted into young recipients became innervated by cholinergic sympathetic fibers with a density appropriate for the age of the donor tissue (Cowen *et al.*, 1996). Thus, the age-related changes in sudomotor function reflect a loss of sympathetic innervation probably due to changes in local neurotrophic support provided by the sweat glands themselves.

The elderly are, in general, more susceptible to heat stress than are the young, and during passive heating core body temperature may rise to a greater extent in older individuals (Inoue & Shibasaki, 1996). This difference in body temperature is, in part, secondary to lower sweating rates, which are apparent in both animals and human subjects, particularly in women (Navarro & Kennedy, 1990; Low *et al.*, 1990), and to diminished   cutaneous   vasodilation (Inoue *et al.*, 1999). These effects of age on sweating and cutaneous blood flow are greater in some regions of the body than others and represent both decreased sweat output per gland as well as decreased density of sweat glands (Inoue *et al.*, 1991; Inoue, 1996). Because an individual's capacity for neurally mediated sweating is programmed early in life by the temperature of the environment to which the individual is exposed (Diamond, 1991), interindividual differences in heat tolerance among elderly subjects may represent the long-term consequences of developmental modification of sympathetic sudomotor function.

VIII. Summary and Conclusions

Although most of the indices used to monitor SNS activity in humans (plasma NE levels and NE kinetics, urinary NE, and microneurography) suggest that aging is associated with increased SNS activity, the findings from animal studies are more equivocal. As discussed previously, a number of the approaches used in human studies potentially are confounded by the putative decrease in density of sympathetic innervation. A decrease in cardiac sympathetic innervation may explain the diminished neuronal re-uptake of NE, which is responsible for increased NE spillover from the heart. Whether similar reductions in sympathetic innervation in other regions contribute to diminished plasma NE clearance or to a compensatory increase in nerve impulse traffic in vasomotor nerves to skeletal muscle is likely, but unproven. Consequently, the indices of SNS activity discussed in this review must be interpreted in the light of the age-related changes in the anatomy of the SNS that may affect the relationship between a particular index and neurotransmitter release at the nerve ending.

An important determinant of sympathetic function near the end of life is the conditions that were present near the beginning. Because the early phases of sympathetic development involve cell proliferation followed by apoptotic elimination of neurons unable to establish connections with appropriate peripheral tissues, the number of sympathetic neurons present in adult animals is dependent upon events during fetal or neonatal life. On the basis of current information, the preservation of sympathetic innervation in maturity relies upon neurotrophic and other factors that controlled the formation of this system initially. This process of neuronal plasticity continues throughout life, and its presumed deterioration in later years (with or without the involvement of adult disease) probably contributes to the selective reductions in sympathetic innervation that characterize aging animals.

Changes in SNS regulation with aging reflect the interplay of three independent factors. First, the innervation in specific subdivisions undergoes involutional change represented by loss of sympathetic neurons and, to a greater extent, by a decrease in the number of nerve endings per neuron. Second, the innervated tissues may become less responsive to adrenergic stimulation, the mechanisms for which remain to be fully defined. Third, the activity of the remaining sympathetic neurons may become more active consequent to the first two factors. Because preservation of sympathetic neurons in mature animals is dependent upon tissue factors that may be influenced by neural mechanisms, the possibility exists that these three factors may be intimately related. Moreover, the changes that take place in the SNS with aging probably are not unlike those that occur within the CNS itself, but they are more accessible for study because of their peripheral location. Better understanding of the sequence of events leading to sympathetic denervation may permit the development of strategies to forestall such changes and maintain the processes of homeostatic regulation well into old age.

References

Abdel-Rahman, T. A., Collins, K. J., Cowen, T., & Rustin, M. (1992). Immunohistochemical, morphological and functional changes in the peripheral sudomotor neuro-effector system in elderly people. *Journal of the Autonomic Nervous System*, 37, 187–198.

Abdel-Rahman, T. A., & Cowen, T. (1993). Neurodegeneration in sweat glands and skin of aged rats. *Journal of the Autonomic Nervous System*, 46, 55–63.

Åkerstedt, T., Gillberg, M., Hjemdahl, P., Sigurdson, K., Gustavsson, I., Daleskog, M., & Pollare, T. (1983). Comparison of urinary and plasma catecholamine responses to mental stress. *Acta Physiologica Scandinavica*, 117, 19–26.

Amenta, F., Bronzetti, E., Ferrante, F., & Ricci, A. (1990). The noradrenergic innervation of spinal cord blood vessels in old rats. *Neurobiology of Aging*, 11, 47–50.

Amiel, S. A., Maran, A., Powrie, J. K., Umpleby, A. M., & Macdonald, I. A. (1993). Gender differences in counterregulation to hypoglycemia. *Diabetologia*, 36, 460–464.

Anderson, D. J. (1993). Cell fate determination in the peripheral nervous system: the sympathoadrenal progenitor. *Journal of Neurobiology*, 24, 185–198.

Avakian, E. V., & Horvath, S. M. (1982). Influence of aging and tyrosine hydroxylase inhibition on tissue levels of norepinephrine during stress. *Journal of Gerontology*, 37, 257–261.

Baker, D. M., & Santer, R. M. (1988). Morphometric studies on pre- and paravertebral sympathetic neurons in the rat: changes with age. *Mechanisms of Ageing and Development*, 42, 139–145.

Baker, D. M., Watson, S. P., & Santer, R. M. (1991). Evidence for a decrease in sympathetic control of intestinal function

in the aged rat. *Neurobiology of Aging*, 12, 363–365.

Barnes, R. F., Raskind, M., Gumbrecht, G., & Halter, J. B. (1982). The effects of age on the plasma catecholamine response to mental stress in man. *Journal of Clinical Endocrinology and Metabolism*, 54, 64–69.

Bellinger, D. L., Ackerman, K. D., Felten, S. Y., & Felten, D. L. (1992). A longitudinal study of age-related loss of noradrenergic nerves and lymphoid cells in the rat spleen. *Experimental Neurology*, 116, 295–311.

Bertin, R., Mouroux, I., De Marco, F., & Portet, R. (1990). Norepinephrine turnover in brown adipose tissue of young rats: effects of rearing temperature. *American Journal of Physiology*, 259, R90–R96.

Black, I. B., DiCicco-Bloom, E., & Dreyfus, C. F. (1990). Nerve growth factor and the issue of mitosis in the nervous system. *Current Topics in Developmental Biology*, 24, 161–192.

Brock, J. A., & Cunnane, T. C. (1993). Neurotransmitter release mechanisms at the sympathetic neuroeffector junction. *Experimental Physiology*, 78, 591–614.

Cabot, J. B. (1990) Sympathetic preganglionic neurons: cytoarchitecture, ultrastructure, and biophysical properties. In A. D. Loewy, & K. M. Spyer (Eds.), *Central Regulation of Autonomic Functions*. (pp. 44–67). New York: Oxford University Press.

Campenot, R. B. (1994). NGF and the local control of nerve terminal growth. *Journal of Neurobiology*, 25, 599–611.

Cannon, W. B. (1939). *The Wisdom of the Body (2nd ed.)*. New York: W. W. Norton & Co.

Chiueh, C. C., Nespor, S. M., & Rapoport, S. I. (1980). Cardiovascular, sympathetic and adrenal cortical responsiveness of aged Fischer–344 rats to stress. *Neurobiology of Aging*, 1, 157–163.

Christensen, N. J. (1973). Plasma noradrenaline and adrenaline in patients with thyrotoxicosis and myxoedema. *Clinical Science and Molecular Medicine*, 45, 163–171.

Cizza, G., Pacak, K., Kvetnansky, R., Palkovits, M., Goldstein, D. S., Brady, L. S., Fukuhara, K., Bergamini, E., Kopin, I. J., Blackman, M. R., Chrousos, G. P., & Gold,

P. W. (1995). Decreased stress responsivity of central and peripheral catecholaminergic systems in aged 344/N Fischer rats. *Journal of Clinical Investigation, 95,* 1217–1224.

Cleaveland, C. R., Rangno, R. E., & Shand, D. G. (1972). A standardized isoproterenol sensitivity test. The effects of sinus arrhythmia, atropine, and propranolol. *Archives of Internal Medicine, 130,* 47–52.

Clutter, W. E., Bier, D. M., Shah, S. D., & Cryer, P. E. (1980). Epinephrine plasma metabolic clearance rates and physiologic thresholds for metabolic and hemodynamic actions in man. *Journal of Clinical Investigation, 66,* 94–101.

Cowen, T. (1993). Ageing in the autonomic nervous system: a result of nerve-target interactions? A review. *Mechanisms of Ageing and Development, 68,* 163–173.

Cowen, T., Haven, A. J., Wen-Qin, C., Gallen, D. D., Franc, F., & Burnstock, G. (1982). Development and ageing of perivascular adrenergic nerves in the rabbit. A quantitative fluorescence histochemical study using image analysis. *Journal of the Autonomic Nervous System, 5,* 317–336.

Cowen, T., & Gavazzi, I. (1998). Plasticity in adult and ageing sympathetic neurons. *Progress in Neurobiology, 54,* 249–288.

Cowen, T., Thrasivoulou, C., Shaw, S. A., & Abdel-Rahman, T. A. (1996). Transplanted sweat glands from mature and aged donors determine cholinergic phenotype and altered density of host sympathetic nerves. *Journal of the Autonomic Nervous System, 60,* 215–224.

Crowley, C., Spencer, S. D., Nishimura, M. C., Chen, K. S., Pitts-Meek, S., Armanini, M. P., Ling, L. H., MacMahon, S. B., Shelton, D. L., Levinson, A. D., & Phillips, H. S. (1994). Mice lacking nerve growth factor display perinatal loss of sensory and sympathetic neurons yet develop basal forebrain cholinergic neurons. *Cell, 76,* 1001–1011.

Daly, P. A., & Sole, M. J. (1990). Myocardial catecholamines and the pathophysiology of heart failure. *Circulation, 82(Suppl I),* I–35–I–43.

Davy, K. P., Jones, P. P., & Seals, D. R. (1997). Influence of age on the sympathetic neural adjustments to alterations in systemic oxygen levels in humans. *American Journal of Physiology, 273,* R690–R695.

Davy, K. P., Tanaka, H., Andros, E. A., Gerber, J. G., & Seals, D. R. (1998). Influence of age on arterial baroreflex inhibition of sympathetic nerve activity in healthy adult humans. *American Journal of Physiology, 275,* H1768–H1772.

Dawson, R. Jr., & Meldrum, M. J. (1992). Norepinephrine content in cardiovascular tissues from the aged Fischer 344 rat. *Gerontology, 38,* 185–191.

Dering, M. A., Santer, R. M., & Watson, A. H. D. (1996). Age-related changes in the morphology of preganglionic neurons projecting to the rat hypogastric ganglion. *Journal of Neurocytology, 25,* 555–563.

Dering, M. A., Santer, R. M., & Watson, A. H. D. (1998). Age-related changes in the morphology of preganglionic neurons projecting to the paracervical ganglion of nulliparous and multiparous rats. *Brain Research, 780,* 245–252.

Dhall, U., Cowen, T., Haven, A. J., & Burnstock, G. (1986). Perivascular noradrenergic and peptide- containing nerves show different patterns of changes during development and ageing in the guinea- pig. *Journal of the Autonomic Nervous System, 16,* 109–126.

Diamond, J. (1991). Pearl Harbor and the Emperor's physiologists. *Natural History, 12,* 2–7.

Ebert, T. J., Morgan, B. J., Barney, J. A., Denahan, T., & Smith, J. J. (1992). Effects of aging on baroreflex regulation of sympathetic activity in humans. *American Journal of Physiology, 263,* H798–H803.

Eckberg, D. L. (1997). Sympathovagal balance: a critical appraisal. *Circulation, 96,* 3224–3232.

Elayan, H. H., Kennedy, B. P., & Ziegler, M. G. (1990). Cardiac atria and ventricles contain different inducible adrenaline synthesising enzymes. *Cardiovascular Research, 24,* 53–56.

Ernfors, P., Lee, K.-F., Kucera, J., & Jaenisch, R. (1994). Lack of neurotrophin–3 leads to deficiencies in the peripheral nervous system and loss of limb proprioceptive afferents. *Cell, 77,* 503–512.

Esler, M., Skews, H., Leonard, P., Jackman, G., Bobik, A., & Korner, P. (1981).

Age-dependence of noradrenaline kinetics in normal subjects. *Clinical Science, 60,* 217–219.

Esler, M., Kaye, D., Thompson, J., Jennings, G., Cox, H., Turner, A., Lambert, G., & Seals, D. (1995). Effects of aging on epinephrine secretion and regional release of epinephrine from the human heart. *Journal of Clinical Endocrinology and Metabolism, 80,* 435–442.

Esler, M. D., Thompson, J. M., Kaye, D. M., Turner, A. G., Jennings, G. L., Cox, H. S., Lambert, G. W., & Seals, D. R. (1995). Effects of aging on the responsiveness of the human cardiac sympathetic nerves to stressors. *Circulation, 91,* 351–358.

Esler, M. D., Turner, A. G., Kaye, D. M., Thompson, J. M., Kingwell, B. A., Morris, M., Lambert, G. W., Jennings, G. L., Cox, H. S., & Seals, D. R. (1995). Aging effects on human sympathetic neuronal function. *American Journal of Physiology, 268,* R278–R285.

Fagius, J., & Wallin, B. G. (1993). Long-term variability and reproducibility of resting human muscle nerve sympathetic activity at rest, as reassessed after a decade. *Clinical Autonomic Research, 3,* 201–205.

Fariñas, I., Jones, K. R., Backus, C., Wang, X.-Y., & Reichardt, L. F. (1994). Severe sensory and sympathetic deficits in mice lacking neurotrophin–3. *Nature, 369,* 658–661.

Ferrante, F., Bronzetti, E., Cavallotti, C., Ricci, A., & Amenta, F. (1990). The noradrenergic innervation of the ovary in old rats. *Mechanisms of Ageing and Development, 54,* 55–61.

Ferrari, A. U., Grassi, G., & Mancia, G. (1989) Alterations in reflex control of the circulation associated with aging. In A. Amery & J. Staessen (Eds.) *Handbook of Hypertension, Vol. 12. Hypertension in the Elderly* (pp. 39–50). Amsterdam: Elsevier.

Fluckiger, L., Boivin, J.-M., Quilliot, D., Jeandel, C., & Zannad, F. (1999). Differential effects of aging on heart rate variability and blood pressure variability. *Journals of Gerontology. Series A, Biological Sciences and Medical Sciences, 54,* B219–B224.

Franco-Morselli, R., Elghozi, J. L., Joly, E., Di Giuilio, S., & Meyer, P. (1977). Increased plasma adrenaline concentrations in benign essential hypertension. *British Medical Journal, 2,* 1251–1254.

Gabaldón, A. M., Florez-Duquet, M. L., Hamilton, J. S., McDonald, R. B., & Horwitz, B. A. (1995). Effects of age and gender on brown fat and skeletal muscle metabolic responses to cold in F344 rats. *American Journal of Physiology, 268,* R931–R941.

Gavazzi, I., Boyle, K. S., & Cowen, T. (1996). Extracellular matrix molecules influence innervation density in rat cerebral blood vessels. *Brain Research, 734,* 167–174.

Gavazzi, I., Canavan, R. E. M., & Cowen, T. (1996). Influence of age and anti-nerve growth factor treatment on the sympathetic and sensory innervation of the rat iris. *Neuroscience, 73,* 1069–1079.

Gerlo, E. A. M., Schoors, D. F., & Dupont, A. G. (1991). Age- and sex-related differences for the urinary excretion of norepinephrine, epinephrine, and dopamine in adults. *Clinical Chemistry, 37,* 875–878.

Gey, K. F., Burkard, W. P., & Pletscher, A. (1965). Variation of the norepinephrine metabolism of the rat heart with age. *Gerontologia, 11,* 1–11.

Gill, J. S., Hunter, G. J., Gane, G., & Camm, A. J. (1993). Heterogeneity of the human myocardial sympathetic innervation: in vivo demonstration by iodine 123-labeled meta-iodobenzylguanidine scintigraphy. *American Heart Journal, 126,* 390–398.

Goldstein, D. S., Brush, J. E. Jr, Eisenhofer, G., Stull, R., & Esler, M. (1988). In vivo measurement of neuronal uptake of norepinephrine in the human heart. *Circulation, 78,* 41–48.

Gorin, P. D., & Johnson, E. M. Jr (1980). Effects of long-term nerve growth factor deprivation on the nervous system of the adult rat: an experimental autoimmune approach. *Brain Research, 198,* 27–42.

Grassi, G., & Esler, M. (1999). How to assess sympathetic activity in humans. *Journal of Hypertension, 17,* 719–734.

Gribbin, B., Pickering, T. G., Sleight, P., & Peto, R. (1971). Effect of age and high blood pressure on baroreflex sensitivity in man. *Circulation Research, 29,* 424–431.

Guertner, C., Krause, B. J., Klepzig, H. Jr, Herrmann, G., Lelbach, S., Vockert, E. K., Hartmann, A., Maul, F. D., Kranert, T. W., Mutschler, E., Hübner, K., & Hoer, G. (1995). Sympathetic re-innervation after heart transplantation: dual-isotope neurotransmitter scintigraphy, norepinephrine content and histological examination. *European Journal of Nuclear Medicine, 22*, 443–452.

Guyenet, P. G. (1990) Role of the ventral medulla oblongata in blood pressure regulation. In A. D. Loewy, & K. M. Spyer (Eds.) *Central Regulation of Autonomic Functions.* (pp. 145–167). New York: Oxford University Press.

Habecker, B. A., & Landis, S. C. (1994). Noradrenergic regulation of cholinergic differentiation. *Science, 264*, 1602–1604.

Hajduczok, G., Chapleau, M. W., & Abboud, F. M. (1991). Increase in sympathetic activity with age. II. Role of impairment of cardiopulmonary baroreflexes. *American Journal of Physiology, 260*, H1121–H1127.

Hajduczok, G., Chapleau, M. W., Johnson, S. L., & Abboud, F. M. (1991). Increase in sympathetic activity with age. I. Role of impairment of arterial baroreflexes. *American Journal of Physiology, 260*, H1113–H1120.

Hajjar, R. J., Liao, R., Young, J. B., Fuleihan, F., Glass, M. G., & Gwathmey, J. K. (1993). Pathophysiological and bio-chemical characterisation of an avian model of dilated cardiomyopathy: comparison to findings in human dilated cardiomyopathy. *Cardiovascular Research, 27*, 2212–2221.

Hausberg, M., Hoffman, R. P., Somers, V. K., Sinkey, C. A., Mark, A. L., & Anderson, E. A. (1997). Contrasting autonomic and hemodynamic effects of insulin in healthy elderly versus young subjects. *Hypertension, 29*, 700–705.

Hendry, I. A. (1977). Cell division in the developing sympathetic nervous system. *Journal of Neurocytology, 6*, 299–309.

Hendry, I. A., & Campbell, J. (1976). Morphometric analysis of rat superior cervical ganglion after axotomy and nerve growth factor treatment. *Journal of Neurocytology, 5*, 351–360.

Hjemdahl, P., Freyschuss, U., Juhlin-Dannfelt, A., & Linde, B. (1984). Differentiated sympathetic activation during mental stress evoked by the Stroop test. *Acta Physiologica Scandinavica, (Suppl 527)*, 25–29.

Huang, B. S., & Leenen, F. H. H. (1992). Dietary Na, age, and baroreflex control of heart rate and renal sympathetic nerve activity in rats. *American Journal of Physiology, 262*, H1441–H1448.

Huang, M.-H., Friend, D. S., Sunday, M. E., Singh, K., Haley, K., Austen, K. F., Kelly, R. A., & Smith, T. W. (1996). An intrinsic adrenergic system in mammalian heart. *Journal of Clinical Investigation, 98*, 1298–1303.

Inoue, Y. (1996). Longitudinal effects of age on heat-activated sweat gland density and output in healthy active older men. *European Journal of Applied Physiology and Occupational Physiology, 74*, 72–77.

Inoue, Y., Nakao, M., Araki, T., & Murakami, H. (1991). Regional differences in the sweating responses of older and younger men. *Journal of Applied Physiology, 71*, 2453–2459.

Inoue, Y., & Shibasaki, M. (1996). Regional differences in age-related decrements of the cutaneous vascular and sweating responses to passive heating. *European Journal of Applied Physiology and Occupational Physiology, 74*, 78–84.

Inoue, Y., Shibasaki, M., Ueda, H., & Ishizashi, H. (1999). Mechanisms underlying the age-related decrement in the human sweating response. *European Journal of Applied Physiology and Occupational Physiology, 79*, 121–126.

Irwin, M., Hauger, R., & Brown, M. (1992). Central corticotropin-releasing hormone activates the sympathetic nervous system and reduces immune function: increased responsivity of the aged rat. *Endocrinology, 131*, 1047–1053.

Ito, K., Sato, A., Sato, Y., & Suzuki, H. (1986). Increases in adrenal catecholamine secretion and adrenal sympathetic nerve unitary activities with aging in rats. *Neuroscience Letters, 69*, 263–268.

Ivanov, A., & Purves, D. (1989). Ongoing electrical activity of superior cervical ganglion cells in mammals of different size. *Journal of Comparative Neurology, 284*, 398–404.

Iwase, S., Mano, T., Watanabe, T., Saito, M., & Kobayashi, F. (1991). Age-related changes of sympathetic outflow to muscles in humans. *Journal of Gerontology, 46,* M1–M5.

Jaatinen, P., & Hervonen, A. (1994). Reactions of rat sympathetic neurons to ethanol exposure are age-dependent. *Neurobiology of Aging, 15,* 419–428.

Jänig, W., & McLachlan, E. M. (1992a). Characteristics of function-specific pathways in the sympathetic nervous system. *Trends in Neurosciences, 15,* 475–481.

Jänig, W., & McLachlan, E. M. (1992b). Specialized functional pathways are the building blocks of the autonomic nervous system. *Journal of the Autonomic Nervous System, 41,* 3–13.

Jenner, D. A., Harrison, G. A., Prior, I. A. M., Leonetti, D. L., & Fujimoto, W. Y. (1987). 24-h catecholamine excretion: relationships with age and weight. *Clinica Chimica Acta, 164,* 17–25.

Jensen, E. W., Eldrup, E., Kelbæk, H., Nielsen, S. L., & Christensen, N. J. (1993). Venous plasma noradrenaline increases with age: correlation to total blood volume and long-term smoking habits. *Clinical Physiology, 13,* 99–109.

Jensen, E. W., Espersen, K., Kanstrup, I.-L., & Christensen, N. J. (1994). Exercise-induced changes in plasma catecholamines and neuropeptide Y: relation to age and sampling times. *Journal of Applied Physiology, 76,* 1269–1273.

Johnson, E. M., Jr, Gorin, P. D., Osborne, P. A., Rydel, R. E., & Pearson, J. (1982). Effects of autoimmune NGF deprivation in the adult rabbit and offspring. *Brain Research, 240,* 131–140.

Jones, P. P., Davy, K. P., Alexander, S., & Seals, D. R. (1997). Age-related increase in muscle sympathetic nerve activity is associated with abdominal adiposity. *American Journal of Physiology, 272,* E976–E980.

Kawate, R., Talan, M. I., & Engel, B. T. (1993). Aged C57BL/6J mice respond to cold with increased sympathetic nervous activity in interscapular brown adipose tissue. *Journal of Gerontology, 48,* B180–B183.

Kingwell, B. A., Thompson, J. M., Kaye, D. M., McPherson, G. A., Jennings, G. L., & Esler, M. D. (1994). Heart rate spectral analysis, cardiac norepinephrine spillover, and muscle sympathetic nerve activity during human sympathetic nervous activation and failure. *Circulation, 90,* 234–240.

Kiritsy-Roy, J. A., Halter, J. B., Smith, M. J., & Terry, L. C. (1992). Selective impairment of neuroendocrine and hemodynamic responses to a mu-opioid peptide in aged rats. *Journal of Gerontology, 47,* B89–B97.

Kjeldsen, S. E., Eide, I., Christensen, C., Westheim, A., & Müller, O. (1982). Renal contribution to plasma catecholamines— effect of age. *Scandinavian Journal of Clinical Laboratory Investigation, 42,* 461–466.

Kohata, S., Ninomiya, I., Shimizu, J., Furukawa, K., & Matsuura, Y. (1997). Effects of acute arterial bleeding on renal sympathetic nerve activity in young and old anesthetized rats. *Hiroshima Journal of Medical Sciences, 46,* 87–92.

Kopin, I. J., Rundqvist, B., Friberg, P., Lenders, J., Goldstein, D. S., & Eisenhofer, G. (1998). Different relationships of spillover to release of norepinephrine in human heart, kidneys, and forearm. *American Journal of Physiology, 275,* R165–R173.

Korsching, S. (1993). The neurotrophic factor concept: a reexamination. *Journal of Neuroscience, 13,* 2739–2748.

Korsching, S., & Thoenen, H. (1983). Nerve growth factor in sympathetic ganglia and corresponding target organs of the rat: correlation with density of sympathetic innervation. *Proceedings of the National Academy of Sciences of the United States of America, 80,* 3513–3516.

Kregel, K. C. (1994). Influence of aging on tissue-specific noradrenergic activity at rest and during nonexertional heating in rats. *Journal of Applied Physiology, 76,* 1226–1231.

Kreiner, G., Wolzt, M., Fasching, P., Leitha, T., Edlmayer, A., Korn, A., Waldhäusl, W., & Dudczak, R. (1995). Myocardial *m*-[^{123}i]iodobenzylguanidine scintigraphy for the assessment of adrenergic cardiac innervation in patients with IDDM.

Comparison with cardiovascular reflex tests and relationship to left ventricular function. *Diabetes, 44,* 543–549.

Kurosawa, M., Sato, A., Sato, Y., & Suzuki, H. (1987). Undiminished reflex responses of adrenal sympathetic nerve activity to stimulation of baroreceptors and cutaneous mechanoreceptors in aged rats. *Neuroscience Letters, 77,* 193–198.

Low, P. A., Opfer-Gehrking, T. L., Proper, C. J., & Zimmerman, I. (1990). The effect of aging on cardiac autonomic and postganglionic sudomotor function. *Muscle and Nerve, 13,* 152–157.

Mabry, T. R., Gold, P. E., & McCarty, R. (1995). Age-related changes in plasma catecholamine responses to chronic intermittent stress. *Physiology and Behavior, 58,* 49–56.

Madden, K. S., Sanders, V. M., & Felten, D. L. (1995). Catecholamine influences and sympathetic neural modulation of immune responsiveness. *Annual Review of Pharmacology and Toxicology, 35,* 417–448.

Malliani, A., Pagani, M., Lombardi, F., & Cerutti, S. (1991). Cardiovascular neural regulation explored in the frequency domain. *Circulation, 84,* 482–492.

Malliani, A., Pagani, M., Montano, N., & Mela, G. S. (1998). Sympathovagal balance: a reappraisal. *Circulation, 98,* 2640–2643.

Mäntysaari, M., Kuikka, J., Mustonen, J., Tahvanainen, K., Vanninen, E., Länsimies, E., & Uusitupa, M. (1992). Noninvasive detection of cardiac sympathetic nervous dysfunction in diabetic patients using [^{123}I]metaiodobenzylguanidine. *Diabetes, 41,* 1069–1075.

Martinez, J. L. Jr, Vasquez, B. J., Messing, R. B., Jensen, R. A., Liang, K. C., & McGaugh, J. L. (1981). Age-related changes in the catecholamine content of peripheral organs in male and female F344 rats. *Journal of Gerontology, 36,* 280–284.

Matsukawa, T., Sugiyama, Y., & Mano, T. (1996). Age-related changes in baroreflex control of heart rate and sympathetic nerve activity in healthy humans. *Journal of the Autonomic Nervous System, 60,* 209–212.

Matsukawa, T., Sugiyama, Y., Watanabe, T., Kobayashi, F., & Mano, T. (1998). Baroreflex control of muscle sympathetic

nerve activity is attenuated in the elderly. *Journal of the Autonomic Nervous System, 73,* 182–185.

Mazzeo, R. S., & Horvath, S. M. (1987). A decline in myocardial and hepatic norepinephrine turnover with age in Fischer 344 rats. *American Journal of Physiology, 252,* E762–E764.

Mazzeo, R. S., & Grantham, P. A. (1989). Sympathetic response to exercise in various tissues with advancing age. *Journal of Applied Physiology: Respiratory, Environmental and Exercise Physiology, 66,* 1506–1508.

Mazzeo, R. S., Colburn, R. W., & Horvath, S. M. (1986). Effect of aging and endurance training on tissue catecholamine response to strenous exercise in Fischer 344 rats. *Metabolism: Clinical and Experimental, 35,* 602–607.

Mazzeo, R. S., Rajkumar, C., Jennings, G., & Esler, M. (1997). Norepinephrine spillover at rest and during submaximal exercise in young and old subjects. *Journal of Applied Physiology, 82,* 1869–1874.

McCarty, R. (1984). Effects of 2-deoxyglucose on plasma catecholamines in adult and aged rats. *Neurobiology of Aging, 5,* 285–289.

McCarty, R. (1985). Sympathetic-adrenal medullary and cardiovascular responses to acute cold stress in adult and aged rats. *Journal of the Autonomic Nervous System, 12,* 15–22.

McDonald, R. B., Hamilton, J. S., & Horwitz, B. A. (1993). Influence of age and gender on brown adipose tissue norepinephrine turnover. *Proceedings of the Society for Experimental Biology and Medicine, 204,* 117–121.

McLean, M. R., Goldberg, P. B., & Roberts, J. (1983). An ultrastructural study of the effects of age on sympathetic innervation and atrial tissue in the rat. *Journal of Molecular and Cellular Cardiology, 15,* 75–92.

Melander, A., Sundler, F., & Westgren, U. (1975). Sympathetic innervation of the thyroid: variation with species and with age. *Endocrinology, 96,* 102–106.

Meneilly, G. S., Minaker, K. L., Young, J. B., Landsberg, L., & Rowe, J. W. (1985). Counterregulatory responses to insulin-induced hypoglycemia in the elderly. *Journal of Clinical Endocrinology and Metabolism, 61*, 178–182.

Meneilly, G. S., Cheung, E., & Tuokko, H. (1994). Altered responses to hypoglycemia of healthy elderly people. *Journal of Clinical Endocrinology and Metabolism, 78*, 1341–1348.

Messerli, F. H., Frohlich, E. D., Suarez, D. H., Reisin, E., Dreslinski, G. R., Dunn, F. G., & Cole, F. E. (1981). Borderline hypertension: relationship between age, hemodynamics and circulating catecholamines. *Circulation, 64*, 760–764.

Milakofsky, L., Harris, N., & Vogel, W. H. (1993). Effect of repeated stress on plasma catecholamines and taurine in young and old rats. *Neurobiology of Aging, 14*, 359–366.

Mione, M. C., Cavallotti, C., Collier, W. L., & Amenta, F. (1987). The noradrenergic innervation of the vasa nervorum in old rats: a fluorescence histochemical study. *Journal of the Autonomic Nervous System, 18*, 177–180.

Mione, M. C., Dhital, K. K., Amenta, F., & Burnstock, G. (1988). An increase in the expression of neuropeptidergic vasodilator, but not vasoconstrictor, cerebrovascular nerves in aging rats. *Brain Research, 460*, 103–113.

Mione, M. C., Erdö, S. L., Kiss, B., Ricci, A., & Amenta, F. (1988). Age-related changes of noradrenergic innervation of rat splanchnic blood vessels: a histofluorescence and neurochemical study. *Journal of the Autonomic Nervous System, 25*, 27–33.

Miwa, C., Mano, T., Saito, M., Iwase, S., Matsukawa, T., Sugiyama, Y., & Koga, K. (1996). Ageing reduces sympatho-suppressive response to head-out water immersion in humans. *Acta Physiologica Scandinavica, 158*, 15–20.

Morris, J. L., & Gibbins, I. L. (1992) Co-transmission and neuromodulation. In G. Burnstock, & C. H. V. Hoyle (Eds.), *Autonomic Neuroeffector Mechanisms.* (pp. 33–119). Chur, Switzerland: Harwood Academic Publishers.

Morrow, L. A., Linares, O. A., Hill, T. J., Sanfield, J. A., Supiano, M. A., Rosen, S. G., & Halter, J. B. (1987). Age differences in the plasma clearance mechanisms for epinephrine and norepinephrine in humans. *Journal of Clinical Endocrinology and Metabolism, 65*, 508–511.

Moyer, T. P., Jiang, N.-S., Tyce, G. M., & Sheps, S. G. (1979). Analysis for urinary catecholamines by liquid chromatography with amperometric detection: methodology and clinical interpretation of results. *Clinical Chemistry, 25*, 256–263.

Navarro, X., & Kennedy, W. R. (1990). Changes in sudomotor nerve territories with aging in the mouse. *Journal of the Autonomic Nervous System, 31*, 101–107.

Ng, A. V., Callister, R., Johnson, D. G., & Seals, D. R. (1993). Age and gender influence muscle sympathetic nerve activity at rest in healthy humans. *Hypertension, 21*, 498–503.

Ng, A. V., Callister, R., Johnson, D. G., & Seals, D. R. (1994). Sympathetic neural reactivity to stress does not increase with age in healthy humans. *American Journal of Physiology, 267*, H344–H353.

Ng, A. V., Johnson, D. G., Callister, R., & Seals, D. R. (1995). Muscle sympathetic nerve activity during postural change in healthy young and older adults. *Clinical Autonomic Research, 5*, 57–60.

Oki, H., Inoue, S., Makishima, N., Takeyama, Y., & Shiokawa, A. (1994). Cardiac sympathetic innervation in patients with dilated cardiomyopathy—immunohisto-chemical study using anti-tyrosine hydroxylase antibody. *Japanese Circulation Journal, 58*, 389–394.

Olsson, T., Viitanen, M., Hägg, E., Asplund, K., Grankvist, K., Eriksson, S., & Gustafson, Y. (1991). Catecholamine excretion in old age. *Aging, 3*, 263–268.

Oppenheim, R. W. (1985). Naturally occurring cell death during neural development. *Trends in Neurological Sciences, 8*, 487–493.

Palmer, G. J., Ziegler, M. G., & Lake, C. R. (1978). Response of norepinephrine and blood pressure to stress increases with age. *Journal of Gerontology, 33*, 482–487.

Pedersen, E. B., & Christensen, N. J. (1975). Catecholamines in plasma and urine in patients with essential hypertension determined by double-isotope derivative techniques. *Acta Medica Scandinavica, 198*, 373–377.

Pellegrini, A., Soldani, P., Breschi, M. C., Martinotti, E., & Paparelli, A. (1990). Adrenergic innervation of the ductus deferens in young and aging rats: a morpho-functional investigation. *Acta Histochemica, 89*, 67–74.

Pellegrini, A., Soldani, P., Paparelli, A., Breschi, M. C., Scatizzi, R., Nieri, P., Campagni, A., & Del Bianchi, S. (1994). Noradrenergic innervation and receptor responses of cardiovascular tissues from young and aged rats after acute microwave exposure. *International Journal of Neuroscience, 76*, 165– 175.

Pfeifer, M. A., Weinberg, C. R., Cook, D., Best, J. D., Reenan, A., & Halter, J.B. (1983). Differential changes of autonomic nervous system function with age in man. *American Journal of Medicine, 75*, 249–258.

Pierpont, G. L., Einzig, S., Pierpont, M. E., Staley, N. A., Reynolds, S. J., & Noren, G. R. (1992). Catecholamines in turkeys with alcohol-induced cardiomyopathy. *Journal of Applied Physiology, 73*, 1259–1264.

Pigolkin, Yu. I., Chertok, V. M., & Motavkin, P. A. (1985). Age characteristics of the efferent innervation of the pia mater arteries in the human brain. *Neuroscience and Behavioral Physiology, 15*, 343–350.

Poehlman, E. T., McAuliffe, T., & Danforth, E. Jr (1990). Effects of age and level of physical activity on plasma norepinephrine kinetics. *American Journal of Physiology, 258*, E256–E262.

Poehlman, E. T., Gardner, A. W., Goran, M. I., Arciero, P. J., Toth, M. J., Ades, P. A., & Calles-Escandon, J. (1995). Sympathetic nervous system activity, body fatness, and body fat distribution in younger and older males. *Journal of Applied Physiology, 78*, 802–806.

Pomeranz, B., Macaulay, R. J. B., Caudill, M. A., Kutz, I., Adam, D., Gordon, D., Kilborn, K. M., Barger, A. C., Shannon, D. C., Cohen, R. J., & Benson, H. (1985). Assessment of autonomic function in humans by heart rate spectral analysis. *American Journal of Physiology, 248*, H151–H153.

Pratley, R. E., Coon, P. J., Rogus, E. M., & Goldberg, A. P. (1995). Effects of weight loss on norepinephrine and insulin levels in obese older men. *Metabolism: Clinical and Experimental, 44*, 438–444.

Purves, D., & Hadley, R. D. (1985). Changes in the dendritic branching of adult mammalian neurones revealed by repeated imaging in situ. *Nature, 315*, 404–406.

Purves, D., Hadley, R. D., & Voyvodic, J. T. (1986). Dynamic changes in the dendritic geometry of individual neurons visualized over periods of up to three months in the superior cervical ganglion of living mice. *Journal of Neuroscience, 6*, 1051–1060.

Purves, D., Voyvodic, J. T., Magrassi, L., & Yawo, H. (1987). Nerve terminal remodeling visualized in living mice by repeated examination of the same neuron. *Science, 238*, 1122–1126.

Purves, D., Snider, W. D., & Voyvodic, J. T. (1988). Trophic regulation of nerve cell morphology and innervation in the autonomic nervous system. *Nature, 336*, 123–128.

Ramer, M. S., & Bisby, M. A. (1998). Normal and injury-induced sympathetic innervation of rat dorsal root ganglia increases with age. *Journal of Comparative Neurology, 394*, 38–47.

Rappaport, E. B., Young, J. B., & Landsberg, L. (1980). Impact of age on basal and diet-induced changes in sympathetic nervous system activity of Fischer rats. *Journal of Gerontology, 36*, 152–157.

Reuss, S., Spies, C., Schröder, H., & Vollrath, L. (1990). The aged pineal gland: reduction in pinealocyte number and adrenergic innervation in male rats. *Experimental Gerontology, 25*, 183–188.

Roberts, J., & Goldberg, P. B. (1976). Changes in basic cardiovascular activities during the lifetime of the rat. *Experimental Aging Research, 2*, 487–517.

Rubin, E. (1985). Development of the rat superior cervical ganglion: ganglion cell maturation. *Journal of Neuroscience, 5*, 673–684.

Ruit, K. G., Osborne, P. A., Schmidt, R. E., Johnson, E. M. Jr, & Snider, W. D. (1990). Nerve growth factor regulates sympathetic ganglion cell morphology and survival in the adult mouse. *Journal of Neuroscience,* *10,* 2412–2419.

Rush, R. A., Chie, E., Liu, D., Tafreshi, A., Zettler, C., & Zhou, X.-F. (1997). Neurotrophic factors are required by mature sympathetic neurons for survival, transmission and connectivity. *Clinical and Experimental Pharmacology and Physiology, 24,* 549–555.

Santer, R. M. (1982). Fluorescence histochemical observations on the adrenergic innervation of the cardiovascular system in the aged rat. *Brain Research Bulletin, 9,* 667–672.

Santer, R. M. (1991). Morphological evidence for the maintenance of the cervical sympathetic system in aged rats. *Neuroscience Letters, 130,* 248–250.

Santer, R. M. (1993). Quantitative analysis of the cervical sympathetic trunk in young adult and aged rats. *Mechanisms of Ageing and Development, 67,* 289–298.

Santer, R. M., & Baker, D. M. (1988). Enteric neuron numbers and sizes in Auerbach's plexus in the small and large intestine of adult and aged rats. *Journal of the Autonomic Nervous System, 25,* 59–67.

Santer, R. M., Partanen, M., & Hervonen, A. (1980). Glyoxylic acid fluorescence and ultrastructural studies of neurones in the coeliac-superior mesenteric ganglion of the aged rat. *Cell and Tissue Research, 211,* 475–485.

Sato, A., & Trzebski, A. (1993). The excitatory response of the adrenal sympathetic nerve to severe hypoxia hypoxia decreases in aged rats. *Neuroscience Letters, 161,* 97–100.

Saul, J. P., Rea, R. F., Eckberg, D. L., Berger, R. D., & Cohen, R. J. (1990). Heart rate and muscle sympathetic nerve variability during reflex changes of autonomic activity. *American Journal of Physiology,* *258,* H713–H721.

Scarpace, P.J., Matheny, M., & Borst, S.E. (1992). Thermogenesis and mitochondrial GDP binding with age in response to the novel agonist CGP-12177A. *American Journal of Physiology, 262,* E185–E190.

Scarpace, P. J., Tse, C., & Matheny M. (1996). Thermoregulation with age: restoration of β_3- adrenergic responsiveness in brown adipose tissue by cold exposure.

Proceedings of the Society for Experimental Biology and Medicine, 211, 374–380.

Scherrer, U., Randin, D., Tappy, L., Vollenweider, P., Jéquier, E., & Nicod, P. (1994). Body fat and sympathetic nerve activity in healthy subjects. *Circulation,* *89,* 2634–2640.

Schmidt, R. E., Chae, H. Y., Parvin, C. A., & Roth, K. A. (1990). Neuroaxonal dystrophy in aging human sympathetic ganglia. *American Journal of Pathology, 136,* 1327–1338.

Schmidt, K. N., Gosselin, L. E., & Stanley, W. C. (1992). Endurance exercise training causes adrenal medullary hypertrophy in young and old Fischer 344 rats. *Hormone and Metabolic Research, 24,* 511–515.

Schmidt, R. E., Plurad, S. B., Parvin, C. A., & Roth, K. A. (1993). Effect of diabetes and aging on human sympathetic autonomic ganglia. *American Journal of Pathology,* *143,* 143–153.

Schmidt, R. E., Beaudet, L., Plurad, S. B., Snider, W. D., & Ruit, K. G. (1995). Pathologic alterations in pre- and postsynaptic elements in aged mouse sympathetic ganglia. *Journal Neurocytology, 24,* 189–206.

Schwartz, R. S., Jaeger, L. F., & Veith, R. C. (1987). The importance of body composition to the increase in plasma norepinephrine appearance rate in elderly men. *Journal of Gerontology, 42,* 546–551.

Shelton, D. L., & Reichardt, L. F. (1984). Expression of the β-nerve growth factor gene correlates with the density of sympathetic innervation in effector organs. *Proceedings of the National Academy of Sciences of the USA, 81,* 7951–7955.

Shibata, S., Hattori, K., Sakurai, I., Mori, J., & Fujiwara, M. (1971). Adrenergic innervation and cocaine-induced potentiation of adrenergic responses of aortic strips from young and old rabbits. *Journal of Pharmacology and Experimental Therapeutics, 177,* 621–632.

Shvalev, V. N., Vikhert, A. M., Stropus, R. A., Sosunov, A. A., Pavlovich, E. R., Kargina-Terentyeva, R. A., Zhuchkova, N. I., Anikin, A. Yu., & Maryan, K. L. (1986). Changes in neural and humoral mechanisms of the heart in sudden death due to myocardial abnormalities. *Journal of the American College of Cardiology, 8* (Suppl A), 55A–64A.

Shvalev, V. N., Guski, H., Fernández-Britto, J. E., Sosunov, A. A., Pavlovich, E. R., Anikin, A. Yu., Zhuchkova, N. I., & Kargina-Terentyeva, R. A. (1992). Neurohistochemical and electron microscopic investigations of pathological and age-related changes in the cardiovascular system. *Acta Histochemica—Supplementband, 42,* 345–352.

Silverberg, A. B., Shah, S. D., Haymond, M. W., & Cryer, P. E. (1978). Norepinephrine: hormone and neurotransmitter in man. *American Journal of Physiology, 234,* E252–E256.

Sirviö, J., Lahtinen, H., Riekkinen, P., Jr, & Riekkinen, P. J. (1994). Spatial learning and noradrenaline content in the brain and periphery of young and aged rats. *Experimental Neurology, 125,* 312–315.

Stauss, H. M., Morgan, D. A., Anderson, K. E., Massett, M. P., & Kregel, K. C. (1996). Aging is not accompanied by sympathetic hyperresponsiveness to air-jet stress. *American Journal of Physiology, 271,* H768–H775.

Sugiyama, Y., Matsukawa, T., Shamsuzzaman, A. S. M., Okada, H., Watanabe, T., & Mano, T. (1996). Delayed and diminished pressor response to muscle sympathetic nerve activity in the elderly. *Journal of Applied Physiology, 80,* 869–875.

Sundlöf, G., & Wallin, B. G. (1978). Human muscle nerve sympathetic activity at rest. Relationship to blood pressure and age. *Journal of Physiology, 274,* 621–637.

Talan, M. I., Kirov, S. A., & Kosheleva, N. A. (1996). Nonshivering thermogenesis in adult and aged C57BL/6J mice housed at 22°C and at 29°C. *Experimental Gerontology, 31,* 687–698.

Tanabe, S., & Buñag, R. D. (1989). Age-related central and baroreceptor impairment in female Sprague-Dawley rats. *American Journal of Physiology, 256,* H1399–H1406.

Tanaka, H., Davy, K. P., & Seals, D. R. (1999). Cardiopulmonary baroreflex inhibition of sympathetic nerve activity is preserved with age in healthy humans. *Journal of Physiology, 515,* 249–254.

Thrasivoulou, C., & Cowen, T. (1995). Regulation of rat sympathetic nerve density by target tissues and NGF in maturity and old age. *European Journal of Neuroscience, 7,* 381–387.

Tsuchimochi, S., Tamaki, N., Tadamura, E., Kawamoto, M., Fujita, T., Yonekura, Y., & Konishi, J. (1995). Age and gender differences in normal myocardial adrenergic neuronal function evaluated by iodine-123-MIBG imaging. *Journal of Nuclear Medicine, 36,* 969–974.

Vallbo, Å. B., Hagbarth, K.-E., Torebjörk, H. E., & Wallin, B. G. (1979). Somatosensory, proprioceptive, and sympathetic activity in human peripheral nerves. *Physiological Reviews, 59,* 919–957.

Vaz, M., Rajkumar, C., Wong, J., Mazzeo, R. S., Turner, A. G., Cox, H. S., Jennings, G. L., & Esler, M. D. (1996). Oxygen consumption in the heart, hepatomesenteric bed, and brain in young and elderly human subjects, and accompanying sympathetic nervous activity. *Metabolism: Clinical and Experimental, 45,* 1487–1492.

Vega, J. A., Ricci, A., & Amenta, F. (1990). Age-dependent changes of the sympathetic innervation of the rat kidney. *Mechanisms of Ageing and Development, 54,* 185–196.

Veith, R. C., Featherstone, J. A., Linares, O. A., & Halter, J. B. (1986). Age differences in plasma norepinephrine kinetics in humans. *Journal of Gerontology, 41,* 319–324.

Wallin, B. G., Sundlöf, G., Eriksson, B.-E., Dominiak, P., Grobecker, H., & Lindblad, L. E. (1981). Plasma noradrenaline correlates to sympathetic muscle nerve activity in normotensive man. *Acta Physiologica Scandinavica, 111,* 69–73.

Warburton, A. L., & Santer, R. M. (1993). Localisation of NADPH-diaphorase and acetylcholinesterase activities and of tyrosine hydroxylase and neuropeptide-Y immunoreactivity in neurons of the hypogastric ganglion of young adult and aged rats. *Journal of the Autonomic Nervous System, 45,* 155–163.

Warburton, A. L., & Santer, R. M. (1994). Sympathetic and sensory innervation of the urinary tract in young adult and aged rats: a semi-quantitative histochemical and immunohistochemical study. *Histochemical Journal, 26*, 127–133.

Warburton, A. L., & Santer, R. M. (1995). Decrease in synapsin I staining in the hypogastric ganglion of aged rats. *Neuroscience Letters, 194*, 157–160.

Waterson, J. G., Frewin, D. B., & Soltys, J. S. (1974). Age-related differences in catecholamine fluorescence of human vascular tissue. *Blood Vessels, 11*, 79–85.

Weidmann, P., de Chatel, R., Schiffmann, A., Bachmann, E., Beretta-Piccoli, C., Reubi, F. C., Ziegler, W. H., & Vetter, W. (1977). Interrelations between age and plasma renin, aldosterone and cortisol, urinary catecholamines, and the body sodium/volume state in normal man. *Klinische Wochenschrift, 55*, 725–733.

Yamada, Y., Miyajima, E., Tochikubo, O., Matsukawa, T., & Ishii, M. (1989). Age-related changes in muscle sympathetic nerve activity in essential hypertension. *Hypertension, 13*, 870–877.

Young, J. B., & Landsberg, L. (1998) Catecholamines and the adrenal medulla. In J. D. Wilson, D. W. Foster, P. R. Larsen, & H. Kronenberg (Eds.), *Williams Textbook of Endocrinology (9th ed.).* (pp. 621–705). Philadelphia: WB Saunders.

Young, J. B., & Morrison, S. F. (1998). Effects of fetal and neonatal environment on sympathetic nervous system development. *Diabetes Care, 21 (Suppl 2)*, B156–B160.

Young, J. B., Rowe, J. W., Pallotta, J. A., Sparrow, D., & Landsberg, L. (1980). Enhanced plasma norepinephrine response to upright posture and oral glucose administration in elderly human subjects. *Metabolism: Clinical and Experimental, 29*, 532–539.

Young, J. B., Troisi, R. J., Weiss, S. T., Parker, D. R., Sparrow, D., & Landsberg, L. (1992). Relationship of catecholamine excretion to body size, obesity, and nutrient intake in middle-aged and elderly men. *American Journal of Clinical Nutrition, 56*, 827–834.

Zhou, X.-F., Chie, E. T., Deng, Y.-S., & Rush, R. A. (1997). Rat mature sympathetic neurones derive neurotrophin 3 from peripheral effector tissues. *European Journal of Neuroscience, 9*, 2753–2764.

Ziegler, M. G., Lake, C. R., & Kopin, I. J. (1976). Plasma noradrenaline increases with age. *Nature, 261*, 333–335.

Eleven

Endocrine and Neuroendocrine Regulatory Functions

Andrzej Bartke and Mark Lane

I. Introduction

The neuroendocrine system coordinates body functions, mediates responses to the environment, and plays a central role in the maintenance of homeostasis, starting during fetal development and continuing throughout the life span. Therefore, the list of proven, suspected, and potential interactions between the neuroendocrine system and aging is virtually endless. These interactions can differ between various stages of ontogeny, between genders, and between species, further increasing their complexity. However, we propose that the relationships between neuroendocrine regulatory systems and aging can be grasped more easily if they are viewed within the following three broad categories:

- Effects of aging on the neuroendocrine system, including changes in hormone levels, the temporal pattern of their release, and their effects on the target tissues.
- Consequences of altered endocrine function during aging on susceptibility

to disease and on physical, mental, and reproductive fitness.
- Neuroendocrine-related alterations in metabolism, growth, and reproduction as mediators of the effects of genetic makeup on aging and life span.

These areas of interaction between the neuroendocrine system and aging will be discussed briefly.

A. Neuroendocrine Changes as Correlates of Aging

Concerning the effects of aging on neuroendocrine function, there are numerous and well-documented examples of age-related alterations in

- The rate of hormone production and secretion;
- The transport and clearance of hormones;
- The regulation of temporal variations in hormone release, including pulsatility, diurnal, and seasonal rhythms; and
- The responsiveness of target tissues to hormonal signals.

Examples of many of these changes will be provided in this chapter. Studies of these alterations occupy a special place in basic and clinical gerontology.

Age-related changes in neuroendocrine mechanisms of integration of physiological functions involve most, if not all, of the known hormones and neurotransmitters and can occur without changes in the levels of the corresponding signaling molecules. For example, plasma levels of thyroid-stimulating hormone (TSH), thyroxine (T_4), and triiodothyronine (T_3) do not change during human aging, whereas production of T_3 and T_4 decreases and sensitivity of many target tissues to the action of T_3 declines with age. These alterations in the turnover and action of thyroid hormones may be important because many symptoms of aging resemble clinical manifestations of hypothyroidism (Silverberg & Mooradian, 1998).

B. Neuroendocrine Changes as Putative Mechanisms of Aging

Because the neuroendocrine system serves to integrate body functions and to allow adaptations to changes in both internal and external environment, any alterations in the operation of this system may have far-reaching biological and health-related implications. There is considerable evidence that changes in the neuroendocrine system may represent not only *markers* but also *mechanisms* of age-related changes in organ function. To use a specific example, decline in LH and FSH release and a concomitant increase in prolactin (PRL) release in the aging rat described by Meites and his collaborators several decades ago [Clemens *et al.*, 1969; review in Meites (1983)] reflect age-related reduction in the release of neurotransmitters by the hypothalamus and, thus, serve as a marker of hypothalamic aging (Quadri *et al.*, 1973; Riegle *et al.*, 1977). However, these changes also repre-

sent important endocrine mechanisms of reproductive aging in that reduced FSH and LH release leads to decline of gonadal function, whereas hyperprolactinemia contributes to the suppression of gonadotropin release and to the development of mammary tumors. There are other examples of endocrine changes that are associated with aging and that apparently are also involved in the mechanisms of this process. Thus, in the human, declining release of sex steroids by the gonads, dehydroepiandrosterone (DHEA) and its sulfate (DHEAS) by the adrenals, and growth hormone (GH) by the pituitary during aging is believed to account for, or at least contribute to, many of the concomitant changes in body composition and function. Similarly, some suspect that the age-related reduction in the secretion of melatonin by the pineal contributes to age-related diseases and to aging itself by reducing the protective actions of this antioxidant and by inducing changes in neuroendocrine function, metabolism, and body composition.

With regard to the effects of age-related changes in hormone levels and hormone action on body composition and function, it is important to consider complex interactions between the various components of the neuroendocrine system. Thus, metabolic rate is controlled by thyroid hormones and GH, whereas protein synthesis and catabolism reflect the balance of the effects of GH, insulin, gonadal steroids, and, glucocorticoids. Growth is affected by GH, thyroid hormones, gonadal steroids, and during fetal life, insulin. Plasma glucose levels are influenced by insulin, glucagon, glucocorticoids, GH, and other hormones. In addition to exerting similar or opposing effects on the same cellular target, different hormones influence the rate of each other's release as well as responsiveness of the target cells to the action of other hormonal signals. For example, gonadal steroids influence GH release, whereas GH affects gonadal steroidogenesis; thyroid hormones influence the release of GH, whereas GH influences the thyroid; both glucocorticoids and GH influence responsiveness to insulin, and the levels of LH receptors (and, thus, steroidogenic response to LH) are regulated by FSH, PRL, GH, and LH itself. Some of these interactions are very important during aging. For example, age-related increases in corticosterone levels may contribute to concomitant development of insulin resistance, whereas alterations in GH signaling due to mutations, gene knockout, or overexpression of transgenes produce major changes in sensitivity to insulin that may influence the rate of aging.

C. Neuroendocrine-Related Characteristics as Determinants of Life Span

Comparisons both between and within species suggest that several hormonally controlled characteristics, including metabolic rate, fetal and postnatal growth, age of sexual maturation, and reproductive effort, correlate with longevity. Although numerous exceptions exist, high metabolic rate, early maturation, and rapid rate of reproduction (e.g., a large number of offspring produced per year) generally correlate with short life span. Moreover, within a species, suppression of growth and adult body size can delay aging and extend life span, whereas enhancement growth has the opposite effects (details will be discussed later in this chapter). This indicates that hormone-dependent biological processes are important in mediating the effects of the genetic makeup of a species or an individual on aging and life span. Genetic changes caused by evolutionary pressures, artificial selection, naturally occurring mutations, or targeted gene disruption can alter neuroendocrine control of metabolism, growth, and reproduction with profound consequences on the process of aging. Because aging can be characterized as increased susceptibility to environmental insults and disease, the role of hormone levels and hormone-dependent characteristics (including adult height and weight) as risk factors for cardiovascular disease and cancer [reviewed by Samaras and Elrick (1999)] deserves special emphasis.

The role of endocrine changes as putative mechanisms of aging and as identifiable causes of some of its symptoms is of obvious relevance to the current attempts to devise therapeutic interventions for the aging process. There is good evidence that age-related decline of bone mineral density and muscle mass as well as the age-related increase in adiposity can be reduced, postponed, or reversed by hormonal treatments. There is also little doubt that the use of various hormonal and hormone-related products by the elderly will become increasingly popular. However, the risk:benefit ratios of most of the available hormonal therapies remain to be evaluated thoroughly, and the proof that any treatment can influence the rate of human aging and prolong life is yet to be obtained. Deciphering complex relationships outlined in this section will be important for understanding the mechanisms of aging and for devising interventions that may promote healthy aging and perhaps even extend life.

In this chapter, we will focus on several issues that concern the relationship of hormonally controlled parameters of growth, metabolism, and food intake to aging and are of intense interest. We also will deal briefly with the interrelationships of neuroendocrine system and stress responses during aging. For a comprehensive survey of endocrine and neuroendocrine changes during aging, the reader is referred to Mobbs (1998).

II. Growth Hormone and the Somatotropic Axis

A. Release of Growth Hormone Declines with Age

The progressive decline in plasma growth hormone (GH) levels is among the most striking changes in the function of the neuroendocrine system during aging. In the human, peripheral GH levels are maximal during infancy and during the peripubertal period of rapid growth, and thereafter they begin to decline. The decline in the 24-hr mean serum GH levels is exponential, with a $t_{1/2}$ of approximately 7 years (Giustina & Veldhuis, 1998).

Age-related changes in GH release and the mechanisms responsible for these changes were studied extensively in the rat, dog, and human. Collectively, these studies indicate that the major decline in plasma GH levels with age is due to the increased release of somatostatin (somatotropin release inhibiting factor, SRIF) combined with reduced release of GH-releasing hormone (GHRH) by hypothalamic neurons into the portal blood supply of the anterior pituitary (Müller et al., 1993; Friend et al., 1997). Increased somatostatin "tone" is manifested by reduced responsiveness of pituitary somatotrophs to stimulatory inputs, including GHRH (Iranmanesh et al., 1998). Consequently, the treatment of elderly subjects with GHRH alone usually fails to restore GH secretion to the level typical of young adulthood (Ghigo et al., 1994). Reduction in the levels of the putative endogenous ligand of the receptor of the GH-releasing peptide(s) conceivably could also be involved in the age-related decline of GH release (Arvat et al., 1994).

Complex interplay between the somatotropic GH–insulin-like growth factor-I (GH–IGF-I) axis and the hypothalamic–pituitary–gonadal axis includes stimulatory effects of gonadal steroids on GH secretion (Iranmanesh et al., 1998; Giustina & Veldhuis, 1998). Consequently, age-related decline in plasma testosterone in men and menopausal reduction in estrogen levels in women contribute to the concomitant decrease in the peripheral levels of GH (Weltman et al., 1994).

In the male rat, GH normally is released from the pituitary in discrete, secretory bursts that produce the so-called pulsatile pattern of GH levels in peripheral circulation, consisting of sharp peaks occurring every 3 hr with very low levels between these peaks (Tannenbaum & Martin, 1976). Measurements of GH levels in sequentially collected blood samples provided evidence that these peaks of GH levels are virtually absent from old male rats (Sonntag et al., 1995).

B. Suppression of GH Release During Aging May Contribute to Concomitant Changes in Body Composition

Aging normally is accompanied by changes in body composition, which include increased adiposity, reduced lean body mass primarily due to a decrease in muscle mass, reduced bone mineral content, and thinning of the skin. These changes resemble those occurring in GH deficiency and can be at least partially reversed by treatment with GH in both GH-deficient (de Boer et al., 1995) and elderly subjects (Rudman et al., 1990).

These findings lead to several important conclusions and may have far-reaching therapeutic implications. First, they imply that progressive decline in GH release may be partially, or perhaps predominantly, responsible for age-related changes in body composition. Second, these findings suggest that GH therapy or treatments that stimulate endogenous GH release can postpone, reduce, or perhaps even prevent and reverse some of the symptoms of aging.

Theoretically, the benefits of GH (or GH-releasing) treatment in the elderly could be very substantial because loss of muscle mass and bone density leads to frailty, fractures, and loss of independence, whereas increased adiposity (particularly the abdominal adiposity associated with aging) is a risk factor for cardiovascular disease and diabetes. However, the risks and benefits of prolonged elevation of GH and/or IGF-I levels in the elderly have not been evaluated thoroughly.

In this context, it is interesting to note that, in the human, GH release increases in response to physical activity (Felsing *et al.*, 1992; Weltman *et al.*, 1992). Thus, the well-documented beneficial effects of exercise, including increases in muscle mass and bone mineral density and decrease in body fat, may be mediated, at least in part, by stimulation of endogenous GH release.

Psychological benefits of GH therapy in GH-deficient individuals raise additional issues about the consequences of age-related decline of GH release and the rationale for GH replacement. Growth hormone therapy of GH-deficient patients was reported to improve various measures of cognitive function and psychological well-being, leading to improved "quality of life" (Baum *et al.*, 1998). Because loss of short-term memory and other aspects of cognitive function in aging are well-documented, and because psychological changes in the elderly bear some resemblance to mild depression, these findings provide additional rationale for GH replacement during aging.

The issues of side effects and the risk:benefit ratio of GH therapy are outside the scope of this chapter, and the reader is referred to articles and reviews dealing specifically with this topic (Sacca *et al.*, 1994; de Boer *et al.*, 1995; Papadakis *et al.*, 1996). Moreover, there is evidence that GH release and GH signal-ing may act to reduce longevity and that age-related decline in GH and IGF-I levels can have some "protective" value for the aging individual. This evidence will be discussed later in this chapter.

C. Beneficial Actions of Caloric Restriction May Be Related to Its Effects on the GH-IGF-I Axis

A reduction in the availability of food to 60–70% of the voluntary intake, the so-called caloric restriction (CR), results in an impressive extension of life in laboratory rodents. The evidence that CR delays the development of age-related disease as well as aging itself and that its beneficial effects also apply to many species, including primates, is discussed elsewhere in this volume (Chapter 15). Findings concerning the suspected role of alterations in the GH–IGF-I axis in mediating the effects of CR on aging are difficult to interpret. It is well-known that food deprivation and malnutrition suppress GH release and lead to reduced levels of GH and IGF-I in peripheral circulation. Similar changes were described in CR rats (Breese *et al.*, 1991; Meites, 1993) and are consistent with reduced growth rate and reduced adult body size in these animals. Suppression of the GH–IGF-I axis can be viewed as an important mechanism by which CR delays aging, because in mice both GH deficiency and GH resistance are associated with impressive increases in longevity. There is also increasing evidence of a negative correlation between body size and life span within a species (details will be given in the next section of this chapter). However, Sonntag and his colleagues (Sonntag *et al.*, 1995) reported that, in long-term CR rats, peripheral GH levels are higher, rather than lower, than in the age-matched *ad libitum* (AL) fed controls due to the preservation of pulsatile GH release. These investigators proposed that this maintenance of the "youthful" pattern of GH release contributes to delayed aging of CR animals (Sonntag *et al.*, 1995). In support of this proposal, they presented intriguing evidence that age-related deterioration of vascular density on the surface of the brain can be prevented by CR and partially reversed by GH treatment of AL-fed animals (Sonntag, *et al.*, 1997, 1999; Lynch *et al.*, 1999). They also argued that increased GH levels in old CR animals may exert beneficial effects via stimulation of local (tissue) levels of IGF-I, whereas peripheral IGF-I remains below levels measured in AL controls (Sonntag *et al.*, 1999). Together, the seemingly inconsistent observations on the impact of CR on GH and IGF-I release raise some important and fascinating questions concerning the relationship of this axis to aging. It could be proposed that, during childhood, maturation, and early adulthood, GH may act to reduce life expectancy by stimulating growth and metabolism and as a determinant of adult body size, whereas later in life GH may act to prevent adiposity, loss of lean body mass, and age-associated deterioration of the vascular system and, thus, may correlate positively with life expectancy. This highly speculative proposal bears on the understanding of fundamental relationships between the function of the neuroendocrine system and aging and on the rationale for GH therapy in the elderly and, thus, would seem to deserve critical evaluation in future studies.

The age-related decrease of peripheral IGF-I levels and enhancement of this decline in CR animals are of considerable interest in their own right because of the increasing evidence that IGF-I levels are a risk factor in cancer (Holly *et al.*, 1999). Correlation of peripheral IGF-I levels with the incidence of malignancy in the prostate, breast, and colon raises a very interesting issue of the possible benefit ("protective effect") of the physiological age-related decline in the release of hormones that stimulate cell divisions, growth, and secretory activity of target organs. If reduction in the levels of GH, IGF-I, and gonadal steroids during aging indeed confers protection against cancers, the rationale for replacement therapy with these hormones during aging obviously would be weakened. Deciphering evolutionary mechanisms that may have led to adaptive changes in endocrine function in post-reproductive years offers an interesting challenge and adds to the difficulties in understanding the genetic control of aging and life span.

D. Aging Is Delayed in GH-Deficient and GH-Resistant Animals

Transgenic mice overexpressing human, bovine, ovine, or rat GH under the control of different promoters have reduced life expectancy, with GH transgenic animals in some of the lines living only half as long as their normal siblings (Wolf *et al.*, 1993; Cecim *et al.*, 1994; Rollo *et al.*, 1996). Studies of various functional parameters related to aging, including the replicative potential of cells *in vitro* (Pendergast *et al.*, 1993), brain astrogliosis (Miller *et al.*, 1995), turnover of hypothalamic neurotransmitters (Steger *et al.*, 1993), learning and memory (Meliska *et al.*, 1997), and oxidative processes (Rollo *et al.*, 1996), in these animals suggest that they may age prematurely. This conclusion was somewhat unexpected because the documented increase in the mortality of acromegalic patients is ascribed to greater incidence of cardiovascular disease, diabetes, and cancer rather than to accelerated aging (Bengtsson *et al.*, 1988).

The possibility that physiological levels of GH may act to accelerate aging was raised by observations in GH-deficient and GH-resistant mice. Hypopituitary Ames dwarf mice with combined GH, prolactin (PRL), and thyroid-stimulating hormone (TSH) deficiencies outlive their normal siblings by more than 1 year, i.e., over 50% of their normal life span (Brown-Borg et al., 1996). These animals are homozygous for a mutation at the Prop-1 locus, which prevents the development of GH-, PRL-, and TSH-producing cells in their anterior pituitaries (Sornson et al., 1996). A similar longevity advantage was detected in Snell dwarf mice (Miller, 1999; Harrison & Flurkey, personal communication), which have identical endocrine deficiencies due to mutation at the pit-1 locus on a different chromosome (Li et al., 1990). Data from a human pedigree with mutations at the Prop-1 locus (Krzisnik et al., 1999) suggest that congenital hypopituitarism also may be associated with increased life expectancy in the human.

Kopchick and Laron (1999) reported that mice with targeted disruption of the GH receptor gene (GH-R-KO) and the consequent GH resistance live much longer than their normal siblings. Because GH-R-KO mice are not hypothyroid or hypoprolactinemic (Chandrashekar et al., 1999; Danilovich & Bartke, unpublished observations), these results suggest that prolonged survival of Ames and Snell dwarf mice cannot be explained by hypothyroidism, PRL deficiency, or synergistic interactions between their multiple endocrine defects. This clearly focuses attention on the physiological role of the GH–IGF-I axis in determination of the life span. Prolonged survival of GH-deficient and GH-resistant mice suggests that genes related to the development and function of the somatotropic axis qualify as the first mammalian longevity genes.

Ongoing studies aimed at identification of the mechanisms responsible for prolonged survival and for the apparent delay of aging in Ames dwarf mice and information available from the studies of Snell dwarfs suggest the involvement of multiple factors, including reduced body temperature and metabolic rate (Hunter et al., 1999), reduced number of cell divisions (Winick & Grant, 1968), improved antioxidant defenses (Brown-Borg et al., 1999; Hauck & Bartke, 2000), increased sensitivity to insulin (Borg et al., 1995; Bartke & Turyn, unpublished observations), and differences in the relative level of expression of multiple genes (Miller & Bartke, unpublished observations). In addition, the most obvious phenotypic characteristic of Ames dwarfs, Snell dwarfs, and GH-R-KO mice, namely, reduced body size, may be an important determinant of their prolonged survival. In contrast to the generally longer life span of large compared to small species, the relationship of body size to longevity within the species appears to be inverse rather than direct. Mice selected for small body size live significantly longer than larger mice (Roberts, 1961). Small breeds of domestic dogs outlive large breeds (Patronek et al., 1997), and there is increasing evidence that height is negatively correlated with life expectancy in the human (Samaras et al., 1999). Thus, the influence of neuroendocrine function on aging almost certainly includes actions of hormones on growth during prepubertal development. In other words, the onset and/or the rate of aging may be "preprogrammed" early in life by genes, hormones, and environmental factors that influence growth and adult body size. This notion appears to be counter intuitive, because good nutrition marked by rapid growth generally is associated with positive rather than negative health effects, and the progressive increase of human life expectancy is associated with increased rather than reduced height. However, life expectancy in human populations obviously is influenced by the progress of medicine and public health measures, improved hygiene, and the promotion of healthy lifestyles; the effects of these changes may mask the suspected opposing influence of alterations in adult body size.

The evidence for the longevity advantage of small individuals is impossible to ignore. Caloric restriction, which is the best documented and the most studied method of prolonging life span, reduces growth rate and adult body size and is most effective when it is instituted early in life before the adult size is attained (Weindruch et al., 1982; Yu et al., 1985). Obviously, much further work is needed to uncover the mechanism(s) responsible for the small size–delayed aging relationship. Available evidence suggests that multiple mechanisms and their synergistic interactions are likely to be involved and that small size will prove to be a marker of a particular set of characteristics of oxidative metabolism, food intake, carbohydrate processing, and energy partitioning that predict increased life expectancy.

III. Hormonal Control of Carbohydrate Metabolism

A. Effects of Aging on Insulin Signaling

Disruption of homeostatic control of carbohydrate (primarily glucose) metabolic control ranks among the most widely recognized physiological alterations that occur with aging. Glucose tolerance diminishes with age in animal models and humans, and dysregulation of glucose metabolism eventually may become sufficiently severe, such that the diagnostic criteria for diabetes are met. Indeed, it is widely known that the incidence of diabetes increases with age.

Many hormones have an impact glucoregulation, including insulin, glucagon, glucocorticoids, GH, and epinephrine. Normally, glucose metabolism is regulated tightly by feedback control of the glucagon and insulin that are secreted by the pancreatic islets in response to fluctuations in circulating glucose. Although studies are limited in number, available data suggest that glucagon secretion is not changed with age (Berger et al., 1978; Elahi et al., 1982; Meneilly et al., 1987). In contrast, it is generally accepted that insulin secretion and/or action decline with age.

Much evidence suggests that insulin action declines with age. For example, studies using whole animals and perfused or isolated skeletal muscle suggest that insulin-stimulated glucose utilization diminishes across the life span [reviewed in Halter (1995)]. Similarly, older rodents have reduced glucose utilization; however, most of this reduction occurs in younger animals between 4 and 6 months of age, with little or no additional decline thereafter [reviewed in Cartee et al. (1994)]. In mice, at least one study (Leiter et al., 1988) has suggested that glucose tolerance may indeed increase with age. In humans, there is general agreement that glucose disposal declines progressively with age (DeFronzo, 1979; Fink et al., 1983; Ratzmann et al., 1982; Rowe et al., 1983). Studies in both animal and human model systems suggest that the insulin resistance observed with aging is due to a postreceptor defect in insulin action (Ahren & Pacini, 1998; Chen et al., 1985; Fink et al., 1986, 1992; Jackson, 1990; Nishimura et al., 1988; Rowe et al., 1981).

Figure 1 summarizes several key components of the insulin signal cascade that have been examined in aging studies. Figure 1 also illustrates several important signaling outputs of insulin signal transduction that may be relevant to biological aging processes (discussed next).

Insulin receptor number does not change with age in rodent skeletal muscle (Barnard et al., 1992; Carvalho et al., 1996; Wang et al., 1997; Martineau et al., 1999) or adipocytes (Ruiz et al., 1992). Binding of insulin leads to tyrosine phosphorylation of the receptor and the insulin receptor substrates (IRS). Data regarding changes in tyrosine kinase activity of the

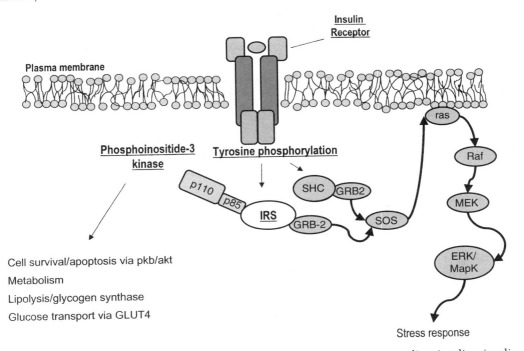

Figure 1. Mammalian insulin signaling pathway. Many genes in the mammalian insulin signaling pathway have been shown to share significant sequence homology with genes that apparently regulate life span in nematodes (see text for details). Several signaling outputs of this pathway may be altered during aging and caloric restriction and may be relevant to processes of biological aging.

insulin receptor during aging are not entirely consistent. For example, studies in rodent adipose tissue report that insulin stimulation of adipose tissue tyrosine kinase is either reduced (Ruiz et al., 1992) or unaltered (Matthaei et al., 1990) in older rats. In contrast, studies of liver (Nadiv et al., 1992) and skeletal muscle (Barnard et al., 1992; Kono et al., 1990) suggest a reduction in insulin-stimulated tyrosine kinase activity with age. However, at least one study (Kono et al., 1990) reported no age impairment of liver tyrosine kinase activity.

Subsequent steps in insulin signaling, such as the activity and amount of insulin receptor substrates (IRS) and phosphoinositide 3-kinase (PI3-K), have not been studied widely in aging model systems. Carvalho et al. (1996) reported that IRS–1 declined in rats by 5 months of age but showed no additional decline in older ages. Basal levels of PI3-K protein in liver and muscle are not different in older compared to younger rodents (Carvalho et al., 1996; Martineau et al., 1999). However, at least one study showed that insulin-stimulated PI3-K activity was reduced significantly in older (20 months) than in younger (2 months) rats (Carvalho et al., 1996). Other than studies of receptor number, it is readily apparent that insufficient data exist upon which to draw conclusions regarding age-associated changes in the early steps of molecular insulin signaling.

B. Age-Related Alterations in Cellular Glucose Transport

Cellular glucose transport is the most extensively studied aspect of insulin action. In rodents, studies at the whole animal level are in agreement that the most notable decline in glucose transport occurs during the first 4 months of life and declines more gradually between 4 and 8–12 months of age. After that, there is little, if any, additional reduction in rodents greater than 12 months of age (Goodman et al., 1983; Gulve et al., 1993; Ivy et al., 1991), suggesting that the reduced glucose in older rodents may not be due to senescence per se. In humans, several studies have reported an age- associated decline in insulin-stimulated glucose disposal (DeFronzo, 1979; Fink et al., 1983; Ratzmann et al., 1982; Rowe et al., 1983). It is apparent that both animal and human studies suggest a defect in cellular glucose transport at the organism level in older subjects.

The primary protein responsible for insulin-stimulated glucose transport in muscle and adipose tissue is the GLUT4 transporter isoform. Age effects on GLUT4 in adipose tissue suggest that both GLUT4 protein and mRNA levels are reduced in older compared to younger rats (Lin et al., 1991. In muscle, changes appear to be muscle-specific, as some muscles show reduced protein levels with age. However, in several studies, GLUT4 protein levels remain stable across the adult life span in rat epitrochlearis (Cartee et al., 1993; Gulve et al., 1993). A study by Barnard et al. (1992) combined several muscles, including gastrocnemius, plantaris, and quadriceps, and reported that GLUT4 protein levels were not different between 2 and 24 months of age.

Few studies have attempted to assess the role of GLUT4 protein in the age-related reduction in glucose uptake/transport in humans. One study by Houmard and co-workers (1995) assessed insulin sensitivity and GLUT4 content of the vastus lateralis and gastrocnemius muscles across a wide age range (18–80 years) in both men and women. They reported that GLUT4 protein declined significantly in vastus lateralis samples from both men and women during aging. However, GLUT4 levels in the gastrocnemius remained stable. This study also showed that vastus lateralis GLUT4 was correlated positively with insulin sensitivity, even after adjusting for differences in central and regional adiposity. In contrast, Dela and co-workers (1994) did not detect a change in GLUT4 protein comparing young men in their twenties to older subjects (over 50 years). It is apparent that the molecular mechanism of age-related changes in glucose transport is not fully understood and will require additional study. In particular, the significance of muscle-specific differences to overall reductions in glucose transport during aging needs to be investigated.

It is not known why some muscles exhibit age-related changes in GLUT4 while others do not. It is possible that differences in contractile activity or fiber type may influence these results. For example, in rodents muscle-specific differences in GLUT4 have been related to fiber type and contractile activity (Hardin et al., 1993; Megeney et al., 1993). In contrast, human studies suggest that GLUT4 content is only minimally or not at all related to fiber type (Houmard et al., 1991, 1993; Andersen et al., 1993). This aspect of age-related changes in insulin action warrants additional research.

C. Effects of Exercise on Carbohydrate Metabolism

Additional insight into age-associated changes in insulin signal transduction can be obtained from studies of exercise intervention. It is well-known that whole body insulin action improves with exercise training in humans (Dela et al., 1996; Cox et al., 1999) and rats (Banks et al., 1992; Goodyear et al., 1991; Rodnick et al., 1992). Most interestingly, several studies have shown that skeletal muscle GLUT4 increases in response to exercise training in middle-aged and older people (Houmard *et al.*, 1991, 1993; Hughes *et al.*, 1993). Similar findings have been reported in some (Youngren & Barnard, 1995), but not all studies (Gulve *et al.*, 1993; Kern *et al.*, 1992) in aged rodents. It is important to consider that the studies reporting no exercise effect were confounded by a relative reduction in exercise capacity in old, compared to young, rats (Youngren & Barnard, 1995). Human studies such as those discussed here have not attempted to address this important issue. In summary, studies of exercise intervention clearly show that age-related declines in GLUT4 are reversible by exercise intervention.

In addition to considering whether age-associated changes are reversible by various interventions, it is important to consider other confounding variables that may influence changes during senescence. It is possible, particularly when considering insulin action during aging, that many other factors may influence experimental outcomes. For example, factors such as body composition, levels of physical activity, and composition of the diet all have well-documented effects on insulin action. In humans, it is widely known that these factors change with age. As such, these factors may influence the outcome of studies designed to assess insulin action during aging. It is imperative that gerontologists consider the influence of these possible confounds when interpreting data or designing studies relating to insulin action and aging. A detailed discussion of these confounds is not possible in the present context, and the reader is referred to several reviews for additional information (Halter, 1995; Muller *et al.*, 1996).

D. Other Actions of Insulin and General Conclusions

Is there evidence that, in addition to its role in glucose metabolism, insulin as a neuroendocrine factor may play an important role in other aging processes? Figure 1 illustrates that several signaling outputs of insulin likely influence several other cellular processes, such as cell growth, apoptosis, metabolism, differentiation, and stress responses. In particular, much evidence has implicated the phosphoinositide 3-kinases in many cellular processes [reviewed in Shepherd *et al.*, (1996)]. Several of these are known to change with age and may be important mediators of aging processes. Given the complexity of cellular signal transduction and the fact that other growth factors also act via this or related pathways, it will be difficult to determine the extent to which insulin influences these signaling outputs. Modulation of cellular metabolism is a well-known effect of insulin; however, it has become recognized that this hormone also regulates the expression of over 100 genes [reviewed in O'Brien and Granner (1996)].

Additional evidence that the insulin signal cascade may play a key role in the biology of aging comes from studies of life span extension by caloric restriction (CR) and genetic manipulation of the life span. Data from CR studies provide only circumstantial evidence that insulin plays a key role in this paradigm. For instance, animal studies show that CR routinely alters fasting insulin and insulin sensitivity in a variety of species and under differing dietary conditions (Reaven *et al.*, 1983; Kalant *et al.*, 1988; Masoro *et al.*, 1989, 1992; Kemnitz *et al.*, 1994; Bodkin *et al.*, 1995; Lane *et al.*, 1995). Fasting insulin remains lower in CR rodents over the entire 24-hr period, including fasting and fed states (Masoro *et al.*, 1992), and in fact insulin levels are reduced over the entire life span in Fischer 344 rats. Finally, studies of short-term CR in both rodent (Dean *et al.*, 1998) and primate models (Lane *et al.*, 2000) show that changes in insulin secretion and responsiveness are among the earliest metabolic adaptations to occur in this paradigm.

More direct evidence that insulin signaling may play a fundamental role in aging comes from studies of the genetic manipulation of life span. Several life span extending mutations in *Caenorhabditis elegans* have been cloned and found to share significant sequence homology with genes in the mammalian insulin-signaling cascade. Specifically, the long-lived mutations *daf–2* and *age-1* (perhaps the same as *daf–23*) share significant sequence homology with the mammalian insulin/growth factor receptors and the PI3-K enzyme complex, respectively (Morris *et al.*, 1996; Kimura *et al.*, 1997). The *daf–18* mutation, which regulates life span effects in both *daf–2* and *age–1* mutants, maps to a mammalian tumor suppressor gene PTEN (Ogg & Ruvkun, 1998; Rouault *et al.*, 1999) that disrupts PI3-K signaling (Myers *et al.*, 1998). Finally, *daf–16* maps to three proteins in the forkhead hepatic nuclear transcription factor (HNF) family in mammals (Lin *et al.*, 1997). These proteins may, in part, mediate insulin's effect on certain hepatic proteins.

A study in transgenic mice has implicated the insulin cascade in mammalian life span control. A transgenic knockout of the p66 isoform of shc (see Fig. 1) exhibited significant extensions of both mean and maximal life span, relative to control mice (Migliaccio *et al.*, 1999). Phosphorylation of shc, an early event in insulin signaling, occurs in response to insulin or growth factor receptor activation. Some caution is warranted in interpreting these studies, given the relatively low number of subjects and the fact that control mice were somewhat short-lived. Other mouse models exhibiting extended life span also implicate insulin or insulin responsiveness. For example, Ames dwarf mice and GH receptor knockout mice have lower fasting insulin levels and/or increased insulin sensitivity (Borg *et al.*,

1995; Turyn, Kopchick, & Bartke, unpublished observations). Genetic manipulation studies in nematodes, and now mammals, provide tantalizing evidence that insulin signal transduction ultimately may be related to more fundamental processes of aging, perhaps even in life span control.

In summary, it is apparent that there is a reduction in insulin action in older individuals, and the available evidence suggests that this decline is due mostly to altered postreceptor events. Unfortunately, this aspect of insulin action has not been studied extensively during aging, and no clear consensus emerges from the limited findings that might help explain the age-associated increase in glucose intolerance. Clearly, more studies of molecular insulin signaling during aging are needed. These studies must also be designed to reduce the possible confounding influences of obesity, physical activity, and dietary differences with aging. Further, care must be taken when selecting animal models for such studies, as evidence in rodents overwhelmingly suggests that glucose utilization changes most during maturation with little additional change during aging. Finally, it seems likely that, in addition to regulation of carbohydrate metabolism, insulin and insulin signal transduction influence many other processes relevant to aging and may even be involved in the regulation of life span.

IV. Neuroendocrine Changes Related to Regulation of Food Intake and Body Composition

Progressive increases in body weight and adiposity accompany aging in many species, including humans. This is due primarily to reduced energy expenditure because food intake is concomitantly declining rather than increasing. In addition to increased adiposity, aging is associated with reduction in lean body mass primarily due to the loss of musculature and bone mineral. Late in life, decline in lean body mass may be accelerated and body weight begins to decline. These changes fail to produce a compensatory increase in food intake, leading to a condition sometimes referred to as "anorexia of aging" (McCue, 1995).

Age-related changes in body composition have been related to alterations in endocrine function and, specifically, to reduced secretion of GH and gonadal steroids. There is also considerable evidence of age-related changes in the levels and actions of peptides involved in the control of food intake, including neuropeptide Y and leptin.

A. Neuropeptide Y

Neuropeptide Y (NPY) acts in the central nervous system to stimulate food intake and to favor peripheral energy storage. It also interacts with other neuronal systems to influence reproductive development and function. In different regions of the rat brain, aging is associated with a loss of NPY immunoreactive neurons and alterations in their morphology (Kowalski et al., 1992; Cha et al., 1996; Huh et al., 1997, 1998) and with reductions in the content of both NPY mRNA and NPY (Higuchi et al., 1988; Gruenewald et al., 1994), as well as in NPY overflow as measured in vivo with the use of push–pull cannulae (Hastings et al., 1998). Fasting leads to an increase in the expression of NPY, and this response is reduced in old, compared to young, rats (Gruenewald et al., 1996). This suggests that impaired stimulation of food intake and slow recovery of body weight after fasting in old rats may be due to the inadequate response of NPY neurons to this stimulus (Gruenewald et al., 1996). It is interesting that reduced NPY mRNA response to food deprivation

was observed as early as 40 weeks of age, that is, in middle-aged rather than old animals (Jhanwar-Uniyal & Chua, 1993).

In addition to age-related decline in the secretory activity of NPY neurons and their physiological responses to food deprivation, the sensitivity of the CNS targets of NPY action may decline with age. Pich et al., (1992) reported that injections of NPY into the paraventricular nucleus were less effective in stimulating eating and drinking in old, compared to young, rats. Reduced responsiveness of feeding behavior to NPY obviously could contribute to the limited capacity of old animals to increase their food intake and to regain body weight after fasting (Gruenewald et al., 1996).

Reduced responsiveness of NPY neurons in old rats is not limited to the central nervous system. Immobilization stress increases the levels of NPY mRNA in the adrenals, a response that declines with aging (Silverstein et al., 1998).

Information on the impact of aging on NPY-producing neurons and on the responsiveness of various cellular targets to NPY in species other than the rat appears to be limited. In the human brain, there is an age-related decline in the NPY content in the gyrus cinguli (Arranz et al., 1996). In the mouse, the effects of NPY on food intake were reported to be similar in young and aged animals (Morely et al., 1987), but the stimulatory effect of NPY on the migration of lymphocytes toward a chemoattractant disappeared during aging (Medina et al., 1998).

B. Leptin

Leptin is a hormone that is involved in the control of food intake, energy metabolism, and body composition. It is produced in adipose tissue and acts to reduce food intake and increase energy expenditure. Mutant mice that do not produce leptin or lack leptin receptor develop extreme obesity early in life.

However, in humans, obesity rarely is due to leptin deficiency and normally is associated with increased rather than reduced levels of leptin in peripheral circulation.

During aging, serum leptin levels in humans generally increase (Perry et al., 1997; Moller et al., 1998; Koistinen et al., 1998; Morley et al., 1999) and are more closely related to the increase in adiposity than to aging per se (Perry et al., 1997; Sumner et al., 1998). The correlation of leptin levels to relative fat mass is weaker in old than in young subjects, and it has been suggested that disruption of this relationship in the elderly might contribute to their tendency toward obesity (Moller et al., 1998).

In elderly men, serum leptin levels are inversely related to serum testosterone (Luukkaa et al., 1998). Studies in young men treated with testosterone (Luukkaa et al., 1998) and longitudinal studies during puberty (Blum et al., 1997; Garcia-Mayor et al., 1997) suggest that testosterone suppresses leptin production. This effect, together with the action of testosterone on body composition, could account for the association of higher testosterone with lower leptin levels in elderly subjects.

In women, serum leptin levels were not affected by menopause or estrogen replacement (Sumner et al., 1998; Castracane et al., 1998), but were inversely correlated to serum GH (Roubenoff et al., 1998). This latter relationship may be related to the well-established lipolytic action of GH. In a prospective study of elderly women, leptin levels were reduced in the subjects who died within 5 years of blood sampling compared to those who lived longer, probably reflecting better nutritional status in the latter group (Koistinen et al., 1998).

In his review of the relationship of leptin to aging, Mobbs (1998) pointed out interesting similarities between endocrine correlates of aging and leptin deficiency or resistance. These include increases in glucocorticoids and insulin and decreases in sex steroids, growth hormone, and thyroid hormones. He further suggested that some underweight elderly individuals could benefit from a diet that increases leptin levels by increasing body fat or from leptin injections.

In the rat, there is considerable evidence that the levels of both leptin mRNA and leptin increase with age (Li et al., 1997, 1998; Wolden-Hanson et al., 1999; Rasmussen et al., 1999). Although these changes are associated with, and most likely due to, age-related increase in adiposity, the age-related increase in leptin expression in the inguinal white adipose tissue was found to be independent of the increase in adiposity (Li et al., 1997). Fasting-induced suppression of serum leptin levels was attenuated in old rats (Li et al., 1998).

In one study, leptin levels in middle-aged rats were reduced to the values encountered in young animals by treatment with melatonin (Rasmussen et al., 1999). The employed regimen of melatonin administration in drinking water resulted in large nocturnal elevations of plasma melatonin, thus mimicking the diurnal pattern of melatonin secretion in young rats. It remains to be determined whether melatonin lowers leptin levels by reducing adipose mass or by inhibiting leptin secretion from the adipocytes. However, in male C57 BL/6 mice, leptin expression did not increase with age but correlated with plasma glucose levels at each of the ages examined (Mizuno et al., 1996).

Parallel increases in adiposity and in leptin levels during aging suggest that the ability of leptin to reduce food intake and fat deposition may be compromised as the animal ages. In strong support of this possibility, the suppressive effects of intracerebroventricular leptin administration on body weight, water intake, weight of fat deposits, number of adipocytes, and various indices of their function were readily detectable in young Sprague–Dawley rats, but were reduced or absent in middle-aged (8-month-old) animals (Qian *et al.*, 1998a,b). Old rats from another, longer living strain were described as "leptin-resistant" (Li *et al.*, 1998). Alterations in responsiveness to leptin during aging could be due to changes in the level of leptin receptors (Gayle *et al.*, 1999).

C. Galanin

Age-related changes in neuroendocrine control of food intake are likely to involve multiple factors in addition to NPY and leptin (Blanton *et al.*, 1999). Galanin is of potential interest in this regard because its multiple effects include food-intake-stimulating (orexigenic) activity. Krzywkowski *et al.*, (1994) reported increased galanin binding in several brain regions of old male Sprague–Dawley rats. In a subsequent study of Fischer 344 male rats, Planas, *et al.*, (1998) detected small but significant age-related reductions in galanin binding in several brain regions, including some of the same regions that were examined by Krzywkowski *et al.*, (1994). Major differences in age-related neuroendocrine changes in different rat strains are discussed elsewhere in this chapter. The possible functional significance of age-related changes in CNS galanin binding is suggested by the report that the GH responses to galanin treatment were reduced in elderly, compared to young, women (Giustina *et al.*, 1993).

V. Hypothalamic–Pituitary–Adrenal Axis

Studies of age-related changes in the function of the hypothalamic–pituitary–adrenal (HPA) axis continue to attract considerable attention. This is primarily related to the importance of this axis for coping with stress and to the role of glucocorticoids in the control of neuronal survival in the aging brain, although effects of the HPA axis on metabolic control also are of obvious relevance.

There is considerable evidence to suggest that cumulative exposure to basal and stress-induced levels of glucocorticoids may contribute to age-related loss of memory and cognitive function, most likely by promoting neuronal loss in the hippocampus (Stein-Behrens *et al.*, 1994; Angelucci, 1997; Reagan & McEwen, 1997). Although evidence for age-related decreases in the number of hippocampal neurons has been questioned (Reagan & McEwen, 1997; Leverenz *et al.*, 1999), there is little doubt that glucorticoids can induce neuronal death (Behl *et al.*, 1997) and that the function of the HPA axis is related to cognitive abilities (Herbert, 1998).

In rats, glucocorticoid receptor (GR) expression (as measured by steady-state levels of GR mRNA) and glucocorticoid binding in the hippocampus and other brain areas decline significantly during aging (van Eekelen *et al.*, 1992; Morano *et al.*, 1994; Cizza *et al.*, 1994; Ferrini *et al.*, 1999; Hassan *et al.*, 1999). These alterations are of functional significance because old rats exhibit reduced sensitivity to negative feedback inhibition of the HPA axis by natural glucocortiocoids or synthetic agonists such as dexamethasone (Morano *et al.*, 1994; Hatzinger *et al.*, 1996; Slotkin *et al.*, 1996; Ferrini *et al.*, 1999). As a result, stress-induced elevations in plasma ACTH and, consequently, corticosterone are "extinguished" less effectively by negative feedback mechanisms and persist longer than in young animals (Morano *et al.*, 1994). Preliminary data suggest a similar situation in transgenic mice overexpressing GH in which life span is reduced drastically (Steger & Bartke, unpublished results). Moreover, old animals have a reduced ability to develop tolerance of the HPA axis to chronic stress (Odio & Brodish, 1989; Spencer & McEwen, 1997). This, together with increased peripheral responsiveness to glucocortiocoids in aging animals (Slotkin et al., 1996; Reagan & McEwen, 1997; Dardevet et al., 1998), could exacerbate the effects of stress on CNS function and body composition in older individuals.

In aging rats, the levels of corticotropin releasing-hormone (CRH) and CRH message decrease (Cizza et al., 1994; Givalois et al., 1997), whereas ACTH responses to CRH are augmented (Cizza et al., 1994; Hatzinger et al., 1996). Consequently, ACTH levels may be elevated (van Eekelen et al., 1992; Hatzinger et al., 1996). There is also evidence of increased adrenal responses to ACTH stimulation (Verkhratsky, 1995). Plasma levels of corticosterone, the principal glucocorticoid in this species, have been reported to be elevated (Yau et al., 1995; Windle et al., 1998), unaltered (van Eekelen et al., 1992; Morano et al., 1994; Ferrini et al., 1999), or reduced in the course of aging (Cizza et al., 1994; Hassan et al., 1999). Although some of these differences may be related to the age of the animals used in the various studies, differential exposure to stress prior to blood collection, time of day, and other experimental factors, there is little doubt that they are due mostly to using animals from different strains (De Kloet et al., 1991). Strains of laboratory rats used in aging research differ widely in their life span, age-related pathological lesions, apparent causes of death, and also the responses of the HPA axis to stress (Windle et al., 1998).

There is interesting evidence that age-related decline in melatonin release and in the amplitude of its diurnal rhythm may contribute to alterations in the function of the HPA axis. In rats given high doses of dexamethasone, chronic treatment with melatonin reduced corticosterone levels and increased sensitivity to glucocorticoid feedback (Konakchieva et al., 1998). The authors concluded that melatonin protects the HPA axis from glucocorticoid-induced deterioration (Konakchieva et al., 1998). In Sprague–Dawley rats, which experience declines in plasma corticosterone with advancing age, long-term treatment of middle-aged animals with melatonin in drinking water increased plasma corticosterone levels and partially or completely reversed age-related changes in plasma insulin levels, body composition, core body temperature, and locomotor activity (Rasmussen et al., 1999). These findings are most intriguing because the employed regimen of melatonin administration was effective in mimicking wide diurnal fluctuations in plasma melatonin levels, which are characteristic of young rats (Rasmussen et al., 1999).

Increases in glucocorticoid levels during aging have been described in other species. In old dogs, ACTH and cortisol levels are increased (Reul et al., 1991). In mice, plasma corticosterone levels increase with age (Miller et al., 1995). This increase is exaggerated in transgenic mice overexpressing GH in which life span is reduced drastically and aging appears to be accelerated (Miller et al., 1995). However, age-related decline in plasma corticosterone levels was detected in animals from another stock (Borg et al., 1995).

Relation of glucocorticoid levels to the process of aging or to the mechanisms involved is very difficult. Catabolic and neurotoxic effects of glucocorticoids as well as their ability to induce insulin resistance would be expected to accelerate various age-related physiological changes and perhaps aging itself. Whereas anti-inflammatory effects of glucocorticoids could be viewed as beneficial, suppression of immune responses could compromise defenses against infection and cancer. However, caloric restriction (CR), which delays aging and prolongs life in laboratory rats and mice, is associated with stimulation rather than suppression of the HPA axis and an increase in peripheral glucocorticoid levels. For a detailed discussion of the effects of CR on neuroendocrine functions, the reader is referred to Chapter 15 in this volume.

In humans, aging is associated with increased plasma cortisol levels (DeKloet et al., 1991), reduced sensitivity to negative glucocorticoid feedback (Cocchi, 1992; Wilkinson et al., 1997), reduced amplitude of the diurnal rhythm of ACTH and cortisol (Deuschle et al., 1997), and impaired inhibition of the HPA axis during sleep (Born & Fehm, 1998). Importantly, cognitive impairments correlate with elevated plasma cortisol and dysregulation of the HPA axis (Lupien et al., 1994; Meaney et al., 1995). In contrast to the evidence of age-related increase in cortisol levels, adrenal output and peripheral levels of dehydroepiandrosterone (DHEA) and its sulfate (DHEAS) reach a maximum in early adulthood and decline precipitously during aging (Orentreich et al., 1984; Yen & Laughlin, 1998). This may have far-reaching implications, because DHEA is neuroprotective (Kimonides et al., 1998) and can specifically oppose the neurotoxic effects of glucocorticoids (Herbert, 1998). Moreover, DHEA and DHEAS serve as important precursors for peripheral conversion to sex steroids. The current interest in DHEA/DHEAS as antiaging agents and the potential implications of their wide and not medically supervised use in our society are outside the scope of this writing.

Acknowledgements

We thank Mr. Steven Hauck for his help in searching the literature, Ms. Carole Daesch for editing, and Ms. Mae Hilt for typing. Our own studies on this topic were supported by the National Institute on Aging and by the Illinois Council on Food and Agricultural Research.

References

Ahren, B., & Pacini, G. (1998). Age-related reduction in glucose elimination is accompanied by reduced glucose effectiveness and increased hepatic insulin extraction in man. *Journal of Clinical Endocrinology Metablolism, 83,* 3350–3356.

Andersen, P. H., Lund, S., Schmitz, O., Junker, S., Kahn, B. B., & Pedersen, O. (1993). Increased insulin-stimulated glucose uptake in athletes: The importance of GLUT4 mRNA, GLUT4 protein and bibre type composition of skeletal muscle. *Acta Physiologica Scandinavica, 149,* 1393–1404.

Angelucci, L. (1997). Glucocorticoid hormone, aging brain and dementia. *Functional Neurology, 12,* 167–173.

Arranz, B., Blennow, K., Ekman, R., Eriksson, A., Mansson, J. E., & Marcusson, J. (1996). Brain monoaminergic and neuropeptidergic variations in human aging. *Journal of Neural Transmission, 103,* 101–115.

Arvat, E., Gianotti, L., Grottoli, A., Imbimbo, B. P., Lenaerts, V., Deghenghi, R., Camanni, F., & Ghigo, E. (1994). Arginine and growth hormone-releasing hormone restore the limited growth hormone-releasing activity of hexarelin in elderly subjects. *Journal of Clinical Endocrinology and Metabolism, 79,* 1440–1443.

Banks, E. A., Broznick, J. T., Yaspelkis, B. B., Kang, H. Y., & Ivy, J. L. (1992). Muscle glucose transport, GLUT–4 content, and degree of exercise training in obese Zucker rats. *American Journal of Physiology, 263,* E1010–E1015.

Barnard, R. J., Lawani, L. O., Martin, D. A., Youngren, J. F., Singh, R., & Scheck, S. H. (1992). Effects of maturation and aging on the skeletal muscle glucose transport system. *American Physiological Society, 262,* E619–E626.

Baum, H. B. A., Katznelson, L., Sherman, J. C., Biller, B. M. K., Hayden, D. L., Schoenfeld, J. C., Cannistraro, K. E., & Klibanski, A. (1998). Effects of a physiological growth hormone (GH) therapy on cognition and quality of life in patients with adult-onset GH deficiency. *Journal of Clinical Endocrinology and Metabolism, 83,* 3184–3189.

Behl, C., Lezoualc'h, F., Trapp, T., Widmann, M., Skutella, T., & Holsboer, F. (1997). Glucocorticoids enhance oxidative stress-induced cell death in hippocampal neurons *in vitro. Endocrinology, 138,* 101–106.

Bengtsson, B.-Å., Edén, S., Ernest, I., Odén, A., & Sjögren, B. (1988). Epidemiology and long-term survival in acromegaly. *Acta Medica Scandinavica, 223,* 327–335.

Berger, D., Crowther, R. C., Floyd, J. C., Pek, S., & Fajans, S. S. (1978). Effect of age on fasting plasma levels of pancreatic hormones in man. *Journal of Clinical Endocrinology and Metabolism, 49,* 1183–1189.

Blanton, C. A., Horwitz, B. A., & McDonald, R. B. (1999). Neurochemical alterations during age-related anorexia. *Proceedings of the Society for Experimental Biology and Medicine, 221,* 153–165.

Blum, W. F., Englaro, P., Hanitsch, S., Juul, A., Hertel, N. T., Müller, J., Skakkeback, N. E., Heiman, M. L., Birkett, M., Attanaskio, A. M., Kiess, W., & Rascher, W. (1997). Plasma leptin levels in healthy children and adolescents: Dependence on body mass index, body fat mass, gender, pubertal stage, and testosterone. *Journal of Clinical Endocrinology and Metabolism, 82,* 2904–2910.

Bodkin, N. L., Ortmeyer, H. K., & Hansen, B. C. (1995). Long-term dietary restriction in older-aged rhesus monkeys: Effects on insulin resistance. *Journal of Gerontology, American Biological Sciences and Medical Sciences, 50(3),* B142–B147.

Borg, K. E., Brown-Borg, H. M., & Bartke, A. (1995). Assessment of the primary adrenal cortical and pancreatic hormone basal levels in relation to plasma glucose and age in the unstressed Ames dwarf mouse. *Proceedings of the Society for Experimental Biology and Medicine, 210,* 126–133.

Born, J., & Fehm, H. L. (1998). Hypothalamus-pituitary-adrenal activity during human sleep—a coordinating role for the limbic hippocampal system

(review). *Experimental and Clinical Endocrinology, 106,* 153–163.

Breese, C. R., Ingram, R. L., & Sonntag, W. E. (1991). Influence of age and long-term dietary restriction on plasma insulin-like growth factor-I (IGF-I), IGF-I gene expression, and IGF-I binding proteins. *Journal of Gerontology, 46,* B180–B187.

Brown-Borg, H. M., Borg, K. E., Meliska, C. J., & Bartke, A. (1996). Dwarf mice and the ageing process. *Nature, 384,* 33.

Brown-Borg, H. M., Bode, A. M., & Bartke, A. (1999). Antioxidative mechanisms and plasma growth hormone levels: Potential relationship in the aging process. *Endocrine, 11,* 41–48.

Cartee, G. D., Briggs-Tung, C., & Kietzke, E. W. (1993). Persistent effects of exercise on skeletal muscle glucose transport across the life span of rats. *Journal of Applied Physiology, 75,* 972–978.

Cartee, G. D., Kietzke, E. W., & Briggs-Tung, C. (1994). Adaptation of muscle glucose transport with caloric restriction in adult, middle-aged, and old rats. *American Journal of Physiology, 35,* E1443–E1447.

Carvalho, C. R., Brenelli, S. L., Silva, A. C., Nunes, A. L., Velloso, L. A., & Saad, M. J. (1996). Effect of aging on insulin receptor, insulin receptor substrate-1, and phosphatidylinositol 3-kinase in liver and muscle of rats. *Endocrinology, 137(1),* 151–159.

Castracane, V. D., Kraemer, R. R., Franken, M. A., Kraemer, G. R., & Gimpel, T. (1998). Serum leptin concentration in women—effect of age, obesity, and estrogen administration. *Fertility and Sterility, 70,* 472–477.

Cecim, M., Bartke, A., Yun, J. S., & Wagner, T. E. (1994). Expression of human, but not bovine growth hormone genes promotes development of mammary tumors in transgenic mice. *Transgenics, 1,* 431–437.

Cha, C. I., Lee, Y. I., Park, K. H., & Baik, S. H. (1996). Age-related change of neuropeptide Y-immunoreactive neurons in the cerebral cortex of aged rats. *Neuroscience Letters, 214,* 37–40.

Chandrashekar, V., Bartke, A., Coschigano, K. T., & Kopchick, J. J. (1999). Pituitary and testicular function in growth hormone receptor gene knockout mice. *Endocrinology, 140,* 1082–1088.

Chen, M., Bergman, R. N., Pacini, G., & Porte, D. (1985). Pathogenesis of age-related glucose intolerance in man: Insulin resistance and decreased β-cell function. *Journal of Clinical Endocrinology and Metabolism, 60,* 626–634.

Cizza, G., Calogero, A. D., Brady, L. S., Bagdy, G., Bergamini, E., Blackman, M. R., Chrousos, G. P., & Gold, P. W. (1994). Male Fischer 344/N rats show a progressive central impairment of the hypothalamic-pituitary-adrenal axis with advancing age. *Endocrinology, 134,* 1611–1620.

Clemens, J. A., Amenomori, Y., Jenkins, T., & Meites, J. (1969). Effects of hypothalamic stimulation, hormones and drugs on ovarian functions in old female rats. *Proceedings of the Society for Experimental Biology and Medicine, 132,* 561–563.

Cocchi, D. (1992). Age-related alterations in gonadotropin, adrenocorticotropin and growth hormone secretion. *Aging (Milano), 4,* 103–113.

Cox, J. H., Cortright, R. N., Dohm, G. L., & Houmard, J. A. (1999). Effect of aging on response to exercise training in humans: Skeletal muscle GLUT–4 and insulin sensitivity. *Journal of Applied Physiology, 86(6),* 2019–2025

Dardevet, D., Sornet, C., Savary, I., Debras, E., Patureau-Mirand, P., & Grizard, J. (1998). Glucocorticoid effects on insulin- and IGF-I-regulated muscle protein metabolism during aging. *Journal of Endocrinology, 156,* 83–89.

Dean, D. J., Gazdag, A. C., Wetter, T. J., & Cartee, G. D. (1998). Comparison of the effects of 20 days and 15 months of caloric restriction on male Fischer 344 rats. *Aging Clinical and Experimental Research, 10,* 303–307.

de Boer, H., Blok, G. J., & Van der Veen, E. A. (1995). Clinical aspects of growth hormone deficiency in adults. *Endocrine Reviews, 16,* 63–86.

DeFronzo, R. A. (1979). Glucose intolerance and aging; evidence for tissue insensitivity to insulin. *Diabetes, 28,* 1095–1101.

de Kloet, E. R., Sutano, W., Rots, N., van Haarst, A., van den Berg, D., Oitzl, M., van Eekelen, A., & Voorhuis, D. (1991). Plasticity and function of brain corticosteroid receptors during aging. *Acta Endocrinologica (Copenhagen), 125,* 65–72.

Dela, F., Ploug, T., Handberg, A., Petersen, L. N., Larsen, J. J., Mikines, K. J., & Galbo, H. (1994). Physical training increases muscle GLUT4 protein and mRNA in patients with NIDDM. *Diabetes, 43,* 862–865.

Dela, F., Mikines, K. J., Larsen, J. J., & Galbo, H. (1996). Training-induced enhancement of insulin action in human skeletal muscle: The influence of aging. *Journal of Gerontology, 51A,* B247–B252.

Deuschle, M., Gotthardt, U., Schweiger, U., Weber, B., Korner, A., Schmider, J., Standhardt, H., Lammers, C. H., & Heuser, I. (1997). With aging in humans the activity of the hypothalamus-pituitary-adrenal system increases and its diurnal amplitude flattens. *Life Sciences, 61,* 2239–2246.

Elahi, D., Muller, D. C., Tzankoff, S. P., Andres, R., & Tobin, J. D. (1982). Effect of age and obesity on fasting levels of glucose, insulin, glucagon, and growth hormone in man. *Journal of Gerontology, 37,* 385–391.

Felsing, N. E., Brasel, J. A., & Cooper, D. M. (1992). Effects of low and high intensity exercise on circulating growth hormone in men. *Journal of Clinical Endocrinology and Metabolism, 75,* 157–162.

Ferrini, M., Piroli, G., Frontera, M., Falbo, A., Lima, A., & De Nicola, A. F. (1999). Estrogens normalize the hypothalamic-pituitary-adrenal axis response to stress and increase glucocorticoid receptor immunoreactivity in hippocampus of aging male rats. *Neuroendocrinology, 69(2),* 129–137.

Fink, R. I., Kolterman, O. G., Griffin, J., & Olefsky, J. M. (1983). Mechanisms of insulin resistance in aging. *Journal of Clinical Investigation, 71,* 1523–1535.

Fink, R. I., Wallace, P., & Olefsky, J. M. (1986). Effects of aging on glucose-mediated glucose disposal and glucose transport. *Journal of Clinical Investigation, 77,* 2034–2041.

Fink, R. I., Wallace, P., Brechtel, G., & Olefsky, J. M. (1992). Evidence that glucose transport is rate-limiting for *in vivo* glucose uptake. *Metabolism, 41,* 807–902.

Friend, K., Iranmanesh, A., Login, I. S., & Veldhuis, J. D. (1997). Pyridostigmine treatment selectively amplifies the mass of GH secreted per burst without altering the GH burst frequency, half-life, basal GH secretion or the orderliness of the GH release process. *European Journal of Endocrinology, 137*, 377–386.

Garcia-Mayor, R. V., Andrade, M. A., Rios, M., Lage, M., Dieguez, C., & Casanueva, F. F. (1997). Serum leptin levels in normal children: Relationship to age, gender, body mass index, pituitary-gonadal hormones, and pubertal stage. *Journal of Clinical Endocrinology and Metabolism, 82*, 2849–2855.

Gayle, D., Hyin, S. E., Romanovitch, A. E., Peloso, E., Satinoff, E., & Plata-Salaman, C. R. (1999). Basal and IL–1 beta-simulated cytokine and neuropeptide mRNA expression in brain regions of young and old Long-Evans rats. *Molecular Brain Research, 70*, 92–100.

Ghigo, E., Ceda, G. P., Valcavi, R., Goffi, S., Zini, M., Mucci, M., Valenti, G., Cocchi, D., Mueller, E. E., & Camanni, F. (1994). Low doses of either intravenously or orally administered arginine are able to enhance growth hormone releasing hormone in elderly subjects. *Journal of Endocrinological Investigation, 17*, 113–117.

Giustina, A., & Veldhuis, J. D. (1998). Pathophysiology of the neuroregulation of growth hormone secretion in experimental animals and the human. *Endocrine Reviews, 19*, 717–797.

Giustina, A., Licini, M., Bussi, A. R., Girelli, A., Pizzocolo, G., Schettino, M., & Negro-Vilar, A. (1993). Effects of sex and age on the growth hormone response to galanin in healthy human subjects. *Journal of Clinical Endocrinology and Metabolism, 76*, 1369–1372.

Givalois, L., Li, S. Y., & Pelletier, G. (1997). Age-related decrease in the hypothalamic CRH MRNA expression is reduced by dehydroepiandrosterone (DHEA) treatment in male and female rats. *Molecular Brain Research, 48*, 107–114.

Goodman, M. S., Dluz, S., McElaney, M., Belur, E., & Ruderman, E. (1983). Glucose uptake and insulin sensitivity in rat muscle: Changes during 3–96 weeks of age. *American Journal of Physiology, 244(7)*, E93–E100.

Goodyear, L. J., Hirshman, M. F., Smith, R. J., & Horton, E. S. (1991). Glucose transporter number, activity, and isoform content in plasma membranes of red and white skeletal muscle. *American Journal of Physiology, 261*, E556–E561.

Gruenewald, D. A., Naai, M. A., Marck, B. T., & Matsumoto, A. M. (1994). Age-related decrease in neuropeptide-Y gene expression in the arcuate nucleus of the male rat brain is independent of testicular feedback. *Endocrinology, 134(6)*, 2383–2389.

Gruenewald, D. A., Marck, B. T., & Matsumoto, A. M. (1996). Fasting-induced increases in food intake and neuropeptide Y gene expression are attenuated in aging male brown Norway rats. *Endocrinology, 137*, 4460–4467.

Gulve, E. A., Henriksen, E. J., Rodnick, K. J., Youn, J. H., & Holloszy, J. O. (1993). Glucose transporters and glucose transport in skeletal muscles of 1- to 25-mo-old rats. *American Journal of Physiology, 264(27)*, E319–E327.

Halter, J. B. (1995). Carbohydrate metabolism. In E. J. Masoro (Ed.), *Handbook of Physiology: Section 11, Aging* (pp. 119–145). New York: Oxford University Press.

Hardin, D. S., Dominguez, J. H., & Garvey, W. T. (1993). Muscle-group specific regulation of GLUT4 glucose transporters in control, diabetic, and insulin-treated diabetic rats. *Metabolism, 42*, 1310–1315.

Hassan, A. H., Patchev, V. K., von Rosenstiel, P., Holsboer, F., & Almeida, O. F. (1999). Plasticity of hippocampal corticosteroid receptors during aging in the rat. *FASEB Journal, 13*, 115–122.

Hastings, J. A., McClure-Sharp, J. M., & Morris, M. J. (1998). In vitro studies of endogenous noradrenaline and NPY overlow from the rat hypothalamus during maturation and ageing. *Naunyn Schmiedebergs Archives of Pharmacology, 357(3)*, 218–224.

Hatzinger, M., Reul, J. M. H. M., Landgraf, R., Holsboer, F., & Neumann, I. (1996). Combined dexamethasone/CRH test in rats: Hypothalamo-pituitary-adrenocortical system alterations in aging. *Neuroendocrinology, 64*, 349–356.

Hauck, S. J., & Bartke, A. (2000). Effects of growth hormone on hypothalamic catalase and Cu/Zn superoxide dismutase. *Free Radical Medicine Biology, 28(6)*, 970–978.

Herbert, J. (1998). Neurosteroids, brain damage, and mental illness. *Experimental Gerontology, 33*, 713–727.

Higuchi, H., Yang, H. Y., & Costa, E. (1988). Age-related bidirectional changes in neuropeptide Y peptides in rat adrenal glands, brain, and blood. *Journal of Neurochemistry, 50*, 1879–1886.

Holly, J. M. P., Gunnell, D. J., & Smith, G. D. (1999). Growth hormone, IGF-I and cancer. Less intervention to avoid cancer? More intervention to prevent cancer? *Journal of Endocrinology, 162*, 321–330.

Houmard, J. A., Egan, P. C., Neufer, P. D., Friedman, J. E., Wheeler, W. S., Israel, R. G., & Dohm, G. L. (1991). Elevated skeletal muscle glucose transporter levels in exercise-trained middle-aged men. *American Journal of Physiology, 261*, E437–E443.

Houmard, J. A., Shinebarger, M. H., Dolan, P. L., Leggett-Frazier, N., Bruner, R. K., McCammon, M. R., Israel, R. G., & Dohm, G. L. (1993). Exercise training increases GLUT-4 protein concentration in previously sedentary middle-aged men. *American Journal of Physiology, 264*, E896–E901.

Houmard, J. A., Weidner, M. D., Dolan, P. L., Leggett-Frazier, N., Gavigan, K. E., Hickey, M. S., Tyndall, G. L., Zheng, D., Alshami, A., & Dohm, G. L. (1995). Skeletal muscle GLUT4 protein concentration and aging in humans. *Diabetes, 44*, 555–560.

Hughes, V. A., Fiatarone, M. A., Fielding, R. A., Kahn, B. B., Ferrara, C. M., Shepherd, P., Fisher, E. C., Wolfe, R. R., Elahi, D., & Evans, W. J. (1993). Exercise increases muscle GLUT–4 levels and insulin action in subjects with impaired glucose tolerance. *American Journal of Physiology, 264*, E855–E862.

Huh, Y., Kim, C., Lee, W., Kim, J., & Ahn, H. (1997). Age-related change in the neuropeptide Y and NADPH-diaphorase-positive neurons in the cerebral cortex and striatum of aged rats. *Neuroscience Letters, 223(3)*, 157–160.

Huh, Y., Lee, W., Cho, J., & Ahn, H. (1998). Regional changes of NADPH-diaphorase and neuropeptide Y neurons in the cerebral cortex of aged Fischer 344 rats. *Neuroscience Letters, 247(2–3)*, 79–82.

Hunter, W. S., Croson, W. B., Bartke, A., Gentry, M. V., & Meliska, C. J. (1999). Low body temperature in long-lived Ames dwarf mice at rest and during stress. *Physiology and Behavior, 67*, 433–437.

Iranmanesh, A., South, S., Liem, A. Y., Clemmons, D., Thorner, M. O., Weltman, A., & Veldhuis, J. D. (1998). Unequal impact of age, percentage body fat, and serum testosterone concentrations on the somatotropic, IGF-I, and IGF-binding protein responses to a three-day intravenous growth-hormone-releasing hormone (GHRH) pulsatile infusion. *European Journal of Endocrinology, 139*, 59–71.

Ivy, J. L., Young, J. C., Craig, B. W., Kohrt, W. M., & Holloszy, J. O. (1991). Ageing exercise and food restriction: Effects on skeletal muscle glucose uptake. *Mechanisms of Aging Development, 61*, 123–133.

Jackson, R. A. (1990). Mechanisms of age-related glucose intolerance. *Diabetes Care, 13(2)*, 9–19.

Jhanwar-Uniyal, M., & Chua, Jr, S. C. (1993). Critical effects of aging and nutritional state on hypothalamic neuropeptide Y and galanin gene expression in lean and genetically obese Zucker rats. *Brain Research Molecular Brain Research, 19(3)*, 195–202.

Kalant, N., Stewart, J., & Kaplan, R. (1988). Effect of diet restriction on glucose metabolism and insulin responsiveness in aging rats. *Mechanisms of Ageing and Development, 46 (1–3)*, 89–104.

Kemnitz, J. W., Roecker, E. B., Weindruch, R., Elson, D. F., Baum, S. T., & Bergman, R. N. (1994). Dietary restriction increases insulin sensitivity and lowers blood glucose in rhesis monkeys. *American Journal of Physiology, 266 (4 Pt. 1)*, E540–E547.

Kern, M., Dolan, P. L., Mazzeo, R. S., Wells, J. A., & Dohm, G. L. (1992). Effect of aging and exercise on GLUT–4 glucose transporters in muscle. *American Journal of Physiology, 263*, E362–E367.

Kimura, K. D., Tissenbaum, H. A., Liu, Y., & Ruvkun, G. (1997). *daf–2*, an insulin receptor-like gene that regulates longevity and diapause in *Caenorhabditis elegans*. *Science, 277*, 942–946.

Kimonides, V. G., Khatibi, N. H., Svendsen, C. N., Sofroniew, M. V., & Herbert, J. (1998). Dehydroepiandrosterone (DHEA) and DHEA-sulfate (DHEAS) protect hippocampal neurons against excitatory amino acid-induced neurotoxicity. *Proceedings of the National Academy of Sciences of the USA, 95*, 1852–1857.

Koistinen, H. A., Kolvisto, V. A., Karonen, S. L., Ronnemaa, T., & Tilvis, R. S. (1998). Serum leptin and longevity. *Aging (Milano), 10(6)*, 449–454.

Konakchieva, R., Mitev, Y., Almeida, O. F. X., & Patchev, V. K. (1998). Chronic melatonin treatment counteracts glucocorticord-induced dysregulation of the hypothalmic-pituitary-adrenal axis in the rat. *Neuroendocrinology, 67*, 171–180.

Kono, S., Kuzuya, H., Okamoto, M., Nishimura, N.,Kosaki, A., Kakehi, T., Okamoto, M., Inoue, G., Maeda, I., & Imura, H. (1990). Changes in insulin receptor kinase with aging in rat skeletal muscle and liver. *American Journal of Physiology, 259*, E27–E35.

Kopchick, J. J., & Laron, Z. (1999). Is the Laron mouse an accurate model of Laron Syndrome? (minireview). *Molecular Genetics and Metabolism, 68*, 232–236.

Kowalski, C., Micheau, J., Corder, R., Gaillard, R., & Conte-Devolx, B. (1992). Age-related changes in cortico-releasing factor, somatostatin, neuropeptide Y, methionine enkephalin and β-endorphin in specific rat brain areas. *Brain Research, 582*, 38–46.

Krzisnik, C., Kolacio, Z., Battelino, T., Brown, M., Parks, J. S., & Laron, Z. (1999). The "Little People" of the island of Krk—revisited. Etiology of hypopituitarism revealed. *The Journal of Endocrine Genetics, 1*, 9–19.

Krzywkowski, P., Lagny-Pourmir, I., Jazat, F., Lamour, Y., & Epelbaum, J. (1994). The age-related increase in galanin binding sites in the rat brain correlates with behavioral impairment. *Neuroscience, 59*, 599–607.

Lane, M. A., Ball, S. S., Ingram, D. K., Cutler, R. G., Engel, J., Read, V., & Roth, G. S. (1995). Diet restriction in rhesus monkeys lowers fasting and glucose-stimulated glucoregulatory end points. *American Journal of Physiology, 268*, E941–E948.

Lane, M. A., Tilmont, E. M., DeAngelis, H. D., Handy, A., Ingram, D. K., Kemnitz, J. W., & Roth, G. S. (2000). Short-term calorie restriction improves disease-related markers in older male rhesus monkeys. *Mechanisms of Ageing and Development, 112*, 185–196.

Leiter, E. H., Premdas, F., Harrison, D. E., & Lipson, L. G. (1988). Aging and glucose homeostasis in C57BL/6J male mice. *FASEB Journal, 2*, 2807–2811.

Leverenz, J. B., Wilkinson, C. W., Wamble, M., Corbin, S., Grabber, J. E., Raskind, M. A., & Peskind, E. R. (1999). Effect of chronic high-dose exogenous cortisol on hippocampal neuronal number in aged nonhuman primates. *Journal of Neuroscience, 19*, 2356–2361.

Li, S., Crenshaw, III, B. E., Rawson, E. J., Simmons, D. M., Swanson, L. W., & Rosenfeld, M. G. (1990). Dwar flocus mutants lacking three pituitary cell types result from mutations in the POU-domain gene pit-1. *Nature, 347*, 528–533.

Li, H., Matheny, M., Nicolson, M., Tumer, N., & Scarpace, P. J. (1997). Leptin gene expression increases with age independent of increasing adiposity in rats. *Diabetes, 46*, 2035–2039.

Li, H., Matheny, M., Tumer, N., & Scarpace, P. J. (1998). Aging and fasting regulations of leptin and hypothalamic neuropeptide Y gene expression. *American Journal of Physiology, 275(3 Pt. 1)*, E405–E411.

Lin, J. L., Asano, T., Shibasaki,Y., Tsukuda, K., Katagiri, H., Ishihara, H., Takaku, F., & Oka, Y. (1991). Altered expression of glucose transporter isoforms with aging in rats—selective decreases in GluT4 in the fat tissue and skeletal muscle. *Diabetologia, 34(7)*, 477–482.

Lin, K., Dorman, J. B., Rodan, A., & Kenyon, C. (1997). daf–16: An HNF–3forkhead family member that can function to double the life-span of *Caenorhabditis elegans*. *Science, 278*, 1319–1322.

Lupien, S., Lecours, A. R., Lussier, I., Schwartz, G., Nair, N. P., & Meaney, M. J. (1994). Basal cortisol levels and cognitive deficits in human aging. *Journal of Neuroscience, 14*, 2893–2903.

Luukkaa, V., Pesonen, U., Huhtaniemi, I., Lehtonen, A., Tilvis, R., Tuomilehto, J., Koulu, M., & Huupponen, R. (1998). Inverse correlation between serum testosterone and leptin in men. *Journal of Clinical Endocrinology and Metabolism, 83*, 3243–3246.

Lynch, C. D., Cooney, P. T., Bennett, S. A., Thornton, P. L., Khan, A. S., Ingram, R., & Sonntag, W. E. (1999). Effects of moderate caloric restriction on cortical microvascular density and local cerebral blood flow in aged rats. *Neurobiology of Aging, 20*, 191–200.

Martineau, L. C., Chadan, S. G., & Parkhouse, W. S. (1999). Age-associated alterations in cardiac and skeletal muscle glucose transporters, insulin and IGF–1 receptors, and PI3-kinase protein contents in the C57BL/6 mouse. *Mechanisms of Ageing Development, 106(3)*, 217–232.

Masoro, E. J., Katz, M. S., & McMahan, C. A. (1989). Evidence for the glycation hypothesis of aging from the food-restricted rodent model. *Journal of Gerontology, 44*, B20–B22.

Masoro, E. J., McCarter, R. J. M., Katz, M. S., & McMahan, C. A. (1992). Dietary restriction alters characteristics of glucose fuel use. *Journal of Gerontology and Biological Science, 47*, B202–B208.

Matthaei, S., Benecke, H., Klein, H. H., Hamann, A., Kreymann, G., & Greten, H. (1990). Potential mechanism of insulin resistance in ageing: Impaired insulin-stimulated glucose transport due to a depletion of the intracellular pool transporters in Fischer rat adipocytes. *Journal of Endocrinology, 126(1)*, 99–107.

McCue, J. D. (1995). The naturalness of dying. *Journal of the American Medical Association, 273*, 1039–1043.

Meaney, M. J., Odonnell, D., Rowe, W., Tannenbaum, B., Steverman, A., Walker, M., Nair, N. P., & Lupien, S. (1995). Individual differences in hypothalamic-pituitary-adrenal activity in later life and hippocampal aging. *Experimental Gerontology, 30*, 229–251.

Medina, S., Del Rio, M., Manuel, V. V., Hernanz, A., & De la Fuente, M. (1998). Changes with ageing in the modulation of murine lymphocyte chemotaxis by CCK–8S, GRP and NPY. *Mechanisms of Aging and Development, 102*, 249–261.

Megeney, L. A., Neufer, P. D., Dohm, G. L., Tan, M. H., Blewett, C. A., Elder, G. C. B., & Bonen A. (1993). Effects of muscle activity and fiber composition on glucose transport and GLUT4. *American Journal of Physiology, 264*, E583–E593.

Meites, J. (1983). *Neuroendocrinology of Aging*. New York: Plenum Press.

Meites, J. (1993) Anti-aging interventions and their neuroendocrine aspects in mammals. *Journal of Reproduction and Fertility, 46*, 1–9.

Meliska, C. J., Burke, P. A., Bartke, A., & Jensen, R. A. (1997). Inhibitory avoidance and appetitive learning in aged normal mice: Comparison with transgenic mice having elevated plasma growth hormone levels. *Neurobiology of Learning and Memory, 68*, 1–12.

Meneilly, G. S., Minaker, K. L., Elahi, D., & Rowe, J. W. (1987). Insulin action in aging man: Evidence for tissue-specific differences at low physiologic insulin levels. *Journal of Gerontology, 42*, 196–201.

Migliaccio, E., Giorgio, M., Mele, S., Pelicci, G., Reboldi, P., Pandolfi, P. P., Lanfrancone, L., & Pelicci, P. G. (1999). The p66[shc] adaptor protein controls oxidative stress response and life span in mammals. *Nature, 402*, 309–313.

Miller, R. A. (1999). Kleemeier Award Lecture: Are there genes for aging? *Journal of Gerontology, 54A*, B297–B307.

Miller, D. B., Bartke, A., & O'Callaghan, J. P. (1995). Increased glial fibrillary acidic protein (GFAP) levels in the brains of transgenic mice expressing the bovine growth hormone (bGH) gene. In Bartke, A., & Falvo, R. (Eds.), *Experimental Gerontology*. Vol. 30, (pp. 383–400), Amsterdam: Elsevier Science.

Mizuno, T., Bergen, H., Kleopoulos, S., Bauman, W. A., & Mobbs, C. V. (1996).

Effects of nutritional status and aging on leptin gene expression in mice—importance of glucose. *Hormone and Metabolic Research, 28,* 679–684.

Mobbs, C. V. (1998). Leptin and aging. In C. V. Mobbs, & P. R. Hof, (Eds.). *Functional Endocrinology of Aging* (pp. 228–240). New York: Karger.

Moller, N., Obrien, P., & Nair, K. S. (1998). Disruption of the relationship between fat content and leptin levels with aging in humans. *Journal of Clinical Endocrinology and Metabolism, 83,* 931–934.

Morano, M. I., Vazquez, D. M., & Akil, H. (1994). The role of the hippocampal mineralocorticoid and glucorcorticoid receptors in the hypothalamo-pituitary-adrenal axis of the aged Fisher rat. *Molecular and Cellular Neurosciences, 5,* 400–412.

Morely, J. E., Hernandez, E. N., & Flood, J. F. (1987). Neuropeptide Y increases food intake in mice. *American Journal of Physiology, 253,* R516–R522.

Morley, J. E., Perry, H. M., Baumgartner, R. P., & Garry, P. J. (1999). Commentary: Leptin, adipose tissue and aging—Is there a role for testosterone? *Journals of Gerontology Series A-Biological Sciences and Medical Sciences, 54,* B108–B109.

Morris, J. Z., Tissenbaum, H. A., & Ruvkun, G. (1996). A phosphatidylinositol-1-OH kinase family member regulating longevity and diapause in *Caenorhabditis elegans. Nature, 382,* 536–539.

Müller, E. E., Cella, S. G., De Gennaro Colonna, V., Parenti, M., Cocchi, D., & Locatelli, V. (1993). Aspects of the neuroendocrine control of growth hormone secretion in ageing mammals. *Journal of Reproduction and Fertility, Suppl. 46,* 99–114.

Muller, D. C., Elahi, D., Tobin, J. D., & Andres, R. (1996). The effect of aging on insulin resistance and secretion: A review. *Seminars in Neurobiology, 16(4),* 289–298.

Myers, M. P., Pass, I., Batty, I. H., & Tonks, N. K. (1998). The lipid phosphatase activity of PTEN is critical for its tumor suppressor function. *Proceedings of the National Academy of Science USA, 95,* 13513–13518.

Nadiv, O., Cohen, O., & Zick, Y. (1992). Defects of insulin's signal transduction in old rat livers. *Endocrinology, 130(3),* 1515–1524.

Nishimura, H., Kuzuya, H., Okamoto, M., Yoshimasa, Y., Yamada, K., Ida, Y., Kakehi, T., & Imura, H. (1988). Change of insulin action with aging in conscious rats determined by euglycemic clamp. *American Journal of Physiology, 254,* E92–E98.

O'Brien, R. M., & Granner, D. K. (1996). Regulation of gene expression by insulin. *The American Physiological Society, 76(4),* 1109–1161.

Odio, M., & Brodish, A. (1989). Age-related adaptation of pituitary-adrenocortical responses to stress. *Neuroendocrinology, 49,* 382–388.

Ogg, S., & Ruvkun, G. (1998). The *C. elegans* PTEN homolog, DAF–18, acts in the insulin receptor-like metabolic signalling pathway. *Molecular Cell, 2,* 887–893.

Oka, Y., Asano, T., Lin, J. L., Tsukuda, K., Katagiri, H., Ishihara, H., Inukai, K., & Yazaki, Y. (1992). Expression of glucose transporter isoforms with aging. *Gerontology, 38 Suppl 1,* 3–9.

Orentreich, N., Brind, J. L., Rizer, R. L., & Vogelman, J. H. (1984). Age changes and sex differences in serum dehydrioepiandrosterone sulfate concentration throughout adulthood. *Journal of Clinical Endocrinology and Metabolism, 59,* 551–555.

Papadakis, M. A., Grady, D., Black, D., Tierney, M. J., Gooding, G. A., Schambelan, M., & Grunfeld, C. (1996). Growth hormone replacement in healthy older men improves body composition but not functional ability. *Annual of Internal Medicine, 124,* 708–716.

Patronek, G. J., Waters, D. J., & Glickman, L. T. (1997). Comparative longevity of pet dogs and humans: Implications for gerontology research. *Journal of Gerontology, 52A,* B171–B178.

Pendergast, W. R., Li, Y., Jiang, D., & Wolf, N. S. (1993). Decrease in cellular replicative potential in "giant" mice transfected with the bovine growth hormone gene correlates to shortened life span. *Journal of Cellular Physiology, 156*, 96–103.

Perry, H. M., Morley, J. E., Horowitz, M., Kaiser, F. E., Miller, K. K., & Wittert, G. (1997). Body composition and age in African-American and caucasian women—relationship to plasma leptin levels. *Metabolism: Clinical and Experimental, 46*, 1399–1405.

Pich, E. M., Messori, B., Zoli, M., Ferraguti, F., Marrama, P., Biagini, G., Fuxe, K., & Agnati, L. F. (1992). Feeding and drinking responses to neuropeptide Y injections in the paraventricular hypothalamic nucleus of aged rats. *Brain Research, 575(2)*, 265–271.

Planas, B., Kolb, P. E., Raskind, M. A., & Miller, M. A. (1998). Galanin receptors in the hippocampus and entorhinal cortex and aged Fischer 344 male rats. *Neurobiology of Aging, 19*, 427–435.

Qian, H., Azain, M. J., Hartzell, D. L., & Baile, C. A. (1998). Increased leptin resistance as rats grow to maturity. *Proceedings of the Society for Experimental Biology and Medicine, 219(2)*, 160–165.

Qian, H., Hausman, G. J., Compton, M. M., Azain, M. J., Hartzell, D. L., & Baile, C. A. (1998). Down-regulation of CCAAT/enhancer binding proteins alpha, beta and delta in adipose tissue by intracerebroventricular leptin in rats. *Biochimica et Biophysica Acta, 1442(2–3)*, 245–251.

Quadri, S. K., Kledzik, G. S., & Meites, J. (1973). Reinitiation of estrous cycles in old constant estrous rats by central acting drugs. *Neuroendocrinology, 11*, 248–255.

Rasmussen, D. D., Boldt, B. M., Wilkinson, C. W., Yellon, S. M., & Matsumoto, A. M. (1999). Daily melatonin administration at middle age suppresses male rat visceral fat, plasma leptin, and plasma insulin to youthful levels. *Endocrinology, 140*, 1009–1012.

Ratzmann, K. P., Witt, S., Heinke, P., & Schulz, B. (1982). The effect of ageing on insulin sensitivity and insulin secretion in non-obese healthy subjects. *Acta Endocrinology, 100*, 543–549.

Reagan, L. P., & McEwen, B. S. (1997). Controversies surrounding glucocorticoid-mediated cell death in the hippocampus. *Journal of Chemical Neuroanatomy, 13*, 149–167.

Reaven, E., Wright, D., Mondon, C. E., Solomon, R., Ho, H., & Reaven, G. M. (1983). Effect of age and diet on insulin secretion and insulin action in the rat. *Diabetes, 32*, 175–180.

Reul, J. M., Rothuizen, J., & De Kloet, E. R. (1991). Age-related changes in the dog hypothalamic-pituitary-adrenocortical system: Neuroendocrine activity and corticosteroid receptors. *Journal of Steroid Biochemistry, 40*, 63–69.

Riegle, G. D., Meites, J., Miller, A. E., & Wood, S. M. (1977). Effect of aging on hypothalamic LH-releasing and prolactin inhibiting activities and pituitary responsiveness to LHRH in the male laboratory rat. *Journal of Gerontology, 32*, 13–18.

Roberts, R. C. (1961). The lifetime growth and reproduction of selected strains of mice. *Heredity, 16*, 369–381.

Rodnick, K. J., Piper, R. C., Slot, J. W., & James, D. E. (1992). Interaction of insulin and exercise on glucose transport in muscle. *Diabetes, 15*, 1679–1689.

Rollo, C. D., Carlson, J., & Sawada, M. (1996). Accelerated aging of giant transgenic mice is associated with elevated free radical processes. *Canadian Journal of Zoology, 74*, 606–620.

Rouault, J. P., Kuwabara, P. E., Sinilnikova, O. M., Duret, L., Thierry-Mieg, D., & Billaud, M. (1999). Regulation of dauer larva development in *Caenorhabditis elegans* by daf-18, a homologue of the tumor suppressor PTEN. *Current Biology, 25*, 329–332.

Roubenoff, R., Rall, L. C., Veldhuis, J. D., Kehayias, J. J., Rosen, C., Nicolson, M., Lundgren, N., & Reichlin, S. (1998). The relationship between growth hormone kinetics and sarcopenia in postmenopausal women: The role of fat mass and leptin. *Journal of Clinical Endocrinology and Metabolism, 83(5)*, 1502–1506.

Rowe, J. W., Young, J. B., Minaker, K. L., Stevens, A. L., Pallotta, J., & Landsberg, L. (1981). Effect of insulin and glucose infusions on sympathetic nervous system activity in normal man. *Diabetes, 30,* 219–225.

Rowe, J. W., Minaker, K. L., Pallotta, J. A., & Flier, J. S. (1983). Characterization of the insulin resistance of aging. *Journal of Clinical Investigation, 71,* 1581–1587.

Rudman, D., Feller, A. G., Nagraj, H. S., Gergans, G. A., Lalitha, P. Y., Goldberg, A. F., Schlenker, R. A., Cohn, L., Rudman, I. W., & Mattson, D. E. (1990). Effects of human growth hormone in men over 60 years old. *New England Journal of Medicine, 323,* 1–6.

Ruiz, P., Pulido, J. A., Martinez, C., Carrascosa, J. M., Satrustegui, J., & Andres, A. (1992). Effect of aging on the kinetic characteristics of the insulin receptor autophosphorylation in rat adipocytes. *Archives of Biochemistry and Biophysics, 296(1),* 231–238.

Sacca, L., Cittadini, A., & Fazio, S. (1994). Growth hormone and the heart. *Endocrine Reviews, 15,* 555–573.

Samaras, T. T., & Elrick, H. (1999) Height, body size and longevity. *Acta Medica Okayama, 53,* 149–169.

Samaras, T. T., Elrick, H., & Storms, L. H. (1999). Height, health and growth hormone. *Acta Pædiatrica, 88,* 602–609.

Shepherd, P. R., Nave, B. T., & O'Rahilly, O. (1996). The role of phosphoinositide 3-kinase in insulin signalling. *Journal of Molecular Endocrinology, 17,* 175–184.

Silverberg, A. B., & Mooradian, A. D. (1998). The thyroid and aging. In C. V. Mobbs, & P. R. Hof, (Eds.). *Functional Endocrinology of Aging. Vol 29,* (pp. 27–43). Basel: Karger.

Silverstein, J. H., Beasley, J., Mizuno, T. M., London, E., & Mobbs, C. V. (1998). Adrenal neuropeptide Y MRNA but not preproenkephalin MRNA induction by stress is impaired by aging in Fischer 344 rats. *Mechanisms of Aging and Development, 101(3),* 233–243.

Slotkin, T. A., Thai, L., McCook, E. C., Saleh, J. L., Zhang, J., & Seidler, F. J. (1996). Aging and glucocorticoids—effects on cell signaling mediated through adenylyl cyclase. *Journal of Pharmacology and Experimental Therapeutics, 279,* 478–491.

Sonntag, W. E., Xu, X., Ingram, R. L., & D'Costa, A. (1995). Moderate caloric restriction alters the subcellular distribution of somatostatin mRNA and increases growth hormone pulse amplitude in aged animals. *Neuroendocrinology, 61,* 601–608.

Sonntag, W. E., Lynch, C. D., Cooney, P. T., & Hutchins, P. M. (1997). Decreases in cerebral microvasculature with age are associated with the decline in growth hormone and insulin-like growth factor 1. *Endocrinology, 138,* 3515–3520.

Sonntag, W. E., Cefalu, W. T., Ingram, R. L., Bennett, S. A., Lynch, C. D., Cooney, P. T., Thornton, P. L., & Khan, A. S. (1999). Pleiotropic effects of growth hormone and insulin-like growth factor (IGF) on biological aging: Inferences from moderate caloric restricted animals. *Journal of Gerontology, 54A,* B521–B538.

Sornson, M. W., Wu, W., Dasen, J. S., Flynn, S. E., Norman, D. J., O'Connell, S. M., Gukovsky, I., Carriére, C., Ryan, A. K., Miller, A. P., Zuo, L., Gleiberman, A. S., Anderson, B., Beamer, W. G., & Rosenfeld, M. G. (1996). Pituitary lineage determination by the prophet of pit–1 homeodomain factor defective in Ames dwarfism. *Nature, 384,* 327–333.

Spencer, R. L., & McEwen, B. S. (1997). Impaired adaptation of the hypothalamic-pituitary-adrenal axis to chronic ethanol stress in aged rats. *Neuroendocrinology, 65,* 353–359.

Steger, R. W., Bartke, A., & Cecim, M. (1993). Premature ageing in transgenic mice expressing growth hormone genes. *Journal of Reproduction and Fertility, Suppl. 46,* 61–75.

Stein-Behrens, B., Mattson, M. P., Chang, I., Yeh, M., & Sapolsky, R. (1994). Stress exacerbates neuron loss and cytoskeletal pathology in the hippocampus. *Journal of Neuroscience, 14,* 5373–5380.

Sumner, A. E., Falkner, B., Kushner, H., & Considine, R. V. (1998). Relationship of leptin concentration to gender, menopause, age, diabetes, and fat mass in African Americans. *Obesity Research, 6(2),* 128–133.

Tannenbaum, G. S., & Martin, J. B. (1976). Evidence for an endogenous ultradian rhythm governing growth hormone secretion in the rat. *Endocrinology, 98,* 562–570.

van Eekelen, J. A., Rots, N. Y., Sutano, W., & de Kloet, E. R. (1992). The effect of aging on stress responsiveness and central corticosteroid receptors in the brown Norway rat. *Neurobiology of Aging, 13,* 159–170.

Verkhratsky, N. S. (1995). Limbic control of endocrine glands in aged rats. *Experimental Gerontology, 30,* 415–421.

Wang, Z. Q., Bell-Farrow, A. D., Sonntag, W., & Cefalu, W. T. (1997). Effect of age and caloric restriction on insulin receptor binding and glucose transporter levels in aging rats. *Experimental Gerontology, 32,* 671–684.

Weindruch, R., Cottesman S. R. S., & Walford, R. L. (1982). Modification of age-related immune decline in mice dietarily restricted from or after midadulthood. *Proceedings of the National Academy of Science USA, 79,* 898–902.

Weltman, A., Weltman, J. Y., Schurrer, R., Evans, W. S., Veldhuis, J. D., & Rogol, A. D. (1992). Endurance training amplifies the pulsatile release of growth hormone: Effects of training intensity. *Journal of Applied Physiology, 76,* 2188–2196.

Weltman, A., Weltman, J. Y., Hartman, M. L., Abbott, R. A., Rogol, A. D., Evans, W. S., & Veldhuis, J. D. (1994). Relationship between age, percentage body fat, fitness and 24 hour growth hormone release in healthy young adults: Effects of gender. *Journal of Clinical Endocrinology and Metabolism, 78,* 543–548.

Wilkinson, C. W., Peskind, E. R., & Raskind, M. A. (1997). Decreased hypothalamic-pituitary-adrenal axis sensitivity to cortisol feedback inhibition in human aging. *Neuroendocrinology, 65,* 79–90.

Windle, R. J., Wood, S. A., Lightman, S. L., & Ingram, C. D. (1998). The pulsatile characteristics of hypothalamo-pituitary-adrenal activity in female Lewis and Fischer 344 rats and its relationship to differential stress responses. *Endocrinology, 139,* 4044–4052.

Winick, M., & Grant, P. (1968). Cellular growth in the organs of the hypopituitary dwarf mouse. *Endocrinololgy, 83,* 544–547.

Wolden-Hanson, T., Marck, B. T., Smith, L., & Matsumoto, A. M. (1999). Cross-sectional and longitudinal analysis of age-associated changes in body composition of male brown Norway rats: Association of serum leptin levels with peripheral adiposity. *Journals of Gerontology Series A-Biological Sciences and Medical Sciences, 54(3),* B99–B107.

Wolf, E., Kahnt, E., Ehrlein, J., Hermanns, W., Brem, G., & Wanke, R. (1993). Effects of long-term elevated serum levels of growth hormone on life expectancy of mice: Lessons from transgenic animal models. *Mechanisms of Ageing and Development, 68,* 71–87.

Yau, J. L., Olsson, T., Morris, R. G., Meaney, M. J., & Seckl, J. R. (1995). Glucocorticoids, hippocampal corticosteroid receptor gene expression and antidepressant treatment: Relationship with spatial learning in young and aged rats. *Neuroscience, 66,* 571–581.

Yen, S. S. C., & Laughlin, G. A. (1998). Aging and the adrenal cortex. *Experimental Gerontology, 33,* 897–910.

Youngren, J. F., & Barnard, R. J. (1995). Effects of acute and chronic exercise on skeletal muscle glucose transport in aged rats. *Journal of Applied Physiology, 78(5),* 1750–1756.

Yu, B. P., Masoro, E. J., & McMahan, C. A. (1985). Nutritional influences on aging of Fischer 344 rats: Physical, metabolic and longevity characteristics. *Journal of Gerontology, 40,* 657–670.

Twelve

Immune System Activity

Rita B. Effros

I. Introduction

The notion that aging constitutes a state of unilateral immunodeficiency gradually has been supplanted with descriptions that attempt to encompass the complex and multifactorial changes within the immune system. The terms "remodeling" and "cross wiring," for example, more accurately portray such changes as the *increased* numbers of killer (NK) cells and the *qualitative* shift in the humoral immune system from the production of exquisitely specific high-affinity IgG responses against foreign antigens to the occurrence of natural low-affinity autoreactive IgM antibodies (LeMaoult *et al.*, 1997; Franceschi *et al.*, 1995). Similarly, "regulatory changes" is more appropriate than "dysregulation" to describe age-related cytokine modulations that include *increased constitutive* levels together with both *increased and diminished inducible* production. It is possible, in fact, that what appears as random dysregulation actually may be an appropriate compensatory mechanism or even an ongoing attack on subclinical neoplastic or infectious disease (Meyer

et al., 1996). In any case, it is now eminently clear that such terms as "immunodeficiency," "deterioration," and even "immunosenescence," fail to convey the pleiotropic, and possibly adaptive, nature of alterations in the immune system during aging.

This chapter will review the state of our understanding of immune system activity during aging, focusing on research published since the last edition of this handbook (Miller, 1996). These studies continue to validate the prediction that the immune system constitutes a highly accessible and convenient organ system to elucidate the process of biological aging. Indeed, immunogerontological research has been enhanced considerably by the unique opportunity for synthesis of analyses performed at the level of the individual immune cell with data obtained on the function of that cell in the milieu of the aging individual. The field of gerontology has, in turn, yielded novel and unexpected insights into the normal functioning of the immune system, as evidenced by several advances in the areas of thymic activity and telomere biology.

II. Immune Function and Life Span

The biological significance of immune competence in the context of organismal aging is underscored by research in several areas. First, studies of "successful aging" indicate that a higher proportion of centenarians show well-preserved immune function compared to less elderly cohorts (Franceschi et al., 1995). Conversely, in the very old, the combination of poor T- cell proliferation, high numbers of CD8+ T-cells, low numbers of CD4+ T-cells, and low numbers of B-cells is predictive of poor survival (Ferguson et al., 1995). Autopsy data showing that infections cause the majority of deaths in the over-80 age group further implicate defective immune function in life span determination (Horiuchi & Wilmoth, 1997). The increased longevity of mice that were selectively inbred exclusively according to high antibody responses further highlights the link between immune function and life span (Salazar et al., 1995). Finally, among the genetic components of longevity, the MHC class I and class II loci, which are intimately involved in immune function, arguably are among the most potent in mammalian life span determination (Ivanova et al., 1998; Smith & Walford, 1977; Takata et al., 1987; Rea & Middleton, 1994).

III. T-Cells

A. Oligoclonal Expansions

The most dramatic age-related changes in the immune system are observed within the T-cell compartment, with one of the more striking alterations being the appearance of clonal expansions (Nociari et al., 1999; Ku et al., 1997). Expansions are uncommon in children and young adults, but their prevalence increases

significantly with age, in some cases occupying over 50% of the total T-cell population. The predominance of these expansions within the CD8+ versus CD4+ subset most probably relates to the stronger, more persistent nature of the antigenic drive for CD8+ T-cells responding to chronic systemic intracellular pathogens, in contrast to the more discrete localization of extracellular pathogens recognized by CD4+ T-cells (Maini et al., 1999a). Indeed, the maintenance of specific CD8+ T-cell receptor (TCR) clonotypes at high circulating frequency in humans has been documented in chronic infections such as cytomegalovirus, human immunodeficiency virus (HIV), and Epstein–Barr virus, as well as in repeated infections with influenza, a virus with conserved CD8+ T-cell epitopes (Maini et al., 1999a). In mice too, the presence of CD8+ T-cell clonal populations correlates with chronic mouse hepatitis virus infection (Ku et al., 1997). Importantly, the result of the oligoclonal expansions comprising an increasing proportion of the T-cell pool with age is that the remaining naïve repertoire will be narrowed. The poor response to neo-antigens in the elderly may, in fact, be one clinical manifestation of the more restricted naïve repertoire.

An intriguing aspect of the age-associated T-cell clonal expansions is that they consist predominantly of cells lacking expression of CD28, a molecule critical for delivering the requisite second activatory signal as well as for enhancing cell–cell adhesion. The biological outcome of such expansions is that, in the elderly, the CD28– T-cell population comprises more than 60% of the CD8+ peripheral blood T-cell pool (Boucher et al., 1998), in stark contrast to its negligible representation during early life (Azuma et al., 1993). Importantly, identical TCR clonotypes within the CD28+

and CD28– T-cell compartments from the same donors have been documented, with one report formally demonstrating that the CD28– T-cells actually were derived from the CD28+ T-cells (Posnett et al., 1999). The notion that the CD28+ T-cells are the reservoir for the CD28– T-cells is supported further by the observation that CD28– T-cells show minimal proliferative response to antigen, mitogens, or antibody to the TCR (Azuma et al., 1993; Effros et al., 1996; Perillo et al., 1993) and by telomere length studies (Monteiro et al., 1996). Poor proliferation of the aging-associated T cell clonal populations has also been demonstrated in vivo. For example, murine CD8+ clones transferred into lethally irradiated syngeneic recipients expand at an extremely slow rate despite the adequate "space" in such recipients (Ku et al., 1997). In fact, on the basis of the observation that the number of expanded clones within the CD28– compartment exceeds that in the CD45RO compartment, loss of CD28 has been proposed as a more stringent marker for memory cells than acquisition of CD45RO (Maini et al., 1999a). Similarly, the high-molecular-weight CD45 isoform (i.e., CD45RA) is not viewed as a reliable marker for naïve cells within the CD8+ T-cell subset in mice and humans (Nociari et al., 1999; Zimmerman et al., 1996; Hamann et al., 1997).

B. Shifts in Cellular Composition

Flow cytometric analysis of the cellular composition of peripheral blood of Senieur-compatible subjects has documented a variety of statistically significant changes with age, all of which occur within the T-cell compartment (Stulnig et al., 1995). Specifically, increases in activated (HLA-DR+) CD4+ and CD8+ T-cells and in the proportion of CD4+ and CD8+ T-cells expressing the CD45RO memory marker have been observed. The increase in the ratio of memory to naïve

T-cells, a signature change in the aging immune system in rodents as well, may, in part, result from gradual reduction in the naïve T-cell number emerging from the thymus as well as the ongoing transition of naïve cells into the memory pool upon exposure to environmental pathogens. An additional influence may be the aged environment itself, which in mice has been shown accelerate T-cell maturation from naïve to memory status in the periphery (Thoman, 1997). Analysis of less rigorously screened, albeit healthy, adults showed significant decreases in cells expressing CD3, CD4, CD8 (as well as CD19), and total lymphocytes, with females generally showing less of a decrease than males (Huppert et al., 1998). In contrast to peripheral blood findings, the number of T-cells in the tonsil actually increases with age in humans (Bergler et al., 1999), as do total splenic lymphocyte numbers in mice (Spaulding et al., 1996). Interestingly, there is a circadian rhythm in the proportions of some cell types, as well as in the ratio of CD4+ to CD8+ T-cells (Mazzoccoli et al., 1997). Finally, given that lymphocyte activation status can be influenced by exercise (Gueldner et al., 1997) and that CD8+ T-cell number is correlated with muscle strength (Miller et al., 1997), changes in cellular composition clearly are influenced by factors other than age itself.

C. Early Activation Defects

The effect of aging on T-cell activation is manifested in a multitude of alterations that occur at numerous stages. One of the earliest events in signal transduction via the TCR is a series of protein tyrosine phosphorylations, which are reduced during aging in both mice and humans (Miller et al., 1996; Whisler et al., 1998). In human T-cells, an age-associated reduction in actual protein kinase activity has been documented following activation (Quadri *et al.*, 1996), and among the tyrosine phosphorylated proteins, ZAP-70, which is critical for transducing activating signals, is consistently less phosphorylated (Chakravarti *et al.*, 1998). In old mice, Raf-1 kinase activity declines in both naïve and memory CD4+ T-cells, although to a greater extent in the memory population (Miller *et al.*, 1996). The documented changes in calcium signaling may be due to the age-associated alteration in the P-glycoprotein multidrug transporter (Pilarski *et al.*, 1995). Second messengers, such as inositol triphos-phate and diacylglycerol, have also been shown to decrease in lymphocytes isolated *ex vivo* from aged mice, a change that may, in part, result from the age-associated decrease in phospholipase C (Utsuyama *et al.*, 1997). Reduced levels of enzymatic activity and phosphorylation of the p59fyn and p56lck proteins, respectively, have been reported in the elderly (Whisler *et al.*, 1997; Guidi *et al.*, 1998). An age-related decline in the function of the pleiotropic and ubiquitous transcription factor, NF-κB, which is important in the regulation of IL-2 and IL-2 receptor genes, has been documented in both memory and naïve T-cells from humans and mice (Trebilcock & Ponnappan, 1999). Finally, downstream mitogen-activated kinase (MAPK) signaling pathways involved in normal cell growth and function also are compromised with age (Pahlavani *et al.*, 1998). Even once activated, cells from aged donors still show defects in cell cycle progression, particularly at the G2M/S phase, a problem that has been traced to low levels of cdk1 protein, the associated cyclin B1, and incomplete dephosphorylation (Quadri *et al.*, 1998). Thus, a variety of alterations in signal transduction pathways occur with age, and these undoubtedly contribute to the dramatically modulated T-cell function.

D. Cytokines and T-Cells

IL-2 production, the major outcome of T-cell activation, is influenced profoundly by aging, but is normalized in aged rats subjected to dietary caloric restriction (Pahlavani *et al.*, 1997). Treatment of old mice with exogenous IL-2 also normalizes IL-2 (as well as IL-4) dysregulation (Kirman *et al.*, 1996), although the possibility of this treatment causing *excessive* cell division merits investigation. Reduced IL-2 production during aging is not restricted to memory or replicatively senescent cells: naïve T-cells from old mice also produce significantly less IL-2 in response to both specific antigen and stimulation with antibodies to CD3 and CD28 (Linton *et al.*, 1996). The outcome of this alteration is reduced late phase effector expansion and differentiation. Moreover, even when the initial expansion defect is corrected by the addition of exogenous IL-2, the memory cell progeny resulting from this manipulation also show reduced IL-2 production (Haynes *et al.*, 1999). Alterations in IL-2 levels not only may reflect reduced proliferative responses but may also indirectly impact the survival of T-cells by enhancing apoptosis induced by growth factor withdrawal. Interestingly, T-cells are extremely sensitive to *in vivo* levels of the insulin-like growth factor-1 (IGF-1), a polypeptide mitogen that is reduced with age and regulated by growth hormone. In fact, T-cell proliferation shows a significant correlation with plasma levels of IGF-1 (Krishnaraj *et al.*, 1998)

Aging also is associated with a general shift from Th1 to Th2 cytokines (Shearer, 1997), a change implicated in the increased production of autoantibodies and concomitant reduction in cellular immunity. Indeed, treatment of mice with exogenous IL-12 is associated with restoration of the Th1 responses, resulting in increased CTL-mediated tumor control (Horvath-Arcidiacono *et al.*,

1996). In humans, immunity to infection, which is critically dependent on a Th1 response pattern, may be reduced in the elderly due to increased levels of the Th2 cytokines produced by activated PBMC (Castle et al., 1997).

E. T-Cell Apoptosis

Resolution of normal immune responses involves a finely tuned balance between extensive apoptosis of activated T-cells and the retention of a population of anti-gen-specific memory cells. The dramatic increase in memory T-cells with age therefore might reflect both differences in apoptosis sensitivity between naïve and memory T-cells and the overall effect of aging on the ability to orchestrate and regulate apoptosis. Interestingly, robust T-cell apoptosis and preservation of naïve T-cell numbers are two characteristics that accompany the life span extension, increased viral immunity, and reduced tumor incidence in calorically restricted mice (Spaulding et al., 1996; Fernandes et al., 1997; Chen et al., 1998). In fact, the age-associated lymphopenia in calorically restricted mice (Weindruch et al., 1982) may reflect an ongoing vigorous apoptosis throughout life.

Studies on the effect of aging on T apoptosis have been somewhat inconsistent in their findings, possibly due to differences between subpopulations of T-cells, source of cells, or modes of induction (Cossarizza et al., 1997; Aggarwal et al., 1999; Hosono et al., 1996; Provinciali et al., 1998). Age-related decreased expression of the potent apoptosis inducer, Fas, has been documented in humans and mice, and the diminished apoptosis is corrected in transgenic mice engineered to constitutively express the Fas gene (Mountz et al., 1997; Aspinall et al., 1998). In elderly humans, apoptosis induced by mild irradiation also has been reported to decrease with age (Polyak et al., 1997). In old mice, diminished

superantigen-induced clonal deletion, a process involving apoptosis, has been demonstrated (Kuschnaroff et al., 1997; Kuschnaroff, Goebels, Valckx, Heremans, Matthys, & Waer, 1997). Because IL-6 is protective against apoptosis (Ayroldi et al., 1998), elevated serum levels of this cytokine during aging may contribute to the reduced apoptosis.

Apoptosis differences between CD4+ and CD8+ T-cells may, in part, explain the conflicting reports. For example, age-associated increased viability of CD8+ T-cells following oxidative stress has been reported in mice (Lohmiller et al., 1996), and human CD8+ T-cells that reach replicative senescence in cell culture after multiple rounds of antigen-driven proliferation become resistant to apoptosis (Spaulding et al., 1999). Interestingly, cells with the identical phenotype (i.e., CD8+CD28−) isolated ex vivo also show reduced apoptosis compared to the CD8+CD28+ cells from the same individual (Posnett et al., 1999). Because the proportion of CD8+CD28− T-cells increases dramatically with age (Boucher et al., 1998), studies documenting apoptosis resistance in the elderly may reflect the presence of this subset of cells. In contrast to the CD8+ subset, CD4+ T-cells generally show increased apoptosis with age. For example, peripheral expansion of CD4+ T-cells following chemotherapy is hampered in older persons by an increased susceptibility of activated CD4+ T-cells to apoptosis (Hakim et al., 1997). Similarly, CD4+ T-cells followed in long-term cultures show increased apoptosis at senescence (Pawelec et al., 1996; Lechner et al., 1996).

Divergence in apoptosis patterns between subsets is not observed uniformly: increased TNF-induced apoptosis as well as the expression of Fas has been reported for both CD4+ and CD8+ T-cells within the memory and naïve compartments of elderly individuals

(Aggarwal *et al.*, 1999; Phelouzat *et al.*, 1997). Moreover, even within a single subset, the apoptosis-inducing stimulus may influence the outcome (Telford & Miller, 1999). An important caveat with respect to all of the T-cell apoptosis studies is that the T-cells are not being evaluated in the context of their normal physiological milieu. This point is highlighted in a study showing that T-cells can be rescued from apoptosis by stromal cell-derived IFNβ, a mechanism that may be fundamental to the persistence of T-cells at sites of inflammation (Pilling *et al.*, 1999).

IV. B-Cells

A. Germinal Center Reaction

One of the hallmarks of aging is a qualitative change in the humoral immune response, so that even in cases where the *quantity* of antibody production to specific antigens remains robust, the antibodies are *functionally* insufficient. Increased understanding of molecular basis of this phenomenon has emerged from microdissection and histological studies of murine lymph nodes during the course of an ongoing immune response. The proliferation and migration of activated B-cells to splenic follicles, the so-called "germinal center" (GC) reaction, are altered markedly in aged mice. Specifically, the GC response itself is delayed by 1–2 days, fewer GCs are formed, and the size of the GC is reduced. The underlying cause of these changes is an inability of the GCs induced by antigens in the spleens of aged mice to support the extensive level of immunoglobulin (Ig) gene hypermutation that is characteristic of young mice (Zheng *et al.*, 1997). Analysis of the relative contribution of cell types to the GC reaction by using adoptive cell transfer techniques has shown that it is the aged CD4+ T-cell subset rather than the aged

B-cells that is responsible for the reduced GC number and the skewing of the variable (V) gene utilization. By contrast, both T-cells and B-cells have been implicated in the decreased mutation frequency (Yang *et al.*, 1996). Additional qualitative changes in the antibody response may also be due to altered expression of costimulatory molecules (Zheng *et al.*, 1997), as well as reduced inducible expression of the receptor for IgD on T-cells, a change that correlates with the inability to produce high antibody titers to influenza after vaccination (Swenson & Thorbecke, 1997).

B. Intrinsic B-Cell Changes

Whereas many of the alterations in the humoral response during aging can be traced to the influence of T-cells, there are also several striking changes that are intrinsic to the B-cells. For example, the half-life of mature B-cells in the spleen has been estimated to increase severalfold during aging, based on the incorporation of radioactivity in various subsets of B-cells of mice fed BrdU (Kline *et al.*, 1999). The progressive increase in the longevity of mature B with age is accompanied by an approximately tenfold decrease in the proportion of recent bone marrow emigrés in the spleen as well as a reduction in the number of pre-B-cells (Sherwood *et al.*, 1998; Stephan *et al.*, 1997). Increased levels of dexamethasone-induced apoptosis (Souvannavong *et al.*, 1998), as well as the apoptosis-promoting Bcl-xL protein in pre-B-cells from old mice, may also contribute to the reduced numbers of these cells (Kirman *et al.* 1998).

C. CD5+ B-Cells

An intriguing aspect of age-associated changes in B-cells is the appearance of oligoclonal expansions (van Arkel *et al.*, 1997). The expansions in mice are stable, persisting for at least 2 months, and are present in the spleens of 85% of 18-month-old C57BL/6 mice. Because the B-cells from these mice have the potential to mount an exceedingly diverse antibody response when stimulated *in vitro*, it is possible that the aged environment is in some way favoring the more restricted clonal repertoire. Interestingly, the clonal populations are predominantly within the CD5+ B-cell population (Ben-Yehuda, *et al.*, 1999), a subset that increases in proportion during aging and that is responsible for the majority of autoantibodies produced in elderly mice. One possible mechanism for the emergence of autoreactive B-cells during aging is the loss of suppressive CD8+ T-cell influence, mediated by TGFβ, which during youth keeps the autoreactivity in check (Crisi *et al.*, 1998). Although the increased autoantibody response generally has not been associated with pathophysiological consequences, two examples of a negative outcome are increased levels of anti-T-cell autoantibodies that bind to developing thymocytes (Adkins & Riley, 1998) and the penetration by some of these antibodies of living mononuclear cells resulting in activation (Portales-Paerez *et al.*, 1998). In addition to being the major source of autoantibody production in aged mice, the B-cell clonal populations have been proposed as the precursors of two types of neoplasms that are dominated by CD5+ B-cells or plasma cells (B-cell chronic lymphocytic leukemia and multiple myeloma, respectively) (LeMaoult *et al.*, 1999).

V. Natural Killer (NK) Cells

With the increasing awareness of the interdependence between the early, rapid, nonspecific reactivity to foreign pathogens and the exquisitely specific adaptive immune response, research on innate immunity and its relation to aging

has expanded greatly. Most of the studies on this facet of immunological aging are concerned with NK cells, large granular lymphocytes involved in the recognition and lysis of tumor or virally infected cells. Although, on a per cell basis, cytolytic activity of NK cells is decreased in aged humans and rodents (Solana *et al.*, 1999; Hsueh *et al.*, 1996), both the percentage and absolute number of CD3–CD56+ NK cells actually increase with age (Borrego *et al.*, 1999), and in the healthy elderly, the overall NK activity remains stable with age. Similarly, many other aspects of NK function, such as Fc-mediated antibody-dependent cellular cytotoxicity (ADCC) and cytokine-induced antitumor MHC-unrestricted killing, are preserved in the healthy elderly. The relevance of NK function to aging is highlighted by the observations that centenarians have well-preserved NK cytotoxicity (Cossarizza *et al.*, 1997) and that, within the oldest old, high NK cell numbers and cytolytic function correlate with a variety of measures indicative of good health and autonomy (Mariani *et al.*, 1998). Conversely, low NK function has been proposed as a mortality predictor, based, in part, on its correlation with severe infection or death due to infection in a group of elderly subjects (Heller *et al.*, 1998). Interestingly, influenza immunity in mice, involving both NK and T-cells, is completely abrogated by stress (Padgett *et al.*, 1998). This finding, together with a host of environmental, lifestyle, and neurological factors that affect the level of NK function in the elderly, suggests that specific interventions might enhance innate immune function during aging (Woods *et al.*, 1998; Santos *et al.*, 1998; Mariani *et al.*, 1998).

VI. Macrophages

Macrophages, the second component of the innate immune system, undergo changes with age that are independent of NK function, such as reduced production of reactive oxygen and nitrogen intermediates, both of which are essential for intracellular killing of microorganisms and tumor cell lysis (McLachlan *et al.*, 1995). In addition, reduced tumor binding and production of oncostatin-M and dysregulation in expression of the neurotrophin receptor TrkB have been observed in aged rodents (Khare *et al.*, 1999). Altered regulation in the production of pro-inflammatory cytokines by macrophages has been reported, with increases documented in aged rodents and humans. In some cases, these changes correlate with the prolonged *in vivo* inflammatory response to pneumococcal infection in humans (Bruunsgaard *et al.*, 1999c). Some of the macrophage changes, such as increased IL-12 mRNA in aged mice, may, in turn, result in alterations in NK function (Spencer & Daynes, 1997). Finally, alterations in prostaglandin secretion and cyclooxygenase activity by macrophages from aged mice, which are changes possibly linked to concomitantly increased corticosterone and its receptor, may contribute to immune dysfunction of both T-cells and dendritic cells (Wu *et al.*, 1998; Fraifeld *et al.*, 1995).

A stringent *in vivo* test of integrated innate immunity is the early response to infection with parasites, whose elimination is effected by activated macrophages in response to factors produced by NK cells. In two different parasitic infections that have been analyzed in aged mice, profound dysregualtion in the protective response was observed. In the murine model of *Trypanisoma musculi*, aged mice have increased parasitemia, longer duration of infection, and a higher rate of mortality (Albright & Albright, 1998). Diminished protection of aged mice to *Trypanisoma cruzi* has also been documented, and involves reduced macrophage catabolism

of the parasite, a change that may also affect antigen presentation and hence, specific immunity as well (Plasman *et al.*, 1995).

VII. Telomerase Involvement in the Immune System

Ever since publication of the seminal findings of Hayflick (1965) regarding the finite replicative capacity of normal human somatic cells, gerontologists have sought to link cellular senescence with organismal aging. Ironically, it was only recently that lymphocytes, a cell type whose function is uniquely dependent on extensive clonal expansion, have been examined rigorously with respect to telomere dynamics and replicative senescence (Effros & Pawelec, 1997). Results of this relatively new area of immunogerontology have yielded new insights not only on immunological aging but also on the unexpected role of telomerase in normal immune function. Telomerase, the telomere-extending enzyme that maintains telomere length in tumor cells and was believed to be absent from normal somatic cells, is now known to be highly active during T-cell development and following antigenic stimulation, thereby at least partially compensating for telomere length attrition during cell division (Weng *et al.*, 1997; Hiyama *et al.*, 1995). Longitudinal analysis of telomere/telomerase dynamics of the same T-cell population over time, feasible only in cell culture, has shown that telomere shortening in T-cells occurs at a rate of 50–100 bp/cell division (Vaziri *et al.*, 1993). The high telomerase activity that coincides with early activation seems to retard or even counteract telomere shortening during the first wave of proliferation (Bodnar *et al.*, 1996). However, the telomerase activity of memory T-cells declines with each subsequent antigenic stimulation (Valenzuela & Effros, 2000), and as

T-cells progress in long-term culture to replicative senescence, there is an overall telomere shortening from the original 10–11 kb size to 5–7 kb (Vaziri *et al.,* 1993). Several *in vivo* studies on sequential samples of antigen-specific CD4+ and CD8+ T-cells provide data that are consistent with the *in vitro* findings, showing that telomerase activity is also associated with telomere length maintenance *in vivo*, at least in the period immediately following antigenic exposure (Hathcock *et al.,* 1998; Maini *et al.,* 1999b). Increased telomerase activity and retardation of telomere shortening have also been documented in naïve T-cells exposed to IL-7 and are associated with retention of the naïve (CD45RA+RO–) phenotype (Soares *et al.,* 1998). Finally, high telomerase activity, leading to telomere elongation, has been observed in B-cells within the GC (Weng *et al.,* 1997), although the effect of aging on these processes remains to be investigated.

Measurements of telomere length on *in vivo* derived lymphocyte samples from different age groups suggest that the rate of lymphocyte telomere shortening is not linear over the entire life span and declines progressively in old age (Rufer *et al.,* 1999; Frenck *et al.,* 1998). From these cross-sectional data, it is impossible to determine whether this putative reduction in the rate of telomere loss per year in the elderly reflects a reduced rate of cell turnover, a smaller number of telomeric base pairs lost per cell division, a lower proportion of cells undergoing cell division, reduced telomerase activity, or a gradual anatomical shift in lymphocyte populations. Indeed, the potential confounding influence of lymphocyte migration/recruitment on *in vivo* telomere analysis is highlighted in a report showing apparent telomere "shortening" in peripheral blood T-cells *immediately* following exercise (Bruunsgaard *et al.,* 1999b). Additional potential influences

on telomere dynamics in the elderly include oxidative stress, ionizing radiation and DNA damage (Kruk *et al.,* 1992; von Zglinicki *et al.,* 1995; Crompton, 1997).

Irrespective of the mechanism underlying altered telomere size dynamics in the elderly, because the telomere length of a cell is predictive of its overall replicative potential, a major conclusion from the telomere length measurements is that lymphocytes from older persons have reduced replicative potential compared to lymphocytes from younger persons. Thus, in the elderly, smaller clonal populations of T-cells of the requisite specificity can be generated upon antigenic stimulation, and, similarly, the pool from which memory cells can develop is reduced. Interestingly, the two cell populations that have been shown to have the shortest telomeres are memory T-cells and CD28– T-cells (Vaziri *et al.,* 1993; Weng *et al.,* Monteiro *et al.,* 1996). The proportions of these same two populations increase dramatically during aging, suggesting that these cells may account, at least in part, for the overall shorter mean telomere length in the elderly.

The antigenic stimulus responsible for the increased cell division experienced by CD8+ T-cells in the elderly has not been identified. However, on the basis of the observation that accelerated telomere shortening and loss of CD28 expression in CD8+ T-cells occurs in younger persons chronically infected with HIV (Effros *et al.,* 1996), it seems likely that some of the cells with shortened telomeres in the elderly may have been driven to proliferate by latent viruses or recurrent infection with viruses sharing T-cell epitopes. Indeed, the incidence of herpes zoster increases with age (Arvin, 1996), and both natural and vaccine-induced influenza immunity is markedly reduced in the elderly (Bernstein *et al.,* 1999; Bender *et al.,* 1998; Klinman *et al.,* 1998; Remarque, 1999).

VIII. Thymic Involution Revisited

The paradigm that thymic involution is the major cause of age-associated alterations in T-cell function is undergoing a progressive shift, with the emerging consensus being that the human thymus still functions quite adequately even late in life. Two studies have been instrumental in reformulating concepts on thymic potential during aging. By using an innovative assay based on the presence of excision circles created during TCR rearrangements (TRECs) that are present exclusively in those naïve T-cells that have not yet undergone any cell division, thymic output in humans has been evaluated (Douek *et al.*, 1998). High levels of TRECs were found in elderly individuals, and the values obtained for different age individuals are consistent with quantitative data on remaining lymphoid mass. That these recent thymic emigrants were also capable of responding to costimulatory signals and that adult thymic stroma can support thymocyte viability in organ culture provide further evidence that the thymus retains the ability to orchestrate normal T-lymphopoiesis even late in life (Jamieson *et al.*, 1999). Moreover, at least at age 56, the latest time point tested, the distribution of TCR Vβ gene families is comparable to that seen in fetal thymi. Although data on immune reconstitution following chemotherapy suggest that aging does influence thymic function (Mackall *et al.*, 1995), because of the confounding effects of the underlying disease, this effect may not be intrinsic to the aging process itself. In mice, reconstitution experiments using bone marrow from TCR transgenics showed that old mice could still generate about half the number of mature T-cells as the young mice (Mackall *et al.*, 1998). Clearly the interaction between T-cells and thymic stroma may be crucial to the maintenance of thymic integrity with aging, as

demonstrated by the finding that TCR transgenics that do not need to rearrange their TCR genes and that are bred on a RAG–knockout background do not show thymic involution (Aspinall & Andrews, 2000). One component of the thymus that does change with age is the function of thymic stromal cells, which have been shown to exert an inhibitory influence on the thymocyte expression of recombinase activation genes, RAG-1 and RAG-2, and TCR Vβ rearrangement (Ben-Yehuda *et al.*, 1998). Another potential influence on the thymus that merits further investigation is the neuroendocrine axis, particularly in light of the increased numbers of noradrenergic sympathetic nerves and the 15-fold increase in norepinephrine concentration in the thymi of old mice (Nonaka, 1996).

IX. Influence of Hematopoiesis

Alterations in both adaptive and innate immune function may, in part, be the outcome of age-related changes in the early maturation and development within the bone marrow, encompassing altered function in both the stem cells and the stromal cell microenvironment. In humans, increased constitutive production of the pro-inflammatory cytokine, IL-6 (Cheleuitte *et al.*, 1998), and a marked reduction in colony-stimulating factor (Nilsson-Ehle *et al.*, 1995), for example, have been implicated in some of the age-related changes in hematopoiesis. However, even in the presence of recombinant cytokines, mobilization of CD34+ stem cells *in vivo* is reduced in old versus young donors (Anderlini *et al.*, 1997), suggesting certain inherent defects of aged stem cells. The notion of certain defects being intrinsic to the stem cells themselves is consistent with experiments in mice showing that the environment of a young thymus is not able to correct the aged stem cell defects in promoting the normal developmental pathway of T-cells (Globerson, 1997). In addition to developmental alterations, the proliferative potential of bone marrow stem cells is reduced with age, as demonstrated by the progressive shortening with age of the telomeres of CD34+ stem cells (Vaziri et al., 1994) and the delayed T-cell reconstitution and recovery of function observed in older bone marrow transplant recipients (Small et al., 1997). The transient increase in telomerase activity is only partially able to compensate for the telomere loss (Chiu et al., 1996), suggesting that methods of retarding telomere shortening, such as genetic manipulation of telomerase activity, prolonging telomerase activation or reducing oxidative stress, may be of use therapeutically (Bodnar et al., 1996; Furumoto et al., 1998). An example of putative "remodeling" that may be a component of normal aging is the increase in the relative and absolute stem cell number with age in mice, possibly compensating for reduced efficiency of thymic maturation or the reduced homing and engrafting efficiency that has been documented for aged stem cells (Morrison et al., 1996). Interestingly, in a study on eight different mouse strains, a strong inverse correlation was observed between life span and the number of autonomously cycling progenitors, a trait that maps to a chromosomal region syntenic to a human region involved in various human hematological malignancies (de Haan & Van Zant, 1997).

Altered regulation of B-cell generation within the bone marrow during aging is influenced strongly by cytokines. Pro-B-cells (precursors of pre-B-cells) in the bone marrow of aged mice show a reduced ability to enter into the cell cycle in response to the stromal-cell-derived cytokine, IL-7, and even those that can be induced to enter the cycle by using high doses of IL-7 are poorly functional

(Stephan et al., 1997). Expression of the recombination-activating genes RAG-1 and RAG-2, which are required for surface Ig expression and maturation of B-cells, decreases with age (Ben-Yehuda et al., 1999), with mRNA levels undetectable in bone marrow cultures of 18-month-old mice. The reconstitution of RAG-1 expression both in vitro and in vivo with recombinant IL-7 indicates that the potential for activating RAG-1 is retained in old bone marrow, although the functional consequences of this activation remain to be verified (Ben-Yehuda et al., 1999). IL-16, a cytokine produced by activated CD8+ T-cells, is also critical for RAG-1 expression, and the impaired B-cell development associated with aging can, in fact, be partially reversed by the injection of nanogram qunatities of recombinant IL-16 (Szabo et al., 1998). The correlation of decreasing levels of RAG-1 with thymic involution, together with the involvement of IL-16, reinforces the notion that T-cells have a specific influence on B-cell development.

Studies in humans have not always been consistent with observations in mice and, in fact, have shown that bone marrow B-cell generation and Ig gene combinatorial rearrangements are undiminished in the elderly (Nuanez et al., 1996). Flow cytometric analysis of marrow cells derived from rib specimens of donors ranging from age 1 to 80 showed that the relative frequencies of pro-B-cells, pre-B-cells, and their immature B-cell progeny are maintained throughout life. In further contrast to the results in mice, the expression of RAG-1 and RAG-2 persists in humans who are age 62 (Nuanez et al., 1996). These striking differences between humans and mice may reflect species divergence, inbred versus outbred populations, differences between rib and femur bone marrow biology, or the fact that the extremely old persons have not yet been analyzed.

X. Effects of Antigen Presentation/Accessory Cell Function

Alterations in T-cell functions with age may reflect changes in antigen presentation function or other accessory cell activities. The unresponsiveness of aged mice to pneumococcal vaccines, for example, has been traced to an adherent cell population that could be removed by passage through a Sephadex G-10 column, suggesting that it is a macrophage (Garg et al., 1996). In elderly humans, there is a significant decrease in the proportion and function of alveolar macrophages, a factor that may contribute to the increased risk of pulmonary infections in the elderly (Zissel et al., 1999). Monocytes from elderly donors may also be compromised in their accessory function due to their reduced IL–1 secretion, cytotoxicity, and protein kinase translocation (McLachlan et al., 1995). Langerhan cell changes may play a role in the reduction in both barrier function and T-cell activation in aged epidermis (Haratake et al., 1997). In response to stimulation with inactivated influenza virus, elderly-donor-derived dendritic cells (DCs), the most potent type of antigen-presenting cell (APC), are inferior in terms of class II and CD54 upregulation and triggering a Th1 response (Wick & Grubeck-Loebenstein, 1997a,b). Interestingly, improved APC function has been reported in certain influenza vaccine preparations that happen to upregulate expression of the CD86 molecule on APC (Sambhara et al., 1998). Age-associated decreases in follicular dendritic cell antigen trapping and cell–cell adhesion have also been observed (Sato & Dobashi, 1998).

Not all reports claim that APC function is reduced with age. In fact, the response of Staphylococcus enterotoxin-specific T-cell clones actually is *increased*

in the presence of old versus young irradiated PBMC (Castle et al., 1999). Moreover, DCs obtained from elderly persons are able to present antigen as least as well as DCs from young donors (Steger et al., 1996). In addition, aging has no effect on the in vitro cytokine-induced maturation and expansion of monocytes into DCs (Steger et al., 1996). It must be noted, however, that because the production of GM-CSF is reduced in the elderly, the process of generating DCs from monocytes in vivo may be compromised with age. Moreover, new data documenting that monocyte-derived DCs are inferior to CD34+ stem-cell-derived DCs with respect to the activation of antigen-specific CD8+ T-cells suggest that a more rigorous evaluation of the functional competency of DCs during aging is required (Ferlazzo et al., 1999). Finally, in addition to activating T-cells, optimal DC function requires migration through tissues and the ability to trigger IL-10 and IFN production, functions that do seem to be compromised with age (Wick & Grubeck- Loebenstein, 1997a,b).

XI. Physiological Effects of Aging That May Impact Immune Function

Some immune changes may actually be secondary to alterations that occur on an organismic level, affecting a broad range of processes that include, but are not restricted to, the immune system. Even earlier in life, characteristics such as sex and parity influence immune cytokine production and spleen cell composition, suggesting that an age-associated decline in sex hormones exerts an influence on immune function. Other physiological changes, such as altered lipid homeostasis during aging (Rivnay et al., 1979), may also have profound influences on the immune system. Indeed, on a single-cell basis, lymphocytes from Senieur- screened elderly display a higher membrane viscosity than lymphocytes from young controls, and there is an inverse correlation between membrane viscosity and T-cell responses to mitogen (Wick & Grubeck-Loebenstein, 1997a,b).

A hallmark of aging is the reduced capacity to respond to a variety of stressors. The response to thermal stress by rapid production of heat-shock proteins (hsp) is reduced with age in a variety of cell types, including those of the immune system. Age-related decreases have been documented in rat alveolar macrophages, rat splenocytes, human lymphocytes, and senescent human T-cell cultures (Rao et al., 1999; Gutsmann-Conrad et al., 1999; Effros et al., 1994). Oxidative stress, another well-documented physiological change during aging, may specifically influence such diverse immune-related parameters as telomere shortening (von Zglinicki et al., 1995), lymphocyte lipid peroxidation (Tian et al., 1995), protein damage (Garcaia-Arumai et al., 1998), lung viral load (Meydani et al., 1998), and the PPAR family of nuclear steroid hormone receptors, which are expressed in immune cells and influence NF-κB signal transduction (Poynter & Daynes, 1998). Oxidative stress may also be related to diminished pulmonary function, a biomarker that is, in fact, predictive of mortality in the elderly (Ljungquist et al., 1996). Altered redox potential and oxidative stress may, in turn, be related to metabolic and energy changes, which affect growth, thermoregulation, cell maintenance, and heat-induced apoptosis (Volloch et al., 1998), and can have profound effects on the energy available to mount an immune response. Metabolic alteration has, in fact, been proposed as an underlying mechanism of the life extension effect and improved immunity associated with caloric restriction (Walford & Spindler, 1997), and

altered oxidative stress responses are associated with increased life span (Migliaccio et al., 1999).

Proteasomes are involved in a host of cellular functions, including the heat-shock response, degradation of cyclins involved in cell cycle regulation, and breakdown of proteins into peptides for antigen processing. A decline in proteasome function is observed in hepatocytes of aged rats (Anselmi et al., 1998), neural tissue with high levels of β-amyloid protein (Gregori et al., 1997), and T-cells from aged humans (Trebilcock & Ponnappan, 1999). In the T-cells, the age-related decrease in the degradation of the inhibitor of NF-κB leads to multiple downstream DNA-binding and gene transcription defects that occur in both memory and naïve T-cells Diminished proteasome efficiency as well as other changes in protein degradation (Chapter 3 in this volume) may also impact immune function by enhancing the opportunity for protein modifications that can elicit aberrant immune autoreactivity. Finally, a critical proteasome change with age is the reduced capacity to generate antigenic peptides in antigen-presenting cells (Anselmi et al., 1998). This feature of proteasome aging might also contribute to the reduced number of HLA molecules per cell in monocytes, B-cells and T-cells derived from elderly persons (Le Morvan et al., 1998).

The mucosal surfaces of the body continuously are exposed to a myriad of foreign antigens that are acquired during eating, breathing, and physical contact with others. Indeed, given that the gastrointestinal tract represents more than 50% of the human immune system, it is not unexpected that aging is associated with a significant increase in the incidence and severity of gastrointestinal infectious diseases. Alterations in the gut microenvironment, such as reduced acid secretion, may compromise the gut's "self-sterilizing" function, increasing the incidence of viral, bacterial, or parasitite-induced diarrhea (Ratnaike & Jones, 1998). Increased use of medications by elderly individuals may either interfere with gut motility or reduce protection by commensal bacteria, which may, in turn, confer added stress to an immune system already functioning suboptimally.

Surprisingly, mucosal immunity in aged organisms is an underinvestigated area. It is noteworthy that the predominant cell type within the intraepithelial lymphocyte compartment in mice that are not even old has the same phenotype (CD8+CD28–) as a T-cell population that increases with age in the periphery and is associated with responses to pathogens (Arosa et al., 1998). Furthermore, the accessibility of many mucosal surfaces and the efficacy of oral/nasal vaccine delivery in inducing both mucosal and systemic immune responses suggest that more precise characterization of the alterations in mucosal immunity with age would yield immediate gains in terms of improving vaccine efficacy (Ben-Yedidia et al., 1998). Age-associated reduction of immune responses to cholera toxin and *Escherichia coli* enterotoxin, which are adjuvants frequently used in mucosally delivered vaccine preparations, and age-associated reduction in the amounts of secretory IgA, the major immunoglobulin class produced in the mucosal tissues, suggest that changes in the mucosal immune system may have broad implications on overall health and preventative medicine in the elderly (Schmucker et al., 1996).

XII. Immune System Involvement in Diseases of Aging

The major challenge for immunologists over the next few years will be to translate the plethora of immune changes into an integrated model of physiological *in vivo* aging that incorporates the major age-associated disease entities. Cancer, for which old age is the greatest risk factor, has been linked theoretically to altered immune surveillance, with some experimental validation documented in prostate and skin cancers (Alexander et al., 1998; Galvaao et al., 1998), but detailed mechanistic information is lacking. On the other hand, for several other age-associated diseases, more precise immune mechanisms have been documented, as will be discussed below.

A. Alzheimer's Disease (AD)

AD lesions are characterized by the accumulation of a number of cells and proteins associated with the immune system. There is increasing evidence that interactions between the pro-inflammatory cytokine IL-6 and β-amyloid may play an active role in the development of AD neuropathology. IL-6, produced by astrocytes and microglia cells and elevated in the CNS of AD patients (Blum-Degen et al., 1995), affects neuron differentiation (Satoh et al., 1988), decreases the integrity of the blood–brain barrier (de Vries et al., 1996), and is directly involved in regulation of the Alzheimer's β-amyloid precursor protein (APP) production (Brugg et al., 1995). An integral role of IL-6 in AD also is suggested by the association of a particular variant allele of IL-6 with delayed onset and reduced risk of AD (Papassotiropoulos et al., 1999). The correlation between serum IL-6 levels and severity of dementia suggests that, at the very least, IL-6 may serve as a biomarker of disease progression (Kaalmaan et al., 1997). Other proteins, such as IL-1 and those of the classical complement pathway, are closely connected with β-amyloid deposits, and the high plasma concentration of TNFα is associated with dementia in centenarians (Bruunsgaard et al., 1999a).

Involvement of a specific immune response in AD has also been forthcoming. Activated microglia express high levels of MHC class II glycoproteins, and T-lymphocytes infiltrate the diseased tissue. Interestingly, activation of T- and B-cells is associated with high levels of surface APP expression, suggesting that the immune system may be regularly exposed to this AD precursor protein (Bullido et al., 1996). The T-cell proliferation, production of IL-2, and increased IL-2 receptor expression in response to APP peptides present in normals but absent from AD patients raise the intriguing possibility that cellular immunity normally may function to protect against AD by helping to eliminate potentially amyloidogenic substances and AD occurs when the system fails (Trieb et al., 1996). Investigation of possible mechanisms involved in antigen presentation or processing, such as down-regulation of MHC class II expression in DCs exposed to APP (Schmitt et al., 1997), will be the challenge for future research in this area. Further analysis of the role of dysregulated T-cell apoptosis (Lombardi et al., 1999) may also help elucidate the putative specific immune component in AD. Finally, the inhibition of amyloid plaque and its associated dystrophic neurite formation induced in mice in response to Aβ peptide immunization and the retardation of disease progression associated with anti-inflammatory drugs and estrogen provide cogent support for the role of the immune system in AD (Schenk et al., 1999; McGeer & McGeer, 1996).

B. Cardiovasular Disease

Data from both epidemiological and experimental sources suggest immune involvement in cardiovascular disease (CVD). The presence of T-cells in atherosclerotic lesions (Seko et al., 1997) and the demonstrated interaction of CD40 on T-cells with vascular endothelial cells, smooth muscle cells, and macrophages (Mach et al., 1997) strongly implicate cell-mediated immune involvement in CVD. Chronic infections have been hypothesized to increase the risk of CVD by causing systemic inflammation or by triggering autoimmunity, for example, by cross-reactivity of hsp60 with bacterial antigens (George et al., 1996). Indeed, clinically healthy volunteers with sonographically documented carotid artery atherosclerosis have significantly increased antibody titers to hsp65 compared to controls with no lesions, and in follow-up studies, those with the highest titers showed the highest mortality (Xu et al., 1999). An increasing body of epidemiological evidence links immune reactivity, Chlamidia pneumoniae, and cytomegalovirus with CVD, consistent with studies showing that antibiotics might reduce risks of CVD events. In animal studies, immunization with myosin peptides that resemble those present in Chlamidia induces antigen-specific T-cells that were able to transfer heart disease to fresh mice, consistent with an autoimmune response based on antigenic mimicry (Bachmaier et al., 1999). Involvement of stress proteins is illustrated by hsp60-induced innate immune cell production of TNFα and nitric oxide, induction of Th1-promoting cytokines IL-12 and IL-15, and ability of hsp65 to increase the severity of atherosclerotic lesions induced by a high-cholesterol diet alone (Chen et al., 1999). Blocking of the hsp65 effect by T-cell immunosuppressive agents further implicates specific immunity in the pathogenesis of atherosclerosis (Metzler et al., 1998), although reports on lesions in SCID and RAG knockout mice are in conflict with this notion (Dansky et al., 1997). The challenge during the next few years will be to identify the mechanism that links the classic risk factors, pathogens, and the immune system to this major disease of aging.

XIII. Concluding Remarks

Analysis of immunological aging continues to provide novel insights into both the process of aging itself and the integral role of the immune system in health and disease. With the development of increasingly sophisticated molecular, genetic, and biochemical technology, future research in this dynamic area of gerontology promises to yield insights into potential immunomodulatory strategies to increase the period of good health and independence in the rapidly increasing aged population.

Acknowledgments

Much of the work from the author's laboratory has been supported by NIH Grant AG 10415, the Seigel Life Foundation, and the University of California BioSTAR Program. The author thanks Dr. Amiela Globerson for reviewing the manuscript.

References

Adkins, B., & Riley, R. L. (1998). Autoantibodies to T-lineage cells in aged mice. *Mechanisms of Ageing and Development, 103,* 147–164.

Aggarwal, S., Gollapudi, S., & Gupta, S. (1999). Increased TNF-alpha-induced apoptosis in lymphocytes from aged humans: changes in TNF-alpha receptor expression and activation of caspases. *Journal of Immunology, 162,* 2154–2161.

Albright, J. W., & Albright, J. F. (1998). Impaired natural killer cell function as a consequence of aging. *Experimental Gerontology, 33,* 13–25.

Alexander, R. B., Brady, F., Leffell, M. S., Tsai, V., & Celis, E. (1998). Specific T cell recognition of peptides derived from prostate-specific antigen in patients with prostate cancer. *Urology, 51,* 150–157.

Anderlini, P., Przepiorka, D., Lauppe, J., Seong, D., Giralt, S., Champlin, R., & Keorbling, M. (1997). Collection of peripheral blood stem cells from normal donors 60 years of age or older. *British Journal of Haematology, 97,* 485–487.

Anselmi, B., Conconi, M., Veyrat-Durebex, C., Turlin, E., Biville, F., Alliot, J., & Friguet, B. (1998). Dietary self-selection can compensate an age-related decrease of rat liver 20 S proteasome activity observed with standard diet. *Journal of Gerontology: Biological Sciences, 53,* B173–B179

Arosa, F. A., Irwin, C., Mayer, L., de Sousa, M., & Posnett, D. N. (1998). Interactions between peripheral blood CD8 T lymphocytes and intestinal epithelial cells (iEC). *Clinical and Experimental Immunology, 112,* 226–236.

Arvin, A. M. (1996). Varicella-zoster virus: overview and clinical manifestations. *Seminars in Dermatology, 15,* 4–7.

Aspinall, R., & Andrews (2000). Thymic involution in *Journal of Clinical Immunology,* in press.

Aspinall, R., Carroll, J., & Jiang, S. (1998). Age-related changes in the absolute number of CD95 positive cells in T cell subsets in the blood. *Experimental Gerontology, 33,* 581–591.

Ayroldi, E., Zollo, O., Cannarile, L., D' Adamio, F., Grohmann, U., Delfino, D. V., & Riccardi, C. (1998). Interleukin-6 (IL-6) prevents activation-induced cell death: IL-2- independent inhibition of Fas/fasL expression and cell death. *Blood, 92,* 4212–4219.

Azuma, M., Phillips, J. H., & Lanier, L. L. (1993). CD28- T lymphocytes: antigenic and functional properties. *Journal of Immunology, 150,* 1147–1159.

Bachmaier, K., Neu, N., de la Maza, L. M., Pal, S., Hessel, A., & Penninger, J. M. (1999). Chlamydia infections and heart disease linked through antigenic mimicry [see comments]. *Science, 283,* 1335–1339.

Ben-Yedidia, T., Abel, L., Arnon, R., & Globerson, A. (1998). Efficacy of anti-influenza peptide vaccine in aged mice. *Mechanisms of Ageing and Development, 104,* 11–23.

Ben Yehuda, A., Friedman, G., Wirtheim, E., Abel, L., & Globerson, A. (1998). Checkpoints in thymocytopoiesis in aging: expression of the recombination activating genes RAG-1 and RAG-2. *Mechanisms of Ageing and Development, 102,* 239–247.

Ben-Yehuda, A., Wirtheim, E., Abdulhai, A., Or, R., Slavin, S., Babaey, S., & Friedman, G. (1999). Activation of the recombination activating gene 1 (RAG-1) transcript in bone marrow of senescent C57BL/6 mice by recombinant interleukin-7. *Journal of Gerontology: Biological Sciences, 54,* B143–B148.

Bender, B. S., Ulmer, J. B., DeWitt, C. M., Cottey, R., Taylor, S. F., Ward, A. M., Friedman, A., Liu, M. A., & Donnelly, J. J. (1998). Immunogenicity and efficacy of DNA vaccines encoding influenza A proteins in aged mice. *Vaccine, 16,* 1748–1755.

Bergler, W., Adam, S., Gross, H. J., Heormann, K., & Schwartz-Albiez, R. (1999). Age- dependent altered proportions in subpopulations of tonsillar lymphocytes. *Clinical and Experimental Immunology, 116,* 9–18.

Bernstein, E., Kaye, D., Abrutyn, E., Gross, P., Dorfman, M., & Murasko, D. M. (1999). Immune response to influenza vaccination in a large healthy elderly population. *Vaccine, 17,* 82–94.

Blum-Degen, D., Meuller, T., Kuhn, W., Gerlach, M., Przuntek, H., & Riederer, P. (1995). Interleukin-1 beta and interleukin-6 are elevated in the cerebrospinal fluid of Alzheimer's and de novo Parkinson's disease patients. *Neuroscience Letters, 202,* 17–20.

Bodnar, A. G., Kim, N. W., Effros, R. B., & Chiu, C. P. (1996). Mechanism of telomerase induction during T cell activation. *Experimental Cell Research, 228,* 58–64.

Borrego, F., Alonso, M. C., Galiani, M. D., Carracedo, J., Ramirez, R., Ostos, B., Peana, J., & Solana, R. (1999). NK phenotypic markers and IL2 response in NK cells from elderly people. *Experimental Gerontology, 34,* 253–265.

Boucher, N., Defeu-Duchesne, T., Vicaut, E., Farge, D., Effros, R. B., & Schachter, F. (1998). CD28 expression in T cell aging and human longevity. *Experimental Geronology, 33,* 267–282.

Brugg, B., Dubreuil, Y. L., Huber, G., Wollman, E. E., Delhaye-Bouchaud, N., & Mariani, J. (1995). Inflammatory processes induce beta-amyloid precursor protein changes in mouse brain. *Proceedings of the National Academy of Sciences of the USA, 92,* 3032–3035.

Bruunsgaard, H., Andersen-Ranberg, K., Jeune, B., Pedersen, A. N., Skinhj, P., & Pedersen, B. K. (1999). A high plasma concentration of TNF-alpha is associated with dementia in centenarians. *Journal of Gerontology: Medical Sciences, 54,* M357–M364.

Bruunsgaard, H., Jensen, M. S., Schjerling, P., Halkjaer-Kristensen, J., Ogawa, K., Skinhoj, P., & Pedersen, B. K. (1999). Exercise induces recruitment of lymphocytes with an activated phenotype and short telomeres in young and elderly humans. *Life Sciences, 65,* 2623–2633.

Bullido, M. J., Muanoz-Fernandez, M. A., Recuero, M., Fresno, M., & Valdivieso, F. (1996). Alzheimer's amyloid precursor protein is expressed on the surface of hematopoietic cells upon activation. *Biochimica et Biophysica Acta, 1313,* 54–62.

Castle, S., Uyemura, K., Wong, W., Modlin, R., & Effros, R. B. (1997). Evidence of enhanced type 2 immune response and impaired upregulation of a type 1 response in frail elderly nursing home residents. *Mechanisms of Ageing and Development, 94,* 7–16.

Castle, S. C., Uyemura, K., Crawford, W., Wong, W., & Makinodan, T. (1999). Antigen presenting cell function is enhanced in healthy elderly. *Mechanisms of Ageing and Development, 107,* 137–145.

Chakravarti, B., Chakravarti, D. N., Devecis, J., Seshi, B., & Abraham, G. N. (1998). Effect of age on mitogen induced protein tyrosine phosphorylation in human T cell and its subsets: down-regulation of tyrosine phosphorylation of ZAP-70. *Mechanisms of Ageing and Development, 104,* 41–58.

Cheleuitte, D., Mizuno, S., & Glowacki, J. (1998). In vitro secretion of cytokines by human bone marrow: effects of age and estrogen status. *Journal of Clinical Endocrinology and Metabolism, 83,* 2043–2051.

Chen, J., Astle, C. M., & Harrison, D. E. (1998). Delayed immune aging in diet-restricted B6CBAT6 F1 mice is associated with preservation of naive T cells. *Journal of Gerontology: Biological Sciences, 53,* B330–B337.

Chen, W., Syldath, U., Bellmann, K., Burkart, V., & Kolb, H. (1999). Human 60-kDa heat-shock protein: a danger signal to the innate immune system. *Journal of Immunology, 162,* 3212–3219.

Chiu, C. P., Dragowska, W., Kim, N. W., Vaziri, H., Yui, J., Thomas, T. E., Harley, C. B., & Lansdorp, P. M. (1996). Differential expression of telomerase activity in hematopoietic progenitors from adult human bone marrow. *Stem Cells, 14,* 239–248.

Cossarizza, A., Ortolani, C., Monti, D., & Franceschi, C. (1997). Cytometric analysis of immunosenescence. *Cytometry, 27,* 297–313.

Crisi, G. M., Chen, L. Z., Huang, C., & Thorbecke, G. J. (1998). Age-related loss of immunoregulatory function in peripheral blood CD8 T cells. *Mechanisms of Ageing and Development, 103,* 235–254.

Crompton, N. E. (1997). Telomeres, senescence and cellular radiation response. *Cellular and Molecular Life Sciences, 53,* 568–575.

Dansky, H. M., Charlton, S. A., Harper, M. M., & Smith, J. D. (1997). T and B lymphocytes play a minor role in atherosclerotic plaque formation in the apolipoprotein E-deficient mouse. *Proceedings of the National Academy of Sciences of the USA, 94,* 4642–4646.

de Haan, G., & Van Zant, G. (1997). Intrinsic and extrinsic control of hemopoietic stem cell numbers: mapping of a stem cell gene. *Journal of Experimental Medicine, 186,* 529–536.

de Vries, H. E., Blom-Roosemalen, M. C., van Oosten, M., de Boer, A. G., van Berkel, T. J., Breimer, D. D., & Kuiper, J. (1996). The influence of cytokines on the integrity of the blood- brain barrier in vitro. *Journal of Neuroimmunology, 64,* 37–43.

Douek, D. C., McFarland, R. D., Keiser, P. H., Gage, E. A., Massey, J. M., Haynes, B. F., Polis, M. A., Haase, A. T., Feinberg, M. B., Sullivan, J. L., Jamieson, B. D., Zack, J. A., Picker, L. J., & Koup, R. A. (1998). Changes in thymic function with age and during the treatment of HIV infection [see

comments]. *International Immunology, 396,* 690–695.

Effros, R. B., & Pawelec, G. (1997). Replicative senescence of T lymphocytes: Does the Hayflick limit lead to immune exhaustion? *Immunology Today, 18,* 450–454.

Effros, R. B., Zhu, X., & Walford, R. L. (1994). Stress response of senescent T lymphocytes: reduced hsp70 is independent of the proliferative block. *Journal of Gerontology: Biological Sciences, 49,* B65–B70.

Effros, R. B., Allsopp, R., Chiu, C. P., Wang, L., Hirji, K., Harley, C. B., Villeponteau, B., West, M., & Giorgi, J. V. (1996). Shortened telomeres in the expanded CD28-CD8+ subset in HIV disease implicate replicative senescence in HIV pathogenesis. *AIDS/Fast Track, 10,* F17–F22.

Ferguson, F. G., Wikby, A., Maxson, P., Olsson, J., & Johansson, B. (1995). Immune parameters in a longitudinal study of a very old population of Swedish people: a comparison between survivors and nonsurvivors. *Journals of Gerontology: Biological Sciences, 50,* B378–B382.

Ferlazzo, G., Wesa, A., Wei, W. Z., & Galy, A. (1999). Dendritic cells generated either from CD34+ progenitor cells or from monocytes differ in their ability to activate antigen-specific CD8+ T cells. *Journal of Immunology, 163,* 3597–3604.

Fernandes, G., Venkatraman, J. T., Turturro, A., Attwood, V. G., & Hart, R. W. (1997). Effect of food restriction on life span and immune functions in long-lived Fischer–344 × Brown Norway F1 rats. *Journal of Clinical Immunology, 17,* 85–95.

Fraifeld, V., Kaplanski, J., Kukulansky, T., & Globerson, A. (1995). Increased prostaglandin E2 production by concanavalin A-stimulated splenocytes of old mice. *Gerontology, 41,* 129–133.

Franceschi, C., Monti, D., Sansoni, P., & Cossarizza, A. (1995). The immunology of exceptional individuals: the lesson of centenarians [see comments]. *Immunology Today, 16,* 12–16.

Frenck, R. J., Blackburn, E. H., & Shannon, K. M. (1998). The rate of telomere sequence loss in human leukocytes varies with age.

Proceedings of the National Academy of Sciences, 95, 5607–5610.

Furumoto, K., Inoue, E., Nagao, N., Hiyama, E., & Miwa, N. (1998). Age-dependent telomere shortening is slowed down by enrichment of intracellular vitamin C via suppression of oxidative stress. *Life Sciences, 63,* 935–948.

Gafni, A. (2000). Protein structure and turnover. In E. Masoro & S. Austad (Eds.), *Handbook of the Biology of Aging.* San Diego: Academic Press.

Galvaao, M. M., Sotto, M. N., Kihara, S. M., Rivitti, E. A., & Sabbaga, E. (1998). Lymphocyte subsets and Langerhans cells in sun-protected and sun-exposed skin of immunosuppressed renal allograft recipients. *Journal of the American Academy of Dermatology, 38,* 38–44.

Garcaia-Arumai, E., Andreu, A. L., Laopez-Hellain, J., & Schwartz, S. (1998). Effect of oxidative stress on lymphocytes from elderly subjects. *Clinical Science, 94,* 447–452.

Garg, M., Luo, W., Kaplan, A. M., & Bondada, S. (1996). Cellular basis of decreased immune responses to pneumococcal vaccines in aged mice. *Infection and Immunity, 64,* 4456–4462.

George, J., Harats, D., Gilburd, B., & Shoenfeld, Y. (1996). Emerging cross-regulatory roles of immunity and autoimmunity in atherosclerosis. *Immunologic Research, 15,* 315–322.

Globerson, A. (1997). Thymocytopoiesis in aging: the bone marrow-thymus axis. *Archives of Gerontology and Geriatrics, 24,* 141–155.

Gregori, L., Hainfeld, J. F., Simon, M. N., & Goldgaber, D. (1997). Binding of amyloid beta protein to the 20 S proteasome. *Journal of Biological Chemistry, 272,* 58–62.

Gueldner, S. H., Poon, L. W., La Via, M., Virella, G., Michel, Y., Bramlett, M. H., Noble, C. A., & Paulling, E. (1997). Long-term exercise patterns and immune function in healthy older women. A report of preliminary findings. *Mechanisms of Ageing and Development, 93,* 215–222.

Guidi, L., Antico, L., Bartoloni, C., Costanzo, M., Errani, A., Tricerri, A., Vangeli, M., Doria, G., Gatta, L., Goso, C., Mancino, L.,

& Frasca, D. (1998). Changes in the amount and level of phosphorylation of p56(lck) in PBL from aging humans. *Mechanisms of Ageing and Development, 102,* 177–186.

Gutsmann-Conrad, A., Pahlavani, M. A., Heydari, A. R., & Richardson, A. (1999). Expression of heat shock protein 70 decreases with age in hepatocytes and splenocytes from female rats. *Mechanisms of Ageing and Development, 107,* 255–270.

Hakim, F. T., Cepeda, R., Kaimei, S., Mackall, C. L., McAtee, N., Zujewski, J., Cowan, K., & Gress, R. E. (1997). Constraints on CD4 recovery postchemotherapy in adults: Thymic insufficiency and apoptotic decline of expanded peripheral CD4 cells. *Blood, 90,* 3789–3798.

Hamann, D., Baars, P. A., Rep, M. H., Hooibrink, B., Kerkhof-Garde, S. R., Klein, M. R., & Van Lier, R. A. (1997). Phenotypic and functional separation of memory and effector human CD8+ T cells. *Journal of Experimental Medicine, 186,* 1407–1418.

Haratake, A., Uchida, Y., Mimura, K., Elias, P. M., & Holleran, W. M. (1997). Intrinsically aged epidermis displays diminished UVB-induced alterations in barrier function associated with decreased proliferation. *Journal of Investigative Dermatology, 108,* 319–323.

Hathcock, K. S., Weng, N. P., Merica, R., Jenkins, M. K., & Hodes, R. (1998). Antigen- dependent regulation of telomerase activity in murine T cells. *Journal of Immunology, 160,* 5702–5706.

Hayflick, L. (1965). The limited in vitro lifetime of human diploid cell strains. *Experimental Cell Research, 37,* 614–636.

Haynes, L., Eaton, S. M., & Swain, S. L. (1999). The defects in effector generation assocatied with aging can be reversed by addition IL-2 but not other related gamma-c receptor binding cytokines. *Vaccine, 18,* 1649–1653.

Heller, D. A., Ahern, F. M., Stout, J. T., & McClearn, G. E. (1998). Mortality and biomarkers of aging in heterogeneous stock (HS) mice. *Journals of Gerontology. Series A, Biological Sciences and Medical Sciences, 53,* B217–B230

Hiyama, K., Hirai, Y., Kyoizumi, S., Akiyama, M., Hiyama, E., Piatyszek, M.

A., Shay, J. W., Ishioka, S., & Yamakido, M. (1995). Activation of telomerase in human lymphocytes and hematopoietic progenitor cells. *Journal of Immunology, 155,* 3711–3715.

Horiuchi, S., & Wilmoth, J. R. (1997). Age patterns of the life table aging rate for major causes of death in Japan, 1951–1990. *Journals of Gerontology. Series A, Biological Sciences and Medical Sciences, 52,* B67–B77

Horvath-Arcidiacono, J. A., Mostowski, H. S., & Bloom, E. T. (1996). IL-12 administered in vivo to young and aged mice. Discrepancy between the effects on tumor growth in vivo and cytotoxic T lymphocyte generation ex vivo: Dependence on IFN-gamma. *International Immunology, 8,* 661–673.

Hosono, M., Hosokawa, T., Aiba, Y., & Katsura, Y. (1996). Termination by early deletion of V beta 8 + T cells of aged mice in response to staphylococcal enterotoxin B. *Mechanisms of Ageing and Development, 87,* 99–114.

Hsueh, C. M., Chen, S. F., Ghanta, V. K., & Hiramoto, R. N. (1996). Involvement of cytokine gene expression in the age-dependent decline of NK cell response. *Cellular Immunology, 173,* 221–229.

Huppert, F. A., Solomou, W., O'Connor, S., Morgan, K., Sussams, P., & Brayne, C. (1998). Aging and lymphocyte subpopulations: Whole-blood analysis of immune markers in a large population sample of healthy elderly individuals. *Experimental Gerontology, 33,* 593–600.

Ivanova, R., Haenon, N., Lepage, V., Charron, D., Vicaut, E., & Schachter, F. (1998). HLA-DR alleles display sex-dependent effects on survival and discriminate between individual and familial longevity. *Human Molecular Genetics, 7,* 187–194.

Jamieson, B. D., Douek, D. C., Killian, S., Hultin, L. E., Scripture-Adams, D. D., Giorgi, J. V., Marelli, D., Koup, R. A., & Zack, J. A. (1999). Generation of functional thymocytes in the human adult. *Immunity, 10,* 569–575.

Kaalmaan, J., Juhaasz, A., Laird, G., Dickens, P., Jaardaanhaazy, T., Rimanaoczy, A., Boncz, I., Parry-Jones, W. L., & Janka, Z. (1997). Serum interleukin-6 levels correlate with the severity of dementia in Down syndrome and in Alzheimer's disease. *Acta Neurologica Scandinavica, 96,* 236–240.

Khare, V., Sodhi, A., & Singh, S. M. (1999). Age-dependent alterations in the tumoricidal functions of tumor-associated macrophages. *Tumour Biology, 20,* 30–43.

Kirman, I., Zhao, K., Tschepen, I., Szabo, P., Richter, G., Nguyen, H., & Weksler, M. E. (1996). Treatment of old mice with IL-2 corrects dysregulated IL-2 and IL-4 production. *International Immunology, 8,* 1009–1015.

Kirman, I., Zhao, K., Wang, Y., Szabo, P., Telford, W., & Weksler, M. E. (1998). Increased apoptosis of bone marrow pre-B cells in old mice associated with their low number. *International Immunology, 10,* 1385–1392.

Kline, G. H., Hayden, T. A., & Klinman, N. R. (1999). B cell maintenance in aged mice reflects both increased B cell longevity and decreased B cell generation. *Journal of Immunology, 162,* 3342–3349.

Klinman, D. M., Conover, J., Bloom, E. T., & Weiss, W. (1998). Immunogenicity and efficacy of a DNA vaccine in aged mice. *Journals of Gerontololology: Biological Sciences, 53A,* B281–B286

Kohen, F., Abel, L., Sharp, A., Amir-Zaltsman, Y., Seomjen, D., Luria, S., Mor, G., Knyszynski, A., Thole, H., & Globerson, A. (1998). Estrogen-receptor expression and function in thymocytes in relation to gender and age. *Developmental Immunology, 5,* 277–285.

Krishnaraj, R., Zaks, A., & Unterman, T. (1998). Relationship between plasma IGF-I levels, in vitro correlates of immunity, and human senescence. *Clinical Immunology and Immunopathology, 88,* 264–270.

Kruk, P. A., Rampino, N. J., & Bohr, V. A. (1992). DNA damage and repair in telomerase: Relation to aging. *Proceedings of the National Academy of Sciences of the USA, 258,* 262.

Ku, C. C., Kotzin, B., Kappler, J., & Marrack, P. (1997). CD8+ T-cell clones in old mice. *Immunological Reviews, 160,* 139–144.

Kuschnaroff, L. M., Goebels, J., Valckx, D., Heremans, H., Matthys, P., & Waer, M. (1997). Increased mortality and impaired clonal deletion after staphylococcal enterotoxin B injection in old mice: Relation to cytokines and nitric oxide production. *Scandinavian Journal of Immunology, 46,* 469–478.

Lechner, H., Amort, M., Steger, M. M., Maczek, C., & Grubeck-Loebenstein, B. (1996). Regulation of CD95 (APO-1) expression and the induction of apoptosis in human T cells: changes in old age. *International Archives of Allergy and Immunology, 110,* 238–243.

LeMaoult, J., Manavalan, J. S., Dyall, R., Szabo, P., Nikolic-Zugic, J., & Weksler, M. E. (1999). Cellular basis of B cell clonal populations in old mice. *Journal of Immunology, 162,* 6384–6391.

LeMaoult, J., Szabo, P., & Weksler, M. E. (1997). Effect of age on humoral immunity, selection of the B-cell repertoire and B-cell development. *Immunological Reviews, 160,* 115–126.

Le Morvan, C., Cognae, M., Troutaud, D., Charmes, J. P., Sauvage, P., & Drouet, M. (1998). Modification of HLA expression on peripheral lymphocytes and monocytes during aging. *Mechanisms of Ageing and Development, 105,* 209–220.

Linton, P. J., Haynes, L., Klinman, N. R., & Swain, S. L. (1996). Antigen-independent changes in naive CD4 T cells with aging. *Journal of Experimental Medicine, 184,* 1891–1900.

Ljungquist, B., Berg, S., & Steen, B. (1996). Determinants of survival: an analysis of the effects of age at observation and length of the predictive period. *Aging, 8,* 22–31.

Lohmiller, J. J., Roellich, K. M., Toledano, A., Rabinovitch, P. S., Wolf, N. S., & Grossmann, A. (1996). Aged murine T-lymphocytes are more resistant to oxidative damage due to the predominance of the cells possessing the memory phenotype. *Journals of Gerontology: Biological Sciences, 51,* B132–B140

Lombardi, V. R., Garcaia, M., Rey, L., & Cacabelos, R. (1999). Characterization of cytokine production, screening of lymphocyte subset patterns and in vitro apoptosis in healthy and Alzheimer's disease (AD) individuals. *Journal of Neuroimmunology, 97,* 163–171.

Mach, F., Scheonbeck, U., Sukhova, G. K., Bourcier, T., Bonnefoy, J. Y., Pober, J. S., &

Libby, P. (1997). Functional CD40 ligand is expressed on human vascular endothelial cells, smooth muscle cells, and macrophages: Implications for CD40-CD40 ligand signaling in atherosclerosis. *Proceedings of the National Academy of Sciences of the USA, 94,* 1931–1936.

Mackall, C. L., Fleisher, T. A., Brown, M. R., Andrich, M. P., Chen, C. C., Feuerstein, I. M., Horowitz, M. E., Magrath, I. T., Shad, A. T., & Steinberg, S. M. (1995). Age, thymopoiesis, and CD4+ T-lymphocyte regeneration after intensive chemotherapy [see comments]. *New England Journal of Medicine, 332,* 143–149.

Mackall, C. L., Punt, J. A., Morgan, P., Farr, A. G., & Gress, R. E. (1998). Thymic function in young/old chimeras: Substantial thymic T cell regenerative capacity despite irreversible age- associated thymic involution. *European Journal of Immunology, 28,* 1886–1893.

Maini, M. K., Casorati, G., Dellabona, P., Wack, A., & Beverley, P. C. (1999a). T-cell clonality in immune responses. *Immunology Today, 20,* 262–266.

Maini, M. K., Soares, M. V., Zilch, C. F., Akbar, A. N., & Beverley, P. C. (1999b). Virus- induced CD8+ T cell clonal expansion is associated with telomerase up-regulation and telomere length preservation: A mechanism for rescue from replicative senescence. *Journal of Immunology, 162,* 4521–4526.

Mariani, E., Ravaglia, G., Meneghetti, A., Tarozzi, A., Forti, P., Maioli, F., Boschi, F., & Facchini, A. (1998). Natural immunity and bone and muscle remodelling hormones in the elderly. *Mechanisms of Ageing and Development, 102,* 279–292.

Mazzoccoli, G., Correra, M., Bianco, G., De Cata, A., Balzanelli, M., Giuliani, A., & Tarquini, R. (1997). Age-related changes of neuro-endocrine-immune interactions in healthy humans. *Journal of Biological Regulators and Homeostatic Agents, 11,* 143–147.

McGeer, P. L., & McGeer, E. G. (1996). Anti-inflammatory drugs in the fight against Alzheimer's disease. *Annals of the New York Academy of Sciences, 777,* 213–220.

McLachlan, J. A., Serkin, C. D., Morrey, K. M., & Bakouche, O. (1995). Antitumoral properties of aged human monocytes. *Journal of Immunology, 154*, 832–843.

Metzler, B., Xu, Q., & Wick, G. (1998). The role of (auto-) immunity in atherogenesis. *Wiener Klinische Wochenschrift, 110*, 350–355.

Meydani, M., Lipman, R. D., Han, S. N., Wu, D., Beharka, A., Martin, K. R., Bronson, R., Cao, G., Smith, D., & Meydani, S. N. (1998). The effect of long-term dietary supplementation with antioxidants. *Annals of the New York Academy of Sciences, 854*, 352–360.

Meyer, K. C., Ershler, W., Rosenthal, N. S., Lu, X. G., & Peterson, K. (1996). Immune dysregulation in the aging human lung. *American Journal of Respiratory and Critical Care Medicine, 153*, 1072–1079.

Migliaccio, E., Giorgio, M., Mele, S., Pelicci, G., Reboldi, P., Pandolfi, P. P., Lanfrancone, L., & Pelicci, P. G. (1999). The p66[shc] adaptor protein controls oxidative stress response and life span in mammals. *International Immunology, 402*, 309–313.

Miller, R. A. (1996). Aging and the immune response. In E. L. Schneider, & J. W. Rowe (Eds.), *Handbook of the Biology of Aging* (pp. 157–180). New York: Academic Press.

Miller, R. A., Garcia, A., Kirk, C. J., & Witkowski, J. M. (1996). Early activation defects in T lymphocytes from aged mice. *Immunological Reviews, 160*, 79–90.

Miller, R. A., Bookstein, F., Van der Meulen, J., Engle, S., Kim, J., Mullins, L., & Faulkner, J. (1997). Candidate biomarkers of aging: age-sensitive indices of immune and muscle function covary in genetically heterogeneous mice. *Journals of Gerontology: Biological Sciences, 52*, B39–B47.

Monteiro, J., Batliwalla, F., Ostrer, H., & Gregersen, P. K. (1996). Shortened telomeres in clonally expanded CD28-CD8+ T cells imply a replicative history that is distinct from their CD28+CD8+ counterparts. *Journal of Immunology, 156*, 3587–3590.

Moore, S. A., Lopez, A., Richardson, A., & Pahlavani, M. A. (1998). Effect of age and dietary restriction on expression of heat shock protein 70 in rat alveolar macrophages. *Mechanisms of Ageing and Development, 104*, 59–73.

Morrison, S. J., Wandycz, A. M., Akashi, K., Globerson, A., & Weissman, I. L. (1996). The aging of hematopoietic stem cells [see comments]. *Nature Medicine, 2*, 1011–1016.

Mountz, J. D., Wu, J., Zhou, T., & Hsu, H. C. (1997). Cell death and longevity: implications of Fas-mediated apoptosis in T-cell senescence. *Immunological Reviews, 160*, 19–30.

Nilsson-Ehle, H., Swolin, B., & Westin, J. (1995). Bone marrow progenitor cell growth and karyotype changes in healthy 88-year-old subjects. *European Journal of Haematology, 55*, 14–18.

Nociari, M. M., Telford, W., & Russo, C. (1999). Postthymic development of CD28-CD8+ T cell subset: age-associated expansion and shift from memory to naive phenotype. *Journal of Immunology, 162*, 3327–3335.

Nonaka, K.O. (1996). Some aspects of the pineal gland function. *Revista Brasileira de Biologia, 56*, 339–344.

Nuanez, C., Nishimoto, N., Gartland, G. L., Billips, L. G., Burrows, P. D., Kubagawa, H., & Cooper, M. D. (1996). B cells are generated throughout life in humans. *Journal of Immunology, 156*, 866–872.

Padgett, D. A., MacCallum, R. C., & Sheridan, J. F. (1998). Stress exacerbates age-related decrements in the immune response to an experimental influenza viral infection. *Journals of Gerontology: Biological Sciences, 53*, B347–B353.

Pahlavani, M. A., Harris, M. D., & Richardson, A. (1997). The increase in the induction of IL-2 expression with caloric restriction is correlated to changes in the transcription factor NFAT. *Cellular Immunology, 180*, 10–19.

Pahlavani, M. A., Harris, M. D., & Richardson, A. (1998). Activation of p21ras/MAPK signal transduction molecules decreases with age in mitogen-stimulated T cells from rats. *Cellular Immunology, 185*, 39–48.

Papassotiropoulos, A., Bagli, M., Jessen, F., Bayer, T.A., Maier, W., Rao, M.L., & Heun, R. (1999). A genetic variation of the inflammatory cytokine interleukin-6 delays the initial onset and reduces the risk for sporadic Alzheimer's disease. *Annals of Neurology*, 45, 666–668.

Pawelec, G., Sansom, D., Rehbein, A., Adibzadeh, M., & Beckman, I. (1996). Decreased proliferative capacity and increased sucsepibility to activation-induced cell death in late- passage human CD4+ TCR2+ cultured T cell clones. *Experimental Gerontology*, 31, 665–668.

Perillo, N. L., Naeim, F., Walford, R. L., & Effros, R. B. (1993). The in vitro senescence of human lymphocytes: Failure to divide is not associated with a loss of cytolytic activity or memory T cell phenotype. *Mechanisms of Ageing and Development*, 67, 173–185.

Phelouzat, M. A., Laforge, T., Arbogast, A., Quadri, R. A., Boutet, S., & Proust, J. J. (1997). Susceptibility to apoptosis of T lymphocytes from elderly humans is associated with increased in vivo expression of functional Fas receptors. *Mechanisms of Ageing and Development*, 96, 35–46.

Pilarski, L. M., Paine, D., McElhaney, J. E., Cass, C. E., & Belch, A. R. (1995). Multidrug transporter P-glycoprotein 170 as a differentiation antigen on normal human lymphocytes and thymocytes: modulation with differentiation stage and during aging. *American Journal of Hematology*, 49, 323–335.

Pilling, D., Akbar, A. N., Girdlestone, J., Orteu, C. H., Borthwick, N. J., Amft, N., Scheel- Toellner, D., Buckley, C. D., & Salmon, M. (1999). Interferon-beta mediates stromal cell rescue of T cells from apoptosis. *European Journal of Immunology*, 29, 1041–1050.

Plasman, N., Guillet, J. G., & Vray, B. (1995). Impaired protein catabolism in Trypanosoma cruzi-infected macrophages: Possible involvement in antigen presentation. *Immunology*, 86, 636–645.

Polyak, K., Wu, T. T., Hamilton, S. R., Kinzler, K. W., & Vogelstein, B. (1997). Less death in the dying. *Cell Death & Differentiation*, 4, 242–246.

Portales-Paerez, D., Alarcaon-Segovia, D., Llorente, L., Ruaiz-Argeuelles, A., Abud-Mendoza, C., Baranda, L., de la Fuente, H., Ternynck, T., & Gonzaalez-Amaro, R. (1998). Penetrating anti-DNA monoclonal antibodies induce activation of human peripheral blood mononuclear cells. *Journal of Autoimmunity*, 11, 563–571.

Posnett, D. N., Edinger, J. W., Manavalan, J. S., Irwin, C., & Marodon, G. (1999). Differentiation of human CD8 T cells: Implications for in vivo presistence of CD8+CD28– cytotoxic effector clones. *International Immunoogyl*, 11, 229–241.

Poynter, M. E., & Daynes, R. A. (1998). Peroxisome proliferator-activated receptor-alpha activation modulates cellular redox status, represses nuclear factor -κB signaling, and reduces inflammatory cytokine prodcution in aging. *Journal of Biological Chemistry*, 32833–32841.

Provinciali, M., Di Stefano, G., & Stronati, S. (1998). Flow cytometric analysis of CD3/TCR complex, zinc, and glucocorticoid-mediated regulation of apoptosis and cell cycle distribution in thymocytes from old mice. *Cytometry*, 32, 1–8.

Quadri, R. A., Plastre, O., Phelouzat, M. A., Arbogast, A., & Proust, J. J. (1996). Age-related tyrosine-specific protein phosphorylation defect in human T lymphocytes activated through CD3, CD4, CD8 or the IL–2 receptor. *Mechanisms of Ageing and Development*, 88, 125–138.

Quadri, R. A., Arbogast, A., Phelouzat, M. A., Boutet, S., Plastre, O., & Proust, J. J. (1998). Age-associated decline in cdk1 activity delays cell cycle progression of human T lymphocytes. *Journal of Immunology*, 161, 5203–5209.

Rao, D. V., Watson, K., & Jones, G. L. (1999). Age-related attenuation in the expression of the major heat shock proteins in human peripheral lymphocytes. *Mechanisms of Ageing and Development*, 107, 105–118.

Rappuoli, R., Pizza, M., Douce, G., & Dougan, G. (1999). Structure and mucosal adjuvanticity of cholera and *Escherichia coli* heat-labile enterotoxins. *Immunology Today*, 20, 493–500.

Ratnaike, R. N., & Jones, T. E. (1998). Mechanisms of drug-induced diarrhoea in the elderly. *Drugs and Aging*, 13, 245–253.

Rea, I. M., & Middleton, D. (1994). Is the phenotypic combination A1B8Cw7DR3 a marker for male longevity? *Journal of the American Geriatrics Society*, 42, 978–983.

Remarque, E. J. (1999). Influenza vaccination in elderly people. *Experimental Gerontology, 34,* 445–452.

Rivnay, B., Globerson, A., & Shinitzky, M. (1979). Viscosity of lymphocyte plasma membrane in aging mice and its possible relation to serum cholesterol. *Mechanisms of Ageing and Development, 10,* 71–79.

Rufer, N., Breummendorf, T. H., Kolvraa, S., Bischoff, C., Christensen, K., Wadsworth, L., Schulzer, M., & Lansdorp, P. M. (1999). Telomere fluorescence measurements in granulocytes and T lymphocyte subsets point to a high turnover of hematopoietic stem cells and memory T cells in early childhood. *Journal of Experimental Medicine, 190,* 157–167.

Salazar, M., Leong, T., Tu, N., Gelman, R. S., Watson, A. L., Bronson, R., Iglesias, A., Mann, M., Good, R. A., & Yunis, E. J. (1995). Life-span, T-cell responses, and incidence of lymphomas in congenic mice. *Proceedings of the National Academy of Science, 92,* 3992–3996.

Sambhara, S., Kurichh, A., Miranda, R., Tamane, A., Arpino, R., James, O., McGuinness, U., Kandil, A., Underdown, B., Klein, M., & Burt, D. (1998). Enhanced immune responses and resistance against infection in aged mice conferred by Flu-ISCOMs vaccine correlate with up-regulation of costimulatory molecule CD86. *Vaccine, 16,* 1698–1704.

Santos, M. S., Gaziano, J. M., Leka, L. S., Beharka, A. A., Hennekens, C. H., & Meydani, S. N. (1998). Beta-carotene-induced enhancement of natural killer cell activity in elderly men: An investigation of the role of cytokines. *American Journal of Clinical Nutrition, 68,* 164–170.

Sato, H., & Dobashi, M. (1998). The distribution, immune complex trapping ability and morphology of follicular dendritic cells in popliteal lymph nodes of aged rats. *Histology and Histopathology, 13,* 99–108.

Satoh, T., Nakamura, S., Taga, T., Matsuda, T., Hirano, T., Kishimoto, T., & Kaziro, Y. (1988). Induction of neuronal differentiation in PC12 cells by B-cell stimulatory factor 2/interleukin 6. *Molecular and Cellular Biology, 8,* 3546–3549.

Schenk, D., Barbour, R., Dunn, W., Gordon, G., Grajeda, H., Guido, T., Hu, K., Huang, J., Johnson-Wood, K., Khan, K., Kholodenko, D., Lee, M., Liao, Z., Lieberburg, I., Motter, R., Mutter, L., Soriano, F., Shopp, G., Vasquez, N., Vandevert, C., Walker, S., Wogulis, M., Yednock, T., Games, D., & Seubert, P. (1999). Immunization with amyloid-beta attenuates Alzheimer-disease-like pathology in the PDAPP mouse [see comments]. *International Immunology, 400,* 173–177.

Schmitt, T. L., Steger, M. M., Pavelka, M., & Grubeck-Loebenstein, B. (1997). Interactions of the Alzheimer beta amyloid fragment (25–35) with peripheral blood dendritic cells. *Mechanisms of Ageing and Development, 94,* 223–232.

Schmucker, D. L., Heyworth, M. F., Owen, R. L., & Daniels, C. K. (1996). Impact of aging on gastrointestinal mucosal immunity [see comments]. *Digestive Diseases and Sciences, 41,* 1183–1193.

Seko, Y., Sato, O., Takagi, A., Tada, Y., Matsuo, H., Yagita, H., Okumura, K., & Yazaki, Y. (1997). Perforin-secreting killer cell infiltration in the aortic tissue of patients with atherosclerotic aortic aneurysm. *Japanese Circulation Journal, 61,* 965–970.

Shearer, G. M. (1997). Th1/Th2 changes in aging. *Mechanisms of Ageing and Development, 94,* 1–6.

Sherwood, E. M., Blomberg, B. B., Xu, W., Warner, C. A., & Riley, R. L. (1998). Senescent BALB/c mice exhibit decreased expression of lambda5 surrogate light chains and reduced development within the pre-B cell compartment. *Journal of Immunology, 161,* 4472–4475.

Small, T. N., Avigan, D., Dupont, B., Smith, K., Black, P., Heller, G., Polyak, T., & O'Reilly, R. J. (1997). Immune reconstitution following T-cell depleted bone marrow transplantation: effect of age and posttransplant graft rejection prophylaxis. *Biology of Blood and Marrow Transplantation, 3,* 65–75.

Smith, G. S., & Walford, R. L. (1977). Influence of the main histocompatibility complex on ageing in mice. *International Immunology, 270,* 727–729.

Soares, M. V., Borthwick, N. J., Maini, M. K., Janossy, G., Salmon, M., & Akbar, A. N. (1998). IL-7-dependent extrathymic expansion of CD45RA+ T cells enables preservation of a naive repertoire. *Journal of Immunology, 161,* 5909–5917.

Solana, R., Alonso, M. C., & Peana, J. (1999). Natural killer cells in healthy aging. *Experimental Gerontology, 34,* 435–443.

Souvannavong, V., Lemaire, C., Andraeau, K., Brown, S., & Adam, A. (1998). Age-associated modulation of apoptosis and activation in murine B lymphocytes. *Mechanisms of Ageing and Development, 103,* 285–299.

Spaulding, C. S., Guo, W., & Effros, R. B. (1999). Resistance to apoptosis in human CD8+ T cells that reach replicative senescence after multiple rounds of antigen-specific proliferation. *Exerimental Gerontoogyl, 34,* 633–644.

Spaulding, C. S., Walford, R. L., & Effros, R. B. (1996). The accumulation of non-replicative, non-functional, senescent T cells with age is avoided in calorically restricted mice by an enhancement of T cell apoptosis. *Mechanisms of Ageing and Development, 93,* 25–33.

Spencer, N. F., & Daynes, R. A. (1997). IL-12 directly stimulates expression of IL–10 by CD5+ B cells and IL-6 by both CD5+ and CD5– B cells: possible involvement in age-associated cytokine dysregulation. *International Immunology, 9,* 745–754.

Steger, M. M., Maczek, C., & Grubeck-Loebenstein, B. (1996). Morphologically and functionally intact dendritic cells can be derived from the peripheral blood of aged individuals. *Clinical and Experimental Immunology, 105,* 544–550.

Stephan, R. P., Lill-Elghanian, D. A., & Witte, P. L. (1997). Development of B cells in aged mice: decline in the ability of pro-B cells to respond to IL–7 but not to other growth factors. *Journal of Immunology, 158,* 1598–1609.

Stulnig, T., Maczek, C., Beock, G., Majdic, O., & Wick, G. (1995). Reference intervals for human peripheral blood lymphocyte subpopulations from "healthy" young and aged subjects. *International Archives of Allergy and Immunology, 108,* 205–210.

Swenson, C. D., & Thorbecke, G. J. (1997). The effect of aging on IgD receptor expression by T cells and its functional implications. *Immunological Reviews, 160,* 145–157.

Szabo, P., Zhao, K., Kirman, I., Le Maoult, J., Dyall, R., Cruikshank, W., & Weksler, M. E. (1998). Maturation of B cell precursors is impaired in thymic-deprived nude and old mice. *Journal of Immunology, 161,* 2248–2253.

Takata, H., Suzuki, M., Ishii, T., Sekiguchi, S., & Iri, H. (1987). Influence of major histocompatibility complex region genes on human longevity among Okinawan-Japanese centenarians and nonagenarians. *Lancet, 2,* 824–826.

Telford, W. G., & Miller, R. A. (1999). Aging increases CD8 T cell apoptosis induced by hyperstimulation but decreases apoptosis induced by agonist withdrawal in mice. *Cellular Immunology, 191,* 131–138.

Thoman, M. L. (1997). Effects of the aged microenvironment on CD4+ T cell maturation. *Mechanisms of Ageing and Development, 96,* 75–88.

Tian, L., Cai, Q., Bowen, R., & Wei, H. (1995). Effects of caloric restriction on age-related oxidative modifications of macromolecules and lymphocyte proliferation in rats. *Free Radical Biology and Medicine, 19,* 859–865.

Trebilcock, G. U., & Ponnappan, U. (1999). Nuclear factor-κ B induction in CD45RO+ and CD45RA+ T cell subsets during aging. *Mechanisms of Ageing and Development, 102,* 149–163.

Trieb, K., Ransmayr, G., Sgonc, R., Lassmann, H., & Grubeck-Loebenstein, B. (1996). APP peptides stimulate lymphocyte proliferation in normals, but not in patients with Alzheimer's disease. *Neurobiology of Aging, 17,* 541–547.

Utsuyama, M., Wakikawa, A., Tamura, T., Nariuchi, H., & Hirokawa, K. (1997). Impairment of signal transduction in T cells from old mice. *Mechanisms of Ageing and Development, 93,* 131–144.

Valenzuela H. F., & Effros R. B. (2000). Loss of telomerase inducibility in antigen-specific memory T cells following multiple encounters with antigen. *Federation Proceedings, 14,* A 991.

Van Arkel, C., Nooij, F. J., van der Sluijs-Gelling, A. J., & Radl, J. (1997). Frequency of clonal dominance in the specific antibody response to DNP-HSA in CBA and C57BL mice reflects their susceptibility to age-associated development of monoclonal gammopathies. *Clinical Immunology and Immunopathology, 83,* 272–280.

Vaziri, H., Dragowska, W., Allsopp, R. C., Thomas, T. E., Harley, C. B., & Lansdorp, P. M. (1994). Evidence for a mitotic clock in human hematopoietic stem cells: loss of telomeric DNA with age. *Proceedings of the National Academy of Science of the USA, 91,* 9857–9860.

Vaziri, H., Schachter, F., Uchida, I., Wei, L., Zhu, X., Effros, R., Cohen, D., & Harley, C. (1993). Loss of telomeric DNA during aging of normal and trisomy 21 human lymphocytes. *American Journal of Human Genetics, 52,* 661–667.

Volloch, V., Mosser, D. D., Massie, B., & Sherman, M. Y. (1998). Reduced thermotolerance in aged cells results from a loss of an hsp-72-mediated control of JNK signaling pathway. *Cell Stress and Chaperones, 3,* 265–271.

von Zglinicki, T., Saretzki, G., Deocke, W., & Lotze, C. (1995). Mild hyperoxia shortens telomeres and inhibits proliferation of fibroblasts: A model for senescence? *Experimental Cell Research, 220,* 186–193.

Walford, R. L., & Spindler, S. R. (1997). The response to calorie restriction in mammals shows features also common to hibernation: A cross-adaptation hypothesis. *Journal of Gerontology: Biological Sciences, 52,* B179–B183.

Weindruch, R. H., Kristie, J. A., Naeim, F., Mullen, B. G., & Walford, R. L. (1982). Influence of weaning-initiated dietary restriction on responses to T cell mitogens and on splenic T cell levels in a long-lived F1-hybrid mouse strain. *Experimental Gerontology, 17,* 49–64.

Weng, N. P., Levine, B. L., June, C. H., & Hodes, R. J. (1995). Human naive and memory T lymphocytes differ in telomere length and replicative potential. *Proceedings of the National Academy of Science of the USA, 92,* 11091–11094.

Weng, N. P., Palmer, L. D., Levine, B. L., Lane, H. C., June, C. H., & Hodes, R. J. (1997). Tales of tails: Regulation of telomere length and telomerase activity during lymphocyte development, differentiation, activation, and aging. *Immunological Reviews, 160,* 43–54.

Whisler, R. L., Bagenstose, S. E., Newhouse, Y. G., & Carle, K. W. (1997). Expression and catalytic activities of protein tyrosine kinases (PTKs) Fyn and Lck in peripheral blood T cells from elderly humans stimulated through the T cell receptor (TCR)/CD3 complex. *Mechanisms of Ageing and Development, 98,* 57–73.

Whisler, R. L., Karanfilov, C. I., Newhouse, Y. G., Fox, C. C., Lakshmanan, R. R., & Liu, B. (1998). Phosphorylation and coupling of zeta-chains to activated T-cell receptor (TCR)/CD3 complexes from peripheral blood T-cells of elderly humans. *Mechanisms of Ageing and Development, 105,* 115–135.

Wick, G., & Grubeck-Loebenstein, B. (1997a). Primary and secondary alterations of immune reactivity in the elderly: Impact of dietary factors and disease. *Immunological Reviews, 160,* 171–184.

Wick, G., & Grubeck-Loebenstein, B. (1997b). The aging immune system: primary and secondary alterations of immune reactivity in the elderly. *Experimental Gerontology, 32,* 401–413.

Woods, J. A., Evans, J. K., Wolters, B. W., Ceddia, M. A., & McAuley, E. (1998). Effects of maximal exercise on natural killer (NK) cell cytotoxicity and responsiveness to interferon- alpha in the young and old. *Journal of Gerontology: Biological Sciences, 53,* B430–B437.

Wu, D., Mura, C., Beharka, A. A., Han, S. N., Paulson, K. E., Hwang, D., & Meydani, S. N. (1998). Age-associated increase in PGE2 synthesis and COX activity in murine macrophages is reversed by vitamin E. *American Journal of Physiology, 275,* C661–C668.

Xu, Q., Kiechl, S., Mayr, M., Metzler, B., Egger, G., Oberhollenzer, F., Willeit, J., & Wick, G. (1999). Association of serum antibodies to heat-shock protein 65 with carotid atherosclerosis: Clinical significance determined in a follow-up study [see comments]. *Circulation, 100,* 1169–1174.

Yang, X., Stedra, J., & Cerny, J. (1996). Relative contribution of T and B cells to hypermutation and selection of the antibody repertoire in germinal centers of aged mice. *Journal of Experimental Medicine, 183,* 959–970.

Zheng, B., Han, S., Takahashi, Y., & Kelsoe, G. (1997). Immunosenescence and germinal center reaction. *Immunological Reviews, 160,* 63–77.

Zimmerman, C., Brduscha-Riem, K., Blaser, C., Zinkernagel, R. M., & Pircher, H. (1996). Visualization, characterization, and turnover of CD8+ memory T cells in virus-infected hosts. *Journal of Experimental Medicine, 183,* 1367–1375.

Zissel, G., Schlaak, M., & Meuller-Quernheim, J. (1999). Age-related decrease in accessory cell function of human alveolar macrophages. *Journal of Investigative Medicine, 47,* 51–56.

Part Four

Models of Retarded Aging

Edited by
George M. Martin

Thirteen

The Genetics of Aging in *Drosophila*

Stephen C. Stearns and Linda Partridge

I. Introduction

We use the genetics of aging to understand the causes of aging. Genetic variation produces heritable differences between individuals in rate and style of aging, whereas changes in gene expression mediate responses of the aging process to drugs and other interventions. The fruit fly, *Drosophila melanogaster*, is one of the leading models in aging research. Its genetics is well-understood, and the complete genome sequence was published in March 2000. Because the genetics of aging in *D. melanogaster* have been ably reviewed (e.g., Charlesworth, 1993; Curtsinger *et al.*, 1995; Finch & Rose, 1995; Rose, 1999; Tatar, 1999; Tower, 1996; Zwaan, 1999), there is little sense in repeating here what others have said clearly elsewhere. We summarize the current state of knowledge and understanding and discuss issues that present a challenge for future work. We begin with the definition and measurement of aging.

A. Definition and Measurement of Aging in Populations

Aging is a decline in state, manifested demographically as a reduction in survival and fecundity at later ages in the adult period. Fisher's residual reproductive value is a natural measure of state at each age, because it combines prospects for survival and reproduction into a single measure (Partridge & Barton, 1996). Many researchers continue to think of aging only in terms of effects on mortality rates: they ignore effects on fecundity, although the effects of aging normally are reflected in age-related declines in fecundity as well as mortality.

Whereas comparison of fecundity rates across age classes needs more emphasis, measurement of differences in intrinsic mortality rates will always be relevant to studies of aging. Age-specific mortality rates are preferable to life span as an indicator of aging, because events at each age can be viewed independently of all other ages. Gompertz equations or other models of mortality trajectories can be useful in the analysis of mortality rates (e.g., Pletcher, 1999), but assumptions about particular forms of change in mortality rate with age should not be forced upon inappropriate data. To measure age-specific mortality rates, especially in the critical older age classes, very large sample sizes are needed, and maximum likelihood is the preferred method for making the estimates [Pletcher, 1999; Promislow et al., 1999; Shaw et al., 1999; see Nusbaum et al. (1996) for the relationship of Gompertz parameters to average and maximum longevity].

B. Questions about Aging

Questions about aging are pitched at two levels: the evolutionary (why did aging originate and why is it maintained in populations?) and the mechanistic (how does aging occur during the lifetime of an individual organism?) (see Chapter 1). The two levels interact: evolutionary explanations for the maintenance of aging in populations help to make sense of the mechanisms of aging in individuals at the levels of molecules and cells, whereas mechanisms of age-related damage and its prevention provide the framework in which aging and its associated modes of genetic effects evolve.

Three main interventions have been shown repeatedly to reduce the rate of aging. The first is reduced reproductive rate, studied mainly by evolutionary biologists using artificial selection experiments, quantitative genetics, and experimental manipulation (e.g., for Drosophila; Rose & Charlesworth 1980; Rose 1984; Luckinbill et al., 1984; Zwaan et al., 1995b; Partridge et al., 1999; Sgrò & Partridge, 1999). The second intervention is caloric restriction, which has been shown to slow aging in taxonomically widespread groups (e.g., Chippindale et al., 1993; Chapman & Partridge, 1996). The third is mutant gene expression (e.g.,

Lin et al., 1998; Sun & Tower, 1999). These last two interventions typically have been investigated by molecular geneticists focusing on biochemical and cellular function. We need to understand how these three interventions act and interact to produce their effects on the rate of aging.

Changes in gene expression during aging, and in response to environmental interventions that affect its rate, are important areas of inquiry (e.g., Helfand & Naprta, 1996; Rogina et al., 1998). More attention is being paid to the ways in which drugs alter patterns of gene expression and modulate the normal aging process. The future of Drosophila genetics will be influenced strongly by genomic approaches to gene expression profiling: DNA microarrays and proteomics will allow expression profiling of all the genes in the genome. Patterns of age-specific expression and responses to interventions can then be characterized without any need for a candidate gene approach. The new methods are going to present a considerable challenge to statisticians and computer scientists.

C. "Why" Questions about Aging: Evolution

Evolutionary geneticists see the causes of aging as the result of selection for genes with one of two characteristics: antagonistic pleiotropy or detrimental expression limited to late life (see Chapter 1 in this volume). Genes involved in antagonistic pleiotropy have opposite effects on fitness early and late in life. We need to understand how these positive and negative effects are connected with one another. One possibility is direct damage: the early life, beneficial processes themselves could cause the damage responsible for aging. Another is neglect of maintenance—if cellular maintenance is neglected to improve reproduction, subsequent performance will suffer (Kirkwood, 1987).

Theory suggests that it is hard to maintain polymorphism by antagonistic pleiotropy alone (Rose *et al.*, 1987; Curtsinger *et al.*, 1994; Hedrick, 1999). One needs strong selection and balanced fitness effects for the early and late advantages. However, spatially or temporally variable selection could both play a role in maintaining genetic variation for the rate of aging.

The second class of genes, those involved in *mutation accumulation*, have effects only late in life and are unconditionally detrimental. Because the contribution of reproduction and survival to fitness late in life is less than that early in life, the ability of selection to eliminate deleterious mutations decreases with age, allowing them to accumulate to a higher level if they are only expressed later rather than earlier in life. Evolutionary geneticists have looked for evidence that the genes involved in aging belong to one or the other of these two classes.

D. "How" Questions about Aging: Mechanisms

Molecular geneticists, on the other hand, have concentrated their search on defects in cellular metabolism that originate and accumulate during the lifetime of single individuals. Their focus has been increasingly on the *free radical* or *oxidative damage hypothesis* (Chapter 2 in this volume), enzymes that scavenge free radicals, such as copper–zinc superoxide dismutase (SOD), and chaperones that protect proteins from damage.

Attention has not been limited to the free radical scavengers. As many other genes could be involved in aging as take part in metabolic processes whose performance decreases with age. Both evolutionary and molecular biologists therefore have accumulated lists of *candidate*

genes, genes for which some kind of evidence indicates an involvement with aging. Evolutionary geneticists have used QTL (quantitative trait loci) techniques to locate chromosomes and parts of chromosomes involved in aging (e.g., Nuzhdin *et al.*, 1997; Vieira *et al.*, 2000). Molecular geneticists have used transgenesis to over-or underexpress genes. We list the major candidates and discuss the evidence supporting their candidacy below.

The concept of candidate genes depends on the assumption that single-gene effects are large enough to make a measurable difference in mortality and fecundity rates in a controlled environment. The nature of the environment in which measurements are made can be critical, as can sex differences (Viera *et al.*, 2000). Like most life history traits, the rate of aging responds to environmental change. This issue can be addressed by studies of gene × environment interactions (see Chapter 16 in this volume).

Our chapter is structured as follows. First we summarize the results of experiments that have tested for the existence of genes with pleiotropic effects, and then we do the same for mutations that might be expressed only in older age classes. Following a review of the evidence for candidate genes, we present criteria for evaluating the reliability and generality of transgenic experiments and then discuss such experiments with specific candidate genes. In closing, we consider how genomics will change research on the genetics of aging in *Drosophila*.

II. Evidence on Antagonistic Pleiotropy

One method to uncover antagonistic pleiotropy is to study correlated responses in artificial selection experiments: select on one trait, such as early reproduction, and analyze the responses in another, such as life span. The pioneering experiments with *Drosophila* (Wattiaux, 1968; Rose & Charlesworth, 1980, 1981; Rose, 1984; Luckinbill *et al.*, 1984) suggested trade-offs between early fecundity on the one hand and life span and late fecundity on the other, which appeared to support the antagonistic pleiotropy hypothesis. Later analysis, however, indicated that some of those connections might be spurious, caused either by indirect selection or by uncontrolled density effects (Leroi *et al.*, 1994a,b).

Two experiments then were designed to avoid these problems. In the first, Zwaan *et al.* (1995b) performed family selection directly on life span and demonstrated a strong and significant connection between lifetime fecundity and life span: long-lived females produced about half the number of offspring of short-lived females and the effect was present in all age classes, not just the early age classes. In the second, Partridge *et al.* (1999) avoided inadvertent selection and controlled larval densities while selecting lines allowed to reproduce only at old or young ages. A cost of reproduction for survival again was apparent, but late-life fecundity was not higher in the old lines than in the young lines or the base stock, suggesting that standing genetic variance with age-specific effects on late-life fecundity may be relatively low.

Evidence for a cost of reproduction in an artificial selection experiment is not the same thing as support for the pleiotropy theory of aging. First, reproduction can be costly purely because it is risky at the time it is undertaken, but with no lasting ill effects and no increase in the rate of aging (e.g., Partridge & Andrews, 1985). In most of the selection experiments, the increased survival of old lines did persist after their reduced reproductive rate had ceased, which rules out risk as an explanation. However, such evidence is consistent with an explanation based on a combination of risk and mutation accumulation: the increased survival rates of the old lines at later ages could occur because the frequency of late-age deleterious mutants is lowered, rather than because of a history of low reproductive rate.

An experiment demonstrated directly that the low early rate of reproduction did cause the greater late-life survival of old lines. In young and old lines made sterile by irradiation or a single-gene mutant, the difference in survival rate between young and old lines was abolished. The difference in early reproductive rate therefore was the sole cause of the difference in mortality rates at late ages (Sgrò & Partridge, 1999). The result also suggests that there was no constitutive up-regulation of repair or defense processes in the old lines.

The current state of the evidence on antagonistic pleiotropy can be summarized as follows (Fig. 1): There is good evidence for negative pleiotropy between mortality rate and either lifetime or early fecundity (P-element-induced mutational covariance also supports this connection; Stearns & Kaiser, 1996). The connection between development time and body size is similarly robust. A trade-off between early and late fecundity is not found consistently and may be the product of inadvertent selection, nor is there a positive connection between development time and life span, as posited by the developmental theory of aging (Chippindale *et al.*, 1994; Zwaan *et al.* 1995a,b; see also Parsons, 1996). The changes in life history traits are consistent with changes in physiological traits: flies that live longer or that have higher fecundity late in life have higher fat and glycogen contents and higher starvation, desiccation, and alcohol resistance and can fly longer than flies with shorter life spans or lower fecundity late in life.

Although complex, Fig. 1 communicates a few reliable messages about correlated responses to selection: rapidly developing flies are smaller (in contrast,

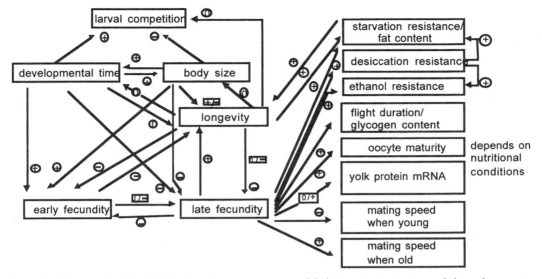

Figure 1. The results of artificial selection experiments on life history traits in *Drosophila melanogaster*. The arrow connects the trait selected to the trait in which a correlated response was measured. The signs by the arrows indicate the sign of the correlated response. Based on results from Carlson and Harshman (1998), Carlson *et al.* (1998), Chippindale *et al.* (1994), Graves *et al.* (1992), Harshman *et al.*, (1999), Hillesheim and Stearns (1991, 1992), Luckinbill *et al.* (1984), Partridge *et al.* (1999), Pletcher *et al.* (1997), Service (1993), Stearns *et al.* (2000), Zwaan (1993, 1999), and Zwaan *et al.* (1995a,b). Modified from a figure provided by B. Zwaan (unpublished results).

flies with hypomorphic mutants in the insulin signaling pathway are slow and small); smaller flies have lower fecundity; and flies that live longer have reduced fecundity. In general, life history traits are connected to each other and cannot respond to selection without changing some other trait that also contributes to fitness. The pattern of changes in life history traits is underlain by consistent changes in physiological traits.

Thus, the first hypothesis for the evolution of aging, antagonistic pleiotropy, is supported by artificial selection experiments and is consistent with physiological changes under selection.

III. Evidence on Mutation Accumulation

Models of mutation accumulation make three assumptions: mutations act addi-

tively on age-specific survival or fecundity, there are mutations that only affect late age classes, and all mutations have equal effects. Testing the mutation accumulation theory is more difficult than testing the pleiotropy theory. Three lines of evidence have been used.

First, under mutation accumulation, additive genetic variation for mortality rate should increase with age (Hughes & Charlesworth, 1994). Initial work suggested that such an increase occurs (Engström *et al.*, 1992; Hughes & Charlesworth, 1994), but subsequent experiments and improved data analysis have shown that genetic variance for age-specific mortality rates decreases at advanced ages (Promislow *et al.*, 1995; Shaw *et al.*, 1999), an effect that may be related to the deceleration of mortality rate at later ages (e.g., Pletcher *et al.*, 1998, Service, in press, S. Pletcher, unpublished data).

A second prediction from mutation accumulation is that inbreeding depression should increase for later age classes, and evidence in support of this idea has been produced (Charlesworth & Hughes, 1996). However, as these authors pointed out, old flies may be phenotypically more susceptible to the effects of inbreeding depression, and the results of this kind of test therefore are ambiguous.

The most direct evidence of mutation accumulation has come from large-scale experiments in which new mutations were allowed to accumulate sheltered from the effects of selection, and their age-specific effects were examined. Whereas some evidence suggests that mutations only affect the mortality rates of particular age classes (Pletcher et al., 1998), that evidence is stronger for the younger than for the older age classes, and, as mutations accumulate, so does the tendency for their combined effects to span several age classes (Pletcher et al., 1999). These experiments have not produced strong evidence for substantial mutational effects on mortality specific to late ages.

However, mortality deceleration and potential cohort heterogeneity may make it unwise to accept this conclusion at face value. An experiment with artificial selection lines suggested that mutants with age-specific effects on mortality at late ages are probably rare. The difference in mortality rates between young and old lines was abolished when the flies were made sterile, whereas if selection on the old lines had lowered the frequency of mutations that increased late-age mortality, their effects would be expected to persist in the absence of reproduction (Sgrò & Partridge, 1999).

Thus, the evidence suggests that mutations can have an important impact on aging, but that impact usually is not additive, is not made up of mutations with equal effects, and is not confined to late age classes (Promislow & Tatar, 1998).

These findings may help to explain why mortality rates do not increase more sharply at very late ages, as would be expected if mutations with age-specific effects at late ages were common. Any correlated effect on fitness at early ages would tend to prevent these mutations from accumulating (Partridge & Barton, 1993; Pletcher & Curtsinger, 1998).

IV. Mortality Plateaus: The Heterogeneity Hypothesis

In *Drosophila melanogaster* (and other organisms), age-specific mortality rates stop increasing well below 100% at advanced ages. Mortality often increases sharply at the onset of aging but then decelerates as the process proceeds. These observations are not consistent with the predictions of simple antagonistic pleiotropy and mutation accumulation models of senescence, which both predict mortality rates near 100% at post-reproductive ages under a range of assumptions. Several solutions for this puzzle have been proposed (Mueller & Rose, 1996; Charlesworth & Partridge, 1997; Pletcher & Curtsinger, 1998; Service et al., 1998; Wachter, 1999).

The leading candidate explanation for mortality plateaus is heterogeneity, i.e., individual variation in the risk of mortality. If individuals differ in "frailty," such that those that die young would have been the ones with higher mortality rates when old and those that survive when young are those that have lower mortality rates when old, then natural selection accounts for the observation that mortality rates do not increase to a 100% post-reproductive maximum: the ones that survive youth are the ones with lower intrinsic mortality rates throughout life (Vaupel & Yashin, 1985; Curtsinger et al., 1992; Carey et al., 1992; Service et al., 1998; Partridge & Mangel, 1999). Service (in press) has simulated these effects and finds that such heterogeneity accounts for the lack of increase in mortality rates in older age classes. Furthermore, heterogeneity predicts the observed decline in mutational variance for mortality rates in older age classes (Pletcher *et al.*, 1998, 1999).

Heterogeneity is a plausible explanation for the observed lack of increases in mortality rates to maximum levels late in life and is a problem to be reckoned with in any study of mortality trajectories. An additional explanation for mortality deceleration is the delayed wave of mortality associated with earlier reproduction. The sharp increase in mortality rates at the onset of aging can result from earlier reproduction. Then, either as the effects of the earlier reproduction wear off or as the less robust members of the cohort succumb to its effects, mortality decelerates (Sgrò & Partridge, 1999).

In the next sections, we review evidence bearing on the biochemical and cellular mechanisms of aging. We pay special attention to evidence for the role of damage by free radicals, which is the leading candidate mechanism (Martin *et al.*, 1996).

V. Evidence for Candidate Genes

A. Evidence Consistent with Free Radical Damage

Oxidatively damaged macromolecules accumulate in almost all organisms as they age (Chapter 2 in this volume), and enzymes have evolved to protect the cell by scavenging them. These include the superoxide dismutases, catalases, and peroxidases. Is there any evidence for a correlation between free radical scavenging enzymes and aging in *Drosophila*?

Tyler and co-workers (1993) showed that *D. melanogaster* populations artificially selected for postponed aging had consistently greater frequencies of the allele at the SOD locus that coded for a more active form of the enzyme, but when they constructed different SOD genotypes in hybrid genetic backgrounds, they could not detect any effect of SOD genotype on longevity or fecundity. Hari and co-workers (1998) developed a polyclonal serum for CuZn SOD that allowed them to measure the quantity of enzyme directly. They used it to demonstrate that their genetically selected long-lived strain had significantly higher levels of CuZn SOD protein than did a control strain.

Schwarze and co-workers (1998 a,b) worked through the components of the oxidative phosphorylation electron transport system in *D. melanogaster* to determine how they changed with age. They found declines in cytochrome *c* oxidase activity (COX, 40% decline) and ATP abundance (15%) and an increase in lipid peroxidation (71%). The gene for COX is located in the mitochondrial genome in a microenvironment with particularly high concentrations of superoxide radicals. In CuZn SOD null mutants, the rate of COX RNA decline was greater than in controls, as it was in hydrogen peroxide treated flies, and the decreased production of COX RNA was reflected in reduced COX enzyme activity. Thus, oxidative stress appears to be associated with reductions in the levels of mitochondrial transcripts of mRNAs involved in key steps in energy metabolism.

Lin *et al.* (1998) screened for mutants with effects on life span by generating a set of P-element insertion lines and focusing on those that outlived the parent strain. One mutant line, methuselah (mth), had a 35% increase in life span and enhanced resistance to starvation, high temperature, and dietary paraquat, which is a free radical generator. The protein predicted for the genes resembles GTP-binding protein. Its coupled seven-transmembrane domain receptors suggest that a signal transduction pathway may be involved in modulating stress resistance and life span.

B. Evidence for Molecular Chaperones

A second class of candidates is genes that code for the molecular chaperones involved in stress responses. One group consists of the so-called heat-shock proteins (HSPs), so named because they were identified first as part of the response to heat shock. Not all members of this family have been cloned, but those that have been cloned appear to function as chaperones: proteins that bind to other proteins to package them during their journey to their functional site, preserve their function in an inappropriate microenvironment, or help them regain their tertiary structure after being damaged.

Some evidence of a role for HSPs in aging is experimental and makes a connection to the free radical hypothesis: Wheeler *et al.* (1995) found that the expression of hsp70 increased in aging flies and was accelerated in flies carrying a mutant for a peroxidase catalase. In young flies mutant for either peroxidase catalase or CuZn SOD, hsp70 expression was also increased, suggesting that hsp70 expression may be, at least in part, a reaction to oxidative damage. Other evidence is still correlational: an increase in expression with age. For example, King and Tower (1999) found that expression levels of hsp22 protein in the head increased by 150-fold as flies aged, that functional heat-shock response elements were required for this change, and that regulation of both transcription and translation was involved.

C. Other Candidates

Khaustova (1995) selected flies for late fecundity and noted that the slow allele for Adh, the form that is less active but

more resistant to inactivation, increased in frequency. Driver and McKechnie (1992) and Nikitin and Woodruff (1995a,b) found that increased movement of P-element transposons decreased life span in *D. melanogaster*; the latter authors observed increased frequencies of somatic cell chromosome breakage in the affected flies. Schwarze *et al.* (1998a) studied aging in flies with mutated mitochondrial genomes; flies still capable of flight at 30 days had 4-fold higher abundance of a mitochondrial-encoded mRNA (COX I) than did individuals that could no longer fly.

Contrary to earlier reports (Shepherd *et al.*, 1989), there is no evidence that peptide synthesis elongation factor (EF–1α) becomes limiting with age (Shikama & Brack, 1996), and it appears that the transgene used in the early overexpression experiments was not expressed (Shikama *et al.*, 1994).

Kann *et al.*, (1998) studied heteroplasmic *Drosophila*—those whose cytoplasm carried a mixture of two mitochondrial variants, one with a short genome and one with a long genome—and found that the mitochondria with the longer genome increased in frequency as the flies aged. This may not have anything to do with aging—it could be interpreted as the result of intracellular reproductive competition favoring the long-genome variant, with no necessary consequences for the aging of the fly phenotype.

D. QTLs

The search for quantitative trait loci (QTLs) casts its net more widely than any candidate gene approach. A QTL analysis of aging asks where chromosome segments can be found in the genome that are correlated with extended life span—for whatever reason.

Curtsinger *et al.* (1998a) screened 1200 randomly chosen chromosome segments defined by RAPD loci markers in two short-lived and two long-lived lines from the Luckinbill *et al.* (1984) experiment. Out of those 1200 segments, 23 showed frequency differences greater than 80% and 5 were greater than 90%. The age-specific effects on survival of those five loci were analyzed in segregating backcross populations. Alleles at four of the five marker loci were associated with extended life span in males; two marker loci had similar effects in females. Both sex-limited and sex-shared effects were observed; they moderated both the level of mortality and the rate at which mortality increased with age.

In that study, one particular chromosome segment, the N14(+) marker, had the largest effect—a 12-day extension of life span in males caused by a decrease in age-specific mortality at all ages. It was not one of the QTLs that had an effect on the rate of increase in mortality with age. Resler *et al.*, (1998) then sequenced the locus. It is noncoding, not obviously regulatory, and hybridizes to 63F/64A on the left arm of chromosome 3, a position that suggests new candidate genes for life span extension, including *ras2*, a gene involved in signaling pathways and related to genes that are implicated in oncogenesis in mammals.

A second type of QTL analysis uses recombinant inbred lines to examine the effects of genetic variants affecting life span. With this approach, Nuzhdin *et al.* (1997) found evidence for five autosomal QTLs with large sex-specific effects on life span and age-specific effects on mortality.

There are two potential problems with the QTL approach, neither insurmountable. The first is inbreeding depression. For a trait related to fitness, as the rate of aging is, the use of inbred genotypes carries the pitfall that the effects of deleterious recessive alleles, not normally expressed, will be studied. The second is that going from QTL to gene has not

proved straightforward, and the candidate gene approach to this problem must be used with circumspection (Keightley *et al.*, 1998).

VI. Transgenic Experiments

A. Critique

The goal of transgenic experiments on aging is, through over- and underexpression of candidate transgenes, to identify the role of single genes in aging. Some transgenic experiments using P-element inserts have not used proper controls (Kaiser *et al.*, 1997). The size of the insert, the position of the insert, and the interactions of the insert with genetic backgrounds have effects on life span as large as those attributed to overexpression; these effects can be as large as responses to several generations of strong directional artificial selection. Thus, some reports of effects of overexpression of transfected genes on life span in *D. melanogaster* probably are experimental artifacts. Credible experiments on the phenotypic effects of transgenesis need proper controls for the effects of insert size and position and should estimate the magnitude of interactions of treatment with genetic backgrounds.

If one is only interested in genetic effects on life span, then measuring age-specific mortality rates suffices. But if one accepts the definition of aging as a decline in residual reproductive value with increasing age (Partridge & Barton, 1996), a parameter in which survival is multiplied by fecundity, then one must measure both fecundity and mortality. If a transgene had detrimental effects on fecundity that were larger than its beneficial effects on survival, then it would not ameliorate aging even though it extended life span. Fecundity is, however, almost never measured in transgenic experiments on aging.

B. Review

We begin with some experiments that did not have proper controls for the effects of insert position or genetic background. The work of Shepherd et al. (1989) with EF–1α was mentioned previously; not only did it lack controls for position and background effects, but the transgene was not expressed. That lack of expression is what allowed Kaiser et al. (1997) to estimate the size of background and position effects.

Fleming et al., (1992) inserted a hybrid gene for CuZn SOD containing the Drosophila actin 5c promoter and the bovine SOD coding region into the D. melanogaster germ line on a P-element; the transformed flies appeared to have better resistance to oxidative stress. Rather than using a gene from a cow, Orr and Sohal (1993) introduced an extra D. melanogaster CuZn SOD gene, measured overexpression, but did not observe any increase in life span. They then simultaneously overexpressed CuZn SOD and catalase (Orr & Sohal, 1994); transgenic flies with three copies of each gene lived up to one-third longer and had less protein oxidative damage, and their physical performance declined less rapidly than that of diploid controls. Thus, both SOD and catalase appeared to be necessary in combination.

As Tower (1996) pointed out, however, Orr and Sohal (1994) did not use an unbiased sample of control strains to compare with their treatment strains—they selected three long-lived treatment lines and compared them to one control line, which may have been short-lived. Tatar (1999) later calculated how many lines needed to be compared, given the variance observed in life span among Orr and Sohal's lines, to detect a 10% difference in genotype longevity when the power of the test is 90% and $\alpha = 0.05$: 15 control lines and 15 treatment lines would be needed.

By overexpressing human SOD1 in motor neurons, Parkes et al., (1998) appeared to have extended Drosophila life span by up to 40%. Their flies had elevated resistance to oxidative stress.

However, none of the preceding studies properly controled for position and background effects (Kaiser et al., 1997). Lack of proper controls does not mean that an effect does not exist, just that experimental artifacts have not yet been ruled out. And in none of these studies was there enough replication of control and treatment lines to allow a reliable statistical conclusion to be reached (Tower, 1996; Tatar, 1999).

The only study of which we are aware in which both position and background effects were controlled and in which there was adequate replication of lines is Sun and Tower's (1999) use of yeast FLP recombinase in a binary transgenic system to induce overexpression of catalase and/or CuZn SOD in adult D. melanogaster with a brief heat shock. In control flies, the heat shock had slightly negative effects on life span. Catalase overexpression significantly increased resistance to hydrogen peroxide but had neutral or slightly negative effects on the mean life span, whereas CuZn SOD overexpression extended mean life span by up to 48%. Simultaneous overexpression of catalase with CuZn SOD had no added benefit, presumably due to a preexisting excess of catalase. Manipulation of the genetic background demonstrated that life span was affected by interactions between the transgene and allele(s) at other loci.

Khazaeli and co-workers (1997) took a different approach to attain overexpression of hsp70: they used lines in which homologous recombination, followed by appropriate crosses, produced allelic strains that differed in the copy number of hsp70 transgenes. In all cases, hsp70 expression was greater in the extra-copy flies. They exposed 4-day-old excision (control) and extra-copy males to a heat shock of 10–135 min and then followed their survival. Flies exposed to 10 or 15 min of heat shock had significantly better survival over the next 2 weeks than did the controls. They also correlated the level of hsp70 expression with the degree of extension of life span, relative to controls, and found a convincingly positive relationship. These results indicate a direct effect of hsp70, a molecular chaperone, on longevity in *Drosophila*.

C. Transgenic Fly Methods

Siegal and Hartl (1996) described a system for placing alternative alleles at identical sites within a single genetic background, a system that Sun and Tower (1999) applied and extended with an induced expression system developed by Struhl and Basler (1993; Basler & Struhl, 1994). The product can be assessed in the presence of, but with and without the expression of, the transgene—in brief, with proper control for position effects.

Another method was developed by Helfand and Naptra (1996), who found that the ability to express a reporter protein, β-galactosidase, was preserved in at least some cells of aging flies. Bieschke *et al.*, (1998) followed up on this idea, coupling the β-gal reporter gene to doxycycline-induced transgene expression. They were able to use doxycycline to induce β-gal expression in all tissues and in larvae and young and old adults. Such induction had no detectable effect on life span in their statistical design, suggesting that the system could be used for testing specific genes for effects on aging.

D. Comments on Transgenesis

Transgenic methods in *Drosophila* have become quite sophisticated, can be used once a candidate gene is identified, and predispose one to think that single genes can cause large differences in life span.

However, they do not normally reveal the full range of consequences of over-or underexpression of a gene product, nor do they reveal the causal network in which a gene is embedded. Gene expression profiling does not solve the problem of genetic causation, but does put the problem in an entirely new light and place it in a much more general, and better informed, context.

VII. Microarrays

Microarray technology is developing rapidly, and it would be pointless to describe here the details of a technology that will have changed considerably before this volume is published. A good review can be found in *The Chipping Forecast* (supplement to *Nature Genetics* **21**, January, 1999). Whatever the details of the technology used, microarrays are having dramatic effects on *Drosophila* genetics (e.g., White *et al.*, 1999).

First, microarrays give us a picture of the level of expression of all of the genes in the genome, a picture that can now be made for an age class in a pooled line and will soon be made for a specific tissue type in an individual. This shifts the focus from changes in the frequency of alleles to differences in the expression of genes and the control thereof.

Second, microarrays change our impression of genetic causation, because they allow us to see clearly and quantitatively how a change in intrinsic mortality rates is associated with differences in the levels of expression of hundreds of genes at once. Single genes certainly have a role in such expression patterns, but they cannot be the whole story; microarrays give us a picture of what the whole story might be. In so doing, they redefine what is to be explained. By placing the patterns of expression of hundreds of genes at the center of our attention, microarrays naturally suggest that those patterns be correlated with candidate genes, QTLs, and the phenotypes studied—the mortality rates, fecundity rates, growth patterns, and physiological traits that form the aging pattern to be explained. That step directly leads to a conception of genetic causation that involves a network of interacting genes with effects distributed across several levels—within and among cells, within and among organs, and direct and indirect effects on whole-organism traits.

Third, microarrays naturally and easily deliver long lists of candidate genes, and that very fact calls into question what it means to be a "candidate." It is one thing to be a candidate for a presidential office and another to be a candidate for membership in a parliament with hundreds of members. The weight that we give to the involvement is completely different in the two cases. This is not to deny Miller's (1999) comment, "although the form aging takes can be affected by variations at many genetic loci, the number of loci that moderate the pace of synchronized decay may be far smaller," but it does mean that microarrays force us to confront how, and whether, changes in a few loci regulate hundreds of others.

References

Basler, K., & Struhl, G. (1994). Compartment boundaries and the control of *Drosophila* limb pattern by hedgehog protein. *Nature, 368,* 208–214.

Bieschke, E. T., Wheeler, J. C., & Tower, J. (1998). Doxycycline-induced transgene expression during *Drosophila* development and aging. *Molecular and General Genetics, 258,* 571–579.

Carey, J. R., Liedo, P., Orozco, D., & Vaupel, J. W. (1992). Slowing of mortality rates at older ages in large medfly cohorts. *Science, 258,* 457–461.

Carlson, K. A., & Harshman, L. G. (1998). Extended longevity lines of *Drosophila melanogaster*: Abundance of yolk protein gene mRNA in fat body and

ovary. *Experimental Gerontology, 34,* 173–184.

Carlson, K. A., Nusbaum, T. J., Rose, M. R., & Harshman, L. G. (1998). Oocyte maturation and ovariole number in lines of *Drosophila melanogaster* selected for postponed senescence. *Functional Ecology, 12,* 514–520.

Chapman, T., & Partridge, L. (1996). Female fitness in *Drosophila melanogaster*: An interaction between the effect of nutrition and of encounter rate with males. *Proceedings of the Royal Society of London, Series B, 263,* 755–759.

Charlesworth, B. (1993). Evolutionary mechanisms of senescence. *Genetica, 91,* 11–19.

Charlesworth, B., & Hughes, K. A. (1996). Age-specific inbreeding depression and components of genetic variance in relation to the evolution of senescence. *Proceedings of the National Academy of Science of the USA, 93,* 6140–6145.

Charlesworth, B., & Partridge, L. (1997). Aging: Levelling of the grim reaper. *Current Biology, 7,* R440–R442.

Chippindale, A. K., Leroi, A. M., Kim, S. B., & Rose, M. R. 1993. Phenotypic plasticity and selection in *Drosophila* life-history evolution. I. Nutrition and the cost of reproduction. *Journal of Evolutionary Biology, 6,* 171–193.

Chippindale, A. K., Hoang, D. T., Service, P. M., & Rose, M. R. (1994). The evolution of development in *Drosophila melanogaster* selected for postponed senescence. *Evolution, 48,* 1880–1899.

Curtsinger, J. W., Fukui, H. H., Townsend, D. R., & Vaupel, J. W. (1992). Demography of genotypes: Failure of the limited life-span paradigm in *Drosophila melanogaster*. *Science, 258,* 461–463.

Curtsinger, J. W., Service, P. M., & Prout, T. (1994). Antagonistic pleiotropy, reversal of dominance, and genetic polymorphism. *American Naturalist, 144,* 210–228.

Curtsinger, J. W., Fukui, H. H., Khazaeli, A. A., Kirscher, A., Pletcher, S. D., Promislow, D. E. L., & Tatar, M. (1995). Genetic variation and aging. *Annual Review of Genetics, 29,* 553–575.

Curtsinger, J. W., Fukui, H. H., Resler, A. S., Kelly, K., & Khazaeli, A. A. (1998a).

Genetic analysis of extended life span in *Drosophila melanogaster*. I. RAPD screen for genetic divergence between selected and control lines. *Genetica, 104*, 21–32.

Driver, C. J. I., & McKechnie, S. W. (1992). Transposable elements as a factor in the aging of *Drosophila melanogaster*. *Annals of the New York Academy of Science, 673*, 83–91.

Engström, G., Liljedahl, L.-E., & Björklund, T. (1992). Expression of genetic and environmental variation during aging. 2. Selection for increased lifespan in *Drosophila melanogaster. Theoretical and Applied Genetics, 85*, 26–32.

Finch, C. E., & Rose, M. R. (1995). Hormones and the physiological architecture of life history evolution. *Quarterly Review of Biology, 70*, 1–52.

Fleming, J. E., Reveillaud, I., & Niedzwiecki, A. (1992). Role of oxidative stress in *Drosophila* aging. *Mutation Research, 275*, 267–279.

Graves, J. L., Toolson, E. C., Jeong, C., Vu, L. N., & Rose, M. R. (1992). Desiccation, flight, glycogen, and postponed senescence in *Drosophila melanogaster. Physiological Zoology, 65*, 268–286.

Hari, R., Burde, V., & Arking, R. (1998). Immunological confirmation of elevated levels of CuZn superoxide dismutase protein in an artificially selected long-lived strain of *Drosophila melanogaster. Experimental Gerontology, 33*, 227–237.

Harshman, L. G., Hoffmann, A. A., & Clark A. G. (1999). Selection for starvation resistance in *Drosophila melanogaster*: physiological correlates, enzyme activities and multiple stress responses. *Journal of Evolutionary Biology, 12*, 370–379.

Hedrick, P. W. (1999). Antagonistic pleiotropy and genetic polymorphism: A perspective. *Heredity, 82*, 126–133.

Helfand, S. L., & Naprta, B. (1996). The expression of a reporter protein, β-galactosidase, is preserved during maturation and aging in some cells of the adult *Drosophila melanogaster. Mechanics of Developoment, 55*, 45–51.

Hillesheim, E., & Stearns, S. C. (1991). The responses of *Drosophila melanogaster* to artificial selection on body weight and its phenotypic plasticity in two larval food environments. *Evolution, 45*, 1909–23.

Hillesheim, E., & Stearns, S. C. (1992). Correlated responses in life-history traits to artificial selection for body weight in *Drosophila melanogaster. Evolution, 46*, 745–752.

Hughes, K. A., & Charlesworth, B. (1994). A genetic analysis of senescence in *Drosophila. Nature, 367*, 64–66.

Kaiser, M., Gasser, M., Ackermann, R., & Stearns, S. C. (1997). P-element inserts in transgenic flies: a cautionary tale. *Heredity, 78*, 1–11.

Kann, L. M., Rosenblum, E. B., & Rand, D. M. (1998). Aging, mating, and the evolution of mtDNA heteroplasmy in *Drosophila melanogaster. Proceedings of the National Academy of Science of the USA, 95*, 2372–2377.

Keightley, P. D., Morris, K. H., Ishikawa, A., Falconer, V. M., & Oliver, F. (1998). Test of candidate gene quantitative trait locus association applied to fatness in mice. *Heredity, 81*, 630–637.

Khaustova, N. D. (1995). The *Drosophila melanogaster* Adh locus upon selection for delayed aging. *Genetika, 31*, 646–651.

Khazaeli, A. A., Tatar, M., Pletcher, S. D., & Curtsinger, J. W. (1997). Heat-induced longevity extension in *Drosophila*. I. Heat treatment, mortality, and thermotolerance. *Journal of Gerontology, Biological Sciences 52A*, B48–B52.

King, V., & Tower, J. (1999). Aging-specific expression of *Drosophila* Hsp22. *Developmental Biology, 207*, 107–118.

Kirkwood, T. B. L. (1987). Immortality of the germ line versus disposability of the soma. In *Evolution of Longevity in Animals* In A. D. H. Woodhead, & K. H. Thompson (Eds.), New York: Plenum.

Leroi, A. M., Chen, W. R. & Rose, M. R. 1994b. Long-term laboratory evolution of a genetic life-history trade-off in *Drosophila melanogaster*. 2. Stability of genetic correlations. *Evolution, 48*, 1258–1268.

Leroi, A. M., Chippindale, A. K. & Rose, M. R. 1994a. Long-term laboratory evolution of a genetic life-history trade-off in *Drosophila melanogaster*. 1. The role of genotype-by-environment interaction. *Evolution, 48*, 1244–1257.

Lin, Y. J., Seroude, L., & Benzer, S. (1998). Extended life-span and stress resistance in the *Drosophila* mutant *methuselah*. *Science, 282,* 943–946.

Luckinbill, L. S., Arking, R., Clare, M. J., Cirocco, W. C., & Buck, S. (1984). Selection for delayed senescence in *Drosophila melanogaster. Evolution, 38,* 996–1003.

Martin, G. M., Austad, S. N., & Johnson, T. E. (1996). Genetic analysis of aging: Role of oxidative damage and environmental stresses. *Nature Genetics, 13,* 25–34.

Miller, R. A. (1999). Kleemeier award lecture: Are there genes for aging? *Journals of Gerontology Series A. Biological Sciences and Medical Sciences, 54,* B297–B307.

Mueller, L. D., & Rose, M. R. (1996). Evolutionary theory predicts late-life mortality plateaus. *Proceedings of the National Academy of Science of the USA, 93,* 15249–15253.

Nikitin, A. G., & Woodruff, R. C. (1995). P DNA element movement in somatic cells reduces lifespan in *Drosophila melanogaster*: Evidence in support of the somatic mutation theory of aging. *Mutation Research, 338,* 35–42

Nikitin, A. G., & Woodruff, R. C. (1995). Somatic movement of the mariner transposable element and lifespan of *Drosophila* species. *Mutation Research, 338,* 43–49.

Nusbaum, T. J., Mueller, L. D., & Rose, M. R. (1996). Evolutionary patterns among measures of aging. *Experimental Gerontology, 31,* 507–516.

Nuzhdin, S. V., Pasyukova, E. G., Dilda, C. L., Zeng, Z. B., & Mackay, T. F. C. (1997). Sex-specific quantitative trait loci affecting longevity in *Drosophila melanogaster. Proceedings of the National Academy of Science of the USA, 18,* 9734–9739.

Orr, W. C., & Sohal, R. S. (1993). Effects of copper zinc superoxide dismutase overexpression on life span and resistance to oxidative stress in transgenic *Drosophila melanogaster. Archives of Biochemistry and Biophysics, 301,* 34–40.

Orr, W. C., & Sohal, R. S. (1994). Extension of life-span by overexpression of superoxide dismutase and catalase in *Drosophila melanogaster. Science, 263,* 1128–1130.

Parkes, T. L., Elia, A. J., Dickinson, D., Hilliker, A. J., Phillips, J. P., & Boulianne, G. L. (1998). Extension of *Drosophila* lifespan by overexpression of human SOD1 in motorneurons. *Nature Genetics, 19,* 171–174.

Parsons, P. A. (1996). Rapid development and a long life: An association expected under a stress theory of aging. *Experientia, 52,* 643–646

Partridge, L., & Andrews, R. (1985). The effect of reproductive activity on the longevity of male *Drosophila melanogaster* is not caused by an acceleration of senescence. *Journal of Insect Physiology, 31,* 393–395.

Partridge, L., & Barton, N. H. (1993). Evolution of aging: Testing the theory using *Drosophila. Genetica, 91,* 89–98.

Partridge, L., & Barton, N. H. (1996). On measuring the rate of aging. *Proceedings of the Royal Society of London, Series B, 263,* 1365–1371.

Partridge, L., & Mangel, M. (1999). Messages from mortality: The evolution of death rates in the old. *Trends in Ecology and Evolution, 14,* 438–442.

Partridge, L., Prowse, N., & Pignatelli, P. (1999). Another set of responses and correlated responses to selection on age at reproduction in *Drosophila melanogaster. Proceedings of the Royal Society of London, Series B, 266,* 255–261.

Pletcher, S. D. (1999). Model fitting and hypothesis testing for age-specific mortality data. *Journal of Evolutionary Biology, 12,* 430–439.

Pletcher, S. D., & Curtsinger, J. W. (1998). Mortality plateaus and the evolution of senescence: Why are old-age mortality rates so low? *Evolution, 52,* 454–464.

Pletcher, S. D., Fukui, H. H., & Curtsinger, J. W. (1997). Mating behavior in *Drosophila melanogaster* selected for altered longevity. *Evolution, 51,* 303–307.

Pletcher, S. D., Houle, D., & Curtsinger, J. W. (1998). Age-specific properties of spontaneous mutations affecting mortality in *Drosophila melanogaster. Genetics, 148,* 287–303.

Pletcher, S. D., Houle, D., & Curtsinger, J. W. (1999). The evolution of age-specific mortality rates in *Drosophila melanogaster*: Genetic divergence among unselected lines. *Genetics, 153,* 813–823

Promislow, D. E. L., & Tatar, M. (1998). Mutation and senescence: Where genetics and demography meet. *Genetica, 102–103,* 299–314.

Promislow, D. E. L., Tatar, M., Khazaeli, A. A., & Curtsinger, J. W. (1995) Age-specific patterns of genetic variation in *Drosophila melanogaster*. I. Mortality. *Genetics, 143,* 839–848.

Promislow, D. E. L., Tatar, M., Pletcher, S., & Carey, J. R. (1999). Below threshold mortality: Implications for studies in evolution, ecology and demography. *Journal of Evolutionary Biology, 12,* 314–328.

Resler, A. S., Kelly, K., Kantor, G., Khazaeli, A. A., Tatar, M., & Curtsinger, J. W. (1998). Genetic analysis of extended life span in *Drosophila melanogaster*. II. Replication of the backcross test and molecular characterization of the N14 locus. *Genetica, 104,* 33–39.

Rogina, B., Vaupel, J. W., Partridge, L., & Helfand, S. L. (1998). Regulation of gene expression is preserved in aging *Drosophila melanogaster*. *Current Biology, 8,* 475–478.

Rose, M. R. (1984). Laboratory evolution of postponed senescence in *Drosophila melanogaster*. *Evolution, 38,* 1005–1010.

Rose, M. R. (1999). Genetics of aging in *Drosophila*. *Experimental Gerontology, 34,* 577–585.

Rose, M. R., & Charlesworth, B. (1980). A test of evolutionary theories of senescence. *Nature, 287,* 141–142.

Rose, M. R., & Charlesworth, B. (1981). Genetics of life history in *Drosophila melanogaster*. II. Exploratory selection experiments. *Genetics, 97,* 187–196.

Rose, M. R., Service, P. M., & Hutchinson, E. W. (1987). Three approaches to trade-offs in life-history evolution. In V., Loeschke, (Ed.), *Genetic Constraints on Adaptive Evolution* (pp. 91–105). Berlin: Springer.

Schwarze, S. R., Weindruch, R., & Aiken, J. M. (1998a). Decreased mitochondrial RNA levels without accumulation of mitochondrial DNA deletions in aging *Drosophila melanogaster*. *Mutation Research, 382,* 99–107.

Schwarze, S. R., Weindruch, R., & Aiken, J. M. (1998b). Oxidative stress and aging reduce cox I RNA and cytochrome oxidase activity in *Drosophila*. *Free Radical Biology and Medicine, 25,* 740–747.

Service, P. M. (1993). Laboratory evolution of longevity and reproductive fitness components in male fruit flies: Mating ability. *Evolution, 47,* 387–399.

Service, P. M. (2000). Heterogeneity in individual mortality risk and its importance for evolutionary studies of senescence. *American Naturalist, 156,* 1–13.

Service, P. M., Michieli, C. A., & McGill, K. (1998). Experimental evolution of senescence: An analysis using a "heterogeneity" mortality model. *Evolution, 52,* 1844–1850.

Sgrò, C. M., & Partridge, L. (1999). A delayed wave of death from reproduction in *Drosophila*. *Science, 286,* 2521–2524.

Shaw, F. H., Promislow, D. E. L., Tatar, M., Hughes, K. A., & Geyer, C. J. (1999). Toward reconciling inferences concerning genetic variation in senescence in *Drosophila melanogaster*. *Genetics, 152,* 553–566.

Shepherd, J. W. C., Walldorf, U., Hug, P., & Gehring, W. J. (1989). Fruit flies with additional expression of the elongation factor EF–1α live longer. *Proceedings of the National Academy of Science of the USA, 86,* 7520–7521.

Shikama, N., Ackermann, R., & Brack, C. (1994). Protein synthesis, elongation factor EF-1α expression, and longevity in *Drosophila melanogaster*. *Proceedings of the National Academy of Science of the USA, 91,* 4199–4203.

Shikama, N., & Brack, C. (1996). Changes in the expression of genes involved in protein synthesis during *Drosophila* aging. *Gerontology, 42,* 123–136.

Siegal, M. L., & Hartl, D. L. (1996). Transgene coplacement and high efficiency site-specific recombination with the *Cre/loxP* system in *Drosophila*. *Genetics, 144,* 715–726.

Stearns, S. C., & Kaiser, M. (1996). Effects on fitness components of P-element inserts in *Drosophila melanogaster*: Analysis of trade-offs. *Evolution, 50,* 795–806.

Stearns, S.C, Ackermann, M., Doebeli, & Kaiser, M. 2000. Experimental evolution of aging, growth and reproduction in fruitflies. *Proceedings of the National Academy of Science of the USA*, 97, 3309–3313

Struhl, G., & Basler, K. (1993). Organized activity of wingless protein in *Drosophila*. *Cell*, 72, 527–540.

Sun, J., & Tower, J. (1999). FLP recombinase-mediated induction of Cu/Zn-superoxide dismutase transgene expression can extend the life span of adult *Drosophila melanogaster* flies. *Molecular and Cellular Biology*, 19, 216–228.

Tatar, M. (1999). Transgenes in the analysis of life span and fitness *American Naturalist*, 154, S67–S81.

Tower, J. (1996). Aging mechanisms in fruit flies. *Bioessays*, 18, 799–807.

Tyler, R. H., Brar, H., Singh, M., Latorre, A., Graves, J. L., Mueller, L. D., Rose, M. R., & Ayala, F. J. (1993). The effect of superoxide dismutase alleles on aging in *Drosophila*. *Genetica*, 91, 143–149.

Vaupel, J. W., & Yashin, A. I. (1985). Heterogeneity's ruses: some surprising effects of selection on population dynamics. *American Statistician*, 39, 176–195.

Vieira, C, Pasyukova, E. G., Zeng, ZB., Hackett, J. B., Lyman, R. F., & Mackay T. F. C. (2000). Genotype-environment interaction for quantitative trait loci affecting life span in *Drosophila melanogaster*. *Genetics*, 154, 213–227.

Wachter, K. W. (1999). Evolutionary demographic models for mortality plateaus. *Proceedings of the National Academy of Science of the USA*, 96, 10544–10547.

Wattiaux, J. M. (1968). Cumulative parental age effects in *Drosophila subobscura*. *Evolution*, 22, 406–421.

Wheeler, J. C., Bieschke, E. T., & Tower, J. (1995). Muscle-specific expression of *Drosophila* hsp70 in response to aging and oxidative stress *Proceedings of the National Academy of Science of the USA*, 92, 10408–10412.

White, K. P., Rifkin, S. A., Hurban, P., & Hogness, D. S. 1999. Microarray analysis of *Drosophila* development during metamorphosis. *Science*, 286, 2179–2184.

Zwaan, B. J. (1993). Aging and development in *Drosophila melanogaster*: An evolutionary approach. *Netherlands Journal of Zoology*, 43, 375–381.

Zwaan, B. J. (1999). The evolutionary genetics of aging and longevity. *Heredity*, 82, 589–597.

Zwaan, B., Bijlsma, R., & Hoekstra, R. F. (1995a). Artificial selection for developmental time in *Drosophila melanogaster* in relation to the evolution of aging: Direct and correlated responses. *Evolution*, 49, 635–648.

Zwaan, B., Bijlsma, R., & Hoekstra, R. F. (1995b). Direct selection on life span in *Drosophila melanogaster*. *Evolution*, 49, 649–659.

Fourteen

Genetics of Increased Longevity and Retarded Aging in Mice

Richard A. Miller

I. Aging and Longevity

People live longer than horses, dogs, and mice and are, in general, pleased with this state of affairs. The broad outline of mammalian senescence is easy to recognize in 3-year-old mice, 12-year-old dogs, 20-year-old horses, 35-year-old chimpanzees, and 75-year-old humans and features diminished reproductive, musculoskeletal, and immune performance, diminished visual and auditory abilities, reproducible changes in gene expression, hormonal regulation, and tissue structure, and exponentially increasing risks of neoplastic, infectious, and other forms of potentially lethal illness. Not all of these ill effects occur in each person and not all features are equally salient in each species, of course, but the patterns are sufficiently similar that, should a new species of mammal be discovered in some hidden, edenic grotto, there would be no difficulty in sorting the population, with reasonable accuracy, into young and old adults. Given adequate motivation—a pot of gold at the top of a long hill, for example, or its species-specific equivalent—a

population of humans, horses, dogs, or Martians will sort itself nicely into age classes during the race to the prize.

For convenience, in this chapter we will use the term "aging" to describe the process that turns the young adults into the older ones. The rate at which this process works clearly is species-specific, in a sense whose quantitative details will be teased apart a few paragraphs further on.

This formulation—aging as a process that creates a similar suite of degenerative changes, but does so at wildly varying rates across (mammalian) species—raises two key challenges for biological gerontologists: learning the mechanism that synchronizes these ill effects within each species and figuring out the basis, obviously genetic, for the species-specific disparities in aging rate. There are no obvious differences among mammalian species in body plan, organ count, tissue organization, or cell structure—sections of lung, liver, kidney, eye lens, and lymph node from young mice and young chimps are almost indistinguishable except to specialist pathologists, and a Golgi is a Golgi is a Golgi.

The myth that interspecies differences in longevity are simply attributable to variation in metabolic rate has been exploded by careful quantitative analyses (Austad & Fischer, 1991; Miller & Austad, 1999). Evolutionary arguments show how decelerated aging may lead to selective benefits in species whose large body size, ability to fly, predator-free environment, or education-dependent lifestyle provides a payoff for decelerated maturation and reproductive scheduling. These explanations, though satisfying in their own terms, are sadly silent as to how, in molecular terms, Darwinian pressures actually alter aging rate. The trick must be a fairly simple one, in that Nature has performed it over and over again, creating relatively long-lived primates, bats, opossums, birds, turtles, naked mole-rats, elephants, and tuna, among others, each from a separate shorter lived predecessor.

Although it is clear both from mortality curves and from the rate of change of multiple age-sensitive traits that humans, dogs, and mice age at different rates, the question of whether members of the same species age at different rates is more tendentious. If it could be shown that among 60-year-old people there existed a subset with stronger muscles, better immunity, superior vision, hearing, and balance, higher insulin sensitivity, undiminished endurance, and unwrinkled skin, and that members of this class tended to die at ages above 85, we would feel safe concluding that they were younger, biologically, than the other, less fortunate members of their birth cohort. An intervention that, when imposed from ages 20 to 60, guaranteed that treated subjects would become members of this youthful subset justifiably would be considered to have retarded the aging rate, whether or not we knew the molecular basis for its effects.

Genetic variations that lead to improved longevity in mammals—the topic of this chapter—have begun to play a major role in testing ideas about the aging process: how it is timed within a species, why it takes so much longer in some species than in others, and how aging produces its effects—the signs of aging—in rough synchrony. The first clear evidence of a single gene mutant that extends life span in a mammal was published only in 1996, and the published literature to date contains only three other examples plus fragmentary hints about a few others. In examining the implications of the work to date—and the much greater potential for future work in this area—it will be necessary to make a clear distinction between life span and aging.

It is clear from inspection of the obituary pages that individuals die at different ages. It is not yet known, however, whether individual members of a mammalian species age at different rates (except for a few illustrative examples that are the central focus of this chapter). Despite a few provocative findings (Miller et al., 1997; Short et al., 1997; Benson et al., 1988), as yet there is no compelling systematic evidence that middle-aged adults with stronger immune systems or greater muscular endurance tend to have fewer cataracts, better reflexes, youthful patterns of gene expression, less pathology, and longer life expectancies. Indeed, some authorities have cogently argued (Costa & McCrae, 1995) that statistical attempts to calculate a "biological age" have stumbled into tautology and have further argued that all such attempts are doomed to failure. Although this latter conclusion is important enough to be worth additional empirical testing, at present there is no agreed-upon method for determining which of two middle-aged mice or humans more closely resembles younger individuals.

For these reasons, assessment of whether a particular mutant mouse stock ages more slowly than controls should be based upon two kinds of evidence:

whether the population's survival curve shows substantially increased longevity (in one of several ways discussed below), and whether mice in the stock exhibit relatively slow changes in many age-dependent traits. Although ideally both kinds of evidence should be pursued, in practice most investigators to date have produced life table data only, relying on the assumption that a mutation that gives a substantial increase in maximal longevity is likely to have done so by retardation of aging per se. This assumption, while plausible, is not always safe: a rat strain in which a specific illness—kidney disease, for example, or a lupus-like autoimmune disease—might show improved longevity if genetic or environmental manipulation made the specific lethal illness less severe. Studies of caloric restriction provide a useful analogy: evidence that low-calorie diets led to increased longevity was gradually, over a 50-year period, supplemented with increased evidence that these diets retarded most of the age-related changes in organ and system function, cell biology, and gene expression, as well as neoplastic and degenerative diseases. Compared to analysis of caloric restriction, the study and exploitation of long-lived stocks of mammals are now at a much earlier stage of development, with a real need for data on pathology and physiology to supplement the slowly developing actuarial data sets.

The remainder of this chapter covers two principal topics: first, what is now known about the genetic control of longevity and aging rate in mammals; and second, how can these and similar results be analyzed and interpreted.

II. Mutations at Single Genes

A. The Ames Dwarf Mouse

Proper development of the anterior pituitary gland depends, in the mouse, on the activity of the *Pit1* gene, whose expression is in turn dependent on expression of *Prop1*. A mutation of the *Prop1* locus on chromosome 11, formerly termed *df* (dwarf) and now referred to as *Prop1df*, leads, in homozygous form, to a phenotype characterized by small body size and diminished production of growth hormone (GH), prolactin (PRL), and thyroid-stimulating hormone (TSH). As young adults, Ames dwarf mice are about one-third the body size of sibling controls, although they consume more calories per gram of body mass than control mice. Bartke and his colleagues (Brown-Borg *et al.*, 1996) have shown that Ames dwarf mice (*df/df*) have increases in both mean and maximal longevity when compared to nonmutant controls (*df/+* and +/+) of the same stock. In males, mean age at death was extended by 49% from 723–1076 days, and in females mean longevity was extended by 68% from 718–1206 days; these differences are each statistically significant at $p < 0.001$. Maximal life span was also extended: no control mouse ($N = 23$) lived beyond 1150 days, but two *df/df* mice (from $N = 34$) survived beyond 1460 days. The experiment was carried out in a conventional colony for which the possible presence of infectious agents was not reported. The background stock, derived from a cross of the "the Goodale large mouse stock to a pink-eyed stock" (Mouse Genome Database, 2000), is not formally inbred, but is a closed breeding colony from which much of the original genetic heterogeneity is likely to have been eliminated (A. Bartke, personal communication).

The basis for the extended longevity of the Ames dwarf mouse is not known, and its elucidation presents important challenges and opportunities for biogerontologists. The defect in the *Prop1* gene and its resulting (Gage *et al.*, 1996) defect in *Pit1* expression (see Snell dwarfs in Section IIB) lead to a complex suite of traits including small body size, infertility, hypothyroidism, and a still only partially charac-terized set of endocrinologic abnormali-ties and alterations in hormone-depen-dent gene expression. The infertility of the female dwarfs can be restored by surgical implantation of PRL-producing pituitary grafts (Bartke, 1965a), and a course of injections of GH, particularly in combination with thyroid hormone, can restore much of the difference in body weight and length and overcome male infertility if begun early in life (Bartke, 1965b). It is not yet known which of these hormonal treatments, if any, might over-come the difference in longevity between the dwarfs and their nondwarf siblings.

At present, essentially nothing is known about the extent to which the superior longevity of the Ames dwarf mice is accompanied by deceleration of the typical age-dependent changes in physiological cell, tissue, and organ func-tion or about late-life pathology of this mutant mouse.

B. The Snell Dwarf Mouse

A mutation of the *Pit1* gene on chromo-some 16 gave rise to the *dw* mutation (*Pit1^{dw}*), first reported in 1929 (Snell, 1929) and has been maintained on the inbred DW/J background. A second muta-tion, *Pit1^{dw-J}*, occurring on the C3H/HeJ background, was reported in 1980 (Eicher & Beamer, 1980). The phenotype of the *dw/dw* homozygote, the Snell dwarf mouse, is very similar to that of the Ames dwarf *df/df*, featuring small body size—about one-third the adult weight of normal siblings—and defects in GH, TSH, and PRL, as would be expected from the known role of *Prop1* as the stim-ulus for *Pit1* expression in the developing pituitary.

An early publication (Fabris *et al.*, 1972) reported that life span in the Snell dwarf mouse was much shorter than that of control animals and that they exhib-ited an immune defect that could be

corrected by injection of GH. In this study, untreated *dw/dw* mice were found to live only 4.5 months, compared to 20 months for nonmutant controls. Other laboratories, however, were not able to confirm the reported immune defects (Cross *et al.*, 1992; Dumont *et al.*, 1979; Schneider, 1976) and a survival study in a specific-pathogen free colony of the Jackson Laboratory (Eicher & Beamer, 1980) found no evidence for diminished longevity of *dwJ/dwJ* homozygotes. These reports, as well as the data on dwarf mouse survival from other colonies discussed later, make it seem likely that the life span of animals in this colony was shortened by inadequacies in husbandry conditions, possibly including infectious agents.

In contrast, two laboratories have now observed extended longevity in mice with mutant *Pit1* alleles. Our own group has observed a 55% increase in mean longevity of *dw/dwJ* males, i.e., from 764–1188 days, and a 36% increase in *dwJ/dw* females compared to nondwarf sibling controls, i.e., from 858–1163 days. These mice were bred as a cross between C3H-HeJ–*dwJ*/+ mothers and DW/J–*dw*/+ fathers. At the time of death of the longest lived of the 33 control mice at 1060 days, 19 of the 25 dwarf mice were still alive, and the longest lived dwarf died at 1451 days of age (R. Miller, unpub-lished data). The differences in mean longevity were significant for both sexes, and there was not a significant effect of gender per se; pooling across genders, the genotype effect is significant by the log-rank test at $p < 0.00001$. In good agree-ment with these findings, Flurkey and Harrison and their colleagues (K. Flurkey, personal communication) have observed a 36% increase in mean longevity in male *dwJ/dw* mice (from 786–1068 days) and a 20% increase in females (from 931–1116 days; these mice were subject to a sham operation because of their use in other experimentation). In a separate study,

Flurkey and Harrison (unpublished) noted a 40% increase in mean longevity of *dw/dw* females on the DW/J background; on this background, however, even the longest lived *dw/dw* female survived less than 1100 days, with all nondwarf controls dying prior to 810 days of age. In both laboratories, the dwarf mice were maintained in a specific-pathogen-free colony, using a husbandry system in which each cage containing dwarf mice also housed at least two nondwarf females; housing the dwarfs together with normally sized mice serves to prevent hypothermia in the dwarf animals.

Flurkey and his colleagues have also performed a number of experiments to determine whether age-sensitive traits change at a slower pace in Snell dwarf mice than in control animals. They have reported, for example, that T-cell *in vitro* proliferative responses to the plant lectins Con A and PHA decline, as expected, by 20–30% by 15 months of age in nonmutant DW/J control mice, but actually increase by ~50% over the same period in *dw/dw* homozygotes (Flurkey & Harrison, 1990), suggesting that functional immune senescence is slowed in the *dw/dw* dwarfs. In unpublished studies, these investigators have also observed a retardation in the rate at which tail tendon denaturation time increases with age between 6 and 18 months in *dwJ/dw* and in *dw/dw* mice and also noted deceleration in the rate at which the dwarf mice accumulate T-cells of the age-dependent CD4 and CD8 memory cell populations. Accumulation of CD4 and CD8 T-cells expressing the age-dependent surface marker P-glycoprotein (Witkowski & Miller, 1993) was also found to occur more slowly in dwarf mice (K. Flurkey *et al.*, unpublished results). These biochemical and immunological findings are consistent with the suspicion that Snell dwarf mice, and by implication probably also Ames dwarf mice, eventually will be shown to have diminished rates of change

in a wide range of age-dependent cellular and physiological traits, although a comprehensive descriptive study has yet to be performed.

C. Other Mutations in the GH Pathway

Ames and Snell dwarf mice show multiple endocrine abnormalities, including deficiencies in the production of GH, as well as deficits in the production of thyroid hormones and prolactin. To examine the effects of isolated alteration in GH-dependent pathways, several laboratories have conducted survival experiments using mice homozygous for the *lit* ("little") mutation of the growth-hormone-releasing hormone receptor gene, *Ghrhr*, on mouse chromosome 6. Homozygous *lit/lit* mice are about two-thirds of normal size as young adults and have lower than normal levels of plasma GH because their pituitary somatotrophs do not respond appropriately to hypothalamic GHRH. Early studies of the life span of C57BL/6–*lit/lit* mice, reviewed in Flurkey and Harrison (1990) produced inconsistent results, with some evidence of modest (13–23%) increases in median longevity in females, but much smaller increases in males. A more recent study, however, has documented a statistically significant increase in mean longevity in *lit/lit* mice (K. Flurkey & D. Harrison, unpublished results), with both males and females affected (27 and 22%, respectively; *N* = 12–18 of each gender per genotype).

Kopchik's group has produced and studied homozygous mice with disruptions in the gene for *Ghr*, the growth hormone receptor on mouse chromosome 15 (Zhou *et al.*, 1997) These mice show severe proportionate growth retardation in early life, with mutants averaging 45% of normal body weight from 10 weeks of age through at least 1 year. The mice show elevated serum GH levels along with very low levels (90% reduction) of the GH-dependent mediator insulin-like growth factor–1 (IGF–1). These GHR-knockout mice are reported (Kopchick & Laron, 2000) to show normal levels of blood glucose, but low levels of insulin, and to have increased insulin sensitivity. Females show delayed puberty and reduced litter size. Although a detailed survival curve has not yet been published, the investigators have reported that at least 80% of the GHR-deficient mice survive beyond 24–30 months, an age at which 90% of the controls have already died. Humans with defects in the growth hormone receptor have been studied extensively by Laron and his colleagues (Laron, 1999); they exhibit many of the same features of the *Ghr*-knockout mice, although they appear to be insulin-resistant. It will be of interest to determine whether individuals with Laron syndrome are also long-lived relative to their nonmutant siblings.

Mice with increased expression of growth hormone have also been studied and have much shorter life spans than nontransgenic controls (Wolf *et al.*, 1993).

Taken together, the studies of *df*, *dw*, *Ghrhr*, and *Ghr* mutants make a consistent case that diminished production of GH can lead to life span extension in mice. Much additional work needs to be done to elucidate the mechanism and implications of these initial observations. For one thing, it is not yet clear to what extent the deficits in thyroid hormone and PRL in the Snell and Ames dwarf mutants contribute to the improved longevity in these two models; indeed, it has not yet been shown formally that the alterations in pituitary hormone production (rather than effects of *Pit1* in other tissues, for example) are the sole mediator of the longevity effect. If we assume, however, that alterations in GH pathways, with or without abnormal TSH and PRL function, are a critical component of the life span effect, it will be important to establish at what stage the hormonal

changes are most effective. Experiments in which GH (and other hormones) is administered, or in which GH secretion is triggered through transgenic methods, at various times and for varying intervals in the juvenile or adult periods will be needed to establish whether the longevity effect can be overcome by brief exposure (sufficient to generate normal body size, for example) or only by hormonal effects in later life. Studies of age-dependent changes in multiple cell types and organ systems, and detailed terminal necropsy series, will be needed to determine which aspects of aging are altered by these mutations and, thus, to clarify whether they are as compelling a model for delayed aging as the better-studied caloric restriction system. These descriptive studies, including tests of gene expression and metabolic factors, will also identify points of similarity and contrast with other models of exceptional longevity, including caloric restriction, and thus help point investigators toward common factors that might underlie disease resistance and improved longevity induced by these distinct ways.

D. p66^{shc} Knockout Mice

Migliaccio and colleagues (Migliaccio *et al.*, 1999) have presented a life span analysis of knockout mice that fail to express the 66-kDa form of the signal transduction coupling protein Shc. The Shc locus encodes three proteins distinguished by differential splicing. The 46- and 52-kD a forms have been studied extensively for their role in signal transduction through Ras and the MAP kinase pathways. The Migliaccio group has shown that the 66-kDa form, p66^{shc}, becomes phosphorylated when cells are exposed to UV light or hydrogen peroxide and that genetic ablation of the p66 form (leaving the 46- and 55-kDa forms intact) rendered fibroblast cells relatively resistant to apoptosis induced by either UV or H_2O_2. These cells did not differ in their resistance to growth arrest induced by γ-irradiation, suggesting that the abnormal phenotype of cells from the knockout mice to UV light reflected alterations in responses to the UV-induced oxidation damage rather than to DNA damage per se. Mice with the defect in p66[shc] expression were also found to be resistant to ordinarily lethal doses of paraquat, an inducer of oxidation damage. These data thus suggest that elimination of p66[shc]-dependent pathways can prevent lethal levels of apoptotic cell death in response to oxidation damage, although the preservation of these pathways in normal mice suggests that they are likely to provide a fitness advantage in some, unknown, circumstances (Guarente, 1999).

Mice with this defect in p66[shc] expression are reported to have a significant increase in longevity (Migliaccio et al., 1999). Median survival in the homozygous knockout mice, 973 ± 37 days, was 28% higher than the median survival of wild-type controls (761 ± 19 days), and differences in the survival curves were significant by log-rank test at p = 0.0002 (N = 14–15 mice/group). All of the 14 wild-type mice died before 28 months of age, but 8 of 15 knockout mice survived beyond this point, with the oldest dying at 36 months. Interestingly, median survival of a group of eight heterozygotes was intermediate (815 ± 37 days) between the two homozygous groups; it would be worthwhile to learn more about the biochemistry and cell biology of fibroblasts from these heterozygotes. This provocative paper leaves a number of technical questions unanswered. Migliaccio et al. (1999) state that there are no significant differences between knockout and control mice in body weight or food consumption, but more data would be needed to see whether the groups differ in rate of weight gain or ultimate adult body weight, even if these differences may not be statistically significant in studies of small size. It would also be helpful to determine whether the groups tested for longevity contained equal numbers of male and female animals. The colony was reported to include carriers of mouse hepatitis virus, and it would be useful to know whether the findings could be repeated in specific-pathogen-free animals. Necropsy data would also be useful in order to clarify whether mice of the (unspecified) wild-type stock tended to die of a particular form of illness; if, for instance, lymphoma were the usual cause of death in the wild-type mice, one would need to consider the hypothesis that the p66[shc]-defective mice were protected against lymphoma but not against other forms of late-life illness. If these results are confirmed, however, it will be of great interest to determine which aspects of the aging phenotype are decelerated in the p66[shc] knockout mice.

E. Urokinase-Type Plasminogen Activator Transgenic Mice

Miskin and Masos (1997) have noted extended life span in a stock of transgenic mice in which the urokinase type of plasminogen activator (uPA) is over expressed in the paraventricular nucleus of the hypothalamus, an element of the system that regulates appetite in normal mice. The construct, in which uPA was driven by the α-crystallin promoter (αMUPA), was developed to study the effects of uPA in the eye, but unexpectedly was found to cause uPA expression in many elements of the central nervous system, including brain, retina, and spinal cord. These mice consume about 20% less food than the inbred FVB/N controls and are, on average, 20–25% lighter than controls between the ages of 4 and 15 months. The survival curves of the two groups were significantly different (p = 0.0001), with the median survival extended by 16% from ~29 to ~33 months. The oldest animals in each group were euthanized for other purposes, and so maximal longevity was not estimated. Blood glucose levels in the transgenic mice are diminished by about 9% compared to wild-type controls. The authors propose that the mechanism of life span extension in these mice is similar to that induced by caloric restriction, although it is noteworthy that control mice fed the same amount of food as that consumed by the transgenic mice were lighter and had lower glucose levels than *ad libitum* fed transgenics. The tangled relationships among size, food consumption, and longevity will be considered again toward the end of this chapter.

F. Congenic Lines Differing at the H–2 and H-16 Loci

Another approach to the genetic dissection of longevity is to compare the survival curves of animals differing only at a single genetic region, one chosen on theoretical grounds because of its potential influence on aging or late-life diseases. An early example (Smith & Walford, 1977) of this strategy involved comparison of congenic mouse lines that differed at the major histocompatibility locus H–2, corresponding to the human HLA locus. In a series of seven mouse lines that differed at H-2 but shared (nearly) all other alleles with the C57BL/10 inbred stock, maximal survival, estimated as the mean for the tenth decile, varied between 139 and 170 weeks for males and between 143 and 165 weeks for females. The shortest lived stock, B10.AKM (H-2 allele m), was significantly different from each of the five longest lived stocks, and the longest lived stock B10.RIII (H-2 allele r) lived significantly longer than any of the others. The data on mean longevity were largely consistent with the conclusions drawn from survival of the oldest deciles. At face value, this result would suggest that

polymorphisms of the H-2 locus play a major role in the control of longevity and perhaps of the aging process.

There are, however, at least two important caveats. First, the effects of the H-2 alleles were shown in this paper (Smith & Walford, 1977) to be contingent on the background stock. Thus, a series of H-2 congenic lines constructed using the A/J background or the C3H/He background in place of C57BL/10 also showed significant differences among the various H-2 alleles, but with a different rank order. The "b" allele of H-2, for example, produced the shortest life span on the A/J background but the longest lived animals in the C3H/He stock; on the C57BL/10 background, H-2(b) males ranked second only to B10.RIII, but H-2(b) females fifth among the seven tested stocks. Thus, the effect of the H-2 alleles seems to depend upon interaction with unknown genetic elements in the background stocks. Secondly, interpretation of these results is difficult in the absence of necropsy data. If, for example, the short-lived B10.AKM mice tended to die, early in life, of a specific form of lethal illness (e.g., an aggressive lymphoma) from which other mice in the C57BL/10 series were protected because of their H-2 alleles, the longevity data might emerge as a consequence of an effect on lymphoma per se, rather than on other aspects of the aging process. Information as to whether H-2 alleles also influence other age-sensitive traits in parallel to their effects on longevity would also help to evaluate the idea that aging, rather than just a few specific diseases, has been altered in these congenic series.

Interestingly, Boerrigter and his colleagues (unpublished results) have observed differential longevity in male mice differing only in the region surrounding the minor histocompatibility locus H-16 on mouse chromosome 4. Figure 1 presents the proportion of surviving mice as a function of age in C57BL/6

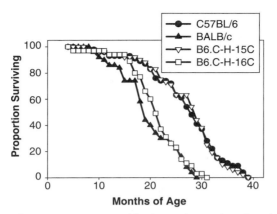

Figure 1. Survival curves for B6.C-H-16C resemble those of BALB/c rather than the C57BL/6 mice with which B6.C-H-16C shares nearly all of its genotype. The graph also shows another congenic strain, B6.C-H–16C, that does not differ significantly from its C57BL/6 progenitor. Each point shows the proportion of mice surviving at the indicated age. The initial cohorts contained 35–50 male mice. (Unpublished data of Dr. Michael Boerrigter.)

mice and in B6.C-H16-C, which are identical to the C57BL/6 mice except for the H-16 allele, derived from the shorter lived BALB/c stock. A negative control line, B6.C-H15-C, which differs from C57BL/6 at the more distal H-15 locus, is also shown. Data of this sort do not reveal which of the many loci in the region near H–16 influence longevity in this collection of inbred strains, but studies of these and other congenic and recombinant inbred lines (see later discussion) may provide valuable tools for dissecting the genetics and pathophysiology of the aging process.

III. Mice Selectively Bred for Variation in Early Life Growth Rate

As noted earlier, small body size is seen together with longer life span in several varieties of dwarf mice, as well as in the uPA transgenic stock; these two traits are also produced, non genetically, through caloric restriction (Weindruch & Walford, 1988) and, possibly, by limitation of the amino acid methionine (Orentreich et al., 1993). The construction, through selec-

tive breeding (Atchley et al., 1997), of stocks of genetically heterogeneous mice differing in early life growth trajectories and, consequently, in adult body size has provided an opportunity to test the generality of this relationship. Starting with a large group of genetically heterogeneous mice, Atchley and his colleagues have produced, by >16 generations of selection, three lines of mice in which progenitors are chosen at each generation for relatively slow weight gain between 0 and 10 days of age, combined with normal growth rates in the second month of life (the ES = early small lines). Three other stocks (LS = late small) were produced selecting for slow weight gain from 28–56 days of age, with normal growth at earlier ages. Three LB and three EB stocks (late big and early big, respectively) were produced by breeding from parents showing unusually large weight gains at the corresponding neonatal and juvenile periods. These intervals were selected on the grounds that weight gain from 0–10 days of life is thought to reflect genetically controlled variation in cell number, whereas gain from 28–56 days is thought to reflect variation in cell size. Finally, three control (C) stocks were produced

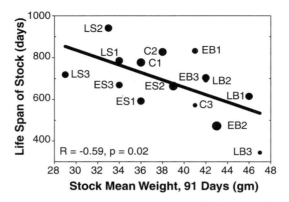

Figure 2.   Correlation of mean longevity versus mean body weight for 15 stocks of mice bred for differences in early life growth rates. Each symbol indicates a stock, and the area of the symbol is proportional to the number of individual female mice tested, varying between 4 and 23 mice. Stock names are explained in the text. (From Miller *et al.* (2000 b). With permission).

without respect to weight gain trajectories; these controls are expected to evolve only by random loss or fixation of alleles.

Figure 2 shows the association between the mean longevity of these 15 stocks and the body weight for the stock measured at 3 months of age. There is a strong and significant correlation between the size and life span, with smaller stocks tending to be longer lived ($R = -0.59$, $p = 0.02$). Thus, about 35% (0.59^2) of the variation in longevity among stocks appears to be associated with factors that regulate growth in weight within the first three months of life. Mean longevity ($R = 0.69$, $p = 0.004$) and maximal longevity ($R = 0.74$, $p = 0.002$) also were correlated strongly with weight at 6 months of age (Miller *et al.*, 2000b). These relationships seem to reflect a pleiotropic effect, in which genes selectively retained because of their effects on early life weight gain have a secondary effect, years later, on longevity and disease. Necropsy data showed that the proportion of deaths due to neoplasia varied among the stocks (between 20 and 86%) and that the relationship between weight and longevity remained strong when only mice dying of neoplastic illnesses were considered ($R = -0.68$, $p = 0.007$). Among the mice dying

of non-neoplastic illnesses, the relationship was still strong, but not quite significant ($R = -0.49$, $p = 0.07$). Thus, the necropsy data are consistent with the idea that the factors that influence early life growth trajectory may help to time multiple forms of late life illnesses. Nothing is known yet about differences among these stocks in other age-sensitive outcomes, such as immune function or cataract progression. Mice in one of the large, short-lived stocks (EB2) tended to die because of pituitary adenoma (16 of 19 mice), but there was no evidence of pituitary adenomas in the other 14 stocks (except for 2/14 cases in stock LS1). It will be interesting to examine these mice, at early and later ages, to determine whether they exhibit abnormalities of the hormones that mediate small body size in the Ames and Snell dwarf lines.

V. Analyses of Recombinant Inbred Mouse Lines

A cross between two different inbred mouse lines produces an F1 hybrid stock, within which each individual is genetically identical to every other and is heterozygous at each locus at which the two parental inbreds are distinct. A cross between two animals of the same F1 stock produces an F2 stock in which each animal is genetically different, having inherited a different selection of alleles from the two starting inbred lines. On average, each F2 mouse receives about 50% of its inheritance from the two starting strains, and the alleles are inherited at random except for the tendency of closely linked alleles to be inherited together. When two F2 mice are mated to produce an F3 generation, their offspring will inherit a subset of the original pool of genetic alleles. Each particular family at the F3 generation—the progeny of any single pair of mated F2 animals—will inherit only a subset of the alleles present in the F1 mice; any alleles that happen, by chance, not to be present in the founding pair of F2 mice of course will not be passed down to any of their progeny. Siblings chosen from a specific family of F3 mice can then be mated to produce F4 animals, and here, too, a certain proportion of the original alleles will, by chance, be lost. Successive generations manufactured by this sibling mating system will eventually—by about the 20th generation—produce mice that can be considered fully inbred, because all mice will have become homozygous at essentially all alleles. Each mouse within this recombinant inbred (RI) line will be identical to all others in the same RI line; on average, each mouse will have inherited about 50% of its alleles from one of the two starting stocks and the other 50% from the alternate progenitor.

Researchers at the Jackson Laboratories and elsewhere have produced large collections of RI lines from selected inbred progenitors. The collection of BXD RI lines, for example, produced from an initial mating of C57BL/6 (B) to DBA/2 (D) mice, provides a valuable resource for mapping genes that influence traits for which C57BL/6 and DBA/2 mice differ. Once preliminary work has established, for each RI stock in the collection, which portions of which chromosomes are of B and which are of D origin, new traits of interest can be mapped simply by determining the pattern of the trait within the collection of RI lines, although the sensitivity and accuracy of this procedure depend greatly on several factors: the degree to which the factor is under genetic control; the number of loci of interest; the presence or absence of gene–gene and gene–environment interactions; and the precision with which the trait can be measured.

By using this system, Gelman and her collaborators (Gelman *et al.*, 1988) measured longevity in 10–20 female mice in each of 20 RI stocks from the BXD collection. The mean longevity values among these RI stocks ranged from 493–904 days. Genetic effects, i.e., differences among the strains, accounted for a mere 29% of the interanimal variation in life span, consistent with other evidence that nongenetic factors also play a major role in determining longevity in mammals. Comparisons among the strains showed that one strain, BXD-19, had a significantly longer life span than any of the other 19 and that two strains, BXD-2 and BXD-14, had significantly shorter life spans than the other stocks examined.

By comparing the strain distribution pattern of known genetic markers with the pattern of longevity data, they attempted to determine which chromosomal segments had the greatest association with longevity. The region with the largest independent effect on longevity was located approximately 7 cM (centimorgans) from the centromere of chromosome 7. A proportional hazards model indicated that combinations of six loci were optimal, in the sense that adding an additional locus did not lead to a statistically significant improvement in the ability to predict strain life span. The optimal combination included loci on chromosomes 1, 2, 7, and 12, but the authors noted that many other combinations of six loci were nearly as good as the combination with highest predictive ability. It is important to note that the test statistic used is sensitive to mortality risk at all stages of the life span; genes that regulate early life mortality risk were as important a factor in the mapping result as genes that regulate mortality risk in the later stages of the life table. The optimal combination included three alleles from the relatively long-lived C57BL/6 progenitor strain and three from the DBA/2 progenitor. No information was provided about whether these RI stocks differed in the rate of change of any age-sensitive variable, such as collagen cross-linking, for example, or cataract formation or immune function. Necropsy data were obtained on only 62 of the 360 mice in the study, making it impossible to determine whether the genes with effects on life span had significant effects on the risk of specific causes of death, or whether they had effects on the life span of mice dying of specific illnesses.

A reanalysis of the Gelman data set by de Haan and van Zant (1999) produced some interesting new results. These authors were able to take advantage of much new fine-scale mapping of the BXD stocks that had not been available to Gelman, as well as new statistical methods for estimating the strength of gene–trait associations in RI series. These workers reported two loci that met the significance levels conventionally considered (Lander & Kruglyak, 1995) to be "suggestive" though not definitively significant; these were located at position 69 cM on chromosome 2 and position 6 cM on chromosome 7. Two other loci, at position 31 cM on chromosome 11 and position 40 cM on chromosome 4, were also found to have weaker associations with life span among these RI stocks. The authors tested each of the RI stocks using an assay that detects the turnover rate of hematopoietic stem cells and noted a strong correlation, among the stocks, between high longevity and relatively slow stem cell turnover rates.

These authors also noted a previously unnoticed feature of the longevity data reported by Gelman et al. (1988), i.e. differences, among the strains, in the variation of life span among mice within each individual strain. Seven of the RI stocks showed a very large interval (800–1000 days) between the first death and the last death in the population, whereas 13 others showed a much shorter range (300–700 days). Nearly all of the strains with the high interstrain variation bore C57BL/6 alleles near the centromere of chromosome 11, whereas nearly all of those with lower variation carried the alternate, DBA/2-derived, alleles. There was no relationship between this index of variance and the mean longevity of the stock. The effect of the chromosome 11 gene on intrastrain variance was not simply due to an influence on early life illness, because a nearly equal effect was seen when the mapping analysis was conducted using the slope of the survival curve after the first death as the measure of variation. The mechanism of the effect is unknown, but presumably represents genetically determined differences in sensitivity to nongenetic factors with major influences on aging and disease risk. It would be of great interest to examine other traits within this RI series to determine which of these show the same pattern of strain-specific variance to provide further clues as to the mechanism of the variance effect and the way in which it leads to alterations in longevity. It would be of particular interest if these studies revealed the same pattern of variance, among the RI strains, in some (but not all) of the traits implicated as putative indices of aging and timers of late life disease—telomere lengths, immune status, accumulation of somatic cell mutations or oxidation damage, and stem cell turnover rates.

V. Selection—Natural and Artificial

A. Variation Attributable to Natural and Artificial Selection: Dogs, Opossums, and Mice

The study of naturally occurring populations of mammals has great, though largely untapped, potential for providing additional insight into the genetic control of aging and longevity. Although laboratory selective breeding projects typically are of fairly short duration (a few years or decades, corresponding to 5–50 mouse generations), natural selection typically has had hundreds to thousands of generations to work, in parallel, in some cases on large numbers of reproductively isolated subpopulations of the species of interest. In addition, selective breeding of domestic mammals—horses, dogs, etc.— has in some cases generated variants differing greatly in the expression of genes controlling behavior, growth, and other life history traits of interest to gerontologists. Studies of fish in high- and low-predation ecological niches, for example, have shown that size at maturity—typically associated, across species, with differences in maturation rate and longevity—is under remarkably plastic genetic control, with major differences able to evolve within 10–20 generations (Reznick et al., 1997). Three mammalian examples will be presented to give some perspective on how resources of this kind might be exploited in aging research.

Dogs have been selected by human breeders, for at least 4000 and perhaps as long as 15,000 years (Clutton-Brock, 1999), for variations in temperament and body size and configuration. Statistics on body weight and age at death have been collected from veterinary archives for domestic pet dogs from 17 breeds (Li et al., 1996), and a regression analysis (Miller, 1999) of these data has shown that there is a very strong relationship (R^2 = 0.56, p = 0.0005) between adult body weight and mean longevity across the collection of breeds. Thus, about 56% of the variation among dog breeds in life span is attributable to factors—almost entirely genetic—that modify stature and body weight. The effects on longevity are pleiotropic, in the sense that genes selected for early life developmental effects have secondary effects on late-life events that were not molded by selective pressures. Although the biochemical basis for differences among dog breeds in body size is not fully defined, it is noteworthy that, in the two cases analyzed so far, comparative analysis of related breeds has suggested that these size differences reflect alterations in IGF–1 levels (Eigenmann et al., 1984, 1988), a striking parallel to the dramatic decline in IGF–1 seen in the long-lived Snell and Ames dwarf mice. The consistently longer life span of smaller breeds of dogs represents a sizable challenge to the popular, but oversimplistic (Austad & Fischer, 1991), theory that higher metabolic rate is the cause of short life span in smaller animals. Slow but steady progress in dog genetics eventually may allow a more informative analysis of the genetic and molecular basis for longevity differences in this highly diverse species.

Samaras and his colleagues (Samaras & Storms, 1992; Samaras & Elrick, 1999) have reviewed the provocative but controversial evidence that short humans are longer lived than taller humans, once the confounding effects of socioeconomic status and early childhood nutrition are accounted for. Other groups (Davey et al., 2000), incorporating adjustments for socioeconomic factors into their models, find height in humans to be associated with lower risks of mortality for cardiovascular and respiratory diseases, but higher risks for several forms of cancer not linked to smoking. These workers make the plausible suggestion that cancer resistance and short stature might be a result of caloric restriction in childhood, but the hypothesis that genetic factors contribute to both outcomes should also be considered in future studies.

Austad's study of an island opossum population provides a second example of the way in which natural selection can mold longer lived genotypes in a time span that is relatively brief by evolutionary standards (Austad, 1993). The separation of Sapelo Island from the U.S. mainland ~4000 years ago left on the island a reproductively isolated opossum population that was no longer able to exchange alleles with the larger mainland population and thus was able to evolve in response to the island's own ecological niche, in which predators were much less common. Biodemographic theory postulates that, under such low hazard conditions, genotypes that produce large early litters were no longer at an advantage over genotypes that favor reproductive performance spaced over longer intervals. Austad demonstrated that island opossums, compared to their mainland cousins, showed a slower rate of aging as measured by mortality risk curves. The island opossums also showed a decelerated rate of accumulation of cross-links in tail tendon collagen and devoted a smaller fraction of their reproductive effort to their first year of life. This study makes a strong case for the hypothesis that genotypes with extended longevity can evolve fairly quickly in a population that finds itself isolated in an appropriate niche. It is difficult to imagine this happening as the result of a series of mutational changes at a very large number of genetic loci, but it seems more likely to represent alteration and fixation at a small number of loci that time the pace of multiple age-associated processes.

Opossum populations can be studied in laboratory conditions, but are not as apt for laboratory study and manipulation as mice. Miller and co-workers (2000a) therefore have initiated a program based on stocks of miniature mice (of the species *Mus musculus*, i.e., the same species as laboratory mouse lines) collected from equatorial islands. Two lines, one from Pohnpei and one from Majuro, have been converted to specific-pathogen-free status and shown to be approximately 50% of the adult body weight of mice from a genetically heterogeneous stock derived from common laboratory inbred lines. Litter sizes of the Pohnpei and Majuro lines are also much smaller than those of laboratory-adapted stocks, i.e., ~4 pups/litter compared to ~10, consistent with the idea that the island-derived stocks have been selected for different reproductive schedules than the laboratory mice typically used for aging research. No information is available yet about the longevity of these wild-derived mouse stocks, although preliminary data (R. Miller, R. Dysko, & S. Austad, unpublished results) suggest that they show a slower decline, with age, in *in vitro* tests of immune function. In view of the associations noted earlier between small body size and extended longevity in dogs and mice, it may prove informative to study crosses between these wild-derived mice and standard laboratory stocks to determine to what extent their dramatic differences in body size, litter size, immune responsiveness, and adrenal steroid (Miller *et al.*, 2000a) levels reflect variation in genes with effects on life span.

B. Selective Breeding for Altered Immune Function

Biozzi and his collaborators, toward the goal of defining the genetic basis for differences in immune responsiveness, have created a series of mouse stocks in which a genetically heterogeneous starting population was bred selectively, over multiple generations, for either strong or weak antibody production when immunized early in life, typically about 2 months (Biozzi et al., 1979; Puel & Mouton, 1996). Mice selected for higher early-life antibody responses were found (Covelli et al., 1989) to live, on average, 612 ± 148 days ($N = 134$), as compared to the much shorter life span of mice selected for weaker immune responses (346 ± 110 days, $N = 123$). These values, even for the longer lived stock, are lower than longevity values typically seen in specific-pathogen-free colonies of inbred mice (Fox & Witham, 1997). The maximal longevity, estimated as the age at death of the longest lived 5% of the population, was also different between the two stocks (822 versus 522 days). In a segregating backcross population of 102 mice, those mice with highest antibody production were found to have highest longevity; the relationship between the decile for longevity and the decline for antibody titer gave $R = 0.76$, $p < 0.01$ for the IgG antibodies. It is possible that this association reflected a direct effect of poor immunity on either infectious or neoplastic disease in this conventional (i.e., not specific-pathogen-free) colony or alterations in immune architecture that both diminished immune responses and also rendered the animals susceptible to early death from lymphoid malignancy. Nonetheless, is it noteworthy that 27–45% of the mice in the various stocks and crosses died of solid tumors and that the age-adjusted incidence of solid tumors was lower in the high-immunity stocks than in the low-immunity stocks. Analysis of the variation among the segregating crosses suggested that the number of loci contributing to inter-stock differences in longevity was fairly small, i.e., 4.5 ± 1.5. Variance analysis showed that the heritability of longevity was about 30%, consistent with a range of other studies in mammals and invertebrates (Curtsinger et al., 1995). Heritability was larger, however, when calculated using the subset of mice that showed the longest

survival, rising to 45% when calculated for the longest lived 10% of the animals. Analysis of polymorphic markers in the Biozzi lines (Puel et al., 1996) has documented loci on chromosomes 4, 8, 12, and 18 with significant effects on antibody titers, with suggestive evidence for loci on chromosomes 6 and 10. The hypothesis that some of these loci also contribute to longevity differences is consistent with the evidence but has not been tested formally.

C. Selective Breeding for Longevity-Associated QTL

Attempts to map polymorphisms that influence life span in mice by genome scanning provide an alternate, though still untested, route toward the development of mouse stocks with extended longevity. Analysis of segregation patterns in mice bred as the progeny of (BALB/c × C57BL/6)F1 mothers and (C3H/He × DBA/2)F1 fathers has documented several alleles with significant effects on longevity, including a chromosome 9 locus associated with extended survival in males only, a pair of loci on chromosomes 2 and 16 that together predict life span in females only, and a chromosome 12 locus associated with life span in males and females (A. Jackson, A. Galecki, D. Burke, & R. Miller, unpublished data). The two loci whose effects can be seen in male mice reach statistical significance only when mice dying at relatively early ages (in this case in the first 20% of deaths) are excluded from the calculation, consistent with the idea that genetic effects on diseases that kill early in the life span may complicate the search for genes with an effect on aging and late-life illnesses. These results suggest that it may be possible, by genotyping mice at a few loci, to identify soon after birth cohorts of mice that are very likely to be long-lived compared to their siblings. Animals of this kind could be an important resource for testing mechanistic theories of aging, helping to support (or refute) hypotheses that specific differences in hormone levels, enzyme expression, cell turnover rates, or gene expression patterns are intimately involved in timing aging and slowing down or speeding up its physiological and clinical effects. A comprehensive analysis of gene combinations in this four-way cross population (P. Hanlon, A. Jackson, A. Galecki, *et al.*, unpublished results) has shown that a set of four loci, on chromosomes 2, 4, 16, and 19, can identify a population of virgin female mice whose mean longevity, 1001 ± 105 days, is 23% longer than the mean longevity of the other $^{15}/_{16}$ths of the population (815 ± 158 days), and experiments are under way attempting to replicate the longevity results and to determine which aspects of the aging process distinguish these genetically selected mice from their sisters.

Similarly, Klebanov, Harrison, and their colleagues (unpublished results) have developed evidence for loci on chromosomes 8 and 10 that influence longevity in segregating populations in which one of the progenitor strains is genetically distant from the progenitors of the common laboratory mouse. Most common strains of laboratory mice are derived from an amalgam of *Mus musculus musculus* and *Mus musculus domesticus*. The experiments in question made use of mice derived by a breeding scheme in which 75% of the genetic alleles came from common laboratory inbred stocks and the remaining 25% from either MOLD/Rk or CAST/Ei. These two progenitor strains, MOLD/Rk and CAST/Ei, were derived from subspecies *Mus musculus molossinus* and *Mus musculus castaneus*, whose lineage diverged from that of *Mus musculus musculus* approximately 500,000 years ago. The MOLD/Rk and CAST/Ei strains were, in addition, derived from wild-captured mice without an extensive period of genetic selection in

a laboratory environment. The results of Klebanov and his colleagues suggested that, in these circumstances, the effects of genetic variation on longevity were much stronger when examined in the longest lived subset of the progeny animals than when tested in the entire cohort. The work of Klebanov and Harrison is consistent with the idea that laboratory adaptation prior to inbreeding may eliminate alleles with instructive influences on aging and longevity and suggests that gene mapping in populations derived, in part, from wild-derived mice may be necessary to develop a more comprehensive picture of how genetic variation alters longevity via effects on aging (Miller *et al.*, 1999).

VI. Analysis and Interpretation of Longevity Gene Experiments

The question of whether a specific genetic allele or allele combination affects aging seems, at first glance, to be easy to answer, but it is not. Complications include the weaknesses of relying on demographic data alone, the lamentable paucity of data beyond the demographic minimum, the difficulties of separating the effects of genes on aging from their effects on specific diseases, and the challenges of disentangling the relationships among genes, size, and life span.

A. Demographic Indices of Retarded Aging

Because so much of the current work on long-lived mutants is restricted to life table analysis, a brief discussion of the strengths, limitations, and complications of demographic approaches to aging is in order. Traditional (Kirkwood, 1985) and more iconoclastic reviews of this topic (Vaupel *et al.*, 1998; Horiuchi & Wilmoth, 1997) are easily accessible and (along with Chapter 1 in this volume) should be consulted for alternative points of view. Most discussions start with a presentation of the Gompertz relationship, an empirical observation originally derived from analysis of human survivorship curves, which notes that the logarithm of the rate of mortality is a linear function of age over most of the adult life span. The slope of this line often is used as an approximation of the "aging rate;" thus, a smaller slope (e.g., for humans compared to mice or for calorically restricted mice compared to those on a control diet) is taken as evidence that humans, and calorically restricted mice, age more slowly than normal mice.

Because the mortality in the neonatal period typically is much higher than in the period just after puberty, calculations of the Gompertz slope typically exclude mortality rates at ages prior to the point of minimum mortality risk. In some species, including humans, the life table also shows an interval of relatively high mortality early after the attainment of adulthood, attributable to the risks of childbirth (in females) or intermale conflict. Documentation of deceleration in the rise of mortality risks at extremely advanced ages in flies and worms (Carey et al., 1992; Curtsinger et al., 1992; Vaupel et al., 1994) has helped to remind gerontologists that the Gompertz relationship, though useful for some kinds of comparisons, is empirical rather than grounded in fundamental biophysical laws. It should be understood, however, that these late-life departures from the Gompertz curve, though reproducibly observable in sufficiently large populations of invertebrates, have not been documented in mammals, except perhaps in a very small proportion of (exceptionally old) humans. Chapter 1 in this volume has additional material on the disparities between invertebrate and mammalian species in the tendency to exhibit non-Gompertzian survival rates in later life.

Even without the complications of late-life mortality rate deceleration, life table data can yield, in principle, estimates of several parameters: (a) the slope of the log mortality risk curve (or its equivalent the mortality rate doubling time, MRDT); (b) the intercept of this curve, related to the initial mortality rate; and (c) the more traditional statistics of mean, median, and maximal longevity. Application of these demographic tools to practical situations, in this case the analysis of life tables of putatively long-lived mutant mice, can sometimes lead to ambiguous results that require careful interpretation and judgment. The data shown in Fig. 3 provide a useful illustration of some of these difficulties. The results show the life table of a population of (DW × C3H)F1–dw/dw (Snell dwarf) mice compared to their nondwarf siblings (R. Miller et al., unpublished). Each cage contained both dwarf and control mice, with control animals replaced by substitute females ("babysitter" mice, not part of the experimental group) as they died off. Because differences between males and females were small and not statistically significant, data from both genders have been pooled. The group consisted of 25 dwarf mice and 33 sibling controls. The upper left panel shows the survival curve, and it is apparent that the dw/dw mice live longer than controls; there is a 42% increase in mean longevity (p = 0.00001 by log-rank test) and a 41% increase in maximal life span, estimated as the mean longevity of the longest lived 20% of each group.

Does this difference reflect a change in the "aging rate" as demographers estimate it on the basis of the slope of the mortality risk curve? The upper right panel shows, for each genotype, the plot of the logarithm of the mortality risk as a function of age, using a smoothing algorithm (Remlau-Hansen, 1983) often employed in studies of aging flies. After the death of one mouse in each group at

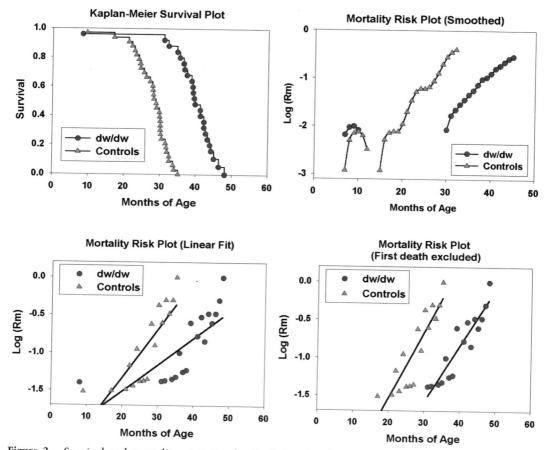

Figure 3. Survival and mortality statistics for Snell dwarf and sibling control mice on the (C3H/He × DW)F1 background. Upper left: survival curve. Each symbol indicates one mouse dying at the indicated age. Upper right: logarithm of mortality risk as a function of age, smoothed using a 6-month window. Each point represents an estimate of the mortality risk at the indicated age. Lower left: log mortality risk at each age; the lines represent the linear regression fit. Lower right: same as in the lower left panel, except that the two mice dying at the earliest ages (one in each group) have been excluded.

8–10 months of age, there is an increase in mortality starting at 17 months in the control group and at about 31 months in the dwarf group. Within the limitations imposed by the small sample size, the plots of log of mortality against age seem acceptably linear, i.e., Gompertzian, but it appears that the increase in mortality risk does not begin to rise in the *dw/dw* mice until an age at which about 75% of the controls have already died.

The two lower panels present, in graphical form, estimates of the slope of the

Gompertz line, the demographic gold standard for differences in aging rate. The plot at the lower left includes all of the data points and supports the conclusion that these two groups differ in the rate of aging: the slope in the controls, 0.147 unit/month on a $\log_{10}$ scale, is about 1.8-fold steeper than the slope (0.082 unit/month) in the dwarf mice. This conclusion, however, stands on shaky ground: each group of mice contains one outlier dying early. Removal of these two outliers, as in the lower right panel, supports the opposite conclusion, i.e., that the slopes are very similar. The accepted demographic criterion—aging rate as estimated by Gompertz slope or its analog the MRDT—provides little guidance in this situation. It is possible that a much larger sample size could generate sufficiently precise estimates of the slope and intercept of the mortality rate plot, but it is also plausible that the shape of the mortality curve in early life may be influenced by factors that are not germane to aging, i.e., to the process that converts young adults to old ones. The most attractive and straightforward interpretation of the data in Fig. 3 is that the *dw/dw* mice and control mice age at the same rate but that the process starts later in the *dw/dw* animals. This interpretation is not well-modeled by the Gompertz equation and its usual variants, but it is considered in some detail in Finch's discussion (Finch, 1990). Studies of patterns of gene expression in dwarf and control mice are likely to provide support for or help to refute this interpretation.

Figure 4 provides a second example of the practical difficulties in relying on life table data alone for answering questions about aging. The data are extracted from a study (R. Miller, D. Burke, C. Chrisp, & A. Jackson, unpublished results) of the genetic bases for longevity in a group of heterogeneous siblings bred as the progeny of (BALB/c × C57BL/6)F1 mothers and (C3H/HeJ × DBA/2)F1 fathers. Analysis of the correlation between longevity and genotype revealed that male mice that inherited the C3H (C3) allele at the ninth chromosome locus D9Mit110 had an unusual survival pattern, as illustrated in the upper panels of Fig. 4: compared to their brothers inheriting the DBA/2 (D2) allele, they had higher mortality rates at early ages, i.e., prior to about 24 months of age, but lower mortality rates at more advanced ages. By using the rubric suggested by Finch

(1990), one would conclude that the C3 allele conferred both a higher initial mortality rate and a longer mortality rate doubling time. By demographic criteria, mice with the C3 allele appear to be "aging" more slowly, although they do not differ from their D2 brothers in mean, maximal, or median survival.

Necropsy data help to clarify this situation. About 30% of the male mice in this population die, relatively early in life, from a single specific disease, the mouse urinary syndrome, termed MUS, which is characterized by urethral plugging and bladder distension or rupture (Tuffery, 1966; Everitt *et al.*, 1988). This syndrome is seen only in group-housed males and is thought to be a result of adjustments in dominance hierarchy. The lower panels of Fig. 4 present the same data set after the exclusion of mice known to have died of MUS. Although the small sample size precludes any definitive conclusions, the data suggest that the higher mortality rate in mice with the C3 allele largely reflects an acceleration of the urinary syndrome and that this allele is also associated with lower mortality risks at later ages. Necropsy data thus can help to distinguish genetic effects on diseases that kill early in life from those late-life illnesses whose timing is influenced by aging. The impression of a plateau, at very advanced age, in the mice with the D2 allele may simply be due to chance effects in a small sample, but deserves reexamination in a replicate sample.

These examples suggest that survival statistics alone are, in practical cases, often unable to provide a simple and compelling answer to the question of whether two groups of genetically distinct animals are aging at different rates. The common assumption that differences in the slope of the mortality risk curve are the only indication of altered aging patterns fails to do justice to the complexity of life table patterns, particularly when survival statistics

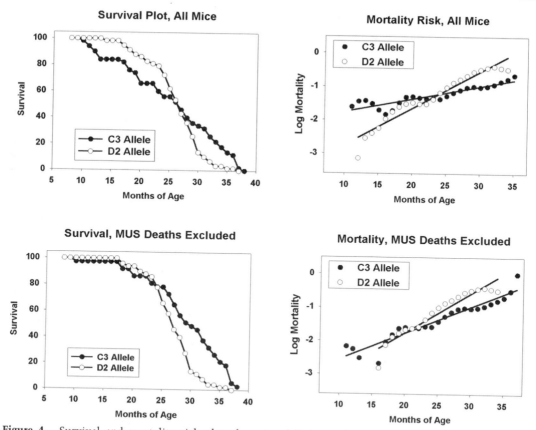

Figure 4. Survival and mortality risk plots for mice differing at locus D9Mit110. Mice are the male progeny of a cross between (BALB/c × C57BL/6)F1 mothers and (C3H/He x DBA/2)F1 fathers. The groups represent the populations that inherit either the C3H (C3) or the DBA/2 (D2) allele at D9Mit110. In the upper left panel, each point represents a mouse dying at the indicated age. The upper right panel shows the corresponding mortality risk plot, smoothed using a 6-month window. The lines show the best fit by linear regression. The lower plots show the survival and mortality risk plots excluding mice that were found, at necropsy, to have died from mouse urinary syndrome. The C3 allele is associated with increased mortality risks in those mice dying of urinary syndrome, most of which die early, but is also associated with lower mortality risks, from multiple lethal illnesses, at older ages. (Data from unpublished studies of A. Jackson, D. Burke, C. Chrisp, A. Galecki, and R. Miller.)

reflect the combined effects of aging and other contributors to death rates, including diseases that kill at relatively early ages. Furthermore, data sets limited to a few scores or a few hundred individuals often are insufficient to provide statistically precise estimates of mortality risks that may vary in a nonlinear fashion across the life course.

Information about age-sensitive traits is likely to provide a much more informative picture than that derivable from life tables by themselves. It will, for example, be of great interest to determine whether mice in any of the long-lived groups listed previously—the dwarf mice, the p66[shc] knockout, H-2 and H-16 congenics, the various RI lines, and mice differentiated by sets of polymorphic alleles—show decelerated rates of change in a wide range of age-dependent biochemical and physiological indicators. This kind of evidence was the most persuasive indication that caloric restriction was a plausible model for decelerated aging and provides good support for the claim that mice, dogs, and people age at differing rates. Collection of such evidence is at a very early stage—limited to just a few unpublished experiments on Snell dwarf mice—and its acquisition is the kind of unglamorous activity typically scorned by review groups. Because dramatic extension of maximal longevity requires the coordinated postponement of potentially lethal changes in multiple organ systems, it seems likely that genes that extend the life span of the longest-lived subset of the population are doing so through effects on aging per se. The point, however, is sufficiently important and sufficiently controversial to be worth more direct examination. Compilation of a listing of similarities and differences among these various longevity genotypes, particularly including data on mice early in adult life, will help to identify changes in affected traits that are common to all long-lived models and, thus, more likely to be causative rather than incidental to the longevity phenotype. Data using high-throughput systems to quantitate gene expression could be an important component of this characterization program.

B. Genes that Affect Both Body Size and Life Span.

Genes that increase life span while decreasing size pose another category of complication. Gerontologists aware of the powerful effect of food restriction on rodent longevity have learned to be suspicious of intervention protocols, for example, those in which a chemical is added to the food or water, that lead to both increased longevity and diminished food intake and body weight. It seems plausible to interpret findings of this kind as artifactual, as merely another variety of food restriction imposed not by direct limitation of food availability but rather by making the food so unpalatable that the mice voluntarily consume less of it. The traditional control is to use a pair-fed group, limited to the amount of food intake consumed by the treated group; if the pair-fed group and the treated group do not differ in life span, this is taken as evidence that the treatment has no effect on life span except insofar as it alters food consumption.

This straightforward line of inference can lead, however, to a tempting misinterpretation of data, such as that presented earlier for the Snell and Ames dwarf models, in which the longevity of small mice is seen as a consequence of low food intake. It is true that dwarf mice have lower food consumption than their normal sized siblings and also true that genetically normal mice restricted to the level of food ordinarily consumed by dwarf mice would exhibit the extended longevity produced by caloric intake. It is a logical error, however, to infer from this that small body size or low food intake is the *cause* of life span extension in dwarf mice. Low food intake can cause small body size, and, conversely, small body size, whether as a consequence of genetic inheritance and perhaps nongenetic factors such as early life nutrition, can itself lead to low food intake. The small size of chihuahuas compared to wolfhounds, or of rats compared to cows, is not caused by caloric restriction, but instead leads to differences in food requirements and food consumption levels. No one would argue that the long life span of chihuahuas compared to wolfhounds is due to food restriction, and similar arguments about the cause of longevity in Snell and Ames dwarf mice are equally unconvincing.

There may well be cases in which genetic alteration does lead to extended longevity because of alterations in appetite and food intake: the uPA transgenic mice (Miskin & Masos, 1997) are the most likely example. In other cases, though, voluntary restriction of food intake seems a dubious explanation. In the Atchley mouse series, for example (Miller et al., 2000b), artificial selection was imposed on growth rate in the first 56 days of life, and the correlation between body weight and life span is equally strong when weight is measured in young adults as in obese older mice. In Ames dwarf mice, food consumption per gram of body mass is higher than in nonmutant siblings, consistent with the need of smaller animals to expend comparatively more energy on maintenance of body temperature; elderly Ames and Snell dwarf mice typically are obese, in contrast to the remarkable leanness of calorically restricted rodents. There may, however, be interesting similarities in hormonal profiles, metabolic adaptations, and gene expression patterns between young adult dwarf mice, young mice in the first few months of a calorie restriction protocol, and adult mice whose genotypes are associated with both extended longevity and small body size. Further analysis of these patterns may provide clues as to the way in which alterations in growth patterns at various stage of life influence, at later ages, vulnerability to multiple forms of illnesses and other concomitants of the aged phenotype.

C. Appropriate Choice of Comparison Group

Valid inferences about the effects of specific genes and gene combinations on aging also require careful consideration of the choice of an appropriate control group. A demonstration, for example, that a line of mice in which all animals died of hemophilia at 6 months of age showed extended longevity when supplemented with a gene encoding a clotting factor would not be taken as evidence that clotting factors regulate aging. Similarly, a demonstration that life span of B10.F mice could be prolonged by an

H-2 allele that prevented the early life lymphoma to which B10.F animals are subject should not be taken as evidence for a general effect of H-2 on the aging process. In other circumstances, however, the question of the appropriateness of the chosen control group may be more difficult to decide. When one documents differences in life span in a series of RI mice (de Haan & Van Zant, 1999; Gelman et al., 1988), or within the Atchley series of size-selected stocks (Miller et al., 2000b), it is not clear whether the critical genetic factors are leading to exceptionally slow aging in the longest lived members of the series or instead producing early death from causes that play little role in the regulation of aging. In some cases (Covelli et al., 1989), even the longest lived group has a reported life span that is shorter than that noted for typical inbred stocks (Fox & Witham, 1997) in modern specific-pathogen-free facilities; in these cases, it is reasonable to guess that husbandry conditions may have limited the life span in the tested group and difficult to predict what effects, if any, the genetic differences might have on life span in a lower risk vivarium. Comparisons of this kind to historical controls are themselves potentially misleading, however, because life span determinations made in different years on the same strain, in the same specific-pathogen-free laboratory often can vary dramatically. Mean longevity for male BALB/cJ mice at the Jackson Laboratory, for example, seems to have increased by 45% from 447–648 days between 1969 and 1975, and reports of life span in CBA/J males vary between 527 and 749 days (Fox & Witham, 1997). On balance, contemporaneous controls provide greater confidence, provided that they are at least as long-lived as published historical controls from the strain of interest. Genetic systems in which transgenes or loss-of-function mutants are studied on a genetically heterogeneous background, such as that typically generated from the progeny of F1 hybrid mice, create further complications to ensure that the effects of interest do not merely reflect uncontrolled differences in background alleles.

D. Assessment of Claims for Altered Aging Rate in Experimental Mammals: Suggested Criteria

Considering these difficulties, how should one assess the hypothesis that a particular stock of mice or rats shows decelerated aging? The following criteria seem reasonable:

1. Maximal longevity, estimated operationally as the mean life span of mice in the longest lived decile, should be significantly longer compared to mice in a control group differing only in the gene(s) of interest.

2. A wide range of age-sensitive changes, monitored within the middle half of the lifespan, should show a slower rate of change in the experimental stock compared to the control stock. Ideally, such a study would include the examination of changes in multiple organ systems, cell types, and extracellular materials: demonstration that the experimental group shows slowed cataract development, slowed immune senescence, and slower rates of change in liver and muscle gene expression patterns should make it difficult to rebut the inference that the loci in fact act by an effect on aging per se.

3. The characterization of age-sensitive changes should include both cross-sectional and terminal pathology to document the claim that the loci in question slow down pathologically evident changes in many tissues, including those that typically lead to death. If the terminal pathology indicates that a single cause of death—a particular neoplasm or a form of autoimmune disease, for example—is extremely frequent in the control population, then the inference that the alleles modify aging, rather than a single disease process, should be greeted with skepticism.

4. Studies of body size and caloric consumption should provide useful insights into possible links between appetite, hormone profiles, metabolic variables, diseases, and longevity. Findings that a particular long-lived stock is smaller than controls should not be interpreted reflexively as merely another example of caloric restriction; the investigators need to consider the possibility that genes may affect both size and life span directly, with alterations in food consumption being the result, rather than the cause, of diminutive stature.

VII. Summary and Prospectus

To date, work on genes that increase longevity in mice has settled a few old questions, raised a few new ones, and provided a glimpse of a largely unexplored landscape of new experimental opportunities. The work on dwarf mice has shown that changes in single mammalian genes can lead to dramatic increases in mean and maximal longevity, raising substantial obstacles to models that portray the aging process as timed by a large number of essentially unlinked sources of physiological damage. The provocative finding that genes involved in responses to members of the insulin and insulin-like growth factor families are implicated in life span extension in dogs (Eigenmann *et al.*, 1984, 1988), mice (Brown-Borg *et al.*, 1996; Miller, 1999), and nematodes (Kimura *et al.*, 1997), though still possibly coincidental, suggests that additional attention to these hormonal pathways is likely to be rewarding. At the same time, observations that life span in both mice (Migliaccio *et al.*, 1999) and nematodes (Johnson *et al.*, 1996) can be increased by genes that modify stress resistance should prompt additional attention to factors that govern cellular responses to chemical and physical injuries. Studies of mice that differ from one another in stature and early life growth rates will help to clarify the ways in which genes that alter preadult developmental pathways lead, later in life, to different rates of aging.

Gerontologists for years have been stuck with only a single method, caloric restriction, for slowing down aging. Studies of calorically restricted rodents have documented a number of alterations that could, in principle, explain or at least contribute to its effect on longevity, including ideas about insulin sensitivity, altered hormonal and gene expression patterns, and changes in exposure to and defense against oxidation damage. The effects of caloric restriction are so numerous, however, that it has proven difficult to discriminate changes that are important to longevity from those that are incidental to the antiaging effect. Studies of single-gene mutants that alter aging, and of polygenic modulators of the aging process, should be able to help sort out those factors that are common to extended longevity from those that are specific to the individual models of life span extension. It is possible that the resulting improvement in our understanding of intraspecies differences in longevity and aging may give helpful leads to the more difficult problem of explaining the far more dramatic differences in life span among mammalian species.

Acknowledgments

I thank David Harrison, Simon Klebanov, Kevin Flurkey, and Michael Boerrigter for sharing unpublished data with me; my colleagues David Burke, Anne Jackson, Andrzej Galecki, and the late Clarence Chrisp for their contributions to our collaborative studies; and Jim Curtsinger for assistance with the demographic analyses and for the program, Mortal 1.0, used for calculating the mortality risks shown in Figs. 3 and 4. The unpublished data included in this review were obtained with the support of NIA Grants AG11687, AG13283, and AG08808.

References

Atchley, W. R., Xu, S., & Cowley, D. E. (1997). Altering developmental trajectories in mice by restricted index selection. *Genetics, 146,* 629–640.

Austad, S. N. (1993). Retarded senescence in an insular population of Virginia opossums (*Didelphis virginiana*). *Journal of Zoology, 229,* 695–708.

Austad, S. N., & Fischer, K. E. (1991). Mammalian aging, metabolism, and ecology: evidence from the bats and marsupials. *Journal of Gerontology: Biological Sciences, 46,* B47-B53.

Bartke, A. (1965a). Influence of luteotrophin on fertility of dwarf mice. *Journal of Reproduction and Fertility, 10,* 93–103.

Bartke, A. (1965b). The response of two types of dwarf mice to growth hormone, thyrotropin, and thyroxine. *General and Comparative Endocrinology, 5,* 418–426.

Benson, W. H., Farber, M. E., & Caplan, R. J. (1988). Increased mortality rates after cataract surgery. A statistical analysis. *Ophthalmology., 95,* 1288–1292.

Biozzi, G., Mouton, D., Sant'Anna, O. A., Passos, H. C., Gennari, M., Reis, M. H., Ferreira, V. C. A., Heumann, A. M., Bouthillier, Y., Ibanez, O. M., Stiffel, C., & Siqueira, M. (1979). Genetics of immunoresponsiveness to natural antigens. *Current Topics in Microbiology and Immunology, 85,* 31–98.

Brown-Borg, H. M., Borg, K. E., Meliska, C. J., & Bartke, A. (1996). Dwarf mice and the ageing process. *Nature, 384,* 33–33.

Carey, J. R., Liedo, P., Orozco, D., & Vaupel, J. W. (1992). Slowing of mortality rates at older ages in large medfly cohorts. *Science, 258*, 457–461.

Clutton-Brock, J. (1999). *A Natural History of Domesticated Mammals, 2 ed.* Cambridge, UK: Cambridge University Press.

Costa, P. T., & McCrae, R. R. (1995). Design and analysis of aging studies. In E. J. Masoro (Ed.), *Handbook of Physiology. Section 11: Aging*, New York: Oxford University Press.

Covelli, V., Mouton, D., Di Majo, V., Bouthillier, Y., Bangrazi, C., Mevel, J. C., Rebessi, S., Doria, G., & Biozzi, G. (1989). Inheritance of immune responsiveness, life span, and disease incidence in interline crosses of mice selected for high or low multispecific antibody production. *Journal of Immunology, 142*, 1224–1234.

Curtsinger, J. W., Fukui, H. H., Khazaeli, A. A., Kirscher, A., Pletcher, S. D., Promislow, D. E., & Tatar, M. (1995). Genetic variation and aging. *Annual Review of Genetics, 29*, 553–575.

Curtsinger, J. W., Fukui, H. H., Townsend, D. R., & Vaupel, J. W. (1992). Demography of genotypes: failure of the limited life-span paradigm in Drosophila melanogaster. *Science, 258*, 461–463.

Cross, R. J., Bryson, J. S., & Roszman, T. L. (1992). Immunologic disparity in the hypopituitary dwarf mouse. *Journal of Immunology, 148*, 1347–1352.

Davey, S. G., Hart, C., Upton, M., Hole, D., Gillis, C., Watt, G., & Hawthorne, V. (2000). Height and risk of death among men and women: Aetiological implications of associations with cardiorespiratory disease and cancer mortality. *Journal of Epidemiology and Community Health, 54*, 97–103.

de Haan, G., & Van Zant, G. (1999). Genetic analysis of hemopoietic cell cycling in mice suggests its involvement in organismal life span. *FASEB Journal, 13*, 707–713.

Dumont, F., Robert, F., & Bischoff, P. (1979). T and B lymphocytes in pituitary dwarf Snell-Bagg mice. *Immunology, 38*, 23–31.

Eicher, E. M., & Beamer, W. G. (1980). New mouse dw allele: genetic location and effects on lifespan and growth hormone levels. *Journal of Heredity, 71*, 187–190.

Eigenmann, J. E., Amador, A., & Patterson, D. F. (1988). Insulin-like growth factor I levels in proportionate dogs, chondrodystrophic dogs and in giant dogs. *Acta Endocrinologica, 118*, 105–108.

Eigenmann, J. E., Patterson, D. F., & Froesch, E. R. (1984). Body size parallels insulin-like growth factor I levels but not growth hormone secretory capacity. *Acta Endocrinologica, 106*, 448–453.

Everitt, J. I., Ross, P. W., & Davis, T. W. (1988). Urologic syndrome associated with wire caging in AKR mice. *Laboratory Animal Science, 38*, 609–611.

Fabris, N., Pierpaoli, W., & Sorkin, E. (1972). Lymphocytes, hormones and ageing. *Nature, 240*, 557–559.

Finch, C. E. (1990). *Longevity, Senescence, and the Genome.* Chicago: University of Chicago Press.

Flurkey, K., & Harrison, D. E. (1990). Use of genetic models to investigate the hypophyseal regulation of senescence. In D. E. Harrison (Ed.), *Genetic Effects on Aging II* (pp. 437–456). Caldwell, NJ: The Telford Press.

Fox, R. R., & Witham, B. A. (1997). *Handbook on Genetically Standardized JAX Mice. (5 ed.).* Bar Harbor, ME: The Jackson Laboratory.

Gage, P. J., Brinkmeier, M. L., Scarlett, L. M., Knapp, L. T., Camper, SA, & Mahon, K. A. (1996). The Ames dwarf gene, df, is required early in pituitary ontogeny for the extinction of Rpx transcription and initiation of lineage-specific cell proliferation. *Molecular Endocrinology, 10*, 1570–1581.

Gelman, R., Watson, A., Bronson, R., & Yunis, E. (1988). Murine chromosomal regions correlated with longevity. *Genetics, 118*, 693–704.

Guarente, L. (1999). Mutant mice live longer. *Nature, 402*, 243, 245.

Horiuchi, S., & Wilmoth, J. R. (1997). Age patterns of the life table aging rate for major causes of death in Japan, 1951–1990. *Journals of Gerontology, Series A, Biological Sciences and Medical Sciences, 52*, B67–B77.

Johnson, T. E., Lithgow, G. J., & Murakami, S. (1996). Hypothesis: interventions that increase the response to stress offer the potential for effective life prolongation and increased health. *Journals of Gerontology A, Biological Sciences Medical Sciences, 51*, B392–5.

Kimura, K. D., Tissenbaum, H. A., Liu, Y., & Ruvkun, G. (1997). daf–2, an insulin receptor-like gene that regulates longevity and diapause in *Caenorhabditis elegans. Science, 277*, 942–946.

Kirkwood, T. B. L. (1985). Comparative and evolutionary aspects of longevity. In C. E. Finch, & E. L. Schneider (Eds.), *Handbook of the Biology of Aging, 2 ed.*, (pp. 27–44). New York: Van Nostrand Reinhold Company.

Kopchick, J. J., & Laron, Z. (2000). Is the Laron mouse an accurate model of Laron Syndrome? *Molecular Genetics and Metabolism, 68*, 232–236.

Lander, E., & Kruglyak, L. (1995). Genetic dissection of complex traits: guidelines for interpreting and reporting linkage results. *Nature Genetics, 11*, 241–247.

Laron, Z. (1999). The essential role of IGF-I: lessons from the long-term study and treatment of children and adults with Laron syndrome. *Journal of Clinical Endocrinology and Metabolism, 84*, 4397–4404.

Li, Y., Deeb, B., Pendergrass, W., & Wolf, N. (1996). Cellular proliferative capacity and life span in small and large dogs. *Journals of Gerontology, Series A, Biolological Sciences and Medical Sciences, 51*, B403–408.

Migliaccio, E., Giorgio, M., Mele, S., Pelicci, G., Reboldi, P., Pandolfi, P. P., Lanfrancone, L., & Pelicci, P. G. (1999). The p66shc adaptor protein controls oxidative stress response and life span in mammals. *Nature, 402*, 309–313.

Miller, R. A. (1999). Kleemeier Award Lecture: Are There Genes for Aging? *Journals of Gerontology, Biological Sciences, 54A*, B297–B307.

Miller, R. A. & Austad, S. N. (1999). Large animals in the fast lane. *Science, 285*, 199–199.

Miller, R. A., Austad, S., Burke, D., Chrisp, C., Dysko, R., Galecki, A., & Monnier, V. (1999). Exotic mice as models for aging research: polemic and prospectus. *Neurobiology of Aging, 20*, 217–231.

Miller, R. A., Chrisp, C., & Atchley, W. R. (2000b). Differential longevity in mouse stocks selected for early life growth trajectory. *Journals of Gerontology: Biological Sciences, 55A*, B455–B461.

Miller, R. A., Chrisp, C., & Galecki, A. (1997). CD4 memory T cell levels predict lifespan in genetically heterogeneous mice. *FASEB Journal, 11*, 775–783.

Miller, R. A., Dysko, R., Chrisp, C., Seguin, R., Linsalata, L., Buehner, G., Harper, J. M., & Austad, S. (2000a). Mouse (Mus musculus) stocks derived from tropical islands: new models for genetic analysis of life history traits. *Journal of Zoolology, 250*, 95–104.

Miskin, R., & Masos, T. (1997). Transgenic mice overexpressing urokinase-type plasminogen activator in the brain exhibit reduced food consumption, body weight and size, and increased longevity. *Journals of Gerontology, Series A, Biological Sciences and Medical Sciences, 52*, B118–24.

Mouse Genome Database (MGD) (2000). Mouse Genome Informatics Web Site, Jackson Laboratory, Bar Harbor, ME [On-line]. Available: http://www.informatics.jax.org/

Orentreich, N., Matias, J. R., DeFelice, A., & Zimmerman, J. A. (1993). Low methionine ingestion by rats extends life span. *Journal of Nutrition, 123*, 269–274.

Puel, A., & Mouton, D. (1996). Genes responsible for quantitative regulation of antibody production. *Critical Reviews in Immunology, 16*, 223–250.

Puel, A., Mevel, J. C., Bouthillier, Y., Feingold, N., Fridman, W. H., & Mouton, D. (1996). Toward genetic dissection of high and low antibody responsiveness in Biozzi mice. *Proceedings of the National Academy of Sciences of the USA, 93*, 14742–14746.

Remlau-Hansen (1983). Smoothing counting process intensities by means of kernel functions. *Annals of Statistics, 11*, 453–466.

Reznick, D. N., Shaw, F. H., Rodd, F. H., & Shaw, R. G. (1997). Evaluation of the rate of evolution in natural populations of guppies (Poecilia reticulata). *Science, 275*, 1934–1937.

Samaras, T. T., & Elrick, H. (1999). Height, body size and longevity. *Acta Medica Okayama*, 53, 149–169.

Samaras, T. T., & Storms, L. H. (1992). Impact of height and weight on life span. *Bulletin of the World Health Organization*, 70, 259–267.

Schneider, G. B. (1976). Immunological competence in Snell-Bagg pituitary dwarf mice: response to the contact-sensitizing agent oxazolone. *American Journal of Anatomy*, 145, 371–393.

Short, R., Williams, D. D., & Bowden, D. M. (1997). Circulating antioxidants as determinants of the rate of biological aging in pigtailed macaques (Macaca nemestrina). *Journals of Gerontology: Biological Sciences*, 52A, B26–B38.

Smith, G. S., & Walford, R. L. (1977). Influence of the main histocompatibility complex on aging in mice. *Nature*, 270, 727–729.

Snell, G. D. (1929). "Dwarf," a new Mendelian recessive character of the house mouse. *Proceedings of the National Academy of Sciences of the USA*, 15, 733–734.

Tuffery, A. A. (1966). Urogenital lesions in laboratory mice. *Journal of Pathology and Bacteriology*, 91, 301–309.

Vaupel, J. W., Johnson, T. E., & Lithgow, G. J. (1994). Rates of mortality in populations of Caenorhabditis elegans. *Science*, 266, 826–826.

Vaupel, J. W., Carey, J. R., Christensen, K., Johnson, T. E., Yashin, A. I., Holm, N. V., Iachine, I. A., Kannisto, V., Khazaeli, A. A., Liedo, P., Longo, V. D., Zeng, Y., Manton, K. G., & Curtsinger, J. W. (1998). Biodemographic trajectories of longevity. *Science*, 280, 855–860.

Weindruch, R. & Walford, R. L. (1988). *The Retardation of Aging and Disease by Dietary Restriction*. Springfield, IL: Charles C Thomas.

Witkowski, J. M., & Miller, R. A. (1993). Increased function of P-glycoprotein in T lymphocytes of aging mice. *Journal of Immunology*, 150, 1296–1306.

Wolf, E., Kahnt, E., Ehrlein, J., Hermanns, W., Brem, G., & Wanke, R. (1993). Effects of long-term elevated serum levels of growth hormone on life expectancy of mice: lessons from transgenic animal models. *Mechanisms of Ageing and Development*, 68, 71–87.

Zhou, Y., Xu, B. C., Maheshwari, H. G., He, L., Reed, M., Lozykowski, M., Okada, S., Cataldo, L., Coschigamo, K., Wagner, T. E., Baumann, G., Kopchick, & JJ. (1997). A mammalian model for Laron syndrome produced by targeted disruption of the mouse growth hormone receptor/binding protein gene (the Laron mouse). *Proceedings of the National Academy of Sciences of the USA*, 94, 13215–13220.

Fifteen

Dietary Restriction: An Experimental Approach to the Study of the Biology of Aging

Edward J. Masoro

I. Introduction

It is more than 60 years since McCay and his colleagues (McCay *et al.*, 1935) published their landmark paper showing that restricting food intake of rats soon after weaning increases the length of life. In the ensuing years, this finding has been confirmed repeatedly. In addition, the life-extending action has also been shown in mice and hamsters as well as in nonmammalian species, such as fish, flies, and water fleas. The life extension appears to be due to the slowing of the aging processes. Indeed, this phenomenon, which is often referred to as the antiaging action of dietary restriction (DR) or caloric restriction (CR), has been and is one of the most active areas of research in biological gerontology. Detailed coverage of the research on DR prior to 1993, including references to the original literature, can be found in a review article by Masoro (1993) and an encyclopedic book by Weindruch and Walford (1988). This chapter will focus on more recent findings; however, earlier work will be discussed as needed to provide a proper context.

II. Rodent Models

Studies on rats and mice, the animal models most used in DR research, have provided detailed information on DR's antiaging actions, as well as insights on possible underlying biological mechanisms. In these studies, the food intake of the DR group ranged from 50–70% of that of a control group; in most but not all studies, the control groups were fed *ad libitum*.

A. Antiaging Actions of Dietary Restriction

The mortality characteristics of populations of rats and mice undergoing DR have provided strong support for an antiaging action. The effects of DR on age changes in physiological processes and on the occurrence and progression of age-associated diseases have supplied additional support.

1. Mortality Characteristics

As already stated, the findings of McCay et al. (1935) have been confirmed repeatedly in these numerous studies, both genders of several different genotypes of rats and mice have been used. In this regard, a study on the influence of DR on the survival characteristics of three rat genotypes and four mouse genotypes simultaneously maintained at the National Center for Toxicological Research in Jefferson, AR, is particularly impressive (Turturro et al., 1999).

In addition, it has been found that life prolongation is robust even when DR is initiated in young adult life rather than soon after weaning (Yu et al., 1985). Indeed, it has been found that DR initiated during early middle age significantly increases longevity in mice, though not as markedly as when started at earlier ages (Weindruch & Walford, 1982). This finding makes it clear that life prolongation by DR is not secondary to the prolongation of immaturity, a view initially proposed by McCay and his colleagues and long held by many. However, it is important to note that findings show that DR is not effective in prolonging life when initiated during late middle age or old age; when DR was started at 18 or 26 months of age in F344 × BN F1 hybrid male rats, there was no increase in longevity (Lipman et al., 1998).

In addition to reducing the amount of food eaten, DR also changes the temporal pattern of food intake, with a meal-eating pattern replacing a nibbling pattern. This raises the possibility that the altered pattern of food intake rather than the reduced amount of food consumption is responsible for the antiaging action. This possibility was investigated, and the findings clearly show that reduced food intake is the factor responsible (Masoro et al., 1995).

Gompertzian analyses of mortality characteristics of ad libitum fed and dietary restricted rat populations also strongly support the view that life prolongation by DR is due to its antiaging action. The analysis of mortality data from four rat studies, in which ingested food was about 60% of the ad libitum intake, showed that the mortality rate doubling time of the ad libitum fed rats ranged from 99–104 days and that of the dietary restricted rats ranged from 187–210 days (Holehan & Merry, 1986).

2. Physiological Functions

At advanced ages, most physiological processes of mice and rats on a DR regimen remain in a youthful state. Indeed, the number of functions thus affected by DR is so great that it is neither possible nor appropriate to provide anything approaching an encylopedic coverage in a chapter of this length. Rather, our discussion will be limited to those effects that, in the author's opinion, may play an important part in the antiaging action.

DR modulates several fundamental cellular processes that may be intimately involved in aging. For example, it is quite likely that damage to DNA plays an important role in aging. In response to ultraviolet irradiation damage, DNA repair decreases with age in mouse splenocytes (Licastro et al., 1988) and in rat liver and kidney cells (Weraarchakul et al., 1989). It is significant that, in these studies, DR was found to retard the age-related decline in DNA repair activity. There is suggestive evidence that DR has a similar action in mouse skin cells (Lipman et al., 1989). Also, cultured hepatocytes from old rats exhibit a compromised coupling of transcription and DNA repair, an age change that is prevented by DR (Guo et al., 1998a,b). It appears that the effect of DR on DNA repair depends on the type of DNA damage (Haley-Zitlin & Richardson, 1993). Indeed, a study indicates that the ability of DR to increase DNA repair is not universal; activities of DNA polymerases (enzymes involved in DNA repair) were found to be increased by DR in some, but not all, brain regions of the rat (Prapurna & Rao, 1996).

There is other evidence that DR helps maintain the stability of the nuclear and mitochondrial genomes with increasing age. DR markedly decreases the age-associated accumulation of mutations at the hypoxanthine phosphoribosyl transferase locus in mice (Dempsey et al., 1993). Also, DR initiated in rats at middle age decreases the accumulation of skeletal muscle mitochondrial deletions and enzyme abnormalities and retards the loss of muscle fibers (Aspnes et al., 1997).

Apoptosis eliminates damaged cells from the organism, and by so doing may protect the organism from deteriorative aspects of aging. Thus, it is significant that DR has been found to promote apoptosis in the liver of aging mice (Muskhelishvilli et al., 1995) and the small intestine and colon of aging rats (Holt et al., 1998). Moreover, apoptosis of preneoplastic cells is enhanced preferentially by DR in rats, thereby protecting them from carcinogenesis (Grasl-Kraup et al., 1994). James and Muskhelishvili (1994) have also linked DR's increase in hepatic apoptosis in mice to a decreased incidence in hepatoma. On the other hand, DR prevents the age-associated increase in the susceptibility of rat hepatocytes to cell death induced by the administration of cycloheximide (Higami et al., 1996).

Damaged proteins accumulate in cells with increasing age, which may well negatively impact cellular function. By degrading such proteins, proteolytic enzymes act to lessen this accumulation. However, protein degradation decreases with increasing age (Van Remmen et al., 1995). DR attenuates the age-associated decrease in proteolysis (Ward, 1988), and this action may well be an important component of its antiaging action. It was suggested that DR's modulation of the age change in proteolysis might be due to alterations in proteosomes; however, studies designed to address this issue indicate that such is not the case (Shibatani et al., 1996; Scrofano et al., 1998).

The functioning of cells is regulated by hormones, cytokines, and neurotransmitters, which bind to cell receptors and alter cellular function by a complex pathway of interlinked chemical reactions collectively referred to as cellular signal transduction. Change with age in receptors and/or signal transduction could cause cellular dysfunction, and such changes do occur with increasing age. For example, cholinergic and dopaminergic stimulation of the formation of inositol phosphates (signal transduction pathway components) is decreased with increasing age in the brain of male F344 rats, and this decrease is prevented by DR (Undie & Friedman, 1993). Also, DR prevents the age-associated impairment in rat brain of the mitogen-activated protein kinase (MAPK) signal pathways (Zhen et al., 1999).

With increasing age, there is a progressive impairment of the signal transduction pathway for growth hormone; DR was found to delay this impairment in mice (Xu & Sonntag, 1996a). Specifically, growth hormone activation of Stat–3 decreases with age, and DR prevents this decrease (Xu & Sonntag, 1996b). Is this action of DR important in its antiaging action? DR retards the age-associated decrease in protein biosynthesis (Van Remmen et al., 1995). DR has been shown to increase the amplitude of growth hormone pulses in old animals (Sonntag et al., 1995) and, by so doing, to sustain insulin-like growth factor-1 (IGF-1), which, in turn, sustains protein synthesis. By delaying age-associated impairment of the signal transduction pathway for growth hormone, DR probably enables increased amplitude of growth hormone pulses to effectively maintain IGF-1 production. This action and the increase by DR of type 1 IGF receptors are probably the major factors involved in the promotion of protein synthesis by DR (D'Costa *et al.*, 1993).

A key process in many cellular signal transduction pathways is the mobilization of intracellular calcium stores, thus increasing the concentration of cytoplasmic calcium ion. The ability of epinephrine to increase cytoplasmic calcium ion concentration in parotid acinar cells declines with advancing age in male F344 rats; DR blunts, but does not prevent, this decline (Salih *et al.*, 1997).

The limited amount of research indicates that modulating age changes in cellular signal transduction may be an important aspect of the antiaging action of DR. Further research in this area should be given high priority.

Because changes in gene expression occur with advancing age, at least some of these changes are likely to play an important role in aging. On the basis of the levels of mRNA transcripts as an index, the expression of some genes decreases and that of others increases, whereas the expression of many other genes does not change with increasing age. For example, the level of mRNA transcripts for both catalase and superoxide dismutase in the liver decrease with age, and DR counters this change (Van Remmen *et al.*, 1995).

The induction of hsp70 in rat hepatocytes in response to heat is the result of increased transcription. This induction, which decreases with increasing age, is enhanced at all ages by DR, an enhancement that correlates with an increase in binding of its transcription factor (Heydari *et al.*, 1993). However, DR decreases the expression of Er_p57, Er_p72, GRP170, calreticulin, and calnexin in

mouse liver (Dhahbi, *et al.*, 1997). DR was found to blunt the age-associated decrease in IL–2 expression in rat splenic T-cells and to increase the binding activity of transcription factor NFAT and the expression of c-fos, a component of the NFAT–protein complex (Pahlavani *et al.*, 1997).

The induction in the fasting state of hepatic gluconeogenic phosphoenolpyruvate carboxykinase decreases with advancing age, and DR prevents this decrease (Van Remmen & Ward, 1998). Whereas the synthesis of p^{53} and its phosphorylation in response to retinoic acid, which damages DNA, decreases with age, DR prevents this decrease (Pipkin *et al.*, 1997).

The information on the relation of gene expression, aging, and DR still is quite limited. Nevertheless, it is already clear that the influence of DR on gene expression increases the ability of the aging rodent to cope more effectively with challenges.

The neuroendocrine system (i.e., the hypothalamic–pituitary system) is a key player in the regulation of organismic function, and thus age-associated alterations in neuroendocrine function could have a major role in aging. Indeed, the neuroendocrine system is known to be involved in the aging of the female rodent's reproductive system. DR delays age-related loss of estrous cycles and promotes gonadotropin secretion by the adenohypophysis of aging female rats (McShane & Wise, 1996). In the female rat arcuate nucleus, DR differentially influences the expression of neuropeptides that regulate reproductive function, increasing neuropeptide Y mRNA per cell, decreasing proopiomelanocortin mRNA per cell, and not changing galanin mRNA per cell (McShane *et al.*, 1999).

DR also influences the neuroendocrine function in male rats. Within weeks of its initiation in young male rats, DR was found to decrease the mRNA content in the pituitary of luteinizing hormone, follicle-stimulating hormone, thyrotrophin, growth hormone, and prolactin, but not that of proopiomelanocortin (Han *et al.*, 1998). Whereas it is obvious that such alterations in pituitary function are almost certain to influence the functioning of many different cell types throughout the body, it is important that this work be extended to include old animals in which DR has been initiated at an early age. Although DR decreases growth hormone pulse amplitude in young rats, long-term DR increases the amplitude in old rats (Sonntag *et al.*, 1995); long-term DR acts by decreasing the translation of hypothalamic somatostatin–mRNA and, thus, the secretion of somatostatin into the hypothalamic–adenohypophyseal portal blood and possibly also by increasing the secretion of hypothalamic growth-hormone-releasing hormone. Long-term DR also increases the number of functional pituitary somatotropes (Shimokawa *et al.*, 1996a). Indeed, Sonntag *et al.*, (1999) propose that, by increasing growth hormone at advanced ages and maintaining low levels of IGF-I throughout life, DR decreases pathologies secondary to dysregulation of cell replication and thereby increases life span.

Much more research is needed on the relation of the neuroendocrine system to aging and its modulation by DR. What has been done to date indicates that such studies will be rewarding, particularly if they are carried out in conjunction with studies on cellular signal transduction pathways, because the action of the hormones of the neuroendocrine system on target cells is dependent on the functioning of these pathways.

Aging of the cardiovascular system causes functional problems for many elderly people. An age-associated loss in the response of the heart to β-adrenergic stimulation is one of these functional problems. This decrease in responsiveness also occurs in the hearts of aging rats, an effect that is countered by DR (Kelley & Herhihy, 1998). Also, studies using membrane preparations from rat ventricular muscle show an age-associated decline in isoproterenol-stimulated adenylyl cyclase activity, and this is attenuated by DR (Gao *et al.*, 1998). In addition, aging is known to reduce the capacity of cardiac adrenergic nerve terminals of male rats to release norepinephrine, and this reduced capacity is attentuated by DR (Snyder *et al.*, 1998).

Deterioration of the immune system occurs in humans and animal models with increasing age, and many gerontologists believe that this plays an important role in organismic aging. DR retards much, but not all, of this deterioration in mice and rats (Miller, 1995). For example, DR retards the age-related decline in the immune response of mice to the influenza A virus (Effros *et al.*, 1991); specifically, the decline in antigen presentation, T-cell proliferation, and antibody production in old mice is attenuated by a long-term DR regimen. Studies provide some insight on mechanisms underlying this protection. DR enhances the apoptotic elimination of nonfunctional T-cells in old mice (Spaulding *et al.*, 1997). In addition, DR delays the decline with age in circulating naive T-cells and in immature T-cell precursors in the thymus (Chen *et al.*, 1998). The extensive literature on the effect of DR on the immune system is available in a review by Pahlavani (1998).

Wound healing in rodents is impaired with increasing age, and long-term DR does not to retard this impairment (Reiser *et al.*, 1995; Roth *et al.*, 1997). A study on mice has shown that DR actually does maintain the youthful capacity to heal wounds, but for this action to be manifest requires an abundant intake of dietary energy just prior to and following the wounding (Reed *et al.*, 1996). Specifically, when provided with *ad libitum* feeding starting 4 weeks prior to wounding, old DR mice heal as rapidly as young *ad libitum* fed mice and much more rapidly than old mice fed *ad libitum* for their entire life. This increased capacity for wound repair appears to relate to an enhancement of collagen biosynthesis and cell proliferation. In regard to the latter, six cell types of male B6D2F1 mice have shown a diminished ability to proliferate by middle age. Whereas DR prevents this decrease in proliferative ability, 4 weeks of *ad libitum* feeding are required for this effect to be manifest (Wolf *et al.*, 1995).

3. Age-associated Diseases

From the late 1930s to the present time, many studies have shown that DR delays or, in some instances, prevents the occurrence of most age-associated diseases. These studies have involved many different rat and mouse genotypes, some with unique age-associated disease processes. The spectrum of such disease processes retarded by DR includes many different spontaneous neoplasms, degenerative diseases such as nephropathy and cardiomyopathy, and autoimmune diseases. For articles that summarize these findings, including citations of the original work, see Keenan *et al.*, (1995a,b), Lipman *et al.*, (1999a), Masoro (1993), and Weindruch and Walford (1988). A paper comparing the influence of DR on age-related lesions in three rat genotypes (F344, BN, and BNF3F1) is particularly informative (Lipman *et al.*, 1999b). Thus, there is no need to review this information in the present chapter, other than to point out a mechanistic study on the anticarcinogenic action of DR. On the basis of a study of bladder cancer in mice, Dunn *et al.*, (1997) propose that DR slows the progression of cancers by decreasing IGF-1 levels, thereby favoring apoptosis over cell proliferation.

The following studies are also worth mentioning. DR slows the development of lens cataracts in the cataract-prone Emory mouse strain (Taylor *et al.*, 1995). DR also retards the age-associated decrease in the proliferative capacity of mouse lens epithelial cells (Li *et al.*, 1997); whether this action plays a role in slowing cataract formation remains to be determined. In addition, DR was found to decrease blood pressure in spontaneously hypertensive, stroke-prone (SHR-SP) rats (Stevens *et al.*, 1998).

B. Nutritional Factor Responsible for Antiaging Action

The antiaging action of DR could be due to decreased intake of a specific nutrient or dietary contaminant or to reduced energy intake. Although manipulation of specific nutrients, such as reducing the intake of protein (Yu *et al.*, 1985), replacing casein with soy protein (Iwasaki *et al.*, 1988), or replacing sucrose with cornstarch (Murtagh-Mark *et al.*, 1995), can influence life span, their effects are small compared to those of DR. The use of semisynthetic diets to evaluate the effect of decreasing specific components has also provided strong evidence that it is the reduction in energy intake that is the major dietary factor underlying the life-prolonging and anticarcinogenic actions of DR (Masoro, 1992; Shimokawa *et al.*, 1996b). Indeed, it is for this reason that dietary restriction often is referred to as caloric restriction (CR).

It is unlikely that the reduced intake of a dietary toxic contaminant is significantly involved in the antiaging action. The findings with the semisynthetic diets, in which the amount of specific dietary components is manipulated as well as the many different food sources used in the different studies, just about preclude such a possibility.

C. Proposed Mechanisms of Antiaging Action

In their initial report, McCay et al. (1935) proposed a mechanism for the life-prolonging action of DR. Since then, many other mechanisms have been proposed. This keen interest in mechanism relates to the insights this knowledge could yield on the basic nature of aging and to the potential database it should provide for the development of antiaging interventions in humans.

1. Overview of Proposed Mechanisms

McCay et al. (1935) proposed that DR increased longevity by retarding growth and development. This view was held widely for quite some time, but further study found DR to be effective in extending life even when not initiated until young adulthood. Since then, other mechanisms have been proposed, many of which focus on the effect of DR on a specific functional characteristic. In addition, several are based on theories of the biological process(es) responsible for aging.

Two facts—that DR reduces the body fat content of rodents and that excess body fat is associated with the premature death of humans—led to the hypothesis that DR extends the length of life of rodents by reducing body fat content (Berg & Simms, 1960). This thinking lost favor when it was found that the life-extending action of DR can be dissociated from its effect on body fat content in rats (Bertrand et al., 1980) and mice (Harrison et al., 1984). However, the reduced body fat hypothesis has been "revisited" because research in the past 5 years has shown that adipose tissue secretes peptides (e.g., leptin) and cytokines (e.g., tumor necrosis factor) with powerful systemic actions that are capable of causing aging if present in excess (Barzilai & Gupta, 1999). By reducing fat content, it

is postulated that DR would decrease the secretion of many of these peptides and, in this way, slow aging. Indeed, DR does decrease plasma leptin levels, presumably by reducing body fat; this finding led Shimokawa and Higami (1999) to hypothesize that the decreased level of this neuroendocrine modulator plays a key role in the antiaging action of DR. Certainly further study is warranted on the association between longevity and total body fat mass as well as the mass of specific fat depots, especially now that noninvasive imaging technology is available. However, until this association is established, the "revisiting" of the reduced body fat hypothesis merely provides a list of potential humoral mechanisms for a phenomenon that may not exist.

As discussed earlier, DR enhances apoptosis. It has been hypothesized that enhanced apoptosis underlies both the antiaging and antitumorigenesis action of DR (Warner et al., 1995). Presumably, the efficient elimination of damaged, and thus probably dysfunctional, cells retards aging, and the elimination of precancerous cells would reduce the occurrence of cancer. However, as of now, there is little empirical evidence to support this hypothesis.

DR decreases body temperature in both mice and rats, though much more markedly in mice than in rats (Weindruch et al., 1995). On the basis of the concept that decreasing body temperature reduces the damage inherent in living processes, it has been postulated that the antiaging action of DR may be due, at least in part, to the reduction in body temperature. However, several lines of evidence indicate that the reduction in body temperature plays, if any, a minor role in the antiaging action. First, DR increases longevity to a similar extent in mice and rats, even though the decrease in body temperature is much greater in mice. Second, although lowering the body temperature of fish extends life span, DR can extend the life span of fish without lowering body temperature, and these two effects are additive (Walford, 1983). Finally, most of the actions of DR occur even in mice maintained in a thermal environment in which DR does not cause a decrease in body temperature (Koizumi et al., 1996). Although the extension of the length of life of the C57BL/6 strain of mouse by DR does not occur in such a thermal environment, this effect was found to be due to the loss in the ability of DR at that ambient temperature to prevent lymphoma development in this lymphoma-prone strain rather than to a loss in the ability to retard aging in general. However, some physiological responses induced by DR do not occur if the rodents are maintained at an environmental temperature that prevents a fall in body temperature (Weindruch et al, 1995). Also, lowering of the ambient temperature of several poikilothermic species has been found to to increase life span (Finch, 1990). Therefore, it seems apparent that one must keep an open mind regarding a possible role for a decrease in body temperature in the antiaging action of DR, although as of now, it seems unlikely that it plays a major role.

DR increases the physical activity of rodents (McCarter, 2000). Because exercise in humans is known to counter many of the effects of aging, the antiaging action of DR may be due, in part, to this effect on physical activity. However, a careful investigation of this possibilty has indicated that increased physical activity probably is not an important factor in the antiaging action of DR in rodents (McCarter et al., 1997).

Currently there are three hypotheses of the antiaging action of DR that appear to be promising; each is based on proximate biological processes that may underlie aging. These hypotheses are worthy of detailed consideration.

2. Oxidative Damage Attenuation Hypothesis

Molecular oxidative damage is due to the interaction of reactive oxygen molecules, such as the hydroxyl and superoxide radicals, with cellular lipids, proteins, and nucleic acids. These reactive oxygen molecules are generated by intrinsic living processes as well as by environmental interactions. The phenomenon is referred to as oxidative stress, and it has been hypothesized that DR retards aging by attenuating oxidative stress (Sohal & Weindruch, 1996). There is much evidence that DR does, indeed, retard the age-associated cellular accumulation of oxidatively damaged molecules (Yu, 1996).

DR suppresses the age-associated increase in the rate of exhalation of ethane and pentane by rats, indicating its attenuation of lipid peroxidation (Matsuo et al., 1993). Also, DR has been shown to slow the increase with age in lipid peroxidation in the kidney, liver, and brain of rats (Cook & Yu, 1998). In what is probably a related action, DR decreases the loss in fluidity of biological membranes with advancing age (Pieri, 1997; Yu et al., 1992).

DR also decreases the age-associated increase in oxidatively damaged proteins in rats (Aksenova et al., 1998; Youngman et al., 1992) and mice (Dubey et al., 1996; Sohal et al., 1994b). Specifically, it attenuates the increase with age in the carbonylation of proteins and also decreases the age-associated loss of sulfhydryl groups of proteins.

DR blunts the age-associated increase in the ratio of 8-hydroxy-2'-deoxyguanosine residues to 2'-deoxyguanosine residues in rats, an indication that it decreases the accumulation of oxidatively damaged DNA (Chung et al., 1992). DR also protects mice from the age-associated accumulation of oxidatively damaged DNA (Sohal et al., 1994a).

This attenuation of the age-associated increase in oxidatively damaged molecules means that DR either (1) decreases the rate of generation of reactive oxygen molecules or (2) increases the effectiveness of protective and repair processes, including removal of damaged molecules and their replacement by biosynthesis. Indeed, a combination of these processes may be involved.

It is often stated that hypometabolism is the mechanism by which DR retards the aging processes. This makes sense because reactive oxygen generation would be expected to decrease in hypometabolic states, and there may well be circumstances in which DR lowers the metabolic rate. However, in both rats and mice, DR shows a marked antiaging action without lowering of the rate of metabolism per unit of lean body mass (Duffy et al., 1991; McCarter & Palmer, 1992). In a report by Greenberg and Boozer (2000), the method of using lean body mass to normalize for body size is cited as the reason DR has been reported not to decrease the metabolic rate. The authors proposed that normalizing for the combined weight of the heart, kidneys, brain, and liver provides more reliable findings. When the authors did this with 22-month-old male F344 rats, it was found that DR did not lower the metabolic rate. They hypothesize that they would have found DR to decrease the metabolic rate if they had studied 6-to 18-month-old rats. Apparently, these authors feel they know the correct answer and now seek the correct model to prove it.

The unsubstantiated claim that DR retards aging by causing hypometabolism has an unfortunate effect. This is well-illustrated by a recent hypothesis on the mechanism by which DR retards aging (Imai et al., 2000). This hypothesis proposes that the DR-induced reduction in metabolic rate decreases the availability of NAD, which causes an up-regula-tion of the deacylation activity of Sir2 proteins and chromatin silencing; it is further postulated that the persistence of genomic silencing slows aging-related processes. Apparently, the proponents of this hypothesis were unaware of the studies showing that DR can retard aging without decreasing the metabolic rate. Alas, both the lay and the scientific press published stories based on the Imai et al. (2000) hypothesis that, worse yet suggested that the way DR increases life span had been uncovered! Clearly, the claim that the antiaging action of DR is due to hypometabolism is misleading and should be avoided.

Moreover, there need not be a decrease in metabolic rate to decrease the generation of reactive oxygen species. Indeed, DR has been found to decrease the rate of mitochondrial generation of superoxide radicals and hydrogen peroxide in the brain, kidney, and heart of mice (Sohal & Dubey, 1994). DR also decreases cyclooxygenase expression and cyclooxy-genase-derived reactive oxygen species (Chung et al., 1999).

The enhancement of antioxidant defenses is another way that DR could decrease molecular oxidative damage (Yu et al., 1989). Early reports on antioxi-dant enzymes supported this possibility (Koizumi et al., 1987; Mote et al., 1991; Rao et al., 1990). However, subsequent studies have not demonstrated DR's consistent enhancement of these enzymes (Gong et al., 1997; Rojas et al., 1993; Sohal et al., 1994b). In fact, DR has been found to attenuate the age-associated increase in rat skeletal muscle antioxidant enzyme activities (Luhtala et al., 1994). This report appears to contradict the finding that DR forestalls the age-associated decrease in the level of liver catalase and superoxide dismutase mRNA (Van Remmen et al., 1995). The apparent discrepancy may be due to differences between muscle and liver or due to the fact that mRNA levels were measured in liver whereas enzyme activities were assessed in skeletal muscle.

Clearly, the effect of DR on antioxidant defenses is complex and requires further study to reconcile apparently conflicting findings. Recent studies provide a good start. Cellular glutathione levels decrease with age but DR maintains youthful levels, particularly of mitochondrial glutathione, into advanced ages, and this may provide a major defense against oxidative damage (Armeni et al., 1998). Also, DR blunts the age-associated increase in the iron content of kidney, brain, and liver, an effect that may well attenuate lipid peroxidation (Cook & Yu, 1998). In addition, long-term DR has been found to protect mouse lens epithelial cells from damage due to exposure to H_2O_2 (Li et al., 1998) and to protect mitochondrial gene transcription against the damage of peroxyl radicals (Kristal & Yu, 1998).

As discussed earlier, DR increases repair processes. It enhances the repair of oxidatively damaged DNA. It also increases the removal of damaged proteins by proteolysis and their replacement with newly synthesized proteins (Van Remmen et al., 1995).

In summary, the evidence that DR protects against oxidative molecular damage is overwhelming; moreover, the processes underlying this protection are understood at least in broad outline. Is this protection the primary mechanism responsible for the antiaging action of DR? To answer this question requires that another question be addressed. Is oxidative stress a major factor responsible for aging in rodents? Whereas many would be inclined to answer this question in the affirmative, clear evidence that such is the case is not yet at hand.

3. Glucose–Insulin Hypothesis

Hyperglycemia and hyperinsulinemia are known to cause aging-like damage (LevRan, 1998; Parr, 1996; Reaven, 1989). Dietary restricted rats have been found to sustain lower plasma glucose concentrations and markedly lower plasma insulin concentrations than rats fed ad libitum, although they utilize glucose fuel at the same rate per gram of body mass to the 3/4 power (Masoro et al., 1992). These findings led to the glucose–insulin hypothesis, that is, maintenance of reduced levels of plasma glucose and insulin without compromising glucose fuel use is, at least in part, responsible for the antiaging action of DR (Masoro, 1996).

Further, it appears that the major factor in the ability of DR rodents to sustain glucose fuel use at reduced plasma glucose and insulin levels relates to enhanced insulin-stimulated glucose transport in the skeletal muscles (Cartee et al., 1994). The glucose transporter GLUT–4 accounts for just about all of the insulin-stimulated glucose transport in muscle. Although DR does not change the level of skeletal muscle GLUT–4, it increases the fraction of the GLUT–4 located at the plasma membrane of the muscle cell during insulin stimulation (Dean et al., 1998a). The reduction in plasma insulin during DR is attributable in large part to decreased insulin secretion by the β-cells of the pancreatic islets (Dean et al., 1998b).

Whereas there has been good progress in defining the mechanisms by which DR decreases plasma glucose and insulin levels while maintaining glucose fuel use, scant evidence has accrued that directly supports the glucose–insulin hypothesis. Specifically, there is little evidence for the retardation of aging because of the sustained reduction in glycemia and insulinemia below that of normoglycemic and normoinsulinemic levels. By decreasing glycation and glycoxidation, lower plasma glucose levels could slow aging. DR has been reported to decrease the formation of advanced glycation end-products in rats (Cefalu et al., 1995;

Reiser, 1994). Another study found that DR decreased the age-associated accumulation of these glycation products in skin collagen, but not aortic collagen (Novelli *et al.*, 1998). It is clear that further research aimed at testing the glucose–insulin hypothesis is needed.

4. Hormesis Hypothesis

Although the oxidative stress attenuation hypothesis and the glucose–insulin hypothesis probably define important aspects of the antiaging action of DR, they may be too tightly focused. The hormesis hypothesis broadens the scope to include protection from a spectrum of damage (Masoro, 1998). In this discussion, hormesis is defined as follows: *Hormesis is the beneficial action(s) resulting from the response of an organism to a low-intensity stressor.*

The first question that needs to be considered is whether DR, as used in experimental gerontology, is a low-intensity stressor. The best evidence that it is a low-intensity stressor can be seen in its effects on the glucocorticoid system. Rats on DR show a modest, but significant, daily elevation in the afternoon peak concentration of plasma-free corticosterone (Sabatino *et al.*, 1991).

Is there evidence that DR has beneficial actions in addition to its antiaging action? Altough there is no evidence available in regard to long-term moderate-intensity stressors, there is abundant evidence that DR protects rodents of all ages from damage due to intense, acute stressors. The following provide examples of the scope of this protection. The acute weight loss in rats following a surgical procedure is reduced markedly by DR (Masoro, 1998). DR attenuates the inflammatory response resulting from injection of carageenan into the foot pad of young mice (Klebanov *et al.*, 1995). The ability of rats to survive a sudden marked increase in environmental temperature is enhanced greatly by DR (Heydari *et al.*, 1993). DR protects rodents from the acute damaging action of toxic drugs (Duffy *et al.*, 1995).

Does DR's increased ability to cope with acute, intense stressors have anything to do with DR's antiaging action? There are two reasons for an affirmative answer. First, genetic manipulations of fruit flies, nematodes, and yeast have yielded genotypes with extended life spans and, thus, presumably a decreased rate of aging; at all ages, these genotypes showed an increased ability to cope with intense stressors (Martin *et al.*, 1996). Second, in all species, the major cause of aging appears to be unrepaired damage due to long-term intrinsic and environmental damaging processes or agents. Thus, hormesis, the increased ability to cope with damaging processes and agents, is likely to be the major factor in the antiaging action of DR.

What are the proximate mechanisms that might underlie the protective actions of hormesis? A spectrum of protective and repair processes probably is involved. Stress response genes are likely candidates. Indeed, DR has been found to enhance the expression of heat-shock proteins in response to stress (Aly *et al.*, 1994; Heydari *et al.*, 1993, 1995; Moore *et al.*, 1998).

Another likely proximate mechanism is the hypothalamic–hypophyseal–adrenal cortical glucocorticoid system, which is known to play an important role in the ability of vertebrates to cope with damage (Munck *et al.*, 1984). Rats undergoing DR maintain elevated maximal daily plasma concentrations of free glucocorticoid throughout the life span (Sabatino *et al.*, 1991). It has been proposed that the elevated levels of glucocorticoid enable the rodent to better cope with the daily insults that cause aging, including damage secondary to the responses of primary defense systems, such as immune and inflammatory reactions. Indeed, it has been shown that the ability of DR to protect against chemically induced tumors is lost if the mice are adrenalectomized (Pashko & Schwartz, 1992).

Clearly, many of the actions of DR, including the antiaging action, are within the realm of hormesis. However, further work is needed to fully define the proximate mechanisms by which hormesis retards the aging processes.

D. Evolution of the Antiaging Actions of Dietary Restriction

Holliday (1989) hypothesized that the antiaging action of DR evolved in nature in response to periods of scant food supply. Specifically, he proposed a survival advantage for those animals that have genomes enabling them to respond to food shortage by diverting energy from reproduction to somatic maintenance. He further postulated that, when there is a sustained reduction in the availability of food (e.g., DR in an experimental setting), the diversion of energy to maintenance continues; in line with the disposable soma theory, this slows the aging processes. Masoro and Austad (1996) expanded this view, emphasizing the role of unpredictable periods of food shortages and the importance for survival of the diversion of energy to cope with enviromental challenges. The expanded version of the evolution of the antiaging action of DR embraces both the disposable soma theory and the hormesis concept.

Walford and Spindler (1997) agree that the antiaging action of DR derives from the evolutionary adaptation to food shortage. Based on metabolic characteristics, they feel the antiaging action is one of a family of such adaptations, which includes hibernation.

Hart and Turturro (1998) proposed an evolutionary concept of the antiaging action of DR similar to that of Holliday, in which they too utilize, without so

stating, the disposable soma theory of aging. The only new contributions from their proposal are the speculations about the cellular and metabolic bases of the antiaging action.

III. Nonhuman Primate Models

Does DR retard aging in humans? This has been debated for a long time. Unfortunately, it is not possible to provide a definitive answer because a carefully designed and executed investigation with human subjects has not been done, nor is it likely such a study will ever be done. In lieu of this, nonhuman primates are being studied in this regard, for if DR retards aging in these animal models, it is likely to do so in humans.

A. Ongoing Studies

There are three major ongoing studies of DR in rhesus monkeys. One is an intramural study conducted by the National Institute on Aging (NIA) (Ingram et al., 1990). In this NIA study of male and female monkeys, DR refers to food intake 30% below that of a control group. DR was initiated at 1–2 years of age, 3–5 years of age, or greater than 15 years of age. (The maximum life span of the rhesus monkey is estimated at 40 years.) Most of the monkeys are utilized in long-term, longitudinal studies, but some are assigned to short-term, cross-sectional studies.

Another study on male and female rhesus monkeys is being carried out at the University of Wisconsin (UW) (Kemnitz et al., 1993). In the UW Study, DR was initiated at 8–14 years of age, but the 30% reduction in food intake is 30% below that of the intake of the same animal during the period just prior to the initiation of DR. Most of the monkeys in this program are used in long-term, longitudinal studies, but some are assigned to short-term, cross-sectional studies.

The third study, the UM study, emerged from ongoing obesity and diabetes mellitus research at the University of Maryland (Hansen & Bodkin, 1993). In this long-term, longitudinal design, DR was initiated in male rhesus monkeys at 11–12 years of age. The level of restriction is that needed to maintain a stable body weight of 10–12 kg. Thus, in this study, the control monkeys are allowed to become obese with increasing age. Indeed, the food intake of the DR monkeys in the UM study is such that their body weight and composition are similar to those of the control group of the NIA study. Therefore, the UM study differs from the NIA study and the UW study in regard to the level of food intake of the DR monkeys, and this difference must be kept in mind when comparing the results of the studies.

B. Dietary Restriction and Body Composition

In the UW study, body composition is assessed semiannually. The results of 7.5 years of such assessment have been reported (Colman et al., 1999). DR resulted in less total body fat and a lower percentage of body fat in the abdominal region. In addition, the animals had a sustained reduction in plasma leptin levels. The DR monkeys also sustained a small, but significantly lower lean body mass than the control group. DR was found to have similar effects on total fat mass and lean body mass in the NIA study (Lane et al., 1997b). As might be expected from the study design, the rhesus monkeys on DR in the UM study have less body fat than the control monkeys (Hansen & Bodkin, 1993).

C. Dietary Restriction and Physiological Characteristics

No attempt will be made here to present all the changes that DR has been found to produce in nonhuman primates. Rather, those changes will be discussed that may indicate a possible antiaging action based on the rodent studies or on current views of the biological nature of mammalian aging.

The effect on metabolic rate is a good starting point. In the NIA Study, metabolic rate per kilogram of lean body mass declined upon initiation of DR, but rose to that of control animals during long-term DR (Lane et al., 1995a). In the UW Study, DR was reported to decrease metabolic rate per kilogram of lean body mass during the first 30 months (Ramsey et al., 1997), but by 42 months it was no longer decreased (Ramsey et al., 1996). In the UM study, the metabolic rate per kilogram of lean body mass remained decreased even after 10 years of DR (DeLaney et al., 1999).

In the NIA study, the influence of DR on motor activity was not consistent, with only one of the two groups of monkeys studied exhibiting an increase in activity (Weed et al., 1997). In the UM Study, DR increased motor activity compared to age-matched controls; however, if activity was adjusted for differences in body size, DR had no effect on motor activity (DeLaney et al, 1999).

In the NIA study, body temperature was decreased by DR (Lane et al., 1996). No such effect on body temperature was observed in the UM study (DeLaney et al., 1999).

In the UW study, long-term DR decreased fasting plasma glucose and insulin levels and increased insulin sensitivity (Kemnitz et al., 1994). The increase in insulin action was not associated with a change in the abundance of GLUT4 glucose transporter, phosphatidylinositol 3-kinase, or insulin receptor substrate (Gazdag et al., 2000). DR also lowered fasting plasma glucose and insulin levels in the monkeys of the NIA study (Lane et al., 1995b). In the UM study, DR lowered fasting plasma insulin levels and increased insulin sensitivity, but did not decrease fasting plasma glucose levels (Bodkin *et al.*, 1995).

DR also influences the plasma lipoproteins of rhesus monkeys. It increases the level of the HDL_2 fraction of plasma high-density lipoproteins (Verdery *et al.*, 1997) and changes the structure of the low-density lipoproteins so as to decrease their interaction with arterial proteoglycans (Edwards *et al.*, 1998).

Whereas other data have been reported on physiological characteristics influenced by DR, the relationship of most of these findings to possible antiaging action is not evident. However, two such findings may have bearing and therefore should be mentioned. First, there is an age-associated decline in serum dehydroepiandrosterone sulfate in the rhesus monkey, and this decline is slowed by DR (Lane *et al.*, 1997a). Second, DR lowers serum insulin-like growth factor-1 and growth hormone in rhesus monkeys (Cocchi *et al.*, 1995).

The major physiologic responses to DR in the three long-term studies of rhesus monkeys are summarized in Table I. Again it must again be emphasized that the design of the UM study differs from that of the NIA and UW studies, in that the food intake of the DR monkeys in the UM study is considerably greater than that in the other two studies. This fact must be kept in mind when comparing the findings of the three studies.

It should also be noted that a short-term DR research program is being carried out on cynomolgus monkeys. Early findings indicate that the effects of DR on body fat and carbohydrate metabolism in this species are similar to those found with rhesus monkeys (Cefalu *et al.*, 1997).

D. Dietary Restriction and Disease Processes

Whereas a great deal of detailed histopathological data on the effects of DR on rodents has been published, such data are not yet available for nonhuman primates. However, the following risk factors for age-associated disease have been assessed: body fat mass and distribution, carbohydrate metabolism, and serum lipoproteins. On the basis of these findings, it appears likely that long-term DR will retard age-associated cardiovascular disease in rhesus monkeys. Moreover, DR prevents the development of type II diabetes in the rhesus monkey (Hansen & Bodkin, 1993). Also, in male rhesus monkeys of ages greater than 18 years, risk factors for cardiovascular disease and diabetes decreased during the first 12 months of DR (Lane *et al.*, 2000).

Table I
Summary of Salient Physiological Responses of Rhesus Monkeys to DR

Physiological characteristic	NIA study	UW study	UM study
Decreased body fat	Yes	Yes	Yes
Decreased lean body mass	Yes	Yes	—
Decreased metabolic rate:			
Short-term	Yes	Yes	Yes
Long-term	No	No	Yes
Decreased body temperature	Yes	—	No
Decreased fasting plasma glucose	Yes	Yes	No
Decreased fasting plasma insulin	Yes	Yes	Yes
Increased insulin sensitivity	—	Yes	Yes

E. Evaluation of Possible Antiaging Action

DR has a broad spectrum of physiological effects in rodents, many of which also occur in nonhuman primates. This provides some indication that DR may have an antiaging action in monkeys similar to that seen in rats and mice. However, this possibility must be tempered by the fact that, in rodents, the relationship between a particular physiological effect and the antiaging action of DR has yet to be established. On a positive note, several of the physiological modifications caused by DR in monkeys decrease known risk factors for age-associated disease. It has been suggested that the antiaging action of DR can be assessed by measuring suitable biomarkers of aging (Roth et al., 1999). Unfortunately, clear evidence of the existence of one or more suitable biomarkers has yet to emerge.

A longevity study using rhesus monkeys is in the planning stage at the National Institute on Aging (Roth et al., 1999). The results of such a study, including histopathological assessments combined with the physiological assessments now underway, should provide a definitive answer to the question of the antiaging action of DR in nonhuman primates. However, it must be noted that it will take 20 or more years to complete all of this work, even if the study is launched in the immediate future.

IV. Insights from Dietary Restriction Studies

The fact that DR has such a marked anti-aging action in rodent models makes it an important tool for learning about the basic biological processes underlying mammalian aging. Uncovering the mechanism or mechanisms by which DR retards aging is likely to yield a database that would be invaluable in the search for human antiaging interventions.

A. Biological Processes Underlying Aging

The findings to date from DR studies provide support for three of the current concepts of the biological basis of aging. That DR protects rodents from an age-associated increase in cellular oxidative damage adds further support for the oxidative stress theory of aging. The fact that rodents on DR regimens sustain lower plasma glucose levels and much lower plasma insulin levels lends credence to the view that glycemia and insulinemia are important factors in mammalian aging. Finally, the ability of DR to protect rodents from a range of stressors, coupled with the genetic evidence on the relation between aging and the resistance to stressors in invertebrate models, points to low-intensity, long-term stressors likely playing a major role in aging.

B. Potential Antiaging Interventions

Even if long-term DR were demonstrated conclusively to have a strong antiaging action in humans, it is not likely that many would make use of it. However, understanding the mechanism(s) underlying the antiaging action of DR in rodents could well yield insights on the kinds of specific interventions likely to retard aging in many mammalian species, including humans. The development of pharmacological agents with antiaging actions similar to those of DR is a particularly promising possibility once the basic mechanism(s) is (are) known.

V. Future Research Directions

The future direction of research on DR in nonhuman primates seems to be outlined clearly. The goal should be to establish, without equivocation, that DR does slow the aging processes in the rhesus monkey and to do so requires determination of its effects on longevity and on the occurrence and progression of age-associated diseases. These are daunting but doable studies.

The rodent model should continue to be used in searching for the mechanism(s) underlying the antiaging action of DR. Transgenic models that overexpress or underexpress specific genes are one approach that is being pursued actively. For such findings to be interpretable, manipulations must alter one or more characteristics in a fashion similar to DR. If the antiaging action of DR is due to the alteration of a specific characteristic, e.g., decreased plasma glucose concentration, then such an approach can yield easily interpretable results. However, because the antiaging action of DR may well be due to the simultaneous alteration of several characteristics, there is a good chance that transgenic technology may provide little insight. Moreover, it is technically challenging to establish that a transgenic model is altered only in regard to the DR characteristic(s) being assessed.

Almost the opposite approach is provided by gene expression profile methodology, in which a broad array of genes is assessed. This approach enables the identification of patterns of genes that change with age and dietary restriction. However, this approach does have pitfalls, as revealed by a report on the effect of DR on gene expression in skeletal muscles of mice (Lee et al., 1999). Of the 6347 genes monitored, the expression of 113 changed with age. Most of these changes were completely or partially prevented by DR. This many genes being affected by DR, even when only a small fraction (5–10%) of the genome is being assessed, presents the investigators with an interpretational dilemma. The authors of this paper tried to make sense of the findings by interpreting the data in terms of alterations of genes expressing enzymes involved in energy metabolism. However, this interpretation is based on a preconceived view of the mechanism of the antiaging action of DR, an approach replete with hazards. Another problem made evident by the report of this study is the need to verify the results of this technology by another independent method; the authors did not do this and, indeed, to do so involves a substantial amount of additional work.

Thus, future research on mechanisms of the antiaging action of DR will not be easy. However, careful, thoughtful application of these new methodologies as well as others that are sure to emerge should bear fruit in the long run.

References

Aksenova, M. V., Aksenov, M. Y., Carney, J. M., & Rutterfield, D. A. (1998). Protein oxidation and enzyme activity decline in old brown Norway rats are reduced by dietary restriction. *Mechanisms of Ageing and Development, 100,* 157–168.

Aly, K. B, Pipkin, J. L., Hinson, W. G., Feuers, R. J., Duffy, P. R., Lyn-Cook, L., & Hart, R. (1994). Chronic caloric restriction induces stress proteins in the hypothalamus of rats. *Mechanisms of Ageing and Development, 76,* 11–23.

Armeni, T., Pieri, C., Marra, M., Saccucci, F., & Principato, G. (1998). Studies on the life prolonging effect of food restriction: Glutathione levels and glyoxylase enzymes in rat liver. *Mechanisms of Ageing and Development, 101,* 101–110.

Aspnes, L. E., Lee, C. M., Weindruch, R., Chung, S., Roecker, E. B., & Aiken, J. M. (1997). Caloric restriction reduces fiber loss and mitochondrial abnormalities in aged rat muscle. *FASEB Journal, 11,* 573–581.

Barzilai, N., & Gupta, G. (1999). Revisiting the role of fat mass in the life extension induced by caloric restriction. *Journal of Gerontology: Biological Sciences, 54A,* B89–B96.

Berg, B. N., & Simms, H. S. (1960). Nutrition and longevity in the rat. II. Longevity and the onset of disease with different levels of intake. *Journal of Nutrition, 71*, 255–263.

Bertrand, H. A., Lynd, F. T., Masoro, E. J., & Yu, B. P. (1980). Changes in adipose tissue mass and cellularity through adult life of rats fed ad libitum or a life-prolonging restricted diet. *Journal of Gerontology, 35*, 827–835.

Bodkin, N. L., Ortmeyer, H.K., & Hansen, B. C. (1995). Long-term dietary restriction in older-aged rhesus monkeys: Effects on insulin resistance. *Journal of Gerontology: Biological Sciences, 50A*, B142–B147.

Cartee, G. D., Kietzke, E. W., & Briggs-Tung, C. (1994). Adaptation of muscle glucose transport with caloric restriction in adult, middle-aged, and old rats. *American Journal of Physiology, 266*, R1443–R1447.

Cefalu, W. T., Bell-Farrow, A. D., Wang, Z. Q., Sonntag, W. E., Fu, M.-X, Baynes, J. W., & Thorpe, S. R. (1995). Caloric restriction decreases age-dependent accumulation of the glycoxidation products, N^e-(carboxymethyl)lysine and pentosidine, in rat skin collagen. *Journal of Gerontology: Biological Sciences, 50A*, B337–B341.

Cefalu, W. T., Wagner, J. D., Wang, Z. Q., Bell-Farrow, A. D., Collins, J., Haskell, D., Bechtold, R., & Morgan, T. (1997). A study of caloric restriction and cardiovascular aging in cynomolgus monkeys (*Macaca fascicularis*): A model for aging research. *Journal of Gerontology: Biological Sciences, 52A*, B10–B19.

Chen, J., Astle, C. M., & Harrison, D. E. (1998). Delayed immune aging in diet-restricted B6CBAT6F1 mice is associated with preservation of naive T cells. *Journal of Gerontology: Biological Sciences, 53A*, B330–B337.

Chung, H.-Y., Kim, H.-J., Shim, K.-H., & Kim, K.-W. (1999). Dietary modulation of prostanoid synthesis in the aging process: Role of cyclooxygenase. *Mechanisms of Ageing and Development, 111*, 97–106.

Chung, M. H., Kasai, H., Nishimura, S., & Yu, B. P. (1992). Protection of DNA damage by dietary restriction. *Free Radical Biology and Medicine, 12*, 523–525.

Cocchi, D., Cattaneo, L., Lane, M. A., Ingram, D. K., Cutler, R. G., & Roth, G. S. (1995). Effect of long-term dietary restriction on the somatotrophic axis in adult and aged monkeys. *Neuroendocrinology Letters, 17*, 181–186.

Colman, R. J., Ramsey, J. J., Roecker, E. B., Havighurst, T., Hudson, J. C. & Kemnitz, J. W. (1999). Body fat distribution with long-term dietary restriction in adult male rhesus macaques. *Journal of Gerontology: Biological Sciences, 54A*, B283–B290.

Cook, C. J., & Yu, B. P. (1998). Iron accumulation in aging: Modulation by dietary restriction. *Mechanisms of Ageing and Development, 102*, 1–13.

D'Costa, A. P., Lenham, J. E., Ingram, R. L., & Sonntag, W. E. (1993). Moderate caloric restriction increases type 1 IGF receptors and protein synthesis in rats. *Mechanisms of Ageing and Development, 71*, 59–71.

Dean, D. J., Brozinick, Jr., J. T., Cushman, S. W., & Cartee, G. D. (1998a). Calorie restriction increases cell surface GLUT–4 in insulin-stimulated skeletal muscle. *American Journal of Physiology, 275*, E957–E964.

Dean, D. J., Gazdag, A. C., Wetter, T. J., & Cartee, G. D. (1998b). Comparison of the effects of 20 days and 15 months of calorie restriction on male Fischer 344 rats. *Aging: Clinical and Experimental Research, 10*, 303–307.

DeLaney, J. P., Hansen, B. C., Bodkin, N. L., Hannah, J., & Bray, G. A. (1999). Long-term calorie restriction reduces energy expenditure in aging monkeys. *Journal of Gerontology: Biological Sciences, 54A*, B5–B11.

Dempsey, J. L., Pfeiffer, M., & Morley, A. A. (1993). Effect of dietary restriction on *in vivo* somatic mutation in mice. *Mutation Research, 291*, 141–145.

Dhahbi, J. M., Mote, P. L., Tillman, J. B., Walford, R. L., & Spindler, S. R. (1997). Dietary energy tissue-specifically regulates endoplasmic reticulum chaperone gene expression in liver of mice. *Journal of Nutrition, 127*, 1758–1764.

Dubey, A., Forster, M. J., Lal, H., & Sohal, R. S. (1996). Effect of age and caloric intake on protein oxidation in different brain regions and on behavioral functions of the mouse. *Archives of Biochemistry and Biophysics, 333*, 189–197.

Duffy, P. H., Feuers, R. J., Leakey, J. E. A., & Hart, R. W. (1991). Chronic caloric restriction in old female mice: changes in circadian rhythms of physiological and behavioral variables. In L. Fishbein (Ed.), *Biological Effects of Dietary Restriction* (pp. 245–263). Berlin: Springer-Verlag.

Duffy, P. H., Feuers, R. J., Pipkin, J. L., Berg, T. F., Leakey, J. E. A., Turturro, A., & Hart, R. W. (1995). The effect of dietary restriction and aging on physiological response of rodents to drugs. In R. W, Hart, D. A. Neuman, & R. T. Robertson (Eds.), *Dietary Restriction: Implications for the Design and Interpretation of Toxicity and Carcinogenicity Studies* (pp. 125–140). Washington, DC: ILSI Press.

Dunn, S. E., Kari, F. W., French, J., Leininger, J. R., Travlos, G., Wilson, R., & Barrett, J. C. (1997). Dietary restriction reduces insulin-like growth factor I levels, which modulates apoptosis, cell proliferation, and tumor progression in p^{53}-deficient mice. *Cancer Research*, 57, 4667–4672.

Edwards, I. J., Rudel, L. L., Terry, J. G., Kemnitz, J. W., Weindruch, R., & Cefalu, W. T. (1998). Caloric restriction in rhesus monkeys reduces low density lipoprotein interaction with arterial proteoglycans. *Journal of Gerontology: Biological Sciences*, 53A, B443–B448.

Effros, R. B., Walford, R. L., Weindruch, R., & Mitcheltree, C. (1991). Influence of dietary restriction on immunity to influenza in aged mice. *Journal of Gerontology: Biological Sciences*, 46, B142–B147.

Finch, C. E. (1990). *Longevity, Senescence, and the Genome*, Chicago: University of Chicago Press.

Gao, E., Snyder, D. L., Roberts, J., Friedman, E., Cai, G., Pelleg, A., & Horwitz, J. (1998). Age-related decline in beta adrenergic and adenosine A_1 receptor function in the heart are attenuated by dietary restriction. *Journal of Pharmacology and Experimental Therapeutics*, 285, 186–192.

Gazdag, A. C., Sullivan, S., Kemnitz, J. W., & Cartee, G. D. (2000). Effect of long-term caloric restriction on GLUT4, phosphatidylinositol-3 kinase p85 subunit, and insulin receptor substrate–1 protein levels in rhesus monkey skeletal muscle. *Journal of Gerontology: Biological Sciences*, 55A, B44–B46.

Gong, X, Shang, F., Obin, M., Palmer, H., Scofrano, M. M., Jahngen-Hodge, J., Smith, D. E., & Taylor, A. (1997). Antioxidant enzyme activities in lens, liver, and kidney of calorie restricted Emory mice. *Mechanisms of Ageing and Development*, 99, 181–192.

Grasl-Kraup, B., Bursch, W., Ruttky-Nedecky, B., Wagner, A., Lauer, B. C., & Schulte-Hermann, R. (1994). Food restriction eliminates preneoplastic cells through apoptosis and antagonizes carcinogenesis in rat liver. *Proceedings of the National Academy of Sciences of the USA*, 91, 9995–9999.

Greenberg, J. A., & Boozer, C. N. (2000). Metabolic mass, metabolic rate, caloric restriction, and aging in male Fischer 344 rats. *Mechanisms of Ageing and Development*, 113, 37–48.

Guo, Z. M., Heydari, A., & Richardson, A. (1998a). Nucleotide excision repair of actively transcribed versus nontranscribed DNA in rat hepatocytes: Effect of age and dietary restriction. *Experimental Cell Research*, 245, 228–238.

Guo, Z. M., Van Remmen, H., Wu, W-T, & Richardson, A. (1998b). Effect of cAMP-induced transcription on the repair of the phosphoenolpyruvate carboxykinase gene by hepatocytes isolated from young and old rats. *Mutation Research*, 409, 37–48.

Haley-Zitkin, V., & Richardson, A. (1993). Effect of dietary restriction on DNA repair and DNA damage. *Mutation Research*, 295, 237–245.

Han, E., Lu, D. H., & Nelson, J. F. (1998). Food restriction differentially affects mRNAs encoding the major anterior pituitary tropic hormones. *Journal of Gerontology: Biological Sciences*, 53A, B322–B329.

Hansen, B. C., & Bodkin, N. L. (1993). Primary prevention of diabetes mellitus by prevention of obesity in monkeys. *Diabetes*, 42, 1809–1814.

Harrison, D. E., Archer, J. R., & Astole, C. M. (1984). Effects of food restriction on aging: Separation of food intake and adiposity. *Proceedings of the National Academy of Sciences of the USA*, 81, 1835–1838.

Hart, R. W., & Turturro, A. (1998). Evolution and dietary restriction. *Experimental Gerontology, 33,* 53–60.

Heydari, A. R., Wu, B., Takahashi, R., Strong, R., & Richardson, A. (1993). Expression of heat shock protein 70 is altered by age and diet at the level of transcription. *Molecular and Cellular Biology, 13,* 2909–2918.

Heydari, A., Conrad, C. C., & Richardson, A. (1995). Expression of heat shock genes in hepatocytes is affected by age and food restriction in rats. *Journal of Nutrition, 125,* 410–418.

Higami, Y., Shimokawa, I., Okimoto, T., Tomita, M., Yuo, T., & Ikeda, T., (1996). Susceptibiliy of hepatocytes to cell death by single administration of cycloheximide in young and old F344 rats. Effect of dietary restriction. *Mutation Research, 357,* 225–230.

Holehan, A. M., & Merry, B. J. (1986). The experimental manipulation of ageing by diet. *Biological Reviews, 61,* 329–368.

Holliday, R. (1989). Food, reproduction and longevity: Is the extended lifespan of calorie-restricted animals an evolutionary adaptation. *BioEssays, 10,* 125–127.

Holt, P. R., Moss, S. F., Heydari, A. R., & Richardson, A. (1998). Diet restriction increases apoptosis in the gut of aging rats. *Journal of Gerontology: Biological Sciences, 53A,* B168–B172.

Imai, S.-I., Armstrong, C. M., Kaeberlein, M., & Guarente, L. (2000). Transcriptional silencing and longevity protein Sir2 is an NAD-dependent histone deacetylase. *Nature, 403,* 795–800.

Ingram, D. K., Cutler, R. G., Weindruch, R., Renquist, D. M., Knapka, J. J., April, M., Belcher, C. T., Clark, M. A., Hatcherson, C. D., Marriott, B. M., & Roth, G. S. (1990). Dietary restriction and aging: the initiation of a primate study. *Journal of Gerontology: Biological Sciences, 45,* B148–B163.

Iwasaki, K., Gleiser, C. A., Masoro, E. J., McMahan, C. A., Seo, E., & Yu, B. P. (1988). The influence of dietary protein source on longevity and age-related disease processes of Fischer rats. *Journal of Gerontology: Biological Sciences, 43,* B5–B12.

James, S. J., & Muskhelishvili, L. (1994). Rates of apoptosis and proliferation vary with caloric intake and may influence incidence of spontaneous hepatoma in C57BL/6 × C3HF$_1$ mice. *Cancer Research, 54,* 5508–5510.

Keenan, K. P., Soper, K. A., Hertzog, P. R., Gumprecht, L. A., Smith, P. F., Mattson, B. A., Ballam G. C., & Clark, R. L. (1995a). Diet, overfeeding, and moderate dietary restriction in control Sprague-Dawley rats. II. Effects on age-related proliferative and degenerative lesions. *Toxicologic Pathology, 23,* 287–302.

Keenan, K. P., Soper, K. A., Smith, P. F., Ballam, G. C., & Clark, R. L. (1995b). Diet, overfeeding, and moderate dietary restriction in control Sprague-Dawley rats: I. Effects on spontaneous neoplasms. *Toxicologic Pathology, 23,* 269–286.

Kelley, G. R. & Herlihy, J. T. (1998). Food restriction alters the age-related decline in cardiac β-adrenergic responsiveness. *Mechanisms of Ageing and Development, 103,* 1–12.

Kemnitz, J. W., Roecker, E. B., Weindruch, R., Elson, D. F., Baum, S. T., & Bergman, R. N. (1994). Dietary restriction increases insulin sensitivity and lowers blood glucose in rhesus monkeys. *American Journal of Physiology, 266,* E540–E547.

Kemnitz, J. W., Weindruch, R., Roecker, E. B., Crawford, K., Kaufman, P. L., & Ershler, W. B. (1993). Dietary restriction of adult male rhesus monkeys: Design, methodology, and preliminary findings from the first year of study. *Journal of Gerontology: Biological Sciences, 48,* B17–B26.

Klebanov, S., Shehab, D., Stavinoha, W. B., Yongman, S., & Nelson, J. F. (1995). Hyperadrenocorticism attenuated inflammation, and the life prolonging action of food restriction in mice. *Journal of Gerontology: Biological Sciences, 50A,* B78–B82.

Koizumi, A., Wada, Y., Tuskada, M., Kayo, T., Naruse, M., Horiuchi, K., Mogi, T., Yoshioka, M., Sasaki, M., Miyamaura, Y., Abe, T., Ohtomo, K., & Walford, R. L. (1996). A tumor preventive effect of dietary restriction is antagonized by high housing temperature through deprivation of torpor.

Mechanisms of Ageing and Development, 92, 67–82.

Koizumi, A., Weindruch, R., & Walford, R. L. (1987). Influence of dietary restriction and age on liver enzyme activities and lipid peroxidation in mice. *Journal of Nutrition,* 117, 361–367.

Kristal, B. S., & Yu, B. P. (1998). Dietary restriction augments resistance to oxidant-mediated inhibition of mitochondrial transcription. *Age,* 21, 1–6.

Lane, M. A., Baer, D. J., Rumpler, W. V., Weindruch, R., Ingram, D. K., Tilmont, E. M., Cutler, R. G., & Roth, G. S. (1996). Calorie restriction lowers body temperature in rhesus monkeys, consistent with a postulated anti-aging mechanism in rodents. *Proceedings of the National Academy of Sciences of the USA,* 93, 4159–2164.

Lane, M. A., Baer, D. J., Tilmont, E. M., Rumpler, W. V., Ingram, D. K., Roth, G. S., & Cutler, R. G. (1995a). Energy balance in rhesus monkeys (*Macaca mulatta*) subjected to long-term dietary restriction. *Journal of Gerontology: Biological Sciences,* 50A, B295–B302.

Lane, M. A., Ball, S. S., Ingram, D. K., Cutler, R. G., Engel, J., Read, V., & Roth, G. S. (1995b). Diet restriction in rhesus monkeys lowers fasting and glucose-stimulated glucoregulatory end points. *American Journal of Physiology,* 268, E941–E948.

Lane, M. A., Ingram, D. K., Ball, S. S., & Roth, G. S. (1997a). Dehydroepiandrosterone sulfate: A biomarker of primate aging slowed by caloric restriction. *Journal of Clinical Endocrinology and Metabolism,* 82, 2093–2096.

Lane, M. A., Ingram, D. K., & Roth, G. S. (1997b). Beyond the rodent model: Calorie restriction in rhesus monkey. *Age,* 20, 45–56.

Lane, M. A., Tilmont, E. M., De Angelis, H., Handy, A., Ingram, D. K., Kemnitz, J. W. & Roth, G. S. (2000). Short-term caloric restriction improves disease-related markers in older male rhesus monkeys (*Macaca mulatta*). *Mechanisms of Ageing and Development,* 112, 185–196.

Lee, C.-K., Klopp, R. G., Weindruch, R., & Prolla, T. A. (1999). Gene expression profile

of aging and its retardation by caloric restriction. *Science,* 285, 1390–1393.

Lev-Ran, A. (1998). Mitogenic factors accelerate later-age disease: Insulin as a paradigm. *Mechanisms of Ageing and Development,* 102, 95–113.

Li, Y., Yan, Q., Pendergrass, W. R., & Wolf, N. (1998). Response of lens epithelial cells to hydrogen peroxide stress and the protective effect of caloric restriction. *Experimental Cell Research,* 239, 254–263.

Li, Y., Yan, Q., & Wolf, N. S. (1997). Long-term caloric restriction delays age-related decline in proliferative capacity of murine lens epithelial cells. *Investigative Opthalmology and Vision Research,* 38, 100–107.

Licastro, F., Weindruch, R., Davis, L. J., & Walford, R. L. (1988). Effect of dietary restriction upon the age-associated decline of lymphocyte DNA repair activity in mice. *Age,* 11, 48–52.

Lipman, J. M., Turturro, A., & Hart, R. W. (1989). The influence of dietary restriction on DNA repair in rodents: A preliminary report. *Mechanisms of Ageing and Development,* 48, 135–143.

Lipman, R. D., Dallal, G. E., & Bronson, R. T. (1999a). Lesion biomarkers of aging in B6C3F1 hybrid mice. *Journal of Gerontology: Biological Sciences,* 54A, B466–B477.

Lipman, R. D., Dallal, G. E., & Bronson, R. T. (1999b). Effects of genotype and diet on age-related lesions in *ad libitum* fed and caloric-restricted F344, BN, and BNF3F1 rats. *Journal of Gerontology: Biological Sciences,* 54A, B478–B491.

Lipman, R. D., Smith, D. E., Blumberg, J. B., & Bronson, R. T. (1998). Effects of caloric restriction or augmentation in adult rats: Longevity and lesion biomarkers of aging. *Aging: Clinical and Experimental Research,* 10, 463–470.

Luhtala, T. A., Roecker, E. B., Pugh, T., Feuers, R. J., & Weindruch, R. (1994). Dietary restriction attenuates age-related increases in rat skeletal muscle antioxidant enzyme activities. *Journal of Gerontology: Biological Sciences,* 49, B231–B238.

Martin, G. M., Austad, S. N., & Johnson, T. E. (1996). Genetic analysis of ageing: Role of oxidative damage and environmental stresses. *Nature Genetics, 13,* 25–34.

Masoro, E. J. (1992). Potential role of the modulation of fuel use in the antiaging action of dietary restriction. *Annals of the New York Academy of Sciences, 663,* 403–411.

Masoro, E. J. (1993). Dietary restriction and aging. *Journal of the American Geriatrics Society, 41,* 994–999.

Masoro, E. J. (1996). Possible mechanisms underlying the antiaging actions of caloric restriction. *Toxicologic Pathology, 24,* 738–741.

Masoro, E. J. (1998). Hormesis and the antiaging action of dietary restriction. *Experimental Gerontology, 33,* 61–66.

Masoro, E. J., & Austad, S. N. (1996). The evolution of the antiaging action of dietary restriction: A hypothesis. *Journal of Gerontology: Biological Sciences, 51A,* B387–B391.

Masoro, E. J., McCarter, R. J. M., Katz, M. S., & McMahan, C. A. (1992). Dietary restriction alters characteristics of glucose fuel use. *Journal of Gerontology: Biological Sciences, 47,* B202–B208.

Masoro, E. J., Shimokawa, I., Higami, Y., McMahan, C. A., & Yu, B. P. (1995). Temporal pattern of food intake not a factor in the retardation of aging proceses by dietary restriction. *Journal of Gerontology: Biological Sciences, 50A,* B48–B53.

Matsuo, M., Gomi, F., Kuramoto, K., & Sagai, M. (1993). Food restriction suppresses an age-dependent increase in exhalation rate of pentane from rats: a longitudinal study. *Journal of Gerontology: Biological Sciences, 48,* B133–B138.

McCarter, R. J. M. (2000). Caloric restriction, exercise, and aging. In C. K. Sen, L. Packer, & O. Hanninen (Eds.), *Handbook of Oxidants and Antioxidants in Exercise,* (pp. 797–829). Amsterdam: Elsevier Science.

McCarter, R. J. M., & Palmer, J. (1992). Energy metabolism and aging: A lifelong study of Fischer 344 rats. *American Journal of Physiology, 263,* E448–E452.

McCarter, R. J. M., Shimokawa, I., Ikeno, Y., Higami, Y., Hubbard, G. B., Yu, B. P., & McMahan, C. A. (1997). Physical activity as a factor in the action of dietary restriction on aging: Effects in Fischer 344 rats. *Aging: Clinical and Experimental Research, 9,* 73–79.

McCay, C., Crowell, M., & Maynard, L. (1935). The effect of retarded growth upon the length of life and upon ultimate size. *Journal of Nutrition, 10,* 63–79.

McShane, T. & Wise, P, M. (1996). Life-long caloric restriction prolongs reproductive life span in rats without interrupting estrous cyclicity: Effects on the gonadotrophin-releasing hormone/luteinizing hormone axis. *Biology of Reproduction, 54,* 70–75.

McShane, T. M., Wilson, M. E., & Wise, P. M. (1999). Effects of lifelong moderate caloric restriction on levels of neuropeptide Y, proopiomelanocortin, and galanin mRNA. *Journal of Gerontology: Biological Sciences, 54A,* B14–B21.

Miller, R. A. (1995). Immune system. In E. J. Masoro (Ed.), *Handbook of Physiology, Section 11, Aging* (pp 555–590). New York: Oxford University Press.

Moore, S. A., Lopez. A., Richardson, A., & Pahlavani, M. A. (1998). Effect of age and dietary restriction on expression of heat shock protein 70 in rat alveolar macrophages. *Mechanisms of Ageing and Development, 104,* 59–73.

Mote, P. L., Grizzle, J. M., Walford, R. L., & Spindler, S. R. (1991). Influence of age and caloric restriction on expression of hepatic genes for xenobiotic and oxygen metabolizing enzymes in the mouse. *Journal of Gerontology: Biological Sciences, 46,* B–95–B100.

Munck, A., Guyre, P. M., & Holbrook, N. J. (1984). Physiological functions of glucocorticoids in stress and their relation to pharmacological actions. *Endocrine Reviews, 5,* 25–44.

Murtagh-Mark, C. M., Reiser, K. M., Harris, Jr., R., & McDonald, R. B. (1995). Source of dietary carbohydrate affects life span of Fischer 344 rats independent of caloric restriction. *Journal of Gerontology: Biological Sciences, 50A,* B148–B154.

Muskhelishvilli, L., Hart, R. W., Turturro, A., & James, S. J. (1995). Age-related changes in the intrinsic rate of apoptosis in livers of diet-restricted and ad libitum-fed B6C3F1 mice. *American Journal of Pathology, 147,* 20–24.

Novelli, M., Masiello, P., Bombara, M., & Bergamini, E. (1998). Protein glycation in aging male Sprague-Dawley rat: Effects of antiaging diet restrictions. *Journal of Gerontology: Biological Sciences, 53A,* B94–B100.

Pahlavani, M. A. (1998). Intervention in the aging immune system: Influence of dietary restriction, dehydroepiandrosterone, melatonin, and exercise. *Age, 21,* 153–173.

Pahlavani, M. A., Harris, M. D., & Richardson, A. (1997). The increase in the induction of Il–2 expression with caloric restriction is correlated to changes in transcription factor NFAT. *Cellular Immunology, 180,* 10–19.

Parr, T. (1996). Insulin exposure controls the rate of mammalian aging. *Mechanisms of Ageing and Development, 88,* 75–82.

Pashko, L. L., & Schwartz, A. G. (1992). Reversal of food restriction induced inhibition of mouse skin tumor promotion by adrenalectomy. *Carcinogenesis, 10,* 1925–1928.

Pieri, C. (1997). Membrane and lipid peroxidation in food restricted animals. *Age, 20,* 71–79.

Pipkin, J. L., Hinson, W. G., James, S. J., Lyn-Cook, L. E., Duffy, P. H., Feuers, R. J., Shaddock, J. G., Aly, K. B., Hart, R. W., & Casciano, D. A. (1997). p^{53} synthesis and phosphorylation in the aging diet-restricted rat following retinoic acid administration. *Mechanisms of Ageing and Development, 97,* 15–34.

Prapurna, D. R., & Rao, K. S. (1996). Long-term effects of caloric restriction initiated at different ages on DNA polymerases in rat brain. *Mechanisms of Ageing and Development, 92,* 133–142.

Ramsey, J. J., Roecker, E. B., Weindruch, R., Baum, S. T., & Kemnitz, J. W. (1996). Thermogenesis of adult male rhesus monkeys: Results through 66 months of dietary restriction. *FASEB Journal, 10,* A726.

Ramsey, J. J., Roecker, E. B., Weindruch, R., & Kemnitz, J. W. (1997). Energy expenditure of adult male rhesus monkeys during the first 30 mo of dietary restriction. *American Journal of Physiology, 272,* E901–E907.

Rao, G., Xia, E., Nadakavukaren, M. J., & Richardson, A. (1990). Effect of dietary restriction on the age-dependent changes in the expression of antioxidant enzymes in rat liver. *Journal of Nutrition, 120,* 602–609.

Reaven, G. M. (1989). *Clinician's Guide to Non-Insulin-Dependent Diabetes Mellitus.* New York: Marcel Dekker.

Reed, M. J., Penn, P. E., Li, Y., Birnbaum, R., Vernon, R. B., Johnson, T. S., Pendergrass, W. R., Sage, E. H., Abrass, I. B., & Wolf, N. S. (1996). Enhanced cell proliferation and biosynthesis mediate improved wound repair in refed, caloric-restricted mice. *Mechanisms of Ageing and Development, 89,* 21–43.

Reiser, K. M. (1994). Influence of age and long-term dietary restriction on enzymatically mediated crosslinks and nonenzymatic glycation of collagen in mice. *Journal of Gerontology: Biological Sciences, 49,* B71–B79.

Reiser, K., McGee, C., Rucker, R., & McDonald, R. (1995). Effects of aging and caloric restriction on extracellular matrix biosynthesis in a model of injury repair in rats. *Journal of Gerontology: Biological Sciences, 50A,* B40–B47.

Rojas, C., Cadenas, S., Perez-Campo, R., Lopez-Torres, M., Pamplona, R., Prat, J., & Barja, G. (1993). Relationship between lipid peroxidation, fatty acid composition, and ascorbic acid in the liver during carbohydrate and caloric restriction in mice. *Archives of Biochemistry and Biophysics, 306,* 59–64.

Roth, G. S., Hengemihle, J., Ingram, D. K., Spangler, E. L., Johnson, L. K., & Lane, M. A. (1997). Effect of age and caloric restriction on cutaneous wound closure in rats and monkeys. *Journal of Gerontology: Biological Sciences, 52A,* B98–B102.

Roth, G. S., Ingram, D. K., & Lane, M. A. (1999). Calorie restriction in primates: Will it work and how will we know? *Journal of the American Geriatrics Society, 47,* 896–903.

Sabatino, F., Masoro, E. J., McMahan, C. A., & Kuhn, R. W. (1991). An assessment of the role of the glucocorticoid system in aging processes and in the action of food restriction. *Journal of Gerontology: Biological Sciences, 46*, B171–B179.

Salih, M. A., Kalu, D. N., & Smith, T. C. (1997). Effects of age and food restriction on calcium signaling in parotid acinar cells of Fischer 344 rats. *Aging: Clinical and Experimental Research, 9*, 419–427.

Scrofano, M. M., Shang, F., Nowell, Jr., T. R., Gong, X., Smith, D. E., Kelliher, M., Dunning, J., Mura, C. V., & Taylor, A. (1998). Aging, calorie restriction and ubiquitin-dependent proteolysis in the livers of Emory mice. *Mechanisms of Ageing and Development, 101*, 277–296.

Shibatani, T., Nazir, M., & Ward, W. F. (1996). Alteration of rat liver 20S proteosome activities by age and food restriction. *Journal of Gerontology: Biological Sciences, 51A*, B316–B322.

Shimokawa, I., & Higami, Y. (1999). A role for leptin in the antiaging action of dietary restriction. *Aging: Clinical and Experimental Research, 11*, 380–382.

Shimokawa, I., Higami, Y., Okimoto, T., Tomita, M., & Ikeda, T. (1996a). Effects of lifelong dietary restriction on somatotropes: Immunohistochemical and functional aspects. *Journal of Gerontology: Biological Sciences, 51A*, B396–B402.

Shimokawa, I., Higami, Y., Yu, B. P., Masoro, E. J., & Ikeda, T. (1996b). Influence of dietary components on the occurrence of and mortality due to neoplasms in male F344 rats. *Aging: Clinical and Experimental Research, 8*, 254–262.

Snyder, D. L., Gayheart-Walsten, P. A., Rhie, S., Wang, W., & Roberts, J. (1998). Effect of age, gender, rat strain, and dietary restriction, on norepinephrine release from cardiac synaptosomes. *Journal of Gerontology: Biological Sciences, 53A*, B33–B41.

Sohal, R. S., & Dubey, A. (1994). Mitochondrial oxidative damage, hydrogen peroxide release, and aging. *Free Radical Biology and Medicine, 16*, 621–626.

Sohal, R. S., & Weindruch, R. (1996). Oxidative stress, caloric restriction, and aging. *Science, 273*, 59–63.

Sohal, R. S., Agarwal, S., Candas, M., Forster, M., & Lal, H. (1994a). Effect of age and caloric restriction on DNA oxidative

damage in different tissues of C57BL/6 mice. *Mechanisms of Ageing and Development, 76*, 215–224.

Sohal, R. S., Ku, H.-H., Agarwal, S., Forster, M. J., & Lal, H. (1994b). Oxidative damage, mitochondrial oxidant generation and antioxidant defenses during aging and in response to food restriction in the mouse. *Mechanisms of Ageing and Development, 74*, 121–133.

Sonntag, W. E., Lynch, D. D., Cefalu, S. T., Ingram, R. L., Bennett, S. A., Thorton, P. L., & Khan, A. S. (1999). Pleiotropic effects of growth hormone and insulin-like growth factor (IGF)–1 on biological aging: Inferences from moderate caloric restricted animals. *Journal of Gerontology: Biological Sciences, 54A*, B521–B538.

Sonntag, W. E., Xu, X., Ingram, R. L., & D'Costa, A. (1995). Moderate caloric restriction alters the subcellular distribution of somatostatin mRNA and increases growth hormone pulse amplitude in aged animals. *Neuroendocrinology, 61*, 601–608.

Spaulding, C. C., Walford, R. L., & Effros, R. B. (1997). The accumulation of non-replicative, non-functional, senescent T cells with age is avoided in calorically restricted mice by an enhancement of T cell apoptosis. *Mechanisms of Ageing and Development, 93*, 25–33.

Stevens, H., Knollema, S., De Jong, G., Korf, J., & Luiten, P. (1998). Long-term food restriction, deprenyl, and nimodipine treatment on life expectancy and blood pressure of stroke-prone rats. *Neurobiology of Aging, 19*, 273–276.

Taylor, A., Lipman, R., Jahngen-Hodge, J., Palmer, V., Smith, D., Padhye, N., Dallal, G. E., Cyr, D. E., Laxman, E., Shepherd, D., Morrow, F., Salomon, R., Perrone, G., Asmundssen, G., Meydani, M., Blumberg, J., Mune, M., Harrison, D. E., Archer, J. R., & Shigenaga, M. (1995). Dietary caloric restriction in the Emory mouse: Effects on lifespan, eye lens cataract, prevalence and progression, levels of ascorbate, glutathione, glucose, and glycohemoglobin, tail collagen break time, DNA and RNA oxidation, skin integrity, fecundity, and cancer. *Mechanisms of Ageing and Development, 79*, 33–57.

Tuturro, A., Witt, W. W., Lewis, S., Hass, B. S., & Hart, R. W. (1999). Growth curves, and survival characteristics of animals used in the biomarkers of aging program. *Journal of Gerontology: Biological Sciences, 54A,* B492–B501.

Undie, A. S., & Friedman, E. (1993). Diet restriction prevents aging-induced deficits in brain phosphoinositide metabolism. *Journal of Gerontology: Biological Sciences, 48,* B62–B67.

Van Remmen, H., & Ward, W. F. (1998). Effect of dietary restriction on hepatic and renal phosphoenolpyruvate carboxykinase induction in young and old Fischer 344 rats. *Mechanism of Ageing and Development, 104,* 263–275.

Van Remmen, H., Ward, W. F., Sabia, R. V., & Richardson, A. (1995). Gene expression and protein degradation. In E. J. Masoro (Ed.), *Handbook of Physiology, (Section 11) Aging* (pp. 171–234). New York: Oxford University Press.

Verdery, R. B., Ingram, D. K., Roth, G. S., & Lane, M. A. (1997). Caloric restriction increases HDL$_2$ levels in rhesus monkeys (*Macaca mulatta*). *American Journal of Physiology, 273,* E714–E719.

Walford, R. L. (1983). *Maximum Life Span,* New York: W. W. Norton.

Walford, R. L., & Spindler, S. R. (1997). The response to calorie restriction in mammals shows features also common to hibernation: A cross-adaptation hypothesis. *Journal of Gerontology: Biological Sciences, 52A,* B179–B183.

Ward, W. F. (1988). Food restriction enhances the proteolytic capacity of rat liver. *Journal of Gerontology: Biological Sciences, 43,* B121–B124.

Warner, H. R., Fernandes, G., & Wang, E. (1995). A unifying hypothesis to explain the retardation of aging and tumorigenesis by caloric restriction. *Journal of Gerontology: Biological Sciences, 50A,* B107–B109.

Weed, J. L., Lane, M. A., Roth, G. S., Speer, D. L., & Ingram, D. K. (1997). Activity measures in rhesus monkeys on long-term calorie restriction. *Physiology & Behavior, 62,* 97–103.

Weindruch, R., & Walford, R. L. (1982). Dietary restriction in mice beginning at 1 year of age: Effect on life span and spontaneous cancer incidence. *Science, 215,* 1415–1418.

Weindruch, R. & Walford, R. L. (1988). *The Retardation of aging and Disease by Dietary Restriction,* Springfield, IL: Charles C Thomas.

Weindruch, R., Kemnitz, J. W., & Uno, H. (1995). Interspecies variations in physiologic and antipathologic outcomes of dietary restriction. In R. W. Hart, D. A. Neuman, & R. T. Robertson (Eds.), *Dietary Restriction: Implications for the Design and Interpretation of Toxicity and Carcinogenicity Studies* (pp. 351–363). Washington, DC: ILSI Press.

Weraarchakul, N., Strong, R., Wood, W. G., & Richardson, A. (1989). Effect of aging and dietary restriction on DNA repair. *Experimental Cell Research, 181,* 197–204.

Wolf, N. S., Penn, P. E., Jiang, D., Fei, R. G., & Pendergrass, W. R. (1995). Caloric restriction: Conservation of *in vivo* cellular replicative capacity accompanies life-span extension in mice. *Experimental Cell Research, 217,* 317–323.

Xu, X., & Sonntag, W. F. (1996a). Moderate caloric restriction prevents the age-related decline in growth hormone receptor signal transduction. *Journal of Gerontology: Biological Sciences, 51A,* B167–B174.

Xu, X., & Sonntag, W. E. (1996b). Growth hormone-induced nuclear translocation of stat–3 decreases with age: modulation by caloric restriction. *American Journal of Physiology, 271,* E903–E909.

Youngman, L. D., Park, J-Y. K., & Ames, B. N. (1992). Protein oxidation associated with aging is reduced by dietary restriction of protein or calories. *Proceedings of the National Academy of Sciences of the United States of America, 89,* 9112–9116.

Yu, B. P. (1996). Aging and oxidative stress: Modulation by dietary restriction. *Free Radical Biology and Medicine, 21,* 651–668.

Yu, B. P., Laganiere S., & Kim, J.-W. (1989). Influence of life-prolonging food restriction on membrane lipid peroxidation and antioxidant states. In M. G. Simic, K. A. Taylor, J. F. Ward, T. von Sonntag (Eds.), *Oxygen Radicals in Biology and Medicine* (pp. 1067–1073). New York: Plenum.

Yu, B. P., Masoro, E. J., & McMahan, C. A. (1985). Nutritional influences on aging of Fischer 344 rats. I. Physical, metabolic, and longevity characteristics. *Journal of Gerontology, 40,* 656–670.

Yu, B. P., Suescun, E. A., & Yang, S. Y. (1992). Effect of age-related lipid peroxidation on membrane fluidity and phospholipase A$_2$: modulation by dietary restriction. *Mechanisms of Ageing and Development, 65,* 17–23.

Zhen, X., Uryu, K., Cai, G., Johnson, G. P., & Friedman, E. (1999). Age-associated impairment in brain MAPK signal pathways and the effect of caloric restriction in Fischer 344 rats. *Journal of Gerontology: Biological Sciences, 54A,* B539–B548.

Part Five

Epilogue

Edited by
Steven N. Austad and Edward J. Masoro

Sixteen

Environment–Gene and Gene–Gene Interactions

Gerald E. McClearn, George P. Vogler, and Scott M. Hofer

I. Introduction

There are several sciences of genetics, and most of them have been deployed in the attempt to understand the processes of aging (McClearn, 1987). Molecular genetics offers a cornucopia of methods and theories with which to approach issues at the level of biochemical and biophysical mechanisms of aging; population and evolutionary genetic theories provide rich contexts for examining the phyletic distributions of longevity and life histories; and quantitative genetics and transmission genetics provide models for examining individual differences in age-related phenomena within a species. It is this last domain—individuality in aging in our own human species and in the various laboratory species that are utilized as model systems—that is the concern of the present chapter.

It is generally accepted that intraspecific genetics plays some role in many age-related traits and in a number of specific anomalies of aging, and an intense and accelerating search is underway for genes that play a role in

dementia, the "abnormally" long life of centenarians, susceptibility to age-related diseases, the assurance of longevity, and other gerontological matters. The theme of this chapter is the importance of considering two general contextual domains—that of environment and that of other genes—in this hot pursuit of "gerontological" genes.

The fact that the consequences of allelic differences at a particular locus might be moderated by the allelic configuration at some other locus or loci is no new discovery; examples were observed early in the exuberant tide of post-rediscovery Mendelian research. Albinism in both animals and plants was an obvious early case, with the influence of all of the other color-affecting loci of the organism obviated by a particular allelic configuration at the one locus that produced albinism. The concept of *epistasis* was elaborated, with numerous subtypes identified, and the notion that "modifier" genes could influence phenotypic expression of a genotype became well-accepted.

Similarly, an influence of environment on the impact of a genetic condition was observed early. In 1933, for one example, Hogben showed a systematic effect of temperature on the phenotypic expression of two genetic conditions affecting eye facet number in *Drosophila* (low bar and ultra bar).

In the century of genetic research that has followed, naturally there has been an emphasis on what might be described as the main effects of genes. Nonetheless, examples of interaction have proliferated, and the pervasiveness of both gene–gene and gene–environment interdependence is becoming clear. As attention is focusing increasingly on complex phenotypes, such as those of aging, interactions are intruding into the limelight and can no longer be treated as occasional special cases. Interactions likely will become compelling considerations in the gerontological genetic research of the new century. Here we shall provide a conceptual scheme that may facilitate the interpretation of these types of interaction, with some examples drawn broadly from a variety of phenotypic domains and further examples that specifically pertain to gerontological science.

II. A "Systems" Perspective on Interactions

In the early days of Mendelian genetics, when the mode of gene action remained utterly mysterious, it was difficult to conceptualize the relationship of genes to phenotypes by much more than a simple unidirectional representation:

GENE → PHENOTYPE

As insights accrued into the mechanism of gene action (e.g., the "one gene–one enzyme hypothesis"), the mode of gene action came into the province of biological chemistry, and the field of molecular biology was launched. In the broadest and simplest terms, these new insights made possible, and required, an elaboration of the scheme to

GENE → MOLECULAR BIOLOGY → PHENOTYPE

Mendelian genetics was, and is, concerned with categorical differences among phenotypes. Whereas the early advances proliferated in respect to this type of dichotomous phenotype, a different tradition was exploring the hereditary basis of continuously distributed phenotypes. A lively intellectual battle ensued between the Mendelians and the biometricians, with the former group increasingly confident about the ubiquity of Mendelian inheritance and the latter group skeptical about the applicability of Mendelian rules of inheritance to normal continuous variability. This dispute essentially was settled by Fisher (1918), who showed that the distribution of continuous phenotypes could be rationalized as a product of the collective contribution of many genetic loci, each of which acts in a Mendelian manner, but each having only a relatively small effect on the phenotype.

The quantitative genetic model was greatly elaborated while transmission genetics advanced and as molecular genetics assumed an increasingly dominant role in genetic science and in biology in general. Figure 1 is one version of a representation that has been useful heuristically in conveying many of the properties of multifactorial inheritance (e.g., Stebbins, 1974; Waddington, 1953). On the left are shown the DNA to RNA to polypeptide routes for seven hypothetical genes that influence a field of causal elements and processes that finally impinge on two phenotypes of interest. Two essential features of quantitative inheritance are depicted clearly: each gene ultimately affects more than one phenotype (pleiotropy), and each phenotype is affected by more than one gene (polygeny; multiple factor inheritance).

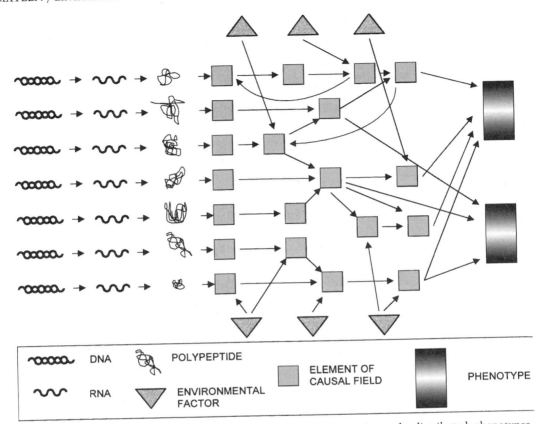

Figure 1. Schema of genetic and environmental influences on continuously distributed phenotypes. Environmental and genetic factors are shown as separate domains, but impinging upon a causal field, the elements of which are interrelated in complex patterns, including feedback relationships. (Modification of Figure 7.1 from T. P. Bresford & E. Gomberg, (Eds.), Alcohol and Aging, Used by permission of Oxford University Press, Inc.)

The "causal field" (Ford, 1987; Mackie, 1974) is also shown as being susceptible to the influence of environmental factors. Contrary to the hoary misconception of "nature versus nurture," genes and environment are shown clearly to be influencing the same causal field in a coacting (and interacting) manner to give rise to the phenotypes. Both genetic and environmental inputs to the causal field are essential to the eventuation in the phenotype. Individuals differ in the alleles they possess at each of the influential loci and also in their exposure to influential environmental factors, with resulting individual differences in phenotypes. One of the functions of quantitative genetic analysis is the estimation of the relative contributions of the genetic differences and of the environmental differences to the observed phenotypic variability. It is important to note that such descriptive statistics apply only to the particular gene pool of the population being studied and to the range of the environmental agencies to which that population is exposed. In a different population with different allelic frequencies and with a different array of environments, the estimates might differ substantially. This point merits emphasis because regarding estimates of heritability or environmentality to be eternal verities has led to much misguided argument and polemic by narrow advocates both of "nature" and of "nurture."

The causal field is the domain of biochemists, physiologists, immunologists, endocrinologists, and neuroscientists (and others) investigating the underpinnings of their primary phenomena. The details of these specialties make clear the enormous complexity of the causal field that is represented in a necessarily greatly oversimplified manner in Fig. 1. Advances in understanding the complex interrelationships within these domains have been truly staggering: compare textbooks of today with their counterparts of a half-century ago. There is, furthermore, an increasing eagerness to apply new modes of conceptualizing and analyzing complex systems. Complexity has long been the target of creative inquiry, but there has been phenomenally escalating interest, with the "sciences of complexity" spreading through academia and spilling over into the popular media. It seems inescapable that insights into gene–gene and gene–environment interactions will be enriched by perspectives from hierarchy theory, information theory, catastrophe theory, chaos theory, and other variants of this lively area. The systems perspectives that have been applied in gerontological research (e.g., Jazwinski, 1999, Jazwinski *et al.*, 1998; Yates *et al.*, 1972) are promissory notes of the inevitable increase in such applications in the future. It requires only some very elementary observations to illustrate the relevance of complex systems topics to the arena of gene–gene and gene–environment interactions in aging processes.

A particularly significant feature of the model is the representation of feedback by the backward-pointing arrows in the causal field. Feedback relationships of this sort frustrate interpretations based on the usual linear, unidirectional, causal models and require circular or network kinds of causal analysis (Sattler, 1986). An especially cogent example is provided by the work of Kacser and Burns (1979), who discuss the situation in which a series of biochemical reactions exists in which the product of each reaction is the substrate for the next, and there is a feedback loop, such as end product inhibition, in the system. Under these circumstances, there is no way of specifying the effect size of an alteration in one of the steps (such as differences in alleles at loci coding for the enzyme of that step) without specifying the prevailing conditions at the other steps. In these circumstances, the explanatory and predictive power of the single elements of the subsystem is constrained, and the most cogent variable may be the flux through the system. Such a conclusion is consistent with a crucial point made by Simon (1973) concerning hierarchical systems: functioning of a particular level may be indifferent to the details of the underlying level depending only upon the output of that level without regard to how that output is accomplished. An important possibility raised by this generalization is that, for many purposes, a collective of genes (those influencing a subsystem), rather than the individual genes of the collective, may be the most powerful and appropriate analytical unit.

Another significant aspect of the causal field is the presence of redundancy. There are multiple routes from genes to phenotype, and with cross-communication between paths, a change in the efficiency of one path may be compensated, partly or totally, by an appropriate change in a parallel path. Thus, the effect of a particular genotype at a given locus in a specific individual can depend greatly upon the genotypic characteristics of elements in the parallel pathway(s) of that individual. This sort of overdetermination and redundancy presumably accounts for many of the manifestations of "lack of penetrance" in linkage and segregation

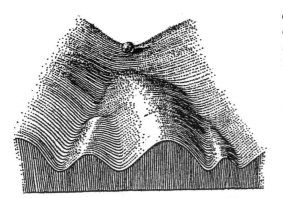

Figure 2. Epigenetic landscape of Waddington (1957). The phenotypic location is represented by the ball that, in developmental time, rolls toward the viewer. The terrain it traverses is shaped by the genes of the organism, and environmental forces act to deflect the ball laterally. (From Waddington, C. H., *The Strategy of the Genes*, The Macmillan Company, ITPs ltd., 1957 with permission.)

analyses that are inexplicable on a simple, single-gene, model and the many unexpected effects, or lack of effects, of gene knockouts and other transgene manipulations of experimental molecular genetics.

In what is now acknowledged (Stein & Varela, 1993) to be a pioneering application of systems perspectives to developmental processes, Waddington (1957) provided a model of great heuristic value—his epigenetic landscape (Fig. 2). In this conception, originally offered as a model of tissue differentiation, the phenotypic location is represented by the ball, which, in developmental time, rolls toward the viewer. The terrain it traverses is shaped by the genes of the organism, and environmental forces act to deflect the ball laterally. The degree and duration of deflection depend upon the steepness of the valley walls and the width of the valley floor at the point at which the environmental agency acts. At certain critical junctures, where two developmental pathways diverge, a modest environmental push can be definitive in committing subsequent development of the tissue to one valley or another. At another time, the same environmental factor would result only in a small deflection, followed by a return to the valley floor. Individual differences in the alleles configuring the landscape result in differences in the extent to which the developmental process is buffered. Although the model was designed to explicate developmental differentiation into distinct tissue types, it can be extrapolated to apply to a quantitatively distributed phenotype and to late-life processes as well as to early development.

A major virtue of the representation is the provision for gene–environment interactions. Individual differences in terrain warn that an environment with a certain effect in one individual may be more or less effective in another individual.

Gene–environment interactions can also have a temporal aspect, waxing or waning during development or aging. The epigenetic landscape accommodates the ideas of critical periods or sensitive periods of developmental biology and developmental psychology and rationalizes differing age of onset of certain age-related diseases (and is an early expression of the notion of the bifurcations of chaos theory). Furthermore, the terrain (and its genetic architecture) differs at different developmental times, and, thus, the influence of a genetic locus at any particular life stage might be greater, less, or totally irrelevant at other times.

III. Interactions Among Genes

Broadly speaking, interactions among genes may involve the regulation of expression of one gene by another or interrelationships among the downstream elements in the causal field that are the products of the genes. The former domain is that of gene regulation, which is at the very apex of advances in molecular and developmental biology and beyond the scope of this presentation. Of special pertinence to the present theme are examples involving polygenic systems and "whole organism" phenotypes.

An instructive example is provided by the *diabetes* locus in mouse, which has been a useful model system for the study of the human disease. Animals homozygous for the recessive allele (*db/db*) are affected with aspects of the human syndrome. Coleman and Hummel (1975), however, have described the dramatically different pathophysiology and symptom pattern in animals of *db/db* genotype, depending upon the context of the rest of the genotype. *db/db* homozygotes on the C57BL/Ks background displayed rapid elevation of blood glucose levels, attaining a value in excess of 400 mg% by 6 months of age. Similar homozygotes on the C57BL/6 background showed a modest rise to about 185 mg% at 4–5 months, with a subsequent drop to 129 mg% at 6 months. The former animals had atrophy of the pancreatic islet cells, whereas the latter displayed hypertrophy. Body weights increased rapidly in both strains until about 3 months of age, when the Ks background animals began to decline. Four of ten females and six of ten males had died by 4 months, and the survivors continued losing weight until 12 months, when the study was terminated. No deaths were described for those mice on the BL/6 background. From further comparisons with F_1 and backcross generations, the authors concluded that a polygenic system, rather than a single locus, was responsible for the syndromic differences.

Similarly, Fowler and Edwards (1961) have shown that a gene, *midget*, with impeccable conformity to Mendelian expectations on the genetically heterogeneous background on which it was described originally, produces distinctly non-Mendelian ratios in a different heterogeneous stock.

Presumably, these results are manifestations of the general point made earlier concerning redundancies and compensatory systems in complex causal fields. They caution against careless assertions about the "effect" of a gene. Thus, descriptions of the effects of allelic differences at a given locus necessarily have an aura of tentativeness, with the implicit reservation that the results could be substantially different if the gene in question were keeping company with a different crowd.

The prospect of all genes being codependent on all others is, of course, a daunting one. It is not likely that we face such a conceptual burden, however. From some cosmological perspectives, everything may, indeed, be ultimately related to everything else, but as Salthe (1985), among others, has pointed out, not equally so. On human scales of time and space, most such relationships are undetectable and irrelevant. So it seems to be in the case of complex genetic systems. From quite different theoretical perspectives, both Bonner (1988) and Kauffman (1993), for example, have given us reason to believe that the number of genes in a coadapted set or epistatic group may be quite modest and analytically manageable. These conclusions argue for the feasibility of the earlier suggestion that, in some cases, dyads or triads of genetic loci might be advantageous basic analytic units.

A tantalizing possible example is provided by the results of Gelman *et al.* (1988) on longevity in the BXD series of recombinant inbred mice. This pioneering study identified several quantitative trait loci (QTLs) affecting duration of life in these animals. With the greater number of markers that have become available since the original analysis, we have reanalyzed and identified eight

QTLs, with marker identifications of *Hdc* (chromosome 2), *Mos*, *Ifna*, and *Ms6-2* (all chromosome 4), *D7Ms1* (chromsome 7), *D10Mc1* (chromosome 10), and *Eif4e-ps* and *Crip* (both on chromosome 12). Loci on the same chromosomes were not closely linked. In an exploration of possible interactions, we examined effect size of the loci (as measured by the inter-

homozygote differences) for each of the QTLs separately for the two homozygote groups for the other loci. Two of the eight analyses are shown. Fig. 3a shows the inter-homozygote differences for the other QTLs when the *Crip* QTL is in the decreasing (0) allelic configuration and when it is in the increasing (1) configuration. Thus, the average effect size of

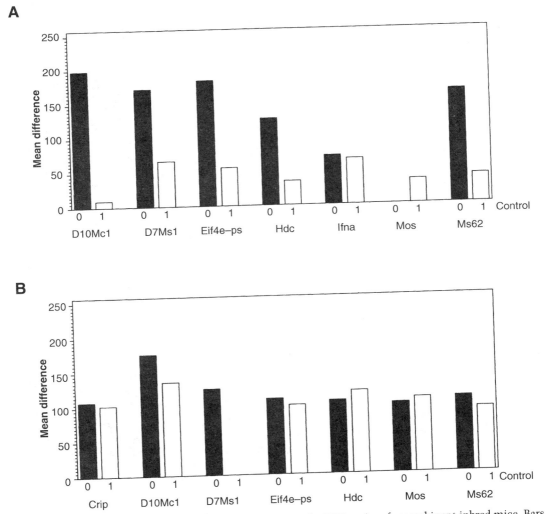

Figure 3. Reanalysis of the data of Gelman *et al.* (1988) in the BXD series of recombinant inbred mice. Bars indicate the effect size of trait loci (as measured by inter-homozygote differences) for each of the QTLs separately for the two homozygote groups at the control locus. (a) Illustrates the presence of interactions using *Crip* as the control locus. (b) Illustrates the absence of interactions using *Ifna* as the control locus.

D10Mc1 is nearly 200 days when *Crip* is homozygous for the decreasing allele and essentially zero when *Crip* is homozygous for the increasing allele. This same general picture is presented for five of the seven comparisons. By contrast, Fig. 3b shows that the effect of allelic substitution at all of the other loci is independent of the condition at the *Ifna* locus.

The limited number of recombinant strains provides relatively little power, of course, but analysis of variance revealed significant interactions of *Crip* with *Eif4e-ps* and with *Ms6-2*. Results are rather mixed when other loci are regarded as control, but no interactions attained significance. With the limited power available, these analyses can only be regarded as provocative of the hypothesis that the *Crip* QTL exerts a key control function in a subsystem affecting longevity. Testing of the hypothesis will require other research designs.

IV. Gene–Environment Interactions

As in the case of gene–gene interactions, we shall provide merely a miscellany of examples, mostly concerning complex phenotypes, to have some empirical data to hang on the theoretical scaffolding of gene–environment interactions.

The classic operon model (Jacob & Monod, 1961) was, of course, an elegant description of gene–environment interactions at the molecular level, with gene expression dependent upon nutrients in the environment. Another classic example involving a single locus may be taken from an early discovery in the genetics of mental retardation. The establishment of the Mendelian transmission of phenylketonuria (PKU), and the subsequent identification of the defective enzyme and the consequent metabolic anomalies (the causal field, which might be called "functional genomics"), permitted the devising

of a rational therapeutic (dietary) environment that greatly ameliorates the devastating effects of the homozygous recessive genotype.

Yet another example that pertains to a broad environmental intervention on gene expression at the molecular level of measurement is change in the gene expression profile of aging mice under conditions of caloric restriction (Lee *et al.*, 1999). The transcription response in mouse gastrocnemius muscle in 5-month-old (adult) and 30-month-old (old) mice demonstrated alterations in gene expression, as assessed by mRNA levels. Caloric restriction appears to decrease the activation of stress response genes that process damaged protein and to lower the activity of metabolic detoxification genes potentially in response to reduced production of toxic byproducts due to lower metabolic rate and to increased biosynthesis and macromolecular turnover.

The widespread occurrence of genetic variation influencing susceptibility to environmental variables is documented in the review by Festing (1979), who cites numerous examples of mouse strain differences in the effects of a wide variety of environmental treatments.

An early demonstration of the dependence of the effect of *polygenic* differences on the environmental milieu was provided by Cooper and Zubek (1958), who examined the maze performance of rat lines generated by selective breeding for maze-learning ability. Performance of animals from the "maze-bright" and "maze-dull" lines that had been reared in environmentally enriched or environmentally impoverished cage conditions was compared to that of animals reared "normally." The impact of environment was dramatic—the number of errors declined from the restricted to normal to enriched conditions. Under the normal condition (under which the strains were bred selectively), the impact of genes (the difference between lines) was equally dramatic. But this line difference was evident only under the normal rearing conditions: under either the impoverished or the enriched conditions, the genes that influenced the phenotypic difference shown in the normal condition were not expressed phenotypically. As a capsule summary, restriction did not appreciably impair the maze-dull rats, and enrichment did not much improve the maze-bright rats.

An example of gene–environment interaction with potential gerontological relevance is provided by Fosmire et al., (1993). The study was motivated by the inconsistent epidemiological evidence concerning aluminum exposure as a risk factor in the etiology of Alzheimer's disease. The speculation was that the impact of environmental aluminum might vary among individuals according to genotype; furthermore, various population study groups could give inconsistent results according to differences among the populations in allelic frequencies at relevant loci. The study utilized five different inbred strains of mice—C57BL/6, C3H/2, BALB/c, A/J, and DBA/2. Samples of young animals of each strain were exposed to a diet with elevated aluminum content for 4 weeks, and compared to controls fed an essentially aluminum-free ration. Four of the strains showed no significant increase in brain aluminum level under the increased dietary aluminum condition. The DBA/2 animals, however, displayed a significant, nearly fourfold, increase. These data obviously do not clarify the issue of the risk factor status of aluminum in Alzheimer's disease; they do, however, serve a heuristic function in illustrating that environmental exposures (either risk factors or presumably beneficial interventions) may have greatly different consequences among individuals depending upon their genotypes.

A study by Falconer (1960) on growth in mice provides a more complicated example. Mice were selected for growth from 3 to 6 weeks under two conditions of nutrition: a "normal" laboratory diet or one diluted with indigestible fiber. Under both the high- and low-nutritional condition, the large line and small line diverged, yielding estimates of heritabilities of 0.41 and 0.36, respectively. Further research showed a genetic correlation of 0.66. This intermediate value indicates that, although some of the same genes were involved in determining the body size differential under both nutritional conditions, much genetic influence was called into play only in one or the other condition.

Many of the environmental variables employed in this type of research can be construed as stressors. Hoffman and Parsons (1991) review a very substantial body of literature supporting the remarkable generalization that heritabilities of a variety of phenotypes increase under conditions of stress. The study by Luckinbill and colleagues (1984) may be an example of special relevance to aging. Selective breeding for early versus late reproduction in Drosophila gave rise to the theoretically expected alteration in longevity if the larvae were maintained in crowded conditions. When larval density in the medium was controlled at a low level, there was little or no response to selection. The former result is an ipso facto demonstration of additive genetic variance under the crowded (stressful?) conditions and its absence under the less crowded condition. Observations in various organisms that heterozygosity for loci affecting specific enzymes is related to phenotypic outcomes only under stressful conditions [for a review of this striking area, see Mitton (1997)] suggest that heterosis may be an important feature of this stress–heritability relationship.

The ubiquity of genotype–environment interactions in respect to life span in Drosophila melanogaster has been demonstrated resoundingly by Vieira and colleagues (2000). Flies were maintained under one of five environmental conditions: standard culture conditions, high or low temperature, heat shock, or starvation stress. Within each sex and within each environment, significant genetic variation was observed, but *all* of this variation appeared in sex × genotype or environment × genotype interaction terms. Seventeen QTLs were identified. *Each* was either sex-specific, environment-specific, or both.

In human populations and naturally occurring environments, a useful conceptualization of the interactive process leading to gene–environment relationships is that of passive, active, and reactive gene–environment correlations (Plomin, 1994; Plomin, *et al.*, 1977; Cattell, 1963, 1965). Passive gene–environment (G–E) correlation occurs when the genes received from, and the environment provided by, an individual's parents both have an effect on a particular phenotype. Active G–E correlation involves the selection or creation of environments conducive to a person's predispositions, whereas reactive G–E correlation arises when environmental influences respond to individual characteristics.

From a systems perspective, these passive, active, and reactive processes operate conjointly and can change over time. For example, it is possible that interactions with the environment that lead to "lack of fit" can provide the impetus to seek environments more conducive to one's genetically related predispositions. Thus, at the population level, an interactive process might be observed as a gene–environment correlation. The potential for particular gene–environment interactions to encourage fit between genetic dispositions and environment may explain some of the difficulties in finding interactions in nonexperimental studies.

With passive G–E correlation, the environment of the child would tend to be correlated with both the child's and parental genotypes, given selection or creation of the environment by the parents. From a developmental perspective, these influences on the child diminish with age as individuals begin to select their environments (Scarr & McCartney, 1983). Nevertheless, it is possible that early influences can affect late-life outcomes, observed as variability due to shared environment (e.g., Gatz *et al.*, 1992).

As individuals mature, the ability for self-direction increases, and the individual selects, shapes, or creates environments that are congruent with his or her genetic predispositions (e.g., abilities, personality, interests). The outcome of this continuous process has been termed "active" gene–environment correlation. For example, individuals may select specific educational and occupational experiences related to their predispositions and abilities. Reactive or evocative gene–environment correlation is produced by the reactive response of the environment (including other people, social institutions) to one's genotypic differences, providing both opportunities and constraints on individual developmental patterns.

Whereas this framework provides a plausible description of potential gene–environment associations, it has proven difficult to disentangle these processes through variance decomposition analysis. The limitations of the decomposition-of-variance approach to understanding complex interactions among anonymous sources of genetic and environmental variability have prompted some researchers to question the validity of heritability models solely based on additive variance assumptions (e.g., Wahlsten & Gottlieb, 1997). However, these concepts are useful for developmental theorists and provide a basis for interpreting and designing developmental and aging studies where genotype and environmental measures are obtained directly (Plomin & Rutter, 1998).

Studies that demonstrate the sensitivity of genetic relatedness to environmental variation typically have relied on stratification across levels of measured environment. For example, in a study of whether parental education acts as a moderator of genetic and environmental influences on verbal IQ in children, genetic influences were found to be lower, and shared environmental influences higher, in less educated families (Rowe et al., 1999). This type of finding emphasizes the degree to which particular environments affect the expression of genetically related traits by restricting or encouraging adaptive responses.

Experimental studies focusing on adaptation or learning also provide evidence for gene–environment interaction. Bouchard et al. (1990) examined individual differences in adaptive response (VO_2 max) to experimentally controlled environmental conditions (exercise training) in a sample of adult MZ twins. Although all individuals showed improvement in VO_2 max following exercise training, the observed training gain was similar within twin pairs (intraclass $r = 0.77$), suggesting that adaptive responses to different environmental influences are, in part, genetically influenced. Such experimental designs provide evidence for gene–environment interactions and urge cautious appraisal in the interpretation of simple additive effects from twin and family studies given variation in naturally occurring environmental conditions.

The interaction of genotype and environmental risk factors on health-related outcomes (Vogler et al., 1997) provides many examples relevant to the increase of disease with aging. The interaction of genes, age, and cardiovascular disease provides a particularly good example of the complex relationships (Sing, et al., 1994). The prediction of parental coronary artery disease (CAD) by age, plasma ApoE

level, and Apo ε4 genotype was examined in a sample of males aged 27–62 years. Main effects for age and plasma ApoE were significant, whereas Apo ε genotype (pooled ε43 and ε44) was not. First-order interactions of Apo ε4 genotype with age and with plasma ApoE also were not significant. However, the second-order interaction of Apo ε4 genotype and plasma ApoE was significant and improved the prediction of parental CAD. The results encourage examination of complex genotype-dependent interactions (Sing et al., 1994).

Measured environmental variables often have been found to have substantial variation associated with genetic differences (Plomin & Bergeman, 1991). Such findings provide indirect evidence for gene–environment associations, such as active or reactive gene–environment correlation. Findings of genetic effects on environmental measures have been discovered in late childhood and adolescence (Plomin & Bergeman, 1991; Plomin et al., 1994; Rowe, 1981, 1983) and in older adults for the occurrence of life events (Plomin et al., 1990) and the availability and perceived adequacy of social support (Bergeman et al., 1990).

Another example of genetic differences accounting for environmental influences is a study of older adults' ratings of their current family environment (Plomin et al., 1989) in twins reared together and reared apart. An average heritability of 24% was obtained for the Family Environment Scales (Moos & Moos, 1981), with evidence for nonadditive effects on several scales. Similar findings were found in a study of retrospective ratings of the early family environment of adult twins (Plomin et al., 1988).

To some degree, however, environmental measures are filtered by perceptions, expectations, memory, motivations, and personality, which might be under more direct genetic influence (Bergeman et al., 1990; Plomin et al., 1990). This may prove to be a particular problem for subjective forms of environmental assessment, such as retrospective reports, ratings of parental treatment, or ratings of the family environment (Rowe, 1981, 1983). However, there is evidence for genetic effects on environmental influences measured by more objective means (e.g., Braungart *et al.*, 1992; Rende *et al.*, 1992). These findings provide support for the complex interactions leading to different developmental and aging trajectories as individuals actively create and select environments that are conducive to their predispositions, and perhaps modifying their behaviors to match their environments (Cattell, 1963). Findings of this sort demonstrate the embeddedness of the genotype within its context and signal the result of processes by which individuals select, create, and conform to their environments.

V. Interactions and Aging

Age-related changes are definitional in gerontological research. It may be tempting to regard the causal factors to be more or less constant (after adult status is achieved, say), with the aging changes simply due to the accumulation of effects from this constellation of causes. If this assumption were veridical, the task of gerontologists would be simplified, because examination of aging mechanisms at any segment of the life span would be revealing for the whole. Observations from the sciences of complexity warn us, however, that it is typical of developing complex systems to undergo saltatory change. As noted earlier, we must be prepared, therefore, for the possibility of temporal heterogeneity of the mix of genetic and environmental influences on aging (and, presumably, of their opportunities for interactions) over the life span. Factors that predominate in the age changes in

the young-old may be inconsequential for nonagenarians; different panels of predictor variables for longevity or health span or other outcome measures may be required for various life stages. Indeed, it is implicit in some theoretical perspectives, such as that of antagonistic pleiotropy, that there will be a change in genetic scenarios between reproductive and post-reproductive life stages (e.g., Rose, 1991).

A particularly pertinent illustration of change in gene expression throughout the life span is provided by the work of Helfand and colleagues (Helfand *et al.*, 1995; Rogina & Helfand, 1995), who employed enhancer traps and reporter genes to evaluate the level of gene expression in the postmitotic tissue of *Drosophila* antennae. Of 49 genes examined, 20% were constitutive, displaying steady expression throughout the 60 days studied. Of the 80% showing change, one pattern is for gradual increase to a midlife peak followed by a decline, another pattern shows gradual increase in expression after a substantial initial delay, and yet another begins with a high level of expression and gradually declines. Furthermore, by altering life span by temperature (Helfand *et al.*, 1995) or by genes (Rogina & Helfand, 1995), it was shown that these temporal patterns were related proportionally to life span rather than to chronological time.

There is a long-standing expectation in gerontology that the accumulated effects of environmental influences should come to play an increasing role in determining individuality as age advances. A graphic demonstration of such an expected outcome is provided by results shown in Fig. 4a concerning triglyceride levels from an adoption-twin study on aging (Heller, 1992). In a moving interval analysis of variance components (in cross-sectional data), the genetic component declines from a high level in midlife to practically nothing in the 70s. This

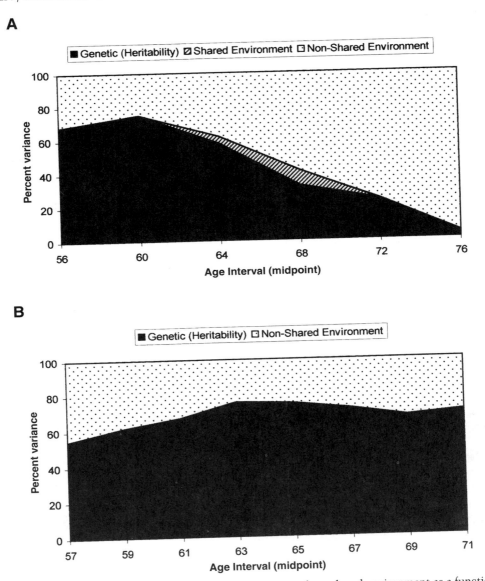

Figure 4. Effects of genetic heritability, shared environment, and nonshared environment as a function of age. Environmental influences play an increasing role in individual differences in serum triglycerides with age (a) [Heller, (1992), used with permission], whereas the pattern of genetic and environmental influences remains stable with age for forced expiratory volume (b) (McClearn *et al.*, 1994).

is not an invariable pattern, however. In the case of forced expiratory volume (Fig. 4b), the heritability (McClearn *et al.*, 1994) remains high throughout the entire age range. Although these observations do not address the issue of whether the same genes are operative throughout the life span for either case, they make it clear that the proportion of genetic influence (and, thus, the proportion of environmental influence) can change. Furthermore, there is no overall rule of thumb—it depends upon the phenotype.

Interactions have been identified in the risk for Alzheimer's disease associated with the ε4–allele of the apolipoprotein E gene (Corder *et al.*, 1994). In a relatively small sample of Nigerians, no evidence was obtained for enhanced risk due to ApoE genotype (Osuntokun *et al.*, 1995). In an African-American population, the risk was found to be less than that reported in Caucasian populations (Sahota *et al.*, 1997). The authors observe that these risk differences may be due to either genetic differences among the populations or the environmental circumstances in which they live. Another study conducted in New York (Tang *et al.*, 1996, 1998) found that the ε4 allele was a significant risk factor in Caucasians but not among African-Americans (with the possible exception of the ε4/ε4 homozygote compared to the ε3/ε3 homozygote). In a metaanalysis of data from 40 groups, Farrer *et al.* (1997) found an ε4-Alzheimer's association in all ethnic groups, but it was weaker in African-Americans and Hispanics and stronger in Japanese relative to Caucasians.

Although empirical documentation of changing genetic influences throughout aging is still sparse, the spectacular advances in molecular developmental genetics might be regarded as making such changes a default expectation when exploring any developmental or aging process.

VI. Quantitative Approaches to Evaluating Gene–Gene and Gene–Environment Interactions: New Opportunities

There is a long history of the development of approaches for evaluating a phenotype for interaction effects, most notably in the context of experimental designs in agricultural or experimental

situations. In these contexts, it is possible to obtain a sufficient degree of experimental control and to obtain data from the very large samples that are required to detect interactions. In general, statistical results from experimental data provide support for the argument that gene–gene interactions (Moreno, 1994; Wright, 1968) and gene–environment interactions are common [for reviews see Kang and Gauch (1995) and Wahlsten (1990)]. Natural populations, including humans, however, present challenges for the detection of interaction effects because of the lack of control over the environment and low statistical power.

Quantitative methods for detecting interaction effects follow from the conceptualization developed by Fisher (1918) of the effects of alleles at a locus and the partitioning of genetic variance into components. Cockerham (1954) and Kempthorne (1954) extended the general least-squares model into a general multilocus model that includes various gene–gene interaction components. A general linear model defines the phenotype as follows:

$$P = G + E + GE,$$

where P is the phenotype (on a scale with a mean of zero), G consists of all genetic effects, E denotes effects of the environment, and GE is the interaction between genotype and environment.

The variance decomposition approach expresses the total genetic variance as:

$$\sigma^2_G = \sigma^2_A + \sigma^2_D + \sigma^2_{AA} + \sigma^2_{AD} + \sigma^2_{DD} + \ldots,$$

which indicates total genetic variance as a function of additive and dominance variance, additive-by-additive interaction, additive-by-dominance interaction, and dominance-by-dominance interaction for two loci. The open-ended form of the equation indicates that there are numerous additional similar terms for the situation described by more than two loci.

The environmental variance, σ^2_E, in the context of a natural population, is a combination of environmental effects. Some are true influences of the environment, and others consist of residual variability that can include random effects such as measurement error.

For a complex phenotype, it is clear that the number of possible interaction effects becomes enormous if more than a handful of loci influence the phenotype. Interestingly, this means that even if individual combinations of alleles produce epistatic effects that are small, the sum of all epistatic effects can be substantial (Cheverud & Routman, 1995). However, the quantitative genetic approach to understanding complex phenotypes, which models variance components as latent unmeasured effects, is likely to be unrealistic for reasonable sample sizes, particularly from natural populations, due to limitations of statistical power. Furthermore, this issue is even more complex for gene–environment interactions because the environmental component may be poorly defined and could consist of numerous real environmental influences in addition to random effects.

Widespread availability of genetic markers provides the opportunity to incorporate information on either candidate genes directly or linked markers into a model of epistasis using techniques based on regression or analysis of variance instead of latent models. The use of measurable genetic influences provides some degree of relief regarding statistical power issues, because the effects are observed rather than latent variables. For exploratory analyses, however, enthusiasm for this approach should be tempered by the fact that the effect of epistasis from any particular measured combination of loci (e.g., specific dyads or triads) might be quite small and difficult to detect even with measured genotype data.

Epistatic interactions between QTLs have been described in mouse for suscep-tibility to lung cancer (Fijneman et al., 1996), epileptic seizure frequency (Frankel et al., 1995), diabetes (Galli et al., 1999), and blood pressure (Rapp et al., 1998), in Caenorhabditis elegans for survival and fertility-related traits (Shook & Johnson, 1999), and in Drosophila for bristle number (Gurganus et al., 1999; Long et al., 1996). Examples of epistatic QTLs have been identified in plant genetics (see Lynch & Walsh, 1998), though studies finding evidence of epistasis from experimental QTL studies are not common and detection is challenging (Gallais & Rives, 1993).

Intriguingly, Damerval et al., (1994) report QTLs for protein volume genes that were not detected through their main effects, but only through their epistatic effect. Because QTL investigations of epistasis generally only consider interactions between loci that exhibit a main effect, it is possible that epistasis is underreported. However, given the issues of practicality and false positive errors, testing for interaction effects among all possible combinations of loci in exploratory studies is not a viable strategy.

The analogous approach of incorporating measured factors is more of a challenge when considering genotype-environment interaction. In health or aging, an important context in which genotype–environment interaction arises is in genetically based individual differences in sensitivity to environmental risk factors or in phenotypic expression which is sensitive to some environmental stimuli at specific periods of development (such as would occur in the Waddington model discussed previously). The challenge is in identifying precisely what the relevant environmental risk factors are for any particular phenotype.

Once relevant aspects of the environment are identified, analysis of variance or regression approaches can be applied to detect interaction effects. Some controversy exists over the precise form of an ANOVA model for genotype–environment interaction effects (Ayres & Thomas, 1990; Fry, 1992). These issues generally concern whether genetic and environmental influences are considered to be fixed or random effects. In general, random effects models assume that the factors are sampled randomly from some larger population of possibilities, whereas fixed effects models assume that the factors are fixed for a specific reason. In general, genotypes are considered appropriately as random effects, and the controversy primarily is focused on the nature of environmental effects. Lynch and Walsh (1998) contrast the alternative assumptions and interpretations of random effects versus mixed-model ANOVA in the context of genotype–environment interaction models. As an alternative, joint-regression analysis [summarized by Lynch and Walsh (1998)] permits partitioning of the genotype interaction effect into the tendency of a genotype to respond to different environments more or less strongly than the average response and residual variance about the regression line that can differ as a function of genotype.

To exploit the opportunities for quantitative assessment of genotype–environment interaction using genetic markers, it is imperative that measures of relevant environmental factors also be developed. In health and aging research, such measures are not always obvious, yet they are critical to the implementation of quantitative genetic models with measured genotypes and environments in order to assess genotype–environment interaction effects.

New opportunities will arise with the rapid expansion of technology to assess gene expression in large numbers of genes using microarrays. Investigation of differential response of genes on alternative genetic backgrounds or in alternative environments will bring us one step closer to potential mechanisms of epistasis or gene–environment interaction. At the same time, this technology will bring greater attention to the issues that arise when many genes are evaluated. It is clear from gene expression results that many genes are likely to be identified as showing differences in alternative conditions. ANOVA or regression-based approaches are ill-equipped to handle such massive amounts of information. New techniques involving pattern recognition or clustering are required. Despite the challenges involved, these procedures ultimately are likely to be closer to causal field analysis than current ANOVA and regression procedures.

VII. Summary and Conclusions

It is abundantly clear that, for many age-related traits and anomalies related to aging, the pattern of genetic and environmental influences is likely to be characterized more by complexity, including interactions, than by simplicity. Consequently, in research designed to understand the full complexity of individual differences in these traits, the quantitative genetic model must be elaborated further to include genetic influences on the influences of the environment and of environmental effects on gene expression.

The extensive set of examples that are available in the literature to demonstrate that the the consequences of an allelic configuration at a particular locus might be modified by the allelic configuration at other loci or under different configurations of environmental factors emphasizes the contextual embeddedness of the "effects of a gene." This has a number of implications at both the conceptual and practical levels.

The simple search for a mechanism using a one gene–one product strategy, though useful at some highly restrictive level, is not sufficient for understanding the full complexity of genetic and environmental influences on phenotypic expression at the whole organism level. For many issues of relevance to aging, it is this higher level that is likely to have the greatest impact in ultimate applications. Whereas the investigation of single-gene effects provides a starting point to identify potential elemental loci and environmental circumstances to include in a more comprehensive investigation without which an integrationist approach would be severely limited, it represents merely a starting point. Future research strategies should, as a rule, ultimately lead to a systems approach that incorporates information in a manner that can be used to characterize complexity. Clearly there are limitations to the ability of quantitative methods to handle complexity in realistic data sets. But consideration of small subsets of factors (dyads or triads) might be sufficient to go far in characterizing complexity. Clearly there remains a place for both reduction and integration in building a comprehensive understanding of age-related traits.

Ultimately, casting of influences of individual loci and environmental factors in a complex network will open up opportunities for conceptualizations that are not normally considered in quantitative genetic analysis. There are likely to be phenotypes where it is appropriate to conceptualize genetic influences as having an impact on the environment, as well as the environment impacting gene expression. Gene expression technology may permit more accurate assessment of more complex mechanisms, including feedback from the environment to the genotype.

Gene–environment and gene–gene interactions have had a place in quantitative genetics nearly from the beginning. Rapid developments in molecular genetics provide expanded opportunities to incorporate these influences in complex models of aging from the genetic perspec-

tive. Equal emphasis should be placed on utilizing appropriate environmental assessments within genetically informative designs. High-quality genetic and environmental assessment will be the key in providing the elements of comprehensive models of complex systems in aging that incorporate gene–environment and gene–gene interactions as integral components.

Acknowledgments

The examples cited from the authors' own work were supported variously by the MacArthur Foundation Research Network on Successful Aging, NIA Grants AG04948, AG09333, AG08861, AG04563, AG10175, and AG14731; NIAAA Grant AA08125, NHLBI Grant HL55976, and funds from the Center for Developmental and Health Genetics.

References

Ayres, M. P., & Thomas, D. L. (1990). Alternative formulations of the mixed-model ANOVA applied to quantitative genetics. *Evolution, 44,* 221–226.

Bergeman, C. S., Plomin, R., Pedersen, N. L., McClearn, G. E., & Nesselroade, J. R. (1990). Genetic and environmental influences on social support: The Swedish adoption/twin study of aging. *Journal of Gerontology, 45,* 101–106.

Blizard, D. A., & Randt, C. T. (1974). Genotype interaction with undernutrition and external environment in early life. *Nature, 251,* 705–707.

Bonner, J. T. (1988). *The Evolution of Complexity.* Princeton, NJ: Princeton University Press.

Bouchard, C., Perusse, L., & Leblanc, C. (1990). Using MZ twins in experimental research to test for the presence of genotype-environment interaction effect. *Acta Geneticae Medicae et Gemellologiae, 39,* 85–89.

Braungart, J. M., Plomin, R., & Fulker, D. W. (1992). Genetic mediation of the home environment during infancy: A sibling adoption study of the HOME. *Developmental Psychology, 28,* 1048–1055.

Cattell, R. B. (1963). The interaction of hereditary and environmental influences. *British Journal of Statistical Psychology,* 16, 191–210.

Cattell, R. B. (1965). Methodological and conceptual advances in evaluating hereditary and environmental influences and their interaction. In S. G. Vandenberg (Ed.), *Methods and goals in human behavior genetics* (pp. 95–139). New York: Academic Press.

Cavener, D. (1979). Preference for ethanol in *Drosophila melanogaster* associated with the alcohol dehydrogenase polymorphism. *Behavior Genetics,* 9, 359–365.

Cheverud, J. M., & Routman, E. J. (1995). Epistasis and its contribution to genetic variance components. *Genetics,* 139, 1455–1461.

Cockerham, C. C. (1954). An extension of the concept of partitioning hereditary variance for analysis of covariances among relatives when epistasis is present. *Genetics,* 39, 859–882.

Coleman, D. L., & Hummel, K. P. (1975). Influence of genetic background on the expression of mutations at the diabetes locus in the mouse. II. Studies on background modifiers. *Israeli Journal of Medical Science,* 11, 708–713.

Cooper, R. M., & Zubek, J. P. (1958). Effects of enriched and restricted early environments on the learning ability of bright and dull rats. *Canadian Journal of Psychology,* 12, 159–164.

Corder, E. H., Saunders, A. M., Risch, N. J., Strittmatter, W. J., Schmechel, D. E., Gaskell, P. C., Jr., Rimmler, J. B., Locke, P. A., Conneally, P. M., Schmader, K. E., Small, G. W., Roses, A. D., Haines, J. L., & Pericak-Vance, M. A. (1994). Protective effect of apolipoprotein E type 2 allele for late onset Alzheimer disease. *Nature Genetics,* 7, 180–184.

Crabbe, J. C., Jr., & Harris, R. A. (1991). *The Genetic Basis of Alcohol and Drug Actions.* New York: Plenum.

Damerval, C., Maurice, A., Josse, J. M., & de Vienne, D. (1994). Quantitative trait loci underlying gene product variation: A novel perspective by analyzing regulation of genome expression. *Genetics,* 137, 289–301.

Deitrich, R. A. (2000). *Bibliography of Short and Long Sleep Mice and High and Low Alcohol Sensitivity Rats (Tech. Report).* Denver, CO: University of Colorado Alcohol Research Center.

Falconer, D. S. (1960). Selection of mice for growth on high and low planes of nutrition. *Genetical Research,* 1, 91–113.

Falconer, D. S., & Mackay, T. F. C. (1996). *Introduction to Quantitative Genetics,* 4th ed.. London: Longman.

Farrer, L. A., Cupples, L. A., Haines, J. L., Hyman, B., Kukull, W. A., Mayeux, R., Myers, R. H., Pericak-Vance, M. A., Risch, N., & van Duijn, C. M. (1997). Effects of age, sex, and ethnicity on the association between apolipoprotein E genotype and Alzheimer disease. A meta-analysis. *Journal of the American Medical Association,* 278, 1349–1356.

Festing, M. F. W. (1979). *Inbred Strains in Biomedical Research.* London: Macmillan.

Fijneman, R. J., de Vries, S. S., Jansen, R. C., & Demant, P. (1996). Complex interactions of new quantitative trait loci, *Sluc1, Sluc2, Sluc3,* and *Sluc4,* that influence the susceptibility to lung cancer in the mouse. *Nature Genetics,* 14, 465–467.

Fisher, R. A. (1918). The correlation between relatives on the supposition of Mendelian inheritance. *Transactions of the Royal Society of Edinburgh,* 52, 399–433.

Ford, D. H. (1987). *Humans as Self-Constructing Living Systems: A Developmental Perspective on Behavior and Personality.* Hillsdale, NJ: Erlbaum.

Fosmire, G. J., Focht, S. J., & McClearn, G. E. (1993). Genetic influences on tissue deposition of aluminum in mice. *Biological Trace Element Research,* 37, 115–121.

Fowler, R. E., & Edwards, R. G. (1961). "Midget," a new dwarfing gene in the house mouse dependent on a genetic background of small body size for its expression. *Genetical Research,* 2, 272–282.

Frankel, W. N., Valenzuela, A., Lutz, C. M., Johnson, E. W., Dietrich, W. F., & Coffin, J. M. (1995). New seizure frequency QTL and the complex genetics of epilepsy in EL mice. *Mammalian Genome,* 6, 830–838.

Fry, J. D. (1992). The mixed-model analysis of variance applied to quantitative genetics: Biological meaning of the parameters. *Evolution,* 46, 540–550.

Gallais, A., & Rives, M. (1993). Detection, number and effects of QTLs for a complex character. *Argonomi, 13*, 723–738.

Galli, J., Fakhrai-Rad, H., Kamel, A., Marcus, C., Norgren, S., & Luthman, H. (1999). Pathophysiological and genetic characterization of the major diabetes locus in GK rats. *Diabetes, 48*, 2463–2470.

Gatz, M., Pedersen, N. L., Plomin, R., Nesselroade, J. R., & McClearn, G. E. (1992). Importance of shared genes and shared environments for symptoms of depression in older adults. *Journal of Abnormal Psychology, 101*, 701–708.

Gelman, R., Watson, A., Bronson, R., Yunis, E. (1988). Murine chromosomal regions correlated with longevity. *Genetics, 118*, 693–704.

Goldman, D. (1993). Recent developments in alcoholism: Genetic transmission. *Recent Developments in Alcoholism, 11*, 231–248.

Gurganus, M. C., Nuzhdin, S. V., Leips, J. W., & Mackay, T. F. (1999). High-resolution mapping of quantitative trait loci for sternopleural bristle number in Drosophila melanogaster. *Genetics, 152*, 1585–1604.

Helfand, S. L., Blake, K. J., Rogina, B., Stracks, M. D., Centurion, A., & Naprta, B. (1995). Temporal patterns of gene expression in the antenna of the adult Drosophila melanogaster. *Genetics, 140*, 549–555.

Heller, D. A. (1992). *Genetic and Environmental Influences on Serum Lipids in Elderly Twins Reared Together and Reared Apart*. Unpublished doctoral dissertation, The Pennsylvania State University, University Park.

Hoffman, A. A., & Parsons, P. A. (1991). Selection for increased desiccation resistance in Drosophila melanogaster: Additive genetic control and correlated responses for other stresses. *Genetics, 122*, 837–845.

Hogben, L. (1933). *Nature and Nurture*. London: Allen and Unwin.

Jazwinski, S. M. (1999). Non-linearity of the aging process revealed in studies with yeast. In V. A. Bohr, B. F. C. Clark, & T. Stevnsner (Eds.), *Molecular Biology of Aging* (pp. 35–44). Copenhagen: Munksgaard.

Jazwinski, S. M., Kim, S., Lai, C,-Y., & Benguria, A. (1998). Epigenetic stratification: the role of individual change in the biological aging process. *Experimental Gerontology, 33*, 571–580.

Jacob, F., & Monod, J. (1961). Genetic regulatory mechanisms in the synthesis of proteins. *Journal of Molecular Biology, 3*, 318–356.

Kacser, H., & Burns, J. A. (1979). Molecular democracy: Who shares the controls? *Biochemical Society Transactions, 7*, 1149–1160.

Kang, M. S., & Gauch, H. G., Jr. (1995). *Genotype-By-Environment Interaction*. Boca Raton, FL: CRC Press.

Kauffman, S. A. (1993). *The Origins of Order*. New York: Oxford University Press.

Kempthorne, O. (1954). The correlation between relatives in a random mating population. *Proceedings of the Royal Society of London B, 143*, 103–113.

Lee, C-K., Klopp, R. G., Weindruch, R., & Prolla, T. A. (1999). Gene expression profile of aging and its retardation by caloric restriction. *Science, 285*, 1390–1393.

Long, A. D., Mullaney, S. L., Mackay, T. F., & Langley, C. H. (1996). Genetic interactions between naturally occurring alleles at quantitative trait loci and mutant alleles at candidate loci affecting bristle number *in Drosophila melanogaster. Genetics, 144*, 1497–1510.

Luckinbill, L. S., Arking, R., Clare, M. J., Cirocco, W., & Buck, S. A. (1984). Selection for delayed senescence in Drosophila melanogaster. *Evolution, 3*, 996–1003.

Lynch, M., & Walsh, B. (1998). *Genetics and Analysis of Quantitative Traits*. Sunderland, MA: Sinauer.

Mackie, J. L. (1974). *The Cement of the Universe*. Oxford: Clarendon Press.

McClearn, G. E. (1987). The many genetics of aging. In A. D. Woodhead, & K. H. Thompson (Eds,), *Evolution of Longevity in Animals: A Comparative Approach* (pp. 135–144). New York: Plenum Press.

McClearn, G. E. (1991). The tools of pharmacogenetics. In J. C. Crabbe, & R. A. Harris (Eds.), *The Genetic Basis of Alcohol and Drug Actions* (pp. 1–23). New York: Plenum Press.

McClearn, G. E., & Kakihana, R. (1981). Selective breeding for ethanol sensitivity: SS and LS mice. In G. E. McClearn, R. A. Deitrich, & V. G. Erwin (Eds.),

Development of Animal Models as Pharmacogenetic Tools (pp. 147–159). Washington DC: U. S. Printing Office (DHEW Publication No. [ADM] 81–113).

McClearn, G. E., Svartengren, M., Pedersen, N. L., Heller, D. A., & Plomin, R. (1994). Genetic and environmental influences on pulmonary function in aging Swedish twins. *Journal of Gerontology: Medical Sciences, 49,* M264–M268.

Mitton, J. B. (1997). *Selection in Natural Populations.* Oxford: Oxford University Press.

Moos, R. H, & Moos, B. S. (1981). *Family Environment Scale Manual.* Palo Alto, CA: Consulting Psychologists Press.

Moreno, G. (1994). Genetic architecture, genetic behavior, and character evolution. *Annual Review of Ecological Systems, 25,* 31–44.

Osuntokun, B. O., Sahora, A., Oguniyyi, A. O., Gureje, O., Baiyewu, O., Adeyinka, A., Oluwole, S. O., Komolafe, O., Hull, K. S., Unverzugt, F. W., Hui, S. L., Yang, M., & Hendrie, H. C. (1995). Lack of an association between apolipoprotein E ε4 and Alzheimer's disease in elderly Nigerians. *Annals of Neurology, 38,* 463–465.

Plomin, R. (1994). *Genetics and Experience: The Interplay Between Nature and Nurture.* Thousand Oaks, CA: Sage Publications.

Plomin, R., & Bergeman, C. S. (1991). The nature of nurture: Genetic influence on "environmental" measures. *Behavioral and Brain Sciences, 14,* 414–424.

Plomin, R., DeFries, J., & Loehlin, J. (1977). Genotype-environment interaction and correlation in the analysis of human development. *Psychological Bulletin, 84,* 309–322.

Plomin, R., Lichtenstein, P., Pedersen, N. L., McClearn, G. E., & Nesselroade, J. R. (1990). Genetic influence on life events during the last half of the lifespan. *Psychology and Aging, 5,* 25–30.

Plomin, R., McClearn, G. E., Pedersen, N. L., Nesselroade, J. R., & Bergeman, C. S. (1988). Genetic influence on childhood family environment perceived retrospectively from the last half of the life span. *Developmental Psychology, 24,* 738–745.

Plomin, R., McClearn, G. E., Pedersen, N. L., Nesselroade, J. R., & Bergeman, C. S. (1989). Genetic influence on adults' ratings of their current family environment. *Journal of Marriage and the Family, 51,* 791–803.

Plomin, R., Reiss, D., Hetherington, E. M., & Howe, G. W. (1994). Nature and nurture: Genetic contributions to measures of the family environment. *Developmental Psychology, 30,* 32–43.

Plomin, R., & Rutter, M. (1998). Child development, molecular genetics, and what to do with genes once they are found. *Child Development, 69,* 1223–1242.

Powell, J. R. (1997). *Progress and Prospects in Evolutionary Biology: The Drosophila Model.* New York: Oxford University Press.

Rapp, J. P., Garrett, M. R., & Deng, A. Y. (1998). Construction of a double congenic strain to prove an epistatic interaction on blood pressure between rat chromosomes 2 and 10. *Journal of Clinical Investigation, 101,* 1591–1595.

Rende, R. D., Slomkowski, C. L., Stocker, C., Fulker, D. W., & Plomin, R. (1992). Genetic and environmental influences on maternal and sibling interaction in middle childhood: A sibling adoption study. *Developmental Psychology, 28,* 484–490.

Rogina, B., & Helfand, S. L. (1995). Regulation of gene expression is linked to life span in adult Drosophila. *Genetics, 141,* 1043–1048.

Rose, M. R. (1991). *Evolutionary Biology of Aging.* New York: Oxford University Press.

Ross, H. (1985). *Evidence for Genetic Factors in Catch-Up Growth.* Unpublished Master's Thesis. University Park; The Pennsylvania State University.

Rowe, D. C. (1981). Environmental and genetic influences on dimensions of perceived parenting: A twin study. *Developmental Psychology, 17,* 203–208.

Rowe, D. C. (1983). A biometrical analysis of perceptions of family environment: A study of twin and singleton siblings. *Child Development, 54,* 416–434.

Rowe, D. C., Jacobson, K. C., & Van den Oord, E. J. (1999). Genetic and environmental influences on vocabulary IQ: Parental education level as moderator. *Child Development, 70*, 1151–1162.

Sahota, A., Yang, M., Gao, S., Hui, S. L., Baiyewu, O., Gureje, O., Oluwole, S., Ogunniyi, A., Hall, K. S., & Hendrie, H. C. (1997). Apolipoprotein E-associated risk for Alzheimer's disease in the African-American population is genotype dependent. *Annals of Neurology, 42*, 659–661.

Salthe, S. N. (1985). *Evolving Hierarchical Systems*. New York: Columbia University Press.

Sattler, R. (1986). *Biophilosophy: Analytic and Holistic Perspectives*. Berlin: Springer-Verlag.

Scarr, S., & McCartney, K. (1983). How people make their own environments: A theory of genotype-environment effects. *Child Development, 54*, 424–435.

Shook, D. R., & Johnson, T. E. (1999). Quantitative trait loci affecting survival and fertility-related traits in *Caenorhabditis elegans* show genotype-environment interactions, pleiotropy and epistasis. *Genetics, 153*, 1233–1243.

Simon, H. A. (1973). The organization of complex systems. In H. H. Pattee (Ed.), *Hierarchy Theory: The Challenge of Complex Systems*. New York: George Braziller.

Sing, C. F., Zerba, K. E., & Reilly, S. L. (1994). Traversing the biological complexity in the hierarchy between genome and CAD endpoints in the population at large. *Clinical Genetics, 46*, 6–14.

Sokolowski, M. B., Bauer, S. J., Wai-Ping, V., Rodriguez, L., Wong, J. L., & Kent, C. (1986). Ecological genetics and behaviour of Drosophila melanogaster larvae in nature. *Animal Behavior, 34*, 403–408.

Stebbins, G. L. (1974). *Flowering Plants: Evolution Above the Species Level*. Cambridge: The Belknap Press of Harvard University.

Stein, W., & Varela, F. J. (1993). *Thinking about Biology*. Reading, MA: Addison-Wesley.

Tang, M. X., Maestre, G., Twai, W. Y., Liu, X. H., Fent, L., Chung, W. Y., Chun, M., Schofield, P., Stern, Y., Tycko, B., &

Mayeux, R. (1996). Effect of age, ethnicity, and head injury on the association between APOE genotypes and Alzheimer's disease. *Annals of The New York Academy of Sciences, 16*, 6–15.

Tang, M. X., Stern, Y., Marder, K., Bell, K., Gurland, B., Lantigua, R., Andrews, H., Feng, L., Tycko, B., & Mayeux, R. (1998). The APOE-epsilon4 allele and the risk of Alzheimer disease among African Americans, whites, and Hispanics. *Journal of the American Medical Association, 279*, 751–755.

Vieira, C., Pasyukova, E. G., Zeng, Z.-B., Hackett, J. B., Lyman, R. F., & Mackay, T. F. C. (2000). Genotype-environment interaction for quantitative trait loci affecting life span in *Drosophila melanogaster. Genetics, 154*, 213–227.

Vogler, G. P., McClearn, G. E., Snieder, H., Boomsma, D. I., Palmer, R., de Knijff, P., & Slagboom, P. E. (1997). Genetics and behavioral medicine: Risk factors for cardiovascular disease. *Behavioral Medicine, 22*, 141–149.

Waddington, C. H. (1953). Genetic assimilation of an acquired character. *Evolution, 7*, 118–126.

Waddington, C. H. (1957). *The Strategy of the Genes*. New York: Macmillan.

Wahlsten, D. (1990). Insensitivity of the analysis of variance to heredity-environment interaction. *Behavioral and Brain Sciences, 13*, 109–120.

Wahlsten, D. (1999). Single-gene influences on brain and behavior. *Annual Review of Psychology, 50*, 599–624.

Wahlsten, D., & Gottlieb, G. (1997). The invalid separation of effects of nature and nurture: Lessons from animal experimentation. In R. J. Sternberg & E. L. Grigorenko (Eds.), *Intelligence, Heredity, and Environment* (pp. 163–192). New York: Cambridge University Press.

Wright, S. (1968). *Evolution and the genetics of populations. I. Genetic and biometric foundations*. Chicago: University of Chicago Press.

Yates, F. E., Marsh, D. J., & Iberall, A. S. (1972). Integration of the whole organism—A foundation for a theoretical biology. In J. A. Behnke (Ed.), *Challenging Biological Problems: Directions Toward their*

Solution (pp. 110–132). Fairlawn, NY: Oxford University Press.

Zeleny, C., & Mattoon, E. W. (1915). The effect of selection upon the "bar eye" mutant of *Drosophila. Journal of Experimental Zoology, 9,* 515–529.

Seventeen

Aging, Health, Longevity, and the Promise of Biomedical Research: The Perspective of a Gerontologist and Geriatrician

William R. Hazzard

I. Aging, Health, Longevity, and the Promise of Biomedical Research: The Perspective of a Gerontologist and Geriatrician

The foregoing chapters elaborate the biological basis of aging at levels of increasing complexity, from the genome itself to subcellular and cellular levels, to organs and organ systems, and to mechanisms of their integration and the maintenance of homeostasis in the steady state and during perturbation, both short term and on a lifelong basis. Other chapters introduce evidence that suggests that longevity may be plastic, with the potential for extension through genetic and environmental manipulation. Beyond the focus of this volume, but of equal relevance to the field of gerontology, are companion bodies of research-based knowledge on the psychological and social dimensions of aging. All of these contributions anticipate ever greater acceleration of scientific progress in gerontology in the new millennium as the fruits of the human genome project, gene and ultrasophisticated pharmacological, medical, and surgical intervention therapy, biomedical imaging, and information technology are increasingly brought to bear on our most ancient fear and fascination, the wonder of life and the certainty of human mortality.

The pace of progress reflected in these chapters can be dizzying. Indeed this explosion of information may threaten to overwhelm the geriatric clinician working with fellow health professionals, patients, and their supporters in an effort to maximize the quality and quantity of the lives of aging people. Whereas the magnitude, complexity, and inevitable need to deal with constraints on resources in the delivery of optimal geriatric care may seem far removed from the world of basic biogerontology, the public that funds much of the basic research clearly is increasingly concerned with the realities of clinical geriatrics, even as they invest hope and considerable resources in

Handbook of the Biology of Aging, Fifth Edition

the promise of breakthroughs from fundamental investigations. Moreover, that public has mixed feelings regarding the implications of such advances for the costs of caring for an ever-aging society. Therefore, a primary goal of this treatise is to strengthen the bridge of understanding between biological gerontology and clinical geriatrics in the interest of enhancing the insight of each discipline into the world of the other and promoting communication and collaboration between the two. Articulation of a philosophy and set of organizing principles in this essay may serve as the foundation for this bridge, with selected examples from human physiology and clinical medicine to illustrate major concepts.

II. Preventive Gerontology: A Lifelong Strategy To Minimize Secondary Aging and Make Successful and Usual Aging Synonymous

Much has been written in the past two decades regarding the universal human goal of successful aging. Put simply, to age successfully is to live a life of highest quality, maximal longevity, and minimal disease and disability. This philosophy received perhaps its most eloquent, yet provocative, articulation in a 1980 essay by James Fries entitled, "Aging, Natural Death, and the Compression of Morbidity" (Fries, 1980). In this seminal treatise, Fries combined elegant prose, at times bordering on poetry and fantasy, with science and common sense. His treatise emphasized that the progressive rise in average longevity in America in the twentieth century took place in parallel with advances in education, housing, transportation, public health, health care, biomedical science, and prosperity in general. This remarkable increase in longevity thus was largely attributable to

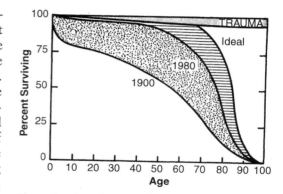

Figure 1. American population survival curves in 1900, 1980, and the future, ideal state per the theory of Fries (1980).

the impact of all of these developments in vastly reducing infant and childhood death that ravaged our underdeveloped nation at the turn of the twentieth century. However, this transformation largely was complete in America by midcentury. Whereas average longevity has continued to rise since 1950, its rate of increase has decelerated as the causes of mortality have shifted to the chronic diseases of middle and, increasingly, old age. These trends have caused a progressive shift of the human survival curve from the semilogarithmic first-order morphology of biblical times (when average longevity was about 30 years) to a more rectangular configuration (Fig. 1) in which death prior to true old age (above 75–85 years) becomes uncommon. A narrow, nearly Gaussian distribution of ages at death evolves from this shift, one only slightly skewed to the left with an average age at death of 85 ± 4 years (Fig. 2) [revised by Fries to ±7 (personal communication)], with well less than 1% of death occurring above age 100. Fundamental to this argument has been the principle that the absolute upper limit of human longevity (sometimes called the maximum life span potential, MLSP) is fixed in the genome of our species at ca. 122.3 years, the current

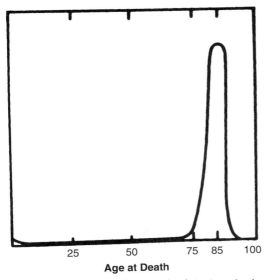

Age at Death

Figure 2. Histogram of ages at death in America in the future, ideal state per the theory of Fries (1980).

record for longevity set in 1997 by Jean Calment, a French woman who died at that age. Thus, barring unforeseen breakthroughs in biotechnology (amply described for nonhuman species in this volume, however), according to Fries' argument, human longevity will be maximized in the mid-twenty-first century at an *average* age at death of 85 years. This contention has been bolstered by subsequent research that has estimated the magnitude of reductions in mortality from the major chronic diseases all too familiar to the geriatric clinician (heart disease, stroke, cancer, and diabetes) that would be required to reach that 85-year average age at death: all causes of death would have to decline by over 60% beyond age 50; indeed, if deaths attributable to cancer, diabetes, and cardiovascular disease were prevented entirely, overall mortality would be reduced by only 75% (Olshansky & Carnes, 1990). Hence, it seems highly unlikely that that an average figure of 85 years will be reached within any current clinician's lifetime. Thus, deceleration in the rate of

rise in average longevity is likely to continue even as the average inches toward the 85-year mark.

A corollary, cardinal feature of the Fries treatise was the concept of a "compression of morbidity" as that barrier to immortality is approached. Thus, when premature death has been minimized, disease, disability, and functional decline will become compressed into a "brief" period before death [acknowledged by Fries, however, to average ca. 3–5 years (personal communication)]. At that point, parallel, irreducible declines in physiological efficiency in all systems proceeding from aging per se will lead to multisystem failure and "natural death" at the age genetically programmed for the individual. Such natural death would be attributable to "primary aging", whereas any death occurring earlier would be defined as premature and (except those proceeding from violence or environmental catastrophes) attributable to a combination of primary and "secondary" aging. The latter are disease processes that may accelerate and, hence, mimic the phenotype of primary aging, but are at least potentially amenable to being retarded through environmental, biomedical, or behavioral interventions. (To disentangle secondary aging from primary aging has preoccupied medical gerontologists and geriatricians ever since these fields were born, an exercise likened by some wags as akin to trying to "sweep the sand off the beach.") In this scenario, effective "preventive gerontology" (Hazzard, 1983, 1997, 1999) represents a strategy to retard pathogenic processes such that death occurs from primary aging per se before the clinical horizon for a given disease has been crossed (Fig. 3). Alternatively, such premature interventions will defer the advent of clinical disease until close to one's genetically determined upper limit of life. At that point, morbidity, often in the form of multiple diseases affecting multiple organs, will emerge

448   W. R. Hazzard

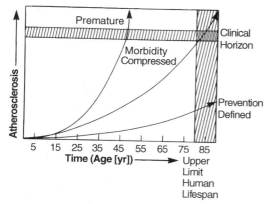

Figure 3. Prototypical course of a chronic progressive disease (atherosclerosis in this illustration) in the various scenarios according to differential success in the application of prevention strategies, per the theory of Fries (1980). (Reproduced with permission from *Atherosclerosis and Aging*, S. R. Bates & E. C. Gangloff, Eds., pp. 75–103, 1987 New York: Springer-Verlag.)

often in the form of the common "geriatric syndromes" (e.g., the five I's of incompetence, incontinence, immobility, impaired homeostasis, and iatrogenesis) during a compressed period of preterminal decline along an ever-accelerating final common pathway of frailty, disability, multisystem failure, and death.

According to this philosophy, applied preventive gerontology becomes translated as detailed by Fries and Crapo (1981) into a menu of personal strategies to enhance vitality in physical, psychological, and social domains, with some differences in points of emphasis specific to each stage of life, but all in the interest of ensuring a life of maximal quality and quantity (Table I). In scanning this list of strategies, certain features become apparent. First, effective preventive gerontology begins before birth and continues throughout life. However, those strategies with the greatest payoff in terms of added longevity are initiated well before old age. Conversely, although it appears that it is never too late to derive some benefit, the least return in

those terms will be from interventions initiated near the end of life. Moreover, given that even such theoretically benign interventions as a change in diet or physical exercise carry the potential for adverse outcomes when begun in old age, careful, individualized evaluation of risk versus benefit of every element of a general preventive strategy is central to expert geriatric practice.

Second, the list of recommended interventions is short when compared with the long list of potential benefits to be derived, e.g., a diet low in fat and of appropriate caloric content would be expected to reduce the risk of heart disease, diabetes, and cancer. Similarly, a program of conscientious, active exercise, both aerobic and resistive, will assist not only in preventing or reversing obesity but also in enhancing muscular strength, bone mineral content, vascular tone and blood flow to critical organs, and agility.

Third, most of the elements of this plan are hardly more than common sense (what might be summarized as "what your grandmother told you"). Yet it is amazing in the real world how uncommon such common sense really is. Hence, the challenge to make preventive gerontology an effective program adopted on a population-wide basis is to mount effective programs of public education and interventions that achieve broad support. To achieve requisite dissemination, these must utilize the media and, increasingly, information technology to promote the healthy behaviors and environmental safeguards that are at the core of this largely public health approach. At the same time, it is incumbent upon the scientific community to undergird this common sense approach with a solid basis in evidence, a daunting and no doubt never-ending challenge. Nevertheless, as will be noted later, that scientific underpinning grows stronger with every passing year.

Table I

A Life-Stage-Specific Schedule for Successful Application of Preventive Gerontology[a]

Prenatal life (maternal strategies)
Maximize fetal growth and development: prevent low birth weight
  Optimal nutrition
  Prenatal blood pressure and glucose regulation
  Avoid unnecessary drugs
  Avoid alcohol
  Avoid tobacco
Appropriate prenatal medical care, labor, and delivery

Infancy and childhood
Breast-feeding to optimize infant nutrition and immunological status
Optimize childhood nutrition: learn lifelong healthy eating habits
  Calories, appropriate distribution among carbohydrates, fats, and protein
  Minerals (especially calcium and iron)
  Vitamins
Vitamin supplements as appropriate
Immunizations
Learn lifelong activity and exercise patterns (build exercise into daily activity, e.g., walking to school, riding bicycle to sports activities)
Learn behavioral and social skills
Begin formal education (including basic health education)
Health care and counseling as appropriate

Adolescence (to age ca. 25 years)
Continue optimal nutrition: Reinforce healthy eating habits
  Provide appropriate substrates for growth and maturation
  Minerals (especially calcium to optimize skeletal growth and iron for marrow reserves, especially for women)
  Vitamins
  Calories: adequate amount to support growth spurt; avoid excess fat and simple carbohydrates (prevent obesity); emphasize complex carbohydrates and fiber
  Proteins
  Avoid extremes of body weight: underweight (from anorexia or exercise to the point of cachexia) is as great a risk as overweight (especially in girls)
Maximize exercise: aerobic and anaerobic in high amounts (prevent obesity and build lean body mass)
Avoid toxic substance exposure and habituation: tobacco, alcohol, mind-altering drugs
Learn behavioral control, obtain emotional stability, maturity, and interpersonal skills
Avoid hazardous behaviors (e.g., risky driving, unprotected sex); practice safety measures (e.g., use seat belts, eliminate careless or hostile firearms use)
Pursue higher undergraduate, graduate, and professional education

Middle age—first half (ca. 25–50 years)
Optimize reproductive health and outcomes (especially in women): appropriate weight gain in pregnancy and postnatal return to desirable weight, enhanced by breast-feeding
Continue optimal nutrition (adopt AHA Step I diet low in fat and cholesterol, moderate in salt and simple sugars); prevent obesity, especially "middle age spread" (upper body "android" obesity, especially in men), optimize glucose and lipid metabolism
Continue regular exercise: incorporate physical exercise into daily activities and optimize metabolism, prevent obesity, e.g., walk to work, shopping; regular exercise to the point of sweating at least 30 min, 3 times weekly
Undergo periodic health screening (blood pressure, cholesterol; in women, pap smears and later mammograms): treat conditions detected as appropriate
Avoid toxic exposures: substance abuse, excessive sunlight, environmental hazards
Continue safe health and behavior practices (safe sex, seat belts, etc.)
Continuous education, including health education

(continues)

Table I   *(Cont'd)*

Balance life challenges and tasks in a healthy manner: work, home, family, personal interests, and leisure

Middle Age—Second Half (ca. 50–75 years)

Continue optimal nutrition: women, avoid postmenopausal weight gain and shift to "android" obesity (emphasize complex carbohydrates and fiber for diverticulosis and possibly colon cancer prevention); men, focus on diet to prevent cardiovascular disease

Continue regular exercise: aerobic and resistive

Avoid toxic exposures: substance abuse, prescription drug dependency, excessive sunlight, environmental hazards

Undergo periodic health screening and clinical examinations: increasing concentration on management of chronic problems with an emphasis on prevention of complications (e.g., hypertension, dyslipoproteinemia, diabetes, cancer detection and early intervention)

Maintain immunization status: tetanus, annual influenza vaccination (with chronic lung or cardiovascular disease and all persons over 65) and one-time pneumococcal vaccination after age 65

Women: have annual mammograms, manage menopause optimally, consider hormone replacement therapy for cardiovascular disease and osteoporosis prevention, calcium and vitamin D supplements for osteoporosis prevention

Men: surveillance of prostate symptoms and digital rectal examinations, with PSAs if at increased risk

Continue education, including health education

Remain socially engaged, negotiate retirement transition as appropriate with forethought and planning (including joint planning by couples for changes in lifestyle, finances, and relationship that retirement will bring)

Old Age (Above 75 years)

Continue optimal nutrition, including calcium, vitamins, adequate calories, protein, and fiber

Continue exercise as possible, both aerobic and resistive

Continue health surveillance and problem management:

  Emphasis upon maintenance of function in social, psychological, and physical domains

  Preventive interventions increasingly focused upon near-term issues:

   Blood pressure

   Blood glucose

   Cardiovascular health: prevent thrombosis (e.g., aspirin)

   Mental health; remain socially and intellectually active, adult education increasingly relevant

   Immunizations

   Maintenance of physical strength and agility through exercise and practice, prevent falls and fractures

  Continue education (e.g. elder hostel for education and social benefits)

  Continue social engagement

  Contemplate relocation for health care, family, social, or financial reasons

[a]A strategy to maximize longevity of highest quality through the practice of effective preventive gerontology. Modified from Hazzard (1999).

Fourth, the role of the formal health care system in this strategy is relatively small. However, with the advancing age of patients and the population at large this role grows progressively, and it will no doubt continue to do so as science continues to provide remarkable ways to diagnose and treat the chronic diseases of old age, even up until very close to the end of life as determined by primary aging. Here geriatricians will join forces with more classically defined specialists and subspecialists both to maximize the health and independence of patients for as long as possible and also to provide expert, sensitive, and sensible care to persons who are in the ineluctable final phase of life, when issues of comfort, freedom from pain, and preservation of dignity become of paramount importance. In this scenario, the geriatrician works hand in hand with patient, family, and other members of a multidisciplinary care team to optimize the outcome of an infinitely complex and subtle process. This delicate professional challenge is, however, ultimately founded in basic biogerontology. Hence, the geriatric physician must constantly stretch him- or herself intellectually to remain in touch with that dynamic scientific base while managing individual patients in an intelligent and informed manner as they negotiate their final path from robust health to frailty and ultimately decline and death. Thus, the expert geriatrician is the consummate professional bridge between effective prevention and acceptance of the consequences of both primary and secondary aging.

The concepts of Fries and preventive gerontology have been expanded further and popularized by John Rowe and Robert Kahn in their works on "Successful Aging" (Rowe & Kahn, 1987, 1998). In these contributions, they have notably expanded the focus of Fries on health-related behaviors to the social realm, emphasizing that sustained, active participation in a dynamic social network and intellectual engagement are as important as physical and medical issues in ensuring a life of maximum quality and vitality.

Data on average longevity, functional status, health-care utilization, and socioeconomic status, gathered in the intervening two decades, have largely supported Fries' thesis. For example, Fries and his colleagues have generated a preliminary confirmation of the validity of the concept of compression of morbidity in prospective studies of an aging cohort of college graduates (Vita *et al.*, 1998). While confirming the progressive course of disease and disability as well as increased death rates of those with adverse health and risk profiles, this study also documents that those with the

most favorable profiles, who nevertheless died during follow-up, remained independent and in vigorous health until shortly before death. The fact that vitality and independence can be sustained until shortly before death has also been supported by population-based studies demonstrating enhanced vigor and decreased health-care utilization (and cost) among present-day Americans over age 80, even surpassing the average remaining survival of their counterparts in societies of the Far East and northern Europe with long traditions of great longevity (Manton & Vaupel, 1995). Also adding to an optimistic view of the future are studies (Lakdawalla & Philipson, 1999) that now project an age-adjusted per capita *decline* in long-term-care requirements (and cost), even as average longevity continues to rise slowly toward the projected maximum age of 85 (it is currently ca. 76 years), the age above which risk of nursing home placement traditionally has risen dramatically. This carries major implications regarding the challenge to our aging American society to provide appropriate care for those at greatest risk by virtue of physical, psychological, social, and functional vulnerability. Of special gerontological significance, given that a spouse of either gender is the source of first resort for support during illness and with deterioration in functional status to a substantial degree, this decline has been attributed to improved health and vitality among older men (as well as the development of community-based alternatives to institutional long-term care). Thus, the ca. 7-year gender gap in longevity that emerged in the United State in the first 70 years of the twentieth century, and was at one time predicted to grow progressively through the mid-twenty-first century, has begun to narrow in the past three decades as gains enjoyed by men have slightly exceeded those by women. Have the messages of preventive gerontology and successful aging begun to penetrate the public consciousness, especially of men, such that the benefits of not smoking, drinking responsibly, eating sensibly, exercising regularly, and detecting and treating risk factors for major diseases are becoming widely appreciated and affecting behaviors accordingly? One might hope so, though the impending epidemic of obesity and its attendant health risks that is emerging in young Americans, especially in teenage girls and in mothers who fail to return to prepregnancy weight following childbirth, is a sobering reminder of just how difficult it is to effect widespread behavioral change, especially when habitual exercise that prevents adipose tissue accumulation is made socially and practically difficult by a style of living built around the automobile.

So how do the scientific contributions of the preceding chapters inform the concepts of preventive gerontology and successful aging? And, vice versa? And, in turn, to geriatrics, the discipline charged with providing health and social care to the elderly? Quite well, it would seem from the perspective of the gerontologist and geriatrician.

First, in daily practice, geriatricians observe the triumphs of successful aging and effective applied preventive gerontology in the burgeoning numbers of vital, robust elderly persons in our practices and especially in our community lives (by definition, the healthiest people have little occasion to visit a physician). Whether by virtue of favored genetic status, favored gender status, favored socioeconomic and educational status, or having practiced a healthy lifestyle across their 80, 90, or 100 years, these inspiring citizens are living proof of the truth of the principles of preventive gerontology.

Second, internists and family physicians, generalists who care for persons across the entire adult life span, are all too familiar with the fate of those who have not lived according to those principles. Such generalists become deeply involved in coping with the impact of the multiple forces that converge to determine the rate of pathogenesis of the chronic diseases that dominate clinical medicine in midlife and beyond: superimposed upon each person's genetic complement (and continually interacting with it), the influences of childhood, adolescent, and adult development, sex hormone physiology, nutrition, physical activity, health behaviors (notably alcohol and cigarette abuse), and environmental forces all modulate the pace of development of cardiovascular disease, cancer, and neurodegenerative and musculoskeletal diseases, the major conditions that preoccupy the clinician who cares for old people. In the latter capacity, rate phenomena that are critical in the pathophysiology of the chronic, progressive diseases of "secondary aging" and, hence, the central role of time in their genesis become a special focus. Here we revisit a fundamental precept of preventive gerontology: rather than seeking, perhaps in vain, to eliminate these disease processes altogether, we can accomplish almost as much by simply retarding their pathogenesis such that symptoms and functional consequences remain below the clinical threshold until shortly before death (the strategy that produces a compression of morbidity) or, in practical terms, preventing them altogether if death from a competing cause or constellation of causes intervenes before their clinical manifestation (Fig. 3). As an example, estrogen replacement therapy (ERT) in postmenopausal women reduces low-density lipoprotein (LDL) and raises high-density lipoprotein (HDL) cholesterol, thereby favorably affecting the cardiovascular risk profile in both the numerator and denominator of the LDL:HDL ratio. Thus, ERT regimens can be designed to avoid the acceleration of atherogenesis that would be predicted to occur with the decline in estrogen secretion across menopause. Of special note, ERT has been suggested to be associated with even greater reductions in cardiovascular disease than would be predicted on the basis of these observed patterns of lipid profiles (Grady et al., 1992). This disparity has led to a widespread search for additional mechanisms of cardiovascular protection conferred by estrogen, focusing upon nitric oxide mediated vascular reactivity as well as possible alterations in the oxidation of LDL and its arterial uptake. Instructive to the discipline of our scientific process, however, these findings, from epidemiological studies and partially controlled clinical trials, especially when combined with data confirming the benefit of ERT in reducing osteoporotic fractures, threatened to foreclose further investigation of ERT and specifically controlled clinical trials that would provide the strongest evidence for the efficacy of this medical intervention. However, the Heart Estrogen Replacement Study (HERS), a secondary prevention trial of ERT in postmenopausal women with established coronary disease, unexpectedly found an early increase in recurrent coronary events and overall no effect over the 4 years of the study (interpreted by optimists as reflecting offsetting effects of estrogen likely to favor ERT with prolonged usage) (Hulley et al., 1998). Thus, the importance of the rigor of conducting formal clinical trials is underscored before the widespread adoption of medical interventions can be recommended. Meanwhile, the results of the Women's Health Initiative remain eagerly awaited to help resolve this important gerontological issue.

Third, the principles of this life span approach to gerontology are consistent with findings from basic research. In the first instance, given that genetics is the foundation of every aspect of biology, it is clear in both population-based research and clinical experience that major genetic abnormalities are prime determinants of abbreviated longevity. Thus, in developed societies in which the major scourges of infections and malnutrition that decimate populations of children have been eliminated, disorders that cause disease, disability, and death in childhood are most likely to reflect serious genetic flaws. As a corollary, when a process such as atherogenesis causes a disease prototypically associated with middle or old age in a child, it most often proceeds from a major genetic abnormality that vastly accelerates that process (e.g., homozygous familial hypercholesterolemia). Indeed, the strategic investigation of such accidents of nature often has produced the most profound insights into the pathogenesis of those disorders because of limited confounders imposed by aging and its inextricable association with the passage of time (e.g., the Nobel prize-winning work of Goldstein and Brown in elucidating the central role of the LDL receptor in regulating hepatic and circulating LDL cholesterol levels and, in turn, the rate of atherogenesis) (Brown & Goldstein, 1986). Thus, insightful gerontological research can capitalize upon every stage of the life span to gain understanding of such processes, coupling research in human genetic disorders with companion investigations utilizing transgenic animals, genetically manipulated cells, and gene and pharmacological interventions to probe the mechanisms of such disorders.

Conversely, diseases that emerge in old age are the least likely to have a major or at least a simple genetic basis. This principle has been amply demonstrated in studies of populations with noteworthy longevity and widespread "successful aging" (Rowe & Kahn, 1998). This tenet, however, has required refinement in investigations that have identified a strong genetic basis even for certain diseases prototypically of late onset (e.g.,

Alzheimer's disease). Thus, whereas most studies of the genetic basis of Alzheimer's disease have verified the principle of early expression of genetic diseases articulated earlier (e.g., major abnormalities in the presenilins and those genes located on chromosome 21, especially those with Down's syndrome and an extra copy of the defective DNA, cause Alzheimer's disease in the 40s and 50s), the serendipitous discovery of the strong association of apolipoprotein E_4 with Alzheimer's disease that passes the clinical horizon after age 65 suggests that even diseases of truly old age may have an important genetic basis. Here, too, however, E_4 seems to accelerate the development of Alzheimer's disease in one otherwise predisposed, but in itself is insufficient to cause the disease even when present in homozygous gene dosage. Thus, multifactorial causation remains the rule for all diseases of aging and especially those of new onset in old age. This principle in turn will better inform interventions designed to forestall the pathogenic process. If the principles of Fries hold true, even if these interventions were only to retard the rate of Alzheimer's pathogenesis, for instance, the projected savings in human misery and economic costs would be monumental, with Alzheimer's disease thereby becoming compressed into a brief final phase of life (if not avoided altogether).

This example also illustrates an emerging emphasis in gerontological research on the complex polygenetic and gene × environment basis of virtually every disease of adulthood. Indeed the genome of each individual is the template upon which every aspect of life and aging is superimposed, including age at death. Thus, contemporary investigations of coronary disease, hypertension, dyslipoproteinemia, and diabetes are revealing an extraordinary complexity in their genetic basis, variable expression at different ages, and the cumulative impact of multiple coincident and interacting disorders at various points in the life span. Even the psychological and social factors that are so important in modulating the impact of diseases of middle and old age, aggravating them in some persons and ameliorating them in others, are being shown to have a major heritable basis. Here the promise of new technologies to unravel this vast network of interacting forces is certain to provide an explosion of important information in this new century: the genome of every individual will be capable of being made known—to the individual, to family members, and possibly to others if codes of privacy are violated. Thus, contemporary discussions already focus on the potential for abuse of the power of the new biogerontology, physicians and other health-care professionals are becoming uneasy at this prospect, and a new discipline of the ethics of biomedical gerontology is emerging (as illustrated by the issue of whether genetic predisposition to Huntington's or Alzheimer's diseases should be determined for those at risk by virtue of a familial predisposition).

Finally, on the genetic front of gerontology, emphasis is now shifting from abnormalities that limit longevity (determinants of "brevigevity," if you will) to those that confer extraordinary longevity. Thus, for reasons reflecting both our traditionally greater fascination with disease than with health in a positive sense, research in medical genetics has long focused on the genetics of disease and premature mortality. Now as we become more sophisticated and impressed by the survival of a substantial number of citizens to age 100 and above, we shall begin to discover genetic as well as behavioral factors that have permitted such extraordinary longevity. Thus, we shall now investigate the genetics of how threats to homeostasis and time-related disorders may be resisted through the blockade of pathogenic processes or compensation for their effects (e.g., how high levels of super-oxide dismutase can prevent damage from accumulated toxic oxidants or how enhanced nitric oxide synthase activity may prevent atherogenesis at the level of the arterial wall).

Here geriatricians will rejoice at the prospect of a shift in their practice from an overwhelming emphasis on chronic, progressive, debilitating disease with its physical, psychological, social, and economic burdens to issues of health in a more positive sense, including optimistic approaches to the prevention and enhancement of vitality even in 90- and 100-year-olds. This will afford a greater balance in their professional activities, even as they maintain their commitment to providing the most expert, compassionate, and comforting care for the very old in terminal decline and the process of dying.

The practice of medicine in the aging and elderly will also be better informed by the advances described in many other contributions to this volume. Adults of all ages and especially seniors already are embracing the potential that consumption of antioxidants may retard or possibly inhibit altogether the many pathogenic consequences of excessive and cumulative exposure to superoxides in various organs and tissues. These "healthy behaviors" are being adapted well ahead of the development of a solid basis in evidence favoring such behavior and no doubt include an element of denial and wishful thinking. Nevertheless, millions are consuming vitamins E and C and even β-carotene as a hedge against ubiquitous damage caused by superoxides. On another front, the remarkable role of folic acid in preventing neural tube defects *in utero* is being extended to its widespread consumption in adults of all ages in an effort to reduce homocysteine levels and, in turn, to retard atherogenesis and coronary disease. Other sophisticated and targeted pharmacological interventions will attempt to retard or reverse the resistance to insulin that seems to accompany aging and accounts for the increase in incidence of type II diabetes in old age. This disease, perhaps the best phenocopy of accelerated aging, is the focus of much gerontological investigation. Here, too, research on the role of exercise in overcoming insulin resistance as well as in the prevention of coronary disease, the osteopenia and sarcopenia of old age, and physical and functional decline even at very advanced ages is especially promising. Finally, insights gained from the remarkable and almost universally confirmed role of caloric restriction in actually prolonging longevity are certain to produce new approaches to increasing the life span and health in old age of many humans. Although it seems unlikely that this strategy will ever receive widespread application in our species, one might predict that we shall instead find a pharmacological or other less ascetic way to achieve the same end, just as we now know that we can largely prevent the consequences of the general hypercholesterolemia that characterizes western society with its habitual high fat, high-calorie diet by widespread intake of the HMG CoA-reductase-inhibiting "statin" drugs that up-regulate the LDL receptor.

Thus, from a clinical gerontologist's perspective, the twenty-first century will be a time of unprecedented promise and excitement. Indeed, during this era a life of great quality, great longevity, and brief, limited disease and preterminal decline may become the norm rather than the exception. Continuing and very likely even accelerating scientific progress will provide the means to make this ideal approachable for millions of people as the fruits of such progress become globally disseminated.

However, just as surely, attitudinal and behavioral barriers to universal acceptance of the principles and practice of preventive gerontology will remain.

These barriers may perhaps even be reinforced by resistance to the behavioral uniformity that widespread adoption of such hygienic practices would introduce, as well as by the ethical dilemmas and challenges to provide care for the very large number of very old people. So, perhaps reassuringly, the diversity of behavior that in large part defines the human species stands in little jeopardy of being lost, even if the key to a life of the greatest duration is discovered in the impending era of exploding biomedical knowledge. The related fields of gerontology and geriatrics will become ever more lively, productive, and fascinating in this new millennium.

Finally—and perhaps most germane to the foregoing chapters—developments in the twenty-first century may challenge the basic premise of Fries' (1980) thesis that the maximum life span potential for humans is immutably fixed in the genome at ca. 122 years. Will advances in basic research, genetic engineering, therapeutics, behavioral norms, or continuing evolution per se alter that concept and possibly raise that upper limit in a way that will shift both maximum and average human longevity to ever higher levels? If so, all bets in this treatise will be off, and future editions of this handbook will deal with a whole new set of challenges that are currently unforeseeable.

References

Brown, M. S., & Goldstein, J. L. (1986). A receptor-mediated pathway for cholesterol homeostasis. *Science, 232*, 34–47.

Fries, J. F. (1990). Aging, natural death, and the compression of morbidity. *New England Journal of [??] Medicine, 303*, 130–135.

Fries, J. F., & Crapo, L. M. (1981). *Vitality and Aging*. San Francisco, CA: Freeman.

Grady, D., Rubin, S. M., Petitti, D. B., Fox, C. S., Black, D., Ettinger, B., Ernster, V. L., & Cummings, S. R. (1992). Hormone therapy to prevent disease and prolong life in postmenopausal women: a review. *Annals of Internal Medicine, 117*, 1016–1037.

Hazzard, W. R. (1983). Preventive gerontology: strategies for healthy aging. *Postgraduate Medicine, 74*, 279–287.

Hazzard, W. R. (1997). Ways to make "usual" and "successful" aging synonymous. *Western Journal of Medicine, 67*, 206–215.

Hazzard, W. R. (1999). Preventive gerontology: a personalized, designer approach to a life of maximum quality and quantity. In W. R. Hazzard *et al.* (Eds.). *Principles of Geriatric Medicine and Gerontology*, 4th ed. (pp. 239–245). New York: McGraw-Hill.

Hulley, S., Grady, D., Bush, T., Furberg, C., Herrington, D., Riggs, B., & Vittinghoff, E. (1998). Randomized trial of estrogen plus progestin for secondary prevention of coronary heart disease in women. *Journal of the American Medical Association, 280*, 605–613.

Lakdawalla, D., & Philipson, T. (1999). Aging and the growth of long-term care, working paper 6980. National Bureau of Economic Research, Inc.

Manton, K. G., & Vaupel, S. W. (1995). Survival after the age of 80 in the United States, Sweden, France, England, and Japan. *New England Journal of Medicine, 333*, 1232–1235.

Olshansky, S. J., & Carnes, B. A. (1990). In search of Methuselah: Estimating the upper limits to human longevity. *Science, 250*, 634–640.

Rowe, J. W., & Kahn, R. L. (1987). Human aging: Usual and successful: A review. *Science, 237*, 143–149.

Rowe, J. W., & Kahn, R. L. (1998). *Successful Aging*. New York: Random House.

Vita, A. J., Terry, R. B., Hubert, H. B., & Fries, J. F. (1998). Aging, health risks, and cumulative disability. *New England Journal of Medicine, 338*, 1035–1041.

Author Index

Author Index

Author Index

511

Subject Index

Subject Index